MW00988151

20L

I am a

I am a
Multi-millionaire

The Miraculous Millionaire
A Sensible Approach to Financial Freedom

We mint millionaires one person at a time.

First Printing

Paperback Edition

ISBN-10: 0988383209

ISBN-13: 978-0-9883832-0-3

LCCN: 2012919855

Cover Design: Kenneth Osong

Layout: Alexia Ayuk

Illustration: Lucielle Ayuk

Principally, *The Miraculous Millionaire* and other Shake-Scene Press books are available for sale at Amazon.com, Barnesandnoble.com, Miraculousmillionaire.com, Princeojong.com, and Millionaireiuniversity.com. Please, we encourage you to contact us for information on book tours, signings, special promotions, corporate training, seminars, and workshops: (301) 593-4897 or (301) 593-4879. For emergencies, please, call us at (240) 330-0839. We are ready to serve you.

There is more to personal finance than the drudgery of debts and budgets.

ABOUT THE AUTHOR

Prince Ojong is a self-made millionaire who lives in the Washington, D.C., area with his family of four. The founder of the Millionaire Club, he is also the president of Millionaire iUniversity. com, and the chief executive officer of OverReacher Empire Corporation. Since he dropped out of Howard University's PhD program in organizational communications in 1990, he has been busy pursuing the American Dream, which has led him to the foray of many lucrative small-business opportunities: word processing, income tax preparation, real-estate sales and investing, loan and mortgage brokering, title insurance agency, bond trading and stock investing, general business consulting, life and health insurance sales, photo and video editing, and movie production.

ACADEMIC BACKGROUND

BA (Hons), English, The University of Yaounde, Cameroon, West Africa.

MA, American, British, and Afro-American Literature, The American University and Howard University, Washington, DC.

PhD candidate, Organizational Communications, Howard University, Washington, DC.

PRINCE OJONG'S PROFESSIONAL TITLES

The Financial Savior of Middle America
The Prophet of the American Dream
The Robin Hood of Personal Finance

Shake-Scene Press
A Division of OverReacher Empire Corporation
11231 Lockwood Drive, Silver Spring, MD 20901
Office #: (301) 593-4897
         (301) 593-4879
Fax #: (240) 241-5137

IN GOD I TRUST

There is more to personal finance than the drudgery of debts and budgets.

PRINCE OJONG'S DAILY PRAYER

Jesus Christ is my salvation.
My Lord, I love you.
My God, I worship you.
I dedicate my life to you;
I consecrate on your altar.
Let my dreams be closer than I think.

My God! My God!
As you were with Moses, so shall you be with me!
As you are with Jesus, so shall you be with me.
So let it be!
So mote it be!

ARE YOU HAPPY WITH YOUR PRESENT FINANCIAL SITUATION?

IF NOT, WHY NOT CHANGE IT TODAY?

THE HOLY BIBLE SAYS YOU WERE BORN WITH THE UNLIMITED AND DIVINE POWER TO CHANGE YOUR LIFE!

YOU SEE, THE DNA OF YOUR CURRENT CIRCUMSTANCES OF LIFE WILL STAY WITH YOU FOREVER, UNLESS YOU TAKE QUICK ACTION TO CHANGE THE BLUEPRINT NOW!

SO IN THE NAME OF JESUS CHRIST OF NAZARETH
I COMMAND YOU TO READ THE BOOK AND CHANGE YOUR LIFE TODAY.

Prince Ojong

The Lord and Financial Savior of Middle America
The Prophet of the American Dream
The Robin Hood of Personal Finance

Email: theafricannation@yahoo.com

Web: http://www.princeojong.com

http://www.miraculousmillionaire.com

http://www.millionaireiuniversity.com

There is more to personal finance than the drudgery of debts and budgets.

YOUR DREAMS ARE CLOSER THAN YOU THINK!

So Discover How to Use $ucce$$tology to Get Rich Quickly & Easily.

THE CLOSELY-GUARDED-MILLIONAIRE- MONEY-MAKING SECRETS OF AMERICA'S SUPER RICH and FAMOUS ARE ABOUT TO BE REVEALED TO YOU.

Imagine......

- Learning to Re-program Your Mind Like a Computer
- Modeling Computer Entrepreneurs and Superstars
- Coding Your Way To Fame and Fortune

In *The Miraculous Millionaire*, in twelve easy steps, Prince Ojong relates how, whether by accident or divine design, he stumbled upon a treasure trove of arcane knowledge that has, until now, been the preserve of America's artificial aristocratic families of millionaires and billionaires.

CHANGING $1.00 INTO $1,000,000

Like a miracle wrought in heaven, Prince Ojong's story will amaze and enthrall you. How did a poor African immigrant change $1.00 into $1,000,000? What is his game? What wealth-building secrets does Prince Ojong possess? Is he the new Alchemist? To discover the truth, please, read *The Miraculous Millionaire*. It is the magic pill of poverty elimination, so swallow it now and feel the excitement!

We mint millionaires one person at a time.

$UCCE$$TOLOGY SYSTEM

Success = (ASP) or (SMT)

A= Art
S= Science
P= Philosophy

S=Skills
M=Methods
T=Thoughts

HERE IS THE SOURCE CODE OF FAME AND FORTUNE

```
<%
Dim $ucce$$tology
$ucce$$tology = "American Dream"
$ucce$$tology= "an Art"
$ucce$$tology="a Philosophy"
$ucce$$tology="a Science"
If $ucce$$tology = "an art, a philosophy, a science" Then
      Response.Write("Secrets of Realizing the American Dream!")
ElseIf $ucce$$tology = "Poverty" Then
      Response.Write("The Millionaire Entrepreneur!")
        Response.Write("Assets=Liabilities + Equity!")
        Response.Write("The Miraculous Millionaire!")

Else
      Response.Write("Follow Prince Ojong, the Prophet of the American
Dream.")

End If
%>
```

There is more to personal finance than the drudgery of debts and budgets.

Dreams Like Mine

America is a dream,
A nation conceived by the spirit of pioneers.
Do you have a dream today?
A dream like mine?
A dream rooted in the American dream?
Dare to dream the American dream!
Hold on to your dream.
Make it happen.
It will never go away;
Your dream is closer than you think

A Dream Deferred
By Langston Hughes

What happens to a dream deferred?
Does it dry up
like a raisin in the sun?
Or fester like a sore--
And then run?
Does it stink like rotten meat?
Or crust and sugar over--
like a syrupy sweet?
Maybe it just sags
like a heavy load.
Or does it explode?

Table of Contents

There is more to personal finance than the drudgery of debts and budgets.

DEDICATION

I dedicate *The Miraculous Millionaire* to my birth parents, Gabriel Ojong-Ayuk and Lucy Tarkang Ojong-Ayuk, my first and original teachers of self-help philosophy. Indeed, I will never be able to thank them adequately for incubating the ideal of the American Dream in my childhood mind.

Besides, it is my conviction that my parents will be happy to share the dedication of the book with the activists of the Occupy Wall Street movement and the real hard-working and ordinary young men and women all across America who are struggling to achieve the American Dream.

ACKNOWLEDGEMENTS

To my wife, Lady Claire, and my two daughters, Lucielle and Alexia: I thank you for tolerating my long hours of work. Writing is a solitary and laborious process from stultification to clarification; it is a labor of love; personally, *The Miraculous Millionaire* is a soothing balm.

DISCLAIMER

The information provided in *The Miraculous Millionaire* is exclusively for informational purpose. It is not financial advice. The author is not engaged in the provision of professional accounting, finance, or investment advice. The book is not a recommendation to buy, sell, or trade securities, or to invest in any specific product, service, or business. The author can buy, sell, or hold any positions in the securities mentioned in the book or website at any time.

Shake-Scene Press
OverReacher Empire Corporation
11231 Lockwood Drive
Silver Spring, MD 20901

Office #: (301) 593-4897
         (301) 593-4879
Fax #: 240-241-5137

Email: theafricannation@yahoo.com

WEB:
http://www.princeojong.com
http://www.miraculousmillionaire.com
http://www.millionaireiuniversity.com

FOREWORD

Words Written in a Country Cemetery

By Dr. Gabriel Ojong-Ayuk

BA Hons, Linguistics, McGill University, Canada

MA, African and French Literature, University of Alberta, Canada

PhD, African Literature, Yaounde University, Cameroon

Kembong, Cameroon, West Africa

November 14, 2012

Few fathers ever live to see the worthy work of raising their children. Among these few I stand. When Prince Ojong approached me a few months ago to write to you, the reader of his book titled *The Miraculous Millionaire*, I was taken aback by the twin emotions of surprise and elation. Surprise because he knows fully well that I had passed through transition on November 14, 1988; elation because I am delighted to assist my only son in all his undertakings. Hence, I took some time off from my busy schedule of preparing for the second coming of my Lord, Jesus Christ, to read the book from cover to cover. I must admit that I have understood the core message of the book quickly because Prince Ojong had already shared some of his ideas with me during our private sessions. I know Prince Ojong; Prince Ojong is my only son. It is unfortunate that I did not live a long life on earth to experience the physical fruition of my son's noble work in pursuing the American Dream.   Nonetheless, I am bearing witness to them as a spirit.

It has been an odyssey. On many occasions, I was tempted to intervene and play the role of a protective father, but my Lord said I should leave my son to his own devices. I prayed for mercy as I transcended the realms of heaven. Today, I thank God for making my son's financial life a tragi-comedy in twelve acts. Verily do I pray that the good Lord protect and keep you always; may your financial dreams also come true. I am referring you to my son, Prince Ojong, in order for you to change your income tax consultant and financial advisor. Trust me! You will fall in love with my son. Your business relationship will blossom into a personal and close friendship. Prince Ojong will motivate you to complete the writing of your goals and design of your financial plan.

There is more to personal finance than the drudgery of debts and budgets.

The book's appeal is unique. Indeed, I am encouraging you to be the first reader. You will appreciate the novelty, profundity, and simplicity of his financial advice. You will learn much from him, as an ordinary reader. I assume you are an average working-class American; you are not a financial expert who is famous for making personal finance difficult or complicated. So you will admire Prince Ojong for making an intricate subject like personal finance to be sensible and down-to-earth for regular working-class people like him. Prince Ojong identifies with middle-class America; he cares about you. You, the target reader of the book, therefore, are neither a big shot nor a financial whiz. Prince Ojong wrote the book for the average person who is serious about building the foundation of their financial house on the bedrock of risk-free investing. The book's narrative tells the amazing story of my beloved son, Prince Ojong, an African immigrant with no connections, who studied and applied the wealth-building secrets of America's rich and famous. In twelve easy-to-follow steps, Prince Ojong shows how you, too, can play and win the big money game of personal finance.

It is no secret to me that you, like people everywhere in America, have been dreaming of riches every day, but, until you met Prince Ojong, you have not yet seen a book like *The Miraculous Millionaire*, which systematically and completely shows you how to get rich successfully. Thanks, Prince Ojong! I know Prince Ojong. Prince Ojong is my only son. He is a real person, not a creation of television or other media. Like me, Prince Ojong is an African immigrant from Cameroon. He came to America to pursue graduate studies, but he had to work very hard as a dishwasher, security guard, and tutor to support himself financially. A voracious reader with an inquisitive mind, Prince Ojong dropped out of Howard University's school of communications and turned his love for learning into a research project fit for a post-doctoral treatise: an inquiry into the nature, causes, and money secrets of America's millionaires and billionaires or an expose of the wealth-building strategies of the rich and famous.

Personally, I believe that by studying and applying the financial methods presented in *The Miraculous Millionaire*, including the step-by-step plan, you can get rich in America without risks. The book brings you the gospel of the American Dream; it shows that in America there is an opportunity for the ordinary person to achieve financial freedom. By reading *The Miraculous Millionaire*, you will realize your dreams and change your life. Most of Prince Ojong's clients and customers have already started applying his ideas; I hope you are poised to begin riding the waves of success from the wings of economic independence. The book will remind you that the price of success is the discipline of capitalizing on your God-given talents, self-study of personal finance, and computer literacy. In fact, I am highly recommending *The Miraculous Millionaire* to you today; it is not because Prince Ojong is my son. By applying Prince Ojong's turn-key program or push-button system, you do not have to depend on other people for success; rather, you have to depend on yourself. It will always be up to you to think and grow rich in America; nobody can do it for you; you have to carry your own cross. Please, review the twelve steps outlined in *The Miraculous Millionaire* below:

Step 1 Pay God first
Step 2 Discover the millionaire's secret
Step 3 Use insurance as your foundation of wealth
Step 4 Teach yourself personal finance
Step 5 Balance your financial book
Step 6 Computerize and research the Internet
Step 7 Acquire entrepreneurial skills
Step 8 Decode the IRS tax codes
Step 9 Play the stock market game
Step 10 Invest in real estate, mortgages, and title insurance
Step 11 Join the Millionaire Club
Step 12 Attend the Millionaire iUniversity

The book is chock-full of content you, as middle-class America, all crave. The book urges you to return to the financial basics of success. It reminds you that time is running out on you, so you should start worrying about your personal finances. The specialized knowledge simplified in the book will reassure you that it is now possible for you to make your dreams come true. The book shows you how to translate your faith in God into the belief in yourself. The book takes you along on a financial journey from your present financial situation to the life you have always dreamed for yourself. The book will inspire you to take action to resolve your financial problems. You will laugh when you arrive at your destination of financial success. As such, Prince Ojong is a credible author because he practices what he preaches to his clients every day. *The Miraculous Millionaire* motivates you to model his excellence. Shift your focus on the urgency to resolve your financial problems once and for all. People may say to you that money is not everything; money is the root of all evil. The truth of the matter is that sooner or later you will find out that money matters. Really! Money is just a medium of exchange in the form of paper or coin with no intrinsic value; people are the ones who confer value to money; for this reason, people's lustful pursuit of money is the root of all evil.

There is more to personal finance than the drudgery of debts and budgets.

What did Jesus Christ say? "Render therefore to Caesar the things that are Caesar's, and to God the things that are God's." Therefore, I ask you to act now; buy and read *The Miraculous Millionaire* today! Your friends and neighbours are using the ideas explained in the book to fix the problems of their lives; they are reconstructing their financial dreams. What about you? Follow Prince Ojong's success blueprint. It is easy. Prince Ojong has given you the blocks you need to build your financial house. He has given you the architectural blueprint you need to construct your edifice; he has given you the map you need to tread upon the treacherous road to financial freedom. His ideas, which are practical and sensible, work in good times and bad times, so, please, look forward to your financial future with confidence and great expectations. Trust in the Lord. May God bless you.

PREFACE

By Prince Ojong
Silver Spring, Maryland
November 30, 2012

The Sermon on the Mount

This book does not need a traditional preface. Why not? The timing is not right to cover the elaborate story of how the book came into being, or how the idea for the book was developed. *The Miraculous Millionaire* is your book; it is not mine. The book is not original, so I cannot take credit for its contents. It is your gift from God. I am merely the instrument God is using to spread the ancient and everlasting truths of nature and the good news for all the 99% working people in America. De jure, the book's contents might be colored by my point of view, yet I regard my personal, professional, and business experiences as reflections of my voice. I beg your indulgence to acknowledge our Father who is in heaven for his guidance and assistance. Nonetheless, I would like to thank all the brothers and sisters in Christ who have, immeasurably and anonymously, helped me during the time of writing the book.

Hearty welcome to the millionaire-ministry of wealth building. Like Angel Gabriel of old, my mission in writing *The Miraculous Millionaire* is to bring good tidings to you. As a servant of God, I want to deliver a message of hope to you. I want to start a conversation with you on God's plan for you with the great American Dream. I want you to hear the good news meant for you. Jesus Christ does not want you to suffer in silence on this earth.

Of course, you may not be aware that before Jesus Christ ascended into heaven he bequeathed you with the treasury of divine wisdom that can soothe you like a balm. All across America, ordinary individuals, like you and me, are wresting this occult or esoteric knowledge from nature; they are enriching their lives; they are living glamorous lives like millionaires and billionaires. What about you?

By contrast, you are wallowing in financial darkness like lost sheep, a motherless child, or a lost soul in hell. Indeed, that is why the good Lord said it is high time somebody exposes the plain truth to you and all the masses of America. If you are serious about making big money and changing your life for the better, then, I am ready to welcome you as God's next millionaire apprentice.

Who am I? I am a humble prophet of the American Dream. Unashamedly, I am a born-again Christian. I am on a crusade to utilize prosperity theology to convert you into Christianity or Roman Catholicism. Jesus loves you. Did you know? I want you to think about putting your financial house in good order. I want you to have the dream of starting your own small business. Does the idea of becoming your own boss sound good to you? Unapologetically, I am here to show you the shimmering rays of divine hope and personal hope. I want to fill your head with great expectations, a miracle program, and the ultimate financial success system called $ucce$$tology: the art, science, and philosophy of realizing the American Dream today.

As I am completing this preface, I urge you to motivate yourself to take quick action to change your life dramatically. May your thoughts flash on the holy Bible. Let them focus like a laser beam on the Sermon on the Mount. Do you remember the Sermon on the Mount? It is a collection of sayings and teachings of Jesus Christ, which emphasizes his moral teaching found in the Gospel of Matthew (chapters 5, 6, and 7). It is the first of the five discourses of Matthew, and it takes place relatively early in the ministry of Jesus, after he has been baptized by John the Baptist and preached in Galilee. *The Miraculous Millionaire* is an amazing book. I encourage you to read it from cover to cover.

PROLOGUE

Who wants to be a millionaire? It is no secret that ordinary people everywhere in America dream of getting rich quickly and easily, but there is no book that systematically and completely shows them, average Americans with neither connections nor memberships in country clubs or the Washington or New York mass-media elite, how it is done successfully. That is, until now, with the publishing of *The Miraculous Millionaire*. Written by Prince Ojong, a West-African immigrant and a frustrated and former security guard, the book presents a step-by-step plan to getting rich without risks. De jure, in evaluating books on personal finance, what sets Prince Ojong's book apart is the fact that readers acknowledge that it is, unquestionably, a real game changer.

Why should you read *The Miraculous Millionaire*? It is a tell-all book on DIY personal finance, which has neither been vetted nor censored by any US power center or authority. Certainly, the scale and magnitude of the book's financial revelations put many classified secrets and little-known wealth accumulation and distribution strategies favored by the rich and famous into the public domain for the consumption of Main Street America. *The Miraculous Millionaire* is revolutionary in altering the business strategy of writing personal finance books; it conceives and introduces an entirely new paradigm. Yet, I do not want to take the credit for this budding revolution. I may be flattered to hear you say that I am a person who is a visionary, but the glory belongs to our Father who is heaven. For this reason, I would like to remind you that whatever amount of money you want can be yours. Please, just ask God, your father who is in heaven. You are the son or daughter of God; as your creator, God made you in his likeness; you have divine qualities that are latent; it is my prerogative to assist you in awakening the giant within you. Did the Holy Bible not tell you so?

"Ask, and it will be given you; search, and you will find; knock, and the door will be opened for you. For everyone who asks receives, and everyone who searches finds, and for everyone who knocks, the door will be opened."
The Holy Bible, Matthew 7:7-8

WELCOME TO THE MILLIONAIRE MINISTRY OF MONEY-MAKING and WEALTH-BUILDING!

Do you want to make more money? Most of us do. We want to raise our standard of living, and we want to even live the American Dream. What about you? If you have seriously been thinking about improving your financial circumstance, then, here is a one-time opportunity of a lifetime. Here is a fair chance for you to learn how to make your dreams come true. $5,000 or more … Picture you in the next few days earning at least $ 5,000 per week. What will you do with your new money? Quit your job and take a vacation to Hawaii or a fantasy island in the Caribbean? Pay off all your bills? Save your money for retirement? Buy a nice car? Purchase your dream home? Allocate funds for your children's education?

There is more to personal finance than the drudgery of debts and budgets.

Please, do not just dream about great riches. Take quick action to make much money for you. If you are reading *The Miraculous Millionaire*, then, you have come to the revolutionary, money-making temple that shows you how to motivate yourself to make nothing but big money.

Here is what you will be able to do after you read the book and join the Millionaire Club:

1. --understand the money secrets of the rich and famous
2. --apply the cosmic laws of financial success and personal achievement
3. --save more money and become debt-free to weather the recession gracefully
4. --capitalize on innovative wealth-building to leverage your way to financial success.

WHAT EVER AMOUNT OF MONEY YOU WANT CAN BE YOURS!

But you must be disciplined in following my soon-to-be millionaire principles. Personally, I recognize the fact that discipline and organization are the major weaknesses of most students on the path to financial success. This fact reflects why I pay much attention to making personal coaching and academic instruction components of my wealth-building system.

Unlike motivational speakers hawking half-baked millionaire programs for a summer season, I promise to be there for you in all kinds of weather to offer you a comprehensive learning system. After buying my book and subscribing to an annual support plan, you will never be left to alone to your own devices.

I will monitor your progress personally; when I am busy, I will delegate the task of monitoring your progress to one of my able assistants. In the end, you will concur that my $ucce$$tology system is the #1 and complete step-by-step technology for the attainment of financial independence and true self-improvement.

BENEFITS OF $UCCE$$TOLOGY

For a brief moment, I want you to sit on a chair and daydream. Visualize the benefits of $ucce$$tology:
1. --Dream and aspire
2. --Set your goals
3. --Believe and achieve
4. --Determine what you really want out of life
5. --Experience the joy of living
6. --Pray and count your blessing
7. --Praise the Lord Jesus Christ and God

WRITING *THE MIRACULOUS MILLIONAIRE*

My dear reader, I am happy to present to you a new book on personal finance and investing written and published by me, a 100% true or real guy, someone who was just like you. What motivated me to write the book is the following question: When shall a good book on personal finance and investing be published for the rest us? I am referring to us, the masses of America, that is, regular or ordinary folks who work hard every day just to pay the bills.

When shall a practical book be published from our own perspective? I mean a book written by one of us, a member of the masses for the masses; I am referring to a book written by the masses, not an armchair writer from the mass-media elite in Washington or New York. You may find comfort in the fact that I have read all the new personal finance books, including the For Dummies and Idiot series, yet these books lack the heart and soul or the consciousness of the average American; if the books are not pedantic and verbose, they are too simplistic and unrealistic.

Therefore, in a desperate attempt to answer the questions raised earlier, in November 2012, I, an average American, a new immigrant from West Africa, set out to publish a new personal finance guide for the masses, the 99% of America. God willing, I know the book will become popular due to the rarity of beginner-friendly personal finance books written from the point of view of poor folks like us who are inspired and motivated to escape the rat race. Although I have focused much attention on the fundamentals of personal finance, I have also interwoven these materials with the narrative of my unique personal experiences.

The book is intended to serve as a non-intimidating money guide for readers like me who are new to the various personal finance and investing topics covered in books published by intellectual elements of the mainstream mass media.

To tell you the truth, since I came to America, I have never taken a college course on personal finance or investing; rather, I buy books like a child in a candy store and read them on my own; I attend money-making seminars often, and I struggle to apply what I have learned from these seminars.

In fact, that is why my prose is simple and direct. I want to reassure you that if I can do it, you can do it, too! I will teach you the fundamentals of personal finance: faith in God, credit cards and debt management, spending and saving, careers and small business, taxes, computers, income taxes, real estate, stocks, and bonds.

HORATIO ALGER VARIETY

There is no personal narrative thread to build the reader's trust. The average American cannot relate to the biography of a billionaire such as Donald J. Trump; the average American cannot relate to the memoir of Barack H. Obama; the average American cannot comprehend books penned by Wall Street money managers from Ivy League MBA schools. The point I am making, in this instance, is that there is no Horatio Alger variety. Those who are familiar with motivational stories might remember Horatio Alger, Jr., January 13, 1832 – July 18, 1899. A prolific 19th-century American author, Horatio Alger, Jr. was best known for his many formulaic juvenile novels about impoverished boys and their rise from humble backgrounds to lives of middle-class security and comfort through hard work, determination, courage, and honesty. His writings were characterized by the "rags-to-riches" narrative, which had a formative effect on America during the Gilded Age. He secured his literary niche in 1868 with the publication of his fourth book Ragged Dick, the story of a poor bootblack's rise to middle-class respectability, which was a huge success. His many books that followed were essentially variations on Ragged Dick and featured a cast of stock characters–the valiant youth, the noble, mysterious stranger, the snobbish youth, and the evil squire. In the 1870s, Alger took a trip to California to gather material for future books, but the trip had little influence on his writing. In the last decades of the 19th century, boys' tastes changed, and Alger's moral tone coarsened accordingly. The Puritan ethic had loosened its grip on America, and violence, murder, and other sensational themes entered Alger's works. Public librarians questioned whether his books should be made available to the young. By the time he died in 1899, he had published around a hundred volumes.

The Miraculous Millionaire! The title of the book is *The Miraculous Millionaire*. In the book you will discover how to use $ucce$$tology to get rich quickly and easily. On the one hand, to individuals unaware of the money secrets of America's rich and famous, the title of the book may sound preposterous like a fairy tale told by an idiot. On the other hand, individuals familiar with the growing body of self-help literature would welcome the book with open arms. Who is a miraculous millionaire? I, the writer of the book, am a miraculous millionaire. It is neither an accident nor a coincidence that today I am living the great American Dream of financial success. I am a West African immigrant from Cameroon. I came to America in 1983 as a poor international student pursuing the Golden Fleece. I was a legal alien on a student visa, but I knew no body to take me in, so I sought shelter and financial help from complete strangers; in fact, it is a miracle that I am still living in the USA.

Today, however, as a Roman Catholic Christian, I am so proud to say that my life is a miracle, a miracle of Jesus Christ. By struggling to maintain my religious faith in the face of adversity and acting programmatically on the business intelligence I have gathered heretofore, I have found favor with God. He has blessed me financially beyond any measure. Hence, I believe in the miracles of Jesus Christ. De jure, miracles were widely believed in around the time of Jesus Christ's life, but I am giving you the reason to believe in them today. The miracles of Jesus are the supernatural deeds of Jesus, as recorded in gospels, in the course of his ministry. According to the Gospel of John, only some of these miracles were recorded. John 21:25 states, "Jesus did many other things as well. If every one of them were written down,　even the whole world would not have room for the books that would be written." These miracles may be categorized into four groups: cures, exorcisms, resurrection of the dead, and control over nature. In the Synoptic Gospels (Mark, Matthew, and Luke), Jesus refuses to give a miraculous sign to prove his authority. In the Gospel of John, Jesus is said to have performed seven miraculous signs that characterize his ministry, from changing water into wine at the start of his ministry to raising Lazarus from the dead at the end. My life is a miracle because I am a miraculous millionaire. Similarly, you, the reader of the book, can become the miraculous millionaire, the next soon-to-be or new millionaire entrepreneur or computer superstar. In fact, that is my message to you; that is why I wrote this book; and that is why I am motivating you to read the book from cover to cover; that is why I am encouraging you to learn and respect the power and glory of God.

OCCUPY WALL STREET

Although I have been gathering the research material of *The Miraculous Millionaire* for over ten years, it was not my intention to publish a do-it-yourself ("DIY") personal finance book this year. However, the Occupy Wall Street protests provided a major impetus for the completion of *The Miraculous Millionaire*. Occupy Wall Street was an ongoing series of demonstrations initiated by the Canadian activist group Adbusters which began September 17, 2011, in Zuccotti Park of New York City's Wall Street financial district. The protests were against what these protesters had perceived to be social and economic inequality, high unemployment, greed, as well as corruption, and the undue influence of corporations—particularly that of the financial services sector—on government.

The protesters' slogan "We are the 99%" referred to what these protesters had perceived to be the growing difference in wealth in the U.S. between the wealthiest 1% and the rest of the 99% of the population. De jure, *The Miraculous Millionaire* is an experimental, practical, and positive message addressed to you and these protesters and other Americans belonging to the class of 99%. *The Miraculous Millionaire* makes the assumption that the majority of protesters and the population of the 99% are computer literate and technology savvy. Certainly, during these recessionary times, the big boys on Wall Street are having some fun; the poor folks on Mean Street are experiencing many financial difficulties.

Please, do not hate the big guys on Wall Street because they are rich, and you are poor. Remember, you are still living in America, the land of opportunity, the citadel of capitalism on planet earth. America is still the best of all possible worlds. I was poring over statistics on international trade last night, and I was comforted to discover that of all the major world economies (Russia, Britain, France, Germany, China, and Japan), America will be the only juggernaut to report positive economic growth for 2012. So my friend, only in America can you, an average individual with no connections, really have the power to become a rich millionaire, what I refer to as "The Miraculous Millionaire," a computer entrepreneur or superstar."

$UCCE$$TOLOGY OR SPECIALIZED KNOWLEDGE

In fact, in America, your dreams are closer than you think. You just have to learn to model the excellence of America's rich and famous folks; you have to rewire your brain so that you can emulate the mental syntax of computer entrepreneurs or the rich people on Wall Street. You have to acquire the specialized knowledge that they possess already; specialized knowledge is power, so understand it and use it. What is actually separating you from the millionaires on Wall Street is the specialized financial knowledge fundamental to realizing the American Dream. I call this specialized knowledge software for your brain or "$ucce$$tology."

You, as a divine creature, have a brain that is bigger than a million-dollar supercomputer. To the Almighty God is the glory! A supercomputer can attempt to emulate human behavior, but a computer cannot think; you can think innately and creatively. What you need to do is unlearn negative behaviors, habits, and rituals.

It is the intention of $ucce$$tology to assist you in re-programming your human mind like a personal computer, so that you can code your way proudly to fame and fortune. I want you to think and grow rich with peace of mind. No more will you be jealous of America's rich and famous folks on Wall Street; you will be more engrossed in thoughts of implementing your own plan of financial success.

OCCUPY WALL STREET VERDICT

Class warfare is un-American; it is anathema. Class warfare is diametrically opposed to the true character of America, the pioneer spirit of the frontiersmen and women of the Old Wild West. This country is neither Russia nor China. It is still possible, fashionable, and acceptable for you to become rich in America. If you are not rich in America, the problem is either your ignorance or lack of personal drive; therefore, it is the purpose of $ucce$$tology to change your life for the better.

As such, *The Miraculous Millionaire* is your financial success bible: beginner's instruction before leaving earth. If you are living in America, all is for the best in the best of all possible worlds. I have weighed and considered the list of the demands of the activists of the Occupy Wall Street movement. I express my support for the 99 percent, agreeing with Occupy Wall Street protesters that the nation's current financial system is seriously harming the US economy. As a result, it is appropriate for protesters to demand greater corporate transparency, restraint of excessive payouts to executives and support for the federal Consumer Financial Protection Bureau.

Philosophically, I sympathize with protesters, but, legally, I disagree with their al-Qaeda tactics and strategies. The goals of Osama bin Laden and his al-Qaeda jihadist network are to destroy the American economy and Western civilization. By disrupting the transaction of daily commerce, Occupy Wall Street protestors are implementing the nefarious and negative lessons they have learned from the Islamic terrorists' playbook. While it is true that it is time for protestors to occupy their own country, it is wrong for them to destroy the economic fabric in place. I mean that they have to protest in the right way; that is, without destroying the infrastructure that has taken us hundreds of years to build. America is a country of laws. It is not a wild jungle where protesters can afford to take the laws into their own hands. If they have any issues that need to be addressed, it behooves them to follow the proper legal procedures. Verily I say unto them, if they are serious about occupying their country, they have to metamorphose from a lone supplier of labor into a capitalist. Instead of engaging in violent street protests, they can fix the broken Wall Street system by becoming players, not spectators; let them join the big boys; they should not get mad and protest; they should get even by learning the rules and changing these rules for their own betterment.

Even in heaven, there is a hierarchy; indeed, that is why Lucifer chose to reign in hell than serve God in heaven; even among angels there are higher and lower angels, so let us all contend with the fact that on Wall Street, or in the USA, all men and women are born equal but some are more equal than others. Do not break the system; use it to get rich. A case in point is Thomas Peterffy, a Hungarian immigrant who owns Interactive Brokers. Thomas Peterffy is a Hungarian-born American entrepreneur who burst into the national scene during the presidential campaign season of 2012 with television advertisements supporting the Republican Party. Some of my friends were laughing at his foreign accent, but I admire Thmas Peterffy very much. He is an American success story. He is the founder and head of Interactive Brokers and played a key role in founding the Boston Options Exchange. Thomas Peterffy arrived in America without the ability to speak the English language. Instead of making excuses for himself as a refugee, he decided to capitalize on all the opportunities that America had to offer; he learned English and bought a premium seat on the American Stock Exchange. If he can do it, you can do it, too! Infact, that is why I am writing this book for you. I want to share the resources you need to become America's next success story.

DO-IT-YOURSELF (DIY) MILLIONAIRE OR COMPUTER ENTREPRENEUR

$ucce$$tology is a new revolution, but $ucce$$tology is a peaceful revolution. $ucce$$tology is a self-help revolution. $ucce$$tology is a do-it-yourself revolution in the realm of personal finance. If you have already rebelled against your station in life, that rebellion is a positive action marking the beginning of your declaration of economic independence, financial freedom, a revolution, which is an economic turnaround; it is a fundamental change in power or organizational structures that takes place in a relatively short period of time. Now $ucce$$tology will act as both a catalyst and agent in motivating you to take concrete steps to change your financial situation. Why should the big boys on Wall Street be having all the fun? Ignore this question! Or rephrase it in the following manner: what can I do to model the big boys on Wall Street and be having some fun, too? Instead of being labeled a spoiler, become a gate crasher of the millionaire party.

There is more to personal finance than the drudgery of debts and budgets.

There are better things you can do with your time; become a DIY (do-it-yourself) millionaire or computer entrepreneur; if you do not do it for yourself, nobody else will. I, Prince Ojong, am a DIY millionaire or computer entrepreneur; you are the next DIY millionaire or computer entrepreneur.

Do it yourself (DIY) is a term used to describe building, modifying, or repairing of something without the aid of experts or professionals. The phrase "do it yourself" came into common usage in the 1950s in reference to home improvement projects which people might choose to complete independently. In recent years, the term DIY has taken on a broader meaning that covers a wide range of skill sets.

DIY is associated with the international alternative rock, punk rock, and indie rock music scenes; indie media networks, pirate radio stations, and the zine community. In this context, DIY is related to the Arts and Crafts movement, in that it offers an alternative to modern consumer culture's emphasis on relying on others to satisfy needs.

$ucce$$tology will teach you the art, science, philosophy of realizing your financial dreams on your own terms. Be prepared to learn how to earn big money. Think like a master entrepreneur or computer superstar; what I call a millionaire entrepreneur is someone who thinks like a good business person. Just like any good business person, you are a capitalist; you want to grow your profits to an unlimited level.

If you are still working for a salary or wages, your employer would be in love with you if you manifest entrepreneurial thinking, you exhibit business consciousness; you make a living based on income from the job; therefore, you work hard and smart to make the business profitable. As much as possible, you begin saving your money for the smallest investments possible.

Thus, if your choices are working more hours to make more money or going back to school to become a doctor, you might opt for the latter due to the much higher earnings down the road by putting in a comparable amount of double and triple-shifts. This brief explanation leads to a golden rule of wealth building: you must invest in yourself if you want to experience true financial freedom. Investing in you means gaining new skills and turning those skills into monetary gain.

Learn millionaire lessons, $ucce$$tology, the so-called millionaire money secrets. Do not be afraid! The lessons are not above your level of understanding or comprehension; indeed, the lessons only require discipline and commitment from the practitioner, you or any down-to-earth people. First, can you decide to be wealthy? I have decided to be wealthy by following Jesus Christ's counsel in business. There is no turning back, so must you decide to be wealthy. Despite chill penury, hardship, and temptations, you must agree not to turn back on your decision to be wealthy.

PERSONAL RESPONSIBILITY

Second, can you take responsibility for your money? By applying my do-it-yourself wealth-building principles and practices, you are taking personal responsibility for your money. Even if financial experts and other professionals are assisting you to complete a task, you must manage the completion of the task yourself. Third, can you keep a portion of everything you earn at work? By consistently cultivating the habit of implementing the 10% saving rule, you are keeping a portion of your money curtailing spending and eliminating debt. I can provide you with lists of moonlighting or sidelines activities for boosting your income.

Fourth, can you go on a debt and financial diet? I want you to win in the margins. The margins are the excess - both the extras you consume and the extras you earn. The idea of making you win in the margins is about living your dream life without sacrificing anything of value. Residence, food, entertainment, and other activities can remain virtually the same, and your current income still allows for the creation of significant wealth. I will reveal the urgency of saving 10% of your money and the miracle of the power of compounding, which is the amazing result of compound interest.

Consider couponing to save money—use store coupons. Fifth, do you agree to give back to your community and God? Someone once made the following remark: "freely giving of our wealth is also the only way to fully protect ourselves from our wealth." Money does not equal joy, but it can help you to be able to help others and to improve the world around you. By following my advice in making God the topmost priority in your life and paying your tithe, you are living your life in accord with the cosmic law of reciprocity; for all the blessings Jesus Christ is showering on you, you have to tithe to show your sense of appreciation. It is your personal responsibility to apply the recommendations stipulated above.

WAYS TO WEALTH IN AMERICA

Generally, there are nine delineable paths to riches in America. These paths have been enumerated below, so choose how to get rich now:

1. Marry Rich.
2. Inherit Wealth
3. Hit the Lottery
4. Steal Money
5. Rub your Lucky Rabbit's foot
6. Look into a Crystal Ball
7. Invent a Product/Provide a Service
8. Join the Millionaire Club
9. Attend Millionaire iUniversity

It is important for you to understand that *The Miraculous Millionaire* does not address the first six paths to riches; by contrast, the book concentrates on paths seven through nine. Hence, choose your way to wealth attentively. If you are dreaming of getting rich by marrying a wealthy guy or girl, *The Miraculous Millionaire* is not for you; if you want to get rich by inheriting big money from an uncle, aunt, or angel, please, put *The Miraculous Millionaire* down and save yourself from some moments of disappointment; if you are daydreaming of winning the lottery and living happily ever after, then, stop reading any further; if you are considering robbing the bank to make your way to wealth, do not read *The Miraculous Millionaire*; as for you rubbing your lucky rabbit's foot, keep at it and forget *The Miraculous Millionaire*; and finally, if you are gazing into a crystal ball to espy a trailer load of money, give up the ordeal of wishful thinking.

EARTHQUAKE WARNING

Please, be forewarned that *The Miraculous Millionaire* can be dangerous to your mind. It is a lethal weapon. It is an atomic bomb. In fact, it is the earthquake that will wake you up from the stupor of your slumber. Like many holy books since the discovery of the dead-sea scrolls, *The Miraculous Millionaire* can change your life forever! Why? *The Miraculous Millionaire* holds the ancient and dead-sea-scroll secrets of the rich and famous. By applying the ideas contained within its pages, you will see a dramatic improvement in your life; spiritually, you will be born again with a new vision, attitude, and outlook. Materially, you will notice people start treating you differently; indeed, you will be treated much better by your colleagues, friends, and family members. In *The Miraculous Millionaire*, I, Prince Ojong, vilified by rich folks as the Robin Hood of personal finance, am giving you money-making formulas for financial success, including focusing on a single goal, prioritizing, avoiding distractions and having both faith and audacity. Underlying all this knowledge is an emphasis on Norman Pearle's *The Power of Positive Thinking* and Napoleon Hill's *Think and Grow Rich* and *The Master-Key to Riches*.

If you hope to find the way to fiscal success, then, welcome with an open mind my foray into the fundamental elements of personal finance, neuro-linguistic programming (NLP), Christian mysticism, metaphysics, and omniscient capitalism. As a book, *The Miraculous Millionaire* is a money manual for the average American who is serious about achieving greatness and success. It posits my thesis on the nature, purpose, and end of realizing the American dream. My success formula is christened "$ucce$$tology." Simply, to achieve financial freedom, you need to discover the money secrets of millionaires and apply their wealth-building principles in your life daily. For this reason, *The Miraculous Millionaire* holds the secrets to my own success. By applying the ideas contained within its pages, you will already seen a dramatic improvement in your life, in your attitude, and in our outlook. You are treating yourself differently and in turn you are being treated much better by colleagues, friends, and family.

TOP 10 PERSONAL FINANCE BOOKS

As I was reviewing, abridging, and revising the one-thousand-page manuscript of *The Miraculous Millionaire* in the comfort of my family library, an article on the Internet titled "Top 10 Financial Books" commanded my attention:

#1 The Total Money Makeover by Dave Ramsey
#2 How to Get Out of Debt, Stay Out of Debt, and Live Prosperously by Jerrold Mundis
#3 Your Money or Your Life by Vicki Robin, Joe Dominguez, and Monique Tilford
#4 All Your Worth: The Ultimate Lifetime Money Plan by Elizabeth Warren and Amelia Warren Tyagi
#5 I Will Teach You to Be Rich by Ramit Sethi
#6 The Random Walk Guide to Investing by Burton G. Malkiel
#7 The Complete Tightwad Gazette by Amy Dacyczyn
#8 The Millionaire Next Door by Thomas Stanley and William Danko
#9 Work Less, Live More: The Way to Semi-Retirement by Billy Clyatt
#10 Why Smart People Make Big Money Mistakes (and How to Correct Them) by Gary Belsky and Thomas Gilovich

Why is Prince Ojong publishing another book on personal finance? In a word, the answer is that I am writing for you, the little guy or girl whose needs have been ignored or overlooked by the big-name authors and vanilla publishers. I care about you because I can identify with your predicament; I am an unknown and self-published author, and you remind me of my past as a struggling guy; I love you as my neighbor, but they claim, like infidels, that you do not exist. Unlike them, I have conducted a needs-assessment study of you, my target audience. I speak to you directly; I have looked into your eyes, and I have sensed the purity of your SOUL. I want to reassure you that I have bought and read all the top ten financial books whose titles have been listed above.

In fact, I have studied the books with a laser beam, like the subject of a scientific experiment on wealth building. At this juncture, the plain truth must be told to you and the reading public; the unvarnished truth is that as much as all the top ten financial books are good on facts and fanciful theories, they lack a sense of identity or uniqueness; as I have discovered in my research, each book regurgitates facts and theories that have been extant in other personal finance books. None of the top ten financial books breaks new grounds or provides you or the average American reader with a "how-to," holistic, gestalt, realistic, and turn-by-turn roadmap from the Main Street of poverty to the Wall Street of riches.

Besides, a critical analysis of all the personal finance books in the marketplace reveals that they have many inherent weaknesses. Empirically, these books do not adequately conceptualize the issue of addressing the masses' personal-finance problem as a researched question. As a result, their solutions and answers are too trite, hackneyed, simplistic, or myopic. First, Dave Ramsey's *The Total Money Makeover* is a good book for neophytes of personal finance whose singular or exclusive mission is debt elimination. However, individuals who are already turning on the right way to wealth dismiss the book's exclusive focus on the theme of budgeting for debt elimination; there is more to personal finance than the drudgery of budgets and debt-reduction or the simplicity of jingles and snowballing games.

There is more to personal finance than the drudgery of debts and budgets.

What do you do after you have become debt-free? Why must you become debt-free for debt's sake? Why? What do you do with your golden touch and surplus money? Should you become King Midas with an ass' ear? Indeed, Dave Ramsey's book is folksy and evangelistic, but it does not foretell how to get the reader to financial peace or the promise land of financial paradise. Man shall not live by Dave Ramsey's debt reduction alone, but on every word that comes from the mouth of Prince Ojong, the prophet of the American Dream! As such, my book provides a map and twelve signposts to financial freedom. While most personal finance books offer the insights of one or two gurus, my book is a synthesis of all the great personal finance ideas that have worked for me and other do-it-yourself millionaire entrepreneurs; I am humble to state that like Prometheus, I did not create anything; I was just sent to deliver the good news and the fire of ancient wisdom to help the suffering masses who could not afford to research many sources like me. In fact, that is why my admirers and detractors call me "the Robin Hood of personal finance."

RICH DAD POOR DAD

In addition to the top ten financial books, I would like to draw your attention to two other popular personal finance books: *Rich Dad Poor Dad* and *The Automatic Millionaire*. In the example of the book entitled *Rich Dad Poor Dad*, Robert Kiyosaki and Sharon Lechter use an effective metaphor in juxtaposing the dichotomy between the poor and the rich, and the authors also make a compelling case for the importance of financial literacy. However, the book does not offer the reader a step-by-step blueprint for walking from the Main Street of poverty to the Wall Street of riches. By contrast, my new book titled *The Miraculous Millionaire* uses the narrative of my quest for the American Dream, which it anchors on wealth-building strategies that have worked, and are still working for me, the emerging author of do-it-yourself success guide. My book is unlike the purely theoretical information from the mind of a Wall Street finance whiz kid who was born with a golden spoon in his mouth and has never struggled.

THE AUTOMATIC MILLIONAIRE

Additionally, in his book titled *The Automatic Millionaire*, David Bach stresses a variety of the 10% saving solution technique; Bach encourages his readers to rely on automatic employee payroll deductions that are credited into the employee's 401(K) account. The merit of David Bach's book is the automation, systemization, and simplification of the difficult task of budgeting and saving money consistently; nevertheless, I disagree with Bach's argument that automatic payroll deductions will make an employee a millionaire. Where? In America? No way! It is impossible for any employee in America to get rich by saving money in a 401(K) account; nobody ever gets rich by working for somebody else. If you want to get rich, you have to learn not only how to budget and save money but how to grow your money through many of the investment vehicles I have mentioned in *The Miraculous Millionaire*. Do not believe David Bach's baloney and hype! Trust me! I, Prince Ojong, should know better.

In fact, *The Miraculous Millionaire* is the first money guide of its kind to address personal, professional, and business success and its attainment through accessible vital skills and processes, using universal theories derived from the Holy Bible and motivational literature. No other guide is easier to understand, implement, or is so universally beneficial. Place yourself into the hands of Prince Ojong, an award-winning international life coach and business facilitator. My book is your secret guide to success. It provides the processes needed for you to benefit from every other personal development book you will ever read. Learn how to implement self-change and grow from me. Each purchase of *The Miraculous Millionaire* also provides you limited access to my amazing Millionaire iUniversity website (http://www.millionaireiuniversity.com) for training and dynamic on-going support, testing, planning and much more to help you define your goals and achieve. Discard the old mindset or conventional wisdom which, in all probability, has been used and discarded by almost every student's parents for generations; namely: get an education, get a job, work hard, buy a house, save for the future in a 401(K) plan, and someday you will be able to retire and live happily ever after as a millionaire.

The Miraculous Millionaire is a way to inform you, or the average citizen, on the current economic crisis, and how you can rise above it. As an author, I am able to communicate effectively with the average person. Why not? Only a few years ago, I was one of them; I was a poor and hungry immigrant from Africa. As much as I was experiencing American hunger, I had big dreams in my big head. Like the Pilgrim Fathers, pioneers of yore, and gamblers of the Old West, I had hedged my bets on the promise of the American frontier, what I had perceived since my childhood to be like Alice's wonderland. I am not a Wall-Street darling or creation, such as the arm-chair personal finance gurus collecting six figure incomes from Wall Street investment banking firms and concerns. Every blessed day, I am living what I preach; almost no other author today can claim to be doing what he or she recommends in books; I am making a daily living buying and selling real estate, trading stocks and investments, selling insurance and more. The writing of the book, therefore, is aimed at reassuring you, and ordinary Americans in the throes of the recession, that things will be all right in the end, but you must commit yourselves to have faith in yourselves and in the America Dream. You must be hungry. I am using hunger as a metaphor intended for you to create metaphysical rebellion; instead of occupying Wall Street, you should dispel the mental poisoning that makes you envy America's millionaires and billionaires; America is still the land of opportunity, so you should channel your anger and hunger into lifting yourself up from these hard times. Hence, that is the reason for the actual writing of *The Miraculous Millionaire*; sometimes the book retains a consumer friendly and conversational tone in order for me to simplify very "do-able" information; I have taken time to create something within the grasp of average Americans.

THE HOLY BIBLE

I maintain that religious faith should be your foundation of building wealth. You should build wealth with a moral imperative. You should build wealth like the wise home builder in the Gospel of Mathew:

"Therefore whosoever heareth these sayings of mine, and doeth them, I will liken him unto a wise man, which built his house upon a rock: And the rain descended, and the floods came, and the winds blew, and beat upon that house; and it fell not: for it was founded upon a rock. And every one that heareth these sayings of mine, and doeth them not, shall be likened unto a foolish man, which built his house upon the sand: And the rain descended, and the floods came, and the

winds blew, and beat upon that house; and it fell: and great was the fall of it."
Matthew 7:24-2

Neither a robber baron nor a Shylock be! Believe in God, and accept Jesus Christ as your savior. Seek ye first the Kingdom of God, and every other thing shall be given to you—be it material success or other. If you follow this precept, then, you are ready spiritually to attract money in abundance. The Holy Bible relates that every human being is made in the image or likeness of God. Hence, you were born with some degree of psychic ability. It is my mission to show you how to access and utilize your in-born and latent psychic abilities; you could succeed at everything you turned your mind to, from solving everyday money problems to enjoying dynamic and fulfilling human relationships. In the next few chapters, my book shows you some fast, easy ways to unleash your personal psychic force in order for you to become a wealthy, happy, healthy, and fully developed human being. The practical exercises in the book will quickly enable you to realize a host of material, spiritual, and natural benefits, from learning how to contact God, Jesus, the Virgin Mary, the saints, or a spirit guide. You can also alert yourself of imminent danger with psychic warnings. These exercises are simple, take little time, and they allow you to design a personal psychic development program and proceed at your own pace.

THE LEGEND OF PRINCE OJONG

Who is Prince Ojong? In the throes of the economic meltdown of 2007, in the lotus comfort of my palatial four-acre Montgomery county mansion, Maryland, I experienced a transfiguration, a nightmare in which God reminded me of the messianic mission to spread the gospel of $ucce$$tology. I was ashamed because I had failed to keep the initial promise I had made to God. Back in 1997, I had signed a goal agreement with God during a séance of cosmic consciousness, in which I had promised to make the knowledge, discipline, and system fundamental to wealth building available to ordinary mortals—every Tom, Dick, and Harry. The conditional clause of the contract that was accelerated pertains to me earning over $1,000,000 in 2004. Why did I renege on my initial promise to expose millionaire money secrets to the masses? The answer, in one word, is procrastination or the pleasure of making big money, which is like the elixir of getting high and higher on an artificial substance. Instead of cursing the day I was born or making excuses, I have set out to obey God: evangelize the gospel of personal finance all across America! I am busy recruiting disciples for my millionaire ministry.

Will you follow me?Ladies and gentlemen, I am here to present the phenomenon and legend of Prince Ojong. Today, it is a truth universally asserted that in African immigrant communities in America I am the new personal finance messiah. As a financial savior, I am motivating African immigrants and Americans to model the financial success of America's rich and famous. As an academic discipline, finance is a complicated subject. As a culture, personal finance is unpopular and unintelligible to the ordinary individual in America. The rich folks can afford to hire professionals such as insurance agents, accountants, lawyers, and financial planners to help them navigate through the maze of their personal finances; by contrast, the poor folks are condemned to continue to wallow in the mediocrity of their own ignorance. Yet, single-handedly, one man has sought to demystify the abstruse world of personal finance for the masses all across America. That man is none other than me, your own Prince Ojong. The complex world of personal finance can often overwhelm the average person. Mortgages, credit, insurance, taxes, investments, real estate, employment, and business carry with them a host of rules, regulations, and pitfalls that seem designed to transfer wealth from the ignorant to the informed. Neither money nor personal finance comes with user manual. A variety of magazines and books have offered instructions on how to control expenditures and build personal wealth. But, by any measure, the all-time best-selling book on personal finance has come from one man: Prince Ojong.

Once again, let me ask the question: Who is Prince Ojong? How can an ordinary mortal, an African immigrant, possess the power to emerge as a phenomenon of personal finance in America? Why is the self-taught genius modeling Jesus Christ to revolutionize the world of personal finance? The story of my rise to financial fame provides lessons for all of us. If I can do it, you can do it, too! See you at the top! In the beginning, I read every book or magazine on personal finance. I attended every moneymaking seminar and workshop. As my business savvy matured, I formed my own company to teach my hard-learned success strategies to others. The focus of my efforts shifted primarily to readily usable financial strategies accessible by common people. My stated mission was to stamp out financial ignorance and illiteracy in America. In a pioneering effort, I offered one-stop shopping for a variety of low-cost financial services along with a readily available financial hotline to get fast answers to tough questions. My policy offered a money-back guarantee to new members of the Millionaire Club. If members attempted to use the strategies within 30 days of purchase and failed to save the cost of their initial membership fee, then, they could obtain a refund of that fee. All of my effectiveness as a personal financial planner served me well in the years following my rise to fame.

Today, I am at the peak of my personal-finance career. I personally spend 40 weeks per year touring the U.S.A. to sell membership in my organization. During my sales pitch, I, the flamboyant Prince Ojong, introduce myself as someone who had made and lost over a million dollars two times as a young man before finally learning how to build wealth. My story consists of the narrative of attempting to build a luxurious single-family housing business in Beltsville and Laurel, Maryland, only to have the whole project collapse to the ground without anything for me to show for it.

As I explain in the chapter on real-estate investing, the bitter lesson I have learned is that excessive financial leverage or speculation in real-estate investments is very bad, if not dangerous; the crash of my real-estate business consumed all of my capital. A book agent, I shall not name, with a famous vanity publishing company attended one of my personal-finance seminars and encouraged me to publish, print-on-demand, a series of seminars and workshops on wealth and success titled *The Miraculous Millionaire*, which quickly became a top seller across the USA in immigrant communities, and I embarked on a whirlwind tour of talk shows around the country to promote my message. My success and the persuasive message of my book are leading many people to join the Millionaire Club. The seminars and workshops formed the foundations of what is known today as *The Miraculous Millionaire*.

Finally, what lessons can you learn from me and personal finance? I am not in the business of providing legal or accounting advice. The materials in this book serve as general information only. For this reason, responsibility for the defense and growth of personal wealth and wellness fall ultimately upon the individual. Please, remember that sound advice if not always soundly followed, can result in financial risks. People who fail to implement good advice properly will often blame the originator of that advice rather than accept personal accountability for their own shortcomings. I am warning you to protect myself from the US government, whose laws sometimes unintentionally support jealousy and envy at the expense of the productive capacity of rich folks like me and the continuous improvement of poor folks like average Americans. Generally, in a court of law, what are the so-called facts established under the law frequently have nothing to do with reality and everything to do with self-serving fictions. It becomes the melodramatic fiction that can be subsumed in the following manner: if you cannot kill the message, kill the messenger.

Who Is Prince Ojong? I am Prince Ojong. I am the name behind $ucce$$tology. I welcome you heartily to my fairy tale world, which begins at Kembong Palace or Ayukland, the new principality of Africa's crowned prince of personal finance atop a mountain of a hill known as Clematis Drive. Come and see American wonders! My admirers describe me as the very definition of the American success story, continually setting the standards of excellence while expanding my business interests in real estate, gaming, sports, and entertainment. I am the archetypal businessman, a deal maker without peer and an ardent philanthropist.

Do you know Prince Ojong? Maybe yes. Maybe no. If not, you will pretty soon, especially if you are reading *The Miraculous Millionaire* and are serious about investing and getting ahead financially. I am a guy who may turn you on—green with ENVY--, or I may just turn you OFF—black with JEALOUSY. Prince Ojong is my name. Making big money in real estate, stocks, insurance, and other investments is the secret. Flaunting my sexy toys is the game. What mystical power do I possess? African witchcraft? Black magic? Voodoo? What? Why do many of my students claim I am the chosen one?

How did a regular guy like me become the millionaire next door? The answer is simple. I became a millionaire by mustering the courage to decide to become rich and use $ucce$$tology as a wealth-building guide. I was and I am still doing what I am preaching to you: thinking, learning, and acting; by thinking about my dreams; by learning creative principles of dream fulfillment; by acting on simple strategies to implement my ideas.

Will you be like me, Prince Ojong? Will you put your money where your mouth is? Will you open your mind to new ideas about changing your financial future for the better? Will you submit to the do-it-yourself technologies of *The Miraculous Millionaire*?You see, nobody understands the power of do-it-yourself investing like me. Interestingly, a few years ago, I, an investing colossus was only a frustrated dishwasher and heart-broken security guard stranded on the shores of fantasy and limping by the ocean of broken American dreams. Tired of daydreaming and making flimsy excuses for myself, I resolved to model myself after a character in Daniel Defoe's novel titled *Robinson Crusoe*.

I decided to get rich. First, I was born again; the Holy Bible and motivational books became my soothing balm. Second, I attended all the free money-making seminars in the country and slept in public libraries. Because I could not afford to buy any seminar promotional packages, I borrowed them from acquaintances that had bought and abandoned these materials in their living rooms.

36

Third, I used my newly-acquired knowledge to operate many computer-service businesses from my dingy apartment. A computer enthusiast, I joined the Capital PC User Group and taught myself BASIC and ACCESS programming! Some of the software I developed included Badchecks Doctor for check-cashing businesses and Smart Collector for debt-collection enterprises. Fourth, I started investing my profits in mutual funds and real estate. Fifth, I taught myself how to trade stocks without the help of any full-service brokers. I invented statistically rational analysis (SRA) to achieve superior stock-trading performance. News of my success resulted in the formation of the Millionaire Club, an investment club I used to teach my friends and family members how to trade stocks profitably in all markets—bull or bear. Today, I want to keep a promise I had made to myself during my days in the wilderness: to share my investment knowledge with any human being who is serious about achieving the American dream: "After I start making an average of $1,000 a day, I said, "I will teach my methods to my fellow beings." I said that I wanted the whole world to know that what happened to me can also happen to you. I am dying to share my trading secrets with you. And so *The Miraculous Millionaire* was born!

THE MASTERY OF SUCCESS

The mastery of financial success involves the possession of a blueprint for achieving the American Dream. 99% of the people living in America have no plan to organize the chapters of their lives; indeed, they are merely living a humdrum existence of surviving on jobs; that is, living from one paycheck to another paycheck. They lack a financial safety net like an emergency saving fund to cover living expenses for at least six months. The problem is that the average person is too overwhelmed by the pressures of daily living to afford a respite to consider an important issue like the organization of their personal finances. The problem is that 99% of Americans feel like they are puppets of fate, flip-floppers turning and tossing in the winds of personal finance. What about you? Please, you do not have to accept your predicament as a puppet of fate; you have to rebel against your fate as a victim of financial circumstances. There is no such thing as providence governing human and financial affairs in America. Learn the mystical power of harnessing the forces of wealth. You are a child of God. Your heavenly Father wants you to be rich, so you have to choose to make your financial life anew; choose the better life of riches.

Do what 1% of America is doing to get ahead financially. Learn the art, science, and philosophy of building wealth. Become a student of $ucce$$tology. A life of wealth awaits you, but you have to prove yourself worthy. You have to obey the natural and cosmic laws governing the universe. For example, the spiritual law stipulates that God is a spirit, an infinite force of divinity who created you in his own likeness. Because you are God's likeness, you have to use the mystical techniques of cosmic consciousness to communicate with God. This advice may sound esoteric, but the goal of $ucce$$tology is about teaching you to create your own miracles;

There is more to personal finance than the drudgery of debts and budgets.

it is about showing you how you can harness the invisible forces in the cosmos for your own betterment in business or home; it is about thinking, learning, and acting. It is about taking action after developing the skills you need to have your financial dreams come true. That is the solution of $ucce$$tology. Imagine riding the waves of investing success today! What will you do with your new wealth? The teaching of $ucce$$tology is that each soul is an integral part of God, which is seeking to gain experience by repeated existences in gradually improving material bodies and that, therefore, it passes into and out of material existences many times; that each time it gathers a little more experience than it previously possessed and in time is nourished from nescience to omniscience--from impotence to omnipotence--by means of these experiences.

A GOAL OF MULTIPLE GOLD MINES

The true secret to building wealth is to understand you need to set the goal of having multiple gold mines. Each goldmine provides a form of financial security to your life. What would you do if you lost your main source of income today? As one of my students, you will learn to create many millionaire mountains to protect yourself, like:

1 Establishing your personal wealth-building machine
2 Earning $100,000 to $250,000 a year for life
3 Growing your own money tree
4 Profiting from massive trends that will make you the new millionaires
5 Developing multiple streams of income
6 Starting your very own multi-million dollar business from your kitchen table
7 Starting a home-based business for less than a thousand dollars
8 Creating a money-making machine that runs 24 hours a day, 365 days a year
9 Developing streams of income without overheard, officers, or employees
10 Tapping into the essential secrets for finding the most powerful home-based business.
11 Investing creatively in real estate
12 Modeling the examples of millionaires who made their fortunes in real estate
13 Implementing real-estate strategies that work
14 Buying a house or condo and selling it and walking away with a cash profit
15 Executing OPM, that is, the buying of millions in real estate with none of your own money.
16 Walking away from real-estate settlements with lots of cash from the table
17 Buying a home but paying no mortgage interest.
18 Seducing motivated sellers to let you live in a million dollar mansion for free
19 Profiting from government loans and grants
20 Selling information online

INFORMATION POWER

It is easy for you to become an infopreneur. I can teach you how to sell your ideas for royalties, the hottest millionaire making trend. How can you become a money-making infopreneur? In today's networked world, it easy for you to become a millionaire selling information on the Internet. Some entrepreneurs are making a thousand dollars a day selling "How To" information booklets, courses, and manuals. Here is your turn to watch how total strangers practically line up and literally beg you to take their money for your information product. You can also make money from writing. You can make $20 a word every time you sit down to write. In fact, writing is the fastest way to turn an idea into cash. If you are reading this, chances are you paid money for it, or you borrowed it from one of my customers.

STOCK MARKET MIRACLES

Have you ever considered stock investing? The smart money on Wall Street makes money whether the stock market is up or down; the foolish money on Wall Street loses money irrespective of the direction of the stock market. In this book, you will learn how to make money consistently on Wall Street, regardless of what the stock market does. You will study my stock-picking system called SRA, statistically rational analysis.

INTERNET MILLIONS

You do not have to be Mark Zuckerberg to make big money online. In fact, there are many Internet enterprises you can start from the comfort of your kitchen table and make $94,000 online in 24 hours. In my seminars and workshops, I plan to discuss my unique Internet cash strategies. I will show you how to build a small or not so small fortune on the Internet. You will be happy to moonlight at home and double your income and work less hours in your regular job. In this book, I have provided detailed information on the list of search engines, and I will share search-engine optimization techniques with you at a workshop near your hometown. I will help you build a web site, and I will reveal the secret strategies for getting people to your website.

Information is the easiest product to sell on the Internet; I promise to show you how to do it. If you believe you have what it takes to succeed with my guidance, I am going to do something special for you that you will admit is absolutely unheard of; remember, I have promised to help you by any legal means necessary to succeed; and I assume you have accepted my public challenge, so I am emphasizing that I am willing to do practically anything to help you succeed! Do you want to stop living from paycheck to paycheck? Then, this conversation is a unique and one-time opportunity for you to rise to the occasion.

Here is your chance; success is calling you, today! Will you answer the call? Stop suffering in silence. Help is only a phone call away. Dial the magic number NOW!
(301) 593-4897

DREAMING OF GETTING RICH?

Stop dreaming! Start thinking! Start growing! Start learning! Learn the magic secrets of realizing the American Dream today! Life is too short. Then, why wait to get rich in America? Now you are holding and reading the most important document that has the mystical power to change your financial life and future for the better! THE CLOSELY GUARDED MILLIONAIRE MONEY MAKING SECRETS OF AMERICA'S SUPER RICH and FAMOUS ARE ABOUT TO BE REVEALED TO YOU.

Name them: Bill Hewlett, David Packard, Bill Gates, Steve Jobs, Steve Wozniak, Alan C. Ashton, Bruce Bastian, Mitchell David Kapor, Meg Whitman, Zuckerberg, Jeff Bezos, MARC Lowell ANDREESEN, Pierre Omidyar, Steve Case, Jim Clark, Michael Dell, Larry Ellison, Andrew Carnegie, J.P. Morgan, John D. Rockefeller, Cornelius and William Vanderbilt, Henry Ford, John Paul Getty, Jay Gould, Napoleon Hill, Donald Trump, Bill Cosby, Oprah Winfrey, John H. Johnson, and others. They have all used these secrets to get rich! What about you? That is why I, Prince Ojong, the millionaire mentor, am bringing these good tidings to you.

Like Angel Gabriel, Prince Ojong is a messenger of the ancient and arcane wisdom of millionaire money-making secrets. In fact, the quest for these cosmic secrets compelled me to abandon my PhD studies in favor of the Dead Sea scrolls and philosopher stone. With Prince Ojong, the money magician, all things are possible.

Let Prince Ojong, the master Alchemist, display his King Midas' touch. Come and see the wonder of a security guard turning a $1.00 investment into a portfolio of over $1,000,000. Come to the shrine of $ucce$$tology! Become a votary at the temple of millionaire success. Learn the mystery of making big money in America. A world of riches awaits you; get the master key to riches from Prince Ojong; become God's millionaire apprentice! Are you ready to unlock the treasury of Eldorado for infinite opportunities? Dial the magic number: (301) 593-4897.

LETTER TO PROSPECTIVE WEALTH BUILDER

Dear Prospective Wealth Builder, my name is Prince Ojong. I am a former dishwasher and security guard who became a self-made millionaire by applying the money-making secrets of America's rich and famous. When I was starting out, I took an oath to emulate the examples of Prometheus and Robin Hood; I swore I would divulge the secrets of building wealth to anyone who would be interested in thinking and growing rich.

First, I created the Millionaire Club to share knowledge of investing with my fellow human beings. In fact, over the last decade, I have trained individuals JUST LIKE YOU to become financially independent through investing in real estate, stock market, insurance, and business.

Today, I am introducing $ucce$$tology, a better-organized technology of building wealth, and the Millionaire Club. When you join the Millionaire Club, you will benefit from two powerful programs of $ucce$$tology: service America and business America. You will learn how to make money without having any money. You will discover that financial independence is closer than you think.

You will see the road to the promise land, and you will know how to get there. With service America, you will begin making money from our referral network of discounted services. With business America, you will learn the money-making secrets of the rich and famous, what we have christened $ucce$$tology. Building wealth is a science, a philosophy, and an art; building wealth requires a judicious application of the principles of $ucce$$tology.

In fact, $ucce$$tology's business America program will expose you to

- ☐ Rehabbing properties and making cosmetic improvements
- ☐ Dealing with motivated buyers and sellers
- ☐ Creating cash flow and reinvesting profits into more real estate
- ☐ Finding investments through goldmine ads
- ☐ Utilizing pre-foreclosure techniques for investment
- ☐ Identifying good properties for investment
- ☐ Exploiting the higher-and-better-use technique
- ☐ Benefiting from government grants and loans
- ☐ Buying your first income-producing property in a few days
- ☐ Learning forced appreciation techniques and building sweat equity
- ☐ Selling *The Miraculous Millionaire* to your friends and family members

The above stipulation is all about making intelligent choices, based on improving cash flow and accumulating wealth through capitalizing on property equity. This idea is not exactly revolutionary, is it? It is not. What is different here is that I have developed a systematic approach that has worked for me and made me a multi-millionaire.

I am about to let you in on the techniques that I learned, and I can save you from the pain of making many of the mistakes that I made. If nothing else, after today I hope that you get a sense of the potential you have to become anything you want to be in life; all you have to do is create a system that works, and do it! You are about to learn about a program that can make you realize your financial dreams.

THINKING LIKE A MILLIONAIRE

Beginning right now, I want you to start DREAMING and THINKING like a millionaire. Are you not happy to become the next success story? The SUCCESS train is leaving the station. Would you be left behind? Here is the final call of opportunity! My Dear Potential Millionaire, I am Prince Ojong. Chances are you must have already heard my amazing and graceful story. I am a former dishwasher and security guard who parlayed the money-making secrets of the rich and famous into a large multi-million dollar fortune in real estate, stocks, bonds, technology, and business ventures. Tired of being poor and making excuses for myself, I resolved to change my financial situation. From a victim of circumstance, I became a master of my financial destiny.

Today, I live the American Dream: lots of toys that money can buy, a multi-million dollar residence atop a hill in Montgomery county fit for the principality of a prince, nice cars, bank accounts with lots of money, and many rental properties producing mountain streams of passive income.

What about you? Do not be jealous! Will you get on the way to success? Will you accept with an open mind the secrets of success conditioning? In fact, I would like to welcome you to join the Millionaire Club, where you can learn how to build wealth and amass your own personal fortune. I am talking about wealth without risk; I am talking about a lifetime of financial security and comfort for you and your family. By teaching you how to think and grow rich, I will prove to you how any individual without connections or money can rise to the level of a millionaire. Specialized knowledge, desire, and action are the objects and tools that distinguish millionaires from you. If you have the desire to be rich, I will give you the specialized knowledge you need to succeed and live a better life. I will teach you to think positive like a millionaire; I will teach you to become creative; I will teach you the philosophy of sweet are the uses of risk and adversity; I will teach you the program of success mapping and modeling. In short, here is what you will be able to do with my professional assistance:

1. Uncover surefire ways to stop living from paycheck to paycheck
2. Generate at least $1,000 in cash within 1 week
3. Establish the groundwork for a six-figure annual income in consulting
4. Erase bad credit legally and get up to $100,000 loan;
5. Obtain a $100,000 credit line
6. Build your credit power to the level of a millionaire
7. Get out of debt in 90 days
8. Buy a home with no money down and pocket up to $5,000 at your first closing or settlement
9. Start a home-based business and generate $5,000 to $10,000 in monthly income
10. Buy a car for FREE by using a simple business tip
11. Use government wealth fare, free money, giveaways, grants, and freebies
12. Build your way to wealth without any risks
13. Reduce or slash your taxes

If you have read this chapter so far, then, the odds are that for some time you may have been trying to achieve the American Dream of financial independence, but perhaps without much success and with limited funds. Perhaps you are wondering how an average guy with big dreams can start making big money. Well, I, Prince Ojong, can help you solve all your money problems. When I was struggling financially, some people dismissed me as a backstreet guy, but I did not give up on my dreams. I did not want my dreams to die like raisins in the sun. As far as I am concerned, old dreams may fade away, but old dreamers like me never die; indeed, they lie buried in the ash heap of despair, forgetfulness, and neglect. So will you bootstrap your way to riches? It all depends on you. Is success not a personal choice? Today, I am urging you to board the train of financial success, which is about to leave the station. Will you? Or will you not? See you in the paradise of the investment-club meeting for soon-to-be millionaires.

THE PRINCE OJONG STORY

The Prince Ojong story revolves around the plot of how I turned the daily habit of saving and investing $1.00 into $1,000,000. My Fellow American, I care about you. I love you. I really do! That is why I want to share the secrets of building wealth with you. In fact, you are like my neighbor; the Holy Bible exhorts me: "You shall love your neighbor as yourself." I cannot begin discussing the miracles of building wealth from just a dream of riches without telling you my life story in brief. Why? I want to reassure you that it is still possible for you to create your own American Dream of financial success. Hence, please, grant me the permission to be the first individual to address you with the title miraculous millionaire or soon-to-be millionaire. In fact, this title is not a borrowed robe; rather, it is my recognition of your hunger for success; it is my acknowledgement of the confidence that the mission of your quest will be fulfilled. After reading my story and modeling my excellence, you will find financial peace. You will be able to move financial mountains.

The American Dream! In $ucce$$tology, I explore every aspect of how to live your life in such a way that you will have security and the confidence that comes from knowing that what you have cannot be taken away from you. I focus on the most challenging money problems that make it difficult, if not impossible, for you to realize the American Dream of home, family, career, and retirement. Specifically, these challenges comprise of poverty, dreams, retirement, debts, illness, and disability. My dear friend, I have good news for you; I have a plan for you. My plan is unlike what you have seen before. Almost all self-help books consist of two varieties: pedantic theory of making money or armchair Wall Street advisor's how-to manual. My book is different; it presents a money-making system that is suffused with theory and practice that is genuine. After introducing you to theory, I introduce solutions in the form of a plan of action. Are you ready to welcome my ideas of money-making with an open mind? Are you ready to master your financial destiny? Then, let me schedule your date with destiny; let me show you the fast lane to wealth.

There is more to personal finance than the drudgery of debts and budgets.

POETRY OF IDENTITY

Who am I? My name is Prince Ojong. I am a new West African immigrant from Cameroon. I came to the United States of America on August 28, 1983, to attend graduate studies in English at The American University, 4400 Massachusetts Avenue, NW, Washington, DC 20016. Why did I choose to come to America? The plain and unvarnished truth is that I had a dream, an American Dream. Ever since I was a little boy of four years, I had nursed a burning and an unquenchable desire to come to America, the promise land of my childhood.

As I remember now, the year was 1966. In Malende, a small village located in the African nation of Cameroon, a young couple unwittingly and unknowingly introduced their young son to the ideal of the American Dream. Every week end, they took their son to a Cameroon Development Corporation (CDC) plantation to watch the movies of Charlie Chaplin and other actors of the early 1960s. The couple topped the week-end film outings with a gift to their lone son of a kiddie slide projector, which became their son's most-prized possession. Their son was enamored of beautiful cities such as New York and Los Angeles, which he had viewed on his toy projector:

"Daddy, what place is this?" [Pointing a left finger to the lens of the slide projector]

"Son, it is America!"

"America? It is very beautiful. Daddy, I want to go to America when I grow up."

To the little boy's bewilderment, his parents burst into a paroxysm of laughter. Their son swallowed hard. He told his parents he had named his toy "fine country," a Pidgin English word for America as a beautiful land. So the little boy's fascination with the images of a beautiful America gave birth to his burning desire to come to America, the land of his dreams and wonders, and start a new life in the land of opportunity. By the way, the son in question is Prince Ojong, the writer of *The Miraculous Millionaire*.

Initially, however, I had to defer my big dream because my parents did not support it. I was dying for them to take me seriously. While they had perceived my American Dream to be a childhood fantasy that would fade away like dew in the morning sun, I decided to cherish and nurture my dream.

For many years, I held the dream in the bosom of my heart; for many years I carried my dream in my soul; for many years, the dream flowed in the valleys of my mind like a river in the Amazon rainforest. All day long, I would sit alone and daydream; I would visualize the image of myself walking in America; all night long, I would dream of living a glamorous life in America.

The next time I heard the word America was at a magic show; the magician was punctuating his act with the following song: "Come and see American wonders......." As I dreamed on, I started researching America. I listened attentively to tales from Cameroonians who had studied or lived in America. As for my parents, they started using America as a gimmick to motivate me to study hard and do well in school. My father said, "If you get excellent grades in the GCE ordinary level exam, I shall send you to America." When I rushed and obtained excellent grades in the GCE ordinary level exam, my father raised the bar by one notch: "You are still young, son. Why rush to go to America? If you get excellent grades in the GCE advanced level exam, I shall send you to America." I performed a great feat; instead of spending two years in high school, I spent less than six months and sat for the GCE advanced level exam. I passed the exam with flying colors. Instantaneously, I became a local hero in Yaounde, the capital city of Cameroon. Wherever I went, I attracted the attention of parents whose children were struggling to obtain good grades in school. These parents regarded me as a wonderful role model to their children who were sometimes older than me.

I became a celebrity because of my overnight academic success, but I did not enjoy the fame for long. I became despondent when my father confessed to me that he was not yet ready for his only son to leave Cameroon for America. As I sobbed for many weeks, my father comforted me by promising to allow me to travel to America if we could reach a mutual agreement on the following terms: If I travel to America, I would return to Cameroon upon completion of my studies; during my stay in America I promise not to become politically active or marry a negress or a white girl; finally, I must obtain a bachelor's degree from Cameroon's bilingual university located in Yaounde—summa cum laude. I signed the deal grudgingly. Although I did not like the pact I signed with my father, in my mind, I calculated that a bad deal was far better than no deal at all. So long as a contract contained the provision that I would go to America, I would sign it, albeit grudgingly. Thereupon, I focused like a laser beam on completing my undergraduate studies in English at the Department of Arts and Social Sciences.

FASCINATION WITH AMERICAN PROFESSORS

During this interim, I struck up friendship with an American Fulbright scholar known as Professor George Hagerty, who introduced me to American literature and weekly reels of CBS news; he also assisted me with the process of applying for graduate admission into American universities. Professor George Hagerty used to visit my family home. On one occasion when he was visiting us, my father made the following observation to him: "You see, my son is crazy about America; I have been to New York many times when I was studying in Canada; I do not know what is wonderful about America. The students there work a lot, so I prefer that my son should stay here and study here." I also had a fascination for Dr. Linda LaRue, a sociologist who taught me a course on the poetry of identity. To this day, I remember her forays into Freudian psychology and psychoanalysis, insights I have tapped in $ucce$$tology to shed light on the workings of money and the human mind. There was also Dr. Pinkie Gordon Lane, another American professor who made a lasting impression on me. She was a fine poet. In fact, the racial undertones of her poems jerked me into the reality of America's color line before I crossed the Atlantic Ocean. In all innocence, she awakened me to the fact even in paradise there was trouble. Hence, she reminded me that there were no roses without thorns.

There is more to personal finance than the drudgery of debts and budgets.

Upon completion of studies for my first degree in 1982, I was disappointed again because, with all my excellent grades, I could not obtain admission into an American university with either a scholarship or graduate assistantship. My father advised me to enroll in the graduate program in Cameroon, but I refused because I was tired of living in Cameroon. Although I decided to accept a teaching job offer from the Cameroon government to save money for postgraduate studies, my mind was no longer in Cameroon; my physical body was in Cameroon, but my spirit was already roaming the landscape all across America. Vividly do I remember August 25, 1983; that was my lucky day; that was the day I left Cameroon to paradise. Upon I arrival in the USA, I was not completely prepared for the situation of things: culture shock. I had to grapple with the reality of making a living without the resources that had sustained me in Cameroon; verily, I was culture shocked. As I slept on the floor during those nights, I overheard echoes of the following headline reverberating huge noises and a question into my consciousness: Is coming to America an experiment that failed? I remembered Robert Frost's poem titled *Stopping by the Woods on a Snowy Evening*. I had literarily appreciated the poem many times back in Cameroon; once again, I was rehearsing the lines of the poem mechanically:

Whose woods these are I think I know.
His house is in the village though;
He will not see me stopping here
To watch his woods fill up with snow.

My little horse must think it queer
To stop without a farmhouse near
Between the woods and frozen lake
The darkest evening of the year.

He gives his harness bells a shake
To ask if there is some mistake.
The only other sound's the sweep
Of easy wind and downy flake.

The woods are lovely, dark and deep.
But I have promises to keep,
And miles to go before I sleep,
And miles to go before I sleep.

If you want to capture my state of mind during that period, I would like to refer you to my collections of poems titled *Valleys of My Mind*. Frost's poem helped me to resist the temptation of wallowing into self-pity. As I trudged on to my studies at American University, and eventually Howard University, I was always reminded of the need to put my financial house in order. But I kept on making flimsy excuses for myself because I was still a student.

AN EARTHQUAKE AND AN EPIPHANY

When my father, the primary family breadwinner, died suddenly of a heart attack, I could not continue making excuses anymore. I felt like an earthquake had hit me, and I was fortunate to be alive. From November 14, 1988, my father's date of death, I knew I had to rely exclusively on myself for financial survival in this world. My father was my anchor, my door to the world, so I had to pray to God to open a window for me to pull myself by my own bootstraps.

Before November 14, 1988, I was a boy who was almost a man. After my father's transition, I had to become a man crying *thanatopsis*. My American Dream was long deferred by my pursuit of academic knowledge. When a new seminar promoter called Russ Whitney quibbled to my Howard university professor that if making big money in America depended on academic knowledge professors would be the richest people in the country, I experienced an epiphany. Here was I attending a money-making seminar in a five-star hotel ballroom rented for $15,000 by Russ Whitney, a high-school dropout.

In fact, the *Rich Dad Poor Dad* metaphor was not lost on me here. My Howard University professor was my poor father; Russ Whitney was my rich father. While my Howard University professor held a PhD and lived poorly like me, from one paycheck to another paycheck, Russ Whitney was rich enough to afford the luxury of flying in airplanes all over America pitching his wealth-building strategies. For this reason, I made the fateful decision of suspending my doctoral studies in organizational communications and concentrating on wealth-building.

My Howard University professor had warned me that I was making a terrible mistake; my mother and sisters lamented my stubbornness and calamity, but I was adamant in my decision to refocus my research efforts to an investigation into the nature and causes of the wealth of individuals in America.

Jasper Ojongtambia, a family friend who was operating a computer services business in New York City, had just sent me an audiotape of Napoleon Hill's book titled *Think and Grow Rich*. As I listened to the audiotape, I was enthralled by the awesome power of the speaker's message and the simplicity of the delivery. I decided to buy Napoleon Hill's book; I also bought Dennis Kimbro's book. When I put down the sum of $125,000 to buy my first home in 1997, my sisters and mother were flabbergasted; indeed, my naysayers were too stunned to think. When I sold four rental properties in 2004 to buy a multi-million dollar mansion atop a hill in Maryland, my celebrity status as a mogul in the African community was established forever. Sometimes in my cheerful hour, when I look back now, I give thanks to God for making my dreams come true. I remind God that I will always to keep the promises I had made in my goal contract: if I ever succeed to become a millionaire in America, I will spend time evangelizing the success secrets of America's rich and famous so that all ambitious folks who are poor can rise up from poverty. That is my story in brief, but I am busy writing my complete story in a memoir titled *Dreams of America: the Memoir of an African Child*.

There is more to personal finance than the drudgery of debts and budgets.

So let me ask you a question rooted in the American Dream. You believe in the great American Dream. Do not you? It happened to me, a poor immigrant from Africa who still speaks English with a heavy accent, so it could happen to you. By patronizing my business, buying and reading *The Miraculous Millionaire*, you are supporting your own American dream. America! What a country! Sometimes dreams do come true if you try to work hard and follow the wealth principles presented in *The Miraculous Millionaire*.

How did I become a self-made millionaire? In fact, my claim to fame is that working as a security guard I parlayed the love of voracious reading with the daily habit of saving and investing $1.00, which grew into over $1,000,000 in less than ten years. Although my original plan was to accomplish this investment feat in seven years, I was sidetracked by the failure of my first business: the publishing of a magazine called *The Black Shopper*. As a result, I had to file for chapter 7 bankruptcy because I could no longer afford to pay my business and personal debts. I did not have the money to pay a lawyer, so I taught myself how to prepare my case pro se.

Why did my first business fail? I prefer not to blame the recession that occurred immediately after the first Gulf War; I would like to assume personal responsibility for my business failings; I had learned how to build and use consumer credit to finance my magazine business, but I did not know how to operate a magazine for profit. As a case in point, I knew how to get many new subscribers for the magazine by appealing to businesses and individuals in the African and African-American community, but I did not know how to build effective operations for distribution and advertising. As a consequence, the magazine was losing money, and I was using credit cards to prop it up. In the end, I had to close my publishing offices and return to my dingy apartment in disgrace.

While looking for a fresh financial start, I spent much time analyzing my personal and business failures. First, I learned that it was foolish to start a publishing business simply because I love writing; rather, I was supposed to ascertain that there was an adequate market need for the magazine. Second, I learned the potentially disastrous consequences of consumer debt. I had spent time learning creative and nonconventional strategies to build my credit power to a high level; I had used those credit cards to finance the purchase of a lot of furniture and computer equipment: chairs, tables, IBM PCs, printers, scanners, and software. Unfortunately, I was not making any money, so I had to start withdrawing cash advances from my credit cards.

Third, by learning how to deal with my own financial problems, I realized many of my friends and family members were wrestling with debt issues; they started treating me like a personal-finance professional. Although I was flattered by their compliments, I recognized the need to absorb as much knowledge on personal finance as I could at that time. Although I worked two jobs as a security guard and desk clerk, I spent my spare or leisure time in the public library. The underlying lesson I learned throughout my study in public libraries is the urgency to become a producer instead of a consumer to attain wealth.

As I have said already, the catalyst that catapulted me on the way to building wealth is the sudden death of my father. For so long I have been making excuses about building wealth by deceiving myself that I would return to Africa and enjoy my father's wealth. If I have been stranded on the shores of procrastination because I was pretending to be a postgraduate student, the death of my father became the earthquake that woke me up. My father's death, or its aftermath, was a moment of decision for me. This was a moment in my life when someone just turned on the switch of a light bulb; if you are looking forward to induce a similar moment of financial decision, please, look no further than my book, which shows you the expressway to extraordinary wealth that can burn a trail to financial independence faster than any road out there.

My book exposes the truth about money. It explains why jobs, 401(K)s, mutual funds, and 40-years of mindless frugality will never make you rich. You have to apply the wealth-building technology of $ucce$$tology to attain your goals. Apply the real mystical laws of wealth; leverage these laws and you will magnetize wealth to you. The leading cause of poverty is negativity; change your attitude toward money; everything around you will change.

The possession of a positive mental attitude is how the rich really get rich; indeed, a positive mental attitude has nothing to do with a fat paycheck or a huge 401(K) account. I will teach you a few lessons on the success gurus' vaunted grand deity called compounding, which is the aggregation of compound interest; compounding is a multiplier of investment returns and a potent wealth accelerator. Compounding is the fast lane of the expressway of wealth. The game of compounding works with time. In regard to your dream of riches, time is your greatest asset. Time is your friend. Time is not a tyrant. Time will make it possible for you to grow your money.

EXPRESSWAY TO WEALTH

Wealth building is a journey to a particular destination. As a soldier of fortune, I urge you to drive on the express lane, an alternative to the slow road to wealth. Please, tread on the road to riches; one that actually ignites dreams and creates millionaires young or old like you. If you are sick and tired running the race on the slow lane, please, change lanes; move over to the fast lane of success and find your explosive wealth accelerator.

That is the purpose of writing *The Miraculous Millionaire*; I want to assist you, like a teacher, coach, and mentor to hit the fast lane; crack the computer code to wealth; live rich for a lifetime. If you are a novice, my book is an excellent eye opener to the world of personal finance. The truth about personal finance is that money does not come with an instruction manual. When it comes to money, nobody is your friend. The people you typically get advice from have their hands in your pockets: brokers, bank loan officers, financial planners, auto and life insurance salespeople, and car sales people.

But I am different; my goal is to raise your level of perception. My book teaches what the average American votary at the shrine of financial success needs to understand to financially protect them in a volatile economic environment. The book sets the premise that you never learn to deal with money successfully until you overcome your fear of money: of not having enough and fear of taking action with your money. It is about how to make money work for you so you have more than enough because you learn to devote energy, time, and understanding, to money. Indeed, as *The Miraculous Millionaire* shows, I have researched America's financial elite and how they became very rich. My book is great because it allows you to revisit human psychology and explore the teachings of Sigmund Freud on the working of the human mind: the id, ego, superego, the subconscious, and your childhood money messages that are sabotaging your chance of becoming wealthy.

The recurrent theme of my book is the premise that your mind is the incubation of thoughts that can make you rich. Thoughts are energy; thoughts can be transmitted in the form of energy. Your thoughts can lead you to action; by contrast, your thoughts can result in inaction, like the example of William Shakespeare's *Hamlet*. Too much thinking leads to inaction or procrastination. My book is great because it is replete with excellent examples of real life scenarios, as well as my personal experiences. As a self-made millionaire, I am teaching you how to become rich. As a votary at the shrine Christian mysticism, I believe fervently that thoughts lead to feelings, which lead to actions, which lead to results.

Hence, the master key to riches or attaining great wealth begins in the conscious mind and subconscious mind with thinking and growing. That is the lesson I learned from Napoleon Hill; that is the lesson all rich people claim to be true. After reading my book, you will discover the new technology of success conditioning, which I have christened $ucce$$tology: the art, philosophy, and science of recreating the American Dream today. In fact, new ways of thinking and acting will lead you to new, positive, and different results. My thesis is the proposition that financial success is a learnable skill; financial success is a game; you, too, can learn to succeed at anything if you put your mind in it. My book regurgitates the principles for amassing wealth that lie buried in many voluminous tomes of personal-finance literature. Finally, I have to plug an obvious infomercial for my seminars, coaching sessions, and training workshops. If you are serious about implementing the ideas propounded in my book, please, come to my seminars. Indeed, even if you disagree with all of my ideas, you will be honest in admitting that my book offers thought-provoking advice and valuable insight.

STUDENT WEAKNESSES

I am afraid to tell you that your financial foible is a kind of mental illness, one I already have a ready set of cures. Let us travel on memory lane to your childhood. I want to address the potentially disastrous results of your superego. Think back to your childhood days! Imagine and visualize those days. Identify the money lessons you passively learned from your parents and society.

For this reason, your slavish attitude toward money is rooted in your childhood socialization process. Your parents and society allowed a negative attitude toward money to enter your mind. As you grew older, this negativism became material in your life, a self-fulfilling prophecy. This is the reason why I am encouraging you to admire the rich and famous; do not resent them! Be positive! Do not wallow in self-abnegation and small-mindedness. I will offer insights into millionaires' pinch-penny ways, so that you should learn to model their financial excellence.

I will focus much attention on the key characteristics that explain how the elite club of millionaires became wealthy. As a surprise, you will discover that the fundamental qualities of these millionaires are diametrically opposed to today's earn-and-consume popular culture of living above your financial means. I will show you how to allocate your funds efficiently in ways that build wealth. I will advise you to ignore your friends who are keeping up with the Joneses; I will dissuade you from engaging in conspicuous consumption. If you are in the wrong profession, I will counsel you to be proficient in targeting marketing opportunities and choosing the right occupation. It is evident that anyone can accumulate wealth, if they are disciplined enough, determined to persevere, and have the merest of luck. Ordinary folks can accumulate wealth. Do the ideas presented in the book work for average or ordinary working-class folks? You bet! Yes! The average Joe, Jack, and Jill can benefit from $ucce$$tology. In fact, secretaries, dishwashers, security guards, desk clerks, firefighters, retired naval officers, housewives, construction workers, schoolteachers, and pharmacists can become wealthy if they change their daily money habits per the recommendations of the book. Remember that these ideas were honed when I was fighting in the trenches of poverty as a laboring dishwasher in Washington, DC, and a security guard in Alexandria, Virginia.

Additionally, while I was pursing my PhD in organizational communications, I was spending my spare time in university and county libraries studying the wealth-making habits of America's rich and famous. In the course of my business career, I have shared my winning methods and practical money formula with hundreds of ordinary Americans.

Today, I am revealing my findings in this extraordinary book that outlines in twelve easy, practical steps the secrets to achieving and maintaining wealth. Here you will find a lifetime of wealth-building experience from people just like me -- people who have figured out how to arrange their finances and make wise investment decisions so that they can reach their goals and achieve financial security.

MILLIONAIRE TRIBE

Who wants to be a millionaire? If you asked the average American who wants to be a millionaire, he or she will jump high and scream ME. Then he or she will probably imagine and dream about the millionaire lifestyle. *The Miraculous Millionaire* is real life, not a reality television show. Instead of quizzing you about trivia, I have to bombard you with real-life questions pertaining to the arcane discipline of personal finance. Parlez vous Quicken? What is the famous accountant's secret?

Can you solve the following equation: ASSETS=LIABILITIES+EQUITY? Are you a gambler? Are you divorce-prone? Do you savor conspicuous consumption? What is the difference between a profit and loss and an income statement? What is a balance sheet? How many millionaires shop at Brooks Brothers? Millionaires! Who are they? What success factor made them wealthy in one generation? What part did luck and school grades play in their success? How do they find the courage to take financial risks? How did they find the ideal vocations? What are their spouses like and how did they choose them? How do they run their households? How do they buy and sell their homes? What are their favorite leisure activities? What is the millionaire's secret? What is the meaning of the word wealthy?

Have you ever entertained thoughts of becoming wealthy? The meaning of wealthy indicates a great deal about who you are. A few years ago, a friend invited me to the Montgomery Country Club, Chevy Chase, Maryland, for a meeting with some high net worth individuals. The wealthy at country clubs talk about a person's net worth, but the members of the middle class at other environments talk about getting a raise; and the poor folks talk about making it by playing the lottery. The same folks pretend that "Oh! Money is not that important." My natural reaction is predictable: I tap the palm of my left hand on my forehead as I say, "Oh! I get it. You are broke!"

RICH AND POOR VISION

Shall we compare the rich to the poor? The most common assertions of comparison are the following:

1. While rich people believe in recreating the realities of their lives, poor people believe life happens to them.
 2. Whereas rich people play the money game offensively to win, poor people, who assume defensive postures, play the money game to not lose.
3. While rich people are committed to being rich, poor people want or wish to be rich.
4. Whereas rich people think big, poor people think small.
5. Rich people focus on opportunities; by contrast, poor people focus on obstacles.
 6. Rich people admire rich and successful people, but poor people resent rich and successful people.
7. Rich people associate with positive, successful people, but poor people associate with negative or unsuccessful people.
8. While rich people are willing to promote themselves and their values, poor people think negatively about selling and self-promotion.
9. Rich people think they are bigger than their problems, but poor people feel they are smaller than their problems.
10. Rich people are excellent receivers; poor people are poor receivers.
11. Rich people choose to get paid based on results, but poor people choose to get paid based on time.
12. Rich people think in terms of the duality of both, but poor people think in terms of either/or.
13. Rich people create their living balance sheet and focus on their net worth. Poor people, who fail to plan or balance their books, focus on their working income.
14. Rich people manage their money well; poor people mismanage their money well.

15. Rich people have their money work hard for them. Poor people work hard for their money.
16. Rich people act in spite of fear. Poor people let fear stop them.
17. Rich people constantly learn and grow. Poor people think they already know.

WEALTH CREATION PLAN

How can an average guy in the world of today get money to become rich in America? Of course, my personal experience and research in personal finance shows that there are three ways of getting money in this world: first, you can get a job and work for money; second, you can inherit big money by marrying rich or you can receive a gift from an angel; third, you can begin by developing the good financial habit of saving at least $1.00 per day and investing the money you save like me. In fact, the cultivated and consistent habits of saving and investing are the most powerful and respectful ways to get rich by pulling yourself up by your own bootstraps. Like the number of the disciplines of Jesus Christ, I have presented twelve steps that will guide you to financial freedom:

Step 1 Pay God first
Step 2 Discover the millionaire's secret
Step 3 Use insurance as your foundation of wealth
Step 4 Teach yourself personal finance
Step 5 Balance your financial book
Step 6 Computerize and research the Internet
Step 7 Acquire entrepreneurial skills
Step 8 Decode the IRS tax codes
Step 9 Play the stock market game
Step 10 Invest in real estate
Step 11 Join the Millionaire Club
Step 12 Attend the Millionaire iUniversity

A PYRAMID OF RICHES

Paychecks make it difficult for you to climb the pyramid of riches. There is a millionaire inside of you. I want to show you how to get him or her out, The secret of how to become rich is to stop climbing pyramids, running the rat race and living from paycheck to paycheck. Start building a pyramid of riches. Pyramid builders get rich; pyramid climbers go broke, so help spread the gospel the good news of $ucce$$tology $ecret$. Stop the prostitution of Monday through Friday! Get off the slow lane of working jobs; get on the fast lane of business prosperity. The average person sacrifices his or her hands to work for money, smart people use tools, systems, and machines. I am offering a push-button system. Motivational gurus sell you a collection of useless manuals; indeed, that is slave labor, a trade of your precious time for money in a job you most likely hate; that is like telling you to climb a pyramid.

There is more to personal finance than the drudgery of debts and budgets.

My solution is to offer you a chance to build and own the pyramid. If you choose my pyramid building system, then, you slave to create a machine THAT WILL DO THE WORK FOR YOU. You can be disciplined, passionate, committed, and positive, as every motivational speaker says, but all those motivational feel-good pieces are irrelevant without the idea of building and ownership. What are you doing different today to build and own the future? Do you know the big secret behind making money? It has nothing to do with money! People always talk about making big money, but no one ever talks about the economics and physics of money; that is, what really causes money to exchange hands. If you want to make money, the law of nature states that there is no such thing as getting something for nothing; you have to create value in the marketplace and convince someone to open their wallet and give it to you.

THE CASE OF BILL GATES

Do you want to become as rich as Bill Gates? Lesson one is that you should choose your grandparents carefully. In this wise, there are three ways to make money: you can inherit it; you can marry it; or you can steal it. As an example, William Henry Gates III made his best decision on October 28, 1955, the night he was born. He chose J.W. Maxwell as his great-grandfather. Maxwell founded Seattle's National City Bank in 1906. His son, James Willard Maxwell was also a banker and established a million-dollar trust fund for William (Bill) Henry Gates III. In some of the later lessons, you will be encouraged to take entrepreneurial risks. You may find it comforting to remember that at any time you can fall back on a trust fund worth many millions of 1998 dollars.

Lesson two is that you should, like Bill Gates, choose your parents carefully. They must be affluent. William Henry Gates, Jr. and Mary Maxwell were among Seattle's social and financial elite. Bill Gates, Jr. was a prominent corporate lawyer while Mary Maxwell was a board member of First Interstate Bank and Pacific Northwest Bell. She was also on the national board of United Way, along with John Opel, the chief executive officer of IBM who approved the inclusion of MS/DOS with the original IBM PC. Remind your parents not to send you to public school. Bill Gates went to Lakeside, Seattle's most exclusive preparatory school where tuition in 1967 was $5,000. Bill Gates' parents had sent him to Harvard University; Harvard tuition that year was $1760. Typical classmates of Bill Gates included the McCaw brothers, who sold the cellular phone licenses they obtained from the U.S. Government to AT&T for $11.5 billion in 1994. When the children there wanted to use a computer, they asked their mothers to hold a rummage sale and raise $3,000 to buy time on a DEC PDP-10, the same machine used by computer science researchers at Stanford and MIT.

A second example of choosing a good family is Donald J. Trump. It is important for you to recall that in the 1980s America venerated Donald Trump and studied his book titled *The Art of the Deal*. If Donald Trump had taken the millions he inherited from his father and put it all into mutual funds, you would never have had to suffer through the indignities of one of his books. But he would be just about as rich today.

Lesson three is for you to acquire research results by hiring and buying valuable tools. As an example, conventional economic wisdom holds that monopolies should spend heavily on research because they are in a position to capture the fruits of the research. But if you want to become as rich as Bill Gates, you have to remember that it is cheaper to wait for a small company like Netscape to come up with something good and then buy or destroy them. In the old days, antitrust laws kept monopolies from buying potential competitors. But not anymore! When Microsoft products were threatened by network computers and web-based applications, they simply bought Hotmail. Another good strategy is to hire the right people. Some of the guys who wrote Microsoft Windows had previously worked on window systems at Xerox PARC, so Xerox paid for the research; Microsoft paid only for development. In the long run, a technology company without research facilities probably cannot sustain its market leadership, so you will eventually need to build something like research.microsoft.com.

Lesson four is for you to let other people do the programming. If you are a great engineer, it can be frustrating to rely on other people to translate your ideas into reality. However, keep in mind that the entire Indian subcontinent is learning Java, and that if Microsoft, Oracle, SAP, and Sun products simply worked and worked simply, half of the world's current IT workers would be out of a job. You are not going to get rich being just a coder, especially working in painful low-level imperative languages such as C or Java. It might be worth writing your own SQL queries and HTML pages since these tend to be compact and easier than precisely specifying the work for another person to do. But basically you need to get good at thinking about whether a piece of software is doing something useful for the adopting organization and end-user. Bill Gates does code reviews, not coding. If you are not sure that you need to be filthy rich and like to do some coding, remember you are the big boss.

Lesson five is for you to train your new CEO to replace you in the end. That is what Steve Jobs did with Apple before his demise. If you are an intelligent and curious person, it can be painful to run a company of more than 50 people. You spend more time than you would like repeating yourself, sitting in boring meetings, skimming over long legal documents in which you know there are errors but you are not sure how serious. The temptation is to hand over the reins to the first professional manager who comes along. And that is what the standard venture capitalist formula dictates, but Bill Gates did not do that; he hired Steve Ballmer in 1980 and gave him the CEO job 20 years later. Making money in the software products business requires domain expertise and a commitment to solving problems within that domain. Great technology companies are seldom built by non-technical management or professional managers who are not committed to anything more than their paycheck. Adobe is a third example. The two founders were PhD computer science researchers from Xerox PARC who were passionate about solving problems in the publishing and graphics world. They are still guiding operations at Adobe. Remember that this is a principle that Old Economy companies have long understood; for instance, Jack Welch joined GE in 1961 and became CEO 20 years later. Sometimes an Old Economy company may invite a few outsiders to senior positions but, because they have such stable bureaucracies underneath, they can more easily afford this than startups.

Lesson six is for you to focus on profit. Remembering to make a profit was tough in the dotcom 1990s but it turns out that Hewlett and Packard's ideas were right; most of the management teams at dotcom businesses, by being disorganized, unintelligent, and ignorant, were subtracting value from the resources that they controlled. How does one make money in the software products business? Simple! The necessary step is to build something that becomes part of information systems that generate value for organizations and end-users. Once you have created value you can extract a portion in lots of ways. You can be closed-source and charge a license fee. You can be open-source and charge for training, service, support, and extensions. But if you are not getting your software product into important information systems, you do not have a prayer, no matter how slick are your marketing materials. If you are creative and diligent, the software products business is extremely lucrative. If you are losing money, ask yourself what you are doing wrong. The answer is probably plenty.

Lesson seven is for you to let the venture capitalists schmooze Wall Street, but do not let them run your company. A profitable Microsoft Corporation brought in venture capitalists at the last minute. They did not need or spend the money but used the venture capitalists to boost their valuation at the initial public offering, thus getting more money for the shares that they sold. Venture capitalists are dangerous because even the most successful might not know anything about business. Remember that there are tens of thousands of venture capitalists in this world. Assuming that they make random choices of companies in which to invest there will be a Gaussian curve of performance. Some firms will do consistently better than average even if everyone is guessing. The bottom line is that successful software products companies spend most of their time listening to their customers and users rather than to venture capitalists.

MEANING OF $UCCE$$TOLOGY

Welcome to the magical world of $ucce$$tology. In your hands you are holding the master key to riches. $ucce$$tology is a new technology of personal achievement developed by me, Prince Ojong. A drop-out of the Howard University PhD program in organizational communications, I am an American success story. A poor immigrant from Africa, today, I have succeeded in realizing the American dream. Starting out as a dishwasher and secrity guard, I have succeeded in rising from poverty to the level of a self-made millionaire. How? By applying millionaire secrets in my personal life! In fact, these money-making secrets were revealed to me by divine design, personal experience, and self-study.

Tired of making excuses for myself, I decided to learn the money-making secrets of the rich and famous. In publicizing the secrets that worked for me, I christened these esoteric truths and specialized knowledge $ucce$$tology. The nature, end, and purpose of $ucce$$tology is to train students to become God's millionaire apprentices. What is $ucce$$tology? A Science! A Philosophy! An Art! $ucce$$tology is the science, philosophy, and art of achieving the American dream of success.

$UCCE$$TOLOGY AS A SCIENCE

If science is perceived to be an orderly or systematic study of nature, then, $ucce$$tology is a science. $ucce$$tology utilizes the scientific method to demonstrate how an average individual can apply the moneymaking secrets of America's rich and famous folks: observation, classification, and analysis. My dictionary tells me that the word *science* is a noun: in Middle English, *science* is knowledge and learning, that is, from Old French and Latin *scientia*. Therefore, science is the observation, identification, description, experimental investigation, and theoretical explanation of phenomena. Similarly, $ucce$$tology pertains to such activities restricted to a class of natural phenomena, or such activities applied to an object of inquiry or study. $ucce$$tology uses methodological activity, discipline, and study. In fact, I have packed a suitcase replete with moneymaking secrets down to a science. Hence, if you want to succeed, you have to adhere to activities that appear to require study. When I open it, you will acquire knowledge, especially the variety of specialized knowledge that is gained through experience.

$UCCE$$TOLOGY AS A PHILOSOPHY

$ucce$$tology is a philosophy. My dictionary tells me that the word philosophy is a noun: Middle English philosophie, from Old French. Literally, therefore, philosophy is the love of, including the search after, wisdom; in actual current usage, philosophy is the knowledge of phenomena as explained by, and resolved into, causes and reasons, powers and laws. Philosophy is a belief, or system of beliefs, accepted as authoritative by some group or school. Philosophy is a doctrine or a school of thought; philosophy is the rational investigation of questions about existence and knowledge and ethics; philosophy is any personal belief about how to live or how to deal with a situation.

When applied to any particular department of knowledge like $ucce$$tology, philosophy denotes the general laws or principles under which all the subordinate phenomena or facts relating to that subject are comprehended. Thus philosophy, when applied to God and the divine government, is called theology; when applied to material objects, it is called physics; when it treats of man, it is called anthropology and psychology, with which are connected logic and ethics; when it treats of the necessary conceptions and relations by which philosophy is possible, it is called metaphysics.

$UCCE$$TOLOGY AS AN ART

$uce$$tology is an art. Fundamentally, art is the creation of natural beauty. An artist, like God, is the creator of beauty—the artificer. My dictionary tells me that art is a noun. Synonyms of art include craft, expertise, knack, know-how, and technique. These nouns denote skill in doing or performing that is attained by study, practice, or observation: the art of rhetoric; pottery that reveals an artist's craft; political expertise; a knack for teaching; mechanical know-how; a precise diving technique.

Art is a human effort to imitate, supplement, alter, or counteract the work of nature. Art is the conscious production or arrangement of sounds, colors, forms, movements, or other elements in a manner that affects the sense of beauty, specifically the production of the beautiful in a graphic or plastic medium. Art is the study of the activities mentioned above. Art is the product of these activities; art is a human work of beauty considered as a group. Art is the aesthetic value and high quality of conception or execution, as found in works of beauty; there are fields or categories of art, such as music, ballet, or literature. Art can also denote a system of principles and methods employed in the performance of a set of activities: the art of building.

Similarly, a trade or craft that applies such a system of principles and methods may be considered as art; for example, the art of the lexicographer, the art of painting, the art of writing, and the art of $ucce$$tology. Skills that are attained by study, practice, or observation of a master artist of wealth-creation may be defined as art. With the study of $ucce$$tology, you, my student is like an apprentice studying the art of the baker or the blacksmith's art. A skill arising from the student or apprentice exercising his or her intuitive faculties is art.

It takes long time for artists to learn, practice, and perfect their craft or hone their skills. It took me many years of trial-and-error drudgery to master the art of making big money, but today I can teach them to you in a very short time. These artful devices, stratagems, contrivances, and tricks are what people refer to as the cunning secrets of the artist. Now that I have introduced you to the meaning of the building blocks of $ucce$$tology, I have almost set the ground game to reveal the millionaire's secret to you. As you study the superstructure of the American capitalist society, please, pay attention to its artistic import. In fact, you can see it in the three stages of the American capitalism: agrarian economy, industrial economy, and information economy. May this artistic beauty attract you to establish a home-based business with low-capital services.

Step 1
PAY GOD FIRST

"To want as little as possible is to make the greatest approach to God."

What should you do to model my success in do-it-yourself personal finance? PAY GOD FIRST. First and foremost, you must accept an invitation to God. As a child of God, your first initiative must be to take the faltering step of walking into the presence of your heavenly Father; you will not be walking alone; in fact, the Holy Spirit will be with you. However, if you are already a devout Christian, you must commit yourself to be born again; that is, fulfilling Jesus Christ's mission on earth. Perhaps it is appropriate for me to underscore the primacy of God with a prayer. Why? In my mind, prayer is the best way to introduce you to the first chapter of *The Miraculous Millionaire*:

I confess to almighty God, and to you, my brothers and sisters, that I have sinned through my own fault, in my thoughts and in my words, in what I have done, and in what I have failed to do; and I ask blessed Mary, ever virgin, all the angels and saints, and you, my brothers and sisters, to pray for me to the Lord our God.

There is more to personal finance than the drudgery of debts and budgets.

I believe in God. I am passionate about Jesus Christ. In step two, you will discover the mysterious millionaire's money-making secret, but step one is the most important chapter in *The Miraculous Millionaire*. In the first chapter, I discuss the importance of God and the sources of my enabling belief. Unquestionably, in reshaping our lives for the better, faith in God is the superlative belief. Show me a very successful individual who does not believe in God, and I will show you a clever fool. As a case in point, even the self-effacing Governor Willard Mitt Romney has had to proclaim, hesitatingly, his strong faith in God. He is a Mormon (The Church of Jesus Christ of Latter-day Saints), but I, like many other Americans, love and accept him with open arms as my brother in Jesus Christ. Similarly, I am a Roman Catholic Christian. I was born a Catholic, and I will die a Catholic. All my life, as a mystic, I have labored to be a charismatic believer in Jesus Christ; I have sought to comprehend the mystery of life and transcend the infinite cosmos and the oneness of God; I believe in the holy trinity; that is, God is a triumvirate: God the Father, God the Son, and God the Holy Spirit. I believe in the fall of the first man and woman in the Garden of Eden; I believe in original sin and the holy sacraments; I do not worship the Virgin Mary, but I venerate the mother of Jesus Christ, and I am looking forward to the second coming of our savior and Lord Jesus Christ.

Unlike pompous financial gurus, I am telling you, humbly, that I am unworthy to coach you to become a miraculous millionaire. In fact, I need divine intervention to help you realize your financial goal. Those who are familiar with self-help literature may remember the following rule of personal finance: pay yourself first. Indeed, it is rare to read a financial book without the author recommending that you should pay yourself first. Usually, the technique has many variations; while some authors advise you to allocate 10% of your income to savings, others require you to save as much as 25%. Today, I, Prince Ojong, have decided to challenge that conventional wisdom. To say the least, it is lunacy to take care of your needs without recognizing the primacy of God, your creator. God must be first; you must be second. How can you receive preferment from God if you reduce your own maker to the status of a second-class citizen? My canon, therefore, is PAY GOD FIRST! When you receive your income, pay God first; give 10% of your income to your church before worrying about yourself. I have the authority of the scriptures to justify my first law of personal development or self achievement:

Mathew 6:26-34
Look at the birds of the air, that they do not sow, nor reap nor gather into barns, and yet your heavenly Father feeds them. Are you not worth much more than they? And who of you by being worried can add a single hour to his life? And why are you worried about clothing? Observe how the lilies of the field grow; they do not toil nor do they spin, yet I say to you that not even Solomon in all his glory clothed himself like one of these. But if God so clothes the grass of the field, which is alive today and tomorrow is thrown into the furnace, will He not much more clothe you? You of little faith! Do not worry then, saying, 'What will we eat?' or 'What will we drink?' or 'What will we wear for clothing?' For the Gentiles eagerly seek all these things; for your heavenly Father knows that you need all these things. But seek first His kingdom and His righteousness, and all these things will be added to you. So do not worry about tomorrow; for tomorrow will care for itself. Each day has enough trouble of its own.

Are you still in doubt? Fine! If you are in doubt, I urge you to discuss this matter with your priest or pastor. Whatever he or she tells you, please, remember that the Holy bible makes the requirements of tithing and offering. I would like to share a few quotes with you:

2 Corinthians 9:7
"Each one must give as he has decided in his heart, not reluctantly or under compulsion, for God loves a cheerful giver."

Malachi 3:10
"Bring the full tithe into the storehouse, that there may be food in my house. And thereby put me to the test, says the Lord of hosts, if I will not open the windows of heaven for you and pour down for you a blessing until there is no more need."

Proverbs 11:24
"One gives freely, yet grows all the richer; another withholds what he should give, and only suffers want.."

Mark 12:41-44
"And he sat down opposite the treasury and watched the people putting money into the offering box. Many rich people put in large sums. And a poor widow came and put in two small copper coins, which make a penny. And he called his disciples to him and said to them, "Truly, I say to you, this poor widow has put in more than all those who are contributing to the offering box. For they all contributed out of their abundance, but she out of her poverty has put in everything she had, all she had to live on."

2 Corinthians 9:6-7
"The point is this: whoever sows sparingly will also reap sparingly, and whoever sows bountifully will also reap bountifully. Each one must give as he has decided in his heart, not reluctantly or under compulsion, for God loves a cheerful giver."

Luke 6:38
"Give, and it will be given to you. Good measure, pressed down, shaken together, running over, will be put into your lap. For with the measure you use it will be measured back to you."

Proverbs 3:9
"Honour the Lord with your wealth and with the first fruits of all your produce."

Malachi 3:8-10
"Will man rob God? Yet you are robbing me. But you say, 'How have we robbed you?' In your tithes and contributions. You are cursed with a curse, for you are robbing me, the whole nation of you. Bring the full tithe into the storehouse, that there may be food in my house. And thereby put me to the test, says the Lord of hosts, if I will not open the windows of heaven for you and pour down for you a blessing until there is no more need."

There is more to personal finance than the drudgery of debts and budgets.

Matthew 6:1-4
"Beware of practicing your righteousness before other people to be seen by them, for then you will have no reward from your Father who is in heaven. "Thus, when you give to the needy, sound no trumpet before you, as the hypocrites do in the synagogues and in the streets, that they may be praised by others. Truly, I say to you, they have received their reward. But when you give to the needy, do not let your left hand know what your right hand is doing, so that your giving may be in secret. And your Father who sees in secret will reward you."

Proverbs 3:9-10
"Honour the Lord with your wealth and with the first fruits of all your produce; then your barns will be filled with plenty, and your vats will be bursting with wine."

Malachi 3:8-12
"Will man rob God? Yet you are robbing me. But you say, 'How have we robbed you?' In your tithes and contributions. You are cursed with a curse, for you are robbing me, the whole nation of you. Bring the full tithe into the storehouse, that there may be food in my house. And thereby put me to the test, says the Lord of hosts, if I will not open the windows of heaven for you and pour down for you a blessing until there is no more need. I will rebuke the devourer for you, so that it will not destroy the fruits of your soil, and your vine in the field shall not fail to bear, says the Lord of hosts. Then all nations will call you blessed, for you will be a land of delight, says the Lord of hosts."

Acts 20:35
"In all things I have shown you that by working hard in this way we must help the weak and remember the words of the Lord Jesus, how he himself said, 'It is more blessed to give than to receive.'"

Psalm 4:5
"Offer right sacrifices, and put your trust in the Lord."

1 Corinthians 16:2
"On the first day of every week, each of you is to put something aside and store it up, as he may prosper, so that there will be no collecting when I come."

Leviticus 27:30
"Every tithe of the land, whether of the seed of the land or of the fruit of the trees, is the Lord's; it is holy to the Lord."

Luke 16:10
"One who is faithful in a very little is also faithful in much, and one who is dishonest in a very little is also dishonest in much."

Luke 21:1-4
"Jesus looked up and saw the rich putting their gifts into the offering box, and he saw a poor

widow put in two small copper coins. And he said, "Truly, I tell you, this poor widow has put in more than all of them. For they all contributed out of their abundance, but she out of her poverty put in all she had to live on."

Matthew 6:33
"But seek first the kingdom of God and his righteousness, and all these things will be added to you."

Genesis 14:20
"And blessed be God Most High, who has delivered your enemies into your hand!" And Abram gave him a tenth of everything."

Philippians 4:19
"And my God will supply every need of yours according to his riches in glory in Christ Jesus."

Romans 13:7
"Pay to all what is owed to them: taxes to whom taxes are owed, revenue to whom revenue is owed, respect to whom respect is owed, honour to whom honour is owed."

2 Corinthians 8:1-9:15
"We want you to know, brothers, about the grace of God that has been given among the churches of Macedonia, for in a severe test of affliction, their abundance of joy and their extreme poverty have overflowed in a wealth of generosity on their part. For they gave according to their means, as I can testify, and beyond their means, of their own accord, begging us earnestly for the favour of taking part in the relief of the saints— and this, not as we expected, but they gave themselves first to the Lord and then by the will of God to us."

Luke 11:42
"But woe to you Pharisees! For you tithe mint and rue and every herb, and neglect justice and the love of God. These you ought to have done, without neglecting the others."

Job 41:11
"Who has first given to me, that I should repay him? Whatever is under the whole heaven is mine."

Deuteronomy 14:22
"You shall tithe all the yield of your seed that comes from the field year by year."

Malachi 3:8
"Will man rob God? Yet you are robbing me. But you say, 'How have we robbed you?' In your tithes and contributions."

Leviticus 27:30-34
"Every tithe of the land, whether of the seed of the land or of the fruit of the trees, is the Lord's; it is holy to the Lord. If a man wishes to redeem some of his tithe, he shall add a fifth to it. And

every tithe of herds and flocks, every tenth animal of all that pass under the herdsman's staff, shall be holy to the Lord. One shall not differentiate between good or bad, neither shall he make a substitute for it; and if he does substitute for it, then both it and the substitute shall be holy; it shall not be redeemed."

Deuteronomy 14:22-29
"You shall tithe all the yield of your seed that comes from the field year by year. And before the Lord your God, in the place that he will choose, to make his name dwell there, you shall eat the tithe of your grain, of your wine, and of your oil, and the firstborn of your herd and flock, that you may learn to fear the Lord your God always. And if the way is too long for you, so that you are not able to carry the tithe, when the Lord your God blesses you, because the place is too far from you, which the Lord your God chooses, to set his name there, then you shall turn it into money and bind up the money in your hand and go to the place that the Lord your God chooses and spend the money for whatever you desire—oxen or sheep or wine or strong drink, whatever your appetite craves. And you shall eat there before the Lord your God and rejoice, you and your household."

Matthew 6:21
"For where your treasure is, there your heart will be also."

Genesis 14:18-20
"And Melchizedek king of Salem brought out bread and wine. (He was priest of God Most High.) And he blessed him and said, "Blessed be Abram by God Most High, Possessor of heaven and earth; and blessed be God Most High, who has delivered your enemies into your hand!" And Abram gave him a tenth of everything."2 Corinthians 8:1-5
"We want you to know, brothers, about the grace of God that has been given among the churches of Macedonia, for in a severe test of affliction, their abundance of joy and their extreme poverty have overflowed in a wealth of generosity on their part. For they gave according to their means, as I can testify, and beyond their means, of their own accord, begging us earnestly for the favour of taking part in the relief of the saints— and this, not as we expected, but they gave themselves first to the Lord and then by the will of God to us."

Matthew 23:23
"Woe to you, scribes and Pharisees, hypocrites! For you tithe mint and dill and cumin, and have neglected the weightier matters of the law: justice and mercy and faithfulness. These you ought to have done, without neglecting the others."

Hebrews 7:1-9
"For this Melchizedek, king of Salem, priest of the Most High God, met Abraham returning from the slaughter of the kings and blessed him, and to him Abraham apportioned a tenth part of everything. He is first, by translation of his name, king of righteousness, and then he is also king of Salem, that is, king of peace. He is without father or mother or genealogy, having neither beginning of days nor end of life, but resembling the Son of God he continues a priest forever. See how great this man was to whom Abraham the patriarch gave a tenth of the spoils! And those descendants of Levi who receive the priestly office have a commandment in the law to take

tithes from the people, that is, from their brothers, though these also are descended from Abraham."

Psalm 50:7-12
"Hear, O my people, and I will speak; O Israel, I will testify against you. I am God, your God. Not for your sacrifices do I rebuke you; your burnt offerings are continually before me. I will not accept a bull from your house or goats from your folds. For every beast of the forest is mine, the cattle on a thousand hills. I know all the birds of the hills, and all that moves in the field is mine. "

Numbers 18:21
"To the Levites I have given every tithe in Israel for an inheritance, in return for their service that they do, their service in the tent of meeting. "

Hebrews 7:1-28
"For this Melchizedek, king of Salem, priest of the Most High God, met Abraham returning from the slaughter of the kings and blessed him, and to him Abraham apportioned a tenth part of everything. He is first, by translation of his name, king of righteousness, and then he is also king of Salem, that is, king of peace. He is without father or mother or genealogy, having neither beginning of days nor end of life, but resembling the Son of God he continues a priest forever. See how great this man was to whom Abraham the patriarch gave a tenth of the spoils! And those descendants of Levi who receive the priestly office have a commandment in the law to take tithes from the people, that is, from their brothers, though these also are descended from Abraham."

Malachi 3:1-18
"Behold, I send my messenger, and he will prepare the way before me. And the Lord whom you seek will suddenly come to his temple; and the messenger of the covenant in whom you delight, behold, he is coming, says the Lord of hosts. But who can endure the day of his coming, and who can stand when he appears? For he is like a refiner's fire and like fullers' soap. He will sit as a refiner and purifier of silver, and he will purify the sons of Levi and refine them like gold and silver, and they will bring offerings in righteousness to the Lord. Then the offering of Judah and Jerusalem will be pleasing to the Lord as in the days of old and as in former years. "Then I will draw near to you for judgment. I will be a swift witness against the sorcerers, against the adulterers, against those who swear falsely, against those who oppress the hired worker in his wages, the widow and the fatherless, against those who thrust aside the sojourner, and do not fear me, says the Lord of hosts."

Genesis 28:20-22
"Then Jacob made a vow, saying, "If God will be with me and will keep me in this way that I go, and will give me bread to eat and clothing to wear, so that I come again to my father's house in peace, then the Lord shall be my God, and this stone, which I have set up for a pillar, shall be God's house. And of all that you give me I will give a full tenth to you."

There is more to personal finance than the drudgery of debts and budgets.

Numbers 18:26
"Moreover, you shall speak and say to the Levites, 'When you take from the people of Israel the tithe that I have given you from them for your inheritance, then you shall present a contribution from it to the Lord, a tithe of the tithe."

1 Corinthians 9:13-14
"Do you not know that those who are employed in the temple service get their food from the temple, and those who serve at the altar share in the sacrificial offerings? In the same way, the Lord commanded that those who proclaim the gospel should get their living by the gospel."

Nehemiah 10:38
"And the priest, the son of Aaron, shall be with the Levites when the Levites receive the tithes. And the Levites shall bring up the tithe of the tithes to the house of our God, to the chambers of the storehouse."

Philippians 2:17
"Even if I am to be poured out as a drink offering upon the sacrificial offering of your faith, I am glad and rejoice with you all."

Exodus 25:2
"Speak to the people of Israel, that they take for me a contribution. From every man whose heart moves him you shall receive the contribution for me."

2 Chronicles 31:5-12
"As soon as the command was spread abroad, the people of Israel gave in abundance the first fruits of grain, wine, oil, honey, and of all the produce of the field. And they brought in abundantly the tithe of everything. And the people of Israel and Judah who lived in the cities of Judah also brought in the tithe of cattle and sheep, and the tithe of the dedicated things that had been dedicated to the Lord their God, and laid them in heaps. In the third month they began to pile up the heaps, and finished them in the seventh month. When Hezekiah and the princes came and saw the heaps, they blessed the Lord and his people Israel. And Hezekiah questioned the priests and the Levites about the heaps."

Mark 7:9-13
"And he said to them, "You have a fine way of rejecting the commandment of God to establish your tradition! For Moses said, 'Honour your father and your mother'; and, 'Whoever reviles father or mother must surely die.' But you say, 'If a man tells his father or his mother, "Whatever you would have gained from me is Corban"' (that is, given to God)— then you no longer permit him to do anything for his father or mother, thus making void the word of God by your tradition that you have handed down. And many such things you do."

Philippians 1:5
"Because of your partnership in the gospel from the first day until now."

Luke 18:12
"I fast twice a week; I give tithes of all that I get."

Hebrews 7:8
"In the one case tithes are received by mortal men, but in the other case, by one of whom it is testified that he lives."

2 Corinthians 8:12
"For if the readiness is there, it is acceptable according to what a person has, not according to what he does not have."

Deuteronomy 14:28-29
"At the end of every three years you shall bring out all the tithe of your produce in the same year and lay it up within your towns. And the Levite, because he has no portion or inheritance with you, and the sojourner, the fatherless, and the widow, who are within your towns, shall come and eat and be filled, that the Lord your God may bless you in all the work of your hands that you do."

Leviticus 27:32
"And every tithe of herds and flocks, every tenth animal of all that pass under the herdsman's staff, shall be holy to the Lord."

1 Timothy 5:17-18
"Let the elders who rule well be considered worthy of double honour, especially those who labour in preaching and teaching. For the Scripture says, "You shall not muzzle an ox when it treads out the grain," and, "The labourer deserves his wages."

Amos 4:4
"Come to Bethel, and transgress; to Gilgal, and multiply transgression; bring your sacrifices every morning, your tithes every three days."

Genesis 4:1-26
"Now Adam knew Eve his wife, and she conceived and bore Cain, saying, "I have gotten a man with the help of the Lord." And again, she bore his brother Abel. Now Abel was a keeper of sheep, and Cain a worker of the ground. In the course of time Cain brought to the Lord an offering of the fruit of the ground, and Abel also brought of the firstborn of his flock and of their fat portions. And the Lord had regard for Abel and his offering, but for Cain and his offering he had no regard. So Cain was very angry, and his face fell."

Haggai 2:8
"The silver is mine, and the gold is mine, declares the Lord of hosts."

Isaiah 1:16-20
"Wash yourselves; make yourselves clean; remove the evil of your deeds from before my eyes;

There is more to personal finance than the drudgery of debts and budgets.

cease to do evil, learn to do good; seek justice, correct oppression; bring justice to the fatherless, plead the widow's cause. "Come now, let us reason together, says the Lord: though your sins are like scarlet, they shall be as white as snow; though they are red like crimson, they shall become like wool. If you are willing and obedient, you shall eat the good of the land; but if you refuse and rebel, you shall be eaten by the sword; for the mouth of the Lord has spoken."

Deuteronomy 14:23
"And before the Lord your God, in the place that he will choose, to make his name dwell there, you shall eat the tithe of your grain, of your wine, and of your oil, and the firstborn of your herd and flock, that you may learn to fear the Lord your God always."

Genesis 28:22
"And this stone, which I have set up for a pillar, shall be God's house. And of all that you give me I will give a full tenth to you."

Acts 11:27-29
"Now in these days prophets came down from Jerusalem to Antioch. And one of them named Agabus stood up and foretold by the Spirit that there would be a great famine over all the world (this took place in the days of Claudius). So the disciples determined, everyone according to his ability, to send relief to the brothers living in Judea."

John 3:16
"For God so loved the world, that he gave his only Son, that whoever believes in him should not perish but have eternal life."

Luke 18:10-14
"Two men went up into the temple to pray, one a Pharisee and the other a tax collector. The Pharisee, standing by himself, prayed thus: 'God, I thank you that I am not like other men, extortioners, unjust, adulterers, or even like this tax collector. I fast twice a week; I give tithes of all that I get.' But the tax collector, standing far off, would not even lift up his eyes to heaven, but beat his breast, saying, 'God, be merciful to me, a sinner!' I tell you, this man went down to his house justified, rather than the other. For everyone who exalts himself will be humbled, but the one who humbles himself will be exalted."

Matthew 28:19-20
"Go therefore and make disciples of all nations, baptizing them in the name of the Father and of the Son and of the Holy Spirit, teaching them to observe all that I have commanded you. And behold, I am with you always, to the end of the age."

2 Corinthians 1:1-24
"Paul, an apostle of Christ Jesus by the will of God, and Timothy our brother, To the church of God that is at Corinth, with all the saints who are in the whole of Achaia: Grace to you and peace from God our Father and the Lord Jesus Christ. Blessed be the God and Father of our Lord Jesus Christ, the Father of mercies and God of all comfort, who comforts us in all our affliction, so that we may be able to comfort those who are in any affliction, with the comfort with which

we ourselves are comforted by God. For as we share abundantly in Christ's sufferings, so through Christ we share abundantly in comfort too."

1 Corinthians 13:3
If I give away all I have, and if I deliver up my body to be burned, but have not love, I gain nothing."

Acts 4:34-35
"There was not a needy person among them, for as many as were owners of lands or houses sold them and brought the proceeds of what was sold and laid it at the apostles' feet, and it was distributed to each as any had need."

Isaiah 40:9
"Get you up to a high mountain, O Zion, herald of good news; lift up your voice with strength, O Jerusalem, herald of good news; lift it up, fear not; say to the cities of Judah, "Behold your God!"

Psalm 24:1
"A Psalm of David. The earth is the Lord's and the fullness thereof, the world and those who dwell therein."

Acts 15:4-5
"When they came to Jerusalem, they were welcomed by the church and the apostles and the elders, and they declared all that God had done with them. But some believers who belonged to the party of the Pharisees rose up and said, "It is necessary to circumcise them and to order them to keep the law of Moses.""

Malachi 3:3
"He will sit as a refiner and purifier of silver, and he will purify the sons of Levi and refine them like gold and silver, and they will bring offerings in righteousness to the Lord."

Psalm 1:3
"He is like a tree planted by streams of water that yields its fruit in its season, and its leaf does not wither. In all that he does, he prospers."

1 Samuel 8:11-18
"He said, "These will be the ways of the king who will reign over you: he will take your sons and appoint them to his chariots and to be his horsemen and to run before his chariots. And he will appoint for himself commanders of thousands and commanders of fifties, and some to plow his ground and to reap his harvest, and to make his implements of war and the equipment of his chariots. He will take your daughters to be perfumers and cooks and bakers. He will take the best of your fields and vineyards and olive orchards and give them to his servants. He will take the tenth of your grain and of your vineyards and give it to his officers and to his servants."

Numbers 18:24
"For the tithe of the people of Israel, which they present as a contribution to the Lord, I have

given to the Levites for an inheritance. Therefore I have said of them that they shall have no inheritance among the people of Israel."

Numbers 18:20-24
"And the Lord said to Aaron, "You shall have no inheritance in their land, neither shall you have any portion among them. I am your portion and your inheritance among the people of Israel. "To the Levites I have given every tithe in Israel for an inheritance, in return for their service that they do, their service in the tent of meeting, so that the people of Israel do not come near the tent of meeting, lest they bear sin and die. But the Levites shall do the service of the tent of meeting, and they shall bear their iniquity. It shall be a perpetual statute throughout your generations, and among the people of Israel they shall have no inheritance. For the tithe of the people of Israel, which they present as a contribution to the Lord, I have given to the Levites for an inheritance. Therefore I have said of them that they shall have no inheritance among the people of Israel."

Genesis 14:1-24
"In the days of Amraphel king of Shinar, Arioch king of Ellasar, Chedorlaomer king of Elam, and Tidal king of Goiim, these kings made war with Bera king of Sodom, Birsha king of Gomorrah, Shinab king of Admah, Shemeber king of Zeboiim, and the king of Bela (that is, Zoar). And all these joined forces in the Valley of Siddim (that is, the Salt Sea). Twelve years they had served Chedorlaomer, but in the thirteenth year they rebelled. In the fourteenth year Chedorlaomer and the kings who were with him came and defeated the Rephaim in Ashteroth-karnaim, the Zuzim in Ham, the Emim in Shaveh-kiriathaim."

Philippians 3:3-6
"For we are the circumcision, who worship by the Spirit of God and glory in Christ Jesus and put no confidence in the flesh— though I myself have reason for confidence in the flesh also. If anyone else thinks he has reason for confidence in the flesh, I have more: circumcised on the eighth day, of the people of Israel, of the tribe of Benjamin, a Hebrew of Hebrews; as to the law, a Pharisee; as to zeal, a persecutor of the church; as to righteousness under the law, blameless."

Deuteronomy 14:2
"For you are a people holy to the Lord your God, and the Lord has chosen you to be a people for his treasured possession, out of all the peoples who are on the face of the earth."

Deuteronomy 26:12
"When you have finished paying all the tithe of your produce in the third year, which is the year of tithing, giving it to the Levite, the sojourner, the fatherless, and the widow, so that they may eat within your towns and be filled."

Deuteronomy 18:4
"The first fruits of your grain, of your wine and of your oil, and the first fleece of your sheep, you shall give him."

Numbers 18:28
"So you shall also present a contribution to the Lord from all your tithes, which you receive from the people of Israel. And from it you shall give the Lord's contribution to Aaron the priest."

Numbers 18:26-28
"Moreover, you shall speak and say to the Levites, 'When you take from the people of Israel the tithe that I have given you from them for your inheritance, then you shall present a contribution from it to the Lord, a tithe of the tithe. And your contribution shall be counted to you as though it were the grain of the threshing floor, and as the fullness of the winepress. So you shall also present a contribution to the Lord from all your tithes, which you receive from the people of Israel. And from it you shall give the Lord's contribution to Aaron the priest."

Exodus 19:5
"Now therefore, if you will indeed obey my voice and keep my covenant, you shall be my treasured possession among all peoples, for all the earth is mine."

Revelation 2:1-29
"To the angel of the church in Ephesus write: 'The words of him who holds the seven stars in his right hand, who walks among the seven golden lampstands. "'I know your works, your toil and your patient endurance, and how you cannot bear with those who are evil, but have tested those who call themselves apostles and are not, and found them to be false. I know you are enduring patiently and bearing up for my name's sake, and you have not grown weary. But I have this against you, that you have abandoned the love you had at first. Remember therefore from where you have fallen; repent, and do the works you did at first. If not, I will come to you and remove your lampstand from its place, unless you repent."

1 Timothy 6:10
"For the love of money is a root of all kinds of evils. It is through this craving that some have wandered away from the faith and pierced themselves with many pangs."

1 Corinthians 16:1-2
"Now concerning the collection for the saints: as I directed the churches of Galatia, so you also are to do. On the first day of every week, each of you is to put something aside and store it up, as he may prosper, so that there will be no collecting when I come."

Matthew 7:21-23
"Not everyone who says to me, 'Lord, Lord,' will enter the kingdom of heaven, but the one who does the will of my Father who is in heaven. On that day many will say to me, 'Lord, Lord, did we not prophesy in your name, and cast out demons in your name, and do many mighty works in your name?' And then will I declare to them, 'I never knew you; depart from me, you workers of lawlessness."

Deuteronomy 14:28
"At the end of every three years you shall bring out all the tithe of your produce in the same year and lay it up within your towns."

There is more to personal finance than the drudgery of debts and budgets.

Deuteronomy 14:22-26
"You shall tithe all the yield of your seed that comes from the field year by year. And before the Lord your God, in the place that he will choose, to make his name dwell there, you shall eat the tithe of your grain, of your wine, and of your oil, and the firstborn of your herd and flock, that you may learn to fear the Lord your God always. And if the way is too long for you, so that you are not able to carry the tithe, when the Lord your God blesses you, because the place is too far from you, which the Lord your God chooses, to set his name there, then you shall turn it into money and bind up the money in your hand and go to the place that the Lord your God chooses and spend the money for whatever you desire—oxen or sheep or wine or strong drink, whatever your appetite craves. And you shall eat there before the Lord your God and rejoice, you and your household."

Deuteronomy 8:17-18
"Beware lest you say in your heart, 'My power and the might of my hand have gotten me this wealth.' You shall remember the Lord your God, for it is he who gives you power to get wealth, that he may confirm his covenant that he swore to your fathers, as it is this day."

Numbers 18:25-31
"And the Lord spoke to Moses, saying, "Moreover, you shall speak and say to the Levites, 'When you take from the people of Israel the tithe that I have given you from them for your inheritance, then you shall present a contribution from it to the Lord, a tithe of the tithe. And your contribution shall be counted to you as though it were the grain of the threshing floor, and as the fullness of the winepress. So you shall also present a contribution to the Lord from all your tithes, which you receive from the people of Israel. And from it you shall give the Lord's contribution to Aaron the priest. Out of all the gifts to you, you shall present every contribution due to the Lord; from each its best part is to be dedicated."

2 Timothy 3:16-17
"All Scripture is breathed out by God and profitable for teaching, for reproof, for correction, and for training in righteousness, that the man of God may be competent, equipped for every good work."

Galatians 3:10
"For all who rely on works of the law are under a curse; for it is written, "Cursed be everyone who does not abide by all things written in the Book of the Law, and do them.""

1 Corinthians 11:30
"That is why many of you are weak and ill, and some have died."

Romans 11:35
"Or who has given a gift to him that he might be repaid?"

Acts 2:1-47
"When the day of Pentecost arrived, they were all together in one place. And suddenly there

came from heaven a sound like a mighty rushing wind, and it filled the entire house where they were sitting. And divided tongues as of fire appeared to them and rested on each one of them. And they were all filled with the Holy Spirit and began to speak in other tongues as the Spirit gave them utterance. Now there were dwelling in Jerusalem Jews, devout men from every nation under heaven."

John 20:17
"Jesus said to her, "Do not cling to me, for I have not yet ascended to the Father; but go to my brothers and say to them, 'I am ascending to my Father and your Father, to my God and your God.'"

John 5:24
"Truly, truly, I say to you, whoever hears my word and believes him who sent me has eternal life. He does not come into judgment, but has passed from death to life."

Matthew 5:23
"So if you are offering your gift at the altar and there remember that your brother has something against you."

Isaiah 53:5-6
"But he was wounded for our transgressions; he was crushed for our iniquities; upon him was the chastisement that brought us peace, and with his stripes we are healed. All we like sheep have gone astray; we have turned—every one—to his own way; and the Lord has laid on him the iniquity of us all."

Nehemiah 12:44
"On that day men were appointed over the storerooms, the contributions, the first fruits, and the tithes, to gather into them the portions required by the Law for the priests and for the Levites according to the fields of the towns, for Judah rejoiced over the priests and the Levites who ministered."

Deuteronomy 14:22-27
"You shall tithe all the yield of your seed that comes from the field year by year. And before the Lord your God, in the place that he will choose, to make his name dwell there, you shall eat the tithe of your grain, of your wine, and of your oil, and the firstborn of your herd and flock, that you may learn to fear the Lord your God always. And if the way is too long for you, so that you are not able to carry the tithe, when the Lord your God blesses you, because the place is too far from you, which the Lord your God chooses, to set his name there, then you shall turn it into money and bind up the money in your hand and go to the place that the Lord your God chooses and spend the money for whatever you desire—oxen or sheep or wine or strong drink, whatever your appetite craves. And you shall eat there before the Lord your God and rejoice, you and your household."

James 1:27
"Religion that is pure and undefiled before God, the Father, is this: to visit orphans and widows in their affliction, and to keep oneself unstained from the world."

Acts 15:19-20
"Therefore my judgment is that we should not trouble those of the Gentiles who turn to God, but should write to them to abstain from the things polluted by idols, and from sexual immorality, and from what has been strangled, and from blood."

Isaiah 1:1-31
"The vision of Isaiah the son of Amoz, which he saw concerning Judah and Jerusalem in the days of Uzziah, Jotham, Ahaz, and Hezekiah, kings of Judah. Hear, O heavens, and give ear, O earth; for the Lord has spoken: "Children have I reared and brought up, but they have rebelled against me. The ox knows its owner, and the donkey its master's crib, but Israel does not know, my people do not understand." Ah, sinful nation, a people laden with iniquity, offspring of evildoers, children who deal corruptly! They have forsaken the Lord, they have despised the Holy One of Israel, they are utterly estranged. Why will you still be struck down? Why will you continue to rebel? The whole head is sick, and the whole heart faint."

Genesis 28:1-22
"Then Isaac called Jacob and blessed him and directed him, "You must not take a wife from the Canaanite women. Arise, go to Paddan-aram to the house of Bethuel your mother's father, and take as your wife from there one of the daughters of Laban your mother's brother. God Almighty bless you and make you fruitful and multiply you, that you may become a company of peoples. May he give the blessing of Abraham to you and to your offspring with you, that you may take possession of the land of your sojournings that God gave to Abraham!" Thus Isaac sent Jacob away. And he went to Paddan-aram, to Laban, the son of Bethuel the Aramean, the brother of Rebekah, Jacob's and Esau's mother."

Galatians 6:16
"And as for all who walk by this rule, peace and mercy be upon them, and upon the Israel of God."

Luke 16:13-15
"No servant can serve two masters, for either he will hate the one and love the other, or he will be devoted to the one and despise the other. You cannot serve God and money." The Pharisees, who were lovers of money, heard all these things, and they ridiculed him. And he said to them, "You are those who justify yourselves before men, but God knows your hearts. For what is exalted among men is an abomination in the sight of God."

Malachi 4:4
"Remember the law of my servant Moses, the statutes and rules that I commanded him at Horeb for all Israel."

Malachi 3:9
"You are cursed with a curse, for you are robbing me, the whole nation of you."

Deuteronomy 27:1-26
"Now Moses and the elders of Israel commanded the people, saying, "Keep the whole commandment that I command you today. And on the day you cross over the Jordan to the land that the Lord your God is giving you, you shall set up large stones and plaster them with plaster. And you shall write on them all the words of this law, when you cross over to enter the land that the Lord your God is giving you, a land flowing with milk and honey, as the Lord, the God of your fathers, has promised you. And when you have crossed over the Jordan, you shall set up these stones, concerning which I command you today, on Mount Ebal, and you shall plaster them with plaster. And there you shall build an altar to the Lord your God, an altar of stones. You shall wield no iron tool on them."

Galatians 3:24
"So then, the law was our guardian until Christ came, in order that we might be justified by faith."

Romans 1:16
"For I am not ashamed of the gospel, for it is the power of God for salvation to everyone who believes, to the Jew first and also to the Greek."

Acts 15:1-2
"But some men came down from Judea and were teaching the brothers, "Unless you are circumcised according to the custom of Moses, you cannot be saved." And after Paul and Barnabas had no small dissension and debate with them, Paul and Barnabas and some of the others were appointed to go up to Jerusalem to the apostles and the elders about this question."

John 1:1-15
"In the beginning was the Word, and the Word was with God, and the Word was God. He was in the beginning with God. All things were made through him, and without him was not anything made that was made. In him was life, and the life was the light of men. The light shines in the darkness, and the darkness has not overcome it."

Matthew 10:8
"Heal the sick, raise the dead, cleanse lepers, cast out demons. You received without paying; give without pay."

Psalm 50:12
"If I were hungry, I would not tell you, for the world and its fullness are mine."

Job 19:25
"For I know that my Redeemer lives, and at the last he will stand upon the earth."

There is more to personal finance than the drudgery of debts and budgets.

Deuteronomy 26:13
"Then you shall say before the Lord your God, 'I have removed the sacred portion out of my house, and moreover, I have given it to the Levite, the sojourner, the fatherless, and the widow, according to all your commandment that you have commanded me. I have not transgressed any of your commandments, nor have I forgotten them.'"

Exodus 20:15
"You shall not steal."

1 Corinthians 9:14
"In the same way, the Lord commanded that those who proclaim the gospel should get their living by the gospel."

John 19:30
"When Jesus had received the sour wine, he said, "It is finished," and he bowed his head and gave up his spirit."

Matthew 15:1-9
"Then Pharisees and scribes came to Jesus from Jerusalem and said, "Why do your disciples break the tradition of the elders? For they do not wash their hands when they eat." He answered them, "And why do you break the commandment of God for the sake of your tradition? For God commanded, 'Honour your father and your mother,' and, 'Whoever reviles father or mother must surely die.' But you say, 'If anyone tells his father or his mother, "What you would have gained from me is given to God.""

Galatians 6:9
"And let us not grow weary of doing good, for in due season we will reap, if we do not give up."

1 Samuel 8:1-22
"When Samuel became old, he made his sons judges over Israel. The name of his firstborn son was Joel, and the name of his second, Abijah; they were judges in Beersheba. Yet his sons did not walk in his ways but turned aside after gain. They took bribes and perverted justice. Then all the elders of Israel gathered together and came to Samuel at Ramah and said to him, "Behold, you are old and your sons do not walk in your ways. Now appoint for us a king to judge us like all the nations.""

2 Corinthians 6:9
"As unknown, and yet well known; as dying, and behold, we live; as punished, and yet not killed."

Ecclesiastes 5:4-5
"When you vow a vow to God, do not delay paying it, for he has no pleasure in fools. Pay what you vow. It is better that you should not vow than that you should vow and not pay."

Psalm 34:19
"Many are the afflictions of the righteous, but the Lord delivers him out of them all."

3 John 1:2
"Beloved, I pray that all may go well with you and that you may be in good health, as it goes well with your soul."

1 Kings 17:8-24
"Then the word of the Lord came to him, "Arise, go to Zarephath, which belongs to Sidon, and dwell there. Behold, I have commanded a widow there to feed you." So he arose and went to Zarephath. And when he came to the gate of the city, behold, a widow was there gathering sticks. And he called to her and said, "Bring me a little water in a vessel, that I may drink." And as she was going to bring it, he called to her and said, "Bring me a morsel of bread in your hand." And she said, "As the Lord your God lives, I have nothing baked, only a handful of flour in a jar and a little oil in a jug. And now I am gathering a couple of sticks that I may go in and prepare it for myself and my son, that we may eat it and die."

Acts 10:2
"A devout man who feared God with all his household, gave alms generously to the people, and prayed continually to God."

Matthew 7:11
"If you then, who are evil, know how to give good gifts to your children, how much more will your Father who is in heaven give good things to those who ask him!"

Deuteronomy 16:17
"Every man shall give as he is able, according to the blessing of the Lord your God that he has given you."

Genesis 22:2
"He said, "Take your son, your only son Isaac, whom you love, and go to the land of Moriah, and offer him there as a burnt offering on one of the mountains of which I shall tell you.""

John 10:10
"The thief comes only to steal and kill and destroy. I came that they may have life and have it abundantly."

Haggai 1:2-4
"Thus says the Lord of hosts: These people say the time has not yet come to rebuild the house of the Lord." Then the word of the Lord came by the hand of Haggai the prophet, "Is it a time for you yourselves to dwell in your panelled houses, while this house lies in ruins?""

1 Kings 1:1-53
""Now King David was old and advanced in years. And although they covered him with clothes, he could not get warm. Therefore his servants said to him, "Let a young woman be sought for

There is more to personal finance than the drudgery of debts and budgets.

my lord the king, and let her wait on the king and be in his service. Let her lie in your arms, that my lord the king may be warm." So they sought for a beautiful young woman throughout all the territory of Israel, and found Abishag the Shunammite, and brought her to the king. The young woman was very beautiful, and she was of service to the king and attended to him, but the king knew her not. Now Adonijah the son of Haggith exalted himself, saying, "I will be king." And he prepared for himself chariots and horsemen, and fifty men to run before him.""

If you have read the biblical quotes above, it means that you are ready now to apply the theories and principles postulated in step one, PAY GOD FIRST. As far as I am concerned, the first step of getting rich is the establishment of a close relationship with God, the infinite force of divinity. The labor of getting rich is an odyssey that surpasses the potential of an ordinary mortal; you must summon the millionaire inside your being; you must seek the help of an external or supepower: divine assistance; you must stop being earth-bound like the unworthy; you must aspire to touch the miraculous curtain of heaven. You must ask God to become the driver of your automobile of financial success. You are a mortal human being. Your spirit may be willing to soar and touch the skies, but your body is weak. You are incapable of driving the car of riches on your own. As your Father, God is able and willing to drive the car for you. Just ask God to do it for you. Dial His cellular phone number. Pay God First! Surrender yourself to God. Please God!

Literally, you have to discover your spirituality. As a human being, you are a duality: you have a physical dimension and a spiritual self. As a human being, you are like the battery of an automobile; like a battery, you need to be charged from time to time; God is the electrical charger. Your vital life force attunes you to God's invisible cosmos. Vital life force is an electric nerve energy, which is vibratory in nature. As a human entity, your human aura reveals you are a generator of psychic energy; your thoughts are a form or expression of psychic energy. If you are not aware of these experiences and facts, it is because you are still stuck in the time warp of the physical dimension of being. Yet, you have to cultivate the unlimited power of your spiritual self. I call this process psychic development, the cultivation of your autonomic nervous system to such high attunement that it becomes more and more sensitive to all higher rates of vibrations from within and from without your human body.

The specialized knowledge in this book is the master key you need to start up or jump start your psychic system. Like a car key, *The Miraculous Millionaire* can show you how to use your fingers to touch zones of your anatomy that are very sensitive in a spiritual sense; you can begin igniting the fire of your psychic energy. I will reveal simple experiments you can use to build your spiritual potential. I know the most sensitive areas of the human anatomy that generate psychic energy.

Time, space, and mind have to be in concord agreement with the laws of the cosmic, emanating from divine consciousness. By this explanation, I am stressing the primordial essence of the divine in your personal success. If you want to become the architect of your spiritual destiny today, you must begin to pay God first. By making God the priority of your life, you are paying God first; by living your daily life in accord with the natural laws of the cosmos, you are truly paying God first; by allocating 10% of your income to God (tithing), you are putting God first; you are making God the driver of the car of your life.

Why pay God first? As a human being, you owe your existence to the will, grace, and providence of God. The heavenly Father is your maker. Like the choirs of angels singing at heaven's gate, you have to demonstrate you love God the way God loves you. Before you can re-program your brains like a human computer and code your way to fame and riches, you must ask for God's blessings. If you do not seek divine permission, then, you are behaving like the foolish man who built his house on sandy soil.

God made you. He created you to function better than any supercomputer made by IBM and Apple on planet earth; as a human being making use of his or her brains, you can think naturally and creatively; by contrast, even the best supercomputers cannot compare with your raw human power, Every day, please, thank God for giving you the gift of life. Thank God for giving you a natural and infinite mind that beats the computer. You are better than a supercomputer. With all the progress and advances made in science, technology, engineering, and mathematics, we have yet to break the barrier of cloning a perfectly natural brain. In fact, all neural studies have failed and fallen short of intuitively imitating the human mind.

LAW OF SACRIFICE

God's universe operates like a clock. In order for you to derive many benefits from the universe, you must understand the natural laws that bind you to the visible and invisible cosmos. One such canon is the law of sacrifice; by offering tithes to God, therefore, you are starving yourself; you are acting and behaving in accord with the law of sacrifice. Hence, to want as little as possible is to make the greatest approach to God, your mission on planet earth.

Did you know your life is a mission? Did you know you ought to be a missionary of, by, and for Jesus Christ? Are you fulfilling God's purpose on earth? Well, think about it. In a few weeks, it will be December 25, 2012, and we shall, as usual, be celebrating Christmas, the birthday of Jesus Christ of Nazareth. Like many Christians, I have developed a love affair with Christmas from years of childhood. Year after year, I have awaited Christmas with the devotion and unbroken concentration of a Christian mystic at prayer. I have looked forward to gifts from Santa Claus. I have savored the pleasures of gifts from many well-wishers, too.

By contrast, in retrospect, as a little boy, I was perturbed by my parents' refusal to enjoy Christmas like me. I remembered I once told my parents I never wanted to grow up because I wanted to continue enjoying Christmas. Indeed, most Christian children of my generation and beyond have been corrupted by a materialist interpretation of Christmas. Although years of adolescence and adulthood in Africa diverted my attention away from preoccupation with the crass materialism of Christmas celebrations, many years of living in America took me back to the time of hectic celebration of Christmas. The materialism of modern American society has hijacked Christmas, giving the nativity of Jesus Christ, a spiritual event, a wholly material hew and orientation. Many businesses, especially retailers, herald Christmas season as their most profitable time of the year.

I think Christmas should be a time of love, reflection, meditation, and spiritual preoccupation. As a departure from tradition, this year my family has decided to reduce the scale of our Christmas celebration. Although we plan to be merry and buy gifts for all our guests, we have decided also to downsize our Christmas budget. As one of my college professors once told me, "to want as little as possible is to make the greatest approach to God."

Additionally, we have decided to implement one subtle change, too: to impress upon our guests the religious significance of Christmas. As we remember and celebrate the birthday of Jesus, let us also recommit ourselves to be better disciples of Jesus Christ. As apostles of Christ, let us submit ourselves to the will of God and live our lives according to the Holy bible, the true word of God. In this vein, the bible teaches us that there is a duality in Christian life: the material and the spiritual. Since we have spent the entire year engrossed in materialism, let us spend the remaining days of 2012 engrossed in spiritual reflection.

Practically, I am asking you to receive an assignment from me: stand and look in the mirror and tell me what you see. You may see the reflection of either a man or woman. Do you like the image in the mirror? If the image has been fulfilling God's mission on earth, in this life, you would, certainly, love that image. Chances are that the man or woman in the mirror is still a sinner, a plaything of fate tossing in the wild wind of the wicked wilderness. In fact, that is why I want to show you how to become the architect of your true and spiritual destiny. The mastery of life comes to those who have learned how to harness the divine forces of the infinite cosmos. Spiritual illumination and cosmic consciousness come to votaries at the shrine of the ancient and arcane wisdom of the sages.

Indeed, that is the secret knowledge I teach in my money-making seminars titled $ucce$$tology. Are you happy with your relationship with God? Have you learned how to live your daily life in concord relationship with the metaphysics of God's natural laws? Will you welcome $ucce$$tology with an open mind? You see, $ucce$$tology is the art, philosophy, and science of success conditioning in all phases of life. If you are hankering after spiritual enlightenment, you would appreciate this chapter of $ucce$$tology entitled "PAY GOD FIRST." Meaningful success can only come to those who worship God; hence, success is by the HOLY BIBLE. Are you not tired of living your life like a victim of circumstances? There should be no such thing as providence governing your human affairs. You should be in charge of your life.

Buoyed on by this explanation, before December 25, 2012, I have chosen to introduce you to a few divine laws germane to assisting you rise from the status of a blind puppet of fate to a clairvoyant and master of life. First, there is the law of cosmic creation, the law of Moses. Do you abide by the law of cosmic creation? The Book of Genesis must have taught you much about the origin of the creation. You must have learned how God created the world. The universe is akin to God's clock, and you can espy the transcendentalist and invisible hands of divinity in the manner in which natural phenomena work themselves out. But have you ever cogitated on the art, philosophy, and science of the holy creation? How much do you know of Moses? Did you know Moses wrote more than five books? While giving you some food for thought, I would like to refresh your memory with the Ten Commandments:

""And God spake all these words, saying, I am the LORD thy God, which have brought thee out of the land of Egypt, out of the house of bondage. Thou shalt have no other gods before me. Thou shalt not make unto thee any graven image, or any likeness of anything that is in heaven above, or that is in the earth beneath, or that is in the water under the earth. Thou shalt not bow down thyself to them, nor serve them: for I the LORD thy God am a jealous God, visiting the iniquity of the fathers upon the children unto the third and fourth generation of them that hate me; And shewing mercy unto thousands of them that love me, and keep my commandments. Thou shalt not take the name of the LORD thy God in vain; for the LORD will not hold him guiltless that taketh his name in vain. Remember the Sabbath day, to keep it holy. Six days shalt thou labor, and do all thy work: But the seventh day is the Sabbath of the LORD thy God: in it thou shalt not do any work, thou, nor thy son, nor thy daughter, thy manservant, nor thy maidservant, nor thy cattle, nor thy stranger that is within thy gates: For in six days the LORD made heaven and earth, the sea, and all that in them is, and rested the seventh day: wherefore the LORD blessed the Sabbath day, and hallowed it. Honor thy father and thy mother: that thy days may be long upon the land which the LORD thy God giveth thee. Thou shalt not kill. Thou shalt not commit adultery. Thou shalt not steal. Thou shalt not bear false witness against thy neighbor. Thou shalt not covet thy neighbor's house, thou shalt not covet thy neighbor's wife, nor his manservant, nor his maidservant, nor his ox, nor his ass, nor any thing that is thy neighbor's. And all the people saw the thunderings, and the lightnings, and the noise of the trumpet, and the mountain smoking: and when the people saw it, they removed, and stood afar off. And they said unto Moses, Speak thou with us, and we will hear: but let not God speak with us, lest we die. And Moses said unto the people, Fear not: for God is come to prove you, and that his fear may be before your faces, that ye sin not. And the people stood afar off, and Moses drew near unto the thick darkness where God was. And the LORD said unto Moses, Thus thou shalt say unto the children of Israel, Ye have seen that I have talked with you from heaven. Ye shall not make with me gods of silver, neither shall ye make unto you gods of gold. An altar of earth thou shalt make unto me, and shalt sacrifice thereon thy burnt offerings, and thy peace offerings, thy sheep, and thine oxen: in all places where I record my name I will come unto thee, and I will bless thee. And if thou wilt make me an altar of stone, thou shalt not build it of hewn stone: for if thou lift up thy tool upon it, thou hast polluted it. Neither shalt thou go up by steps unto mine altar, that thy nakedness be not discovered thereon.""

There is more to personal finance than the drudgery of debts and budgets.

Second, there is the law of cosmic consciousness. Through biblical immersion, spiritual attunement, and psychic development you can achieve cosmic consciousness. How aware are you about the existence of God? WHAT ON EARTH ARE YOU HERE FOR? WHAT IS THE MEANING OF LIFE? SHOULD HUMAN LIFE BE AN ABSURD DRAMA? Heaven helps those who ask and seek, so why do some people choose to suffer in silence? Please, spend a few minutes to rationalize and address the above stipulated questions. In fact, such a mental exercise might become the genesis of your extrasensory initiation, the goal of this chapter of *The Miraculous Millionaire*. If, after reading this book, you can learn to rise from the earthly plane of existence to the celestial sanctum, the realm of a higher consciousness, I would be happy to have contributed toward your oneness with God, the infinite force of divinity. Oneness with God is one of the fundamental doctrines of $ucce$$tology. The thesis of $ucce$$tology is that each soul is an integral part of God, which is seeking to gain purifying experience by repeated initiatives in gradually improving material deeds and that, therefore, it passes into and out of spiritual spheres many times; that each time it gathers a little more experience than it previously possessed and in time is nourished from nescience to omniscience--from impotence to omnipotence--by means of these spiritual experiences.

The most basic question you face in life right now is the following: Why am I here? What is my purpose? Self-help books suggest that you should look within, at your own desires and dreams, but I am saying the starting place must be with God and the divine or eternal purposes for your life. Real meaning and significance come from understanding and fulfilling God's purposes for putting us on earth. In *The Miraculous Millionaire*, I want to take this groundbreaking message of God and go deeper and deeper; applying it to your lifestyle as an individual Christian. I want you to understand God's incredible plan for your life. I want to enable you see to the big picture of what life is all about and begin to live the life God created you to live. Hence, I want you to welcome this chapter as a manifesto for Christian living today, I am advocating a lifestyle based on God's eternal purposes, not the debased spiritual or cultural values prevalent in the Sodom and Gomorrah of our time. Let biblical stories in the Holy Bible speak for themselves.

According to Rick Warren, I want you to remember God's five purposes for you:

1.   -- You were born for God's pleasure, so your first purpose is to offer real worship.
2.   -- You were trained for God's family, so your second purpose is to enjoy real fellowship.
3.   -- You were raised to become like Christ, so your third purpose is to learn real discipleship.
4.   -- You were educated to serve God, so your fourth purpose is to practice real ministry.
5.   -- You were placed on earth for a mission, so your fifth purpose is to live out real evangelism.

Third is the law of cosmic compensation. This is the law of reward. This law teaches us that there is no such thing as something for nothing. Do not be fooled by the American mass media's deceptive advertising to expect something for free. Nothing in life is free. In life you get what you pay for. There is a season for everything. There is a time for sowing, and there is a season for reaping. Heaven helps those farmers who help themselves by doing their homework very well.

In conclusion, you reap what you sow. If you would like to receive blessings from heaven, you must work hard to deserve such blessing. You cannot sleep peacefully like a baby and wake up to expect divine favor. Heaven helps those who help themselves. If you do good deeds, God will shower you with heavenly rewards; if you do bad deeds, you will pay the price with the wrath of God. In other words, cosmic compensation is the law of karma-- the law of preparation.

Fourth is the law of prayer. In the mind of a television generation, prayer may be perceived to be the remote control you need to flip celestial channels in order to interact with your maker; or prayer is the magic cellular phone number you dial to ask God for divine intercession of grace and mercy. Even Jesus Christ emphasizes the power of prayer; for example, in recognition of the value of prayer, Jesus, the Christ, used the Lord's Prayer to teach us how to pray:

Our Father, who art in heaven,
Hallowed be thy Name.
Thy kingdom come.
Thy will be done,
On earth as it is in heaven.
Give us this day our daily bread.
And forgive us our trespasses,
As we forgive those who trespass against us.
And lead us not into temptation,
But deliver us from evil.
For thine is the kingdom, and the power, and the glory, for ever and ever.
Amen.

If you are on the path of spiritual enlightenment, prayer should be an important tool in your arsenal. For over twenty years, I have collected a library of prayers, and I have been learning how to apply the law of prayer. Praying is about communion, creating miracles. It is about concentrating, dreaming, visualizing, thinking, learning, and acting. It is about taking action after developing the skills you need to have your spiritual dreams come true. Then, you have learned how to become the architect of your spiritual destiny. Then you are ready to become a student of $ucce$$tology. The above stipulation is just the tip of the iceberg. If you would like to learn how $ucce$$tology can change your life, please contact us at (301) 593-4897. As a Roman Catholic mystic, I promise to help you unleash your spiritual potential. I will aid you discover the mysteries of religious faith and peace profound. Before I say farewell to you, I want to belabor the importance of belief to a Christian; if you belief in Jesus Christ as your savior, you can move mountains. Please, recite The Apostle's Creed to yourself aloud:

I believe in one God,
the Father almighty,
maker of heaven and earth,
of all things visible and invisible.

I believe in one Lord Jesus Christ,
the Only Begotten Son of God,

There is more to personal finance than the drudgery of debts and budgets.

born of the Father before all ages.

God from God, Light from Light,
true God from true God,
begotten, not made,
consubstantial with the Father;
through him all things were made.
For us men and for our salvation
he came down from heaven,
[At the words that follow up to and including 'and became man,' all bow.]

and by the Holy Spirit
was incarnate of the Virgin Mary, and became man.
For our sake he was crucified under Pontius Pilate,
he suffered death and was buried,
and rose again on the third day
in accordance with the Scriptures.
He ascended into heaven
and is seated at the right hand of the Father.
He will come again in glory
to judge the living and the dead
and his kingdom will have no end.

I believe in the Holy Spirit,
the Lord, the giver of life,
who proceeds from the Father and the Son,
who with the Father and the Son
is adored and glorified,
who has spoken through the prophets.

I believe in one, holy,
catholic and apostolic Church.
I confess one baptism
for the forgiveness of sins
and I look forward to the resurrection of the dead
and the life of the world to come. Amen.

I believe in God, the Father Almighty, Creator of heaven and earth; and in Jesus Christ, His only Son, our Lord: Who was conceived by the Holy Spirit, born of the Virgin Mary; suffered under Pontius Pilate, was crucified, died and was buried. He descended into hell; the third day He rose again from the dead; He ascended into heaven, is seated at the right hand of God the Father Almighty; from thence He shall come to judge the living and the dead. I believe in the Holy Spirit, the Holy Catholic Church, the communion of Saints, the forgiveness of sins, the resurrection of the body, and life everlasting. Amen.

I urge you to pray many times per day. The starting place for financial success must be with God and his eternal purposes for each life. Real meaning in life comes from fulfilling God's purposes for putting you on this earth. I hope I have enabled you to see the big picture of what life is all about; you will embark on the quest for financial success by praying for God's blessings. You will begin to live the life God created you to live. If you are not yet a devout or born-again Christian, then, I urge you to change your lifestyle for God. Before desiring financial success, change your lifestyle by making God the center of your universe. You should declare a 40-day and a 40-night devotional campaign of purpose-driven living. After praying and fasting forty days and forty nights, you will be hungry.

My favorite prayers are the Lord's Prayer and the Holy Rosary.

The Lord's Prayer
Our Father, which art in heaven,
Hallowed be thy Name.
Thy Kingdom come.
Thy will be done in earth,
As it is in heaven.
Give us this day our daily bread.
And forgive us our trespasses,
As we forgive them that trespass against us.
And lead us not into temptation,
But deliver us from evil.
For thine is the kingdom,
The power, and the glory,
For ever and ever.
Amen.

THE HOLY ROSARY

The Rosary is a devotional prayer to the Virgin Mary, who is the mother of Jesus Christ. Many people neglect to honor her, but Jesus wishes for us to seek His mother. She deserves our devotion for this reason. She gave birth to Jesus, raised Him, and then watched at the foot of the cross when He died. Jesus gave His mother to us while He was suffering on that very cross. For this prayer, you need a Rosary, which is a string of beads with a crucifix. A short string of five beads is attached to the crucifix, which is joined to a circular string of beads consisting of five sets of one large bead and ten smaller beads, known as "decades." Each decade is recited in honor of a mystery of the life of our Lord and His Blessed Mother, beginning with the Annunciation of the Incarnation and ending with Mary's triumphal Coronation in heaven.

There are four sets of mysteries: the five Joyful Mysteries, the five Sorrowful Mysteries, the five Glorious Mysteries, and the five Luminous Mysteries. Although the entire Rosary consists of twenty decades, it is customary to recite five decades at a time, while meditating on one set of mysteries.

There is more to personal finance than the drudgery of debts and budgets.

To say the rosary, make the Sign of The Cross. Take the crucifix of the rosary and pray the Apostles' Creed. Move to the first large bead and pray the Our Father. For the three small beads, say one Hail Mary per bead, followed by the Glory Be To The Father.

For the next large bead, announce and meditate on the first mystery, then say the Our Father. Move to the circular section of the rosary and say a Hail Mary for each of the ten small beads, followed by the Glory Be To The Father and the Fatima Decade prayer (the prayer that Our Lady asked the Fatima children to add after each decade). This completes one decade of the rosary. Proceed to the next mystery (the next large bead) and repeat the process until five decades of the rosary have been said. Conclude with the Hail, Holy Queen prayer.

STEP-BY-STEP INSTRUCTIONS FOR PRAYING THE ROSARY

Begin by holding the crucifix, saying "In the Name of the Father and of the Son and of the Holy Spirit," (making the sign of the Cross while doing that), then say the Apostles Creed. On the single bead just above the cross, pray the "Our Father." This and all prayers of the rosary are meditative prayers.

The next cluster has 3 beads. The "Hail Mary" prayer is said on these three beads. You pray the 3 Hail Marys while meditating on the three divine virtues of faith, hope, and love/charity. On the chain or cord after the three beads, say the "Glory be..."

On the next bead, which is a single bead, you announce the first divine mystery of contemplation. For example, if it were a Monday, you would say the first Joyful Mystery is "The Annunciation", at this point you pray the "Our Father" prayer.

Now this will bring you to the first decade, or set of 10 beads of the Rosary. You will then pray 10 Hail Marys while contemplating the first mystery, example: The Annunciation. After the 10th Hail Mary you will have completed the first of 5 decades which make up a Chaplet of the Rosary. You now come to another single bead, at this point, you pray the... Glory be to the Father... then (on the same bead) pray the O My Jesus... then (on the same bead) announce the next or second mystery. For example: if its Monday and your praying the Joyful Mysteries, the second Joyful Mystery is The Visitation. At this point you pray the Our Father....

You will now come to the second decade or group of 10 beads, you will now pray the 10 Hail Marys while contemplating the appropriate mystery. You continue to pray the rosary the same way throughout. If your intention is to pray a Chaplet (a single set of mysteries) at the end of the fifth mystery you will come back to the joiner, this is where the decades all join with the lower part of the rosary which contains the cross. When you come to the joiner, you decide whether or not you wish to say another Chaplet or end. If you decide to say another Chaplet you simply announce the next mystery and continue. If you wish to end, you simply say the Glory Be To The Father, the O My Jesus, The Our Father and end the rosary with the Hail Holy Queen and the sign of the Cross........

VARIOUS ROSARY PRAYERS IN APPROXIMATE ORDER AS PRAYED IN THE ROSARY

THE APOSTLE'S CREED: I believe in God, the Father Almighty, Creator of heaven and earth and in Jesus Christ, His only Son, our Lord; Who was conceived by the Holy Spirit, born of the Virgin Mary, suffered under Pontius Pilate, was crucified, died, and was buried, He descended into hell; the third day He arose again from the dead; He ascended into Heaven, sitteth at the right hand of God, the Father Almighty, from thence He shall come to judge the living and the dead. I believe in the Holy Spirit, the Holy Catholic Church, the communion of saints, the forgiveness of sins, the resurrection of the body, and life everlasting. Amen.

THE OUR FATHER: Our Father, Who art in Heaven, hallowed be Thy name; Thy Kingdom come, Thy will be done on earth as it is in Heaven. Give us this day our daily bread; and forgive us our trespasses as we forgive those who trespass against us; and lead us not into temptation, but deliver us from evil. Amen.

THE DOXOLOGY: Glory be to the Father, the Son, and the Holy Spirit. As it was in the beginning is now and ever shall be, world without end. Amen. (this prayer is optional and may be said after all Glory Be to the Fathers.....)

O my Jesus, have mercy on us. Forgive us our sins. Save us from the fires of hell. Take all souls into heaven, especially, those most in need of thy mercy. Amen.
THE HAIL MARY: Hail Mary, full of grace, the Lord is with thee, blessed art thou amongst women and blessed is the fruit of thy womb, Jesus. Holy Mary Mother of God, pray for us sinners now and at the hour of our death. Amen.

DECADE PRAYER

(prayer for priests): God, our Father, please send us holy priests, all for the sacred and Eucharistic heart of Jesus, all for the sorrowful and immaculate heart of Mary, in union with saint Joseph. Amen.

THE SALVE REGINA (Hail Holy Queen): Hail Holy Queen, Mother of Mercy, our life our sweetness and our hope. To thee do we cry, poor banished children of Eve; To thee do we send up our sighs, mourning and weeping in this valley of tears. Turn then, most gracious advocate, thine eyes of mercy toward us and after this our exile show unto us the blessed fruit of thy womb, Jesus. O clement, O loving, O sweet Virgin Mary!
V: Pray for us, O Holy Mother of God
R: That we may be made worthy of the promises of Christ.

LET US PRAY: O God, by the life, death and resurrection of Your only begotten Son, You purchased for us the rewards of eternal life; grant, we beseech You that while meditation on these mysteries of the Holy rosary, we may imitate what they contain and obtain what they promise. Through the same Christ our Lord. Amen.

There is more to personal finance than the drudgery of debts and budgets.

FATIMA PRAYER

Most Holy Trinity - Father, Son, and Holy Spirit - I adore thee profoundly. I offer Thee the most precious Body, Blood, Soul and Divinity of Jesus Christ, present in all the tabernacles of the world, in reparation for the outrages, sacrileges and indifferences whereby He is offended. And through the infinite merits of His Most Sacred Heart and the Immaculate Heart of Mary, I beg of Thee the conversion of poor sinners.
"Let this prayer be echoed all over the world."

FATIMA PRAYER

My God, I believe, I adore, I hope, and I love You. I beg pardon of You for those who do not believe, do not adore, do not hope, and do not love You.
Mary, Queen of the Holy Rosary, pray for us. Mary, Queen of Peace, pray for us. Mary, Our Loving Mother, pray for us.

MEMORARE

Remember, O most gracious Virgin Mary that never was it known that anyone who fled to Your protection, implored Your help, or sought Your intercession was left unaided. Inspired with this confidence, we fly to you, O Virgin of virgins, our Mother. To You we come; before You we stand, sinful and sorrowful. O Mother of the Word Incarnate, despise not our petitions, but in Your mercy, hear and answer us. Amen.

THE FIFTEEN PROMISES OF MARY TO CHRISTIANS WHO RECITE THE ROSARY

Whoever shall faithfully serve me by the recitation of the rosary, shall receive signal graces.
I promise my special protection and the greatest graces to all those who shall recite the rosary.
The rosary shall be a powerful armor against hell, it will destroy vice, decrease sin, and defeat heresies.

It will cause virtue and good works to flourish; it will obtain for souls the abundant mercy of God; it will withdraw the heart of men from the love of the world and its vanities, and will lift them to the desire of eternal things. Oh, that souls would sanctify themselves by this means.

The soul which recommend itself to me by the recitation of the rosary, shall not perish. Whoever shall recite the rosary devoutly, applying himself to the consideration of its sacred mysteries shall never be conquered by misfortune. God will not chastise him in His justice, he shall not by an unprovided death; if he be just he shall remain in the grace of God, and become worthy of eternal life. Whoever shall have a true devotion for the rosary shall not die without the sacraments of the Church. Those who are faithful to recite the rosary shall have during their life and at their death the light of God and the plenitude of His graces; at the moment of death they shall participate in the merits of the saints in paradise.

I shall deliver from purgatory those who have been devoted to the rosary. The faithful children of the rosary shall merit a high degree of glory in heaven. You shall obtain all you ask of me by the recitation of the rosary. All those who propagate the holy rosary shall be aided by me in their necessities.

I have obtained from my Divine Son that all the advocates of the rosary shall have for intercessors the entire celestial court during their life and at the hour of death.
All who recite the rosary are my son, and brothers of my only son Jesus Christ.

The devotion of the rosary is a great sign of predestination. Why do I pray the daily Rosary? It is my obligation as a Roman Catholic Christian. As Catholics, we make Jesus Christ proud by venerating his mother. In fact, the Virgin Mary, Our Lady, has 117 titles. She selected this title at Fatima: "I am the Lady of the Rosary." St. Francis de Sales said the greatest method of praying is to pray the Holy Rosary. St. Thomas Aquinas preached forty straight days in Rome, Italy on just the Hail Mary. St. John Vianney, patron of priest, was seldom seen without a rosary in his hand. Pope Adrian VI said that the rosary is the scourge of the devil; Pope Paul V said the rosary is a treasure of graces; Padre Pio, the stigmatic priest, said that the Holy Rosary is the weapon. Pope Leo XIII wrote nine encyclicals on the rosary. Pope John XXIII spoke thirty-eight times about our Lady and the Holy Rosary; he prayed fifteen decades daily. St. Louis Marie Grignion de Montfort wrote the following words: "The rosary is the most powerful weapon to touch the Heart of Jesus, Our Redeemer, who so loves His Mother."

JESUS, MARY, AND JOSEPH ARE PATRIARCHS OF THE HOLY FAMILY. MARY IS THE QUEEN OF THE HOLY ANGELS. I AM ASKING HER TO PRAY FOR YOU!

IN THE NAME OF OUR FATHER WHO IS IN HEAVEN, SAY "JESUS AND MOTHER MARY, I LOVE YOU; PLEASE, SAVE MY SOUL. MAKE ME A MILLIONAIRE"

GOD BLESS YOU!

Step 2

DISCOVER THE MILLIONAIRE'S SECRET

My dear reader, please, allow me to address you as a miraculous millionaire. Why? By completing a reading of the prologue and PAY GOD FIRST, you have gone through a rite of passage. You have demonstrated that you are worthy to join the Millionaire Club; you deserve to discover the famous millionaire's secret. I hope you do not have second thoughts or conclude that I have been making much ado about nothing. As you may be aware now, I am a former dishwasher and security guard who used the famous millionaire's secret, the teachings of $ucce$$tology, to become a self-made millionaire. If you are reading this material, it means you have just bought a copy of my book, so I am happy you have joined the ranks of prospective or soon-to-be millionaires.

Welcome to the Millionaire Club. As a potential member, I want to raise your level of financial consciousness, so open your eyes and lend me your ears. By reading this chapter thoroughly, you will motivate yourself to begin making nothing but big money.

Did you know that every twelve minutes in America, someone becomes millionaire; the individual attains millionaire status by taking consistent action to set up a financial system that results in the creation of mind-staggering wealth. Right now, as you read this book, thousands of Soon-to-be Millionaires, individuals like you, have just begun their journey to financial success. Soon twelve more minutes will elapse, and another American will become a millionaire again. Why should this nouveau riche not be YOU?

You may be wondering and doubting the possibility of becoming a millionaire when the economy is in a persistent recession. It is true that the recession has been around for a while. Curiously, as I travel around the country, I observe two diametrically opposed approaches to the recession that are dividing Americans into two distinct groups; while some Americans who cannot cope with the vagaries in the economy feel the recession is bad news, others who have been minding their financial business well think they can handle the cruelest price the recession can exact on them.

What accounts for the difference in the perceptions of these two groups? In one word, it is a positive mental attitude or preparedness. On the one hand, the individuals in group A who say the recession is bad news are unprepared. These individuals are negative, but they are not stupid; in fact, they are intelligent, hardworking , and apparently successful in keeping up with the Joneses, but they are broke; these individuals have been busy following conventional wisdom, which stipulates that if one works hard one would earn enough money to retire. Because these individuals have been busy working hard for a living, the recession has caught them unaware. Hence, they are justified in being pessimistic about recessionary times.

On the other hand, the individuals in group B, who extol the benefits of the recession as good news, are prepared. Like the individuals in group A, the Americans in group B are hard working. The latter, nevertheless, recognizes that working hard is inadequate; one must work smart and anticipate downturns in the economy. For this reason, the individuals in group B are entitled to having an optimistic perception of the looming recession. If you were given a choice, where will you rather be, in group A or B? If you say group A, please read no further; pass the book you have been reading to someone else, who might be interested in improving his or her financial circumstance.

If, however, you would rather belong to group B, then, *The Miraculous Millionaire* is for you. Do you want to be the next American millionaire? Think about it seriously. Actually, you could be the next American to join the Millionaire Club, if you are really serious about economic independence; $ucce$$tology, my financial system, shows the practical steps you should use to bring about the outcome in question.

WHAT IS $UCCE$$TOLOGY?

I have already defined it in the prologue of this book. To recapitulate, $ucce$$tology is the first universal theory of financial success conditioning. It is the most innovative, revolutionary, and straightforward wealth-building program for the new millennium and the future.

There is more to personal finance than the drudgery of debts and budgets.

A simple, practical, and realistic approach to wealth creation, $UCCE$$TOLOGY unselfishly confides the details of my financial success; I am giving you the proven method of playing and winning the money game, not garbage stuff such as academic theory and outdated textbook material. $ucce$$tology is pragmatic, sensible, and timeless wisdom that works effectively in the REAL WORLD.

Some of my students call it the poor man's money machine. $ucce$$tology is the art, science, and philosophy of studying and realizing the American Dream. As an income-opportunity seeker, $ucce$$tology provides the specialized knowledge you need to cut the learning curve. When I was starting out, I bought every money-making plan that was advertised in the media. $ucce$$tology, therefore, reflects an integration of the strengths of these programs into the principles that actually proved almost 100% effective in my quest for financial independence. As a new technology, $ucce$$tology is unlike anything you have already seen in the marketplace. If you are thinking about comparing it with other programs, save your comparisons until you have tested the programs.

Unlike other self-improvement packages, that promise you heaven and earth but give you hell, $ucce$$tology is a new technology of the mind that works, works, and works. Nurses, doctors, pharmacists, engineers and average Americans have used it successfully; indeed, the unparalleled financial gains these individuals have derived from $ucce$$tology makes it the complete, surest, and most powerful wealth-building tool for the new millennium and the future.

But do not merely take my word for it. Try $ucce$$tology in the comfort of your apartment or home. If you are like average income opportunity seekers, you have spent much money buying self-improvement brochures, books and cassettes. Unfortunately, most of them have not worked very well. $ucce$$tology is not one of them! I think that no financial package, except one written by God, can actually produce miraculous results. A good program, like $ucce$$tology, uses what you have received already from God to coach you to get what you really want out of life. And this difference is what distinguishes $ucce$$tology from all the expensive and get-rich-quick packages in the market. There is a brain in your head, and $ucce$$tology will show you simple techniques that can result in the discovery of your true human potential, your psychic or personal power.

If you have read this far, I appreciate your sincere interest in turning your financial situation around. I want to repeat the question I asked you earlier: Do you actually want to make more money, or are you going to waste the next twelve minutes like the ignorant individuals in group A? Do not spend your time worrying about the past, or what you should have done to achieve financial success. The past is gone, and gone forever. What is really significant is what you can do in the next twelve minutes: NOW! Will you take advantage of the millionaire's secret revealed by $ucce$$tology and change your life to win the future, or will you dwell on remembrance of past things? Dispel the myth that you may not have the right stuff. I know that you have what it takes.

$ucce$$tology will show you that your mind is like a trillion dollar computer; it simply needs a plan, or software such as $ucce$$tology, to process and realize your goals. Take it from me, a foreign-born individual who has overcome the greatest odds to achieve the American Dream. Talking about the American Dream, it still exists. But you have to know where to look for it. It is either right under your nose or just a phone call away. Perhaps, as a foreign-born person, I am predisposed to see financial opportunities more clearly than my fellow Americans. Why do you think I came to America? Why?

Even as I talk to you about financial opportunities in your own backyard, I know your mind may revert to thinking about imaginary problems, such as "no credit, no job, no money, and the recession." My book will show you how to get around what you perceive to be potential problems. No credit? No problem! No job? No problem! Recession? No problem! My example and the cases of my students show that you do not have to inherit wealth to live the American Dream of financial success. Model our examples. Success leaves clues, so pick up the clues. Apply the lessons of success; indeed, Aristotle once said that we learn by imitation. Children learn to speak English by modeling their parents and other adults. Imitate me!

Why not model yourself after me? Learn from me; by purchasing *The Miraculous Millionaire*, you have bought the brains of a self-made millionaire; for ten years, I labored in storm and stress to think my way out of the coffin of poverty. Instead of experimenting in the dark with methods that will leave you frustrated and broke, why not take advantage of the moneymaking secrets I had learned from the lives of rich and famous Americans? Now the choice is yours to learn and apply THE MILLIONAIRE'S SECRET. Finally, I am ready to tell you the truth about the millionaire mind, the millionaire's secret. I am happy to pinpoint elements of the millionaire's secret:

FREE

Millionaires have expurgated the word *free* from their dictionary. Free is against the law of nature. God created nature. After the fall of man from the Garden of Eden, God affixed a price to every commodity in nature. Even the air that you breathe is not free. You pay for it by pleasing God. Millionaires know that free is not sacrosanct. Everything in life has a price. Advertisers from Madison Avenue understand that 99% of the population of America is gullible. By contrast, millionaires have deleted the word free from their vocabulary. Hence, the first millionaire secret is that nothing in life is free. YOU HAVE TO SPEND MONEY TO MAKE MONEY. Think!

You have to buy my coaching package to succeed. The book is theoretical and inadequate. Sometimes it is advisable to act like a penny-pincher. But why should you be like the fool who, in attempting to save pennies, lost his wealth? Think about it! Visualize the terrible things that will happen if you do not buy my support plan package: loss, failure, regret, and frustration. Do you want these terrible things to happen to you? Learn a bitter lesson; form a mental picture of the world of opportunity that awaits you: gain, success, satisfaction, and happiness. I am confident of your sense of judgment. I know you will use $ucce$$tology to motivate yourself to make nothing but big money. Think again about it. See you at the top of the money mountain.

SELF-EDUCATION

Are you ready for the second millionaire secret? If you dream about millionaire riches, please, cultivate the self-education habit of highly effective rich folks; they perceive their mind to be a garden, and they use self-education to cultivate it daily. The unvarnished truth about money is that you should ascribe fundamental value to self-education, the acquisition of specialized knowledge. Millionaires possess specialized knowledge; poor folks like university professors possess general knowledge. Knowledge is power, but specialized knowledge is actionable and powerful; general knowledge is power, but specialized knowledge is powerful. Hear it also from Napoleon Hill in chapter five of his book entitled *Think and Grow Rich*:

There are two kinds of knowledge. One is general, the other is specialized. General knowledge, no matter how great in quantity or variety it may be, is of but little use in the accumulation of money. The faculties of the great universities possess, in the aggregate, practically every form of general knowledge known to civilization. Most of the professors have but little or no money. They specialize on teaching knowledge, but they do not specialize on the organization, or the use of knowledge. KNOWLEDGE will not attract money, unless it is organized, and intelligently directed, through practical PLANS OF ACTION, to the DEFINITE END of accumulation of money. Lack of understanding of this fact has been the source of confusion to millions of people who falsely believe that "knowledge is power." It is nothing of the sort! Knowledge is only potential power. It becomes power only when, and if, it is organized into definite plans of action, and directed to a definite end. This "missing link" in all systems of education known to civilization today, may be found in the failure of educational institutions to teach their students HOW TO ORGANIZE AND USE KNOWLEDGE AFTER THEY ACQUIRE IT.

Additionally, I want you to consider the views of Gina Rinehart, an Australian mining heiress, worth $19 billion and earlier this year thought to be the world's richest woman. Unlike her politically correct peers, she has the courage to dare and tell the truth about the millionaire mindset of specialized knowledge. Rinehart has sparked another controversy in her latest column in *Australian Resources and Investment* magazine. Rinehart rails against class warfare, and she challenges the non-rich to stop attacking the rich and go to work: "There is no monopoly on becoming a millionaire," she writes. "If you are jealous of those with more money, do not just sit there and complain. Do something to make more money yourself -- spend less time drinking, or smoking and socializing and more time working." The type of work Rinehart is referring to is a derivative of specialized knowledge. For instance, the publishing of *The Miraculous Millionaire* is an interesting example of specialized knowledge. First, I decided to research the process of book publishing in America today. As a result of my findings, I chose the option of self-publishing.

Second, because I wanted to maintain complete control of the publishing project, l sought to acquire the specialized knowledge required to produce the book; I polished my business-writing skills; I researched the new canons of book layout and typesetting; I taught myself how to use Adobe's InDesign software; and I formatted the manuscript in PDF for my printer. In the end, the specialized knowledge I have embedded in *The Miraculous Millionaire* will attract money because I have worked hard to organize it as a marketable product, and I have directed my creative efforts intelligently through the practical plan of action to the definite end of the accumulation of money. Hence, your goal must be to obtain all the specialized knowledge you can afford in your entire life. You cannot afford the price of ignorance. Invest in yourself. Invest in self-education. Like the technique of paying God first, hire yourself first. Sometimes you should imagine that you are your own doctor; you have the money blues, but you have to learn how to cure yourself. Before calling a financial expert, use the resources in Millionaire iUniversity, step 12, to begin the process of looking for a solution to your money problems. You are the best financial person that you can hire. If you need help in making a critical decision, it is advisable for you to hire objective advisors, conflict-free advisors, who charge you a specific fee for their time. While you work in tandem with the financial advisors, please, do not abdicate control. Cultivate the daily habit of reading magazines, newspapers, and other financial publications that have high-quality standards in their objectivity and recommendations.

GOALS

Are you ready for the third millionaire secret? Goals! On my web site, I have compiled a long list of good books on goal setting. Please, use it to learn how to set your goals. Millionaires understand that life is a mission. They know their mission; they set goals to fulfill their mission. Because you are reading *The Miraculous Millionaire*, it can be assumed that your goal is to resolve financial questions or problems. Fine! Please, do not be vague. Define your goals precisely, and prioritize your financial goals and start working toward them. Be patient. Success leaves clues, so focus on your accomplishments; learn from your past mistakes. Emulate people who are your role models. If you do not know them personally, please, research them methodically.

HEALTH

Are you ready for the fourth millionaire secret? Health! Invest in your health. Use health insurance to protect yourself. Follow the advice of your physician. I meet many individuals who refuse to buy health insurance. They prefer to use the money to buy big cars. According to me, these individuals are penny wise and pound foolish. Maintain cordial relationships with your family and friends. What is the point in having much money if you do not have good health and people with whom to share your good fortune? Please, allocate a portion of your time and money to good causes that make society and the world better.

There is more to personal finance than the drudgery of debts and budgets.

TRANSIENCE

Are you ready for the fifth millionaire secret? Transience! Transience is a dominant theme in art. Literature, for example, refers to the brevity of life. As soon as a human being is born, he or she dies. Nothing seems to stay the same. There is no condition that is permanent in life; life is like a number endowed with motion; cycles of recession are punctuated by cycles of boom. After experiencing a recession, an economic upturn prevails. Millionaires are philosophical enough to comprehend that change is a fact of life, so be prepared for changes in life. If you have learned how to prepare and maintain a monthly budget, then, you are better off handling the shocks of economic slumps; you are better off anticipating life's changes. As a result, you will be better off financially and emotionally.

If you are married, please, recognize your spouse as a partner in wealth building. Allocate family time to discuss joint financial goals, issues, and concerns. Be considerate of your spouse; appreciate your partner's money personality; learn the lessons of compromising with your spouse; manage your personal finance issues as a team. Take charge of your finances. Procrastinating is detrimental to your long-term financial health. Do not wait for an earthquake, a crisis, or catastrophic life event to compel you to organize you financial house. Whether you believe it or not, transience is like a thief who comes to your house in the dead of night without warning. Hence, you should protect yourself: study $ucce$$tology; join the millionaire club, attend Millionaire iUniversity, and start implementing your financial plan now!

EMOTIONS

Are you ready for the sixth millionaire secret? Emotions! Millionaires have learned how to control their emotions. Emotions are out of place in the realm of personal finance. Avoid making financial decisions based on your emotions; apply your faculty of logic. For example, stock investing will impress on you the foolishness of relying on your emotions; an investor who panics and sells his or her stock holdings during or after a major market correction will miss what Warren Buffett and other smart and value investors call buying opportunities. While these amateur investors are ruled by the emotions of greed and fear, the Warren Buffetts of the investment world are shrewd and calculating in executing their trading plans. By the same token, be especially careful in making important financial decisions after major life changes, such as a marriage, divorce, job loss, or death in your family. Make your investing decisions based upon your needs and the long-term fundamentals of the stock or asset you are buying. Ignore the predictive advice offered by financial prognosticators on CNBC like Jim Kramer. Nobody has a working crystal ball. If you make knee-jerk decisions based on financial news headlines, you will lose your shirt.

SAVING

Are you ready for the seventh millionaire secret? Saving! I ascribe fundamental importance to saving money. Frankly, saving money is a major element of financial management. I have devoted two chapters of my book to the habit of saving money effectively: teaching yourself personal finance and balancing your financial book.

In fact, these two chapters are, perhaps, the best treatment of the importance of saving money and the potentially disastrous consequences of debt. I recommend these chapters highly. No financial program can help you get out of poverty if it does not address the significance of budgeting and saving money. Saving money and budgeting are not sexy; indeed, they are monotonous and boring. Yet, they are necessary evils. But, as you will discover soon, there is more to personal finance than the drudgery of debts and budgets.

My additional recommendation to you to save money is the consideration of the usefulness of automatic employee payroll deductions credited into a 401(K) account. If you are undisciplined, risk averse, unmotivated, and satisfied with a comfortable retirement, then, the automatic 401(K) capitalization is appropriate. Yet I submit that it will not make you an automatic millionaire. Have you ever seen someone become a millionaire through a 401(K) account? If you have big dreams to become a millionaire, then, you owe it to yourself to become a miraculous millionaire; please, explore the treasury of wealth-building instruments in my book. My saving solution is the 10% pay yourself rule; you use the fruit of your savings to invest to become a millionaire. There is a chock full of financial vehicles for you to exploit in my book. Save and invest 10 percent of your income. You can invest through a retirement savings account or a private equity bank of your own to reduce your taxes and ensure your future financial independence.

The sine qua non of saving is living within or below your financial means. It is a tragedy for you to try to keep up with your co-workers, neighbors, and peers who are the envious emulators of the Smiths and the Joneses. The Smiths and the Joneses are America's royal or made-for-television family; by contrast, your co-workers, neighbors, and peers who engage in conspicuous consumption are borrowing against their future; they must end up bankrupt. Unlike them, control your spending. You should avoid impulsive shopping and purchases; use credit cards only for convenience, not for carrying debt. Personally, for over ten years, I use only debit cards and cash. If you have a tendency to run up credit card debt, then, get rid of your cards and use only cash, checks, and debit cards. Do not buy consumer items, such as cars, clothing, vacations, and so on that lose value over time on credit. Use debt only to make investments in things that gain value, such as real estate, a business, or an education. I believe in the guns theory of money; the rest of the 99% believes in the butter theory of money. I buy things that appreciate in value, but my friends of the 99% buy items that depreciate in value, like the automobile.

INVESTING

Are you ready for the eighth millionaire secret? Investing! Investing is the awful watchword of millionaires. For example, a few weeks ago, I was examining and comparing the federal income tax returns of President Barack Obama and Governor Willard Mitt Romney. While the president makes much of his money from the executive job of running the country, the governor's income is derived from complex instruments; in accounting terms, much of the president's income is earned, but all of the governor's income is unearned.

The governor makes the president look like either a pauper or a perfect welfare case. Step 8 of the book treats the subject of US income taxation thoroughly; it shows you how the big boys of Wall Street leverage mastery of US tax laws for their own betterment. It is a fact that you can never get rich by saving the paltry sums of money you earn from your job. If you want to argue with me, then, I am going to challenge you to show me just one millionaire who has done that successfully!

Rather, you want the millionaire's investing secret of compounding to work for you. Compounding is just a fanciful word for the power of compound interest, as opposed to simple interest, working itself out to make you quadruple your capital. Imagine turning a $10,000 investment into $150,000 in seven years. What will it take to obtain such results? Read on! After you have saved enough money to allocate some for investing, invest the majority of your long-term money in ownership instruments or vehicles that have appreciation potential, such as stocks, real estate, and your own business. What about lending vehicles like bonds and bank accounts? They are fine.

In step 9, I show you how to play and win the stock market game; also, I teach you how to manage bonds and bank investing. It is important for you to note, however, that when you invest in bonds or bank accounts, you are simply lending your money to financial institutions and others; the return you earn probably will not keep you ahead of inflation and taxes. Yet, for the purpose of diversification, it is necessary for you to have exposure in bonds and lending.

Avoid financial products that carry high commissions and expenses. The culprits here are loaded mutual funds. Companies that sell their products through aggressive sales techniques generally have the worst financial products and the highest commissions. Peter Lynch taught me the importance of investing in what you know. Warren Buffett adheres to a similar philosophy; this fact explains why for so long he has taken a dim look at investing in technology companies. Berkshire Hathaway's recent purchase of IBM stock is an exception to Buffett's rule of investing. Perhaps, there is something about the IBM business franchise that Warren Buffett understands that remains mysterious to the foolish crowd of investors on Wall Street. Hence, do not purchase any financial product that you do not understand. Research the facts; ask questions, and compare what you are being offered using the investigative resources in $ucce$$tology.

Please, refer to the suggested reading list located at Millionaire iUniversity section of the book: step 12. Always research a product or service before you buy it. You should never ever purchase a financial product or service on the basis of the opinions of your friends, family members, or salespersons.

PSYCHOLOGY FOR MONEY BEHAVIOR MODIFICATION

Are you ready for the ninth millionaire secret? Money behavior modification! If you want to become a millionaire, you must modify your money behavior to be in concord relationship with the millionaire mindset.

It is not easier said than done; I am going to hold your hand; please, feel free to lean on me. We shall walk in locked steps, hand-in-hand. The psychology of human money behavior can be cultural, spiritual, sociological, economical, emotional, physical, and historical.

In other words, our perceptions of money may be attributed to the way of life of our people or tribe; our religious faith (Catholic, Presbyterian, Methodist, Baptist, Buddhist, Hindu, or Muslim) and idiosyncratic beliefs also shape our perspectives on money; similarly, the level of development of our society also impacts on our thinking about money; our financial status in society also influences our thoughts about money; money arouses different emotions or feelings in human beings; while citizens of developed societies are comfortable with the electronic form of money, the liquidity preference of citizens of developing countries is physical; in the end, the passing of time also influences people's perceptions of money. Hence, in this narrow context, when I use the word psychology, I am referring to money with the above-mentioned contexts of the workings of the human mind.

In this wise, money behavior modification is a psychological term that refers to the process of changing your old perceptions of money in order for you to learn and adapt to new behaviors that are at congruence with positive results in personal finance. Money behavior modification teaches you how to manipulate your mind by applying effective psychological techniques and strategies. Money behavior modification is a process of normalizing the ideas in your mind so that your mind can function like the minds of America's rich and famous. I have not studied the human anatomy like medical students, but I can assure you that physicians agree with me that your mind is like a computer; like a preprogrammed personal computer network, your human anatomy (respiratory and circulatory system) depends on the mind, which serves as the brain of the human server and network.

Money behavior modification pertains to the mastery of your mind. It is a remedy involving you taking control of the operations of your mind. Indeed, your mind is a living computer. Your mind is a kingdom, your kingdom. You are the king, so command your mind to do your bidding. Your mind is a storehouse of vibratory experiences and a reservoir of knowledge. Since you were born, your mind has been storing all the experiences you have had and all the knowledge you have acquired from your environment. Your experiences about money have been deposited in the library of your mind. Therefore, your money behavior is a reflection of these myriad experiences. Money behavior is a reflection of your mental state. The kind of money behavior you exhibit is the result of either a positive or negative state of mind. While some people use drugs to alter their mental state, my book will show you how to do that without inhaling any artificial drugs; in fact, the tools of my trade are the strategic solutions of art, science, philosophy, mysticism, and neuro-linguistic programming.

As a human being, you are endowed by your maker with five senses, that is, five methods of perception: hearing, sight, touch, smell, and taste. Your experience of the phenomenon of reality is colored by your five senses. In the same vein, your senses affect the manner in which you perceive reality; so does it also have an impact on your money behavior, personality, and attitudes. That is how I also experience reality.

So in talking about me, how was it that Prince Ojong, a poor and laboring immigrant from Africa, could have conditioned his mind to dream big and act to achieve financial freedom? In short, the simple answer is my implementation of the psychological ideas of money behavior modification. The power to magically change your financial destiny lies in using neuro-linguistic programming (NLP) to modify your money behavior. The founders of NLP are Richard Bandler and John Grinder. As a personal development technology, NLP is capable of addressing problems such as addictions, phobias, depression, habit disorder, psychosomatic illnesses, and learning disorders. The stated aim of NLP is to find ways of helping people live better, fuller, and richer lives.

Bandler and Grinder have demonstrated that if the effective patterns of behaviour of exceptional people could be modeled, then, these patterns could be acquired by others. NLP has been adopted by private therapists, including hypnotherapists, and in management workshops and seminars marketed to business and government. Most of us are finding it difficult to make enough money to quit the rat race of working jobs because we are stuck in the rote of negative money habits and attitudes we have acquired from childhood. Indeed, these negative money behaviors sabotage any meaningful effort we make to break the cycle of poverty. NLP can provide us with a catharsis.

For instance, the experience of a calamitous event like the Wall Street crash of the 1930s has shaped the money outlook of many investors who came of age during that epoch; Donji Finch is a case in point; although she does not make much money working as a pharmacy technician for Kaiser Permanente, she has been able to build wealth as a result of the penny-pinching ways she had learned from her parents who had grown up during the American Great Depression. Generally, the Great Depression was a severe worldwide economic depression in the decade preceding World War II. The timing of the Great Depression varied across nations, but in most countries it started in about 1929 and lasted until the late 1930s or early 1940s. It was the longest, most widespread, and deepest depression of the 20th century. In the 21st century, the Great Depression is commonly used as a measure of how far down the world's economy can decline.

The depression originated in the U.S., starting with the fall in stock prices that began around September 4, 1929, and became worldwide news with the stock market crash of October 29, 1929, known as Black Tuesday. From there, it quickly spread to almost every country in the world. The Great Depression had devastating effects in virtually every country, rich and poor. Personal income, tax revenue, profits and prices dropped, while international trade plunged by more than 50%. Unemployment in the U.S. rose to 25%, and in some countries it rose as high as 33%. Cities all around the world were hit hard, especially those dependent on heavy industry. Construction was virtually halted in many countries. Farming and rural areas suffered as crop prices fell by approximately 60%. Facing plummeting demand with few alternate sources of jobs, areas dependent on primary sector industries such as cash cropping, mining and logging suffered the most. Some economies started to recover by the mid-1930s; in many countries the negative effects of the Great Depression lasted until the start of World War II.

In this regard, to Donji Finch, the word Great Depression is a trigger and an anchor. The mere mention of the word conjures up images of economic hardship from her subconscious mind, but she has learned to associate the term with the urgency to save much money every paycheck for a rainy day. In fact, that is how come she has been able to buy a nice house in a pricey neighborhood. Although Donji Finch is not as formally educated as the pharmacists she works with, she has been able to foster a belief in the acquisition of self-taught knowledge through reading books on personal finance, newspapers, and magazines; she also enjoys watching films and movies that are not only entertaining but also educational.

Although she is not very well educated, she is a very self-confident lady; her success in applying the lessons of saving and investing has fostered her high self-esteem. Perhaps more important is her motivational nature; she is a positive thinker who believes she has the power to create in her mind the results she desires in the future as if these results were here now. As she says, if you are a negative thinker, you will only manifest harmful money behaviors. Your reality is the painting you create of your world; if you perceive the world to be beautiful, your positivity will attract success, but if you complain that the world is ugly, money and success will run away from you. Hence, nothing is either good or bad, but thinking makes it so.

As you can see, rich people are positive people. They know that there are no roses without thorns. They know the truth about financial success and life. No matter what happens to them, they always try to see a silver lining in the cloud. No matter how negative the feedback they receive from their environment, they manage to remain perpetual optimists like Candide in a French novel by Voltaire. *Candide, ou l'Optimisme* is a French satire first published in 1759 by Voltaire, a philosopher of the Age of Enlightenment. The novella has been widely translated, with English versions titled *Candide: or, All for the Best* (1759); *Candide: or, The Optimist* (1762); and *Candide: or, Optimism* (1947). It begins with a young man, Candide, who is living a sheltered life in an Edenic paradise and being indoctrinated with Leibnizian optimism by his mentor, Pangloss.

The work describes the abrupt cessation of this lifestyle, followed by Candide's slow, painful disillusionment as he witnesses and experiences great hardships in the world. Voltaire concludes the novella with Candide, if not outright rejecting optimism, advocating an enigmatic precept, "we must cultivate our garden," in lieu of the Leibnizian mantra of Pangloss, "all is for the best in the best of all possible worlds."

Candide is characterized by its sarcastic tone, as well as by its erratic, fantastical and fast-moving plot. A picaresque novel with a story similar to that of a more serious bildungsroman, it parodies many adventure and romance clichés, the struggles of which are caricatured in a tone that is mordantly matter-of-fact. Still, the events discussed are often based on historical happenings, such as the Seven Years' War and the 1755 Lisbon earthquake. As philosophers of Voltaire's day contended with the problem of evil, so too does Candide in this short novel, albeit more directly and humorously. Voltaire ridicules religion, theologians, governments, armies, philosophies, and philosophers through allegory; most conspicuously, he assaults Leibniz and his optimism.

There is more to personal finance than the drudgery of debts and budgets.

Emphatically, my argument is that if you use the technologies of $ucce$$tology to reshape your money perceptions, you can embark on the thrilling journey to grow rich. To assist you in mapping out your way to millions, I plan to introduce you to the art, philosophy, and science of psychology. I am focusing briefly on specialized knowledge, what is germane to money-making, not academic gibberish. I am underscoring the ideas of money behavior normalization to the stage of the average millionaire in America. What separates you from America's rich and famous is not really millions, but the dichotomy of positive and negative money behavior. I am helping you to unlearn negative money behaviors; I am helping you to learn positive money attitudes and habits that you can use every day to make nothing but big money like America's rich and famous.

If you can bear with me and change your money behavior, then, I promise to make it easy for you to begin building wealth with my bulletproof system known as $ucce$$tology. You see, $ucce$$tology is a new technology intended to rewire the workings of your warped mind that is still undergoing the processes of brainwashing; it is my goal to free you from the bondage of mental poverty and slavery. I want you to begin controlling your own mind. $ucce$$tology is the cure of your disease. $ucce$$tology means changing and enhancing the lives of individuals like you. No more do you have to continue living with the sin, disease, and sickness of poverty. $ucce$$tology, therefore, is a form of therapy, a psychological intervention or support system intended to cure the sin, disease, and sickness of poverty. By applying the principles of behavior modification you will grow rich; $ucce$$tology is here to enable you to achieve your potential and contribute as a confident individual to your community. Let us get rid of poverty; poverty is a sin; poverty is a sin because it is the will of God that you should be rich. In fact, that is why God made you in his own image. That is why Jesus said you are divine. There is divinity in you; instead of allowing this divinity to lie dormant, program it to build wealth; you will experience financial peace and happiness.

MONEY PERSONALITY

Are you ready for the tenth millionaire secret? Money personality! What is your money personality? If you are not rich, it means you do not have the millionaire blood type or money personality. Money personality is like what we call blood types in genetics: O, A, B, AB. In some ways, every person's blood is the same. But, when analyzed under a microscope, distinct differences are visible. In the early 20th century, an Austrian scientist named Karl Landsteiner classified blood according to those differences. He was awarded the Nobel Prize for his achievements. Similarly, every individual's money personality is the same, but differences become apparent upon a close examination of these individuals. The mere mention of the word money conjures images in your mind: addictions (alcohol, womanizing, shopping, gambling, smoking, drugs, sex, and Internet), emotions, decisions, actions, habits, personality, and problems (death, birth, divorce, separation, in- laws, extended family, unemployment, business failure, recession, and illness). For your information, economists tell us that money is a tool. Unlike gold, money is a piece of paper with no intrinsic value. Indeed, what confer value on the US dollar in the marketplace are its multivariate functions: a medium of exchange; a store of value; a measure of value; a mode of deferred payment; and a standard of value.

MONEY PERSONALITY TYPES

Do you know your money personality type? I have isolated eight archetypes of money personalities for you to weigh and consider where you belong:
1. The Guardian—the money behavior of the guardian is marked by alertness and the desire to keep money.
2. The Pleasure-Seeker—the money behavior of the pleasure seeker is marked by the lustful pursuit of pleasure for its own sake.
3. The Idealist—the money behavior of the idealist is marked by the use of money to achieve idealistic goals such as social good or world peace.
4. The Saver—the money behavior of the saver is marked by the compulsive desire to save money for financial security.
5. The Star—the money behavior of the star is marked by the use of money for publicity and recognition.
6. The Innocent—the money behavior of the innocent is marked by the deliberate avoidance of money issues with the pretext that life will take care of itself.
7. The Caretaker—the money behavior of the caretaker is marked by the lending and borrowing of money to express compassion and generosity.
8. The Empire Builder—the money behavior of the empire builder is marked by the strife for power and innovation.

Do you know your beliefs and attitudes toward money? While a positive mental attitude attracts money, a negative attitude repels money. Money comes with much emotion and sentiments (greed, fear, irrationality, hate): worry, seriousness, security, coldness, warmth, and dumbness. While negative emotion is represented by the lack of money, positive emotion is represented by the possession of money. Many social studies have shown that people who have money exhibit a better self-image; people who do not have money manifest a negative self-image. Make a decision to take control of your money behavior today.

According to me, the scientific process of money behavior normalization is as easy and simple as A, B, C. A stands for Antecedents; B refers to Behavior; and C stands for Consequences. Antecedents, the first phase of the scientific method, deals with observation of your money behavior; identify your money personality type by asking the following question: What comes before and during the observation of your money behavior? Define your money behavior problems. What is causing your money behavior problems? As for the B, for Behavior, you have to address the following question: What does your money behavior look like? List the money behaviors and organize them in order of security; explain the money-making skills lacking in you by subject. Describe it in detail. Diagnose and classify your money personality based on the eight archetypes I have enumerated before. As for C, for consequences, analyze the consequences of your money behavior. Study the consequences of your money behavior. List how the money-making skills will be taught. List the consequences of breaking the good rules of money-making. I would suggest the following color scheme for the warning process: green, yellow, and red; red is for the most severe situation; yellow is for a mild situation; green is for the normal situation. What is the longevity of the behavior modification? When does the plan begin, and when does it end? Review the plan, and judge its success or failure.

There is more to personal finance than the drudgery of debts and budgets.

TREATMENT

As for treatment, a plan needs to be established that incorporates the best route to modifying your money behavior. If your money behavior is negative, disruptive, dangerous, or out of control, you can intervene in two ways: increasing the frequency of good money behaviors and decreasing the frequency of bad money behaviors. Briefly, I am enumerating ways you can increase the frequency of good money behaviors: satiation, reward or gift, positive reinforcement, alteration of current environment to help you function properly and learn personal finance, apply good principles of applied behavior learning, including operant and classical conditioning. As for decreasing the frequency of your bad money behavior, I recommend the following solutions: removal or extinction of bad money behavior by devoting less time to shopping; punishment of self; breaking tasks into components to be taught through chaining; using neuro-linguistic programming (NLP) to trigger alternative money behaviors that are positive; capitalizing on collaborative goal setting; relying on contingency alternative money behaviors that are positive; and adopting contingency money management to eliminate problems as a last resort.

ACTIONS AND DECISIONS

Are you ready for the eleventh millionaire secret? Learn to associate the actions of executing personal finance tasks with pleasure; learn to associate procrastination and the deferment of personal finance chores with pain. The Christian doctrine of sin, especially the crime of sin and the punishment of death in hell, is as an example of applying the pain principle. While people who obey the commandments of God will go to heaven, sinners will be forbidden from entering the Kingdom of God. Sinners will die in the ball of hellfire. For this reason, the majority of the people on earth are struggling to ensure that they obtain a passport to paradise. Is this not the reason why all of us, Christians, are still waiting for God? Indeed, our action and decision to await the second coming of Christ has been fictionalized in Samuel Beckett's play titled Waiting for Godot; movies such as *2012* and *Apocalypse* have dramatized this human condition of pain, so learn to associate procrastination and the deferment of money-making actions and decisions with pain. In fact, the sale of life insurance is another good example, in this regard. Life insurance is a product that turns a lot of immigrants off; most people hate to be reminded of their own mortality.

A few months ago, I visited a Muslim business associate in Silver Spring, Maryland. The purpose of my visit was to convince him to buy a life insurance policy prior to his departure to Mecca, Saudi Arabia, for a pilgrimage. After my presentation and illustration, he objected to the idea of life insurance; he argued that life insurance was inimical to the teachings of Islam; he could purchase health and auto insurance, but he would never buy life insurance. I retorted by painting a phantasmagoria of his demise in an aircraft on his way to Mecca. His wife swallowed hard and asked him to buy the life insurance for the sake of their six children. He did. Now, after I have painted a rosy picture of his children attending Ivy League colleges in America, he is talking to me about the possibility of converting his policy from term to an option B equity indexed universal life product.

As an example of applying the pleasure principle, learn to derive pleasure from the drudgery of preparing your monthly budget. You can fool your subconscious mind in the same way that advertisers do every day, using the mass media to associate a boring activity with pleasure. Linking pleasure with the action and decision of planning your personal finances can become a very effective and positive habit. For example, there is nothing enjoyable about the nasty habit of smoking, but advertisers have been bombarding you with the romantic message that smoking is as pleasurable as the act of sexual intercourse.

An interesting example, in this regard, is the cigarette advertisement of Benson and Hedges. Cigarette advertisement is an almost perfect example representing the effective way of applying the pain and pleasure principles of mental association. I will focus your attention on Benson and Hedges because I love their ads. Benson & Hedges is a British brand of cigarettes owned by the Gallaher Group, which became a subsidiary of Japan Tobacco in 2007. They are registered in Old Bond Street in London, and are manufactured in Lisnafillen, Ballymena, Northern Ireland for the UK and Irish markets.

Generally, the subconscious message that the Benson and Hedges cigarette advertisement is conveying is positive and pleasurable. If you smoke their brand of cigarettes, you are going to look beautiful and feel so good, too. The advertisement appeals to your five senses and the subconscious. The black and white 7 1/4" x 10 1/2" ad displays this cigarette as a quality cigarette shortly after the brand became available in the United States. The picture in the ad shows the unique way that the cigarette pack works and calls the product "Top Drawer." The text reveals that the outer wrap held all of the information, such as the product name, and when it was removed it became your own personal case. It explains too that the filter was recessed into the mouthpiece so that it never was able to touch your lips or intrude on your enjoyment. It also bragged about the blend of the world's choicest tobaccos and that this is a limited edition cigarette. The final claim is that "With Benson & Hedges you pay more...you get more."

BENSON AND HEDGES IN POPULAR CULTURE

American popular culture also exhibits the projection of the reach of Benson & Hedges. For instance, Oasis members Noel and Liam Gallagher smoked Benson and Hedges during the 1990s, with Noel naming his two cats "Benson" and "Hedges." Oasis released a collection of their singles up until their second album. What is the Story, Morning Glory? The singles were sold in a special box shaped and colored like Benson & Hedges cigarette packets. British indie band Carter the Unstoppable Sex Machine referenced the brand in the song "England," from their 1992 album titled The Love Album, with the lyrics: "I have been GBH'd and ABH'd for a packet of B&H." In the film Mike Bassett: England Manager, Bassett, played by Ricky Tomlinson, writes down his squad for a match against Belgium on a packet of Benson and Hedges; his PA unwittingly includes two players with the surnames Benson and Hedges to the squad. A pair of twins in New Zealand was named "Benson" and "Hedges" after the brand and was cited by a New Zealand judge amongst a list of inappropriate children's names, alongside names like "Fish and Chips," "Black child," or "nigger." "Benson Hedges" is the name of the second track on the album Aim and Ignite from the New York power pop band Fun.

There is more to personal finance than the drudgery of debts and budgets.

WINSTON CIGARETTE ADVERTISING

I hope you do not feel like I am picking on Benson & Hedges. Let me turn your attention to Winston cigarettes. You should have heard the following slogan: "Winston tastes good like a cigarette should."

"Winston tastes good like a cigarette should" is an enduring slogan that appeared in newspaper, magazine, radio, and television advertisements for Winston cigarettes from the brand's introduction in 1954 until 1972. It is one of the best-known American tobacco advertising campaigns. In 1999, Advertising Age ranked the jingle eighth-best out of all the radio and television jingles that aired in the United States in the 20th century.

The deliberate use of "like" rather than "as" was provided by the William Esty Ad Agency, and the overall campaign was directed by Esty executives Wendell Adams and Arline Lunny, Lunny serving as producer/director of most of the visual and recording production related to the campaign in its initial years. Adams was a classically-trained musician in his own right, but singer/model/pianist Margaret Johnson ghost wrote the Jingle and, along with her husband, Travis Johnson, recorded it with their group, the Song Spinners. Johnson's insertion of the two quick hand claps before the word "cigarette" caught America's ear by surprise and had much to do with the jingle's success.

A second Winston jingle by Johnson, using the folk tune "Skip to my Lou," has faded into obscurity. In a departure for the time, the advertising campaign was also used to target distinct niche groups apart from its core clientele of Caucasian smokers, such as American Jews and African Americans. A catchy jingle and ad campaign, it has come to embody a piece of Americana, and has even seeped into the consciousness of people who were too young, or not even alive, to remember the campaign when it occurred.

The slogan was so well-remembered that it was added to Simpson's Contemporary Quotations in 1988. In the radio and television advertisements, the slogan is presented in a sing-song fashion with a noticeable two-beat clap near the end, so the jingle would sound like Winston tastes good like a [clap clap] cigarette should. The "clap" noise was sometimes substituted for actors in the commercials knocking twice against a truck carrying Winston cigarettes, or an actor flicking his lighter twice to the same conceit.

Winston cigarettes were sponsors of such television series as The Beverly Hillbillies and The Flintstones. The former series would show stars Buddy Ebsen, Irene Ryan, and Nancy Kulp extolling the virtues of Winston's while smoking them and reciting the jingle. The latter series would later come under fire for advertising cigarettes on an animated series watched by many children, but Winston pulled their involvement with the series after the Pebbles Flintstone character was born in 1963.

What about the grammar controversy? In reference to the grammar controversy, during the campaign's long run in the media, many viewers criticized the slogan as grammatically incorrect and that it should say, "Winston tastes good as a cigarette should." Ogden Nash, in The New Yorker, published a poem that ran "Like goes Madison Avenue, like so goes the nation." Walter Cronkite, then hosting The Morning Show, refused to say the line as written, and an announcer was used instead. Malcolm Gladwell, in The Tipping Point, says that this "ungrammatical and somehow provocative use of 'like' instead of 'as' created a minor sensation" in 1954 and implies that the phrase itself was responsible for vaulting the brand to second place in the U.S. market. Winston overtook Pall Mall cigarettes as the #1 cigarette in the United States in 1966, while the advertising campaign continued to make an impression on the mass media.

In the fall of 1961, a small furor enveloped the literary and journalistic communities in the United States when Merriam-Webster published its Third New International Dictionary. In the dictionary, the editors refused to condemn the use of "like" as a conjunction, and cited "Winston tastes good like a cigarette should" as an example of popular colloquial use. After publication of Webster's Third, The New York Times called the edition "Bolshevik," and the Chicago Daily News wrote that the transgression signified "a general decay in values." When the players in The Beverly Hillbillies spoke the line, they stretched the grammatical boundaries further: Jed: Winston tastes good...Granny: Like a cigarette had ought-a!

In 1970 and 1971, Winston sought to revamp its image and chose to respond to many grammarians' qualms with the slogan, "What do you want, good grammar or good taste?" MAD Magazine published a parody of this on the back cover of its January 1971 issue; set in a cemetery, it featured four tombstones who spoke in the past tense: "What did you want, good grammar or lung cancer?" With the new slogan in wide use, "Winston tastes good like a cigarette should" was retired permanently in 1972. In 1981, actor James Garner claimed responsibility for the wording of the slogan during an interview with Playboy magazine. Garner, who narrated the original commercial, stated that his first action ever to be captured on film was to misread the line that had been provided to him. However, as noted above, the advertisements first appeared in print before their debut on television, which would cast doubt on Garner's claim.

BEGIN WRITING MONEY ADVERTISEMENTS TO YOURSELF IN THE THIRD PERSON

Have you seen the success of Madison Avenue advertising in the above-mentioned discussion? I want you to emulate the advertising professionals. Watch the ads of President Barack H. Obama and Governor Romney in the 2012 presidential campaign. Do you observe how these two titans use ads tactfully to persuade the voters? God has given you a brain; God has given you a body. Run your own brain; run your own body. Stop allowing Madison Avenue to fool you into looking for pleasure for pleasure's sake; change your money behavior so that you can begin associating the act of making money and building wealth with pleasure, instead of pain. If you do not know how to do it, I will advise you to begin by making the decision to talk to yourself positively about building wealth; recite your self-messages many times daily; write marketing and money advertisements to yourself by employing Madison Avenue's own technique of AIDCAS.

There is more to personal finance than the drudgery of debts and budgets.

AIDCAS is an acronym used in marketing that describes a common list of events that may be undergone when a person is selling a product or service. The term and approach are attributed to American advertising and sales pioneer, E. St. Elmo Lewis. In 1898 Lewis created his AIDA funnel model on customer studies in the US life insurance market to explain the mechanisms of personal selling. Lewis held that the most successful salespeople followed a hierarchical, four layer process using the four cognitive phases that buyers follow when accepting a new idea or purchasing a new product. Act now! Quick action is required! Indeed, decision and action go hand in hand. The decision to act is the goad that will drive you to success city. Action produces quick results. My hero, Anthony Robbins, says that "...the greatest gift that extraordinarily successful people have over the average person is their ability to get themselves to take action." Indeed, procrastination is anathema, even when they toil in "sturm und drang," turbulence and stress or urgency.

AIDCAS

What does AIDCAS stand for? A=Attention; I=Interest; D=Desire; C=Confidence; A=Action; and S=Satisfaction.

A=Attention: A - Attention (Awareness): attract the attention of the customer.

I=Interest: I - Interest: raise customer interest by focusing on and demonstrating advantages and benefits (instead of focusing on features, as in traditional advertising).

D=Desire: D - Desire: convince customers that they want and desire the product or service and that it will satisfy their needs.

C=Confidence: C-make the customer to develop confidence in the product or service

A=Action: A- Action: lead customers towards taking action and/or purchasing.

S=Satisfaction: S-Satisfaction - satisfy the customer so they become a repeat customer and give referrals to a product.

Using a system like AIDCAS gives you a general understanding of how Madison Avenue targets the market effectively. You can apply these same principles in your daily life; pretend to talk to yourself; if you practice this exercise for thirty days, you will develop an uncanny ability to program your mind with positive messages. Now AIDCAS is an excellent weapon of power communication in your arsenal. Please, exploit it in your life: home, business, school, and community. By exploiting AIDCAS, you can manage your emotional states. To produce positive feelings in your environment, please, I urge you to think about positive experiences and discuss them with yourself subliminally. You are the movie director of your own life; you can choose to direct either a tragedy or a comedy, so you have the power to create your own reality. You can manipulate the movie set of your life like James Cameron in *The Titanic* and *Avatar*.

POWER OF MENTAL ASSOCIATION

Are you ready for the twelfth millionaire secret? In my linguistics classes, my professors taught me that words, especially abstract nouns, tended to have associations. Words like chair, table, and bed refer to a tangible object that can be felt or visualized; we call these words concrete nouns. By contrast, words such as love, war, or sea are indefinite; they have many shades of meaning; as a result, they have many and different associations to people with different cultural backgrounds and experiences. Abstract nouns are those words which have varying definitions and cannot be identified using the five senses (sight, hearing, smell, taste, touch). More examples of abstract nouns are the following: duty, honor, country, love, friendship, luxury, freedom, peace, bravery, hero, faith, hope, love, charity, redemption, victim, power, success, failure, joy, happiness, honesty, loyalty, humor, pain, health, health care, comfort, home, generosity, education, knowledge, wisdom, truth, art, beauty, memory, victory, survivor, control, attractive, and romance.

Experts of neuro-linguistic programming (NLP), like me, know how to use anchors and triggers to manipulate these abstract nouns. Why am I succeeding in personal finance? I have mastered the power of mental association. I have developed the ability to use anchors and triggers to manipulate my mind to link or delink pleasure or pain with personal finance tasks. Anchors are commands and actions that you summon to reinforce your nerves and confidence while thinking or talking. I am practicing the power of mental association. Because the mind consists of three parts, the action of triggering mental associations might be voluntary and deliberate; as in the case of Sigmund Freud referring to the unconscious or preconscious mind, the action might also be involuntary and accidental.

I have learned how to tap from the waters of the eternal and natural spring of divinity. I have practiced the art of running my own brain; I have perfected the science of running my own body. Like in real-estate and insurance sales, my success is attributable to my almost perfect understanding of human psychology, motivation, and hierarchy of needs. Indeed, I gleaned much of my knowledge of human psychology from the observation of nature, college courses on art, literature, philosophy, sociology, anthropology, and self-study. Always prefigure what people want by reading their body language and listening to what they say or do not say; then I figure out how Abraham Maslow's concept of hierarchy of needs applies to the person.

Summarily, Abraham Maslow's theory of human motivation consists of the following stages: physiological, safety, love or belonging, self-esteem, and self-actualization. Before you pitch a product or service to someone, know their level of motivation. Below is a more detailed explanation of the steps in Abraham Maslow's theory of human motivation: physiological, safety, love or belonging, self-esteem, and self-actualization. I am emphasizing them because they would tell you the truth about your response to the success system I am presenting to you.

If you are preoccupied primarily with daily survival and safety, my material may not be for you, but if you are driven by the volcanic ambition to realize your true human potential, then, you are ready for my message: financial literacy plus change in money habits will make you rich; my wealth-building system plus your discipline of following my methods will make it possible for you to achieve financial independence.

PHYSIOLOGICAL NEEDS

For the most part, physiological needs are obvious — they are the literal requirements for human survival. If these requirements are not met, the human body simply cannot continue to function. Air, water, and food are metabolic requirements for survival in all animals, including humans. Clothing and shelter provide necessary protection from the elements. The intensity of the human sexual instinct is shaped more by sexual competition than maintaining a birth rate adequate to survival of the species.

SAFETY NEEDS

With his or her physical needs relatively satisfied, the individual's safety needs take precedence and dominate physiological behavior. In the absence of physical safety -- due to terrorist attack, war, natural disaster, or, in cases of family violence, childhood abuse, etc. -- people (re-) experience post-traumatic stress disorder and trans-generational trauma transfer. In the absence of economic safety -- due to economic crisis and lack of work opportunities - these safety needs manifest themselves in such things as a preference for job security, grievance procedures for protecting the individual from unilateral authority, savings accounts, insurance policies, reasonable disability accommodations, and the like. Safety and security needs include: personal security, financial security, health and well-being. Safety implies security against accidents/illness and their adverse impacts.

LOVE AND BELONGING

After physiological and safety needs are fulfilled, the third layer of human needs is social; it involves feelings of belongingness. The social need is especially strong in childhood and can over-ride the need for safety as witnessed in children who cling to abusive parents. Deficiencies with respect to this aspect of Abraham Maslow's hierarchy - due to hospitalism, neglect, shunning, ostracism etc. -- can impact individual's ability to form and maintain emotionally significant relationships in general, such as: friendship, intimacy, and family.

Humans need to feel a sense of belonging and acceptance, whether it comes from a large social group, such as clubs, office culture, religious groups, professional organizations, sports teams, gangs, or small social connections (family members, intimate partners, mentors, close colleagues, confidants). They need to love and be loved (sexually and non-sexually) by others. In the absence of these elements, many people become susceptible to loneliness, social anxiety, and clinical depression. This need for belonging can often overcome the physiological and security needs, depending on the strength of the peer pressure; an anorexic, for example, many people ignore the need to eat and the security of health for a feeling of control and belonging.

ESTEEM

All humans have a need to be respected and to have self-esteem and self-respect. Esteem presents the normal human desire to be accepted and valued by others. People need to engage themselves to gain recognition and have an activity or activities that give the person a sense of contribution, to feel self-valued, be it in a profession or hobby. Imbalances at this level can result in low self-esteem or an inferiority complex. People with low self-esteem need respect from others. They may seek fame or glory, which again depends on others. Note, however, that many people with low self-esteem will not be able to improve their view of themselves simply by receiving fame, respect, and glory externally, but must first accept themselves internally.

Psychological imbalances such as depression can also prevent one from obtaining self-esteem on both levels. Most people have a need for a stable self-respect and self-esteem. Abraham Maslow noted two versions of esteem needs, a lower one and a higher one. The lower one is the need for the respect of others, the need for status, recognition, fame, prestige, and attention. The higher one is the need for self-respect, the need for strength, competence, mastery, self-confidence, independence and freedom. The latter one ranks higher because it rests more on inner competence won through experience. Deprivation of these needs can lead to an inferiority complex, weakness and helplessness. Abraham Maslow also states that even though these are examples of how the quest for knowledge is separate from basic needs, he warns that these "two hierarchies are interrelated rather than sharply separated." This explanation means that this level of need, as well as the next and highest level, is not strict, separate levels but closely related to others, and this is possibly the reason that these two levels of need are left out of most textbooks.

SELF-ACTUALIZATION

There is a saying that "What a man can be, he must be." This saying forms the basis of the perceived need for self-actualization. This level of need pertains to what a person's full potential is and realizing that potential. Abraham Maslow describes this desire as the desire to become more and more what one is, to become everything that one is capable of becoming.

This is a broad definition of the need for self-actualization, but when applied to individuals the need is specific. For example, one individual may have the strong desire to become an ideal parent, in another it may be expressed athletically, and in another it may be expressed in painting, pictures, or inventions. As mentioned before, to reach a clear understanding of this level of need one must first not only achieve the previous needs, physiological, safety, love, and esteem, but master these needs.

SIGMUND FREUD

While Abraham Maslow posits a theory of human motivation, Sigmund Freud lays threadbare the workings of the human mind. For this reason, much of the knowledge that I have retained in human psychology that is germane to personal finance is the teaching of Sigmund Freud. Who is he? Sigmund Freud was an Austrian neurologist who founded the discipline of psychoanalysis. Freud is best known for his theories of the unconscious mind and the mechanism of repression, and for creating the clinical method of psychoanalysis for investigating the mind and treating psychopathology through dialogue between a patient (or "analysand") and a psychoanalyst.

Freud postulated that sexual drives were the primary motivational forces of human life, developed therapeutic techniques such as the use of free association, discovered the phenomenon of transference in the therapeutic relationship and established its central role in the analytic process; he interpreted dreams as sources of insight into unconscious desires. He was an early neurological researcher into cerebral palsy, aphasia and microscopic neuroanatomy, and a prolific essayist, drawing on psychoanalysis to contribute to the history, interpretation and critique of culture.

In his early work on psychoanalysis, Sigmund Freud propounded the theories of the conscious, unconscious, and preconscious mind. Conscious is the region of the mind pertaining to self-awareness. Unconscious is the realm of a higher consciousness like dreams or trances. Preconscious refers to the interlude between sleep and waking. In his later work, Sigmund Freud divided the human mind into three parts: the ego, the superego, and the id. The ego is the region of the mind that deals with the sense of self; the superego is the area of the mind that handles morality, tradition, culture, and social convention; and the id is the realm of impulses.

As Napoleon Hill recommends, if you want your unconscious, the subconscious mind, to work for you so that you can think and grow rich, issue it precise verbal commands. For instance, tell your unconscious, the subconscious mind, to assist you in enjoying the study of personal finance; repeat this message to yourself daily before you fall asleep. Like a miracle, while you are sleeping, your unconscious will start working for you. In fact, this exercise will assist you in attuning with the realm of higher consciousness.

Trust me! When I was planning to get rich, I started applying these assertions, affirmations, and mystical principles, which I had learned not only from Napoleon Hill, but also from Christian mystics, Tuesday Lobsang Rampa, the Rosicrucians, and occult books such as *6 & 7 Books of Moses*, *Secrets of the Psalms*, *7 Keys to Power*, *7 Steps to Power*, *Telecult Power*, and *Mystics at Prayer*.

In an exercise to define my goal precisely to my subconscious mind, in 1997, I had affixed a replica of a million dollar bill on a wall in my study; I had written the following slogan above the bill: "Prince Ojong, your dreams are closer than you think." I was implementing the psychological techniques of imagination and visualization. My friends started laughing at me. As an exemplary student of Napoleon Hill, I had the self-confidence to dismiss their laughter as the mockery of "skellum, a blethering, blustering, drunken blellum; that frae November till October."

I had borrowed the words in the quotation above from an old Scottish poem in the Gaelic dialect that I used to like in middle school; here is the translation in modern English: "a waster, a rambling, blustering, drunken boaster, that from November until October" of next year will be idling around. Hence, you must be bold in implementing your plan of building wealth. When I made it into the big-time, all my detractors were green with envy; for once and for all, I dismissed them as losers. So learn to talk to yourself and your subconscious; the results can be as therapeutic and effective as divine communion.

Why did Sigmund Freud propose that the human psyche could be divided into three parts: Id, Ego, and Superego? Freud discussed this model in the 1920 essay *Beyond the Pleasure Principle*, and fully elaborated upon it in *The Ego and the Id* (1923), in which he developed it as an alternative to his previous topographic schema (i.e., conscious, unconscious, and preconscious). The id is the impulsive, child-like portion of the psyche that operates on the "pleasure principle" and only takes into account what it wants and disregards all consequences.

Freud acknowledged that his use of the term Id (das Es, "the It") was derived from the writings of Georg Groddeck. The super-ego is the moral component of the psyche, which takes into account no special circumstances in which the morally right thing may not be right for a given situation. The rational ego attempts to exact a balance between the impractical hedonism of the id and the equally impractical moralism of the super-ego; it is the part of the psyche that is usually reflected most directly in a person's actions. When overburdened or threatened by its tasks, it may employ defense mechanisms including denial, repression, and displacement. This concept is usually represented by the "Iceberg Model." This model represents the roles the Id, Ego, and Super Ego play with conscious and unconscious thought.

Are you ready to get rich? Then, you must learn how to make conscious use of your ego, superego, and id. Like a magician, command them to do your bidding. Like a movie director, create the picture of your new life, goals, hopes, wishes, and dreams.

Now that you have an idea of the psychology of money behavior modification, I would like to shift your focus to $ucce$$tology's ultimate money success formula: first, identify what you want or choose a successful role model; the second step is to take concrete action to create the results you have constructed and seen with your mind's eyes; the third step is to leverage what you have learned in this chapter pertaining to the syntax of the human mind, the power of mental association, the hierarchy of needs, money personality, positive attitudes, communication, divinity, dreams, imagination, visualization, and advertising.

There is more to personal finance than the drudgery of debts and budgets.

SEVEN LITTLE IDEAS

In addition to the above stipulations, I would like to introduce you to seven little ideas: passion, belief, strategy, clarity of values, energy, bonding power, and mastery of communication.

As you will soon discover, especially in my discussion of Napoleon Hill's *Think and Grow Rich*, passion is the fuel that can alight the fire of your ambition.; you must believe ardently in your goal almost like a religious fanatic; you must define the strategy you will employ to get rich; you must clarify your goal, so that your ambition is very clear and precise in your mind; condition your mind and body so that you are brimming with high octane energy; you must know how to bond with other human beings; if you are having problems, I would invite you to one of my workshops; until then, pick up a copy of Dale Carnegie's book titled *How to Win Friends and Influence People*. Summer 1972 was the first time I read Dale Carnegie's book; I have read this book several times since then. Similarly, I have read *How to Stop Worrying and Start Living* many times. Indeed, these books are perennial classics of motivational literature.

Since the most successful people are masters of the art and science of communication, you should polish your non-verbal and verbal communication skills; if you are a leader, achiever, and master communicator, like Ronald Reagan, you can persuade people to assist you in succeeding. Hence, begin communicating your goals to yourself. Choose the person you want to be your role model, and learn all what you can learn about them until you know precisely how they made it into the big time.

As Anthony Robbins says, success leaves clues, so you can follow the tracks of the success of your role model; try to duplicate the precise steps of your role model; if you want to model the excellence of your role model, you must learn his or her belief system: doctrines, creeds, guiding principles, dictum, faith, and passion. Beliefs open a channel of communication between you and your nervous system, so use your nervous system to communicate with your mind; use your nervous system to send success signals to your mind. Your brain simply does what you ask it to do.

You may be unaware that from childhood you begin hiding away your ego, your inner self. Your superego forces you to learn to adapt and survive in the family, church, school, work, and the outside world. For instance, your family and peers teach and prescribe socially acceptable behavior to you. Similarly, your educational system teaches you the technical and social skills you need to sustain a material life. As an adult, you are thrust into a society geared towards crass materialism, copy-cat socialization, standardization, and maintenance of the status quo.

Rarely, especially in your early formative years, are you taught inner psychic development, with an emphasis on intuition, the subconscious mind, independent thinking, self-esteem, self-confidence, psychic, or inner spiritual growth. Then, is it any wonder to you that your inner self has become lost in the rat-race business of the outer world? Yet despite all this, your ego, the inner self, does remain dormant and alive in you.

Are you ready to heed its call? That is why I am writing *The Miraculous Millionaire* to publicize $ucce$$tology and set you free financially; I cannot take credit for the invaluable material in the $ucce$$tology system; the material may be invaluable, but it lacks originality; except for forays I have made into my personal experiences; indeed, most of the ideas in $ucce$$tology have been in existence today and have been for centuries, offering rich people a way to realize their own infinitely powerful and divine nature. I am the Robin Hood of personal finance; I am Prometheus; for your sake, I have stolen the fire of knowledge from all the quarters of the earth. Open your mind to receive new, positive feedback from $ucce$$tology. Let me re-program your mind that has been damaged by societal influences. Join my new money revolution. Let me teach you how to earn big money every day without having any connections or angels. My book is your master key to riches, so use it to think and grow rich with peace of mind.

SIMPLIFY YOUR LIFESTYLE WITH MONEY BEHAVIORAL GUIDEPOSTS

Are you ready for the thirteenth millionaire secret? Values! Did you know that millionaires have a set of values? Millionaires not only have a set of values, but they establish a values hierarchy they live by year by year, month by month, week by week, day by day, hour by hour, minute by minute, and second by second. Your values are things that are very important to you in this life. The hierarchy of values is the strongest determinant of your behavior. It outlines the order of your priorities; it evinces the set of principles you consider to be very important. Therefore, your values hierarchy is a ranking of the items that are important to you. You can emulate my values hierarchy; my values hierarchy is in the following order: God first, family second, business and personal finance third:

1. God-- Believe in God and pray
2. Family
3. Business and Personal Finance
4. Freedom
5. Love
6. Growth
7. Support
8. Challenge
9. Creativity
10. Respect
11. Spirituality
12. Honesty
13. Ecstasy
14. Communication
15. Beauty
16. Attraction
17. Fun

There is more to personal finance than the drudgery of debts and budgets.

KEEP A JOURNAL

Are you ready for the fourteenth millionaire secret? Millionaires like keeping records, so they keep a journal to create a paper trail of the drama of life. A journal is a good way to express and record your thoughts, aspirations, dreams, and worries.

At the end of the day, after saying your prayers, please, spend a few minutes to reflect on your day. Brainstorm and free write your houghts and feelings.

SET YOUR GOALS

Are you ready for the fifteenth millionaire secret? To become financially independent, it is important for you to set the goals that you want to achieve. Please, be specific about what you want to accomplish. In my case, I had set the goal to make a million dollars and become financially independent in 10 years; that is, from 1997 to 2007. Officially, I began the journey in 1997, but I was fortunate to achieve my goal in 2004, a few years sooner. I thank God for his favor.

CALENDARS AND DAILY PLANNERS

Are you ready for the sixteenth millionaire secret? Simplify your lifestyle with a manual calendar and daily planner. When I was starting out, I bought a daily planner from a local supermarket called Giant Foods. The planner was crucial to my strategy of time management. I have never believed in the idea of colored people's time; I like to be punctual because punctuality is the soul of business. First, I isolated all the national holidays in my planner. Federal law (5 U.S.C. 6103) establishes many public holidays for Federal employees. Please note that most Federal employees work on a Monday through Friday schedule. For these employees, when a holiday falls on a non-workday -- Saturday or Sunday -- the holiday usually is observed on Monday (if the holiday falls on Sunday) or Friday (if the holiday falls on Saturday).

HOLIDAY CALENDAR

New Year's Day	January 1
Martin Luther King Day	third Monday in January
President's Day	third Monday in February
Memorial Day	last Monday in May
Independence Day	July 4
Labor Day	first Monday in September
Columbus Day	second Monday in October
Veterans Day	November 11
Thanksgiving Day	fourth Thursday in November
Christmas Day	December 25

I can use my electronic calendar to visualize my schedule by minute, hour, day, week, month, or year. What do you plan to do on a particular holiday? Time is money, so do not waste it in idleness. I use holiday time to travel and spend time with friends. Traveling is not only a leisure activity but also a form of education in and itself. If I decide not to travel during a particular holiday, I spend my time in solitude, reading at home or in a library.

Computerize your lifestyle with a desktop organizer or a web day planner. If you are a computer enthusiast, like me, I would recommend a desktop or web daily planner to you. An organizer provides all the tools I need to organize my personal and professional life. I started out with a desktop organizer, but I have since switched to a web day planner. I prefer web-based organizers because they sport an intuitive and familiar interface plus thousands of calendar designs and synchronization with a plethora of my mobile devices. I have everything I need in one place.

I always stay up to date, even when I am on the go. I synch my schedule, tasks, and address book to my handheld, mobile devices. Indeed, a web organizer works the way I like to simplify my life and daily activities.

In addition, I save valuable time. As for programming my to-do-lists, I prioritize my tasks, without worrying about conflict of appointments. I accomplish more in less time, without missing important deadlines or losing track of my daily progress.

As for my address book, I use it to record information about my customers, acquaintances, friends, peers, prospects, partners, and colleagues. My address book helps me communicate with the individuals in my circle of influence effortlessly. As a result, I build stronger relationships and stay in constant touch with customers and family members. I value the people in my circle of influence; I like to stay in touch with them; my address book facilitates this process.

SOCIALIZE FOR FUN

Are you ready for the seventeenth millionaire secret? My father used to tell me that it is important to study hard. He did not forget, however, to remind me about the importance of interspersing work with play. As he used to say, too much work without play makes Jack a dull boy. Hence, I urge you to work and allocate time for entertainment. Please, engage in social networking to create your mastermind, but make time for personal socialization. I challenge you to think and grow rich. Millionaires work hard, but they like to have fun, too.

MILLIONAIRE SECRET FROM NAPOLEON HILL'S *THINK AND GROW RICH*

I credit my success to a thorough reading, rereading, comprehension, and implementation of the success system expounded in Napoleon Hill's *Think and Grow Rich*. For your information, the book resulted from the suggestion of Andrew Carnegie, one of America's famous robber barons, to Napoleon Hill, a journalist.

Carnegie's suggestion was for Hill to interview him and other rich folks in America to publish a philosophical system of success for all Americans; I encourage you to buy and read Napoleon Hill's book; if you join the Millionaire Club or attend the Millionaire's iUniversity, you will receive an electronic copy of the book, and I will teach you the wealth-creation formula that had worked for the business magnates who were the peers of Andrew Carnegie.

List of the Most Popular Robber Barons:

- John Jacob Astor (real estate, fur) – New York
- Andrew Carnegie (steel) – Pittsburgh and New York
- Jay Cooke (finance) – Philadelphia
- Charles Crocker (railroads) – California
- Daniel Drew (finance) – New York
- James Buchanan Duke (tobacco) – Durham, North Carolina
- James Fisk (finance) – New York
- Henry Morrison Flagler (railroads, oil) – New York and Florida
- Henry Clay Frick (steel) – Pittsburgh and New York
- John Warne Gates (barbed wire, oil) – Texas
- Jay Gould (railroads) – New York
- Edward Henry Harriman (railroads) – New York
- James J. Hill (railroads) – Minnesota
- Charles T. Hinde (railroads, water transport, shipping, hotels) - Illinois, Missouri, Kentucky, California
- Mark Hopkins (railroads) – California
- Andrew W. Mellon (finance, oil) – Pittsburgh
- J. P. Morgan (finance, industrial consolidation) – New York
- John Cleveland Osgood (coal mining, iron) - Colorado
- Henry B. Plant (railroads) – Florida
- John D. Rockefeller (oil) – Cleveland, New York
- Charles M. Schwab (steel) – Pittsburgh and New York
- Joseph Seligman (banking) – New York
- John D. Spreckels (sugar) – California

- Cornelius Vanderbilt (water transport, railroads) – New York

- Charles Tyson Yerkes (street railroads) – Chicago

COMPREHENSIVE LISTING OF ROBBER BARONS FOR STUDY

Let us pay homage to great men. Below I have provided a comprehensive list of robber barons. I want you to use Internet search engines to study the source of their wealth. It may be a good idea to select someone you would like to be your role model from this list. Later proceed to Amazon.com to ascertain if there are any books on your chosen role model:

Henry M. Flagler
John W. Mackay
Frank W. Woolworth
August Belmont
Richard W. Sears
Charles W. Post
Daniel Drew
Jay Gould
Jacob Schiff
John P. Morgan
John D. Rockefeller
William Vanderbilt
John Jacob Astor
Stephen Girard
Frederick Weyerhaeuser
Marshall Field
Henry Ford
James G. Fair
James Fisk
Henry C. Frick
E. I. DuPont
Levi Strauss
Russell Sage
John I. Blair
Collis Huntington
James C. Flood
Phillip Armour
Leland Stanford
James J. Hill
Claus Spreckels
George Eastman
James B. Duke
George Hearst
William Randolph Hearst

There is more to personal finance than the drudgery of debts and budgets.

Isaac Singer
Adolphus Bush
George Pullman
Johns Hopkins
Cyrus McCormick
Joseph Pulitzer
Cornelius Vanderbilt
Andrew W. Mellon
William Weightman
Edward H. Harriman
Henry H. Rogers
Mark Hopkins
Edward Clark
William Rockefeller
Charles Crocker
Charles Tiffany

THINK AND GROW RICH: A BOOK REVIEW AND SUMMARY

Think and Grow Rich is one of the best-selling and most influential book of all time. It is written by Napoleon Hill, an American author born in October 26, 1883. Hill is one of the earliest producers of personal development, financial success, social achievement, and motivational literature. In fact, Hill is considered as one of the best authors of motivational-success books. *Think and Grow Rich* is a classic of success philosophy and motivation, a book that should be in everyone's success library. Napoleon Hill published *Think and Grow Rich* first in 1937, after twenty-five years of studying over five hundred of America's most successful and wealthiest businessmen of that time, the robber barons.

For your erudition, I have already included people like, Henry Ford, Andrew Carnegie, Theodore Roosevelt, Thomas Edison, Charles Schwab, Arthur Brisbane, Howard Taft, and John Patterson on the lists above. These names represent a small fraction of the hundreds of well-known Americans whose achievements financially, and in all other aspects, prove that those who understand and apply the same success principles reach high stations in life.

THE MAKING OF *THINK AND GROW RICH*

In 1908, Andrew Carnegie   invited Napoleon Hill to a meeting. The former assigned the latter the task of writing a book that will tell the story and summarize the principles of success of the most influential and successful people of America. Andrew Carnegie wanted to bequeath the 99% of the working people of America his financial success formula. As a requirement of the writing mission, Andrew Carnegie also wanted Napoleon Hill to spend more than twenty years to observe and interview the other five hundred successful men at that time and summarize the common mindset, attitudes, principles, and habits that led to their success.

Upon hearing the request of Andrew Carnegie, the young Napoleon Hill felt overwhelmed with the tasks assigned to him, but he still persisted with the task of fulfilling the mission. Today, after more than seventy years since *Think and Grow Rich* was first released in 1937 and more than one hundred years after the idea was born, *Think and Grow Rich* remains the primary source of motivation and success principle for many successful and wealthy people then and now. It remains, unarguably, one of the best-selling books on success up to this time. Its timeless wealth-creation principles are also being used in the teachings of modern-day personal development coaches, writers and trainers, such as John Maxwell.

Although we are going to study *Think and Grow Rich* as a course at Millionaire iUniversity, I would like to summarize the book's content and salient characteristics. *Think and Grow Rich* TEACHES YOU THE SECRET OF MASTERING TRUE AND LASTING PROSPERITY.

INDEED, THE BOOK IS one of my great sources of motivation and inspiration, in my day-to-day quest in living life to the fullest. I urge you to read the book over and over again, to refresh the teachings that can help you achieve your own definition of personal success and happiness in life. Here is a summary of the THIRTEEN SUCCESS PRINCIPLES taught in *Think and Grow Rich*:

1. DESIRE

THE GREATEST ACHIEVEMENT WAS, AT FIRST, AND FOR A TIME, BUT A DREAM. Desire is *Think and Grow Rich*'s first step to riches and success in life. Napoleon Hill has discussed why desire is the starting point of all achievements. Napoleon Hill explains how one sound idea can create change, success, richness, and fulfillment in your life. He has shared the six definite practical steps in transforming your desires or dreams to reality. Also, you will know and understand the difference between wishing and desiring, including what one does to turn dreams into reality.

2. FAITH

THE HOLY BIBLE SAYS FAITH CAN MOVE MOUNTAINS. Napoleon HILL SAYS FAITH IS POWERFUL. THERE ARE NO LIMITATIONS TO THE MIND EXCEPT THOSE WE ACKNOWLEDGE IN CONSCIOUSNESS. POVERTY AND RICHES ARE THE OFFSPRING OF THOUGHT. HAVING FAITH IS SIMILAR TO BELIEVING THE UNSEEN. WE HAVE NOT SEEN GOD, BUT WE BELIEVE IN THE EXISTENCE OF THE INFINITE FORCE OF DIVINITY; WE HAVE NOT SEEN WHAT WE DESIRE, BUT WE IMAGINE SEEING IT IN OUR MIND'S EYE.

Faith is *Think and Grow Rich*'s second step to riches and success in life. It discusses the importance of visualization and belief in the attainment of desire. Napoleon Hill has showed the relation of emotion to faith. How a mind dominated by positive emotions becomes a favorable adobe for the state of mind known as faith. Also, Napoleon Hill has taught the steps in developing faith or belief in oneself of which can help in making desires to reality.

3. AUTO-SUGGESTION

Auto-suggestion is *Think and Grow Rich's* third step to riches and success in life. It is a medium for influencing the subconscious mind. Mr. Hill discusses how powerful our subconscious mind is, and if you learn how to direct your thoughts, things happen. Similar to faith, auto-suggestion is an act on visualizing and having faith that your desires can turn into reality. Also, this chapter taught principles and six steps in developing and practicing auto-suggestion.

4. SPECIALIZED KNOWLEDGE

KNOWLEDGE WILL NOT ATTRACT RICHES AND SUCCESS IN LIFE, UNLESS IT IS ORGANIZED. Have you ever wondered why many smart people are not rich and successful? In this chapter, Napoleon Hill has differentiated general knowledge from specialized knowledge. One personal experience or observation can bring riches and success in life. An "ignorant person" can make fortune compared to a "smart person." It explained why "knowledge is not power" alone. The book explains how special knowledge can be acquired anywhere, if only you are open to seek and use them.

5. IMAGINATION

MAN CAN CREATE ANYTHING HE CAN IMAGINE. Imagination is *Think and Grow Rich's* fifth step towards riches and success in life. It is through imagination wherein desire is crystallized into reality. Napoleon Hill discussed in this chapter how man's only limitation lies in the development and use of his imagination.

He has shared that great leaders of business, industry and finance, great artists, musicians, poets, and writers, became great because they developed the faculty of creative imagination. Also, he has taught the practical use of imagination that leads to success and riches in life.

6. ORGANIZED PLANNING

YOUR ACHIEVEMENT CAN BE NO GREATER THAN YOUR PLANS ARE SOUND. Organized planning is *Think and Grow Rich's* sixth step towards riches and success in life. Napoleon Hill has given his most thoughts and attentions in this chapter. His twenty five years of study have focused on how successful and wealthy people have accumulated their achievements through this principle.

As stated by Napoleon Hill, "The most intelligent man living cannot succeed in accumulating riches and success – not in any other undertaking – without plans which are practical and workable."

In this chapter, Napoleon Hill discusses the characteristics and attitudes of successful and wealthy people, the thirty major causes of failure, twenty self-analysis questionnaire for personal inventory, where and how one may find opportunities, and how to accept and move on from temporary defeat.

7. DECISION

ONE OF THE REASONS MOST MEN AND WOMEN EXPERIENCE FAILURE IS BECAUSE THEY LACK DECISION. Decision is *Think and Grow Rich*'s seventh step towards riches and success in life. It is called the mastery of procrastination. The opposite of decision, procrastination is a common enemy which practically every man must conquer. Napoleon Hill has disclosed in this chapter that people who fail to accumulate riches and success in life, without exception, have the habit of reaching decisions very slowly and of changing these decisions quickly and often. In this chapter you will learn how rich people make the decisions that brought about the riches and success they have accumulated.

8. PERSISTENCE

WILL-POWER AND DESIRE, WHEN PROPERLY COMBINED, MAKE AN IRRESISTIBLE PAIR. Persistence is *Think and Grow Rich*'s eighth step towards riches and success in life. Persistence is a sustained effort necessary to induce faith. In this chapter, Napoleon Hill discusses why a majority of people fail and only a few succeed. He discusses what comprises and creates persistence, the symptoms of lack of persistence, the ways to develop persistence and the steps essential for success in all aspect of life.

9. POWER OF THE MASTER MIND

POWER IS AN ORGANIZED AND INTELLIGENTLY DIRECTED KNOWLEDGE. Power of the Master Mind is *Think and Grow Rich*'s ninth step to riches and success in life. Napoleon Hill has discussed in this chapter the role of power in attainment of any success and riches in life. Power is described differently here than what we usually know about power.

In *Think and Grow Rich*, power is described as organized efforts, sufficient to enable an individual to transmute desire into its desired equivalent. You will learn how to gain power through the master mind, what are the sources of knowledge and learn the story of how the richest and successful men attained their status through their power of the master mind.

10. THE MASTERY OF SEX TRANSMUTATION

THE EMOTION OF SEX BRINGS INTO BEING A STATE OF MIND. The mastery of sex transmutation is *Think and Grow Rich*'s tenth step to riches and success in life. This is not about having sex, per se, but Napoleon Hill uses the term "sex" to describe a state of mind that points out human's greatest desire. If a person is driven by a desire, a deep down burning desire, as powerful as "sex," that is when the person is able to turn his or her dreams dream into reality.

There is more to personal finance than the drudgery of debts and budgets.

In this chapter, Napoleon Hill explains the roles of the senses and stimuli in turning your desires to reality. He also explains how our sixth sense can develop a "genius" within us. In addition, he explains why men seldom succeed before forty and why women are men's greatest motivator in life.

11. THE SUBCONSCIOUS MIND

WHERE ONE IS FOUND, THE OTHER CANNOT EXIST. The subconscious mind is *Think and Grow Rich*'s eleventh step to riches and success in life. Napoleon Hill explains how the subconscious mind can be the connecting link of our desires to reality. It is the connecting link between our finite mind and the infinite intelligence. Also, he discusses how you cannot entirely control your subconscious mind, but you can voluntarily hand over a task to your subconscious mind to plan a strategy for success.

You can communicate your desire or purpose which you wish to transform into reality to your subconscious mind, which supports the belief that what you feed your mind, you conceive it. So if you are thinking negative things, you are bringing negative results. It is the same as if you are thinking positive things, you bring more positive things in your life. This principle explains why you cannot think of negative thoughts and expect to receive positive results in your life.

12. THE BRAIN

THE BRAIN IS THE BROADCASTING AND RECEIVING STATION FOR THOUGHT. This is *Think and Grow Rich*'s twelfth step towards riches and success in life. In this chapter, Napoleon Hill explains the connection between your subconscious mind, creative imagination, and auto-suggestion. The connection sheds light on the greatest intangible forces that are governing our world and how these forces can dramatically change things.

13. THE SIXTH SENSE

THE SIXTH SENSE IS THE DOOR TO THE TEMPLE OF WISDOM. The sixth sense is *Think and Grow Rich*'s last and thirteenth step to riches and success in life. If you have noticed, you may have been feeling a little different once you have reached this stage. I can tell you it is normal and that you deserve to pat yourself for reaching and reading this far. Remember the saying, "Insanity is doing the same things over and over but expecting different result."

If you have been doing and receiving the same things, yet you want to create change in your life, most of the time, there is a need for you to open your mind and accept a new reality. And once you do, you may expect to receive different results in your life. Let the principles, values, and attitudes that great and successful men lived by be an integral part of your life.

In addition, the last chapter of *Think and Grow Rich* discusses the Ghost of Fears that stops people in acting and realizing their dreams. Napoleon Hill presents ways on how to overcome these fears to enable you to start creating and acting upon the success and riches you deserve in your life.

GEMS OF WEALTH WISDOM

You can obtain a FREE copy of *Think and Grow Rich* on my web site: princeojong.com. I regard Napoleon Hill's book as a classic treasury of the words of wisdom of the ancient builders of wealth, such as the earliest captains of America's high finance and industry. I respect these great men; you should respect them, too. In fact, Henry Wadsworth Longfellow said it best in his poem titled A Psalm of Life: "Lives of great men all remind us we can make our lives sublime, and, departing, leave behind us footprints on the sands of time...." Hence, below, I am going to present a few excerpts from Napoleon Hill's book that keep streaming into my consciousness like the refrain of a melody:

"There is no such thing as something for nothing."

"...riches are not beyond your reach that you can still be what you wish to be, that money, fame, recognition, and happiness can be had by all who are determined to have these blessings."

"All achievement, all earned riches, have their beginning in an idea!"

"when a man really desires a thing so deeply that he is willing to stake his entire future on a single turn of the wheel to get it, he is sure to win."

"...the tricks of opportunity. It has a sly habit of slipping in by the back door, and often it comes disguised in the form of misfortune, or temporary defeat. Perhaps this is why so many fail to recognize opportunity."

"Before success comes in any man's life, he is sure to meet with such temporary defeat and, perhaps, some failure."

"One sound idea is all that one needs to achieve success."

"...riches come only to those who work hard and long."

"...riches begin with a state of mind, with definiteness of purpose, with little or hard work."

"Success comes only to those who become success conscious. Failure comes to those who indifferently allow themselves to become failure conscious."

"...see and feel and believe yourself already in possession of the money."

"...that accumulation of money cannot be left to chance, good fortune, and luck. One must realize that all who have accumulated great fortunes first did a certain amount of dreaming. Hoping, wishing, desiring, and planning before they acquired money."

There is more to personal finance than the drudgery of debts and budgets.

"We who desire to accumulate riches should remember the real leaders of the world always have been men who harnessed and put into practical use the intangible, unseen forces of unborn opportunity, and have converted those forces (or impulses of thought) into skyscrapers, cities, factories, airplanes, automobiles, and every form of convenience that makes life more pleasant."

"In planning to acquire your share of the riches, let no one influence you to scorn the dreamer. To win the big stakes in this changed world you must catch the spirit of the great pioneers of the past, whose dreams have given to civilization all that it has of value, the spirit which serves as the lifeblood of our own country."

"If the thing you wish to do is right and you believe in it, go ahead and do it. Put your dreams across.....Practical dreamers do not quit."

"No one is ready for a thing until he believes he can acquire it."

"It is a well-known fact that one comes, finally, to believe whatever one repeats to one's self, whether the statement be true or false."

"Thoughts that are mixed with any of the feelings of emotion constitute a magnetic force, which attracts other similar or related thoughts."

"Your ability to use the principle of autosuggestion will depend, very largely, upon your capacity to concentrate upon a given desire until that desire becomes a burning obsession."

"..the principle of concentration....fix in your own mind the exact amount of money you desire," hold your thoughts on that amount of money by concentration, or fixation of attention, with your eyes closed until you can actually see the physical appearance of the money. Do this at least once each day. As you go through these exercises, follow the instructions given in this chapter on faith, and see yourself actually in possession of the money!"

"Man may become the master of himself, and of his environment, because he has the power to influence his own subconscious mind."

"Knowledge will not attract money, unless it is organized and intelligently directed, through practical plans of action, to the definite end of accumulation of money. Lack of understanding of this fact has been the source of confusion to millions of people who falsely believe that "knowledge is power.""

"Any man is educated who knows where to get knowledge when he needs it, and how to organize that knowledge into definite plans of action."

"...you will require specialized knowledge of the service or merchandise which you intend to offer in return for fortune. Perhaps you may need much more specialized knowledge than you have the ability or the inclination to acquire, and if this should be true, you may bridge your weakness through the aid of your "Master Mind" group.""

"Anything acquired without effort and without cost is generally unappreciated, often discredited; perhaps this is why we get so little from our marvelous opportunity in public schools."

"Desire is thought impulse."

"Ideas are the beginning of all fortunes. Ideas are products of the imagination."

"A quitter never wins—and a winner never quits."

"...all the great fortunes began in the form of compensation for personal services, or from the sale of ideas."

"Men are paid not merely for what they know, but more particularly for what they do with that which they know."

"Your value is established entirely by your ability to render useful service or your capacity to induce others to render such service."

"There is but one dependable method of accumulating and legally holding riches, and that is by rendering useful service."

"Financial independence, riches, desirable business and professional positions are not within reach of the person who neglects or refuses to expect, plan, and demand these things."

"The starting point of all achievement is desire."

"...every failure brings with it the seed of an equivalent advantage."

A LISTING OF NAPOLEON HILL'S TWELVE LAWS OF RICHES

1 Positive mental attitude
2 Sound health
3 Harmony in human relations
4 Freedom from fear
5 Hope of future achievement
6 Capacity for applied faith
7 Willingness to share one's blessings with others
8 Be engaged in a labor of love
9 An open mind towards all subjects and people
10 Complete self-discipline
11 Wisdom to understand people
12 Financial security

There is more to personal finance than the drudgery of debts and budgets.

It is important for you to observe that money comes last in the list I have presented above. For assistance in mastering the laws stipulated above, please, attend Millionaire iUniversity.com.

DENNIS KIMBRO

He is an African-American motivational author who collaborated with Napoleon Hill to write *Think and Grow Rich: A Black Choice*. When Napoleon Hill died, he left behind a manuscript aimed at the specific problems of African-Americans, and the Napoleon Hill Foundation chose an author and entrepreneur known as Dennis Kimbro to complete it.

The purpose of the book is to underscore the fact that success in America is colorless. It does not matter if you are black or white; if you work hard and are smart in reading and applying Napoleon Hill's philosophy, you will become successful; I am an African immigrant from Cameroon, Africa. My success is a positive proof of the possibility of the American dream. The main strength of Dennis Kimbro's book is the author's preponderance in the use of black role models: George Washington Carver, Jesse Jackson, Oprah Winfrey, Michael Jordan, Alex Palmer Haley, Ray Charles, Selma Burke, Leontyne Price, Spike Lee, and Wally Amos.

ANTHONY ROBBINS AND *UNLIMITED POWER*

After you have read Napoleon Hill's books, I recommend *Unlimited Power*, a book written by Anthony Robbins. Did you know that Anthony Robbins is a great success coach? I learned much about the application of success principles by adhering to the teachings of Anthony Robbins. In my objective estimation, after Napoleon Hill, Robbins comes a proud second. Indeed, I have read all his books, and I have been impressed by their quality as motivational and business literature. I will recommend two of his books to you: *Unlimited Power* and *Awaken the Giant Within*.

In a nutshell, *Unlimited Power* theorizes that you, as a human being created by God, have been endowed with limitless potential that you can harness to achieve your dreams. In essence, you are like a personal computer; your framework is guided by input-output, garbage in garbage out; that is, good stuff gets in you and good stuff gets out of you; or, you can be what you want to be; your senses could be likened to a radio transmitting station; if you feed your mind garbage, the result you get will be garbage; if you program your mind with positive material, you will receive successful outcomes. Buy the book and read it; or you can borrow it from your county or public library.

You will be happy to practice some of the exercises of breathing and visualizing presented in the book. As for *Awaken the Giant Within*, it reinforces the themes that Anthony Robbins has already explored in *Unlimited Power*; *Awaken the Giant Within* reminds you of the fact that you are a sleeping giant; the author motivates you to wake up. Central to Anthony Robbins teaching is the concept of the modeling of excellence.

If you want to succeed, model your life after someone who is already achieving the results you want to achieve. In my case, I have had many role models: John H. Johnson of *Ebony* magazine, Earl Graves of *Black Enterprise*, Bill Gates of *Microsoft*, Donald Trump, and Sandy Weill. I have spent so much time researching all these personalities, and I have read all their books, too.

NEURO LINGUISTIC PROGRAMMING

Who is afraid of neuro linguistic programming? I have collected many articles on the subject on my web site: princeojong.com. For now, the following introduction suffices. Anthony Robbins also introduces you to the theory and practice of neuro-linguistic programming (NLP), the science of peak performance and achievement. NLP is the study of the structure of excellence of human beings. It is the modelling of good behaviours and effective habits. It is the structure of the organization of thoughts and senses. Anthony Robbins introduces you to VAKOG: Visual, Auditory, Kinesthetic, Olfactory, and Gustatory.

Also known as sensory modalities, VAKOG is a representational system of NLP. It is a neuro-linguistic programming model that examines how the human mind processes information. It states that for practical purposes, information is, or can be treated as if, processed through the senses. Thus people say one talks to oneself, the auditory sense, even if no words are emitted; one makes mental pictures in one's head when thinking or dreaming, the visual sense, and one considers feelings in the body and emotions, known as the kinesthetic sense.

NLP theorizes that it is crucial in human cognitive processing to recognize that the subjective character of experience is strongly tied into, and influenced by, how memories and perceptions are processed within each sensory representation in the mind. NLP considers that expressions such as "It is all misty" or "I cannot get a grip on it," can often be precise literal unconscious descriptions from within those sensory systems, communicating unconsciously where the mind perceives a problem in handling some mental event.

Within NLP, the various senses in their role as information processors, are known as representation systems, or sensory modalities. As stated above, the model itself is known as the VAKOG model, an acronym from the initial letters of the sensory-specific modalities: Visual, Auditory, Kinesthetic, Olfactory, and Gustatory). Since taste and smell are so closely connected, sometimes as a four-tuple, meaning its four-way sensory-based description.

LEVELS OF NLP

It is an approach to problem solving and an understanding of the core identity belief structures. NLP stands for Neuro-Linguistic Programming, a name that encompasses the three most influential components involved in producing human experience: neurology, language, and programming. The neurological system regulates how our body functions; language determines how we interface and communicate with other people; and our programming determines the kinds of models of the world we create.

Neuro-Linguistic Programming describes the fundamental dynamics between mind, neuro, and language, linguistic, and how their interplay affects our body and behavior, that is, our personal programming. As Anthony Robbins shows, NLP provides tools and skills for the development of states of individual excellence, but it also establishes a system of empowering beliefs and presuppositions about what human beings are, what communication is, and what the process of change is all about. At another level, NLP is about self-discovery, exploring your true identity and mission. It also provides a framework for you to understand the relation between your physical and spiritual human experiences that reach beyond you as an individual connected to family, community, and global system.

NLP is not only about competence and excellence; in fact, it is also about wisdom and vision. Neuro-linguistic programming (NLP) is an approach to psychotherapy and organizational change based on "a model of interpersonal communication chiefly concerned with the relationship between successful patterns of behavior and the subjective experiences, especially patterns of thought, underlying them and "a system of alternative therapy based on this which seeks to educate people in self-awareness and effective communication, and to change their patterns of mental and emotional behavior."

I REALIZE THAT IS THE WIKIPEDIA DEFINITION AND A LOT FOR MOST OF US TO DIGEST. SIMPLY PUT, NLP IS A PRACTICE THAT USES VARIOUS MODALITIES TO GIVE PEOPLE THE TOOLS THEY NEED TO BE SUCCESSFUL, TO OVERCOME ADDICTION, AND TO REPROGRAM THE WAY THEY THINK; NLP DOES NOT NEED TO KNOW WHY THEY HAVE AN ADDICTION OR ARE SUFFERING FROM UNDERACHIEVEMENT IN ANY AREA OF THEIR LIFE. THE REASON A PROBLEM EXISTS IS NOT IMPORTANT TO THE APPLICATION OF NLP, SO THERE IS NO TIME WASTED GETTING TO THE ROOT OF A PROBLEM BUT RATHER JUST ADDRESSING THE ISSUE AT HAND. THERE IS NO DELVING INTO A PERSON'S PAST TO FORCE THEM TO IDENTIFY THE SOURCE OF THE PROBLEM BUT TIME IS MORE EFFICIENTLY SPENT IN ACTIVITIES THAT HELP REPROGRAM THE THOUGHT PATTERNS, ESPECIALLY ON A SUBCONSCIOUS LEVEL. NLP MODALITIES ARE VERY SIMPLE AND EASY TO DO. THEY DO NOT REQUIRE DRUGS, AND THEY ARE PAIN-FREE ACTIVITIES THAT ARE LIFE CHANGING FOR MANY CLIENTS.

AS A FOLLOWER OF ANTHONY ROBBINS, I HAVE FOUND NLP TO BE A HIGHLY EFFECTIVE TOOL. BEFORE I WAS FORTUNATE ENOUGH TO DISCOVER NLP, I HAD ALREADY BEGUN TO LEARN MANY LIFE-CHANGING LESSONS. FOR ONE, I REALIZED NEGATIVE THOUGHTS WERE THE BARRIERS ERECTED BY MANY PEOPLE WHO CLAIM TO BE MAKING AN EFFORT TO GET RICH QUICKLY AND EASILY; BESIDES, I OBSERVED THAT MANY PEOPLE GET STUCK IN A ROUTINE RUT IN TRYING TO GET RICH BECAUSE THEY ALLOW THEIR NEGATIVE THOUGHTS TO OVERPOWER AND OVERWHELM THEIR BEINGS; I KNEW THAT OFTEN NO MATTER WHAT THEY DID, THEY WOULD BE STUCK IN A POVERTY RUT. NLP HAS BEEN THE TOOL THAT HAS HELPED MANY OF MY CLIENTS GET OVER THE HURDLE THAT EXISTED IN THEIR SUBCONSCIOUS MIND, ALLOWING THEM TO GET RICH QUICKLY AND REMAIN FINANCIALLY FIT.

NLP FOUNDERS AND PRACTICE

NEURO-LINGUISTIC PROGRAMMING WAS ORIGINALLY PROMOTED BY ITS CO-FOUNDERS RICHARD BANDLER AND JOHN GRINDER IN THE 1970S AS AN EFFECTIVE AND RAPID FORM OF PSYCHOLOGICAL THERAPY CAPABLE OF ADDRESSING THE FULL RANGE OF PROBLEMS THAT PSYCHOLOGISTS ARE LIKELY TO ENCOUNTER, FROM PHOBIAS, TO DEPRESSION TO LEARNING DISABILITIES. NLP IS OFTEN USED TO HELP WITH ADDICTIONS TO CIGARETTES, AS WELL AS FOOD, AND IS EFFECTIVE IN HELPING MANY PEOPLE LOSE WEIGHT. AS A NLP PRACTITIONER, I UNDERSTAND THAT WE ARE ABLE TO MAKE THOSE HARD-CORE CONSCIOUS DECISIONS THAT WE MAKE WITH NOTHING MORE THAN DETERMINATION ONLY FOR A SHORT PERIOD OF TIME. FOR INSTANCE, IF WE FIND OURSELVES HUNGRY, ANGRY, LONELY, OR TIRED OUR RESOLVE IS WEAKENED AND OUR WILLPOWER IS GONE. THIS IS WHEN WE FALL BACK INTO MAKING DECISIONS AND DOING EXACTLY WHAT WE DO NOT WANT TO DO. MOST OF US HAVE OFTEN TOLD OURSELVES THAT WE WERE GOING TO STOP DOING SOMETHING – WHATEVER IT IS – AND WERE SUCCESSFUL FOR A BRIEF TIME.

HOWEVER, NO MATTER HOW HARD WE TRY WE ALMOST ALWAYS CATCH OURSELVES FALLING BACK INTO OUR OLD WAYS, EVENTUALLY DOING THE SAME OLD THING AND THEN ASKING THE FOLLOWING QUESTION: "WHY DID I DO THAT AGAIN?" OR WE MAY HAVE MADE RESOLUTIONS TO BEGIN DOING SOMETHING DIFFERENTLY ONLY TO FIND THAT NO MATTER HOW HARD WE TRY, WE JUST CANNOT STICK WITH IT, SO WE GIVE UP. THESE FUTILE ATTEMPTS OFTEN LEAVE US FEELING LIKE WE HAVE FAILED AND YET NLP OFFERS US TOOLS TO GET PAST THESE OBSTACLES AND TRULY MAKE LASTING CHANGES IN OUR LIVES. NLP HELPS TO RETRAIN OUR SUBCONSCIOUS MIND SO THAT WHEN WE ARE UNABLE TO MAINTAIN OUR DETERMINATION AND OUR WILLPOWER IS WEAKENED, OUR SUBCONSCIOUS MIND ACTS IN ACCORDANCE WITH OUR CONSCIOUS MIND AND WE DO NOT WIND UP DOING THE SAME THINGS WE DO NOT WANT TO DO OVER AND OVER. REMEMBER HOW YOU SWORE THAT YOU WOULD NEVER KICK THE DOG, CALL THAT EX-BOYFRIEND, OR SWEAR AT SOMEONE WHO CUT YOU OFF IN TRAFFIC -ONLY TO CATCH YOURSELF DOING THE SAME THINGS AGAIN AT A MOMENT OF WEAKNESS.

WHEN WE REALIZE THAT MOST OF OUR DECISIONS ARE DRIVEN FROM OUR SUBCONSCIOUS MIND AND WE USE NLP TO BRING OUR THOUGHTS BOTH SUBCONSCIOUS AND CONSCIOUS TOGETHER, WE ARE ABLE TO FIND SUCCESS. IF YOU FIND YOURSELF IN THE SAME BAD RELATIONSHIPS OVER AND OVER, EATING THE SAME CHOCOLATE CAKE, NO MATTER HOW HARD YOU TRY NOT TO, UNABLE TO GET TO THE NEXT LEVEL OF SUCCESS IN YOUR JOB OR BUSINESS, UNABLE TO QUIT SMOKING FOR MORE THAN A FEW DAYS, MONTHS, OR EVEN YEARS, THEN, NLP COULD CHANGE YOUR LIFE! WHILE NLP CONTINUES TO BE USED IN THERAPY, IT IS EARNING ITS PLACE AS A WONDERFUL TECHNIQUE TO HELP INDIVIDUALS UNLOCK THEIR FULL POTENTIAL AND FIND SELF-DETERMINATION THROUGH OVERCOMING LEARNED LIMITATIONS.

There is more to personal finance than the drudgery of debts and budgets.

NLP HAS BEEN PROMOTED AS A SCIENCE OF EXCELLENCE. TODAY EVERYONE CAN REAP THE BENEFITS OF NLP, WHETHER THEY ARE A HOME-MAKER OR CEO OF A COMPANY. NLP WORKS TO HELP EACH ONE OF US ACHIEVE OUR BEST BY PROGRAMMING OUR LIVES AND THOUGHTS TO MODEL THE MINDSETS, HABITS, AND SKILLS OF HIGHLY-EFFECTIVE AND SUCCESSFUL PEOPLE. THESE SKILLS, HABITS, AND MINDSETS CAN BE LEARNED BY ANYONE TO IMPROVE ONE'S EFFECTIVENESS BOTH PERSONALLY AND PROFESSIONALLY. IF YOU FIND YOURSELF TODAY IN THE SAME OLD GRIND, DOING THE SAME OLD THINGS, OR YOU JUST WANT TO BECOME A BETTER MORE ENLIGHTENED INDIVIDUAL, I ENCOURAGE YOU TO EXPLORE THE AMAZING BENEFITS OF NLP. WHETHER YOU NEED TO LOSE WEIGHT, QUIT SMOKING, IMPROVE ATHLETIC PERFORMANCE, INCREASE YOUR FINANCIAL EARNINGS , OR FIND THE RIGHT RELATIONSHIP, NEURO- LINGUISTIC PROGRAMMING IS FOR YOU!

Awaken the Giant Within

If *Unlimited Power* is Anthony Robbins' theory of self-mastery, then, *Awaken the Giant Within* is the perfect practice of applying the principles of that theory. The book teaches you how to apply the ideas of taking immediate control of your mental, emotional, physical, and financial destiny. Personally, when I was in the trenches fighting the war of financial freedom, *Awaken the Giant Within* taught me how to take immediate control of my mental, emotional, physical, and financial destiny. I regarded the book as a success companion. In fact, the book was like a well-wisher asking me to wake up and take complete control of my life. As I was waking up, the book was showing me how to walk on the stairwell of success. Instead of complaining and making excuses, I had to take control of my life.

Anthony Robbins's thesis is that you can operate at the level of peak performance if you can take control of your life; you can reshape the beliefs and values that are directing how you think, how you feel, and what you can do in every moment; so your decisions, not your conditions, shape your destiny. The book's main argument is that within each of us lies a special gift, talent, a sleeping giant. You are a lion. Please, know thyself! It is a challenge for you to discover your God-given talent. Perhaps, you cannot sing like Michael Jackson. Chances are that you may be the best handyman. Why not explore your hidden talent? I am willing to work with you to investigate the special gift you brought to thids world.

Change your strategy; change your role model. If you want to get to the top, make smart decisions; your decisions shape your destiny. Pleasure and pain are twin influences that affect your actions. People do things in life either to gain pleasure or avoid pain. Anthony Robbins also recognizes the importance belief systems; belief systems shape our destiny; our beliefs direct our decisions and actions. We are what we believe. For instance, because my religious faith is Roman Catholicism, my perception of reality is shaped by the teachings of Jesus Christ and my church. I do not pretend to be an angel, but Jesus Christ's message of love is the common core of my being. Love dictates my perception of reality.

Hence, as far as I am concerned, there is no such thing as environmental determinism. I am not a victim of environmental circumstances. I am not a puppet of fate; I am a master of life. I do not worry about what is happening to me. Whether an experience is good or bad, I accept it with equanimity. NLP, art, science, and philosophy have conditioned me to confront life's challenges. My solace is Jesus Christ. I practice my religion daily, and it guides my thoughts and actions. Let your beliefs shape your decisions and actions. There are many neuro linguistic programming experiments in the book that can help you accomplish this goal.

A BIRD'S EYE VIEW OF *UNLIMITED POWER*

What is the meaning of personal success? What is the millionaire's secret that attracts success to you? As you read Anthony Robbins' *Unlimited Power*, I want to draw your attention to salient elements of the millionaire's secret.

CHAPTER 1:-- SUCCESS
Success means:

☐ To laugh often and much;
☐ To win the respect of people and the affection of children;
☐ To earn appreciation of honest critics;
☐ To endure the betrayal of false friends;
☐ To appreciate beauty; to find the best in others;
☐ To leave the world a bit better, whether by a healthy child, a garden patch, or a redeemed social condition;
☐ To know even one life breathed easier because you have lived.-- Ralph Waldo Emerson
☐ Who you know, where you go and what you own are not the true measure of personal success.
☐ Ongoing process of striving to become more.
☐ It is the opportunity to continue to grow emotionally, socially, spiritually, physiologically, Intellectually and financially, while contributing in some positive way to others.
☐ The road to success is always under construction...it is a progressive course, not an end to be reached.

What is the common thread of successful people? Power! Unlimited Power! Unlimited power is the ultimate power; it is the belief in your ability to produce the results you desire most; in this vein, you create value for others in the process. Bill Gates, Bill Clinton, Kerry Packer, and Rupert Murdoch are examples of powerful individuals; they exude unlimited power, which is different from power as it was understood by Alexander the Great in ancient times; in the old ages, power used to be a physical thing: for example, kings had large armies, so they were perceived to be strong and powerful. Nowadays, the largest sources of power are based on specialized knowledge; Bill Gates became powerful because of the preeminence of Windows and the market dominance of Microsoft, the erstwhile biggest software company in the globe. Today, new high-tech companies such as Google and Apple have eclipsed Microsoft.

Furthermore, we are no longer in an industrial revolution, which was fueled by manufacturing and money; we are in an information epoch marked by a communication revolution which is fueled by new specialized knowledge.

With new communication technologies exploding as they are today, and advanced weapons systems of many countries become irrelevant, power is based now on how countries have developed their communication and knowledge infrastructure. For example, Russia, a country which is rich in resources, agricultural land, and people is now collapsing politically, socially, and economically. Russia needs to import food, minerals, and technology to just survive. Why? Communism has made Russians merciless and senseless; Russians are strangulating under the tyranny of Vladimir Putin and finding miserable graves. As a people, Russians have no power; they have no common goal, common bond; they are moving in different directions.

By contrast, Israel, a very small country consisting mainly of desert, minimal resources, and limited people, is politically, socially, and economically powerful. Why? The people of Israel are the chosen children of God; since the times of the Old Testament; the Israelis have a common goal. Additionally, Israel possesses specialized knowledge. Israelis have been conditioned by their government to use specialized knowledge to overpower their enemies. Specialized knowledge is only part of the Israeli equation. A major part of the Israeli equation and aura of invincibility is quick ACTION. Israeli's swift ACTION against its many neighbors and enemies produces quick results. Hence, unlimited power is, in fact, the ability to act.

COMMUNICATION

Most powerful and effective leaders are masters of the art of communication. Every communication we make is an action, so communication is power. Those who know how to affect the thoughts, feelings, and actions of the majority of us are those who know how to use this tool of power. I can name a few of them for you: Jesus Christ, John Fitzgerald Kennedy, Thomas Jefferson, Mahatma Gandhi, and Winston Churchill.

Your level of communication mastery will determine your level of success with others, personally, emotionally, socially and financially. The level of success you experience internally is based on how you communicate with yourself. How you feel is not the result of what is happening in your life, but what you perceive is happening in your life. How you interpret the results of what is happening is significant. You can interpret any result in a positive way or a negative way. Philosophically, nothing is either good or bad, but your thinking makes it so. As VAKOG shows, the problem is your internal representations of reality. Positive people say the glass of water is half full; negative people say the glass of water is half empty. Life is what you make it; as you make your bed, so shall you lie on it. If you are positive, you attract positive things; if you are negative you repel good luck. That is the law of physics; that is the law of attraction. You can choose to attract positive vibrations, or you can elect to repel good fortune. If you are reading this book, I assume you want to attract positive vibrations.

A friend of mine inherited millions; he was a gifted sportsman; he committed suicide as he believed he had nothing to live for. The quality of our lives is determined by not what happens to us, but rather by what we do about what happens to us. How you react to events that you come across is a measure of your success. You can control your state of mind by adopting a point of view that creates that emotion. You alone control the point of view that you take. It is your power and your prerogative. If you change your mental and physical actions, you can immediately change your emotions and behaviors. You shape your perceptions or someone, like the guy from Madison Avenue, shapes them for you. It is all about how you perceive events; it is all about what you do about these events that makes a difference.

ULTIMATE SUCCESS FORMULA

☐ TARGET – Your target goal is to know your outcome.
☐ ACTION – You must take action that you believe will produce the results you desire.
☐ DREAMS – Your desire will always only be your dreams
☐ DETERMINE RESPONSE - Develop sensory acuity to recognize the responses and results you are getting to determine whether they are moving towards the outcome.
☐ ADAPT AND CHANGE UNTIL DESIRED RESULT IS ACHIEVED - Develop the flexibility to change your action until you get the result you want to achieve your outcome. For example, Colonel Sanders, of the KFC recipe fame, wanted to sell his recipe to restaurants for royalty. He looked for someone to back him; he was kicked by door one thousand times, and then someone backed him. Whenever someone said no to Colonel Sanders, he worked hard to change the results until he gets a yes response from the prospect, so you need to be able to cope with rejection or no and try again. Take actions to achieve your dreams. Success is not a random roll of the dice. There are consistent, logical patterns of action, specific pathways to excellence that are within the reach of us all.

SEVEN FUNDAMENTAL CHARACTER TRAITS OF SUCCESS

1 PASSION

Passion may be defined as a consuming obsessive purpose for you to do what you do to grow and to be more. Passion gives you the fuel that powers your success train and causes you to tap your true potential. Passion causes you to stay late and leave early; passion is what you want in relationships; passion gives you the life power, the juice and meaning for you to be the best.

2 BELIEF

Belief is the possession of faith in God and yourself. Jesus Christ told us much about the power of belief. Faith can move mountains:

"And He said to them, "Because of the littleness of your faith; for truly I say to you, if you have faith the size of a mustard seed, you will say to this mountain, 'Move from here to there,' and it will move; and nothing will be impossible to you."
Mathew 17:20

There is more to personal finance than the drudgery of debts and budgets.

The life of the typical individual is marked by the loss of or nonexistence of faith. His or her belief system is marked by self-doubt and disappointment. By contrast, millionaires possess, or have developed, a positive belief system. There is a huge power of belief and effect of faith on mankind. Our belief in our perception of our true identity shapes our actions and decisions; our beliefs control what we are and what we can be; our beliefs will determine what we will be. If you believe in the magic of a beautiful world, you will live a happy and magical life. If you believe your life is defined by limits, your life will be defined by limits. What you believe is true, and what you perceive to be possible will become what is true and possible. People who succeed know what they want and believe that they can get it. The millionaire secret postulates that all millionaires subscribe to the power of beliefs in reshaping their lives for the better; if you aspire to become a millionaire, therefore, you have to utilize beliefs to draw the masterpiece of the life you have been dreaming about. My reasoning may sound old, Aristotelian, and syllogistic; yet, no modern sophist can challenge me or win the argument that our passion and beliefs provide the rocket fuel, lunar module, and propulsion toward the space of human excellence.

3. STRATEGY

Living is analogical to a game. At the centre of playing the game of life is the notion of winning or losing. Success in life requires the development of a plan with tactics and strategies for winning the game. A strategy is a way of organizing resources to achieve goal. Some people say they want to become millionaires, but they daydream and sleep off like Rip Van Winkle, the fictional protagonist of a short story written by Washington Irving. The story of Rip Van Winkle is set in the years before and after the American Revolutionary War. In a pleasant village, at the foot of New York's "Kaatskill" Mountains, lives the kindly Rip Van Winkle, a colonial British-American villager of Dutch descent. Rip is an amiable though somewhat hermitic man who enjoys solitary activities in the wilderness, but he is also loved by all the people in town, especially the children to whom he tells stories and gives toys. However, a tendency to avoid all gainful labour, for which his nagging wife, Dame Van Winkle, chastises him, allows his home and farm to fall into disarray due to his lazy neglect. One autumn day, Rip is escaping his wife's nagging, wandering up the mountains with his dog, Wolf. Hearing his name being shouted, Rip discovers that the speaker is a man dressed in antiquated Dutch clothing, carrying a keg up the mountain, who requires Rip's help.

Without exchanging words, the two hike up to an amphitheatre-like hollow in which Rip discovers the source of previously-heard thunderous noises: there is a group of other ornately-dressed, silent, bearded men who are playing nine-pins. Although there is no conversation and Rip does not ask the men who they are or how they know his name, he discreetly begins to drink some of their liquor, and soon falls asleep.

In the end, Rip Van Winkle awakes in unusual circumstances: It seems to be morning, his gun is rotted and rusty, his beard has grown a foot long, and Wolf is nowhere to be found. Rip returns to his village where he finds that he recognizes no one. Asking around, he discovers that his wife has died and that his close friends have died in a war or gone somewhere else. He immediately gets into trouble when he proclaims himself a loyal subject of King George III, not knowing that the American Revolution has taken place; George III's portrait on the town inn has been replaced by that of George Washington.

Rip is also disturbed to find another man is being called Rip Van Winkle, though this is in fact his son, who has now grown up. The men he met in the mountains, Rip learns, are rumoured to be the ghosts of Hendrick (Henry) Hudson's crew. Rip is told that he has apparently been away from the village for twenty years.

An old local recognizes Rip and Rip's now-adult daughter takes him in. Rip resumes his habitual idleness, and his tale is solemnly taken to heart by the Dutch settlers, with other hen-pecked husbands, after hearing his story, wishing they could share in Rip's good luck, and have the luxury of sleeping through the hardships of war. In short, the hilarious story teaches us the importance of using your mind to develop a strategy to provide gainful employment to yourself.

I cannot overemphasize the importance of developing a strategy for the game of your life. You want to be a winner. Right? What you need is to formulate a strategy for realizing your dreams; a blueprint of success is what you need to do to achieve your goal. You have to ascertain your needs; you have to know in advance the resources you will use in an effective way to get rich. Use your best talents and ambitions to find the right avenue of success.

4 CLARITY OF VALUES

Your mind is like a house with cobwebs. Clean it so that you should have a clear vision of its true beauty. In fact, clarity of values is fundamental, ethical, and moral judgments you make about what is important to you. A clarity of values will help you identify your belief system. In your mind, clarity of values are the judgments on what makes life worth living.

5 ENERGY

Energy is the physical vitality for you to take action to realize your goals. You must strive to use the hunger and thirst of desire to build the physical, intellectual, and spiritual energy you need to take action to make the most of what you have. You have to maximize your physical vibrancy.

6 BONDING POWER

Bonding power is the ability to create and develop a rapport with different backgrounds and beliefs. Great successes are not on the world stage but in the recesses of your heart. Hence, you need to form long-lasting and loving relationships with other human beings on planet earth and the invisible cosmos of heaven.

7 MASTERY OF COMMUNICATION

It is important for you to become not only a student but a master of the art, philosophy, and science of divine and human communication. The way you communicate with others and yourself will determine the quality of your life. People who shape our lives have an ability to communicate a vision, quest, joy or mission in a way that creates a passion in you to share that vision. It is what makes a great parent, artist, politician, or teacher.

CHAPTER 2:--MODELING

You can achieve the above stipulated goals by exploiting the strategy of the modelling of excellence. Many people have done this modelling before you! Outstanding people tell stories or leave clues pertaining to how they achieved their results. Even if you do not know them personally, you can clone and duplicate the actions and beliefs of these successful folks.

Look at memoirs and autobiographies; these books tell the stories of the success of their authors. I love reading biographies, autobiographies, and memoirs. These works provide me a window or vantage point from where I can mimic the mental state of my subject for only a few dollars. Additionally, I like watching the interviews of successful people on television. A perfect example, in this regard, is Robin Leach's Lifestyles of the Rich and Famous, a television series that aired in syndication from 1984 to 1995. The show featured the extravagant lifestyles of wealthy entertainers, athletes, and business moguls. It was hosted by Robin Leach for the majority of its run. When Leach was joined by Shari Belafonte in 1994, the show was renamed Lifestyles with Robin Leach and Shari Belafonte. Leach ended each episode with a wish for his viewers that became his signature phrase, "champagne wishes and caviar dreams."

If you need to duplicate a successful marriage, model the excellence of a role model who has been married to the same spouse for thirty years or more. Interestingly, most people love the idea of getting advice from their friends and family members who are not even successful. This ineffective habit reminds me of educated Africans who go to the shrines of fortune tellers and black magicians to conjure good graces to them. What is comical to me is the fact that these Africans are blind to the fact that their occult masters are not doing well. The examples above explain why you must follow me. I am qualified to write about the exposure of millionaire money secrets because, as a normal or average individual, I have copied wealth-building systems to climb to the mountaintop of riches. I know my stuff; I know what I am writing about.

First, the dream of a fabulous life of riches brought me to the shores of America.

Second, I sought to comprehend the so-called millionaire secret, which I am exposing to you right now. In my quest for wealth, it dawned upon me that if my mind can conceive the financial success that I strongly desire, and my heart can believe it, then, I know I can achieve it quickly and easily.

Third, I had to proceed by researching the role models whose success I wanted to emulate.

Fourth, I had to use my faith in God, the fruits of my model research, and the techniques of neuro-linguistic programming to become a miraculous millionaire.

In fact, that is what will happen to you if you learn how to duplicate the success of your role models. Do not wish you were rich; rather, adopt actions and beliefs that will produce similar results for you. Find models of personal excellence around you; if they are not there, please, widen the tent; you are a fisherman, so cast a wider net by turning to television and the Internet.

For example, you are overweight in a financial sense; you need to lose weight; you need a total money makeover right now; you need a proven plan of financial fitness, so study people who are financially fit; you are in a financial gym now, so emulate their actions, and you will become fit. Use NLP, neuro-linguistic programming, to reprogram your mind like a personal computer; indeed, programming the language of your brain is the only way for you to achieve outstanding results.

Outstanding results can be achieved by producing specific communication to and through the nervous system. NLP is how to produce optimum results; NLP is how to duplicate human excellence in a short period of time. Modeling is the pathway to excellence. If I identify the traits and habits of highly effective people, my next action is to pay the price of time and effort of a successful athlete, friend, parent, or businessman. I will become a successful athlete, friend, parent, or businessman.

Modeling is at the center of franchising; many successful businesses make money by determining what is successful in one city and duplicating it in another city. For instance, franchising is a form of success modeling. Franchising is the practice of using another firm's successful business model. A franchise is a way of cloning a winning system that has been proven to be successful. America is replete with many examples of thriving franchises: Subway, 7-11, Burger King, Dunkin' Donuts, Jani-King, Servpro, H&R Block, Maaco, Days Inn, and Super 8.

Similar to businesses, human beings can copy the success systems of powerful persons. I define powerful persons as human beings who are successful in mastering life's challenges. Hence, take a proven system from me and duplicate it, and maybe improve upon it. People who do this are virtually guaranteed success. Success modeling is important to business success. The difference between those who succeed and those who fail is not that the former folks have abundant resources; rather, it is what they choose to see and do with their resources and experience of life. Modeling performance patterns is what Anthony Robbins, my hero, calls Optimum Performance Technologies. NLP is a tool to develop your own insights and strategies.

FIND MODELS OF EXCELLENCE

Medicine and automobile manufacturing use the science of modeling, too. You can teach a dog patterns that will improve its behavior. You can do the same with people. Seize the modeling of excellence, and make it your own. Building from the successes of others is one of the fundamental aspects of most learning. When I was in Africa, my parents used to make fun of Japanese cars. In the beginning, that is during the early 1970s, the Japanese did not know how to make the transition from building ugly and shoddy cars to manufacturing sexily-perfect vehicles like American companies such as the following: Chrysler, Chalmers-Detroit/Chalmers, DeSoto, Dodge, Eagle, Imperial, Jeep, Maxwell, Plymouth, Ram, Valiant, Ford, Continental, Edsel, Lincoln, Mercury, General Motors, Buick, Marquette, Cadillac, LaSalle, Cartercar, Chevrolet, Geo, Elmore, Ewing, GMC, Hummer, Oakland, Pontiac, Oldsmobile, Viking, Rainier, Saturn, Scripps Booth, Sheridan, Welch, and Welch-Detroit.

In the end, when I came to America during the early 1980s, I was too stunned to watch Americans flocking in long lines to buy Japanese cars and reciting the jingle of the Japanese miracle and business management. Unbeknownst to me, the Japanese have been coming to America as tourists; the Japanese have been using cameras to take pictures of perfect models of American auto manufacturing. In trade, stealing or business espionage is a bad thing; in personal life, modeling effective habits and behaviors is a good thing. From the rise of Japanese auto manufacturing you can conclude that every advance in technology is based on the foundation of earlier discoveries and breakthroughs. Modeling gives you the fundamental ingredients that must be duplicated to establish any form of human excellence. Our belief system and mental syntax help us organize thoughts and understand how other people organize their thoughts, so unlock the computer code of success. Use physiology to manipulate the way you breathe, hold your body, posture, your movements to reflect the character and posture of your role model.

CHAPTER 3 THE POWER OF STATE

Your mental state is a powerful determinant of success. If you feel you are on a roll, you will be on a roll. If you feel that you cannot win, you will not win. Often there are times that you can do nothing wrong. Other times you can do nothing right. It is like your words become a self-fulfilling prophecy. You are either using your mental state to bless yourself or you are using it to curse yourself. You can stop sabotaging yourself by training yourself to continue to be on a roll by mirroring positive neuro-physiological states, enabling mental states that infuse in you confidence, love, inner strength, ecstasy, and belief; I want you to tap the great wellsprings of your personal power. Dispel the poison of negative or paralyzing mental states. Avoid confusion, depression, fear, sadness, angst, and frustration because they leave you powerless. If you can change a state, you can change a behavior. If you have practiced the habit of changing your mood from negative to positive, then, you have learned how to put yourself into an empowering mental state or behavior.

Generally, your needs and goals are almost always to achieve the state that you would ideally be in. Money will assist you in achieving a feeling of freedom, success, and respect, so this is a state and a feeling. The key to love, power, and joy is the ability to control, direct, and manage your states. You can use states to make yourself either happy or sad, so learn to effectively run your brain. Man has been fascinated for centuries by how to alter his or her mental states using drugs, music, sex, religion, liquor, and chant. These substances all have their uses and limitations, but I must warn you that there is a better and an easier way that is easier, quicker and more precise way to alter your mental state.

What creates the mental state that we are in? The two components are internal representations (the mind) and your physiology (the body). An example of the former is the case of the spouse who returns late to the matrimonial home. A second example is a man worrying about an accident. Third, there can be the case of a woman feeling the dissipation of unconditional love. Fourth, a lady may be concerned about her husband's new habit of gambling or extra-marital affair. As you can see, our beliefs, attitudes, values and past experiences with a person all affect the type of representations we will make about the behaviors.

As for the component of physiology (the body), pay special attention to the following body movements: muscle tension, how you breathe, what you eat, your posture, and how the overall level of biochemical functioning have a huge impact on your mental state. Internal representation and physiology will work together in a cybernetic loop. What effect will one have on the other? If you are feeling ill and tired, your internal representation will be negative; if you are feeling vibrant and on a roll, your internal representation will be positive.

Please, make an effort to learn how to manipulate or change your internal representation and physiology to achieve the results you desire most in your life. Derived from VAKOG, internal representation and physiology determine your behavior every day. Verbal behavior pertains to what you say; physical behavior deals with what you do. As human beings, since we do not know how things really are , but only how we represent them to ourselves, then, it stands to reason that you should make an effort to represent things or phenomena to yourself in a way that empowers you and other living or human creatures in your natural habitat. I urge you to focus your attention on the positive; if you represent to yourself that something is not going to work, it will not work. You have discouraged your mind from working to produce a miracle for you. I am not advising you to engage in exercises of self deception or delusion. Rather, I am encouraging you to always look for something positive in a negative situation. An old English adage states that to every cloud, there is a silver lining. You must adopt a balanced approach in analyzing every situation. I resent the fact that most people focus exclusively on the negative side of things; they trigger negative mental states by looking for all the reasons in the world why something will not work. In my life, I frown upon people who are negative; they irritate me.

By contrast, if you form an internal representation that something will work, you push a button on your head that tells your brain to produce the mental state that will support you in producing positive results. Life is marked by the character of transience; life is not static; life is like a number endowed with motion; life does not obey the laws of gravitational physics; life is like a river; it is moving always. You can be at the mercy of the river and drown, or you can ride the waves of success by steering life in your predetermined course. At the end of the day, all of us will reach the same destination. Many roads lead to heaven; you can choose the path of Roman Catholicism or you can become a protestant. What is the difference? The difference is the knowledge, satisfaction, enjoyment, and added value you have created along the way to heaven. I like following established systems; I do not like to reinvent the wheel. I like modeling. I like modeling the execellence of my role models. What about you?

Follow my program of $ucce$$tology! Always move with the tide; if you move against it, your action is like pushing shit uphill. The tide is determined by Nature and the set of values and beliefs that you hold. Your behavior and actions are a result of your mental state. If your hunch or internal representation warns you that you are going to have an accident, you will have an accident. If your internal representation tells you that you will be successful, you will be successful. The ancestor of every action is a thought. If one changes one's beliefs and internal representations to something positive, one can achieve huge results. There is no such thing as fate or providence governing human affairs.

There is more to personal finance than the drudgery of debts and budgets.

Procrastination and fear make a coward of us all who have never dared to pursue our dreams. Action is the brainchild of thought. There is no power like the power of a resourceful mental state. The kind of behavior people produce is the result of the mental state they are in. How they respond to the state they are in is based on their models of the world. Most people make little conscious effort to direct their states. Mental state change is what most people are after. They want to be in a positive state. Successful people know how to tap into their resourceful states. You can control the state you are in. You do not have to be at the mercy of whatever comes your way. Why must you remain a puppet of fate? If you refuse to get the best in life, you will always get the worst in life. Learn to control your thoughts because they become your dreams fulfilled; control your dreams because they become your actions; control your actions because they become your habits; control your habits because they become your destiny.

CHAPTER 4 BELIEF

Belief is any guiding principle, dictum, faith, or passion that can provide meaning and direction in life. Beliefs are prearranged filters to our perceptions of the world. One person with a belief is equal to a force of ninety-nine individuals who have only an interest. Beliefs are the compass and maps that guide us to our goals; beliefs give us the assurance that we know that we will get there in the end, like the dramatic hero of a religious thriller. To change your behavior, you need to start with your own beliefs. Your beliefs become your reality. Like drugs, beliefs alter your perceptions of reality. You do not need drugs to succeed financially; drugs are not always necessary; belief in recovery always is. Like a digital camera, belief is nothing but a picture of a mental state, an internal representation that governs behavior. If you want to change your life for the better, you must change your beliefs; you must change your internal representation, which will change your behavior for the better. Belief is a choice. Your beliefs form the core of your value system or hierarchy.

SOURCES OF BELIEF

Where do our beliefs come from? When we are born, we enter this world with original sin but without any beliefs. We acquire our beliefs through an osmotic process, as we transcend many experiences of life. My biology teacher had told me that osmosis is the tendency of a fluid, usually water, to pass through a semi-permeable membrane into a solution where the solvent concentration is higher, thus equalizing the concentrations of materials on either side of the membrane.

In this regard, your beliefs are like the diffusion of fluids, and your body and mind are like the membranes or porous partitions through which beliefs enter you physical and spiritual being. Success breeds success, failure breeds failure. Below are the five sources of human beliefs:

1. Environment –the geography where we are born and grow.
2. Events-- small or large events in life can help foster our beliefs.
3. Knowledge—it fosters belief through dogmatism.
4. Results--our past results engender belief of success or failure.
5. Creative imagination-- your mind experiences shape your desires and goals

If you can control your beliefs, you can control the way you model others. You can consciously direct your life; you can change your life. If you are not succeeding in life, your beliefs may be the culprit; they have limited you. Positive beliefs, however, can serve to help you achieve your highest goals in life.

If you do not like your beliefs, you have the miraculous power to change them. In your hands, you hold the master key to your own liberation. Continually remain alert, adjust behaviors, and recalibrate actions to determine where you want to go. The key is to take your beliefs and ensure that they are working for you in a way to achieve your goals and objectives; that is, they are effective and empowering to you.

If you believe in your heart that success is within your grasp, then, you will keep coming back until you succeed. If something does not work, change it until it works. Only a mad man keeps doing the same thing foolishly and getting negative results over and over. If you take responsibility, you can control the agenda. You can generate your own experiences of life; you learn from all of them.

You need to feel that you create your world, else you are at the mercy of others, a plaything for the sport of the gods. Do not get bogged down in the details. Understand the outcome, and what you need to get to the outcome, and have good people around you who are competent at each particular post. Exact the essence from the situation. You do not need to know how a motor engine works to drive an automobile. If you are going to succeed you need to enjoy what you are doing. Make your vocation your vacation.

CHAPTER 5: SEVEN BELIEFS THAT FOSTER EXCELLENCE

1. Everything happens for a reason and a purpose and it serves us.
2. There is no such thing as failure; there are only results.
3. Whatever happens, take responsibility.
4. You do not have to understand everything to use everything.
5. People are your greatest resource. Form the sense of team, purpose, and unity.
6. Work is play.
7. There is no abiding success without commitment.

CHAPTER 6: HOW TO RUN YOUR BRAIN

Your brain is a jukebox. You choose the music to play; reprogram your jukebox. How you produce a state of depression or ecstasy is how you structure your internal representations and physiology. This action is done through the manipulation of your five senses. To get a result, you need an ingredient. For instance, remember a pleasant experience; step into that experience; see what you saw through your eyes, events images, color brightness, and more; hear what you heard; feel what you felt. Imagine the experience as if you are in a movie theater.

There is more to personal finance than the drudgery of debts and budgets.

Which experience feels greater? What is the difference between an associated experience and a disassociated experience? You can change the effect of any experience by changing an associated experience to a disassociated experience. You can implant in your brain the cues you want. A king can direct his kingdom. Your kingdom is your brain. You can direct your brain. There are various methods you can use to command your brain to do your bidding. Be in charge!

CHAPTER 7: THE SYNTAX OF SUCCESS

Syntax is the logical structure or the scheme of things. You can talk of the idea of the syntax of the English language; syntax is the way you order actions or arrange phenomena. The order that we say and do things causes them to register in the brain in a specific way. The strategy you use to arrange and implement your goal is the syntax of success. The order in which we use resources that we have will determine the outcome of our endeavor. Success is like a cooking recipe. If you follow the recipe to the letter, if you model the recipe, you will achieve the same results every time. It is like working in a chemistry laboratory to produce water or salt. If the syntax consists of two molecules of hydrogen with one molecule of oxygen, you will produce water; if the syntax consists of one molecule of sodium and one molecule of chloride, you will produce edible salt.   A recipe is a formula. Once you understand the syntax of success, it easy for you to apply it and obtain the results you desire.

My advice to you is to find people who have financial success and fulfilling relationships; discover their strategy and apply it to achieve similar results, and save tremendous time and effort. That is what Anthony Robbins calls THE POWER OF MODELING. In the baking of human experience, our ingredients are the five senses. We also need how much of the ingredients are needed. We need to know how much visual input, audio or kinesthetic are needed. Like a recipe, it must be the same amounts, same sequence, and same ingredients in order for you to achieve similar results.

Strategies are like the combination numbers to a safe or money vault. Strategy is the order that the numbers are used. This syntax will find the right combination: Visual (V), Auditory (A), Kinesthetic (K), Internal (I), External (E), Digital (D), and Tonal (T). See! Hear! Feel! Recognize what your strategies are, as well as other people's strategies, so you can determine what they react to; presenting information in another person's syntax is a powerful form of rapport. Your communication becomes irresistible, as it automatically triggers certain responses.

There are strategies for Selling, Motivation, Seduction, Learning, Athletics, Depression, or Ecstasy. There are strategies for efficient money management. You need to determine what your strategy is to access your mental state on cue. To achieve a certain mental state or result, find the specific sequence and the specific syntax; take action, and you will create the world as you desire it. Other than the physical necessities of life, like food and water, almost everything else you might want is a mental state. All you have to know is the right syntax and strategy to enable you to get there. Teach an army to shoot a new rifle; find the point of difference of a star, and show others how to model that star. What are their beliefs, their common mental syntax and their strategies? Model their internal representations and their physiology.

Once this is done, I will design a two-day NLP course for you, and you will experience amazing results. If you have an excellent role model, discover what he or she does; duplicate his or her system in order for you to produce similar results in a shorter period of time. My only problem is that I need to know who you are. The biggest problem with success gurus and honest teachers like me is that we do not know the extant capacities of our students. How would our students like to learn? What are the most effective learning strategies of our students? What buttons do I need to push to assist you to learn faster and efficiently? As teachers, we are like builders; if we put the wrong tool in a wrong sequence, you will get the wrong results. In order for you to make it easy for me to assist you proficiently, I ask you to communicate with me. There are forms and my contact information at the back of the book. If you are a salesman, for example, find out what your customers' buying strategy is. If the customer is strongly Kinesthetic, hit him or her with a feeling; if he or she is visual, show him or her the colors. Do you understand me?

CHAPTER 8: HOW TO ELICIT SOMEONE'S STRATEGY

There are methods to elicit anyone's strategy in any situation. Like a actor, you have to become a master communicator. Look for things you were not seeing; hear things you were not hearing; feel things you were not feeling; and asking questions you were not hearing before. Do this elegantly and attentively. People will tell you about their strategies in what they say, how they look, and how they move. Learn to read a person like a map or a book. You can tell what representational system he is using by watching a person's eyes.

LANGUAGE AND COMMUNICATION

Central to NLP is the role of language and communication. Linguistic programming entails the scientific use of language to comunicate with ourselves and other individuals effectively. In order to be understood, we have to learn how to become masters of the English language. The most charismatic figures in history, such as Jesus Christ, Ronald Reagan, and Barack Obama, are master communicators. They use the language instrument as proficiently and artfully as saxophonists, violinists, and pianists to achieve their desired goals and objectives.

LANGUAGE AND PSYCHOLOGY

I ascribe fundamental importance to language and its relation to psychology. Computers speak their own unique language: 010101. In fact, so do human beings. Language is a code. A language is a code which represents a unique culture, civilization, or world view; as such, mastery of a language implies the privilege of gaining access into a unique culture, civilization, or world view. Have you ever imagined the language millionaires and billionaires speak? Money! In Linguistics we used to call it registers, the secret code of millionaires and billionaires; if you cannot decipher the code of millionaires, you cannot comprehend the subject of their conversation. Language, therefore, may refer either to the specifically human capacity for acquiring and using complex systems of communication, or to a specific instance of such a system of complex communication. The scientific study of language in any of its senses is called linguistics.

The approximately three thousand to six thousand languages that are spoken by humans today are the most salient examples, but natural languages can also be based on visual rather than auditory stimuli; two examples are sign languages and written languages. Codes and other kinds of artificially constructed communication systems such as those used for computer programming can also be called languages: HTML, Basic, C, Pascal, Cobol, Unix, and Java.

A language, in this sense, is a system of signs for encoding and decoding information. The English word derives ultimately from Latin lingua, language, tongue, via Old French. This metaphoric relation between language and the tongue exists in many languages and testifies to the historical prominence of spoken languages. When used as a general concept, language refers to the cognitive faculty that enables humans to learn and use systems of complex communication.

The human language faculty is thought to be fundamentally different from and of much higher complexity than those of other species. Human language is highly complex in that it is based on a set of rules relating symbols to their meanings, thereby forming an infinite number of possible innovative utterances from a finite number of elements. Language is thought to have originated when early hominids first started cooperating, adapting earlier systems of communication based on expressive signs to include a theory of other minds and shared intentionality. This development is thought to have coincided with an increase in brain volume.

Language is processed in many different locations in the human brain, but especially in Broca and Wernicke's areas. Humans acquire language through social interaction in early childhood, and children generally speak fluently when they are around three years old. The use of language has become deeply entrenched in human culture and, apart from being used to communicate and share information, it also has social and cultural uses, such as signifying group identity, social stratification and for social grooming and entertainment. The word "language" can also be used to describe the set of rules that makes this possible, or the set of utterances that can be produced from those rules.

LANGUAGE AND CULTURE

The Tower of Babel symbolizes the division of mankind by a multitude of tongues provided through divine intervention. Languages, understood as the particular set of speech norms of a particular community, are also a part of the larger culture of the community that speaks them. Humans use language as a way of signaling identity with one cultural group and difference from others. Even among speakers of one language several different ways of using the language exist, and each is used to signal affiliation with particular subgroups within a larger culture. Linguists and anthropologists, particularly sociolinguists, ethno linguists and linguistic anthropologists have specialized in studying how ways of speaking vary between speech communities. The English spoken in the USA is a variety of the English spoken in Great Britain.

A community's way of using language is a part of the community's culture, or identity, just as other shared practices are; it is a way of displaying group identity. Ways of speaking function not only to facilitate communication, but also to identify the social position of the speaker. Linguists use the term varieties, a term that encompasses geographically or socio-culturally defined dialects as well as the jargons or styles of subcultures, to refer to the different ways of speaking a language.

Linguistic anthropologists and sociologists of language define communicative style as the ways that language is used and understood within a particular culture. For instance, American English and British English do not differ only in pronunciation, vocabulary, and grammar, but they also differ through having different cultures of speaking. Some cultures, for example, have elaborate systems of social deixis, systems of signaling social distance through linguistic means.

In English, social deixis is shown mostly through distinguishing between addressing some people by first name and others by surname, but also in titles such as Mr., Mrs., boy, Doctor, or Your Honor, but in other languages such systems may be highly complex and codified in the entire grammar and vocabulary of the language. For instance, in several languages of east Asia, such as Thai, Burmese, and Javanese, different words are used according to whether a speaker is addressing someone of higher or lower rank than oneself in a ranking system with animals and children ranking the lowest and gods and members of royalty as the highest.

An appreciation of the connection between language and psychology can be useful to a student of financial success. Since God works through people on earth, it stands to reason that mastery of human communication can be an important asset to an individual seeking the favors of others. An understanding of human nature will facilitate your relationship with your fellow human beings. Above all, learn the language of personal finance; do not feel ignored when professionals or your peers are discussing money. I will stress this point again in step five of *The Miraculous Millionaire*, balance your financial book. The ability to communicate with people is essential to selling your success idea. Style and salesmanship are very important to people who are serious about becoming successful. Conventional wisdom exhorts us not to judge a book by its cover, but you and I know that looks matter. An intesting example is network television. Have you seen an ugly guy or girl anchoring the news? Contrary to the traditional view of salesmen, millionaires cite honest attraction as an important factor in their success. If you want to be a millionaire, be an honest salesman and polish your looks and social skills.

POWERFUL WAYS TO PROGRAM YOUR UNCONSCIOUS MIND FOR SUCCESS

"BE MASTER OF YOUR MIND RATHER THAN MASTERED BY MIND." - Zen Poverb

Your unconscious mind works for you 24 hours a day, 7 days a week. It never rests; it never sleeps. It can process millions of messages of sensory information every single second, and contains all of your wisdom, memories, and intelligence. It is the storage of an infinite source of information, and it holds answers to all the questions you have. Your unconscious mind is eager to assist you; it only needs clear directions to follow. Here are three powerful ways of how to program your mind for success in life and work.

There is more to personal finance than the drudgery of debts and budgets.

1. IMAGINE COMPLETING YOUR GOAL

Your unconscious mind does not differentiate between reality and fantasy. Whatever you imagine, your unconscious mind takes it as real. You can use this principle to program your mind for helping you in reaching your personal and work–related goals. Follow these simple steps to use your imagination in the most effective way:

1. Close your eyes and think of what you want to achieve. Imagine yourself succeeding. Make sure you are looking through your eyes and notice what you see around you, what you hear and what you tell yourself, and what you feel. Ponder on this for a little while, and intensify positive feelings in your mind.

2. Now imagine sitting in the cinema and watching the same movie on the screen. This time, you will see your body in that movie. Again, notice what you can see, hear, and feel. Also notice what you say to yourself. Intensify positive feelings related to achievement of your goal in your mind.

3. Repeat steps 1 and 2 as often as possible. The unconscious mind needs repetition for bigger projects and if your goal is really meaningful to you, this should not be problem at all!

4. USE AFFORMATIONS INSTEAD OF AFFIRMATIONS

You have probably heard of affirmations, commonly used for 'programming' your mind. An example of affirmation is: "I am rich." The trouble is that if you are broke and saying to yourself that you are rich, your brain will simply reject it. You may even experience an uncomfortable feeling when repeating these lies to yourself over and over again, in hope to reprogram your mind. But afformations are simple tricks developed by Noah St. John, turning any affirmation into 'why' question, hence displacing the resistance of the unconscious mind.

For example, if you would like to program your mind for "I can see abundance everywhere around me." (affirmation), you can ask yourself instead: " Why can I see abundance everywhere around me?" (afformation). Using afformations is like typing what you want into a search engine. Since your unconscious mind always looks for closure, it will look for answers and evidence to what you asked. Afformations are easy and powerful way to program your unconscious mind for success. Here are few examples of afformations:

Why am I so happy? (if you still feel resistance, add 'BECOMING' after'AM,' for example, Why am I becoming so happy?
Why am I (becoming) so confident?
Why am I so confident on the phone?
Why am I such an excellent sales person?
Why have I such a great relationship with my spouse?
Why am I such a wonderful parent?
Why am I such happy, caring, and giving money magnet?
Why am I so grateful for all that I have?
Why am I losing weight right now?

In order to assist you master the afformation technique, I have reserved a copy of Noah St. John's book ftitled *The Secret Code of Success* for you on my web site: princeojong.com. Please, read it; if you need help, call my office: (301) 593-4897 or (301) 593-4879. My mission is to help you.

Additionally, before you read Noah St. John's book, follow these tips to take full advantage of programming your unconscious mind with afformations:

Write down 10 – 20 most relevant afformations down. Read these afformation at least twice a day, early in the morning and before you go to sleep. You may want to record your own afformations or purchase pre-recorded afformations that you can listen to often. You can get them at http://www.milionaireiuniversity.com. Persist in your experiments. Although you may start noticing first results of programming your unconscious mind very quickly, use afformations for a minimum of 30 days to gain a maximum advantage.

3. START YOUR GRATITUDE JOURNAL

By maintaining a gratitude journal, you can create a massive shift in your thinking and feeling. The following few suggestions can help you start a gratitude journal and establish a whole new outlook on life:

1. Choose a blank notebook or journal to write in every day. Take care to choose a visually-appealing journal, something that you will want to return to daily!

2. Look for things during the day for which you are grateful to God. Make mental notes throughout the day.

3. Write down five things you are grateful for each night before bedtime. Review the day and include anything, however small or great like a baby's smile, a beautiful flower, or the compliment you received. Make the list personal.

4. Begin to look every day for the positive angle in all things. View obstacles as opportunities to appreciate life. Note these ideas down if you can truly appreciate them.

5. Personalize your gratitude journal. Expand it with pictures, photos, and quotes. The most effective time to communicate with and pay attention to programming of your unconscious mind is in the evening before you fall asleep and in the morning before you get up.

These are times when your unconscious mind is the most alert, in other words, you are in a state of light trance, ideal for programming your mind. Understanding how to use the language of your mind correctly, and putting this knowledge into practice, for your own and others' benefit, will put you on the golden path to success, satisfaction, and happiness.

"Life is 10% what happens to you and 90% of how you react to it!" –Chuck Swindoll

RUSS WHITNEY

There is another book I am recommending; you can buy the book at Amazon.com: *Building Wealth: How Anyone Can Make a Personal Fortune Without Money, Credit, or Luck*. The author is Russ Whitney. After I attended Russ Whitney's money-making seminar, I was disappointed because I could not afford to buy his manuals and software, but I was intrigued when I found his book mentioned above in a Border's bookstore in Alexandria, Virginia. I bought the book, and I spent the week-end reading it. I kept asking myself: Why could a high-school dropout learn how to build wealth in America? What about me, a PhD candidate?

What did I learn from Russ Whitney's seminar and book? I learned how to imitate a successful individual's wealth-building system. Indeed, I would like to draw your attention to some of the wisdom and common-sense I have retained from the book. You can become wealthy by reading motivational books and applying the principles in the teachings in your daily life. You have to believe in rags-to-riches stories and your dream of building wealth. You have to search for financial security. Wealth-building is like going on a journey to a distant place; you have to find a vehicle that will transport you to your destination, where you want to be; you are travelling from poverty to success. You have to love what you do; if you do not enjoy working hard to achieve your goal, then, you are not ready psychologically for success. I still remember Russ Whitney's 95% rule of success; it states that 5% of people in this country do what it takes to become rich, but 95% of them have a negative mental attitude.

I remember how Russ Whitney raised my level of perception when he asked us to answer "GREAT!" with a smile to his question: "How are you doing today?" "GREAT!" "GREAT!" "GREAT!" He urged us to think like winners, not losers. In fact, he persuaded us to buy Dr. Walter Doyle Staples' book titled *Think Like a Winner*. I learned from Dr. Walter Doyle Staples that you can become anything you want because the world exists through the power of beliefs. Like Dr. Walter Doyle Staples, Anthony Robbins emphasizes the significance of beliefs. I spent much time in the preceding paragraphs discussing Anthony Robbins' treatment of the subject of beliefs and success conditioning.

For instance, the Holy bible encourages us to establish strong beliefs in Jesus Christ and God. In the synoptic gospels, Jesus Christ tells us that faith in God can move mountains. What is faith? It is a form of belief. If you have faith, your financial life can become a miracle of Christ. You are made in the likeness of God; you have a divine essence, so all the power of the universe is inside you. You can radiate the divine essence if you train your mind to awaken your latent powers.

Russ Whitney's book also taught me not only how to establish good credit but how to build it to the level of a millionaire. I was applying for credit and receiving so many credit cards in the mail to the extent that I became overwhelmed. In fact, I regret the fact that these techniques worked so well for me to the extent that I abused them; I had to file for bankruptcy protection from my creditors. Indeed, I will discuss how I used the ideas I learned from Russ Whitney in step ten, the real-estate investing section of the book.

WARREN BUFFETT

The Oracle of Omaha! I want you to be like Warren Buffett. Warren Buffett is frugal, so why are you not frugal? Warren Buffett, perennially ranked among the world's richest men, lives a lifestyle that has not changed much before he made his billions. He is often referred to as the world's greatest investor, and his long-term track record suggests the title is well deserved. He is also legendarily frugal, residing in the same house in Omaha, Nebraska, that he bought in 1958 for $31,500. He is well known for his simple tastes, including McDonald's hamburgers and cherry Coke, and his disdain for technology, including computers and luxury cars. Underlying his legend is one simple fact: Buffett is a value investor. It is the hallmark trait of both his professional and personal success. In step nine of *The Miraculous Millionaire,* the chapter of the book discussing the stock market and bonds, I have expended many pages shedding light on Warren Buffett's value-investing approach.

TEN SECRETS THAT MILLIONAIRES KEEP

Do you think the wealthy are all smart, friendly, spendthrift, spoiled and privileged? You might be surprised by the real forces behind their success:

1. "You may think I'm rich, but I do not."

Real millionaires are not like the spendthrifts you see on television. They are very frugal. They do not play the part of what the average person perceives to be the millionaire lifestyle with caviar, champagne, and limousines.

2. "I shop at Wal-Mart."

Millionaires may not buy the 99-cent paper towels, but they know what it is to be frugal. About 80% say they spend their money with a middle-class mind-set. Real millionaires are said to be very economical with their money.

3. "But I did not get rich by skimping on lattes."

So how do you join the millionaires club? Regardless of how they build their nest eggs, virtually all millionaires make judicious use of debt. They will take out loans to build their business, avoid high-interest credit card debt and leverage their home equity to finance purchases if their cash flow is inadequate. Nor is their wealth tied up in their homes. Home equity represents just 11% of millionaires' total assets.

4. "I have a concierge for everything."

That hot restaurant may be booked for months, at least when Joe Nobody calls to make reservations. But many top eateries set aside tables for celebrities and A-list clientele, and that is where the personal concierge comes in.

5. "You do not get rich by being nice."

John D. Rockefeller threatened rivals with bankruptcy if they did not sell out to his company, Standard Oil. Bill Gates was ruthless in building Microsoft. Millionaires are not nice guys. Just 12% say that what they want most to be remembered for is their legacy in business. Millionaires are also seemingly undaunted by failure.

6. "Taxes are for little people."

The wealthy tend to derive a higher portion of their income from dividends and capital gains, which are taxed at lower rates than wages (15% for long-term capital gains versus 25% for middle-class wages.

Has Governor Willard Mitt Romney published his taxes yet? I have perused two years of his income taxes: 2010 and 2011. Is Barack Obama waiting for more years? Is he waiting for Godot? Most millionaires do pay taxes. In fact, the top 1% of earners paid nearly 40% of federal income taxes in 2005, that is a whopping $368 billion -- according to the Internal Revenue Service. Also, high-income earners pay social security tax on only their first $97,500 of income, but the big savings come from owning a business and deducting everything related to it. Landlords can also depreciate their commercial properties and expenses such as mortgage interest. And that is without doing any creative accounting.

Then there are the tax shelters, trusts and other mechanisms the superrich use to shield their wealth. An estimated 2 million Americans have unreported accounts offshore, and income from foreign tax shelters costs the U.S. $20 billion to $40 billion a year, according to the IRS. Indeed, an increasing number of people want to establish an offshore fund.

7. "I was a B student."

My father was right when he said that good grades are the key to success, just not necessarily a big bank account. According to the book titled *The Millionaire Mind*, the median college grade-point average for millionaires is 2.9, and the average SAT score is 1,190, that is hardly Harvard material. In fact, 59% of millionaires attended a state college or university. The keys to their success is the fact that millionaires rank hard work first, then education, determination, and treating others with respect. They also say that what they absorbed in class was less important than learning how to study and stay disciplined.

8. "Like my Ferrari? It is a rental."

Why spend $3,000 on a Versace bag that will be out of style as soon as next season when you can rent it for $175 a month? For that matter, why blow $250,000 on a Ferrari when for $25,000 it can be yours for a few weekends a year? Clubs that offer fractional ownership of jets have been popular for some time, and now the concept has extended to other high-end luxuries like exotic cars and fine art. How hot is the trend? More than 50% of millionaires say they plan to rent luxury goods within the next 12 months.

9. "Turns out money can buy happiness."

It may not be comforting to folks who are not minting cash, but the rich really are different. There is no group in America that is happier than the wealthy. Roughly 70% of millionaires say that money created more happiness for them. Higher income also correlates with higher ratings in life satisfaction, according to a new study by economists at the Wharton School of Business. It is not necessarily the Rolls Royce, Bentley, or Manolo Blahniks that lead to bliss; rather, it is the freedom that money buys. Concomitantly, did you know that the rates of depression are lower among the wealthy? According to the Wharton School of Business's study, the rich tend to have better health than the rest of the population. In fact, health and happiness are as closely correlated as wealth and happiness. The wealthy even seem to smile and laugh more often, according to the Wharton study, to say nothing of getting treated with more respect and eating better food. "People experience their day very differently when they have a lot of money. Do you remember Eddie Murphy's movie Trading Places?

10. "You worry about the Joneses. I worry about keeping up with the Trumps."

Wealth may go a long way toward creating happiness, but the middle-class rich still cannot afford the life of the billionaire next door, the guy who writes charity checks for $100,000 and retreats to his own private island. What makes people happy is not how much money they are making; it is how much they are making relative to their peers. Indeed, for all their riches, some 40% of millionaires fear that their standard of living will decline in retirement and that their money will run out before they die, according to Fidelity. Of course, it may not help if their lifestyle is so lavish that they are barely squeaking by on hundreds of thousands a year. You can always be happier with more money. There is no satiation point, but that is the trouble with keeping up with the Trumps. "Millionaires are always looking up, and think it is better up there.

TEN SECRETS OF MILLIONAIRES' MONEY MANAGEMENT

Do you want to know the ten secrets of millionaire money management? Start investing early; create a vision, and live frugally. It turns out millionaires are just like us, but they have a lot more money. When asked about their secrets to success, they do not cite anything magical or rare, but rather the steady application of wise investing strategies, hard work, and, believe it or not, a degree of frugality. Here are the ten secrets of millionaires' money management:

1. Start early to avoid financial pitfalls

People often get into trouble by racking up personal debt early on, which acts as a big drag on their earnings. Learn how to live within your means and how to delay gratification; these are the habits that you need to maintain on the way up, so you can keep your millions when you get there.

There is more to personal finance than the drudgery of debts and budgets.

2. Believe that you can do it.

Before investing in real estate and becoming a millionaire, I read as many biographies and autobiographies of millionaires as I could find. My most memorable reads include the following: John H Johnson, Earl Graves, Carl Icahn, Sam Walton, Donald J. Trump, Steve Jobs, Sandy Weill, Bill Gates, and Warren Buffett. I was searching for a common characteristic that could help me in my own quest. What I found was they all had an incredible self-belief that they would be financially successful. Indeed, embracing that level of self-confidence helped me get to the top of the financial world.

3. Articulate your vision for success.

The saying, "I want to be rich," is too vague. Instead I recommend imagining what your ideal life as a millionaire will look like. I can offer my example: "I want to have $1,000,000 invested so that I can live off of the interest. Then I will plan to quit my job so that I can volunteer my time teaching people how to become financially independent; I will spend some time traveling all over the world, and I will learn how to play tennis and watercolor, and enjoy picnics at the beach with my family.

4. Insure against life's risks.

Life is full of uncertainties, so you must begin transferring the risks to insurance companies. That is what rich people do. If the risk is not caused by your own errors, it may be caused by bankruptcy; indeed, bankruptcy is often caused by divorce, a death in the family, or a disability that renders someone unable to work. Conversely, protecting against those risks through insurance protects wealth. In the book titled *The Quiet Millionaire*, financial planner Brett Wilder writes that many people either fail to get adequate insurance or pay too much for it because they do not understand it.

5. "Work hard—and you will get lucky."

In his new book entitled *Think Like a Champion*, Donald Trump attributes his success to his hard work, which to outsiders often appears to be luck. But Trump says luck only comes from working hard. "If your work pays off, which it most likely will, people might say you are just lucky. Maybe so, because you are lucky enough to have the brains to work hard!" he says. That same concept, of course, was advocated by Benjamin Franklin in the 18th century. He said, "The harder I work, the luckier I get."

6. Practice smart budgeting.

I recommend that you practice perfectly smart budgeting. You must use *Quicken* or forms to track how much you spend each month; in fact, this chore is something I do religiously. Every month, I download my transactions into a *Quicken* spreadsheet to keep my spending on track.

As prosaic as it sounds, maintaining a good credit score is essential to becoming and staying a millionaire. A good credit score can save you thousands of dollars over the course of your lifetime. Dave Ramsey has done a great job in explaining the practice of smart budgeting in his book titled *The Total Money Makeover*; buy it and read it.

7. Do what you love.

Sure, a career in finance might come with a hefty annual salary, but you probably will not excel at something you do not enjoy. That is why I recommend going into the field that you find yourself reading about in your spare time. Do you read fashion magazines? Get a job in fashion. Do you read gossip blogs? Get a job in celebrity-based enterprises. Do you read *Car and Driver*? ESPN.com? Yahoo Pets Forum? Even if the field does not seem lucrative, there are ways to make it to the top, something that is more likely to happen if you love the field or the job.

8. Decide how much money you really want.

For many people, $1 million will not be enough. For most Gen-X and Gen-Yers, retiring with a couple of millions when they are 65 will not be anywhere near enough to maintain even an average lifestyle, because that little pup called inflation is constantly nipping at your heels as you try to run towards building your own retirement nest-egg. A more reasonable goal might be $3 million, an amount that I consider the minimum to be a bare-bones millionaire these days. Consider your ideal lifestyle and what you would like to be able to fund. A mortgage of a certain size? Exotic vacations? College tuition for your children? Having a concrete goal in mind makes it easier to get there; goal setting is too important for you to ignore.

9. Invest against the grain.

Be a contrarian investor like Warren Buffett. Do not follow the foolish crowd on Wall Street. They are like the foolish brides in the New Testament. I recommend you make investment decisions based on the exact opposite of what everyone else is doing. Right now, for example, stocks are relatively cheap because so many people have sold off shares, which means anyone buying can get them at a discount to their values from a year ago. My rule of thumb does not just apply to stocks; it also applies to real estate, so buy a foreclosed house, fill it up with roommates, and you can get a pretty good passive income. In step ten of the book, titled invest in real estate, I have spent time explaining how I invest in all types of properties.

10. Live below your means.

Even Eminem, a celebrity and millionaire, scales back his purchases out of concern for frugality. In February, London's Independent newspaper reported that as Eminem considered buying a $15,000 watch he liked, he started worrying that he should save his money instead. Eminem reportedly said, "I do not want to run out of money; I want my daughter to be able to go to college."

There is more to personal finance than the drudgery of debts and budgets.

And so far, at least, Eminem has not fallen victim to the financial challenges so many other stars, from Aretha Franklin to Annie Leibovitz and Michael Jackson, have faced. On the same note, even though I am a millionaire, no one would know it; I drive my own car, a car-note free 2006 SUV BMW, and that is the point; my wife paid cash for her Chrysler Town and Country van. My children love the automobile to death because I outfitted it with a colored television set and a CD/DVD player. In the beginning, I recommend you save at least 10 percent of your income; you can increase the percentage to 25 after you have whittled down your debts. I also suggest that you should avoid buying status-symbol items, such as fancy sports cars or mansions. After all, bling does not make a millionaire, and in fact, too much of it can prevent you from ever becoming one.

SECRETS OF SELF-MADE MILLIONAIRES

When you think the word millionaire, what image comes to your mind? For many of us, it is a flashy Wall Street banker type who flies a private jet, collects cars and lives the kind of decadent lifestyle that would make Donald Trump proud. But many modern millionaires live in middle-class neighborhoods, work full-time and shop in discount stores like the rest of us. What motivates them is not material possessions but the choices that money can bring. For the rich like us, it is not about getting more stuff.

It is about having the freedom to make almost any decision you want. Wealth means you can send your child to any school or quit a job you do not like. According to the Spectrem Wealth Study, an annual survey of America's wealthy, there are more people living the good life than ever before, the number of millionaires nearly doubled in the last decade. As you can see, the rich are getting richer. To make it onto the Forbes 400 list of the richest Americans, a mere billionaire no longer makes the cut. This year you needed a net worth of at least $1.3 billion. If more people are getting richer than ever, why should you not be one of them? Before I proceed, I am dying to share with you money secrets that have guaranteed me at least a million dollars in liquid assets:

1. Set your sights on where you are going

In 1990, I hardly seemed on the road to wealth. I was living in a dingy apartment in Alexandria, Virginia. I was a university dropout who struggled to support his mother and five sisters, by running a word processing service, working as a security guard, and moonlighting as a part-time English teacher. At times I was so broke I could barely pay my rents. I was tired of eating chicken and sardines. Along the way, I met other guys struggling to make it like spent swimmers crossing the Atlantic Ocean.

Today, however, I am a self-made millionaire savoring the pleasures of financial success. There was one big reason I pulled ahead of the pack: Deep in my broken heart, I always knew someday soon I would be rich. As I can see it, the reality is that 80 percent of Americans worth at least $5 million grew up in middle-class or lesser households, just like me. The vaulting ambition of wanting to be wealthy is a crucial first step.

The biggest obstacle to wealth is fear. Along the way, I met many friends who were deterred from reaching for the skies by the paralysis of fear. Courage has always been my friend; even when I am facing adversity, I muster the courage to deflect negative thoughts.

I always make an effort to practice the magic of thinking big like a winner. Many people around you are afraid to think big, but if you think small, you will only achieve small things. It all started for me when I met a Jewish teacher who introduced me to Ric Rich, a stockbroker, at a Christmas party. Talking to Ric Rich I felt like I was an ancient Greek discovering the fire of specialized knowledge from Prometheus. I started reading finance books and investing magazines. After an initial deposit of $5,000, I began putting $30 a month in a mutual fund managed by Peter Lynch called Fidelity Magellan. I was thrilled to discover in 2007 that my $10,000 investment had grown to the staggering sum of $125,000 in five years; I used the money to buy my first home for $250,000. Next, I organized an investment club to teach my sisters and friends how to play and win the stock market game. Thanks Ric Rich! There were many hard roads for me to travel; I knew I was a struggling man, but what got me through it all was my solid faith, believing with all my heart that I would succeed in the end.

2. Educate yourself

Financial literacy is important. In order for you to make big money, you must be financially literate. Do not worry if at first you do not understand this financial stuff; come to Millionaire iUniversity. Read books and magazines about money management and investing that I have listed in step 12 of *The Miraculous Millionaire* titled attend Millionaire iUniversity. Ask every financial whiz you know or meet to explain things to you. Start applying the lessons you have learned. Specialized knowledge is what you need to think and grow rich. Self-education is the cheapest and most practical way to obtain it.

3. Passion pays off

You must be passionate about your job or the vehicle you need to get rich. According to research conducted by Thomas J. Stanley, the author of *The Millionaire Mind*, over 80 percent of millionaires say they never would have been successful if their vocation was not something they cared about. Love what you do.

4. Grow your money

Most of us know the never-ending cycle of living paycheck to paycheck. The fastest way to get out of that pattern is to make extra money for the specific purpose of reinvesting in yourself; in other words, earmark some money for the sole purpose of investing it in a place where it will grow dramatically—like a business, stocks mutual funds, or real estate. There are endless ways to make extra money for investing; you just have to be willing to do the work: I will show you how to do it in this book. Everyone has a marketable skill. When I started out, I had an English writing tutoring business, assisting foreign students on campus with the mechanics of expository writing.

There is more to personal finance than the drudgery of debts and budgets.

A little moonlighting cash really can grow into a million. If you want to get rich, you need to make extra money and allocate 10% of it to the saving solution, by putting money where it will work hard for you, whether that is in your retirement fund, a side business or investments like real estate.

5. "No guts, no glory."

You must have guts. Success is not for the faint of heart. The bottom-line of the millionaire's secret is that you must separate the fact from the fiction about millionaires. Maybe you have seen a pattern here from the discussion above: today's millionaires are people who live within their means, budget and spend wisely, and focus on financial independence first. These are habits that take discipline to form, but ones you can all adopt to begin growing wealth. If these facts prove anything, it is that every one of us can strive to become a millionaire -- you can start by driving your old car with pride. That is the miracle and magic of changing your financial life.

IMPOSSIBLE

"Most of the things worth doing in the world had been declared impossible before they were done."
- Louis D. Brandeis

CHANGE

"Progress is impossible without a change, and those who cannot change their minds cannot change anything."
~George Bernard Shaw

TWO WAYS TO LIVE YOUR LIFE

"There are only two ways to live your life. One is as though nothing is a miracle. The other is as everything is."
~Albert Einstein

YOU SEE WHAT YOU ARE

"A loving person lives in a loving world. A hostile person lives in a hostile world. Everyone you meet is your mirror."
~Ken Keyes

PROSPERITY

If you want one year of prosperity grow seeds. If you want 10 years of prosperity grow trees. If you want a lifetime of prosperity, grow your mind. ~John Assaraf

SUCCESS FORMULA OF PELE OF BRAZIL

"Success is no accident. It is hard work, perseverance, learning, studying, sacrifice, and most of all, love of what you are doing or learning to do"
— Pele

You can be a champion like Pele! Pele is a Brazilian winner of the money game. Financial success can be compared to game like soccer, basketball, football, boxing, karate, and ballet. According to Pele, below is what it takes to become a money champion:

1-Passion
2-Preparation
3-Strategy
4-Discipline
5-Respect
6-Perseverance

Since childhood, Pele always had his eyes on the football. Even as a boy, Pele knew what it would take to be extraordinary. Today, he shares those lessons with other children. Chances are, you have never heard of Edson Arantes do Nascimento. You probably do not know that he became the most famous athlete of the last century. Not in America! Not in Europe! In the whole world! Little Edson grew up in relative poverty in Três Corações, Brazil. As a boy, he worked as a servant to earn extra money for his family.

But by the time he was 11, people began to notice Edson was special; he could do things with his feet and a ball that people twice his age could not replicate. A local football coach took an interest in Pele, and the coach began to instruct the slender kid, who usually had to practice with a makeshift ball, sock stuffed with newspaper and tied with string. Edson eventually gained a nickname. He is not quite sure how or why it happened possibly because he modeled himself after his favorite player, Bilé, whose name he had trouble pronouncing. Once schoolmates began using the nickname, he could not shake it. Pelé was born.

You have heard of the name Pelé, but his otherworldly skills on the pitch made him the most prominent and successful footballer of all time. In his prime, he transcended borders, politics and race, a man whose mere appearance resulted in a cease-fire of the Nigerian civil war in 1967 so that both sides could see him play. He even captivated audiences in the United States, despite their lack of enthusiasm for his sport, and his admirers came from all walks of life. About Pelé, former Secretary of State Henry Kissinger told ESPN.com, "Heroes walk alone, but they become myths when they ennoble the lives and touch the hearts of all of us. For those who love soccer, Edson Arantes do Nascimento, generally known as Pelé, is a hero."

There is more to personal finance than the drudgery of debts and budgets.

None of Pelé's success happened by chance. As soon as he started to walk, he was playing soccer. While other children were running around the playground, Pelé was working on and honing his craft. By the time he was fourteen, he was already participating in major tournaments and would turn pro just a year later. As he puts it, "I was eager to help my family, and that gave me extra motivation to succeed and make my father proud of me. I was ready to give up things children my age were normally doing. Instead, I spent a lot of time practicing and improving my skills." At 15, Pelé's skills had improved enough that he made the Brazilian professional team Santos. He scored his first goal during a friendly match. The next year, 1957, Pelé started and starred for one of the best professional teams on the planet at the tender age of 16. He led the league in scoring and was quickly named to the Brazilian national team. Not many outside South America knew him, but the world was soon put on notice that the boy who would become known as the King of Soccer had arrived.

The 1958 FIFA World Cup, held in Sweden, was Pelé's first. At 17, he was then the youngest player to ever appear in the World Cup, and he remains the youngest to appear in a final and score a goal. And it was in the final against Sweden that Pelé proved his greatness to a worldwide audience. In the game's 55th minute, Pelé, draped by two defenders, took a pass off his chest, stopping the ball dead and controlling it to his right foot. He immediately popped the ball over the head of an onrushing Swedish defender, raced two yards around his mark, and kicked the ball before it landed, driving it into the net. It is widely considered one of the greatest individual efforts in soccer history. The 1958 win would be the first of three World Cup titles for Pelé, the only player to ever achieve the feat. His other accolades could fill pages. He led his league in scoring 11 times; he won 32 official team trophies (the most ever); he was named Athlete of the Century by the International Olympic Committee; and TIME magazine named him one of the 100 most important people of the 20th century.

LOVE WHAT YOU DO

Much of what Pelé could do simply cannot be taught. His inherent ball skills and quickness are the stuff of legend. But Pelé believes there is no secret formula to being successful in any arena; you do not need to possess physical or mental tools no one can compete with. He says, "I always took care of myself." "Preparation does not start a day or week before the game or event." Beyond just preparing to obtain your goals, Pelé believes it is critical to find a niche that lights a fire inside you and to share that interest with others. "Love what you do," he says. "That passion will give you the strength, discipline, the desire to work hard and the humility to understand you can always improve. Soccer is a sport that you cannot win without the rest of your team. You cannot win a tournament without a good strategy, discipline and perseverance. Apply that in your life, and you will become a winner." After initially retiring from professional play in 1974, he still had one goal he had not yet netted: "The idea was to establish soccer in America. I had left my professional career, but I decided to come back for that great challenge. America is such a great country and should be part of the most-loved game in the world." In 1975, he signed with the New York Cosmos of the fledgling North American Soccer League. In 1977, he led the team to the league title and closed out his career with an exhibition match between the Cosmos and his longtime club Santos. He played a half for each team and (of course) scored a goal.

Today, Pelé lends his name to soccer-related gear and other goods, but that is hardly his focus. "When I started playing professionally, it was important to me to be very good and succeed," Pelé recalls. "Now that I'm no longer an athlete, I want to make sure I'm giving back to my friends all over the world; I want them to have an opportunity to live in a better place and have opportunities in life."

WHAT SUCCESS REQUIRES

In 1992, Pelé was named the United Nations ambassador for ecology and the environment. He works closely with Pequeno Principe Hospital in Curitiba, Brazil, now the largest pediatric hospital in the country and an important research hub. He is also heavily involved in The Prince's Rainforests Project. Prince Charles of England formed the project in 2007 to combat tropical rainforest deforestation, restore the ability to capture carbon dioxide and reduce the effects of climate change. But setting an example for the youth of the world remains Pelé's primary mission after soccer. "I have been [true] to the same values since I was a kid," he says. "If we can teach children from the very beginning the importance of discipline, determination, teamwork and ethics, among other things, we will make a great contribution."

In 2010, he reached out to children via his illustrated children' book *FOR THE LOVE OF SOCCER!* The story follows Pelé as a boy striving to become a great soccer player and a young fan determined to emulate his hero. He wanted to promote his sport, but he also hoped to fill young minds with life lessons. To achieve success, you need determination, hard work, respect for your mates and your adversaries, and, most of all, a love for what you are doing. Not only in football, but for everything in life." Now 70, Pelé has no interest in slowing down. He spends time with his wife and their twin daughter and son, age 14, as well as his three grown children from a previous marriage. But it is his passion for helping others that continues to drive him.

He has several philanthropic projects he plans to announce soon, and he continues to reach out to children all over the world, hoping to spark their interest in soccer and in being good stewards to their planet. "I believe God gave me a gift, and it is natural that I give my best in return to society," he says. "I want to be remembered for the example I set for people and the way I represented my country. I have a wonderful life, and I thank God for it." Judging by his legions of adoring fans across the globe, he is not the only one who is thankful.

TEN COMMANDMENTS OF MILLIONAIRES

For those who continue to believe in the American Dream, the primary sources of wealth listed by affluent households in the U.S. continue to support that dream. Despite the fact that most of us believe that the rich guy down the street inherited it all, only slightly more than a quarter of millionaires inherited any wealth. Below are the ten commandments of millionaires:

1. Choose the right partner and only marry once

2. Live off one income

There is more to personal finance than the drudgery of debts and budgets.

3. Choose the right career

4. Put your money in appreciating assets

5. Do not live the millionaire lifestyle

6. Adopt the millionaire mindset and character traits

7. Work hard and get aggressive with your plan

8. Maintain good health and exercise routinely

9. Set your goals and have patience

10. Start saving and prepare for rainy days

MILLIONAIRE SECRETS EXPOSED

In the final analysis, I am happy and proud to expose millionaire secrets to you. These secrets are what I refer to as $ucce$$tology, the science, philosophy, and art of achieving the American Dream today. If you have traveled around the world, you will be impressed by the fact that America remains the only country on earth without social stratification. For instance, unlike India or Great Britain, America still affords the opportunity for any individual without connections to rise from a life of poverty to one of riches. America does not have a natural aristocratic class.

You do not have to be a descendant of the Rockefellers, Vanderbilts, Morgans, or Kennedys to become rich in America. The evidence I have submitted to you shows that most new millionaires are nouveaux riches—new money, not the progeny of old money. Every day more and more people are deserting their native lands and clamoring Ellis Island and other shores of America.

Why? They know that America is the only oasis of prosperity on earth; America is the only nation on the planet where an individual has the freedom to realize his or her true human potential. The new immigrants, who believe in the American Dream and pursue it doggedly, become true millionaires.

Hence, do not believe the lies that the American Dream is dead! In fact, it is still alive and well. America remains the land of opportunity. It suffices for you to follow your dreams. America is a mint of millionaires. Statistically, every day new individuals, like you, become millionaires. They become millionaires by acquiring and acting upon the millionaire secret. What about you? If you are ready to change your life, I, Prince Ojong, the founder of the millionaire network, am ready to help you.

Who would not want to be worth a million dollars? Many of us dream of achieving this goal, more often than not for the sake of the freedom financial stability would bring. So how can we get there? The answers are actually much easier than you might expect. Here are several easy steps to get you into the millionaires' club. With a little discipline and the help of some powerful savings and investment vehicles, anyone can hit this mark. The following step-by-step guide is your roadmap to financial security. It shows the millionaire club taking you from point A, where you are now, to Point B, where you want to be in the foreseeable future. In short, it is a financial life projection. Are you still worrying about financial security? Below are 12 steps that will take you to financial paradise:

PRINCE OJONG'S ROADMAP TO FINANCIAL SECURITY

#1: Join the Prince Ojong financial organization called The Millionaire Club.

#2: Submit to a session of the club's Financial Audit and Needs Assessment.

#3: Write your financial plan.

#4: Initiate or reinforce your spiritual relationship with God.

#5: Execute your insurance protection plan: life, health, disability, plus P and C, that is property and casualty.

#6: Implement the pay yourself 10% saving plan: save, save, and save.

#7: Moonlight with Millionaire Club.

#8: Explore business opportunities outside the club

#9: Leverage your assets.

#10: Seek professional advice from accountants, planners, and brokers.

#11: Build your credit power.

#12: Start your business successfully!

There is more to personal finance than the drudgery of debts and budgets.

Step 3

USE INSURANCE AS THE FOUNDATION OF WEALTH

Be all you can be in the good olde USA. I want to get you really pumped up by putting visions of dollar signs in your eyes. I want to show you how you can be transformed from the middle class of common laboring and working folks that you are to fabulously wealthy millionaires like me with mansions, yachts, BMWs, Rolls-Royces, and helicopters. I have discovered the money-making secrets of America's millionaires. Whether it is learning to think and grow rich like a millionaire, mastering your personal finances, starting a business, investing in real estate, or trading in the stock market, I have figured out how to do it, making big money without ever losing money! So my friends, I have a system, the money-making secret of America's millionaires from the dead-sea scrolls. Pay me to follow it and you will grow rich!

We mint millionaires one person at a time.

INSURANCE!

I have learned that rich folks ascribe fundamental importance to insurance—financial security. Rich folks insure all their assets (love, blood, and money) so that they do not lose them in a lawsuit if they run someone over. Do you remember O.J. Simpson? Rich folks never adhere to the Primerica mantra; they do not buy term insurance and invest the difference in mutual funds; rather, they invest in permanent insurance for the merits of cash-values.

Financial security through permanent insurance is like opting to buy a house for equity accumulation instead of renting the house only, that is, without any equity build up.

ARE YOU A WISE OR A FOOLISH BUILDER OF WEALTH?

Therefore everyone who hears these words of mine and puts them into practice is like a wise man who built his house on the rock. The rain came down, the streams rose, and the winds blew and beat against that house; yet it did not fall, because it had its foundation on the rock. But everyone who hears these words of mine and does not put them into practice is like a foolish man who built his house on sand. The rain came down, the streams rose, and the winds blew and beat against that house, and it fell with a great crash.
Matthew 7:24-27

Do you remember the parable of the two builders in the Holy bible? Please, refer to Matthew 7:24-27 and Luke 6:47-49--The House Upon Sand and the House Upon Rock. While Jesus was preaching and teaching there were many people who said they would follow Jesus after hearing him preach. They called themselves his disciples but they did not practice what Jesus preached, like loving others and changing their attitude. Jesus then told them it means nothing to say "'Lord, Lord' when you do nothing to follow my commandments or do the will of God". So Jesus decided to tell them a story of how two men built their homes. It is called the parable of the two builders. Here is his parable:

All those who listen to my words and do something about them are like a wise man who builds his house on a rock. The man laid a strong foundation by digging deep into the earth. Then he worked carefully and slowly making sure the building was strong and secure on the rock. And then the rains and floods came and the wind blew hard and beat against the house. But the house did not fall because it was built on a strong foundation. But the person who hears my words and does nothing with them is like a stupid or foolish man who built his house on the sand. This man did not build a strong deep foundation and built his house very quickly. His tall house was built fast and he moved in feeling safe. Soon the rains and floods came and the wind blew beating against the house. The tall house without a strong foundation just could not stand up to the flooding and winds and it cracked and the whole house collapsed.

The crowds were surprised at Jesus' story. Jesus warned them that if the people did not build their life on a deep foundation and follow his teachings then they too would find that their house had fallen down.

There is more to personal finance than the drudgery of debts and budgets.

Below are questions for you to ask yourself:

1) What does the deep foundation in the story represent? What does the house represent?
 2) Do you think that following Jesus' teachings and building your house on a strong foundation is easy or hard? Why?
 3)Why do you think Jesus used the parable about a house as a way to show people they needed to do more than just hear his teachings? Who did the two builders represent?
 4)Why is it important for us to follow Jesus teachings?
God bless you!

In 1995, I stumbled upon the biggest wealth-building secret in America: insurance. Unfortunately, I did not have the money to attend the workshop that followed the seminar; $10,000, the asking price for a seat at the workshop, was too much for a poor African guy like me. I gave up on the quest in frustration. As time wore on, nevertheless, my interest in insurance was rekindled by the meeting of acquaintances who were insurance agents; unfortunately, all of these acquaintances were broke guys like me; they had never heard the kind of stuff I was talking about. I continued, however, researching the insurance secrets of America's rich and famous.

In 2003, I persuaded a friend who had attended Saint Joseph's College with me, to become an insurance agent; I entrusted him with the sinecure mission of investigating how high-networth folks in America use insurance; with the progression of time, he began briefing me weekly with intelligence on the working of the insurance industry in America. Above all, my psychographic studies laid threadbare the dichotomy between the insurance habits of the rich and poor folks. What perpetuates the ignorance of the masses is the presence in the market of companies like Primerica and World Financial Group, who hire many untrained agents who operate like a cabal of thieves whose penchant for brainwashing the poor is limitless and proverbial. Their popular mantra is the following slogan: "Buy term and invest the difference." Eureka! After many years spent serving and observing the rich and famous in country clubs and researching economic data online and offline, I am convinced, beyond any reasonable doubt, that you should not use insurance like poor folks, the average Primerica client who perceives life insurance to be, actually, death insurance; you should model the rich and famous; to the rich and famous, in the aggregate, life insurance is a tool of financial planning; they want to build wealth without the risks of market corrections and uncertainties. The rich want the peace of mind of investing their money and sleeping at night well.

I want to share the investment intelligence of the rich and famous folks with you now. My discovery is that you can use insurance to build the right financial foundation of wealth today. I will show you how to apply the scientific method consisting of observation, classification, and analysis in this experiment.

In the beginning, I am going to present a personal finance questionnaire that you can download on my web site: http://www.princeojong.com or http://www.millionaireiuniversity.com.

We mint millionaires one person at a time.

I had designed the questionnaire to assist my customers to collect information pertaining to their insurance needs; in fact, I use the questionnaire when I meet my insurance clients for the first time; my clients complete the form with my assistance, or I ask them questions and complete the form for them. After the form is completed, I spend some time observing and reviewing the data I have collected from the customer. You might be interested in using this questionnaire, too.

Stage two of my consultative meeting with a customer is the decision to classify the financial problems the customer faces today or tomorrow. As for step three, needs analysis, I leverage the reservoir of my insurance knowledge to recommend common-sense insurance solutions to the customer. I regard you as my potential customer, so proceed to my web sites and download the questioonaire. If you need any help, please, do not hesitate to call my office: (301) 593-4897 or (301) 593-4879. I would be happy to assist you. If you need me to drive or fly to your city, I am ready to accommodate you. I am a man on a mission. Of course, my mission is to serve you; you are the right reason why I am writing this book. The book is your book; use it to learn and master how the rich and famous folks in America capitalize on insurance.

BERNARD BERNANKE

Uncovering the life insurance secrets of America's rich and famous has become my hobby and business. Last week, I spent much time on the world wide web. I was on the web site of the FDIC, Federal Deposit Insurance Corporation for twenty-two hours; I was researching the life insurance tips and tricks of high net worth Americans such as Warren Buffett and Bernard Bernanke, and I was also poring through the balance sheet of financial institutions such as Citibank and Bank of America.

My investment method is simple. I follow the US Federal Reserve like a hawk. When interest rates are high, money becomes expensive for investors to borrow; rich folks do not like to invest their money in equities; they expect Bernard Bernanke to slash interest rates. When interest rates start to fall, rich people switch their money from bonds back into equities, since the relative value of the bond's interest goes up against a backdrop of rising interest rates, making the dollar/trading value of the bond go up; and the rest of the time, let it ride on stocks! I have learned to imitate the rich folks; when in Rome, do what the Romans do. Why waste time following the foolish crowd? Foolishness is a sin; the Holy bible draws our attention to the potentially disastrous consequences of foolishness. Do you remember the story of the foolish virgins in Matthew 25:1-13?

Be wise like the wisemen in the bible, or be like the wise rich folks in America. The first name that comes to my mind is Bernard Bernanke. Do you know him? If not, he is the chairman of the US Federal Reserve. Ben Bernanke , the U.S Federal Reserve Chairman, recently disclosed details of his personal investments. Any lessons on personal investing from the guru of interest rates?

As required by law, Bernard Bernanke and the other Federal Governors file financial disclosure statements annually. 2009 was a good year for the monetary policy expert. Bloomberg calculated that his assets rose as much as 31% in the market rebound of 2009. Though that record beat the Standard & Poor's 23.5% gain for the year, the Fed Chief did not rack up those big numbers by using exotic derivatives or rapid fire trading. Indeed, in Bernard Bernanke's case, his investment style seemed to be as safe and conservative as the dark suits he favored for Congressional hearings. Bernard Bernanke held tight. He did not do a lot of selling in 2009, but rather held on to almost all the same investments he had had the year before.

His portfolio is pretty straight forward. Most of Bernanke's money is invested in two annuities at TIAA-CREF, which is the dominant player in academia with over $426 billion in assets under management. Bernard Bernanke came to Washington from a career in higher education, and his largest holdings are a TIAA traditional guaranteed annuity and a CREF Stock Large Cap Blend variable annuity. He has somewhere between $1 million and $2 million in the two together, and all values are disclosed in ranges on these forms.

According to TIAA-CREF's web site, their Large-Cap Blend investment strategy "seeks a favorable long-term total return through both capital appreciation and investment income, primarily from income-producing equity securities. The investment team believes that in a dynamic marketplace the stock prices of large, historically successful companies do not always reflect their current or long-term values." A chunk of his investments are quite liquid and low risk. Bernanke has more than $100,000 in a Sun Trust Money Market account, earning the usual paltry interest rates those get. He has multiple income streams. In addition to his $196,700 salary as Federal Chairman, Bernanke earns more than $ 200,000 per year in royalties on two textbooks he wrote as well. The Associated Press called Bernanke's investing style "no frills."

WARREN BUFFETT

Warren Buffett, the former hedge fund manager who built Berkshire Hathaway Inc. into a $195 billion company, is well known for his stock market prowess. However, most of his admirers do not know the fact that he uses life insurance as a lethal weapon; Warren Buffett, the Oracle of Omaha, uses life insurance to gain leverage through insurance premiums. Berkshire Hathaway Inc.'s insurance units cover risks from fender benders to asbestos-related hospital bills; insurance units rely upon life insurance to provide new investment funds in the form of float or accumulated premium.

WALT DISNEY

Do you want to pick the brains of Walt Disney? WALT DISNEY USED FUNDS FROM HIS LIFE INSURANCE POLICY TO BEGIN MANIFESTING HIS DREAM. DID YOU KNOW?

Walt Disney, unable to obtain a substantial bank loan, used the cash-value from his whole life policy to build a sprawling theme park that is now known to the world as "the happiest place on earth."

This privatized banking strategy is not about rate of return within the policy as much as it is about access to capital and what you do with that, outside the policy. Walt Disney collateralized money from his life insurance policy and so was able to take a loan after the bank refused to lend him money to start a theme park, which is now the world famous Disney Land. What do you think his internal policy rate of return was compared to his external rate of return? How much profit has Disneyland generated for him?

MCDONALD'S

Working as a milkshake machine distributor in 1954, Ray Kroc, 1902–1984, took notice of a successful hamburger stand in San Bernardino, California, which he called on, intending to sell brothers Dick and Mac McDonald more multimixers. He learned they were interested in a nationwide franchising agent. Kroc, 52 at the time, decided his future was in hamburgers and partnered with the brothers. He opened his first McDonald's in Des Plaines, Illinois, in 1955 and bought out the McDonald brothers in 1961.

Kroc did not take a salary during his first 8 years, and to overcome constant cash-flow problems, Kroc borrowed money from two cash-value life insurance policies, and also his bank, to help cover the salaries of key employees. He also used some of the money to create an advertising campaign around emerging mascot Ronald McDonald. Using a progressive franchising arrangement and striving for consistency and standardization throughout the chain, McDonald's grew to more than 700 restaurants within 10 years. Today, McDonald's serves more than 50 million people each day through more than 30,000 locations in 119 countries.

SENATOR JOHN MCCAIN

A number of years ago, 2008, presidential candidate John McCain secured initial campaign financing by using his $3 million life insurance policy as collateral.

DORIS CHRISTOPHER

In 1980, Doris Christopher used a life insurance loan to launch her struggling kitchen gadget company. In 2002, she sold that company, the Pampered Chef, to Warren Buffett for a reported $900 million.

J.C. PENNEY

Even in the midst of the Great Depression, J.C. Penney used a loan against his $3 million life insurance policy to resuscitate his retail stores after the 1929 crash.

LELAND STANFORD JR. AND STANFORD UNIVERSITY

Pacific Mutual Life, now Pacific Life, ceremoniously issued its first policy to Leland Stanford, the company's first president, in 1868.

There is more to personal finance than the drudgery of debts and budgets.

After his son, Leland Jr., died of typhoid fever in 1884 at the age of 15, the former California governor and U.S. senator and his wife, Jane L. Stanford, determined that because they could no longer do anything for their own child, they would use their wealth to do something for other people's children. With a strong belief in the importance of a practical education for men and women that would prepare them to be productive and successful, six years of planning led them to establish Leland Stanford Jr. University in Palo Alto in 1891, with a pioneer class of 555 students, including Herbert Hoover. Following Leland's death in 1893, the fledgling university's financial support became uncertain, to the point where Jane tried unsuccessfully to sell her treasured jewel collection in 1897. Intent on preserving the university and avoiding a temporary closure, she used her husband's life insurance policy proceeds to help fund operations and pay faculty, allowing Stanford University to weather a dangerous six-year period of financial distress.

FOSTER FARMS

In 1939, a young couple named Max and Verda Foster started Foster Farms by borrowing $1,000 against a life insurance policy. They invested in an 80-acre farm near Modesto, Calif., and began raising turkeys and, eventually, chickens. By the 1960s, the company had outgrown the original farm and moved its corporate headquarters to the small California Central Valley town of Livingston, where it still resides. Today Max and Verda's grandson, Ron Foster, is the CEO of the family run business. Foster Farms is now more than 10,000 employees strong, with operations in California, Oregon, Washington, Colorado, Arkansas, and Alabama; the company has a line of products that are sold globally. Foster Farms specializes in fresh, all-natural chicken products free of preservatives, additives or injected sodium enhancers.

DAVID N. MULLANY, WIFFLE BALL CREATOR

Cash-value life insurance helps tide over left-handed pitcher and wiffle ball Creator, David N. Mullany, in 1953. Twenty years after being saved from unemployment by his reputation as a solid left-handed pitcher, David N. Mullany was once again out of work. Except now, it was 1953 and he had a family to feed, a family that saw him leave the house in the morning and come back in the evening and thought he still had a job. What he was actually doing was looking for one and bringing home the money from his cashed-in life insurance policy. After every fruitless day, he would return to the same scene: his son playing baseball with his buddies in the back yard. Their only care in the world was figuring out how to throw a curve ball:

"My two cents — I was saddened when I saw the words cashed-in life insurance, when I know that he could have borrowed from his cash-value and paid it back after he earned enough to. That way he would have kept his life insurance policy and the cash-value that may have come in handy later. His family would have kept the protection of the death benefit also."

He could throw a lazy curve," said his son David A., now 70 years old. "And I could never do it." Right about then, Mullany's life took a crazier turn than any wiffle ball. The children were playing with plastic golf balls that, try as they might, they could not spin. So the two Davids, father and son, began experimenting.

They wanted to create a ball that would do the work for them. Mullany came across half-spheres of plastic that a perfume company was using in promotional packets and thought they might hold the solution. Over the course of a week, they cut all sorts of patterns into them before finally settling on the now familiar one. "It was good enough to keep the rotten crew that I hung out with busy," said David A. Mullany, who soon began working in his father's factory taping the wooden bat handles. Wiffle ball made skinny wooden bats until 1972 before switching exclusively to plastic.

JAMES STEWART

It is A Wonderful Life — What did George Bailey want to use as Collateral for a Bank Loan? What happened when James Stewart (George Bailey) went to the bank to ask for a loan? He was first asked by the banker (Lionel Barrymore as Mr. Potter), "What collateral do you have?"

His Answer: James Stewart tried to use his life insurance cash-value as collateral for a loan from Mr. Potter but there was not enough available for what he needed. Still, the point is this concept is not new. It has been around since whole life was invented.

The next question asked by Mr. Potter was the following: ""How much equity do you have in it?" Our grandparents and great grandparents' generation knew the value of whole life insurance. They did not have term insurance with zero equity and that runs out or cost too much when they needed it most. Term insurance has its place, but it should not replace properly designed permanent life insurance. If only they were taught to borrow from the life insurance company using their cash-value as collateral though instead of using the policy as equity (cash-value or death benefit) to borrow from someone else's bank.

Some people of that era did know this well-kept secret though; Walt Disney did, that is where he borrowed from to make Disneyland a reality when the bank turned him down for a loan. The way rich folks design their life insurance policies gives them way more collateral capacity than what George Bailey had though, from 15 days after their policies are completed. They allocate 55% of their premiums as cash-value year one. 85% cash-value year two and the percentage of cash-value only increases every year after that. It only gets better as time goes by.

After your policy is capitalized, the amount of premiums paid equals the amount of cash-value available to use as the measure of how much you can borrow while you are alive. Your life insurance is really free in that, even though you still want to pay your premiums, you do not have to and the policy will continue to grow.

While you are alive, you are able to borrow from the life insurance company using your death benefit as collateral. If you set it up properly, you can even use the death benefit to bring down the points on your mortgage. Are you ready to use life insurance as a foundation of wealth building? Then, call me, today, so I can educate you on the multitude of benefits; my office phone number is (301) 593-4897; my direct life insurance phone line is (240-330-0839; de jure, if PROPERLY DESIGNED FOR PERSONAL EQUITY BANKING, a cash-value life insurance policy can cater to all your financial planning needs while you are living.

There is more to personal finance than the drudgery of debts and budgets.

A VISIT TO COLUMBIA COUNTRY CLUB

Are you ready for a personal story of the life insurance secrets of America's rich and famous? In the following pages, I am going to present some of the life insurance secrets of America's rich and famous folks. How did I discover these secrets? I had charmed an old Jewish guy, a rich and retired throat surgeon, at a home birthday party in Potomac, Maryland; after taking a likeness for me, he promised to invite me to a wealth-building and tax-saving seminar at Columbia Country Club, 7900 Connecticut Avenue Chevy Chase, MD 20815. What did I learn from the country club? For one, the rich and famous folks look exactly like you and me; in fact, the only difference is that they have a different approach to thinking about money.

Besides, they welcome with an open mind new ideas pertaining to income tax reduction and wealth-building strategies. The rich are rich because they understand and apply the rules of insurance: risk protection, tax efficiency, and guaranteed income. Particularly, I learned much about using life insurance as stipulated by IRS Code Section 79; above all, I was impressed by what rich folks perceive to be the primary and secondary functions of life insurance.

IDEA OF INSURANCE

Insurance is defined as a co-operative device to spread the loss caused by a particular risk over a number of persons who are exposed to it and who agree to ensure themselves against that risk. Truly, risk is uncertainty of a financial loss. It should not be confused with the chance of loss which is the probable number of losses out of a given number of exposures. It should not be confused with peril which is defined as the cause of loss or with hazard which is a condition that may increase the chance of loss. Finally, risk must not be confused with loss itself which is the unintentional decline in or disappearance of value arising from a contingency. Wherever there is uncertainty with respect to a probable loss, there is risk. Every risk involves the loss of one or other kind. The function of insurance is to spread the loss over a large number of persons who have agreed to co-operate with each other at the time of loss. The risk cannot be averted but loss occurring due to a certain risk can be distributed amongst the agreed persons. They have agreed to share the loss because the chances of loss, that is, the time and amount, to a person are not known. Anyone of them may suffer loss to a given risk, so, the rest of the persons who have agreed will share the loss; the larger the number of such persons the easier the process of distribution of loss. In fact, the loss is shared by them by payment of premium which is calculated on the probability of loss. In olden time, the contribution by the persons was made at the time of loss. The insurance is also defined as a social device to accumulate funds to meet the uncertain losses arising through a certain risk to a person insured against the risk.

FUNCTIONS OF INSURANCE

The functions of insurance can be divided into two parts: (i) primary functions and (ii) secondary functions.

PRIMARY FUNCTIONS:

(i) Insurance provides certainty:
Insurance provides certainty of payment at the uncertainty of loss. The uncertainty of loss can be reduced by better planning and administration, but the insurance relieves the person from such difficult task. Moreover, if the subject matters are not adequate, the self-provision may prove costlier. There are different types of uncertainty in a risk. There is the question of whether the risk will occur or not, when the risk will occur, and how much loss will be incurred. In other words, there are uncertainty of happening of time and amount of loss. Insurance removes this uncertainty, and the insured is given certainty of payment of loss. The insurer charges premium for providing the said certainty.

(ii) Insurance provides protection:
The main function of the insurance is to provide protection against the probable chances of loss. The time and amount of loss are uncertain and at the happening of risk, the person will suffer loss in absence of insurance. The insurance guarantees the payment of loss and thus protects the insured from sufferings. The insurance cannot prevent the happening of risk, but it can provide for losses at the happening of the risk.

(iii) Risk-Sharing:
The risk is uncertain, and therefore, the loss arising from the risk is also uncertain. When risk takes place, the loss is shared by all the persons who are exposed to the risk. The risk-sharing in ancient time was done only at time of damage or death; but today, on the basis of probability of risk, the share is obtained from each and every insured in the shape of premium without which protection is not guaranteed by the insurer.

SECONDARY FUNCTIONS:

Besides the above primary functions, the insurance works for the following functions:

(i) Prevention of Loss:
The insurance joins hands with those institutions which are engaged in preventing the losses of the society because the reduction in loss causes lesser payment to the insured and so more saving is possible which will assist in reducing the premium. Lesser premium invites more business and more business cause lesser share to the insured. So again the premium is reduced, which will stimulate more business for the insurer and more protection to the insured. Therefore, the insurance assists financially the health organization, fire brigade, educational institutions and other organizations which are engaged in preventing the losses of the masses from death or damage.

(ii) Provision of Capital:
The insurance provides capital to the society. The accumulated funds are invested in a productive channel. The dearth of capital of the society is minimized to a greater extent with the help of investment of insurance. The industry, the business, and the individual benefit from the investment and loans of the insurers.

There is more to personal finance than the drudgery of debts and budgets.

(iii) Improvement of Efficiency:

The insurance eliminates worries and miseries of losses at death and destruction of property. The care-free person can devote his body and soul together for better achievement. It improves not only his efficiency, but the efficiencies of the masses are also advanced.

(iv) Foster Economic Progress:

The insurance, by protecting the society from huge losses such as damage, destruction, and death, provides an initiative to the carrier to work hard for the betterment of the masses. The next factor of economic progress, the capital, is also immensely provided by the masses. The property, the valuable assets, the man, the machine and the society cannot lose much at the disaster.

MORTGAGE PROTECTION LIFE INSURANCE

What is mortgage protection insurance? Mortgage protection is an insurance coverage a homeowner can purchase to ensure that, in the event that they lose their job or they are otherwise unable to continue mortgage payments, their mortgage will be paid by the insurer. Nearly 15 million Americans are currently unemployed; that is 15 million people who have suffered a loss of income. If you are willing to protect yourself, your family, and your home from a possible job loss, then, you should consider buying some form of mortgage protection.

HOW TO PROTECT YOURSELF FROM LOSING YOUR HOME

Mortgage protection can offer you a considerable amount of protection on your home. But to guard against coverage gaps, homeowners should include a job-loss rider in the policy. A job-loss rider prevents your home from falling under foreclosure, and it will also allow you to keep your home while you search for new employment.

FACTORS THAT AFFECT MORTGAGE PROTECTION INSURANCE COST

Insurance agents will use several factors to determine what premium you will be charged for your mortgage protection insurance. Some of the factors will depend on the following:

1.--The likelihood that you will become unemployed.

2.--If your employer, your industry, or your local area has been slashing jobs left and right, that may mean your job is even less secure than some. The job market is a significant deciding factor on your mortgage protection premium. The higher the risk that you may lose your job, the more your mortgage protection insurance may cost.

3.--Cost of your mortgage payments: If you are currently making modest mortgage payments, your mortgage protection is most likely going to be significantly more affordable than mine, a homeowner who lives in a million-dollar home. The more affordable your mortgage, the more willing your insurance provider will offer you inexpensive mortgage protection coverage.

4--The Recession. If projections show that the job market and the economy are going to worsen in the near future, that, too, will affect your mortgage protection costs. As the risk goes up for insurance providers, so do the costs to policyholders.

REPORTING FOR DUTY

I am reporting for duty as your insurance consultant or advisor. Please, feel free to contact me to discuss your needs. I will be humbled to review your current insurance. Even if you are out of state, I plan to assist you. It is in your interest to consult me and the national network of my insurance agents! We have many resources that can be invaluable to you. Least of all, we can design the blueprint of your insurance edifice. Call (240) 330-0839 now.

Should you choose to invest in mortgage protection insurance, be aware that it can protect you from losing your home in the face of an unstable economy. With an added job-loss rider, mortgage protection will help pay your mortgage payments in the event that you lose your job and can also cover your mortgage if you are otherwise unable to continue the payments on your own. Mortgage protection insurance may be more important now than ever. These days, job security is a thing of the past for many Americans. Companies that manage to stay afloat in the current market are usually forced to cut staff. Employees, who have worked in the same position for years, even decades, can find themselves out of work. But should a person who has fallen victim to the current economy lose his or her home, too? No! The biggest debt many families suffer from is their home mortgage. It is a perilous time for homeowners; the loss of income can result in the loss of one's home. One of the best ways to prevent that outcome is through mortgage protection.

MORTGAGE PROTECTION INSURANCE AS A HOME INSURANCE ADD-ON IS RARE. THE BEST WAY TO GET MORTGAGE RELIEF, AND THE EASIEST WAY TO QUALIFY, IS TO GET IT ROLLED IN A TERM LIFE ADD-ON. WHY? BECAUSE THIS IS WHAT MOST RICH FOLKS AND INTELLIGENT INSURANCE AGENTS CARRY AND IS THE MOST COST-EFFECTIVE METHOD OF COVERING YOUR LIFE, HOME, AND INCOME ALL BUNDLED INTO ONE POLICY!

BOLI—THE SWEET DEAL OF BIG BANKS

BOLI is an acronym for bank owned life insurance. There is a famous adage that says when in Rome do what the Romans do. If you are living in America, the citadel of capitalism, do what the capitalists do; for example, big banks and their highly-paid executives leverage the financial benefits of BOLI. As a case in point, I am referring you to the web site of the FDIC, http://www.fdic.gov. I want you to discover the big money that your bank generates from trading: buying and selling life insurance products. The secret is on line 41 of your bank's balance sheet. Let us proceed: log on to the FDIC's web site (http://www.fdic.gov); turn to the extreme right of the web page; identify the dialog box with the heading "Find Your Bank;" select the name of your state; next, type the name of you bank in the box below.

Look below the page where the following instruction is presented: For additional information please click on one of the following; click on item number 3: Current Financial data about your bank - Institution Directory – Two years Financial Report (This will open a new window.). Look at line 41, life insurance assets; those are the billions of dollars your bank made from insurance transactions alone.

Do you see why banks and insurance companies are the most profitable and liquid business enterprises on earth? In the case of Bank of America, their first quarter income from BOLI is nineteen billions. Can you believe it? You work hard and give your hard-earned money to the bank; the bank turns around and invests your money for a profit between 3% and 15%; if you are fortunate, the bank gives you less than a measly 1%, when you could have invested this money yourself. Think about.

Below I am explaining BOLI in detail because I want you to get smart and start investing in cash-value insurance on your own. If you still cannot grasp the concept of BOLI after reading this section of the chapter of the book, I am happy to invite you to my wealth-building seminar. BOLI offers banks another "where" to position favored assets. BOLI, due to its tax-advantaged nature, is an efficient method to incorporate various asset classes into a bank's balance sheet. Due to recent innovations in the BOLI market, asset classes such as senior/secured loan funds and hedge funds are newly available within the BOLI structure.

BOLI is a form of life insurance purchased by banks where the bank is the beneficiary, and/ or owner of the policy. This form of insurance is a tax shelter for the administering bank, as it is a tax-free funding scheme for employee benefits. Banks use BOLI contracts to fund ever-increasing employee benefits at a much cheaper rate.

The process works like this: the bank sets up the contract, and then makes payments into a specialized fund set aside as the insurance trust. All employee benefits that need to be paid to particular employees covered under the plan are paid out from this fund. All premiums paid into the fund, as well as all capital appreciation, are tax free for the bank. Therefore, banks can use the BOLI system to fund employee benefits on a tax-free basis.

Bank-owned life insurance (BOLI), encompasses all life insurance that a bank purchases and either owns or in which it has a beneficial interest. For many years, banks have been purchasing life insurance on the lives of directors, officers, and employees with the banks as the owners and beneficiaries of the policies. These policies have been typically acquired to recover all or a part of the costs of the bank's employee compensation and benefit programs. BOLI is most commonly designed as a single premium life insurance contract specifically designed to earn tax-free income. BOLI's tax-free income is generated by the increase in cash-value of the policy and insurance proceeds paid to the bank when an insured dies.

Most traditional bank investments create taxable interest income. In contrast, BOLI results in no current income tax liability for the earnings generated each year. Earnings are sheltered inside the life insurance contract and are therefore tax-deferred. When a death occurs, the bank receives life insurance proceeds tax-free.

By reinvesting funds from traditional portfolio investments into BOLI, a bank can typically increase its yield by 100 to 350 basis points depending upon marginal tax rates, the size of the transaction, the type of policies selected and the demographics of the key employees to be insured.

Bank Owned Life Insurance (BOLI) is an excellent vehicle for financing the cost of employee benefits. BOLI may offset the current and future costs of pre- and post-retirement medical coverage, group life, retirement and many other benefits offered to bank employees. In addition, Bank Owned Life Insurance is a highly effective financing tool and offers a higher after-tax yield than most other investments. BOLI is an effective asset that helps diversify a portfolio and enhances the balance sheet. Furthermore, it has tremendous advantages as an asset-liability-matching tool.

QUESTIONS & ANSWERS OF (BOLI) BANK OWNED LIFE INSURANCE

Q: Why do financial institutions buy Bank Owned Life Insurance (BOLI)?

A: Financial institutions face a wide range of ever-increasing benefit costs. These benefit plans range from qualified plans such as pensions to group health benefit plans and supplemental benefits designed to attract and retain key personnel. BOLI provides a tax-efficient tool to help offset these benefit costs.

Q: Is Bank Owned Life Insurance (BOLI) widely used?

A: Most of the largest financial institutions in the nation have used BOLI for many years. More recently thousands of banks and thrifts as well as community banks throughout the country have purchased BOLI to help finance benefit costs.

Q: How does Bank Owned Life Insurance (BOLI) work?

A: The bank purchases life insurance on a select group of managers, including officers or other key personnel. The bank, who is the owner of the policies, pays all premiums and is the beneficiary of the insurance proceeds. Some banks may choose to share a portion of these proceeds with plan participants.

Q: Why is Bank Owned Life Insurance (BOLI) attractive?

A: Well-designed BOLI can provide higher after-tax returns to the financial institution than other high quality asset alternatives. BOLI can help diversify a bank's portfolio and has tremendous advantages as an asset-liability matching tool.

Q: What is the primary economic benefit of Bank Owned Life Insurance (BOLI)?

A: During the life of the policy, the growth of the cash surrender value is tax-deferred. Ultimately upon mortality, the death proceeds are received tax-free. This combination of economic benefits makes BOLI an excellent tool to offset a variety of existing or new benefit costs.

Q: Does the financial institution need to communicate with its employees about Bank Owned Life Insurance (BOLI)?

A: Insurable interest laws vary by state. However, The Executive Benefits Network advocates obtaining positive, written consent from every employee to be insured even if doing so is not required by law.

Q: How do potential plan participants react to Bank Owned Life Insurance (BOLI) funding of employee benefit programs?

A: As BOLI usage has become more common, many bank officers have become aware of the viability of this financing option, and realize the value BOLI provides to help the bank manage its benefit costs. The Executive Benefits Network can assist you in designing enrollment materials that may help ensure understanding and participation. Historically, 90% or more of potential participants agree to the purchase of BOLI on their lives.

Q: Are employees required to participate?

A: Employees are never required to participate. We believe that the more an employee understands about the uses and benefits of BOLI, the more likely they are to participate. There is no cost to the employees, and for larger plans. There typically is no medical underwriting required.

Q: What happens when a participant retires?

A: The bank retains the policy on the retiree's life since the economics of BOLI are most effective when BOLI is held for the long-term. The Executive Benefits Network will track the Social Security numbers of plan participants. When an insured dies, this tracking system provides information necessary to gather appropriate documents from the bank to file a death claim with the insurance company.

Q: Does the bank benefit from the death of its employees?

A: The greatest value of a BOLI plan is the tax-deferred growth of the cash surrender value. While the bank receives death proceeds when an employee dies, it loses the potential tax-deferred growth of that contract. In addition, many banks choose to share a portion of the ultimate death benefits as an additional benefit to employees' beneficiaries.

Q: What kinds of Bank Owned Life Insurance (BOLI) products are available?

A: Because of our conservative approach, The Executive Benefits Network typically recommends diversification when making BOLI purchases. There are two basic categories of BOLI products:

General Account: These products typically provide minimum interest rate guarantees. Current interest rates are typically credited on a quarterly or annual basis. The net rates credited reflect the overall earnings of an insurance company's general account, as well as any expenses associated with the policies. The policies are backed by the general account of the insurance company; therefore the credit quality of a potential carrier is a critical issue to potential buyers.

Separate Account: The returns of these policies reflect assets in a segregated account that are not subject to the general creditors of the insurance company. Plan returns are subject to market fluctuations. With a separate account product, the policy owner bears the risk of default of assets in the separate account.

Q: Which insurance companies underwrite the products?

A: Most of the major insurance carriers have BOLI products. Like its industry peers, The Executive Benefits Network has access to most major insurance carriers.

Q: Do all general account products work the same way?

A: There are two primary interest crediting methods used by carriers. "New money" product returns reflect current interest yields available at plan inception. Over time, the underlying assets, or a proxy portfolio that reflects them are tracked to determine future crediting rates. "Portfolio" products typically reflect the returns of assets backing a broad group of policies and provide the same rate for all policies. The differences in renewal crediting rates between the two crediting philosophies can be substantial in early plan years, but tend to diminish over time.

Q : Is Bank Owned Life Insurance (BOLI) liquid?

A: BOLI can be surrendered at any time for its cash surrender value. However, doing so may cause adverse tax consequences to the bank. Therefore, to receive the full economic benefits of BOLI, it should be considered a long-term asset.

Q: What are the tax consequences of surrendering Bank Owned Life Insurance (BOLI)?

A: Any gain above the premium that the bank paid would be taxed at the normal rate. In addition, most BOLI policies are classified as Modified Endowment Contracts. These types of policies allow for the most efficient cash surrender value growth possible, but any gain is subject to an additional 10% penalty tax if the policies' cash-values are accessed. However, even with this penalty tax, the net BOLI returns may compare favorably to other financing alternatives over the same time period.

Q: Bank Owned Life Insurance (BOLI) is a long-term asset. How can I manage credit risk?

A: The bank should do a thorough review of the credit worthiness of any potential carrier as part of its due diligence. The Executive Benefits Network can provide you with updated credit information over the life of your BOLI coverage.

Q: What happens if the tax treatment of Bank Owned Life Insurance (BOLI) changes?

A: BOLI's current tax benefits have been unsuccessfully challenged over the years. There are strong bank regulatory guidelines for proper use of BOLI. If the tax treatment is changed, existing plans may be grandfathered. However, if existing policies are not grandfathered, they may be surrendered for their cash surrender values.

Q: How is Bank Owned Life Insurance (BOLI) regulated?

A: The regulations governing Bank Owned Life Insurance (BOLI) depend on the structure of the financial institution:

National Banks: The OCC acts as the primary authority for BOLI usage for national banks. It has updated its guidelines for BOLI usage periodically in recent years. Its most recent declaration is OCC Bulletin 2004-56. This document outlines the ways in which BOLI can be used, as well as the risks that must be addressed prior to plan inception and over the life of the plan.

State Banks: Part 362 of the FDIC's regulations provides the authority for state-chartered banks' use of BOLI. These guidelines largely defer to the parameters outlined in OCC Bulletin 2004-56, although exceptions may be permitted. In addition, state banks must make sure that any BOLI transactions fall within specific guidelines that may be issued by their state banking department.

Thrifts: The most recent pronouncement regarding BOLI usage issued by the OTS is RB 32-26. This document is an update to the prior guidelines, OTS-250. The most recent guidelines largely follow the parameters of OCC Bulletin 2004-56, although some differences do exist. Regardless of a given institution's primary regulator, The Executive Benefits Network can assist you in designing and administering a BOLI program that is in full compliance with all relevant authorities.

Q: Beyond banking regulations, are there limits on how much Bank Owned Life Insurance (BOLI) a bank can purchase?

A: Regardless of an institution's charter, any BOLI program must comply with state insurable interest laws. The Executive Benefits Network can advise you in determining appropriate amounts of coverage based on state law and the composition of a potential insured group.

Q: What other limitations exist to the purchase of Bank Owned Life Insurance (BOLI)?

A: The OCC has been the lead regulator in this area. There are two basic tests: one based on benefits and one based on capital. The OCC has indicated that the gains from BOLI cannot exceed the costs they are intended to offset. The Executive Benefits Network can help you in determining conservative parameters for the purchase of BOLI. In addition, the OCC says that as a general rule, a bank should not invest more than 15% of its Tier I capital with any one company and no more than 25% of its Tier I capital plus 25% of the allowance for loan and lease losses in BOLI as a whole. The OCC views these as guidelines, while the OTS regards them as stricter limitations.

Q: What risks do banking regulators say need to be evaluated when buying Bank Owned Life Insurance (BOLI)?

A: The OCC requires that a bank evaluate six specific risks in its pre-purchase analysis: transaction risk, credit risk, interest rate risk, liquidity risk, compliance risk, and price risk. While the bank is ultimately responsible for its due diligence process, we can assist you in evaluating and documenting the analysis of each of these risks.

Q: Are there additional risks that need to be evaluated?

A: Some areas that could potentially increase the tax risk of BOLI and invite IRS scrutiny include: Borrowing: A bank cannot directly borrow to fund BOLI or it will lose the interest deductions on the funds that were borrowed to do so. A bank should make clear in its documentation that the source of BOLI funding is not direct borrowings.

Business Objective: A bank must have a valid business purpose for its purchase of BOLI. The Executive Benefits Network can assist you in documenting the purpose of your purchase, which is typically to offset a variety of benefit expenses.

Investor Control: This issue is primarily related to separate account plans. A bank may not exercise undue control of the product's underlying investments. The Executive Benefits Network can assist in designing a BOLI purchase that complies with this guideline, and negotiate documentation from the insurance company that the investment control is in compliance with the Code in this area.

Transfer of Risk: In some plans with large groups of participants, a technique known as experience rating is used to relate mortality costs to a specific case, rather than a broad group. Depending on the particular structure, the IRS could argue that the BOLI policies are not life insurance since no risk has actually been transferred to the insurance company. The Executive Benefits Network does not advocate using this technique in any potential BOLI purchase.

Q: How do I account for Bank Owned Life Insurance (BOLI)?

A: BOLI is governed by FASB Technical Bulletin 85-4. This bulletin states that BOLI should be recorded on the balance sheet as an "other asset" and that both the cash surrender value growth and ultimate net insurance proceeds should be recorded as "other income."

THE LIFE INSURANCE GAME

A reading of Ronald Kessler's book titled *The Life Insurance Game: How the Industry Has Amassed Over $600 Billion at the Expense of the American Public* made me become interested in the American insurance industry. Why? Location, location, location! Do you remember Willie Sutton? Willie Sutton is famously known for answering a reporter, Mitch Ohnstad, who asked why he robbed banks. Willie Sutton replied, "because that is where the money is." William "Willie" Sutton, June 30, 1901 - November 2, 1980, was a prolific U.S. bank robber. During his forty year criminal career, he stole an estimated $2 million, and eventually he spent more than half of his adult life in prison. For his talent at executing robberies in disguises, he gained two nicknames, "Willie the Actor" and "Slick Willie." When not disguised, Sutton was an immaculate dresser.

By contrast, life insurance is a legal business which is regulated by all the states of the USA. So why should you not become involved in the insurance business? Before I explain how you can become involved in the insurance business, I would like to complete my discussion on Ronald Kessler's book. Essentially, the book uses the gaming metaphor to shed light on how the key persons in the insurance industry have co-opted the government and bamboozled the 99% of the American public to enrich themselves. According to Kessler, life insurance is a game like football, basketball, gymnastics, racing, and soccer. To every game, there are owners, teams, players, and referees. Despite the avowed political correctness of good sportsmanship, every player wants his or her team to win; every player knows that there can be only a winner and a loser in every game, and the winner takes it all. After a race, you can stand and applaud for the winner, but to be the one for whom people are clapping is the real achievement.

My first objective is to assist you in understanding how to shop for an insurance policy for yourself, friends, and family members. You will learn all the Ws of insurance: why, when, what, when, and who. Who should buy life insurance? Why should you know how to buy insurance? When should you buy insurance? What type of insurance should you buy? When should you buy insurance? How should you buy insurance?

By answering all these questions, you will be ready to secure an insurance policy for yourself and your family. Now in shopping for insurance, you will be in a position to compare rates and products from all companies in the marketplace. Do you know that two out of every three Americans are covered by a life insurance policy, but 95% of these same policy owners do not know the contents of their insurance contracts? As a result of Ronald Kessler's investigative research, you will have a gestalt window where you can espy the whole insurance industry. The book consists of an introduction and ten chapters: the game, the deck, the pitch, the agents, the poor, the new policies, the computers, the investigators, the investments, the regulators, and winning the game. Kessler's argument is the urgency for you to lay threadbare the intricacies of insurance products and services by becoming an intelligent consumer or a smart shopper.

BUILDING YOUR FINANCIAL FUTURE TODAY......IS ALL ABOUT THE RIGHT FOUNDATION!

Once again, I would like to acknowledge that I am an insurance producer, and I love to work for the benefit of my clients. I am a wonderful agent, but I am not like the average guy peddling insurance services. I am different from producers who worship commissions to the detriment of their customers' interests. One of the ways I work for the benefit of my clients is by providing them with good education on insurance products and services. I advise my clients to use insurance as a foundation of building wealth. Unlike other agents, my focus is on educational consulting, not the rush to sell a new policy quickly. I welcome and engage my new customer on navigating the rough financial seas; I take them on a journey to the paradise of financial freedom.

By interviewing a new client, I gather insights into their common worries, hopes, dreams, concerns, and fears. I reiterate the idea that becoming financially successful requires positioning yourself for financial success. Success is not an accident; it does not just happen; you have to plan it. The question my clients ask me time and time again is the following: "When it comes to determining an effective financial strategy to become wealthy, where do I start with insurance products, services, and solutions?" I begin the meeting or interview by presenting the client with a map of possible financial destinations:

1. Protection
2. Financial comfort
3. Guaranteed long-term financial security
4. Passing of assets on to our heirs

Most people are seeking a place of refuge among the ones I have enumerated above. Protection means examining your assets, obligations, and goals; you determine your current risk exposure; you use the right tools (life insurance, disability insurance, retirement, and long-term care protection) to transfer the risk of loss to an insurer. In regard to protection, I discuss death, disability, long-term illness, and the loss of your family's lifestyle.

Next, I present tools of income protection: life insurance, disability insurance, long-term care protection insurance, and riders. I tell the client that riders, which are optional, may be available at an additional cost, and may not be available in all states. Payment of accelerated benefits will reduce the cash-value and the death benefit otherwise payable under the policy. Receipt of accelerated benefits may be a taxable event, and it may affect your eligibility for public assistance programs.

The answer to the problem of maintaining a secure and comfortable lifestyle is a plan of asset accumulation. Ask yourself some soul-searching questions. For instance, below are some of the questions I ask my clients directly:

1. How much money do you have to invest?
2. What is your time horizon?
3. What is your tolerance for risk?

The initial reaction of most people is usually that they do not have any money to invest because they are overwhelmed by a mountain of debts. My customary reply to them is the following:

"The money is there for you to make in insurance, but you just are not looking in the right places."

HERE ARE THREE WAYS FOR YOU TO START SAVING MONEY TO BUILD WEALTH WITH INSURANCE TOOLS:

1. Examine your spending
2. Reduce your debt
3. Apply the 10% saving solution

I am going to list the tools that can help you save more money through insurance:

1. Fixed Annuities
2. Equity Indexed Annuities
3. Variable Annuities
4. Mutual Funds
5. Stock and Bonds
6. Cash-value Life Insurance

What about long-term financial security? I will show you how to plan for retirement. I am presenting retirement income sources below:

1. Pensions
2. Social Security
3. Personal Savings Vehicles
4. Fixed and Variable Annuities
5. Permanent Life Insurance

What about distribution planning strategies?

1. Take advantage of tax-deferral
2. Leverage the combination of annuities
3. Take advantage of fixed immediate annuities

Retirement Planning Summary

--Envision your retirement
--Understand the role of personal savings
--Stress the importance of distribution planning

ESTATE PLANNING STRATEGIES

This is the wealth destination phase of passing assets to family. Of course, you should dispel the myth that estate planning strategies are necessary just for the very wealthy only, not for everyone. Nolo.com has published a good book on the subject that may be good for beginners: *Estate Planning Basics*. Use the book to find out the fundamentals of estate planning, including wills, living trusts, estate taxes and more. In addition to Nolo.com, my web site, millionaireiuniversity.com features many articles on estate planning. Read them now.

Primary Reasons Why Estate Planning Strategies are Important:

1. Allow you to decide who receives your assets
2. Allow you to decide how assets will be distributed
3. Allow you to decide who will manage assets in your absence
4. Allow you to ensure tax-efficiency
5. Allow you to select a guardian for your children
6. Allow you to orchestrate a smooth business succession

Who Needs to Create an Estate Planning Strategy?

1. Anyone with assets exceeding federal tax exemption
2. Anyone who owns a business
3. Anyone who has minor children
4. Anyone with dependents who are handicapped, elderly, or have special needs
5. Anyone who wants to leave a charitable donation

Your Estate Taxes: Where Will The Money Come From?

1. Savings and investments
2. Sale of assets
3. Loans
4. Life insurance

Tools For Preserving & Transferring Your Estate

1. Wills
2. Trusts
3. Charitable gifts
4. Life insurance

Financial Tool Applications: Wills

Specify who receives your assets and the distribution method:

1. Designate a legal guardian
2. Name an executor
3. Set up trusts

Financial Tool Applications : Trusts

1. Avoid probate
2. Pass assets to surviving spouse   (Qualified Terminal Interest Property)
3. Keep insurance proceeds out of your estate
4. Provide for heirs and make a charitable gift (Charitable Remainder Trust)

The use of trusts involves complex tax rules and regulations. Consider enlisting the counsel of an estate planning professional and your legal and tax advisors prior to implementing such sophisticated strategies. The cost and availability of life insurance will depend on factors such as age, health, and the type and amount of insurance purchased.

Financial Tool Applications: Charitable Gifting

Reduce estate tax liability
Shelter assets from creditors
Increase privacy
Provide income to a beneficiary
Reward a favorite charity

Financial Tool Applications: Life Insurance
Estate Taxes Owed: $500,000

Cost of Not Planning for Estate Taxes:
Loss to Heirs: $500,000
Amount Preserved for Heirs: $0

Using Life Insurance as an Estate Preservation Tool:
Death Benefit: $500,000
Premiums Paid

($16,290 x 10 years):   ($162,900)
Amount Preserved for Heirs: $337,100

Premium based on NL Life Builder Whole Life Insurance (form series 8310/8311, 8310(0306)/8311(0306)), as of 12/1/09 for a male, age 40, preferred nonsmoker, underwritten by National Life Insurance Company, Montpelier, VT. Rates are subject to change without notice. Guarantees are dependent upon the claims-paying ability of the issuing company.

INSURANCE SUMMARY

Creating a financial strategy allows you to accomplish the following goals:
1. Protect yourself, your loved ones, and your assets
2. Accumulate assets for the future
3. Ensure assets will last a lifetime
4. Pass assets to heirs in a tax-efficient manner

I thank you for accompanying me on this financial journey. God bless you! Now that I have taken you to the mountain top and your eyes have seen the power and the glory of the promise land of insurance, you are ready to build wealth with insurance. But before much ado about nothing, I would like to dwell on a few facts and think points of wealth building with insurance.

Disability

.45% of 40 year olds will experience a disability during their working years that will last 90 days or more.
80% of today's 20 year olds will experience a disability that will last 90 days or more before age 65.3

STATISTICAL THREATS TO YOUR FINANCIAL FUTURE: ILLNESS

People with different chronic conditions face common problems, including high medical costs that are often not covered by insurance, leading to enormous bills that can mean bankruptcy for some families. By the year 2020, the number of people living with chronic conditions is expected to rise to 157 million.

ACCELERATED LIVING BENEFITS LIFE INSURANCE

At age 65, the odds are nearly 1 in 2 that you will require nursing home services for at least 2.5 years
4% of Americans are underinsured.
Only 47% of U.S. Households own any individual life insurance.
More than 1 in 4 men and 1 in 3 women have no life insurance coverage at all.
Life insurance surpasses all other sources of financial assets or income that Americans expect to use to help pay bills and to maintain their lifestyle if a primary wage earner dies. Yet the average household owns just enough life insurance to replace income for only 2.8 years.

There is more to personal finance than the drudgery of debts and budgets.

RETIREMENT

46% (almost half) of Americans have saved less than $50,000 for retirement
15% say they have saved nothing towards retirement.

YOUR CHALLENGES

You have a significant problem. You have the need to protect your family's income in case of death, disability, chronic, or critical illness.

PRINCE OJONG'S SOLUTIONS

Prince Ojong's solutions, listed below, provide you and your family access to tax-advantaged living benefits and asset protection plans:

Reduce Your Liabilities and Get Out of Debt Sooner.

Review Your Current Financial Situation and Execute Cost-Saving Allocations.

Understand How Money Works.

Deal with Constant Changes in Job, Career, or Business.

Create an Independent Plan and Work Towards Your Financial Goals.

Live a Long Life With Adequate Income.

Develop an Income Stream You Cannot Outlive with Regular Reviews.

Handle Taxes and Inflation.

Employ a Tax-Free Plan that Outpaces Inflation.

SOCIAL SECURITY STUDY

The social security study tracked 100 people from age 25-65yrs:

•56 Retired and Relied on Family, Friends, and the Government
•11 Are Still Working
•25 Were Dead
•92 Dead or Dead Broke
•8 Retired with $30k/year.

HERE IS THE ROAD TO YOUR FINANCIAL FUTURE!

THE NEED

What do you estimate your average annual income is: (a)
How many years have you been working? (b)
Your total lifetime earnings are (Multiply a times b) (c)

Now comes the BIG question: How much of this have you actually saved? If you continue to save at this pace until retirement, how much will you have saved? One of the most effective strategies of turning dreams and goals into financial success is to make small changes in your life!

Why Should You Plan for the Future NOW?

A "convenient" time to save never comes.
Do not let time run out on you.

Can you cut down on the following?

Sodas
Cigarettes
Lattes
Cable
TELEVISION Games
Bottled Water
Sweets
New Gadgets
Shopping
Driving a BIG Car
Eating Out
Partying

Let us do some simple arithmetic or mathematics. What happens if you can make small changes in your spending habits and start saving $1.00 or $10.00 per day? In a month, you should have $300.00 or $3,000 for your investment program. Let us work with the conservative estimate of saving $1.00 per day:

$300.00 per month invested at a return on investment (ROI) of 8% in 30 years = $447,107
$600.00 per month invested at a return on investment (ROI) of 8% in 30 years = $894,214

Can you see that a small but consistent drip has a huge impact? The road to your financial future can be laced with many low-risk or risk-free vehicles: savings accounts, short-term emergency funds, checking accounts, certificate of deposits, money-market accounts, 401(K), 403B, 457, 529, IRA, mutual funds, long-term wealth building tools, tax-deferred annuity, private equity banking, municipal bonds, treasury bills, ROTH IRA, and more.

There is more to personal finance than the drudgery of debts and budgets.

THE RULE OF 72

The road to your financial future is paved with the rate of return on investment based on the RULE of 72. What is the projected return on your investment? A hypothetical example representing the performance of the specific investment based on the Rule of 72 requires you to divide the number 72 by the annual interest rate to estimate the number of years it takes for your money to double; the Rule of 72' is a simplified way to determine how long an investment will take to double, given a fixed annual rate of interest. By dividing 72 by the annual rate of return, investors can get a rough estimate of how many years it will take for the initial investment to double itself.

For example, the rule of 72 states that \$1 invested at 10% would take 7.2 years $((72/10) = 7.2)$ to turn into \$2. In reality, a 10% investment will take 7.3 years to double $((1.10{^\wedge}7.3 = 2))$. When dealing with low rates of return, the Rule of 72 is fairly accurate. This calculation compares the numbers given by the rule of 72 and the actual number of years it takes an investment to double. WOW! This is the money game! Are you winning ? If you are losing it means that you cannot have a solid plan without the right financial foundation.

CALCULATING YOUR INSURANCE NEEDS

How do you estimate the amount of insurance you need? Generally, the insurance industry uses three approaches to calculate the precise amount of insurance you need: family needs approach, human life approach, and income objective approach.

FAMILY NEEDS APPROACH

Family-needs approach is a method of calculating how much life insurance is required by an individual or family to cover their needs. These needs include expenses such as funeral expenses, legal fees, estate and gift taxes, business buyout costs, probate fees, medical deductibles, emergency funds, mortgage expenses, rent, debt and loans, college, child care, private schooling and maintenance costs. The family-needs approach contrasts with the human-life approach. The family-needs approach is really a function of two variables:

1. How much will be needed at death to meet obligations.
2. How much future income is needed to sustain the household.

When calculating your expenses, it is best to overestimate your needs a little. Yes! You will be buying and paying for a little more insurance than you need, but if you underestimate, you will not realize your mistake until it is too late.

THE HUMAN-LIFE APPROACH

The human-life approach is a method of calculating the amount of life insurance a family will need based on the financial loss the family would incur if the insured person were to pass away today.

It is usually calculated by taking into account a number of factors including but not limited to the insured individual's age, gender, planned retirement age, occupation, annual wage, employment benefits, as well as the personal and financial information of the spouse and/or dependent children. Since the value of a human life has economic value only in its relation to other lives such as a spouse or dependent children, this method is typically only used for families with working family members. The human-life approach contrasts with the family-needs approach. Remember, when using the human-life approach, you will want to replace all of the income that is lost when an employed spouse dies. To be more precise, you will want to include only the after-tax pay, and make adjustments for expenses, such as a second car, incurred while earning that income. Also, do not forget to add the value of health insurance or other employee benefits to the income number.

INCOME OBJECTIVE APPROACH

The income-objective approach recognizes that to analyze the insurance needs of either family-needs approach or human-life approach you must also take into account the consideration of the income objective of the proposed insured. Usually, you use two methods of the income objective approach to determine the amount of insurance coverage needed to fill the human life value or needs analysis requirements: capital liquidation and capital conservation or retention.

THE DIME METHOD

The DIME method is only a formula that is used by agents to help them determine a client's insurable need. It is not a one-size-fits-all scenario. Below is a hypothetical example of DIME, but it does not represent the needs of any one person:

D=Debts=how much you own over what you owe
I=Income=your yearly wages times 10
M=Mortgage=what you still owe on your home
E=Education=the cost of financing your children's education

Your Valuables=It is YOU = Money Engine!
Your Valuables=It is Your Ability to Generate Income!

Please, let me, Prince Ojong, be your tour guide on the road to your financial future, without risks, with peace of mind. Knowing what you know now and the importance and value you place on you and your family's financial future, it is certain that you will like to choose the appropriate options now to protect you and your family for a lifetime.

Please, do not wait any longer! NOW IS THE TIME! Be responsible to those you love. Establish a solid plan for them: life insurance, wills, power of attorney, estate planning, and more. Life insurance protects your financial future. It provides the resources your family or business may need to pay immediate and continuing expenses when you die.

There is more to personal finance than the drudgery of debts and budgets.

WHAT YOU SHOULD KNOW BEFORE BUYING LIFE INSURANCE

There are different types of life insurance, and choosing a policy is an important decision. You should begin by evaluating the ongoing and future financial needs of those who depend on you. Set your goals, and write your plan of personal finance. Then become familiar with the various policies available in the marketplace and how they work. Most agents are ignorant about the high-finance or investment grade of insurance, so you should not trust them entirely. Please, do your homework; in fact, this is why I am arming you with an arsenal of lethal weapons. You will be in a better position to make a selection best suited to your financial needs and those of your family. I, Prince Ojong, a licensed insurance producer, have prepared this guide to help you understand the types of life insurance available and the questions to ask when you are buying life insurance.

GETTING STARTED

As you prepare to buy a life insurance policy, evaluate your ongoing and future financial needs and review the products. To begin, ask yourself some basic questions: Why do I need to buy life insurance? What needs can life insurance fill in my life? If someone depends on you financially, like a spouse or young children, the likelihood is that you need life insurance. Life insurance provides cash to your family after you die. The money your beneficiary receives, the death benefit, can be an important financial resource.

It can help cover daily living expenses, pay the mortgage and other outstanding loans; it can fund tuition and ensure that your family is not burdened with debt. Having a life insurance policy could mean your spouse or children would not have to sell assets to pay bills or taxes. Another advantage is that beneficiaries will not have to pay federal income taxes on the money they receive.

HOW MUCH LIFE INSURANCE DO I NEED?

Generally, the insurance industry uses three approaches to calculate the precise amount of insurance you need: family needs approach, human life approach, and income objective approach. Everyone's needs are different. A good life insurance agent or financial advisor, like me, can help you determine what level of protection is right for you and your family based on your financial responsibilities and sources of income. Additionally, there are many online calculators that can help you; however, sitting down with an insurance professional, like me, to review your financial needs can give you a more personalized view of your needs.

In general, deciding how much life insurance you need means deducting the total income that would be lost upon your death from the total sum of your family's ongoing financial needs. Please, consider the following ongoing expenses: day care, tuition, mortgage, or retirement, and immediate expenses such as medical bills, burial costs, and estate taxes. Your family also may need money to pay for a move or the costs of looking for a job.

While there is no substitute for evaluating needs based on your own financial information, some experts suggest that if you own a life insurance policy it should pay a benefit equal to seven to 10 times your annual income. Your need could be higher or lower depending on your situation.

TYPES OF LIFE INSURANCE

What are the different types of insurance? Fundamentally, life insurance is like a tale of two cities: rich city and poor city. There are two basic types of life insurance: permanent and term. Permanent insurance is a more sophisticated financial instrument favored by America's rich and famous folks that you can use for financial planning and it pays your beneficiary whenever you die; in contrast, term insurance is an insurance contract that pays your beneficiary if you die during a specific period of time.

PERMANENT INSURANCE

What is permanent insurance? Permanent insurance is a cash-value product that provides you life-long protection as long as premiums are paid. It may build up cash-value over time and the cash-value grows tax deferred. With all permanent policies, the cash-value is different from the death benefit or face amount.

Cash-value is the amount available if you surrender or cancel your policy before your death. The face amount is the money that will be paid to your beneficiary if you die. Your beneficiary does not receive the cash-value of your policy. If you are paying only the target premium, the cash-value of your policy will take too much time to grow. There is a secret, however, to accelerate the building of your cash-value; your insurance agent needs to structure your policy to take advantage of the MEC limit; that is the preferred strategy of millionaires, billionaires, and other rich and famous folks who do not like waiting endlessly and marking time for their money to compound. MEC is an acronym for modified endowment contract.

As for MEC limit, it is important for you to understand that the Internal Revenue Service limits the amount of premium that you can be put into an insurance contract and keep the distributions taxed-advantaged. Those are the rules of Modified Endowment Contract (MEC), so, as a smart investor, your intelligent goal is to contribute the maximum insurance premium allowed below that MEC limit is attained. In life insurance parlance, the guideline level premium determines the policy face amount. The death benefit is structured as increasing during the accumulation phase and level during the distribution phase. In order for you to enjoy a tax-advantaged policy, your insurance agent has to design your policy to satisfy the income tax and revenue guidelines of the US Treasury Department; otherwise, the Internal Revenue Service will consider your insurance policy as an investment that is taxable as income; in other words, you are required to pay taxes. By giving agents a free desk-top quote calculator software, insurance carriers are not only facilitating the work of their agents, but they are also delivering their agents from the temptation of violating MEC rules. The game is like the use of bi-weekly mortgage in real estate for rapid equity acceleration; you build equity in your home faster by prepaying your mortgage to the extent that you accumulate an extra monthly payment at the end of the year.

There is more to personal finance than the drudgery of debts and budgets.

The old-fashioned approach in the industry is for your insurance agent to watch helplessly as you build cash-value slowly, that is, after you have held the policy for several years. I educate my clients to comprehend their options; those who have the discipline and money choose the path of cash-value acceleration and multiply their wealth; others decide to stay put.

CASH-VALUE OPTIONS

Cash-value insurance can offer you several options: You can borrow from the insurer using your cash-value as collateral. You can get the loan even if you do not have a good credit history. If you do not repay the loan, including interest, it will reduce the amount paid to your beneficiaries after your death. You can use the cash-value to pay your premiums or to buy more coverage. You can exchange the policy by using the cash-value for an annuity that will provide income for life or a specified period. You can cancel, surrender, the policy and receive the cash-value in a lump sum. You would pay taxes on the value that exceeds what you have paid in premiums.

BASIC TYPES OF CASH-VALUE INSURANCE

Generally, there are three variations of cash-value or permanent insurance: whole life, universal life, and variable life.

WHOLE LIFE

Whole life, or ordinary life, is the most traditional type of cash-value insurance. Generally, premiums and death benefits stay the same over the life of the policy. The policy's cash-value grows at a fixed rate.

UNIVERSAL LIFE

Universal life gives you flexibility in setting premium payments and the death benefit. Changes must be made within certain guidelines set by the policy; to increase a death benefit, the insurer usually requires evidence of continued good health. A universal life policy, especially the equity indexed variety, can have an investment or variable component. Many carriers offer policies that mimic the S&P 500, a Wall Street index charting the performance of a collection of five hundred of the best or strongest companies in America. Personally, I have a special bias for or toward universal life insurance. I appreciate the manner in which millionaires and billionaires exploit the flexibility of universal life insurance; if the little guy or girl can afford it, I do not hesitate to recommend universal life insurance.

VARIABLE LIFE

The first piece of information I give my clients and customers about a variable life policy is the fact that it exposes them to stock market fluctuations and risks. If I notice that they have the appetite for taking risks, then, I educate them that with a variable life policy they can choose among a variety of investment instruments offering different risks and rewards: stocks, bonds, combination accounts, or options that guarantee principal and interest.

Death benefits and cash-value will vary depending on the performance of the investments they select. By law, they will be given a prospectus for variable life insurance. This prospectus will include financial statements and outline investment objectives, operating expenses, and risks. The cash-value of a variable life policy is not guaranteed. If the market does not perform well, the cash-value and death benefit may decrease, although some policies guarantee that the death benefit will not fall below a certain level.

TERM INSURANCE

What is term insurance? Term insurance provides protection for a defined period of time—from one to 10, 20, or even 30 years—and pays benefits only if you die during that period. As such, term insurance is, actually, death insurance. Term insurance is often used to cover financial obligations that will disappear over time, such as tuition or mortgage payments.

Premiums for term insurance either can be fixed for the length of the term or can increase at a point specified in the policy. They also can be less expensive than a cash-value policy. Term policies can include a return of premium benefit that will refund all or some of the premiums paid at the end of a term if no death benefit was paid. Term policies with this feature are more expensive than those without it. Some term policies can be renewed at the end of a term. However, premium rates will usually increase upon renewal. Many policies require evidence of insurability to qualify for renewal at the lowest rates. At the end of a term, you also may be able to convert the policy to a cash-value policy. Term policies do not usually build up a cash-value, but policies with a return of premium benefit will have a small cash-value.

WHAT ARE THE ADVANTAGES AND DISADVANTAGES OF EACH TYPE OF INSURANCE?

Advantages of Permanent Cash-value Insurance:

--Life-long protection as long as the premiums are paid.
--Premium costs can be fixed or flexible to meet individual financial needs.
--A policy accumulates a cash-value, which can be borrowed against, surrendered for cash, or converted to an annuity. The cash-value also can be used to pay premiums or to buy more coverage.

Disadvantages:

Cash-value insurance is designed to be kept for the long term. Cancelling a cash-value policy after only a few years can be expensive. For the short term, term insurance may prove a better value.

Advantages of Term Insurance:

--A policy can cover financial obligations that will disappear over time, such as a mortgage or college expenses. When you are young, premiums are generally lower than those for cash-value insurance.

Disadvantages of Term Insurance:

--Provides protection for a specific period of time, not for life. Premiums increase as you grow older and your health status changes. Policies do not usually build up a cash-value.

HOW TO PURCHASE/ CHOOSE A COMPANY OR AGENT

You can buy life insurance at an insurance agency, brokerage firm, bank, or directly from a life insurance company on the Internet, over the phone, or by mail. Most companies have web sites that describe their products and services and some will direct you to a local agent. How do you choose a company? I can assist you by researching and referring the best company in your state, or you can contact your state insurance department directly for a list of companies licensed in your state, then, ask friends and relatives for recommendations based on their own experiences. Please, also feel free to make use of the contact information of members of the Millionaire's Club for references of companies. I may be in a position to help you, too. Call my office at (301) 593-4897.You can talk to an insurance agent or broker like me.

Another option is for you to conduct an Internet search. Except for term insurance, I do not encourage you to buy a complicated product like cash-value insurance on the phone or online. Research companies at a public library, but contact me for further assistance. Generally speaking, many life insurers are in excellent financial health. They are required by law to maintain reserves to guarantee that they can meet obligations to their policyholders. However, you should still verify a company's financial strength. You can check any company's financial condition by looking at its rating. The best known rating agencies include A.M. Best Company, Fitch Ratings, Moody's Investor Services, Standard and Poor's Insurance Rating Service, and Weiss Ratings; assess the financial strength of companies. Rating information is available online or in publications usually found in the business section of your public library.

HOW DO YOU CHOOSE AN AGENT?

Most customers choose me because of knowledge, experience, and reputation, but collect the names of several agents through recommendations from friends, family, and other sources. Find out if an agent is licensed in your state by checking with your state's insurance department. Agents who sell variable products also must be registered with the Financial Industry Regulatory Authority (FINRA), and have an additional state license to sell variable contracts. Ask what company or companies the agent represents and check his or her professional accreditations. Agents often belong to professional associations that offer continuing education and grant professional credentials. The National Association of Insurance and Financial Advisors offers local educational seminars for agents. The Society of Financial Service Professionals and the Financial Planning Association offer similar training for financial planners. Agents may earn such professional designations as Chartered Life Underwriter (CLU) and Life Underwriter Training Council Fellow (LUTCF). Agents who also are financial planners may carry such credentials as Chartered Financial Consultant (ChFC), Certified Financial Planner (CFP), or Personal Financial Specialist (CPA–PFS).

WORKING WITH AN AGENT

What should an agent do for you? The agent should be able and willing to explain the different kinds of policies and other insurance-related matters. You should feel satisfied that the agent is listening to you and looking for ways to find the right type of insurance at an affordable price. After a purchase, your agent also should review your life insurance needs from time to time as your circumstances change, as well as help in the claims process. If you are not comfortable with the agent, or you are not convinced he or she is providing the service you want, interview another agent.

What should you expect during your meeting with an agent? An agent will begin by discussing your financial needs. You should have basic personal financial information available—along with a general idea of your goals—before you meet or talk with an agent. He or she will ask questions about your family income, other financial resources you might have, and any debts. With the information you provide, the agent will be better able to assess your needs.

QUESTIONS YOU SHOULD ASK BEFORE BUYING LIFE INSURANCE

If you are considering a term policy, ask: How long can I keep this policy? If I want to renew it for a specific number of years, or until a certain age, what are the renewal terms? Will my premiums increase? If so, will increases start annually or after five or 10 years? Can I convert to a cash-value policy? Will I need a medical exam if and when I convert? If it has a return of premium benefit, ask: What would the policy cost without this benefit? Will all of the premiums be refunded? Is a policy illustration a legal document, like a contract? No! A policy illustration is not part of the life insurance policy, and it is not a legal document. Legal obligations are spelled out in the policy contract. A policy illustration, however, can help you understand how a policy works.

What is in a policy illustration? A policy illustration shows financial projections for each year you own the policy—including, but not limited to, premium amounts owed, cash-values, and death benefits. For a term policy, the projections extend to the end of the term. With a cash-value policy, projections extend past your 100th birthday. Your actual costs and benefits could be higher or lower than those in the illustration because they depend on the future financial results of the insurance company. However, when figures are guaranteed, the insurance company will honor them regardless of its financial success. Ask your agent which figures are guaranteed and which are not. A policy illustration can be complicated. Your agent or financial advisor can explain information you do not understand.

What types of questions will I be asked? In addition to questions about finances, be prepared to answer questions about your age, medical condition, family medical history, personal habits, occupation, and recreational activities. Always answer questions truthfully; a company will use this information to evaluate your risk and set a premium for your coverage. For instance, you will pay a lower premium if you do not smoke; on the other hand, if you have a chronic illness, you can expect to pay a higher premium.

There is more to personal finance than the drudgery of debts and budgets.

When it is time to submit a claim, accurate and truthful answers will enable your beneficiary to receive prompt and full payment. When you apply for life insurance, you may be asked to take a medical exam. In many instances, a licensed health care professional hired and paid for by the life insurance company will make a personal visit to your home to conduct the exam.

EXAMINING A POLICY

How do I know if a life insurance policy is right for me? Read the policy carefully to make sure it meets your personal goals. Because your policy is a legal document, it is important that you understand exactly what it provides. Ask for a point-by-point explanation for anything that is unclear and make sure the agent explains items you do not understand. If your agent recommends a cash-value policy, ask: Is the premium within my budget? Can I commit to these premiums for a long term? Cash-value insurance provides protection for your entire life. Cancelling a cash-value policy after only a few years can be a costly way to get short-term insurance protection. If you do not plan to keep the policy for the long-term, please, consider another kind of coverage such as term insurance.

What should I look for in a policy illustration? Study the policy illustration to answer the following questions: Is my classification (i.e., smoker/nonsmoker, male/female) correct? When are premiums due—monthly, annually, or according to some other schedule? What amounts are guaranteed and which are not? Does the policy have a guaranteed death benefit or could the death benefit change depending on interest rates or other factors? Does the policy offer dividends or interest credits that could increase my cash-value and death benefit or reduce my premium? Will my premiums always be the same? Could premiums increase if future interest rates or investment returns are lower than the illustration assumes? If the illustration shows that I will not have to make premium payments after a certain period of time, is there any chance I would have to start making payments again at any time in the future?

FREQUENTLY ASKED QUESTIONS

What happens if I miss a payment? If you miss a premium payment, you usually have a 30-or 31-day grace period in which to make your payment without consequences. If you die within the grace period, your beneficiary will receive the death benefit minus the overdue premium. However, the policy will lapse (terminate) if you do not make your payment by the end of the grace period. If you own a cash-value policy, your company, with your authorization, can draw from your policy's cash-value to pay the premium. This method of keeping your policy active can work only as long as your cash-value lasts.

Do I have any recourse if my policy lapses? Some life insurance contracts let you reinstate a lapsed policy within a certain time frame. However, you must prove insurability, pay all overdue premiums, plus interest, and pay off any outstanding policy loans. In addition to the death benefit, are there other features I should be aware of when considering a life insurance policy?

Many policies offer purchase options or riders. Some riders let you buy more insurance without taking a medical exam; others waive premiums if you become disabled. Some policies offer an accidental death benefit that pays an additional amount if death occurs as a result of an accident. Some companies offer accelerated benefits, also known as living benefits. An accelerated benefits rider lets you, under some conditions, receive the death benefits of your life insurance policy before you die. Such conditions may include terminal or catastrophic illness, confinement to a nursing home, or need of other long-term care services. You also may combine a full long-term care insurance policy with a life insurance policy as a rider.

When will my policy take effect? If you decide to buy a policy, find out when the insurance contract becomes effective. That date may be different from the date the policy is issued. How is life insurance taxed? Your beneficiaries will not pay income taxes on death benefits. If you own a cash-value policy, you will not pay income taxes on the cash-value unless you cancel the policy and withdraw the money. Then you will pay taxes on the amount that exceeds what you have paid in premiums.

TIPS AFTER BUYING LIFE INSURANCE

After you have bought an insurance policy, you may have a free-look period, usually 10 days after you receive the policy, when you can change your mind. During that period, read your policy carefully. If you decide not to keep it, the company will cancel the policy and give you an appropriate refund. Information about the free-look period is in your contract. Always check the date the insurance becomes effective. Keep your life insurance policy with your other financial records or legal papers, or anywhere your survivors are likely to look for it. However, do not keep your policy in your safe deposit box. In most states, boxes are sealed temporarily on the death of the owner, delaying a settlement when funds may be needed most. Contact your original company, agent, or financial adviser before canceling your current policy to buy a new one. If your health has declined, you may no longer be insurable at affordable rates. If you replace one cash-value policy with another, the cash-value of the new policy may be relatively small for several years. If you have a complaint about your insurance agent or company, contact the customer service division of your insurance company. If you are still dissatisfied, contact your state insurance department. A state insurance department directory is available on our web site, http://www.millionaireiuniversity.com. Review your policy periodically or when a major event occurs in your life, such as a birth, divorce, remarriage, or retirement, to be sure your coverage is adequate and your beneficiaries are correctly named.

Make sure that you fully understand any policy you are considering and that you are comfortable with the company, agent, and product. Most states require insurers to provide a buyer's guide to explain life insurance terms, benefits, and costs. Ask your agent for a copy of your company's guide and follow the tips below: Ask for outlines of coverage so you can compare the features of several policies. Check with your state insurance department to make sure the company and agent are licensed in your state. Look for a company that is reputable and financially strong. A number of insurance rating services rate the financial strength of companies.

You can get such information from your agent, public or business libraries, or on the Internet. Rating agencies include A.M. Best Company, Fitch Ratings, Moody's Investor Services Inc., Standard & Poor's Insurance Rating Services, and Weiss Ratings. Beware of offers for free or inexpensive life insurance.

SCAMS!!

Investors may approach some seniors to offer them money to buy life insurance and then sell the policy to the investors. The investors expect to profit by receiving the death benefit when the senior dies. Often called stranger-originated life insurance, legislators and regulators are concerned about these transactions because they violate public policies against wagering on human life. Also, there may be hidden pitfalls, such as unexpected taxes, fees, and loss of privacy. Always answer questions on your life insurance application truthfully. Be sure your application has been filled out accurately. Promptly notify your agent or company of errors or missing information. When you buy a policy, make your check payable to the insurance company, not the agent. Be sure to get a receipt. Contact the company or agent if you do not get your policy within 60 days.

COLLEGE PLANNING WITH LIFE INSURANCE

 Life Insurance can be a great tool for saving and paying for college. When you log on to millionaireiuniversity.com or attend my seminars, you will benefit from my presenting materials that should serve as food for thought in helping you explore avenues of using life insurance as a tool for saving and paying for the college education of your children and other family members. As for the college planning agenda, I have designed an in-take form for you. I will do a needs analysis so that you can understand your college needs, determine your family's college Expected Family Contribution, (EFC). I shall also provide you with the keys to understanding financial aid, grants, assistantships, fellowships, and scholarships. As for cash-value life insurance versus 529 plans, I still prefer life insurance.

CHILDREN'S COLLEGE FUNDING & PREPARATORY SURVEY

This survey is intended to identify parents and guardians who desire to establish a comprehensive savings program for the educational expenses of a minor. For more information on college funding visit http://www.princeinsurance1.com or princeojong.com, or you can call my office for advisement:

Office #: (301) 593-4879   (301) 593-4897   Cell. #: 240-330-0839

Do you have children?   { } Yes   { } No

How many?   1   2   3   4   5   6

What age? (circle all ages that apply)   < 1 1   2   3   4 5 6 7 8 9 10

Did you attend a college or university?   { } Yes   { } No

If so, what school?_____

Did you receive a degree?   { } Yes   { } No

If not, why not? (costs, personal challenges, work opportunity)
_____

How did you fund your education? (savings, working, etc.)
_____

What is your occupation?
_____

Do you currently participate in an educational expense savings program? { } Yes { } No

How do you plan to fund your child's future educational expenses?
_____

10. Barring any restraints, what college or university would you like for your child(ren) to attend?
_____

11. If you could fund your child's tuition for 4 years at a major college or university by saving $50-$100 monthly would you be interested?   { } Yes   { } No

Fax this Form to: 240-241-5137

Attention: Prince Ojong, Collegiate Funding Division

Parent/Guardian Name: _____

Phone: (c) _____ (h) _____

Best Time to Call: _____

Address: _____
             Street   City   State   Zip code

Email: _____

There is more to personal finance than the drudgery of debts and budgets.

INSURANCE AS PROTECTION OF WEALTH

I will like to supplement the discussion of life insurance by stressing the use of other forms of insurance for the protection of your wealth. After working hard to create personal wealth, you need to protect it. People acquire insurance to protect themselves from major financial loss. Insurance is simply a promise of reimbursement for a loss in return for a premium paid. When shopping for insurance products, consumers should match their needs with what the product offers and seek out the best deal. A solid credit history is also important because insurers use credit information to price homeowners insurance policies. You can buy insurance to cover all kinds of risks, but basic needs can be met with property, health, and life insurance.

TIPS FOR PROTECTING YOUR WEALTH

There are many types of property, health, and life insurance, so do your research and seek good advice:

• Take advantage of group insurance through your employer or other associations you may have.
• Study the needs of your family and decide how much you can afford to pay.
• Shop around and get at least two quotes.
• Consider a higher deductible to lower your premium.
• Ask about other discounts that may be available (for a good driving record, safety equipment, multiple policies with the same provider, etc.) to reduce your cost of coverage.
• Review your insurance coverage annually to make sure you have appropriate coverage as your situation changes.
• Like all investments, be sure to get all the facts before parting with your hard-earned money.

AUTO INSURANCE

State law requires that all motor vehicles have liability insurance to cover injury to other people or damage to their property. If you have a loan on your vehicle, your lender will also require physical damage coverage on it. You may select a higher deductible, the amount you pay out of pocket before insurance kicks in, and receive a more affordable rate on the premium, the cost of the policy. If you have your emergency savings in place, you will feel more confident about taking out a higher-deductible policy, which will lower your premium costs.

HOME INSURANCE

Homeowners insurance covers your home and possessions. The personal liability coverage in a homeowners policy protects you from loss resulting from any injuries that may occur on your property. Your mortgage lender will require you to carry a certain amount of insurance coverage as long as the mortgage is in place.

You may also consider a higher-deductible insurance plan to save money on your homeowners coverage. Standard homeowners coverage insures your home and its contents against loss from such risks as fire and theft. You may require special insurance for flood, earthquake or other risks specific to your area. Contact your state department of insurance for more information on insurance in high-risk areas.

PROPERTY INSURANCE

"It is unwise to be too sure of one's own wisdom. It is healthy to be reminded that the strongest might weaken and the wisest might err."
Mahatma Gandhi

Another type of household protection, a home warranty, is a service contract that protects the homeowner from unexpected costs for repair or replacement of major systems. These might include heating and air-conditioning, plumbing, electrical systems or a water heater. Sellers will sometimes provide a one-year home warranty to give potential buyers added confidence. The homebuyer then has the option of renewing the warranty at the end of the year. If you are renting your home or apartment, you should purchase renters or contents insurance to cover your possessions against loss from fire or theft. Your landlord's insurance will only cover damage to the building, not its contents. Also, if someone is hurt in your rented home, that liability is yours, not the landlord's.

MEDICAL INSURANCE

Medical insurance pays for some, but not all, of your doctor, hospital and prescription drug costs. Many people have significant levels of debt because they did not have medical insurance or they did not have savings to pay the expenses that were not covered by their health plan. Late payments and defaults on medical debt may be reported on credit reports and affect a person's credit score. Premiums are lower on employer-provided health insurance because risk is spread over a larger group of people. Take advantage of the lower costs that employer-sponsored health plans offer, but expect to pay part of the premium out of your paycheck.

In addition to medical insurance, many employers offer dental and vision plans, often at low cost.

FLEXIBLE SPENDING ACCOUNTS

People who are insured through their employer should consider participating in a flexible spending account (FSA) if it is offered. An employer-sponsored FSA allows employees to save pretax dollars in an account to cover deductibles, co-pays, prescription and over-the-counter drugs, and other health expenses not covered by insurance. Employees need to plan their FSA spending so they have enough saved to cover their uninsured medical expenses but not more than they can use in one year plus two and a half months.

On March 15 every year, money left in an FSA from the previous year is forfeited. If you have health insurance and your employer does not offer a flexible spending account, you should make sure your emergency savings account is adequate to provide a safety net against unexpected medical costs.

HEALTH INSURANCE

Are you familiar with health savings accounts? If you do not have health insurance or you need more affordable insurance, a high-deductible health plan (HDHP), coupled with a health savings account (HSA), provides medical insurance coverage and a tax-free opportunity to save for future medical needs. The premium for an HDHP is generally lower than for traditional health insurance because the deductible (the amount you pay before the insurance kicks in) is higher. That is where the health savings account comes in. HSAs are set up at banks or other financial institutions to pay for current and future health-related costs that occur before the deductible is met and insurance takes over. Contributions to an HSA are tax-deductible, up to certain limits, even if you do not itemize deductions on your income tax return. Interest earned on the HSA account is not taxable, and withdrawals are tax-free if used for qualified medical expenses. An HSA is portable, so it stays with you even if you change jobs or retire. Plus, unspent savings in an HSA can grow year-to-year. For more information about HSAs, go to www.treasury.gov/offices/public-affairs/hsa.

HEALTH INSURANCE FOR CHILDREN

Every state provides free or low-cost health insurance for children in low- to moderate-income households. For more information about state programs, contact the U.S. Department of Health and Human Services at 877-Children Now (877-543-7669) or go to www.insurechildrennow.gov.

DISABILITY INSURANCE

Statistics show that you have a higher risk of becoming disabled than of dying before age 65. Disability insurance helps you pay living expenses if you are sick or injured and unable to work for a long time. Your employer may offer this insurance in its benefits plan. It is a good idea to buy this protection even if you have to pay for part of the premium.

The need for life insurance depends on a person's circumstances. In the event of your death, life insurance pays money to the person you choose (your beneficiary). Life insurance helps give financial protection to your children, spouse, parents or even your business. While some types of life insurance offer savings and investment components to keep the future cost of premiums lower or to increase the death benefit, they are not a substitute for a savings or investment plan. Low-cost term insurance, often available through your employer, can offer protection for young families. Personal accident insurance may also offer a cushion to families if a member dies or is seriously injured in an accident. This kind of insurance is often available through your employer or other provider at relatively low cost.

If you or a family member became very ill and needed a nursing home, who would pay for it? You would, until all your assets, and those of your spouse, are exhausted. Only then would government assistance help cover these needs.

Long-term care insurance is not medical insurance, but it pays for such health-related items as nursing home, assisted living or in-home care. Generally, the need for long-term care comes late in life, but insurance premiums are much less expensive when you are younger. Some employers offer access to long-term care insurance for employees to purchase, but most consumers have to find coverage themselves. Shopping for long-term care insurance takes research, common sense and attention to the policy's details.

LIFE INSURANCE AND LONG-TERM CARE INSURANCE

Buy insurance wisely! Insure U, a web site sponsored by the National Association of Insurance Commissioners representing insurance regulators from across the United States, has more information on buying all types of insurance at www.insureuonline.org.

Step 4

TEACH YOURSELF PERSONAL FINANCE 1.0

"An investment in knowledge always pays the best interest."
Benjamin Franklin

Are you ready for financial education? How does money work? What is personal finance 1.0? When it comes to finances, how much do you know? If you are like most people, you probably know little about personal finance. Perhaps you think long-term security is impossible on your income. But, the truth is, no matter what your income level is, you can achieve financial security. You just have to take the time to learn a few simple principles about how money works. I assert that financial education is for everyone. I am serious about your financial education. I believe that there are no secrets to financial security. Financial education is not just for the wealthy. My goal is to educate hardworking families — just like you — on simple concepts that can change your financial future forever. Do you know when you need life insurance the most? How about saving for retirement? Do you know how much something really costs when you put it on your credit card? Taking a few moments to learn some simple concepts about how money works can save you from financial headaches later. Learn about how money works with the financial concepts in *The Miraculous Millionaire*; they are simple!

Personal finance 1.0

What about the theory of decreasing responsibility? According to the theory of decreasing responsibility, your need for life insurance peaks along with your family responsibilities. When you are young, you may have children to support, a new mortgage payment and many other obligations. Yet, you have not had the time to accumulate much money. This is the time when the death of a breadwinner or caretaker could be devastating and when you need coverage the most. When you are older, you usually have fewer dependents and fewer financial responsibilities. Plus, you have had years to accumulate wealth through savings and investments. At this point, your need for insurance has reduced dramatically, and you have your own funds to see you through your retirement years.

Talking about life insurance, I am willing to provide you with a FREE financial needs analysis. If you are like many people, you are in the dark about your finances. You pay your bills each month and do your best to prepare for the future. But the truth is, there is only so much money to go around and preparing for the future can be overwhelming.

I Can Help YOU! To help families better understand their personal finances, I offer financial needs analysis tools. These tools give me a detailed overview of your current financial situation and suggest a personalized wealth-building strategy for your financial security. The use of these tools is complimentary, confidential, and customized for you and every family that I serve. Could you benefit from the financial needs analysis? You bet! Do you have children? Do you owe any debt? Do you plan to retire someday?

Do you lack a strategy for financial independence? I want to help you:

DEBT SOLUTIONS

I have strategies for paying off your credit cards and loans in the quickest, most efficient manner possible with little or no additional cash outlay.

There is more to personal finance than the drudgery of debts and budgets.

RETIREMENT INCOME

I provide a detailed analysis of how much money you need to prepare for retirement.

EDUCATION FUNDING

Using my quantitative and qualitative analytic tools, I can project the actual costs for specific schools you select for your children. In fact, I will show you several strategies for funding your children's education expenses.

INCOME PROTECTION

I will offer you a variety of strategies to ensure your family's financial future should you die prematurely.

BUILD YOUR FINANCIAL FUTURE

Build your financial future today. If you have the right knowledge, specialized knowhow, the process of building your financial future is as easy as 123 or ABC. I will expose millionaire plans to you. I will pull all your information together into a dynamic balance sheet designed just for you; in the end, I will outline specific steps for you to put your financial plan into action. Trust me; I market only first-rate financial products and services from some of the world's more recognizable companies.

The purpose of this chapter is to introduce you to personal finance 101. My assumption is that you are a very smart person who does not have or has never had the time to learn the basics of individual finance. I have scoured the Internet looking for resources. The truth is that the best and trusted material on personal finance has been published the government: federal, state, or local. Yet, success gurus have a cavalier attitude of behaving like this non-copyrighted material belongs to them through adverse possession. The only problem is that the government does not do a good job of publicizing the existence of these learning materials adequately. In the course of this chapter, please, do not be offended if I call you either a dummy or an idiot. Ok? We live in a credit economy, so I would like to begin by discussing personal credit worthiness.

BUILDING A BETTER CREDIT REPORT

If you have ever applied for a credit card, a personal loan, or insurance policy, there is a file about you. This file is known as your credit report. It is chock full of information on where you live, how you pay your bills, and whether you have been sued, arrested, or filed for bankruptcy. Consumer reporting companies sell the information in your report to creditors, insurers, employers, and other businesses with a legitimate need for it. They use the information to evaluate your applications for credit, insurance, employment, or a lease. Having a good credit report means it will be easier for you to get loans and lower interest rates. Lower interest rates usually translate into smaller monthly payments.

Nevertheless, newspapers, radio, TELEVISION, and the Internet are filled with ads for companies and services that promise to erase accurate negative information in your credit report in exchange for a fee. The scam artists who run these ads not only do not deliver — they cannot deliver. Only time, a deliberate effort, and a plan to repay your bills will improve your credit as it is detailed in your credit report. The Federal Trade Commission (FTC), the nation's consumer protection agency, has written booklets and pamphlets to help explain how to build a better credit report.

In fact, they have six sections:

SECTION 1 explains your rights under the Fair Credit Reporting Act and the Fair and Accurate Credit Transactions Act.
SECTION 2 tells how you can legally improve your credit report.
SECTION 3 offers tips on dealing with debt.
SECTION 4 cautions about credit-related scams and how to avoid them.
SECTION 5 offers information about identity theft.
SECTION 6 lists resources for additional information.

THE FAIR CREDIT REPORTING ACT

The Fair Credit Reporting Act (FCRA) promotes the accuracy, fairness, and privacy of information in the files of the nation's consumer reporting companies. The FTC enforces the FCRA with respect to consumer reporting companies. Recent amendments to the FCRA expand consumer rights and place additional requirements on consumer reporting companies. Businesses that provide information about consumers to consumer reporting companies and businesses that use credit reports also have new responsibilities under the law. Here are some questions consumers have asked the FTC about consumer reports and consumer reporting companies, and the answers.

Q. DO I HAVE A RIGHT TO KNOW WHAT IS IN MY REPORT?

A. You have the right to know what is in your report, but you have to ask for the information. The consumer reporting company must tell you everything in your report, and give you a list of everyone who has requested your report within the past year — or the past two years if the requests were related to employment.

Q. WHAT TYPE OF INFORMATION DO CONSUMER REPORTING COMPANIES COLLECT AND SELL?

A. Consumer reporting companies collect and sell four basic types of information:
☐ Identification and employment information: Your name, birth date, Social Security number, employer, and spouse's name are noted routinely. The consumer reporting company also may provide information about your employment history, home ownership, income, and previous address, if a creditor asks.

☐ Payment history: Your accounts with different creditors are listed, showing how much credit has been extended and whether you have paid on time. Related events, such as the referral of an overdue account to a collection agency, also may be noted.

☐ Inquiries: Consumer reporting companies must maintain a record of all creditors who have asked for your credit history within the past year, and a record of individuals or businesses that have asked for your credit history for employment purposes for the past two years.

☐ Public record information: Events that are a matter of public record, such as bankruptcies, foreclosures, or tax liens, may appear in your report.

Q. IS THERE A CHARGE FOR MY REPORT?

A. Under the Free File Disclosure Rule of the Fair and Accurate Credit Transactions Act (FACT Act), each of the nationwide consumer reporting companies — Equifax, Experian, and Transunion — is required to provide you with a free copy of your credit report once every 12 months, if you ask for it.

These consumer reporting companies are phasing in free reports geographically through September 1, 2005. After that, free reports will be accessible to all Americans, regardless of where they live.

☐ Free reports have been available to consumers in the Western states — Alaska, Arizona, California, Colorado, Hawaii, Idaho, Montana, Nevada, New Mexico, Oregon, Utah, Washington, and Wyoming — since December 1, 2004.

☐ Consumers in the Midwestern states — Illinois, Indiana, Iowa, Kansas, Michigan, Minnesota, Missouri, Nebraska, North Dakota, Ohio, South Dakota, and Wisconsin —have been able to order free reports since March 1, 2005.

☐ Consumers in the Southern states —Alabama, Arkansas, Florida, Georgia, Kentucky, Louisiana, Mississippi, Oklahoma, South Carolina, Tennessee, and Texas — can begin ordering their free reports June 1, 2005.

☐ Consumers in the Eastern states —Connecticut, Delaware, Maine, Maryland, Massachusetts, New Hampshire, New Jersey, New York, North Carolina, Pennsylvania, Rhode Island, Vermont, Virginia, and West Virginia — the District of Columbia, Puerto Rico, and all U.S. territories can begin ordering their free reports September 1, 2005.

Q: HOW DO I ORDER MY FREE REPORT?

A: The three nationwide consumer reporting companies are using one website, one toll-free telephone number, and one mailing address for consumers to order their free annual report. To order, click on www.annualcreditreport.com, call 1-877-322-8228, or complete the Annual Credit Report Request Form and mail it to: Annual Credit Report Request Service, P.O. Box 105281, Atlanta, GA 30348-5281. The form is at the back of this book; or you can print it from ftc.gov/credit. Do not contact the three nationwide consumer reporting companies individually. You may order your free annual reports from each of the consumer reporting companies at the same time, or you can order from only one or two. The law allows you to order one free copy from each of the nationwide consumer reporting companies every 12 months.

Q: WHAT INFORMATION DO I HAVE TO PROVIDE TO GET MY FREE REPORT?

A: You need to provide your name, address, Social Security number, and date of birth. If you have moved in the last two years, you may have to provide your previous address. To maintain the security of your file, each nationwide consumer reporting company may ask you for some information that only you would know, like the amount of your monthly mortgage payment. Each company may ask you for different information because the information each has in your file may come from different sources.

Still, www.annualcreditreport.com is the only authorized online source for your free annual credit report from the three nationwide consumer reporting companies. Neither the website nor the companies will call you first to ask for personal information or send you an email asking for personal information. If you get a phone call or an email — or see a pop-up ad—claiming it is from www.annualcreditreport.com (or any of the three nationwide consumer reporting companies), it is probably a scam. Do not reply or click on any link in the message. Instead, forward any email that claims to be from http://www.annualcreditreport.com (or any of the three consumer reporting companies) to pam@uce.gov, the FTC's database of deceptive spam.

Q: ARE THERE OTHER SITUATIONS WHERE I MIGHT BE ELIGIBLE FOR A FREE REPORT?

A: Under federal law, you are entitled to a free report if a company takes adverse action against you, such as denying your application for credit, insurance, or employment, and you ask for your report within 60 days of receiving notice of the action. The notice will give you the name, address, and phone number of the consumer reporting company. You are also entitled to one free report a year if you are unemployed and plan to look for a job within 60 days; if you are on welfare; or if your report is inaccurate because of fraud, including identity theft. Otherwise, any of the three consumer reporting companies may charge you up to $9.50 for another copy of your report within a 12-month period. To buy a copy of your report, contact:

Equifax
800-685-1111
www.equifax.com

Experian
888-EXPERIAN (888-397-3742)
www.experian.com

Trans Union
800-916-8800
www.transunion.com

Under state law, consumers in Colorado, Georgia, Maine, Maryland, Massachusetts, New Jersey, and Vermont already have free access to their credit reports. For more information, see Your Access to Free Credit Reports at ftc.gov/credit.

There is more to personal finance than the drudgery of debts and budgets.

CREDIT SCORES

Q. WHAT IS A CREDIT SCORE, AND HOW DOES IT AFFECT MY ABILITY TO GET CREDIT?

A: Credit scoring is a system creditors use to help determine whether to give you credit, and how much to charge you for it. Information about you and your credit experiences, like your bill-paying history, the number and type of accounts you have, late payments, collection actions, outstanding debt, and the age of your accounts, is collected from your credit application and your credit report. Using a statistical formula, creditors compare this information to the credit performance of consumers with similar profiles. A credit scoring system awards points for each factor. A total number of points — a credit score — helps predict how creditworthy you are, that is, how likely it is that you will repay a loan and make the payments on time. Generally, consumers with good credit risks have higher credit scores. You can get your credit score from the three nationwide consumer reporting companies, but you will have to pay a fee for it. Many other companies also offer credit scores for sale alone or as part of a package of products. For more information, see Credit Scoring at ftc.gov/credit.

IMPROVING YOUR CREDIT REPORT

Under the FCRA, both the consumer reporting company and the information provider (the person, company, or organization that provides information about you to a consumer reporting company) are responsible for correcting inaccurate or incomplete information in your report. To take advantage of all your rights under the FCRA, contact the consumer reporting company and the information provider if you see inaccurate or incomplete information.

1. Tell the consumer reporting company, in writing, what information you think is inaccurate. Include copies (NOT originals) of documents that support your position. In addition to providing your complete name and address, your letter should clearly identify each item in your report that you dispute, state the facts and explain why you dispute the information, and request that the information be deleted or corrected. You may want to enclose a copy of your report with the items in question circled. Your letter may look something like the one on page 8. Send your letter by certified mail, return receipt requested, so you can document what the consumer reporting company received. Keep copies of your dispute letter and enclosures.

Consumer reporting companies must investigate the items in question — usually within 30 days — unless they consider your dispute frivolous. They also must forward all the relevant data you provide about the inaccuracy to the organization that provided the information. After the information provider receives notice of a dispute from the consumer reporting company, it must investigate, review the relevant information, and report the results back to the consumer reporting company. If the information provider finds the disputed information is inaccurate, it must notify all three nationwide consumer reporting companies so they can correct the information in your file.

When the investigation is complete, the consumer reporting company must give you the written results and a free copy of your report if the dispute results in a change. (This free report does not count as your annual free report under the FACT Act.) If an item is changed or deleted, the consumer reporting company cannot put the disputed information back in your file unless the information provider verifies that the information is, indeed, accurate and complete. The consumer reporting company also must send you written notice that includes the name, address, and phone number of the information provider. If you request, the consumer reporting company must send notices of any correction to anyone who received your report in the past six months. A corrected copy of your report can be sent to anyone who received a copy during the past two years for employment purposes. If an investigation does not resolve your dispute with the consumer reporting company, you can ask that a statement of the dispute be included in your file and in future reports. You also can ask the consumer reporting company to provide your statement to anyone who received a copy of your report in the recent past. Expect to pay a fee for this service.

2. Tell the creditor or other information provider, in writing, that you dispute an item. Be sure to include copies (NOT originals) of documents that support your position. Many providers specify an address for disputes. If the provider reports the item to a consumer reporting company, it must include a notice of your dispute. And if you are correct — that is, if the information is found to be inaccurate — the information provider may not report it again.

SAMPLE DISPUTE LETTER

Date
Your Name
Your Address
Your City, State, Zip Code
Complaint Department
Name of Company
Address
City, State, Zip Code
Dear Sir or Madam:
I am writing to dispute the following information in my file. The items I dispute
also are encircled on the attached copy of the report I received. This item (identify item(s)
disputed by name of source, such as creditors or tax court, and identify type of item, such
as credit account, judgment, etc.) is (inaccurate or incomplete) because (describe what is
inaccurate or incomplete and why). I am requesting that the item be deleted (or request another
specific change) to correct the information.

Enclosed are copies of (use this sentence if applicable and describe any enclosed documentation,
such as payment records, court documents) supporting my position. Please investigate this
(these) matter(s) and (delete or correct) the disputed item(s) as soon as possible.
Sincerely,
Your name
Enclosures: (List what you are enclosing)

ACCURATE NEGATIVE INFORMATION

When negative information in your report is accurate, only the passage of time can assure its removal. A consumer reporting company can report most accurate negative information for seven years and bankruptcy information for ten years. Information about an unpaid judgment against you can be reported for seven years or until the statute of limitations runs out, whichever is longer. There is no time limit on reporting information about criminal convictions; information reported in response to your application for a job that pays more than $75,000 a year; and information reported because you have applied for more than $150,000 worth of credit or life insurance. There is a standard method for calculating the seven-year reporting period. Generally, the period runs from the date that the event took place.

ADDING ACCOUNTS TO YOUR FILE

Your credit file may not reflect all your credit accounts. Most national department store and all-purpose bank credit card accounts are included in your file, but not all. Some travel, entertainment, gasoline card companies, local retailers, and credit unions are among those that usually are not included. If you have been told that you were denied credit because of an "insufficient credit file" or "no credit file" and you have accounts with creditors that do not appear in your credit file, ask the consumer reporting companies to add this information to future reports. Although they are not required to do so, many consumer reporting companies will add verifiable accounts for a fee. However, if these creditors do not generally report to the consumer reporting company, the added items will not be updated in your file.

DEALING WITH DEBT

Having trouble paying your bills? Getting dunning notices from creditors? Are your accounts being turned over to debt collectors? Are you worried about losing your home or your car? You are not alone. Many people face financial crises at some time in their lives. Whether the crisis is caused by personal or family illness, the loss of a job, or simple overspending, it can seem overwhelming. But often, it can be overcome. The fact is that your financial situation does not have to go from bad to worse. If you or someone you know is in financial hot water, consider these options: realistic budgeting, credit counseling from a reputable organization, debt consolidation, or bankruptcy. How do you know which option will work best for you? It depends on your level of debt, your level of discipline, and your prospects for the future.

SELF-HELP DEVELOPING A BUDGET

The first step toward taking control of your financial situation is to do a realistic assessment of how much money you take in and how much money you spend. Start by listing your income from all sources. Then, list your "fixed" expenses — those that are the same each month — like mortgage payments or rent, car payments, and insurance premiums. Next, list the expenses that vary — like entertainment, recreation, and clothing. Writing down all your expenses, even those that seem insignificant, is a helpful way to track your spending patterns, identify necessary expenses, and prioritize the rest. The goal is to make sure you can make ends meet on the basics: housing, food, health care, insurance, and education. Your public library and bookstores have information about budgeting and money management techniques. In addition, computer software programs can be useful tools for developing and maintaining a budget, balancing your checkbook, and creating plans to save money and pay down your debt.

CONTACTING YOUR CREDITORS

Contact your creditors immediately if you are having trouble making ends meet. Tell them why it is difficult for you, and try to work out a modified payment plan that reduces your payments to a more manageable level. Do not wait until your accounts have been turned over to a debt collector. At that point, your creditors have given up on you.

DEALING WITH DEBT COLLECTORS

The Fair Debt Collection Practices Act is the federal law that dictates how and when a debt collector may contact you. A debt collector may not call you before 8 a.m., after 9 p.m. while you are at work if the collector knows that your employer does not approve of the calls. Collectors may not harass you, lie, or use unfair practices when they try to collect a debt. And they must honor a written request from you to stop further contact.

CREDIT COUNSELING

If you are not disciplined enough to create a workable budget and stick to it, cannot work out a repayment plan with your creditors, or cannot keep track of mounting bills, consider contacting a credit counseling organization. Many credit counseling organizations are nonprofit and work with you to solve your financial problems. But be aware that just because an organization says it is "nonprofit," there is no guarantee that its services are free, affordable, or even legitimate. In fact, some credit counseling organizations charge high fees, which may be hidden, or pressure consumers to make large "voluntary" contributions that can cause more debt.

Most credit counselors offer services through local offices, the Internet, or on the telephone. If possible, find an organization that offers in-person counseling. Many universities, military bases, credit unions, housing authorities, and branches of the U.S. Cooperative Extension Service operate nonprofit credit counseling programs. Your financial institution, local consumer protection agency, and friends and family also may be good sources of information and referrals.

Reputable credit counseling organizations can advise you on managing your money and debts, help you develop a budget, and offer free educational materials and workshops. Their counselors are certified and trained in the areas of consumer credit, money and debt management, and budgeting. Counselors discuss your entire financial situation with you, and help you develop a personalized plan to solve your money problems. An initial counseling session typically lasts an hour, with an offer of follow-up sessions.

There is more to personal finance than the drudgery of debts and budgets.

AUTO AND HOME LOANS

Your debts can be secured or unsecured. Secured debts usually are tied to an asset, like your car for a car loan, or your house for a mortgage. If you stop making payments, lenders can repossess your car or foreclose on your house. Unsecured debts are not tied to any asset, and include most credit card debt, bills for medical care, signature loans, and debts for other types of services. Most automobile financing agreements allow a creditor to repossess your car any time you are in default. No notice is required. If your car is repossessed, you may have to pay the balance due on the loan, as well as towing and storage costs, to get it back. If you cannot do this, the creditor may sell the car. If you see default approaching, you may be better off selling the car yourself and paying off the debt: You will avoid the added costs of repossession and a negative entry on your credit report.

If you fall behind on your mortgage, contact your lender immediately to avoid foreclosure. Most lenders are willing to work with you if they believe you are acting in good faith and the situation is temporary. Some lenders may reduce or suspend your payments for a short time. When you resume regular payments, though, you may have to pay an additional amount toward the past due total. Other lenders may agree to change the terms of the mortgage by extending the repayment period to reduce the monthly debt. Ask whether additional fees would be assessed for these changes, and calculate how much they total in the long term. If you and your lender cannot work out a plan, contact a housing counseling agency. Some agencies limit their counseling services to homeowners with FHA mortgages, but many offer free help to any homeowner who is having trouble making mortgage payments. Call the local office of the Department of Housing and Urban Development or the housing authority in your state, city, or county for help in finding a legitimate housing counseling agency near you.

DEBT CONSOLIDATION

You may be able to lower your cost of credit by consolidating your debt through a second mortgage or a home equity line of credit. Remember that these loans require you to put up your home as collateral. If you cannot make the payments — or if your payments are late — you could lose your home. What is more, the costs of consolidation loans can add up. In addition to interest on the loans, you may have to pay "points," with one point equal to one percent of the amount you borrow. Still, these loans may provide certain tax advantages that are not available with other kinds of credit.

BANKRUPTCY

Personal bankruptcy generally is considered the debt management option of last resort because the results are long-lasting and far-reaching. A bankruptcy stays on your credit report for ten years, and can make it difficult to obtain credit, buy a home, get life insurance, or sometimes get a job. Still, it is a legal procedure that offers a fresh start for people who cannot satisfy their debts. People who follow the bankruptcy rules receive a discharge — a court order that says they do not have to repay certain debts.

There are two primary types of personal bankruptcy: Chapter 13 and Chapter 7. Each must be filed in federal bankruptcy court. As of January 2005, the filing fees run about $185 for Chapter 13 and $200 for Chapter 7. Attorney fees are additional and can vary. Chapter 13 allows people with a steady income to keep property, like a mortgaged house or a financed car, that they otherwise might lose. In Chapter 13, the court approves a repayment plan that allows you to use your future income to pay off a default during a three-to-five-year period, rather than surrender any property. After you have made all the payments under the plan, you receive a discharge of your debts.

Chapter 7 is known as straight bankruptcy, and involves liquidation of all assets that are not exempt. Exempt property may include automobiles, work-related tools, and basic household furnishings. Some of your property may be sold by a court-appointed official — a trustee — or turned over to your creditors. You can receive a discharge of your debts through Chapter 7 only once every six years. Both types of bankruptcy may get rid of unsecured debts and stop foreclosures, repossessions, garnishments, utility shut-offs, and debt collection activities. Both also provide exemptions that allow people to keep certain assets, although exemption amounts vary. Note that personal bankruptcy usually does not erase child support, alimony, fines, taxes, and some student loan obligations. And unless you have an acceptable plan to catch up on your debt under Chapter 13, bankruptcy usually does not allow you to keep property when your creditor has an unpaid mortgage or lien on it.

AVOIDING SCAMS

Turning to a business that offers help in solving debt problems may seem like a reasonable solution when your bills become unmanageable. Be cautious. Before you do business with any company, check it out with your local consumer protection agency or the Better Business Bureau in the company's location.

ADS PROMISING DEBT RELIEF MAY REALLY BE OFFERING BANKRUPTCY

Consumer debt is at an all-time high. What is more, a record number of consumers — more than 1.6 million in 2003 — are filing for bankruptcy. Whether your debt dilemma is the result of an illness, unemployment, or overspending, it can seem overwhelming. In your effort to get solvent, be on the alert for advertisements that offer seemingly quick fixes. And read between the lines when faced with ads in newspapers, magazines, or even telephone directories that say: Consolidate your bills into one monthly payment without borrowing! STOP credit harassment, foreclosures, repossessions, tax levies and garnishments! Keep Your Property! Wipe out your debts! Consolidate your bills! How? By using the protection and assistance provided by federal law.

For once, let the law work for you! While the ads pitch the promise of debt relief, they rarely say relief may be spelled b-a-n-k-r-up-t-c-y. And although bankruptcy is one option to deal with financial problems, it is generally considered the option of last resort.

The reason: it has a long-term negative impact on your creditworthiness. A bankruptcy stays on your credit report for 10 years, and can hinder your ability to get credit, a job, insurance, or even a place to live. What is more, it can cost you attorneys' fees.

ADVANCE-FEE LOAN SCAMS

These scams often target consumers with bad credit problems or those with no credit. In exchange for an up-front fee, these companies "guarantee" that applicants will get the credit they want — usually a credit card or a personal loan. The up-front fee may be as high as several hundred dollars. Resist the temptation to follow up on advance-fee loan guarantees. They may be illegal. Many legitimate creditors offer extensions of credit, such as credit cards, loans, and mortgages through telemarketing, and require an application fee or appraisal fee in advance. But legitimate creditors never guarantee in advance that you will get the loan. Under the federal Telemarketing Sales Rule, a seller or telemarketer who guarantees or represents a high likelihood of your getting a loan or some other extension of credit may not ask for or receive payment until you have received the loan.

RECOGNIZING AN ADVANCE-FEE LOAN SCAM

Ads for advance-fee loans often appear in the classified ad section of local and national newspapers and magazines. They also may appear in mailings, radio spots, and on local cable stations. Often, these ads feature "900" numbers, which result in charges on your phone bill. In addition, these companies often use delivery systems other than the U.S. Postal Service, such as overnight or courier services, to avoid detection and prosecution by postal authorities. It is not hard to confuse a legitimate credit offer with an advance-fee loan scam. An offer for credit from a bank, savings and loan, or mortgage broker generally requires your verbal or written acceptance of the loan or credit offer. The offer usually is subject to a check of your credit report after you apply to make sure you meet their credit standards. Usually, you are not required to pay a fee to get the credit. Hang up on anyone who calls you on the phone and says they can guarantee you will get a loan if you pay in advance. It is against the law.

PROTECTING YOURSELF

Here are some tips to keep in mind before you respond to ads that promise easy credit, regardless of your credit history:

☐ Most legitimate lenders will not "guarantee" that you will get a loan or a credit card before you apply, especially if you have bad credit, or a bankruptcy.
☐ It is an accepted and common practice for reputable lenders to require payment for a credit report or appraisal. You also may have to pay a processing or application fee.
☐ Never give your credit card account number, bank account information, or Social Security number out over the telephone unless you are familiar with the company and know why the information is necessary.

CREDIT REPAIR SCAMS

You see the ads in newspapers, on TELEVISION, and on the Internet. You hear them on the radio. You get fliers in the mail. You may even get calls from telemarketers offering credit repair services. They all make the same claims: Credit problems? No problem! We can erase your bad credit or 100% guaranteed. Create a new credit identity legally. We can remove bankruptcies, judgments, liens, and bad loans from your credit file forever! Do yourself a favor and save some money, too. Do not believe these statements. They are just not true. Only time, a conscientious effort, and a plan for repaying your debt will improve your credit report.

THE WARNING SIGNS

If you should decide to respond to an offer to repair your credit, think twice. Do not do business with any company that:

☐ wants you to pay for credit repair services before any services are provided
☐ does not tell you your legal rights and what you can do yourself — for free
☐ recommends that you not contact a consumer reporting company directly
☐ suggests that you try to invent a "new" credit report by applying for an Employer Identification Number from the IRS to use instead of your Social Security number
☐ advises you to dispute all information in your credit report or take any action that seems illegal, such as creating a new credit identity. If you follow illegal advice and commit fraud, you may be subject to prosecution. You could be charged and prosecuted for mail or wire fraud if you use the mail or telephone to apply for credit and provide false information. It is a federal crime to make false statements on a loan or credit application, to misrepresent your Social Security number, and to obtain an Employer Identification Number from the Internal Revenue Service under false pretenses.

THE CREDIT REPAIR ORGANIZATIONS ACT

By law, credit repair organizations must give you a copy of the "Consumer Credit File Rights Under State and Federal Law" before you sign a contract. They also must give you a written contract that spells out your rights and obligations. Read these documents before signing the contract. The law contains specific consumer protections. For example, a credit repair company cannot:

☐ make false claims about their services
☐ charge you until they have completed the promised services
☐ perform any services until they have your signature on a written contract and have completed a three-day waiting period. During this time, you can cancel the contract without paying any fees.

Your contract must specify:

☐ the total cost of the services

There is more to personal finance than the drudgery of debts and budgets.

☐ a detailed description of the services to be performed
☐ how long it will take to achieve the results
☐ any "guarantees" they offer
☐ the company's name and business address.

WHERE TO COMPLAIN

If you have had a problem with any of the scams described here, contact your local consumer protection agency, state Attorney General (AG), or Better Business Bureau. Many AGs have toll-free consumer hotlines. Check with your local directory assistance.

IDENTITY THEFT

An identity thief is someone who obtains some piece of your sensitive information, like your Social Security number, date of birth, address, and phone number, and uses it without your knowledge to commit fraud or theft.

HOW IDENTITY THIEVES GET YOUR INFORMATION

Skilled identity thieves use a variety of methods to gain access to your personal information. For example, they may get information from businesses or other institutions by:
☐ stealing records or information while they are on the job
☐ bribing an employee who has access to these records
☐ hacking these records
☐ conning information out of employees
☐ rummage through your trash, the trash of businesses, or public trash dumps in a practice known as "dumpster diving"
☐ get your credit reports by abusing their employer's authorized access to them, or by posing as a landlord, employer, or someone else who may have a legal right to access your report
☐ steal your credit or debit card numbers by capturing the information in a data storage device in a practice known as "skimming." They may swipe your card for an actual purchase, or attach the device to an ATM machine where you may enter or swipe your card.
☐ steal wallets and purses containing identification and credit and bank cards.
☐ steal mail, including bank and credit card statements, new checks, or tax information
☐ complete a "change of address form" to divert your mail to another location
☐ steal personal information from your home
☐ scam information from you by posing as a legitimate business person or government official

HOW IDENTITY THIEVES USE YOUR INFORMATION

Once identity thieves have your personal information, they may:
☐ go on spending sprees using your credit and debit card account numbers to buy "big-ticket" items like computers that they can easily sell.
☐ open a new credit card account, using your name, date of birth, and Social Security number. When they do not pay the bills, the delinquent account is reported on your credit report.

☐ change the mailing address on your credit card account. The imposter then runs up charges on the account. Because the bills are being sent to the new address, it may take some time before you realize there is a problem.

☐ take out auto loans in your name

☐ establish phone or wireless service in your name

☐ counterfeit checks or debit cards, and drain your bank account

☐ open a bank account in your name and write bad checks on that account

☐ file for bankruptcy under your name to avoid paying debts they have incurred, or to avoid eviction

☐ give your name to the police during an arrest. If they are released and do not show up for their court date, an arrest warrant could be issued in your name.

PROTECTING YOURSELF

Managing your personal information is key to minimizing your risk of becoming a victim of identity theft.

☐ Keep an eye on your purse or wallet, and keep them in a safe place at all times.

☐ Do not carry your Social Security card.

☐ Do not share your personal information with random people you do not know. Identity thieves are really good liars, and could pretend to be from banks, Internet service providers, or even government agencies to get you to reveal identifying information.

☐ Read the statements from your bank and credit accounts and look for unusual charges or suspicious activity. Report any problems to your bank and creditors right away.

☐ Tear up or shred your charge receipts, checks and bank statements, expired charge cards, and any other documents with personal information before you put them in the trash.

HOW TO TELL IF YOU ARE A VICTIM OF IDENTITY THEFT

Monitor the balances of your financial accounts. Look for unexplained charges or withdrawals. Other indications of identity theft can be:

☐ failing to receive bills or other mail signaling an address change by the identity thief;

☐ receiving credit cards for which you did not apply;

☐ denial of credit for no apparent reason; or

☐ receiving calls from debt collectors or companies about merchandise or services you did not buy.

WHAT TO DO IF YOUR IDENTITY'S BEEN STOLEN

If you suspect that your personal information has been used to commit fraud or theft, take the following four steps right away. Follow up all calls in writing; send your letter by certified mail, and request a return receipt, so you can document what the company received and when; and keep copies for your files.

1. Place a fraud alert on your credit reports and review your credit reports. Contact any one of the nationwide consumer reporting companies to place a fraud alert on your credit report. Fraud alerts can help prevent an identity thief from opening any more accounts in your name. The company you call is required to contact the other two, which will place an alert on their versions of your report, too:

Equifax: 1-800-525-6285; www.equifax.com

Experian: 1-888-EXPERIAN (397-3742); www.experian.com

Transunion: 1-800-680-7289; www.transunion.com.

In addition to placing the fraud alert on your file, the three consumer reporting companies will send you free copies of your credit reports, and, if you ask, they will display only the last four digits of your Social Security number on your credit reports.

2. Close the accounts that you know, or believe, have been tampered with or opened fraudulently. Contact the security or fraud department of each company where you know, or believe, accounts have been tampered with or opened fraudulently. Follow up in writing, and include copies (NOT originals) of supporting documents. It is important to notify credit card companies and banks in writing. Send your letters by certified mail, return receipt requested, so you can document what the company received and when. Keep a file of your correspondence and enclosures.

When you open new accounts, use new Personal Identification Numbers (PINs) and passwords. Avoid using easily available information like your mother's maiden name, your birth date, the last four digits of your Social Security number or your phone number, or a series of consecutive numbers.

3. File a report with your local police or the police in the community where the identity theft took place. Get a copy of the police report or, at the very least, the number of the report. It can help you deal with creditors who need proof of the crime. If the police are reluctant to take your report, ask to file a "Miscellaneous Incidents" report, or try another jurisdiction, like your state police. You also can check with your state Attorney General's office to find out if state law requires the police to take reports for identity theft. Check the Blue Pages of your telephone directory for the phone number or check www.naag.org for a list of state Attorneys General.

4. File a complaint with the Federal Trade Commission.
By sharing your identity theft complaint with the FTC, you will provide important information that can help law enforcement officials across the nation track down identity thieves and stop them. The FTC also can refer your complaint to other government agencies and companies for further action, as well as investigate companies for violations of laws that the FTC enforces. You can file a complaint online at www.consumer.gov/idtheft.

FOR MORE INFORMATION

The Federal Trade Commission enforces a number of credit laws and has free information about them: The Equal Credit Opportunity Act prohibits the denial of credit because of your sex, race, marital status, religion, national origin, age, or because you receive public assistance. The Fair Credit Reporting Act gives you the right to learn what information is being distributed about you by credit reporting companies.

The Truth in Lending Act requires lenders to give you written disclosures of the cost of credit and terms of repayment before you enter into a credit transaction.

The Fair Credit Billing Act establishes procedures for resolving billing errors on your credit card accounts.

The Fair Debt Collection Practices Act prohibits debt collectors from using unfair or deceptive practices to collect overdue bills that your creditor has forwarded for collection. The FTC works for the consumer to prevent fraudulent, deceptive, and unfair business practices in the marketplace and to provide information to help consumers spot, stop, and avoid them. To file a complaint or to get free information on consumer issues, visit ftc.gov or call criminal law enforcement agencies in the U.S. and abroad.

BUILDING WEALTH

The information I am presenting here may sound simple or easy, but the simplicity or ease is what a prospective millionaire needs to guide him or her to securing a bright financial future. Brush your negative attitudes aside. Resolve to manage the presence of obstacles on your road to riches: fear, cynicism, laziness, arrogance, procrastination, thoughtlessness, inaction, and other bad habits. Rich folks are creative, positive, thoughtful, and action-oriented. You can be like them by learning the basic lessons of personal finance and joining the Millionaire Club and attending the Millionaire iUniversity. Please, begin applying yourself to this introduction of wealth building. Choose to be rich; flock with people who are serious about getting rich. Birds of the same feather flock together. Let the club program your mind for a lifetime of riches.

INTRODUCTION TO BUILDING WEALTH

Building wealth is the building block of a beginner's guide to securing your financial future. It offers introductory guidance to individuals and families seeking help to develop a plan for building personal wealth. While a comprehensive discussion of accounting, finance and investment options is beyond the scope of my guidebook, however, *The Miraculous Millionaire* presents an overview of personal wealth-building strategies for a neophyte like you. For more detailed information and assistance, please consult the resource guide at the back of the book in the section titled Millionaire iUniversity.

For additional copies of this guidebook, visit the web site of Amazon.com. A workbook and an animated video version of this guide have been developed for individuals to use at their home computer or for multiple users in classrooms and computer laboratories to learn the following: buying a home, saving for retirement or for children's education, or even effectively managing the family budget.

You will be happy to have mastered skills you had thought before required more financial sophistication than ever; you will become a financially literate consumer who makes the financial marketplace work better; you will become a better-informed citizen as well. As far as I am concerned, the definition of wealth is being able to put my children through college; wealth means having enough money to buy a house; wealth means buying my freedom from wage slavery; wealth means securing savings that are adequate for me to live a happy and stress-free retirement.

I am challenging you today to take the knowledge in this chapter and start building wealth. I believe in the American Dream; I also want you to believe in the dream of your fathers and forefathers. I want you to believe in your mind that you can create personal wealth. It is all a mind's game. Think about it seriously. If your mind can conceive it, and your heart can believe it, I know you can achieve it. Start planning on building wealth today. Conceive of a wealth plan; believe in a your wealth plan; achieve your wealth plan.

YES YOU CAN! It is possible for you to meet your financial goals. By choosing to budget, save and invest, you can pay off debt, send your child to college, buy a comfortable home, start a business, save for retirement, and put money away for a rainy day. Through budgeting, saving and investing, and by limiting the amount of debt you incur, all these goals are within your reach.

Some people consider themselves wealthy because they live in a very expensive house and travel around the globe. Others believe they are wealthy simply because they are able to pay their bills on time. What we are talking about here is financial wealth and what it means to you. Stop reading the book for a moment. I want you to pick up a pen and a sheaf of papers. Free write your thoughts. In the following space below, I want you to write your definition of wealth:

1.

2.

3.

Now that you have defined what wealth means to you, how do you acquire it? Building wealth requires having the right information, planning, and making good choices. This guidebook provides you with only basic information and a systematic approach to building wealth. It is based on time-honored principles of the dead-sea scrolls you probably have heard many times before: budget to save; save and invest; control debt; and protect the wealth you accumulate.

DEFINING WEALTH

In personal finance, the market value of a home is an asset; the mortgage is a liability. Let us say your house is worth $120,000, but your mortgage is $80,000. That means your equity in the home is $40,000. Equity contributes to your net worth.

WEALTH CREATION

Please, learn the coded language of personal finance; that is the language of millionaires and billionaires. You want to create personal wealth, right? So does Billy. Billy is 35 and works for a manufacturing company in Harrisburg, Pennsylvania. He looked at his finances and realized that at the rate he was going, there would not be enough money to meet his family's financial goals. So he chose to embark on a personal wealth-creation strategy. His first major step was to pick up a copy of this guidebook at Barnes and Noble for guidance. Billy began by learning the language of wealth creation. The first lesson was to understand the meaning of assets, liabilities, and net worth. They make up this very important formula or accountant's secret of finance:

Assets =Liabilities + Net Worth (Owner's equity)
Assets − Liabilities = Net Worth

If you dream about riches, you must learn to do what the wealthy folks do; they acquire appreciating assets, but not depreciating ones, except possessions such as real estate that they can leverage. A wealth-creating asset is a possession that generally increases in value or provides a return, such as:
•Cash-value life insurance
• A savings account.
• A retirement plan.
• Stocks and bonds.
• A house.

Some possessions, like your car, big-screen television, boat and clothes, are assets, but they are not wealth-creating assets because they do not earn money or rise in value. A new car drops in value the second it is driven off the lot. Your car is a tool that takes you to work, but it is not a wealth-creating asset. A liability, also called debt, is money you owe, such as:

• A home mortgage.
• Credit card balances.
• A car loan.
• Hospital and other medical bills.
• Student loans.

Net worth is the difference between your assets, what you own, and your liabilities, what you owe. Your net worth is your wealth.

Billy

Accumulating wealth, as distinct from just making a big income, is the key to your financial independence. It gives you control over assets, power to shape the corporate and political landscape, and the ability to ensure a prosperous future for your children and their heirs. For instnce, to calculate how much he is worth, Billy used the following formula: Assets – Liabilities = Net Worth. He made a balance sheet listing all his assets and all his liabilities. He listed his wealth-building assets first. Billy discovered his net worth is $21,600.

MATHEMATICS PROBLEM

Using Billy's balance sheet as an example, please, figure your own net worth. Be sure to add any assets and liabilities you have that are not listed here. Remember that net worth is your wealth. Are you worth as much as you want to be?

Billy's Balance Sheet

Wealth-building assets	Amount
Cash	$ 1,500
Savings account	1,000
Stocks, bonds and other investments	5,000
401 (k) retirement plan /IRA	25,000
Market value of home	0
Other assets	
Market value of car	14,000
Total assets	$ 46,500

Your Balance Sheet

Wealth-building assets Amount
Cash
Savings account
Stocks, bonds and other investments
401 (k) retirement plan /IRA
Market value of home
Other assets
Market value of car
Total assets

Liabilities Amount
Home mortgage
Home equity loan
Car loan balance
Credit card balances
Student loan
Child support
Miscellaneous liabilities

Total liabilities
Net worth

EXAMPLES OF BUDGETING

Short-Term Example:

1. In one year, save $500 for my emergency fund.
2. In three years, save $5,000 for a down payment on a house.

Long-Term Example:

1. In eight years, save $15,000 to help my child with college. If you make a good income each year and spend it all, you are not getting wealthier. You are just living high.

Budget to Save

What would you like your net worth to be 5 years from now? $
What would you like your net worth to be 10 years from now? $
Most people who have built wealth did not do so overnight. They received wealthy by setting goals and striving to reach them. Billy set two short-term goals: (1) to save $3,000 a year for three years to have $9,000 for a down payment on a house, and (2) to pay off his $3,000 credit card debt within two years.

Billy also set two long-term goals: (1) to save and invest enough to have $25,000 in 15 years for his children's college education, and (2) to have $5,000 a month to live on when he retires in 30 years.

A personal wealth-creation strategy is based on specific goals. In preparing your goals:
• Be realistic.
• Establish time frames.
• Devise a plan.
• Be flexible; goals can change

In the space provided below, list your top goals.

My short-term goals are:

1.
2.
3.

My long-term goals are:

1.

2.

3.

Now you, like Billy, can choose how to meet those goals. This is where budgeting to save comes into play.

SET YOUR FINANCIAL GOALS

When it comes to finances, people generally fall into the following groups: planners, strugglers, deniers, and impulsives. Where do you fit in? Planners control their financial affairs. They budget to save. Strugglers have trouble keeping their heads above rough financial waters. They find it difficult to budget to save. Deniers refuse to see that they are in financial trouble. So they do not see a need to budget to save. Impulsives seek immediate gratification. They spend today and let tomorrow take care of itself. They could not care less about budgeting to save.

Knowing what kind of financial manager you are will help determine what changes to make. To maximize your wealth-creating ability, you want to be a planner, like Penny. Penny is a single parent with one child. "I have to budget to live on my modest income. I have a little notebook I use to track where every dime goes. Saving is very important to me. When my son was born, I started investing every month in a mutual fund for his college education. I am proud to say that I control my future. I have bought my own home and provided for my son, and I have never bounced a check. You must have common sense regarding money!"

Lazy, by contrast, is an impulsive type. Lazy has a good job; she makes good money; she lives a pretty comfortable life, but her bank statement tells a different story. She has no savings or investments. She owns no property and has no plans for retirement. Plus, she has a lot of credit card debt, lives from paycheck to paycheck and does not budget. You can choose to be like Lazy, or you can follow Penny's road to wealth-creation by learning to budget and save.

A budget allows you to:
• Understand where your money goes.
• Ensure you do not spend more than you make.
• Find uses for your money that will increase your wealth.

To develop a budget, you need to:
• Calculate your monthly income.
• Track your daily expenses.
• Determine how much you spend on monthly bills.

DEVELOP A BUDGET AND LIVE BY IT

Track your day-to-day spending. One day, Lazy, the impulsive, realized that to create wealth she had to become more like Penny and plan her financial future. To start, Lazy analyzed her finances to see how much money she made and how she was spending it. She set a goal to save $125 a month to put toward her wealth-creation goals. First, she calculated her income. Then she added up her monthly bills.

She also carried a little notebook in her purse for jotting down her daily spending, whether by cash or debit card, check or credit card. Here is a page from her notebook below.

A Listing of Lazy's Day-to-Day Spending

1/2 Breakfast, Get-N-Go $ 3.56
1/2 Coffee .90
1/2 Lunch $ 6.75
1/2 Soft drink 1.25
1/2 Gas for car 46.00
1/2 Drinks with friends 10.00
1/2 Groceries 50.00
1/2 Dinner 10.00
1/2 Newspaper .50
1/3 Bacon and eggs, Moonlight Diner 4.95
1/3 Newspaper .50
1/3 Coffee .90
1/3 Lunch with coworkers 5.72
1/3 Dinner 15.00
1/3 Dress 45.00
1/3 Soft drink 1.25
1/3 Trip to the movies 15.00
1/4 Breakfast 3.50
1/4 Coffee .90
1/4 Lunch 5.75
1/4 Cookies 1.25
1/4 Newspaper .50
1/4 Birthday present 15.00
1/4 Dinner 6.77
1/5 Breakfast 3.25
1/5 Coffee .90
1/5 Soft drink 1.25
1/5 Newspaper .90
1/5 Magazine 3.95
1/6 Breakfast 3.25
1/6 Coffee .90
1/6 Newspaper .50

There is more to personal finance than the drudgery of debts and budgets.

1/6 Lunch 4.50
1/6 Cookies 1.25
1/6 Jacket 50.00
1/6 Video rental 3.95

You can study your own spending habits by using this sheet of Lazy's to track daily expenses. Be sure to include items purchased with credit cards, as well as those purchased with cash, debit card, or check.

GET A HANDLE ON INCOME AND EXPENSES

Finally, Lazy decided to learn from her financial mistakes. She used the information from tracking her day-to-day expenses to develop a monthly budget. When Lazy reviewed her budget, she realized she was spending more than she earned. Lazy knew if she were ever going to save $125 a month, she had to cut her expenses, earn more money, or both. She worked overtime at her company, which increased her take-home pay. She bought fewer clothes, discontinued premium cable TELEVISION channels, carpooled to work to cut gas consumption and reduced her spending on eating out and entertainment. Tracking her expenses paid off. Lazy successfully developed a budget that enables her to save $125 each month.

Using Lazy's budget as an example, track your income and expenses. Identify changes you can make to increase your income or decrease your expenses, and develop a new budget that includes more savings. Be sure to make reasonable budget changes that you can live with month to month.

To help you maintain the discipline to save:
• Save every month.
• Have savings automatically deducted from your paycheck or checking account.
• Base your budget on what is left. In other words, get on automatic pilot and stay there.
How much do you currently save each month? $
How much are you going to save each month? $

SAVE AND INVEST

You have now successfully budgeted to save. The next step is saving and investing. You have budgeted and identified an amount to save monthly. Where are you going to put your savings? By investing, you put the money you save to work making more money and increasing your wealth. An investment is anything you acquire for future income or benefit. Investments increase by generating income (interest or dividends) or by growing (appreciating) in value. Income earned from your investments and any appreciation in the value of your investments increase your wealth.

There is an art to choosing ways to invest your savings. Good investments will make money; bad investments will cost money. Do your homework.

Gather as much information as you can. Seek advice from personnel at your bank or other trained financial experts. Read newspapers, magazines and other publications. Identify credible information sources on the Internet. Join an investment club. Check out the information resources listed in the resource guide at the back of this publication. Join my financial education. Attend millionaire iuniversity.

COMPOUNDING

Compound interest helps you build wealth faster. Interest is paid on previously earned interest as well as on the original deposit or investment. For example, $5,000 deposited in a bank at 6 percent interest for a year earns $308 if the interest is compounded monthly. In just 5 years, the $5,000 will grow to $6,744. Let us see how interest compounds on Lazy's savings. Assume that Lazy saves $125 a month for 30 years and the interest on her savings is compounded monthly. A compounding table or chart can illustrate the working of the magic of compounding. It can show how compound interest at various rates would increase Lazy's savings compared with simply putting the money in a shoebox. This is compound interest that you earn. And as you can see from Lazy's investment, compounding has a greater effect after the investment and interest have increased over a longer period.

There is a flip side to compound interest. That is compound interest you are charged. This compound interest is charged for purchases on your credit card "Take Control of Debt!" GET GUIDANCE TAKE ADVANTAGE OF COMPOUND INTEREST. Take the power of compound interest seriously—and then save.

SAVING AND INVESTING

When you are saving and investing, the amount of expected return is based on the amount of risk you take with your money. Generally, the higher the risk of losing money, the higher the expected return.

For less risk, an investor will expect a smaller return. For example, a savings account at a financial institution is fully insured by the Federal Deposit Insurance Corp. up to $250,000. The return—or interest paid on your savings—will generally be less than the expected return on other types of investments. On the other hand, an investment in a stock or bond is not insured. The money you invest may be lost or the value reduced if the investment does not perform as expected. After deciding how much risk you are able to take, you can use the investment pyramid to help balance your savings and investments. You should move up the pyramid only after you have built a strong foundation.

UNDERSTAND THE RISK–EXPECTED RETURN RELATIONSHIP HOW MUCH RISK DO YOU WANT TO TAKE?

Here are some things to think about when determining the amount of risk that best suits you. Financial goals. How much money do you want to accumulate over a certain period of time?

Your investment decisions should reflect your wealth-creation goals. What is your time horizon? How long can you leave your money invested? If you will need your money in one year, you may want to take less risk than you would if you will not need your money for 20 years. Financial risk tolerance is the key determinant of your investing. Are you in a financial position to invest in riskier alternatives? You should take less risk if you cannot afford to lose your investment or have its value fall.

INFLATION RISK

This reflects savings' and investments' sensitivity to the inflation rate. For example, while some investments such as a savings account have no risk of default, there is the risk that inflation will rise above the interest rate on the account. If the account earns 5 percent interest, inflation must remain lower than 5 percent a year for you to realize a profit.

TOOLS FOR SAVING

The simplest way to begin earning money on your savings is to open a savings account at a financial institution. You can take advantage of compound interest, with no risk. Financial institutions offer a variety of savings accounts, each of which pays a different interest rate. The next page describes the different accounts. Find the best one for your situation and compare interest rates and fees. You can choose to use these typical accounts to save for the near future or for years down the road.

Once you have a good savings foundation, you may want to diversify your assets among different types of investments. Diversification can help smooth out potential ups and downs of your investment returns. Investing is not a get-rich-quick scheme. Smart investors take a long-term view, putting money into investments regularly and keeping it invested for 5, 10, 15, 20 or more years.

BONDS—LENDING YOUR MONEY

Let us talk about bonds for a minute. Although the bond market is very large comparatively, stocks draw more attention from the mass media. For most American finance professionals and consumers, bonds do not seem to be a very sexy investing vehicle. When you buy bonds, you are lending money to a federal or state agency, municipality or other issuer, such as a corporation. A bond is like an IOU: I owe you. The issuer promises to pay a stated rate of interest during the life of the bond and repay the entire face value when the bond comes due or reaches maturity. The interest a bond pays is based primarily on the credit quality of the issuer and current interest rates. Firms like Moody's Investor Service and Standard & Poor's rate bonds. With corporate bonds, the company's bond rating is dependent on the status of the corporation and prevailing rates. Indeed, bond investing is very complicated. My recommendation is for you to rely on low-load mutual funds that specialize on bonds-bond funds. Additionally, on my web site, http://www.millionaireiuniversity.com, I have many articles that can educate you on the working of bonds. I also sponsor workshops on bond investing. Make use of all these resources.

TOOLS FOR INVESTING

BONDS

The rating for municipal bonds is based on the creditworthiness of the governmental or other public entity that issues it. Issuers with the greatest likelihood of paying back the money have the highest ratings, and their bonds will pay an investor a lower interest rate. Remember, the lower the risk, the lower the expected return. A bond may be sold at face value (called par) or at a premium or discount. For example, when prevailing interest rates are lower than the bond's stated rate, the selling price of the bond rises above its face value. It is sold at a premium. Conversely, when prevailing interest rates are higher than the bond's stated rate, the selling price of the bond is discounted below face value.

When bonds are purchased, they may be held to maturity or traded. Savings bonds. U.S. savings bonds are government-issued and government-backed. There are different types of savings bonds, each with slightly different features and advantages.
Series I bonds are indexed for inflation. The earnings rate on this type of bond combines a fixed rate of return with the annualized rate of inflation. Savings bonds can be purchased in denominations ranging from $50 to $10,000.

INDIVIDUAL DEVELOPMENT ACCOUNTS

In some communities, people whose income is below a certain level can open an individual development account (IDA) as part of a money-management program organized by a local nonprofit organization. IDAs are generally opened at a local bank. Deposits made by the IDA account holder are often matched by deposits from a foundation, government agency or other organization. IDAs can be used for buying a first home, paying for education or job training, or starting a small business. Training programs on budgeting, saving and managing credit are frequently part of IDA programs. Find out about IDAs by calling CFED at (202) 408-9788, or visit its web site at www.idanetwork.org.

TYPES OF SAVINGS ACCOUNTS IN GENERAL

• Access your money at any time.
• Earn interest.
• Move money easily from one account to another.
• Savings insured by the FDIC up to $250,000.
.Money market account
• Earn interest.
• Pay no fees if you maintain a minimum balance.
• May offer check-writing services.
• Savings insured by the FDIC up to $250,000.
.Certificate of deposit (CD)
• Earn interest during the term (three months, six months, etc.).
• Must leave the deposit in the account for the entire term to avoid an early withdrawal

penalty.
• Receive the principal and interest at the end of the term.
• Savings insured by the FDIC up to $250,000.

TREASURY BONDS, BILLS AND NOTES

The bonds the U.S. Treasury issues are sold to pay for an array of government activities and are backed by the full faith and credit of the federal government. Treasury bonds are securities with terms of more than 10 years. Interest is paid semiannually. The U.S. government also issues securities known as Treasury bills and notes. Treasury bills are short-term securities with maturities of three months, six months or one year. They are sold at a discount from their face value, and the difference between the cost and what you are paid at maturity is the interest you earn.

Treasury notes are interest-bearing securities with maturities ranging from two to ten years. Interest payments are made every six months. Treasury Inflation Protected Securities (TIPS) offer investors a chance to buy a security that keeps pace with inflation. Interest is paid on the inflation-adjusted principal. Bonds, bills and notes are sold in increments of $1,000. These securities, along with U.S. savings bonds, can be purchased directly from the Treasury through TreasuryDirect at http://www.treasurydirect.gov.

REMEMBER A GOOD RULE OF THUMB: The Rule of 72

At this juncture, it is appropriate to remember a good rule of thumb, The Rule of 72, which can help you estimate how your investment will grow over time. Simply divide the number 72 by your investment's expected rate of return to find out approximately how many years it will take for your investment to double in value. Example: Invest $5,000 today at 8 percent interest. divide 72 by 8 and you get 9. Your investment will double every nine years. In nine years, your $5,000 investment will be worth about $10,000, in 18 years about $20,000 and in 27 years, $40,000. The Rule of 72 also works if you want to find out the rate of return you need to make your money double. For example, if you have some money to invest and you want it to double in 10 years, what rate of return would you need? Divide 72 by 10 and you get 7.2. Your money will double in 10 years if your average rate of return is 7.2 percent.

Some government-issued bonds offer special tax advantages. There is no state or local income tax on the interest earned from Treasury and savings bonds. And in most cases, interest earned from municipal bonds is exempt from federal and state income tax. Typically, higher income investors buy these bonds for their tax benefits.

STOCKS—OWNING PART OF A COMPANY

When you buy stock, you become a part owner of the company and are known as a stockholder, or shareholder. Stockholders can make money in two ways—receiving dividend payments and selling stock that has appreciated.

A dividend is an income distribution by a corporation to its shareholders, usually made quarterly. Stock appreciation is an increase in the value of stock in the company, generally based on its ability to make money and pay a dividend.

However, if the company does not perform as expected, the stock's value may fall. There is no guarantee you will make money as a stockholder. In purchasing shares of stock, you take a risk on the company making a profit and paying a dividend or seeing the value of its stock rise. Before investing in a company, learn about its past financial performance, management, products and how the stock has been valued in the past. Learn what the experts say about the company and the relationship of its financial performance and stock price. Successful investors are well informed. Particularly, you need to know precisely when to buy or sell a security. When the big boys on Wall Street are trading a stock, you need to either buy or sell it in tandem. I have invented a winning system to trade stocks known as SRA, statistically rational analysis. Review step 9 of the book.

MUTUAL FUNDS—INVESTING IN MANY COMPANIES

Mutual funds are established to invest many people's money in many firms. When you buy mutual fund shares, you become a shareholder of a fund that has invested in many other companies. By diversifying, a mutual fund spreads risk across many companies rather than relying on just one to perform well. Mutual funds have varying degrees of risk. They also have costs associated with owning them, such as management fees, that will vary depending on the type of investments the fund makes. Before investing in a mutual fund, learn about its past performance, the companies it invests in, how it is managed and the fees investors are charged. Learn what the experts say about the fund and its competitors.

Stocks, bonds and mutual funds can be purchased through a full-service broker if you need investment advice, from a discount broker, or even directly from some companies and mutual funds. Remember, when investing in these products:

• Find good information to help you make informed decisions.
• Make sure you know and understand all the costs associated with buying, selling and managing your investments.
• Beware of investments that seem too good to be true; they probably are.

RETIREMENT

Have you ever thought about how much money you will need when you retire? Will you save enough today to meet your future needs at prices higher than today's due to inflation? Many people do not save enough for retirement. Use the following chart to calculate how much you need to invest today to achieve your retirement goal. For example, suppose you are 20 years old and would like to have $1 million when you retire at age 65. If you can invest $13,719 today, it will grow to $1 million over the next 45 years if it earns a constant 10 percent return, compounded annually. You never have to add another dime to your initial investment. How old are you? How much do you want saved by retirement?

INDIVIDUAL RETIREMENT ACCOUNTS

It is not too early for you to begin investing for retirement. Invest today so that you can meet your retirement goals at age 65. An individual retirement account (IRA) lets you build wealth and retirement security. The money you invest in an IRA grows tax-free until you retire and are ready to withdraw it. You can open an IRA at a bank, brokerage firm, mutual fund or insurance company. IRAs are subject to certain income limitations and other requirements you will need to learn more about, but here is an overview of what they offer, with the maximum tax-free annual contributions as of 2010.

You can contribute up to $5,000 a year to a traditional IRA, as long as you earn $5,000 a year or more. A married couple with only one person working outside the home may contribute a combined total of $10,000 to an IRA and a spousal IRA. Individuals 50 years of age or older may make an additional "catch-up" contribution of $1,000 a year, for a total annual contribution of $6,000. Money invested in an IRA is deductible from current-year taxes if you are not covered by a retirement plan where you work and your income is below a certain limit.

You do not pay taxes on the money in a traditional IRA until it is withdrawn. All withdrawals are taxable, and there generally are penalties on money withdrawn before age 59½. However, you can make certain withdrawals without penalty, such as to pay for higher education, to purchase your first home, to cover certain unreimbursed medical expenses or to pay medical insurance premiums if you are out of work.

A Roth IRA is funded by after-tax earnings; you do not deduct the money you pay in from your current income. However, after age 59½ you can withdraw the principal and any interest or appreciated value tax-free from 401(K) Plans. Many companies offer a 401(K) plan for employees' retirement. Participants authorize a certain percentage of their before-tax salary to be deducted from their paycheck and put into a 401(K). Many times, 401(K) funds are professionally managed and employees have a choice of investments that vary in risk. Employees are responsible for learning about the investment choices offered. By putting a percentage of your salary into a 401(K), you reduce the amount of pay subject to federal and state income tax. Tax-deferred contributions and earnings make up the best one-two punch in investing. In addition, your employer may match a portion of every dollar you invest in the 401(K), up to a certain percentage or dollar amount. Assume an annual investment of $3,000 and an 8 percent rate of return. Invest in an IRA: the sooner you start, the better for you.

As long as the money remains in your 401(K), it is tax-deferred. Withdrawals for any purpose are taxable, and withdrawals before age 59½ are subject to a penalty. Take full advantage of the retirement savings programs your company offers—and understand thoroughly how they work. They are great ways to build wealth. The human resource or payroll department of your employer can give you specific information about IRAs, individual retirement accounts. On my web site, millionaireiuniversity.com, I have invaluable information on IRAs. Please, use it for your own betterment. On the IRS' web site, irs.gov, you can find more information on the use of individual retirement accounts. Read IRS Publication 590.

QUALIFIED PLANS

If you are self-employed, do not worry. There is a retirement plan for you. A qualified plan, formerly referred to as a Keogh plan, is a tax-deferred plan designed to help self-employed workers save for retirement.

The most attractive feature of a qualified plan is the high maximum contribution—up to $49,000 annually. The contributions and investment earnings grow tax-free until they are withdrawn, when they are taxed as ordinary income. Withdrawals before age 59½ are subject to a penalty. Check the IRS web site—www.irs.gov—for current information on tax-deferred investments.

INVESTING IN YOUR HOUSE

Do you remember the poor guy called Billy? I am reminding you of the guy who started reading this guidebook to create wealth? Practicing what he read, Billy reduced his debt, increased his savings and is now ready to buy a house. He has a sizable down payment saved, so right from the beginning he will have equity in his home. Equity, in this case, is the difference between the market value of the house and the balance on Billy's mortgage. As Billy pays his mortgage, he increases his equity. Plus, over time, his house may rise in value—giving him more money if he chooses to sell it. Knowing that the more equity he has in his house, the wealthier he will be, Billy takes a 15-year mortgage rather than the more traditional 30-year mortgage. This will enable him to own his house in 15 years. Of course, Billy will make higher monthly payments on his mortgage than he would have, but he will build equity quicker and ultimately pay less interest. By making higher monthly payments, Billy not only will own his house outright in 15 years, but he will save $106,119 in interest payments. Making higher monthly payments, of course, means budgeting. Billy chose to budget extra money each month out of his paycheck, and make wise spending choices, so he can do just that.

START YOUR OWN BUSINESS

You can also start and invest in your own business as part of a wealth-creation plan. This process requires effort, planning, specialized know-how, savings and an entrepreneurial spirit. Starting a small business can be risky, but it is one of the most significant ways individuals have to create personal wealth. Dudley had a dream, so he wanted to own a business. He worked for a printing company for 10 years and learned every aspect of the business. He and his wife saved every month until they had a sizable nest egg. When they felt the timing was right, they bought a printing press and computer equipment and set up shop in an old warehouse. Dudley's wife kept her job so they would have steady income and benefits while the business got off the ground. For the next five years, Dudley worked long hours and put all the income back into the business to help it grow. He gave his customers good service, attracted more customers and paid close attention to his expenses.

By the sixth year, the business was profitable and Dudley and his wife were well on the way to owning a successful, ongoing enterprise that will increase their personal wealth.

There is more to personal finance than the drudgery of debts and budgets.

None of this would have been possible without budgeting and saving. Dudley was able to use the couple's savings to invest in his talents and entrepreneurial spirit.

OTHER INVESTMENT ALTERNATIVES

You also can invest in other things that may not earn a dividend or interest but may rise in value over time, such as land, rare coins, antiques, and art. If you are knowledgeable about these types of investments, they might be the right choice for you. Now it is time to plan your investment strategy. List the investment options you are going to learn more about and weigh them against your wealth-creation goals, time frame, and risk tolerance:

1.

2.

3.

4.

5.

CONTROLLING DEBT

We have seen that by budgeting to save, saving and investing, wealth can be created. But what if debt limits your ability to save and invest? Next we are discussing the idea of controlling debt. Dudley took control of his debt. Do you still remember the definition of net worth (wealth)?

Assets – Liabilities = Net Worth

Liabilities are your debts. Debts reduce your net worth. Plus, the interest you pay on debt, including credit card debt, is money that cannot be saved or invested—it is just gone. Debt is a tool to be used wisely for such things as buying a house. If not used wisely, debt can easily get out of hand. For example, putting day-to-day expenses, like groceries or utility bills, on a credit card and not paying off the balance monthly can lead to debt overload. Lots of people are mired in debt. In some cases, they could not control the causes of their debt. However, in some instances they could have. Many people get into serious debt because they:

• Experienced financial stresses caused by unemployment, medical bills, or divorce.
• Could not control spending, did not plan for the future, and did not save money.
• Lacked knowledge of financial and credit matters.

TIPS FOR CONTROLLING DEBT

• Develop a budget and stick to it.

• Save money so you are prepared for unforeseen circumstances. You should have at least three to six months of living expenses stashed in your rainy day savings account, because as the poet Henry Wadsworth Longfellow put it, "Into each life some rain must fall." I am a fine poet, and I encourage you to read the full version of Longfellow *The Rainy Day* online.
• When faced with a choice of financing a purchase, it may be a better financial decision to choose a less expensive model of the same product and save or invest the difference.
• Pay off credit card balances monthly.
• If you must borrow, learn everything about the loan, including interest rate, fees, and penalties for late payments or early repayment. Ask many questions: What type people get into trouble with debt I owe? Is this a good loan? What are the terms of the loan?

When you take out a loan, you repay the principal, which is the amount borrowed, plus interest, the amount charged for lending you the money. Do you remember the discussion about earning compound interest earlier in this chapter? The interest on your monthly balance is a good example of compound interest that you pay. The interest is added to your bill, and the next month interest is charged on that amount and on the outstanding balance. The bottom line on interest is that those who know about interest earn it; those who do not, pay it. Planners, like Penny, rarely use credit cards. When they do, they pay off their balances every month. When a credit card balance is not paid off monthly, it means paying interest—often twenty percent or more a year—on everything purchased. So think of credit card debt as a high-interest loan.

CREDIT CARD DEBT

Debt is a sickness or sin. I hate debt. I hate credit card debt more. Indeed, I stopped using credit cards many years ago. I use two debit cards daily. Do you need to reduce your credit card debt? Here are some suggestions for you to weigh and consider:

• Pay cash for most of your purchases.
• Set a monthly limit on charging, and keep a written record so you do not exceed that amount. (Do you remember your daily expense sheet? Use it to keep track of your expenses.)
• Limit the number of credit cards you have. Cut up all but one of your cards. Stash that one out of sight, and use it only in emergencies.
• Choose the credit card with the lowest interest rate and no (or very low) annual fee. But beware of low introductory interest rates offered by mail. These rates often skyrocket after the first few months.
• Do not apply for credit cards to get a free gift or a discount on a purchase.
• Steer clear of blank checks that financial services companies send you. These checks are cash advances that may carry a higher interest rate than typical charges.
• Pay bills on time to avoid late charges or increased interest rates. Speaking of interest, avoid credit card debt. Do you want me to recite the tale of two spenders and the big-screen television?

Do you remember Penny, the planner? She saved up for the "extras." When she had enough money in her savings account, she bought a big-screen TELEVISION for $1,500. She paid cash. Her friend Tim is an impulsive spender. He seeks immediate gratification using his credit cards, not realizing how much extra it costs.

There is more to personal finance than the drudgery of debts and budgets.

Tim bought the same TELEVISION for $1,500 but financed it on a store credit card with an annual interest rate of 22 percent. At $50 a month, it took him almost four years to pay off the balance. While Penny paid only $1,500 for her big-screen television, Tim paid $2,200—the cost of the television plus interest. Tim not only paid an extra $700, he lost the opportunity to invest the $700 in building his wealth.

People can get deep in debt when they take out a loan against their paycheck. They write a post-dated check in exchange for money. When they get paid again, they repay the loan, thus the name payday loan. These loans generally come with very high, double-digit interest rates. Borrowers who cannot repay the money are charged additional fees for an extension, which puts them even deeper in debt. Borrowers can continue to pay fees to extend the loan's due date indefinitely, only to find they are getting deeper in debt because of the steep interest payments and fees. Predatory lenders often target seniors and low-income people they contact by phone, mail, or in person. After her husband died, 73-year-old Pauline received plenty of solicitations from finance companies. She was struggling to make ends meet on her fixed income. To pay off her bills, she took out a $5,000 home equity loan that carried a high interest rate and excessive fees. Soon she found she was even deeper in debt, so she refinanced the loan once, then again, and again, paying fees each time. Pauline's children discovered her situation and paid off the loan.

The lessons learned here are the following:

• Do not borrow from Peter to pay Paul.
• Never respond to a solicitation that makes borrowing sound easy and cheap.
• Always read the fine print on any loan application.
• Seek assistance from family members, local credit counseling services or others to make sure a loan is right for you.

Those who have used credit will have a credit report that shows everything about their payment history, including late payments. The information in your credit report is used to create your credit score. A credit score is a number generated by a statistical model that objectively predicts the likelihood that you will repay your debts on time. Banks, insurance companies, potential landlords and other lenders use credit scores. Credit scores range from under 500 to 800 and above and are determined by payment history, the amount of outstanding debt, length of your credit history, recent inquiries on your credit report and the types of credit in use. Factors not considered in a credit score include age, race or ethnicity, income, job, marital status, education, length of time at your current address, and whether you own or rent your home. BEWARE the peril of payday loan and predatory lenders. Know what creditors say about you, Pauline.

CREDIT REPORT

Have you ever seen your credit report? What is on your credit report? Consumers have the right to receive annually a free copy of their credit report from each of the three major credit reporting companies:

Equifax: 1-800-685-1111; www.equifax.com

Experian: 1-800-397-3742; www.experian.com

Trans Union:1-800-888-4213; www.transunion.com

The three nationwide consumer credit reporting companies, listed above, have set up a toll-free telephone number and one central web site for ordering free reports: 1-877-322-8228; http// www.annualcreditreport.com. A credit report that includes late payments, delinquencies, or defaults will result in a low credit score and could mean not getting a loan or having to pay a much higher interest rate. The higher your score, the less risk you represent to the lender. Review your credit report at least once a year to make sure all information is accurate. If you find an error, the Fair Credit Reporting Act requires credit reporting companies and those reporting information to them to correct the mistake.

To start the process of fixing an error:

• Contact the credit reporting company online, by fax or certified letter, identifying the creditor you have a dispute with and the nature of the error.
• Send the credit reporting company verifiable information, such as canceled checks or receipts, supporting your complaint.
• The credit reporting company must investigate your complaint within 30 days and get back to you with its results.
• Contact the creditor if the credit reporting company investigation does not result in correction of the error. When you resolve the dispute, ask the creditor to send the credit reporting company a correction. If the issue remains unresolved, you have the right to explain in a statement that will go on your credit report.

For example, if you did not pay a car repair bill because the mechanic did not fix the problem, the unpaid bill may show up on your credit report, but so will your explanation. Every month, go back to your budget and plan carefully to ensure your bills are paid before their due dates. Penny, the planner, makes sure she pays her bills on time. Penny gets paid twice a month. She has her paycheck set up for direct deposit so she does not have to scramble to get to the bank on payday. With her first paycheck each month, she pays her mortgage (which she has set up on auto debit), cable TELEVISION and utility bills. Out of the second check, Penny makes her car payment (also on auto debit) and has a monthly deposit automatically made to her savings account. Penny has found that "autopilot" really simplifies budgeting and saving.

If you believe you are too deep in debt:

• Discuss your options with your creditors before you miss a payment.
• Seek expert help, such as Consumer Credit Counseling Services (CCCS), listed in your local telephone directory; you can also use the Google search engine to locate CCCS.
• Avoid "credit repair" companies that charge a fee. Many of these are scams. Keep your good name.

There is more to personal finance than the drudgery of debts and budgets.

WAYS OF BUILDING WEALTH

For the most part, building wealth involves the simple process of making wise financial decisions and taking quick action to implement these decisions. If you have good credit, for instance, you may want to take out a loan to purchase a house or to cover educational expenses—both are investments in the future. But regardless of how the money is spent, a loan is a liability, or debt, and decreases your wealth. So choose loans carefully. Shop and negotiate for the lowest interest rate. The interest you save can be invested to build wealth. Take a good look at the charts on my web site. In these examples, it is obvious that some banks charge the lowest interest rate over the term of a loan. What is not obvious is that your credit score may determine which interest rate you are offered. Use an online auto loan calculator to compare rates. You can save interest expense by increasing your monthly payments or choosing a shorter payment term on your loan.

Penny, the planner, knew her new car would cost more than the sticker price because she would have to pay interest on the loan from the bank. After checking her options, she chose a shorter payment term with higher payments. Penny budgeted enough money each month to make the higher payments. By doing this, she will reduce the amount of interest she ultimately pays. A financial chart would show how shorter terms with higher payments would affect the total amount and interest on Penny's $15,000 car loan. Avoid the trap of getting "upside down"— owing more on the car than it is worth when you sell or trade it in. Penny's car will be paid for in three years, and she plans on driving it for at least eight years. Once her car is paid for, she will continue to budget for the car payment but will invest the money to further build her wealth.

As you can see, a big part of building wealth is making wise choices about debt. You need to maximize assets and minimize liabilities to grow your net worth. In order to manage debt efficiently, you need to know how much money you have and develop strategies and tactics to control it. When Billy decided to reduce his $3,000 credit card debt, he analyzed his debt and developed a strategy. He listed the balance, interest rate, and monthly interest on each credit card.

He checked his credit score and shopped for the best rate on a new credit card. Then he transferred all his balances to that card. He destroyed the old credit cards and used the interest he saved to pay toward the principal balance. He used the new card only for emergencies. What is your credit card debt situation?

Using the chart below, do an analysis of your own credit card debts.

My strategy for reducing credit card debt includes:

1.

2.

3.

Just as you protect the security of your home with locks for your windows and doors, you should take steps to protect your identity. Secure your financial records, Social Security number and card, account numbers, and all passwords and PINs (personal identification numbers). A periodic check of your credit report can alert you if someone is illegally using credit products in your name. If you suspect unauthorized access, contact the three major credit reporting companies and place a fraud alert on your name and Social Security number.

Some Tips to Protect Your Identity:

• Shred or destroy your bank and credit card statements and all other private records before tossing them in the trash.
• Give out your Social Security number only when absolutely necessary, and never carry both your Social Security card and driver's license in your wallet.
• Pick up mail promptly from your mailbox, and never leave outgoing mail with paid bills in an unsecured mailbox.
• Do not give out personal information on the phone, through the mail or on the Internet unless you are sure you know whom you are dealing with. Take steps to control your debt. Guard your identity.

WEALTH-BUILDING RESOURCE GUIDE

The following resources can be used for you to learn more about building personal wealth. The list includes sources of information on financial literacy for adults and youth, budget and debt management, and consumer protection. This guide is not intended to be all-inclusive; there are many additional national, state and local resources that can provide additional information on building wealth for a more secure financial future.

REDEFINING WEALTH

Now that you have read this chapter of the guidebook and thought about the information it contains, how would you define wealth?
In the space provided below, write your definition. Then compare it with the definition you wrote back at the very beginning of the discussion on wealth creation. Has your definition of wealth changed? Reset your financial goals. Now, write your financial goals and compare them with your original goals. Keep these new goals with your definition of wealth. Periodically refer to your goals and measure your dynamic balance sheet:

Assets – Liabilities = Net Worth

Is your wealth-building program still on track? Using key wealth-building strategies, now, write your own strategies for building wealth. Keep in mind the following:

• Educate yourself about money.
• Establish financial goals.
• Create a budget.

There is more to personal finance than the drudgery of debts and budgets.

• Save each month, using automatic deduction.
• Take advantage of compound interest.
• Take advantage of tax-deferred investments.
• Research and learn about the best investments for you based on your financial goals, time horizon, and tolerance for risk.
• Control debt.
• Protect your wealth.

Start budgeting, saving, and investing today. Every day counts in building wealth.

WEALTH EXPERIMENT

Wealth Is:
My short-term goals are:

1.

2.

3.

My long-term goals are:

1.

2.

3.

My strategies for building wealth are:
1.

2.

3.

My strategies for controlling debt are:

1.

2.

3.

Clip the box and put it where you will see it often: inside your checkbook, on your computer monitor, where you pay your bills, on your bathroom mirror. Keep your definition of wealth and your goals firmly implanted in your mind and use your wealth-creating and debt-controlling strategies every day.

ELECTRONIC TRANSFER ACCOUNT

For a low-cost option for direct deposit, consider an ETA account. The Electronic Transfer Account, or ETASM, allows you to have your federal benefit, wage, salary and retirement payments deposited directly into your bank account—automatically, electronically and safely. Open a low-cost ETA at a federally insured bank, credit union, or savings and loan. Financial institutions offering the ETA have decals in their windows or lobbies identifying them as certified ETA providers. To find an ETA provider in your area, visit the ETA web site, www.eta-find.gov, or call toll-free, (888) 382-3311.

DIRECT DEPOSIT AND YOU

Many people who receive federal benefits checks, such as Social Security, Supplemental Security Income, Veterans Affairs or other government checks, enroll in direct deposit. Not only is it safer (no direct deposit has ever been stolen), it is far more convenient, and it gives you more control over your money than a mailed check. Call the toll-free Go Direct helpline at (800) 333-1795 or (800) 333-1792 en Español, or go to www.GoDirect.org for more information and other sign-up options. I hope that you have found this information on the building of wealth to be a useful educational tool. I invite you to visit our web site and send us your building wealth success stories: http://www.millionaireiuniversity.com or http://www.princeojong.com.

FIVE RITUALS OF WEALTH

If you have been reading so far, you should have realized the noble role of savings and debt-management in wealth building. Back in the late 1980s, when I developed the daily habit of saving $1.00, it did not take long before I started whittling the items on my budget to save even more money every pay period.

After attending money-making seminars and reading personal finance books like Tod Barnhart's book titled *The Five Rituals of Wealth*, I stumbled upon the powerful idea of 10% saving solution; the so-called 10% solution should work in the following manner: every pay period, as you pay tithes to God, so shall you pay tithes to yourself, too; allocate 10% of every pay check to your savings and investment program; I repeat: use your savings to invest for your future. Stop keeping up with the Joneses; stop acting rich; TELEVISION millionaires may act rich, but real millionaires are penny pinchers and cheapskates, so begin paying yourself, too. Be respectful of yourself and your money. If you do what needs to be done with money, you will attract money to you. You and your money must keep good company. Credit cards are never good company. Get out of debt. Respect yourself and your money by making every penny work for you.

There is more to personal finance than the drudgery of debts and budgets.

MONEY BEHAVIOR ADJUSTMENT

I love to practice the 10% saving solution concept. It is a good money habit to form or adopt. A book like mine can teach you financial literacy, but you need to change your money behavior to think and grow rich; success in personal finance is the talented ratio of 10/90: 10% financial literacy and 90% active or dynamic behavior adjustment; change your attitudes and actions toward spending money; change your spending lifestyle; act now! Your changed money-saving habit may be based on either an envelope system or piggybank concept. Use a stack of envelopes to distibute money for your budget, or put the money in your piggybank; that means each month, before you are tempted to spend money, commit to putting a good bit of it into a savings account.

You can write out a check to be deposited into your savings account, but it is much easier to arrange with your bank to automatically transfer a certain amount from your paycheck or your checking account into savings. And as you pay your bills, your mortgage and other obligations, take satisfaction in knowing that some of your hard-earned dollars are already saved for you! Start small. By consistently saving small amounts, even $25 out of every paycheck, your savings account will grow and you will be motivated to try to save more.

For your information, even the spare change you put away once a month into a bank savings account can add up faster than you think. Please, review your existing credit and debit accounts and comparison shop for the best deals. Look at what is being offered by your bank and a few competitors. The idea is to make sure the interest rates are competitive and that the fees and features are appropriate for how you use each account. For example, if your money is sitting in a low-rate checking or savings account, consider moving it to a higher-yielding account, perhaps a CD where the earnings can get an extra boost. If you are unimpressed by the paltry returns of CDs, explore the possibilities of tax-advantaged and guaranteed equity indexed investing. I can provide you some specifics; call (301) 593-4897 or (301) 593-4879.

TURN A DEBT PAYMENT INTO A DEPOSIT

Here is how it works: If you pay off a debt, such as the outstanding balance on a credit card, or if you make that last loan payment on your car, put that money to work as part of your savings. If you take the loan amount you had been paying and start putting it directly into savings each month, you will be earning interest, not paying interest, and there will be hardly any noticeable change in cash flow. So, please, save, do not spend, a financial windfall. If you receive a large sum, perhaps from an inheritance, an insurance payment, a tax refund or a bonus at work, please, deposit that money into a savings or investment account before you are tempted to spend it; do not give it to others for safekeeping; trust yourself more than you trust others. Find the little voice inside you; listen to what it has to say. Be open to receive all you are meant to receive. When you are in control of your money and have enough to be generous, money flows to you. Understand the ebb and flow of the money cycle. Money has natural cycles as it ebbs and flows through your life. If you choose to entrust your money to someone else, and you really do not know how money works, unscrupulous people can take advantage of you.

Further, you will discover the thrill that comes from wanting to deal with your money instead of just having to deal with it. Get in touch with your money; delight in spending it as you did as a child, but enjoy choosing not to spend it too; take pleasure in putting some away for later. My twelve-year old daughter, Lucielle, has already formed the habit of saving her money effectively. At home, we refer to her as the treasurer of the family.

Initially, she used to give her money to her mother for safekeeping. Now she trusts only her own self; she keeps some money in her piggy bank, but she saves the rest in a custodial or kiddie bank account. Alexia, her junior sister, is struggling to follow suit; she is learning the truth about money management gradually. Most of us need to spend our money differently. I am not advocating a draconian measure such as living like an Oxford cleric, or the drastic action like a large family getting by with only one car in the home. I am smart enough to know that unrealistic budget cuts, like yoyo diets, do not work and never will work.

Rather, decide to spend $25 to $30 less per month from fifteen or twenty of your spending categories; with each decision you make to spend less, you are gaining power over your money, and you will find creative ways to reduce your spending so you hardly notice. Rather than being dictated by a restriction, your actions are guided by the choices you make. This habit is the hardest step to financial freedom; you become honest with yourself about how you really stand. Spend less by putting your money away before you see it. Pay yourself. It is not what you make, but what you keep.

Time plays an essential role in building future wealth because the longer you contribute to your savings, the more money you will have and with time, the contributions you have already made, do more work for you. What makes time so powerful in wealth accumulation and acceleration is the mystery of compounding. As a wealth multiplier, compounding exhibits the time value of money; as a medium of exchange, money flows through our lives like water; sometimes the money is plentiful; at other times, the money is just a trickle. These transitions of money are exciting or scary, but they are all part of the natural cycles of money.

There are two important reactions to these cycles:

(1) You must take the long view of your financial future.
(2) You must believe that what is happening to you is positive, and let it be.

What is important, in this regard, is for you to understand the nature of money and take the right steps to make it work for you. Recognize true wealth. People cannot be measured by their net worth. Money does not make you financially free; only you can make yourself financially free. What you do with your money can make you financially free.

THE MYTH OF THE 10% SAVING SOLUTION

One of the first books that I ever read on the subject of personal finance was George Samuel Clason's *The Richest Man in Babylon*. If you have not read it, get it from my web sites or Amazon.com; my web sites are princeojong.com or millionaireiuniversity.com.

There is more to personal finance than the drudgery of debts and budgets.

Read it. It is a wonderful primer on the basics of personal finance and the value of the habit saving money consistently. The part of *The Richest Man in Babylon* that stood out for me, which has since been re-popularized by David Bach in his *Automatic Millionaire* series, is the notion of PAYING YOURSELF FIRST, BUT I HAVE MODIFIED IT TO REFLECT TRUE CHRISTIAN VALUES: Seek ye first the kingdom of God, and everything else shall be added unto you.

Pay God first by tithing, and pay yourself second. That is what I mean by the judicious application of the 10% saving solution. What about your God? Without God, nothing is possible. I do not like the notion of pay yourself first, a catchy phrase commonly used in personal finance and retirement planning literature that means to automatically route your specified savings contribution from each paycheck to yourself at the time it is received.

Because the savings contributions are automatically routed from each paycheck to your investment account, this process is said to be "paying yourself first;" in other words, paying yourself before you begin paying your monthly living expenses and making discretionary purchases. I have modified this financial formula by urging my readers and students to pay God first and pay themselves second. Ok?

The 10% SAVING SOLUTION

The 10% saving solution is simple system is touted by many personal finance professionals and retirement planners as a very effective way of ensuring that individuals continue to make their chosen savings contributions month after month. It removes the temptation to skip a given month's contribution and the risk that funds will be spent before the contribution has been made. Regular and consistent savings contributions go a long way toward building a long-term nest egg, and some financial professionals even go as far as calling the 10% saving solution the golden rule of personal finance. You pay your bills every month, maybe even through automatically scheduled payments. However, there might be someone you are forgetting to pay: yourself. Paying yourself second is an important step toward a more secure financial future. Pay your tithes before you apply the 10% saving solution or before you pay your mortgage, credit cards or any other monthly bills. The 10% saving solution starts with a direct deposit into your online or offline savings account, followed by transferring only what you need for monthly bills into your checking or bill-pay account. This saving habit will maximize your earned interest and grow your savings faster.

START WITH YOUR MONTHLY BILLS

When you sit down to pay your bills, the first check you write is to God's house, your church; the second check is to yourself. Is it too hard? Do you think what I am recommending sounds too difficult for you to do or accomplish? If so, then, you must answer this question for yourself: Is the pain of giving up your perks greater than the pain of being in financial bondage? If it is, you need to resign yourself to remaining in the same financial situation for the rest of your life. In fact, if you are prone to using debt as a means of upgrading your lifestyle, the problem will probably grow worse with time. Taking control of your finances creates a sense of empowerment that will reach into every area of your life.

The freedom that comes from knowing that you and your family will be provided for regardless of what may come up cannot be expressed in words. It is something you will experience for yourself when you make the decision that being financially independent and secure is more important than impressing your neighbors with material goods.

HONOR YOUR WORD

Most human beings are very honest, honorable, and trustworthy. To these individuals, their word is their bond; just by giving you their word, you can be assured that the promise they make to you will be kept. Once most people have given their word to someone, they are careful to keep their promise. This maritime brokers' motto does not apply when they make promises to themselves; they have no qualms, however, about lying to themselves. To be successful, you must honor your commitment to yourself. You cannot cut yourself any slack. Budget and pay your bills on time. As soon as you miss one payment, the odds are you will miss another, then another, until you stop saving altogether. The secret to success in this money-saving game is not so much the amount of money you are investing, but the persistence with which you are doing it. I recognize the fact that it is a difficult sacrifice; it is not easy. As human beings, we love pleasure, but we detest pain; saving money is painful, but spending money is pleasurable. The way I accomplish the 10% saving solution is to invoke the miraculous power of NLP, neuro-linguistic programming.

I begin by using NLP exercises to convince myself consciously and subconsciously to believe in the value of consistent saving to realize my financial goal. The power of belief will assist me in using my internal representations and physiology to establish enabling mental states that associate the drudgery of saving money with the positive pleasure of sexual arousal; in contrast, going forward I will associate impulsive spending with the negative emotions of pain and suffering. You have the power to condition the way you feel about something; the rich and famous folks became millionaires by learning the mystery of their environment and using that knowledge to master whatever event they experience in consciousness; instead of wallowing in failure and defeat, they rise above tragedy triumphantly like winning champions; indeed, they use their personal and unlimited power to acquire the specialized knowledge that gives them the flexibility to reshape their experiences with a new reality. As such, general knowledge is weakness, but specialized knowledge is power; the rich and famous folks are curious to know what is happening around them; as far as they are concerned, to know is to form a thought image about an experience; it is to establish an understanding of what is experienced in consciousness. A revision of the materials you learned about NLP might be in order.

NLP EXERCISE

Get as close to eight hours of sleep a night as you can. Schedule some do-not-disturb time with your family as often as possible. As you struggle with the formation of a saving habit, please, weigh every business opportunity against your change in quality of life. Ask for what you are worth, so you can work the right number of hours for respectable pay. Work your core projects first over all external projects. Weigh the negatives and positives of any trip you might be asked to take. Decide accordingly.

There is more to personal finance than the drudgery of debts and budgets.

Spend more time exercising. You should realize that physical fitness boosts your mental fitness. Physiology is one of the enabling mental states, so you should make physical fitness a priority in your life. I exercise every day to control my weight, so in my life physical fitness is a must-have, not a nice-to-have option. Listen to physiological warning signs; your body tells you when you are fumbling with its parameters. Watch your diet. Reduce junk food from your diet; spend more hours resting or sleeping; reduce your consumption of soda; entertain less. Your mind and body deserve the best. Audit how you are spending your time and validate whether it is working for you.

HOW TO IMPLEMENT THE 10% SAVING SOLUTION THE NLP WAY

The best way to use NLP to develop a saving habit is to make the process as painless and pleasurable as possible. Make it automatic; make it invisible. If you arrange to have the money taken from your paycheck before you receive it, you will never know it is missing. Part of your savings plan will probably include retirement, but you should also save for intermediate goals too, such as buying a house, paying for a honeymoon, or purchasing a new car. Here are four easy ways to begin doing this yourself: You can exploit the strategy of private equity banking, which works like a poor man establishing and running his or her own bank like the big shots. If you tell the Internal Revenue Service or the government of your state that you want to open your own bank, the officials will laugh at you. They know that the official requirements are daunting to the extent that only the strong breed of millionaires and billionaires dare propose to open banks.

What if I reveal a little secret you could use to open your own bank? You can! By exploiting little-known revenue laws and insurance contracts, you can open and operate a de facto bank. Soon I will reveal the details to you. If your employer offers a retirement plan, such as a 401(K) or 457B account, enroll in it as soon as possible, especially if the company matches your contributions. Matched contributions are like free money. Starting a traditional or a Roth IRA is one of the smartest moves a young adult can make. These accounts allow your investments to grow tax-free. Because of the extraordinary power of compound interest, and compound returns, regular investments in a Roth IRA from an early age can lead to enormous future wealth. The real barrier to developing this habit of saving is finding money to save. Many people believe it is impossible.

But almost everyone can save at least 1% of their income. That is only one penny out of every dollar. Some people will argue that saving this little is meaningless. Young adults should make it a priority to develop a regular saving plan. Establishing this habit early can lead to increased financial security later in life. In fact, David Bach's 2003 best-seller, *The Automatic Millionaire* is devoted exclusively to the subject of programmatic saving. The entire book is a step-by-step guide to developing the saving habit and making it automatic. If you would like more ideas about how to make this work in your life, this is the place to look. Any good public library will have a copy of the book, so you do not have to worry about spending money to buy it. On my web sites, princeojong.com or millionaireiuniversity.com, you can read materials on David Bach's book.

I know the truth about money habits. It is difficult to work on auto pilot; the reality is that some months you can save some money and some you cannot. Sometimes you have to withdraw money that you have saved to pay the bills. So how can the 10% saving solution actually work? You should always begin your pay period by paying God first. Next, you pay yourself second. Gradually, you will begin to accumulate savings. Remember, the idea of paying yourself second does not involve the creation of any magic. You will still get a bill from the electric company each month, and the electric company will expect you to pay it.

Starting a 10% saving solution program is easiest when you get a raise in pay. Just take the increase and put it in your savings account. You will still have the same amount of money available as you did last week. Do not, nonetheless, let the lack of a pay raise keep you from starting your saving program. You can begin with $5 this month. Most of us spend that much impulsively sometimes during the month. I, Prince Ojong, am willing to continue my efforts designed to help you get wealthy and retire rich, that is, even if you have not started saving money yet. I will continue to show you how to reduce your spending and eliminate debt. I will also continue to offer advice on what you should do with your money.

FOR THOSE WHO HATE BUDGETING

Do you hate budgeting? Your initial reaction, the first step most people will relish, is to throw out your budget. That is right! Please, stick to that budget you created for your own self-improvement. If you cannot stick to a budget, then, make the effort to save whatever amount of money you can save. Ok? Frankly, as long as you are saving a certain portion of your salary, it does not really matter what you do with the rest of your money. So, the key is making your saving automatic by paying yourself after paying God first.

In other words, pay yourself before you pay the mortgage, the credit card company or even your taxes. And make sure it happens automatically each month so you do not have a chance to put that retirement money toward new shoes or golf clubs. The government pays itself automatically each time you get paid. Taxes are taken out of your salary before you even get your check: federal tax, state tax, local tax, social security tax, and, Medicare tax. Hence, you should arrange for money to be taken from your salary and put into a retirement account before you ever get to see it. Most employers make this contribution easy for you through a 401(K) plan. Sign up for your company's 401(K) and you are well on your way to retirement. Spending less and saving more are great ways to jumpstart a retirement fund. But to really turbocharge your savings, you also need to earn more.

STEP-BY-STEP PLAN TO THE 10% SAVING SOLUTION

To implement the 10% saving solution, please, create a special account that is separate from all your other accounts. This special account should be only for a specified goal, usually saving or investing. If possible, choose an account with a higher interest rate; usually these types of accounts limit how often you can withdraw money, which is a good thing because you are not going to be pulling money out of it, anyway.

Determine how much you want to put into the account and at what interval. For example, you can decide to put in $300 per month, or $150 per paycheck. This will depend on what you intend to do with the money. For example, if you want to put a $20,000 down payment on a home in 36 months, three years, you will need to save about $550 per month every month.

Put that money into the account as soon as it is available. If you have direct deposit, have a portion of each paycheck automatically deposited into the separate account. You can also set up an automatic monthly or weekly transfer from your main, active account to your separate account, if you can keep track of your balance enough to avoid overdraft fees. The point is to do this before you spend money on anything else, including bills and rent. Leave the money alone. Do not touch it. Do not pull money out of it. You should have a separate emergency fund for just that: emergencies. Typically, that fund should be enough to cover you for three to six months. Do not confuse an emergency fund with a saving or investing fund. If you find that you do not have enough money to pay your bills, look for other ways to make money or cut expenses. Do not charge them on your credit card.

OWNING YOUR OWN BANK

I am ready to let you in on the so-called banker's secret. Back in 1991, I was living in a dingy apartment in Alexandria, Virginia. In the throes of the recession predating the Bill Clinton expansion, one beautiful morning in May, I stumbled upon a program on network television. It was a discussion on home mortgage reduction strategies. The guest on the show was Marc Eisenson, the publisher of a new book titled *The Banker's Secret*. When the television show was over, I sped to an Egghead store located on Baileys' Crossroads to buy the book.

After reading the book, I was too stunned to think that Congress or the US government was legally allowing banks to charge so much interest on loans; that was usury! My Muslim friends screamed when I explained how banks were making fortunes in the loan business; I subscribed to Marc Eisenson's newsletter titled *The Banker's Secret Bulletin*; as I perused the payment tables and charts in the book, I was excited to recognize the power of compounding and prepayment; I dreamed about owning a bank and making huge profits like mortgage lenders; you borrow $100,000 to buy home, but you end up paying $400,000; you pay the money four-fold because you are paying compound interest to your bank. There should be a better way: owning your own bank and accelerating the building of equity fast.

HOW A BANK REALLY WORKS

The funny thing about how a bank works is that it functions based on the principle of trust, mutual trust. On the one hand, as a customer, you give a bank your money to keep it safe for you in the form of a deposit, and then the bank turns around and gives your money to someone else in the form of a loan to make money for itself, not for you; for example, the bank pays you an interest rate of 1% for keeping your money, but the bank charges a borrower a lending rate between 7% and 28%. Even though we know that banks can legally extend considerably more credit than they have cash, most of us still have total trust in the bank's ability to protect our money and give it to us when we ask for it.

One common explanation is the banks' use of Federal Deposit Insurance Corporation (FDIC) insurance to protect your money up to the limit of $250,000 per account. Why do we feel better about having our money in a bank than we do having it under a mattress at home? Is it just the fact that the banks pay interest on some of our accounts? Is it because we know that if we have the cash in our pockets we will spend it?

Or, is it simply the convenience of being able to write checks and use debit cards rather than carrying cash? Any and all of these may be the answer, particularly with the conveniences of electronic banking today. Now, we do not even have to manually write that check; we can just swipe a debit card or click the pay button on the bank's web site. I know you must be thinking about owning your own bank. Right? Before thinking about owning your own bank, please, imagine or look into the world of banking and see how these institutions work around you. Think! Think about what you would have to do to start your own bank, and why we should, or should not, trust you with our hard-earned cash.

PRIVATE EQUITY BANKING

Now that you have grasped the concept of the banker's secret, I am going to introduce you to private equity banking, a little-known millionaire secret that will help you capitalize on saving money and borrowing your way to riches like the Trumps, Rockefellers, and the Kennedys. The private equity banking concept teaches you to play and win the banking money game like Bank of America, Suntrust, Wells Fargo, and other financial institutions by becoming a banker who owns his or her own bank. Fewer than 5% of retired Americans have income over 3k per month.

Here is the problem! Here is the bad news to you: Even with a 401(K) or IRA, or other tax-deferred vehicles, it is not likely that you are saving enough for retirement, because the concept of tax-deferred still means you paying taxes and upon retirement you may even pay more taxes because of fewer deductions. What that tells you is that your government, that is, the Internal Revenue Service (IRS), gets you at the front end of the money gate and also gets you at the back end of the money gate. But here is the good news! The good tidings is that there are many, little-known (IRS) government regulations that have been grandfathered, plus clauses that have been carefully buried in the US income tax codes.

So in plain kindergarten English, what is the solution? The millionaire secret solution is the judicious employment of the Internal Revenue Service (IRS) Code Section 7702, which allows legal reserve insurance companies to construct long-term, cash-accumulated life insurance contracts that do not require any taxation on the growth of your money. In other words, your money is not tax-deferred like a 401(K), 403B, TSP, or IRA. In fact, your money is tax exempt, like the money you can get out of your home equity tax free. Better still, some advantages of private equity banking over home equity loans are the following: there are no income qualifications, no credit checks, and no rental hikes or mortgage increases. For your information, the private equity banking concept has been used by major US banks, several university endowment programs, and large corporations for decades as a safe long-term bet which provides high rates of returns to fund employees and retirees' benefits.

The equity return from the private equity banking instrument is more competitive than a certificate of deposit (CD), money market, or 401(K)s. Above all, private equity banking has the big and dramatic advantage in that you pay no income taxes ever on your fat gains; indeed, if the insurance contract is structured properly and the withdrawals are done based on the US tax laws, you will enjoy having the umbrella of private equity banking in the stormy weather of the present US recessionary economy.

PRIVATE EQUITY BANKING IN ACTION

The summary below will outline the step-by-step process of implementing the idea of private equity banking, if at all you qualify. A restatement of the problem is in order: Fewer than 5% of retired Americans have income over 3k per month. Even with a 401(K) or IRA, or another tax-deferred vehicle, it is unlikely that you are saving enough for retirement, because tax-deferred still means the payment of taxes and upon retirement you may even pay more taxes because you have fewer exemptions and deductions.

Please, let us assume a scenario where you get paid $100,000 and your tax bracket is 30% like most of the folks belonging to the upper middle class. Your take home pay is about $70,000. Now 95% of the things you buy, gasoline, groceries, Starbucks coffee, chewing gum, clothes, etc., with that $70,000 will cost you another 35% of taxes, which means, in reality, your actual take home pay is about $35,000. This is the exact amount you will have to use to pay mortgage, rents, bills, etc. What that tells you is that the government (IRS) gets you at the front end of the money gate and also gets you at the back end of the same gate. But the good news is that I am going to show you how to deconstruct and decode the US tax codes; I am going to show you how to capitalize on tax shelters and loopholes your government has kept in place to protect rich folks, crooked lawyers, and fat-cat investment bankers, a cabal of thieves whose penchant for stealing from the poor American people with impunity knows no bounds. The devil is in the details of the IRS Code Section 7702.

Is this not the reason why the Occupy Wall Street movement was growing by leaps and bounds? In fact, the cause of the enduring protests was what these protesters and average Americans perceived to be the disenchantment of the 99% of the people living on Main Street with the avariciousness of the 1% of the Americans awash with big money on Wall Street. On August 2, 2011, at the very first meeting of what was to become Occupy Wall Street, about a dozen people sat in a circle in Bowling Green. The self-appointed process committee for a social movement we merely hoped would someday exist, contemplated a moments decision. Their dream was to create a New York General Assembly: the model for democratic assemblies we hoped to see spring up across America. But how would those assemblies actually operate? The anarchists in the circle made what seemed, at the time, an insanely ambitious proposal. Why not let them operate exactly like this committee: by consensus. It was, in the least, a wild gamble, because as far as any of us knew, no one had ever managed to pull off something like this before. The consensus process had been successfully used in spokes-councils — groups of activists organized into separate affinity groups, each represented by a single "spoke"—but never in mass assemblies like the one anticipated in New York City.

Even the General Assemblies in Greece and Spain had not attempted it. But consensus was the approach that most accorded with the principles of the protesters, so they took the leap.

INTERNAL REVENUE SERVICE (IRS) CODE SECTION 7702

Section 7702 of the US tax code allows legal reserve insurance companies to construct long-term, cash accumulated life insurance contracts that do not require any taxation on the growth of your money. The insurance policy is not tax deferred like a 401(K), 403B, TSP, or IRA; it is tax exempt like the money you can get out of your home's equity, tax free. Some advantages of the cash-value policy over a home-equity loan are the following: there is no verification or qualification of your income; there is no check of your consumer credit; and your loan's interest rate or payment does not increase. Major banks like Bank of America, Suntrust, Well Fargo, and Citibank do contribute over $13 billion, 12 billions, 3 billion, and 3 billion, respectively into IRS Code Section 7702 insurance instruments.

In fact, it is a major part of their asset allocation schedule; it trumps real estate. Why? Taxes, Taxes, Taxes! Of course, these insurance contracts allow you to deposit your money into a non-MEC, not a modified endowment contract, that is, a fanciful term for the simple idea that the IRS does not consider the cash-value insurance policy as an investment for tax purposes; in other words, this is a cash-value insurance policy without taxation. Best of all, your money compounds and your interest and dividend earnings grow without taxation; additionally, the pay-out of your retirement income is effectuated without taxation, so long as the rules governing MEC limits are adhered to steadfastly. In fact, an experienced insurance super-agent, like me, can illustrate how much money you can put in a cash-value insurance policy to create your own bank.

Furthermore, your interest earnings from private equity banking are based on a guaranteed, balanced, and diversified market indexed of publicly traded securities in the S&P 500, the Dow Jones Industrial Average, and the NASDAQ. But you do not have to actually buy or sell any stocks. In addition, there are no individual equity allocations because the index is already balanced and diversified. Unlike tax-deferred accounts, such as IRA, 401(K), TSP, etc., there are no loads or management fees, and no hidden charges. Generally, as the US Department of the Treasury's beloved son or the IRS' favorite child, these cash-value insurance policies have a built-in guarantee of 3% to 15% rate of return, in addition to the insured's life protection with generous living benefits and limited risk of loss. For instance, if the S&P 500 stock index underperforms in a particular year, the insurance contract guarantees you a return-on-investment (ROI) payment of 3%, more than the 1% you get typically from your bank today.

By contrast, if the S&P 500 index remains in positive territory by the end of the year and you make gains, your profit is limited to or capped at 15%; customarily, your insurer gets the gains over 15%. What this means is that the cash-value policy has a built-in hedge against market risks; of course, you do not get all of the gains, but you do not also get any of the losses, either. The insurer allows you to keep whatever you earn; the beauty of it all is that you keep the money, and it compounds on a tax-free basis.

In addition, several of these insurance contracts today have in-built living benefits, that is, in case of a serious injury or illness, you do not have to worry about the limited benefits of workman compensation insurance; you can pull the trigger of the clause in your cash-value contract which allows you to use the face amount or value of your policy as a source of emergency funding.

HOW IRS CODE SECTION 7702 ENABLES YOU TO OPEN YOUR OWN BANK

First, you have to sign a life insurance contract with a reputable company. I suggest you find one that is a mutual company as opposed to a stock company. I have a list of some highly-rated insurers to share with you; call my office at (301) 593-4897 or (301) 593-4879. When you contact my office, my professional associates will ascertain whether you qualify for the cash-value insurance policies we have discussed in this chapter. If you qualify for a cash-value insurance contract, I promise to work with you diligently until you understand all the nuances in these policies. As a way to whet your appetite with some sweet money and salivating stuff, I am going to recommend a good insurance book for you to buy and read; for your information, I buy most of my books from my web sites (princeojong.com or millionaireiuniversity.com).

Additionally, I avail myself of either Amazon.com or Barnes and Noble's bookstore. If you have some time to read or would like to join The Millionaire Club, I will send you a copy of Patrick Kelly's book entitled *TAX-FREE RETIREMENT*; the retirement expose will enable you to see the differences among insurance contracts from another perspective: term life, whole life, universal life, and variable life. There are several companies out there that preach half the story and Patrick Kelly did a very good job in outlining the pros and cons of different insurance products. Let me also say that there is no insurance instrument that is a money gold standard; in other words, every insurance product is designed for a target market, so if someone tells you that their product is the best, then, they are telling you lies or old wives' tales.

All state insurance commissioners frown upon producers or agents misrepresenting products to the customer. As such, a good insurance agent or broker should be able to outline to you the differences between or among products of the insurer; they are supposed to show you all the riders you can qualify for. As a rule of thumb, whenever an insurance producer quotes a cheap premium to you, please, be on your guard; be advised that he or she is presenting a policy with limited benefits; in regard to legalities such as loopholes and wiggle rooms, please, do not forget that the states allow these companies a two-year contestability option.

For example, if you are the insured on a life insurance policy and die within the first two years of the issue date, the insurance carrier has the right to contest your claim. Most of the time, what this means is that the carrier will investigate to find out if you made any misrepresentations on your policy application. That is why cancelling some type of policies in the early years may be harmful. My word of caution to you is that you should avoid listening to Uncle Joe or Aunty Mary or anyone who is not a credible and licensed insurance producer with sound knowledge of product portfolios.

You may be investing penny wise but pound foolish because you are trying to please Uncle Joe and Aunty Mary. Ignorance in insurance matters is like divorcing your wife on Main Street and getting married to a concubine on Wall Street who is not in love with you in the first place.

Secondly, you need to capitalize your bank by paying your premium. It could be a one-time dump (single), since IRS Code Section 7702 allows the over funding of your policy up to the MEC limit. This capitalization approach is usually the fastest way to raise your equity, if you have the money. When I was starting out, I was diligent in implementing monthly and annual funding of my bank. Depending on your individual needs and wants, you can follow my example. If you consult a money expert, like me, I promise to guide you on this treacherous road, so that you should stay within your budget. My fear is that if you lack discipline you may make the cash-value policy lapse, but that is not good news, especially during your first few years of banking. Please, let me enumerate efficient sources of capitalization for your new private equity bank: paycheck, savings, bonus, raise, certificate of deposit, mutual fund, individual retirement account, gift, tax refund, inheritance, and money pool.

Thirdly, your broker/agent should be able to show you how to use your bank. This is when a one-on-one meeting is very important. If you have a small business, you can do the same, but the advantages will depend on how the business is set up for tax purposes. You may want your attorney, CPA, or other accountant to be involved in the transaction. In general, small businesses can enjoy huge tax write offs, as another way to keep valuable employees. This private equity banking approach turns out to be far better than regular 401(K), because such tax-deferred accounts only benefit the IRS (Uncle Sam), and stock brokers, and managers. Now is the time for you to implement level two of personal finance, private equity banking. Why now? You might be saying to yourself, "if this were very true, how come I have not heard about it?" Oh no! You have heard about it, certainly, but you did not know how to use it to your advantage.

It is like Steve Jobs introducing the iPhone. The phone is a communication device we have taken for granted since its invention. Alexander Graham Bell is commonly credited as the inventor of the first practical telephone. The classic story of his crying out "Watson, come here! I want to see you!" is a well-known part of American history. Bell was the first person to obtain a patent, in 1876, for an apparatus for transmitting vocal or other sounds telegraphically, after experimenting with many primitive sound transmitters and receivers. Bell was also an astute and articulate business man with influential and wealthy friends. Steve Jobs, however, took a popular device and reconfigured how we are using it today, with Internet features. The same argument is true of the iPod and iPad.

Similarly, cash-value insurance has been in existence for an appreciably long time, but I am the one reconstituting a popular product to function like a commercial bank, with you as the ultimate banker; you are the alpha and omega; you own the bank and make all the decisions because you are in control. Private equity banking is an old commodity that several university-endowment programs, large corporations, and banks have used for decades as a safe and long-term investment; it is a sure bet which provides high rates of returns to fund employees and retirees' benefits.

There is more to personal finance than the drudgery of debts and budgets.

Private equity banking is very competitive as a financial product, and it is more appealing than a certificate of deposit, money market, or 401(K). In fact, private equity banking's superiority over other financial instruments stems from the dramatic advantage of it being a risk-free and tax-free investment; you cannot lose any money as a result of using the private equity banking strategy, and the IRS does not tax your gains. If your cash-value contract is structured properly and your deposits and withdrawals are based on insurance and tax laws, you will appreciate the power of private equity banking.

CASE STUDIES OF PRIVATE EQUITY BANKING

In today's volatile and less secure market with the money-market rate hovering around 1% and the five-year certificate of deposit rate at less than 1.5%, the annual interest rate of return of cash-value products is still in the range of 3% and 15%, and these insurance products have many tax-exemption advantages over tax-deferred accounts such as Roth IRA, traditional IRA, and 401(K). In fact, in the 1930s, as an example, J.C. Penney used cash-value insurance in the form of private equity banking to satisfy the payroll needs of his organization during the great depression. In 1953, as another instance, Walt Disney took advantage of private equity banking, a reconstitution of cash- value insurance, to build Disney world in Orlando, Florida. In 2008, as a third instance, Senator John McCain used his cash-value insurance as a collateral to fund the initial phase of his presidential campaign.

Personally, since 1995, I have opened and maintained four separate cash-value insurance accounts; I operate them like four distinct banks: one for me; one for Lady Claire; one for Lucille; and one for Alexia. What makes me smile is the fact that my money is compounding daily. Even the kiddie accounts sport an annual rate of return that has NEVER fallen below 5%, even during the economic depression of 2008 to present. Even with the AIG debacle, which was not really a true issue, the general insurance industry is still sporting a double AA rating; that is why even when over 50 banks failed in 2009 and 2010, not a single insurance company failed. Why? Because, in reality, banks are just the gate keepers working for insurance companies, which are the true controllers of the money you deposit into your present bank account. You see, insurance companies are legal reserve entities, which unlike banks where your deposits are FDIC insured (maximum 250k), they are required by law to maintain capital reserve (billions) for all their contractual agreements. Best of all, insurance contracts, unlike bank deposits, are protected from law suits and probate; by contrast, cash-value insurance is not considered as an asset in the computing of your children's educational or college planning. This is another reason why cash-value insurance beats your favorite Roth and traditional IRA, municipal bonds, and 529 college plans.

CONCLUSION OF PRIVATE EQUITY BANKING

Since private equity banking is a concept that uses a life insurance tool, not every one may qualify because life insurance takes the applicant's health into account. However, there are legal ways for you to beat or navigate around the system, such as a parent or grandparent opening a private equity bank for a child or grandchild, and managing the insurance affairs as the owner.

Talking to an insurance expert, like me, may be your first step to see if you even qualify. Life insurance of the cash-value variety was never designed to bury dead people; indeed, that is the function of death insurance: that is term policies. True life insurance is not for the dead; rather, it is for the living rich who utilize it as the foundation of building financial and generational wealth. De jure, in the long run, cash-value insurance is the cheapest policy your money can buy. Tax laws set in place in 1914 provided the safety net of using insurance to build wealth. I call private equity banking the great grandfather clause of American income taxation.

Hence, I urge you to begin exploiting the awesome power of private equity banking. Do not hate the rich folks; aspire to be like them; make them your friend. As the old saying goes, birds of the same feather flock together. The rich use their immense wealth to lobby politicians to make tax laws friendly to them. As a consequence, the IRS tax code is their friend; make it your friend, too. Even though the tax loopholes were intended for the rich, now you can use them for your own betterment. Act now to establish your own private equity bank; I can predict that the popularity of my book will orchestrate the fine-tuning of laws pertaining to you owning your own bank. In addition to IRS Code Section 7702, other tax vehicles exist favoring millionaires, billionaires, and other rich and famous folks; some tax vehicles that can be amenable to you are the little-known IRS Code Section 79 for business owners; Section 412 (E) (3) for business owners, and Section 162 for business executives.

I will introduce you to these viable instruments when you attend our seminars, workshops, or MillionaireiUniversity.com. To tell you the truth, these tools can be structured based on your individual or corporate needs. Indeed, if well structured, these tools can be very powerful blocks for building GENERATIONAL WEALTH like the Kennedys and the Rockefellers. These strategies can help you REDUCE TAXES without the need of having a bank account from the likes of Bank of America, Wells Fargo, Suntrust, Capital One, and others. It is your own bank. Use it, Mr. or Mrs. Banker! Thanks for taking your valuable time to follow this presentation on your time!

INTERNAL REVENUE SERVICE'S (IRS) Code Section 79

I describe IRS Code Section 79 as level three of the 10% saving solution. In the next few pages, I am going to introduce you to another millionaire secret, 10% saving solution level three or IRS Code Section 79. Previously, I have shown you two strategies of implementing the pay yourself second tool: saving and investing 10% of your income and private equity banking.

Now I am going to introduce you to a third strategy of paying yourself second, the little-known Section 79 of the Internal Revenue Code, the rich man's welfare or wealth fare. When I stumbled upon this knowledge, I was too stunned to think that it was 100% legal; in fact, it is part and parcel of the IRS loopholes that have been savored by America's rich and famous. Specialized knowledge is power. I learned about the use of IRS Code Section 79 as a wealth-building strategy by eavesdropping on the conversation of three lawyers in a country club located in Montgomery county, Maryland. As the Robin Hood of personal finance, I swore there and then that I was going to share this information with whoever needs it.

After researching IRS Code Section 79 with some mutual friends who were CPAs, I succeeded in developing a 10% saving solution money machine that could leverage this strategy for me and my clients. After I contacted some life insurance agents and they confirmed the viability of my strategy, I began assisting everybody who wanted to use it to build wealth quickly through either legal income tax elimination or minimization. My first target customers were high net worth individuals such as entrepreneurs, athletes, singers, lawyers, doctors, and engineers, who were saddled with the yearly heavy weight of high income tax liabilities.

What is IRS Code Section 79? It is an IRS code that allows taxpayers to use life insurance as a vehicle of income tax effacement or reduction. Section 79 of the Internal Revenue Code allows employers to provide group term life insurance to employees on a pre-tax basis. Premiums paid by employers to fund group life insurance in excess of $50,000 are taxable income to employees (reduced by any amounts paid by the employee toward the cost of the coverage). Employer-paid premiums for spouse or dependent life insurance with a face amount of coverage in excess of $2,000 are also considered taxable income to the employee. Coverage under $2,000 may be excluded as a de minimis fringe benefit under IRC Section 132. The employer must compute the cost of the additional protection and notify the employee of the amount to include in his or her taxable income. In addition, supplemental life insurance coverage amounts are considered towards the $50,000 limit if the plan is carried by the employer.

A plan is considered carried by the employer if:

1. The employer pays any cost of the employee or dependent life insurance, or
2. Premium amounts for at least one employee or dependent subsidize those paid by at least one other employee or dependent. IRS Table 1 rates are used to determine if premium amounts are subsidized. A policy is carried if some rates are equal to or below Table 1 rates and some are equal to or above Table 1 rates.

IRS' Code Section 79 permits employers to offer group life insurance to employees. Life insurance is the only way to fund a Section 79 Plan,. With a specially designed policy, the employee can usually exclude about 35-40% of premium from taxable income. IRS Code Section 79 details the tax consequences and requirements for corporations wishing to install a group-term life insurance plan. A corporation may issue term life insurance policies as benefits to its employees; permanent life insurance may also be offered as an added benefit in a Section 79 plan. Indeed, it is important for you to understand that Section 79 plans are non-qualified as defined by the Internal Revenue Code, but these plans still offer a tax deduction for sponsoring employers. Employees participating in a Section 79 plan offered by a sponsoring corporation may receive up to $50,000 in group term life insurance at no cost, if the plan is non-discriminatory. Any amount over this limit is deemed a permanent benefit.

The employee should realize a portion of the permanent benefit as W-2 taxable income, and pay any applicable taxes accordingly. Contributions to a Section 79 plan are 100% tax-deductible, though for owners, and 2% or more shareholders, contributions are only deductible if paid by, and from, a C Corporation.

In the world income tax preparation, few experts, even CPAs know much about the working or benefits of IRS Section 79. Fewer insurance companies have a product catering to this lucrative and niche market. I am willing to share more detailed and specific information on IRS Section 79 with you free of charge. Although the available number of insurance companies that sell a Section 79 term or permanent product may be limited, I want you to know that a Section 79 benefit program may allow you to enjoy the following income tax benefits:

1-- the ability to purchase term or permanent life insurance with corporate dollars, free of charge to you as an individual entity.
2—the ability to deduct 100% of the life insurance cost to the C Corporation you have created as a business expense.
3—the ability to allow the transfer of corporate dollars to the business owner on a "tax favored" basis.
4—the ability to grow the money in the plan in a tax-deferred setting.
5—the ability to have access to money in the plan that can be achieved through policy loans on a tax-deferred basis.
6—the ability to pass on death benefits to heirs on an income tax-free basis.
7—the absence of regulatory limits on funding for the key participants in the plan.
8—the provision of judgment proofing and asset protection by removing plan assets from the reach of your corporate company's creditors.
9—the provision of insurance benefits irrespective of an employee's minimal rank or employee cost.
10—the insurance cash-values may provide tax-free income as long as the policy is kept in force and withdrawals do not exceed the cost basis.

Do not be oblivious of the fact that policy loans and withdrawals reduce the policies' cash-values and death benefits and may result in a taxable event. Although a Section 79 plan is 100% deductible at the corporate level, contributions to a Section 79 plan also provide an economic benefit to the owner, so an individual income tax will be required on approximately 60% of the contribution.

When can you use Section 79? A Section 79 plan may be used for the following five applications:

1. group life insurance benefits.
2. deductible insurance to fund estate planning needs of the business owner.
3. deductible insurance to provide personal life insurance needs for the owner.
4. deductible insurance to fund a buy-sell agreement or key man policy.
5. future business buyout on a tax-advantaged basis.

How do you determine the death benefit? Death benefits can be determined by a number of different methods at the discretion of the employee: from a minimum coverage of group term insurance to a permanent benefit up to a pre-determined multiple of the employee's reported W-2 income.

The tax consequences and funding commitment to the employee will be impacted by the option they choose within the plan. In the case of an employee making $245,000, if a 10x multiple is used that employee will receive a death benefit equal to $2,450,000 ($245,000 x 10). The resulting contribution depends heavily on what product is being used for funding, as well as the employee's age and health.

How do you calculate your tax liability? In a non-discriminatory Section 79 plan, the first $50,000 of coverage is provided free to all employees. Any group coverage over this amount is deemed a benefit for which the employee must pay. The pure insurance portion is factored using the IRS's published rates. If using permanent insurance the portion calculated as the 'permanent benefit' takes into account premiums paid, accumulated and cash surrender value, and other policy factors.

What are the requirements? There are, generally, four main conditions which must be met when a corporation is installing a Section 79 plan:
--The plan must provide a death benefit excludable from income under Code section 101(a)[5].
--The Section 79 plan must be provided to a group of employees
--The Section 79 plan must be provided under a policy carried directly or indirectly by the employer.
--The Section 79 plan must state that death benefits for each employee should be based on a multiple of compensation.

TIPS FOR PAYROLL ADMINISTRATION

Frequency of reporting (that is, per pay period, weekly, monthly, quarterly) is at the employer's discretion as long as the imputed income is treated as paid by December 31 and is reported on employees' W-2. The imputed income amounts are not subject to federal tax withholding and are subject to FICA. If there are changes to the amount of group term life insurance during the year (for example, due to salary adjustments or changes in supplemental life insurance), the imputed income will need to be calculated for each period. For example, if the calendar year group term insurance is a multiple of salary and there is a salary adjustment effective June 1, then the imputed income for the periods of January 1 through May 31 and June 1 through December 31 will be calculated separately and added together.
Key life insurance which has the company named as a beneficiary is exempt from Section 79.

PROS OF Code Section 79

--It encourages employers to provide life insurance benefits for employees.
--It allows employers and employees to avoid some taxation of life insurance benefits.

CONS OF Code Section 79

--Employer must compute the cost of the additional protection and notify the employee of the amount to include in his or her taxable income.

--If the employer's group-term life insurance plan favors key employees, the entire cost of the insurance must be included in the key employee's income.
--If the voluntary life rates favor any one group, imputed income must be assessed.

QUESTIONS AND ANSWERS ABOUT Section 79

Does the Section 79 maintain its non-discriminate form? In order for a Section 79 plan to maintain its non-discriminatory form, other conditions must be met:
--Cover at least 70% of employees
--No more than 15% of the participants are key employees
--Benefits are based on reasonable classifications

What is deemed a discriminatory Section 79 plan?

It is possible to have what is deemed a discriminatory Section 79 plan. Under a discriminatory plan the first $50,000 of death benefit coverage is not free for owners and key employees. Cost will again be based on the IRS Table I rates. Rank and file employees maintain their free benefit whether or not the plan is discriminatory. Yet another set of requirements comes into play if the company has less than 10 employees.

Do you have under 10 employees? Employees must have six months of full-time employment to be eligible for the plan, and benefits must be based on a uniform percentage of compensation or coverage brackets, such that no bracket is more than 2.5 times the next lowest bracket and the lowest bracket is at least 10% of the highest bracket.

Do you have more than 10 employees? Employees must have 36 months of full-time employment to be eligible.

Do you have excluded employees? The clause is referring to the following: employees under the age of 18 or over the age of 64, part-time or seasonal employees covered under a union contract, provided the group term life insurance benefits were the subject of good faith bargaining, anyone not medically approved, or anyone choosing to opt out of the plan.

What about coverage for spouses and dependents? The cost of employer-provided group-term life insurance on the life of an employee's spouse or dependent, paid by the employer, is not taxable to the employee if the face amount of the coverage does not exceed $2,000. This coverage is excluded as a de minimis fringe benefit. Some cases may allow more.

WHAT TYPES OF EMPLOYERS OFFER IT? All types of employers are required to compute imputed income on life insurance over $50,000.

WHAT SIZE EMPLOYERS OFFER IT? Employers of all sizes.

WHAT ARE THE CRITICAL UNDERWRITING OR PARTICIPATION REQUIREMENTS?

The premium amounts that must be included in employees' taxable income for employer-paid and employee-paid life insurance (for self, spouse or dependents) are based on standard rates put forth by the IRS (Table 1).

These rates are based on the age attained by the employee on the last day of taxable year (Dec 31). They are not in any way related to the current life insurance rates charged by insurance companies. To ensure employees are not charged imputed income, employers should verify that voluntary life insurance rates do not crossover or straddle Table 1 rates.

HOW MUCH DOES IT COST?

IMPUTED INCOME TABLE I RATES	Monthly Rate Per $1,000 of Benefit
Employee Age on December 31	
<25	0.05
25 - 29	0.06
30 - 34	0.08
35 - 39	0.09
40 - 44	0.10
45 - 49	0.15
50 - 54	0.23
55 - 59	0.43
60 – 64	0.66
65 – 69	1.27
70+	2.06

THE Section 79 SOLUTION

How can an IRS Code Section 79 plan work? The only way you can legally pay zero or a little business taxes is to use your C corporation structure to implement the IRS' Section 79 life insurance plan. For instance, Secure Plus Advantage 79 is an excellent business life insurance product that you can use to resolve your tax problems. Secure Plus Advantage 79 is a TAX-ADVANTAGED LIFE INSURANCE FOR BUSINESS OWNERS AND EMPLOYEES.

EXAMPLE 1

A 28-year old employee has $150,000 of employer paid basic coverage. The volume of life insurance over $50,000 is considered taxable income and is multiplied by the applicable Table 1 rate for each month the life volume is over $50,000.

The resulting amount is the taxable income that needs to be included on the employee's W-2. Federal and state income tax liability on this amount will depend on the employee's personal circumstances: income tax filing status and the number of personal exemptions, for example.
$ 150,000 = Total amount carried by employer
- $50,000 Exempt amount
$100,000 =Amount that is considered imputed income
/ 1,000 Per $1,000 of coverage
$100 Imputed income volume
x $.06 Rate for 28-year old employee
$6 imputed (taxable) income per month

EXAMPLE 2

The same 28-year old employee receives $50,000 of employer paid, or carried, basic coverage per year. She is also entitled to $100,000 of optional insurance at her own expense, and all the rates are above or at or below or at Table 1 rates. This plan is not considered carried by the employer. Since the additional amounts are not carried by the employer, the employee does not have imputed income.

$50,000 =Total amount carried by employer
- $50,000 Exempt amount
$0 Amount considered imputed

EXAMPLE 3

The same 28-year old employee receives $50,000 of employer paid, or carried, basic coverage per year. She is also entitled to $100,000 of optional insurance at her own expense. Her optional insurance rate is $.04, which is less than the $.06 amount Table 1. Other employees are charged higher rates than Table 1, making the optional insurance considered carried by the employer. The cost of the $100,000 is included in income, and her contributions are subtracted from the unadjusted imputed income amount.

$ 150,000 Total amount carried by employer
- $50,000 Exempt amount
$100,000 Amount subject to imputed income
/ 1,000 Per $1,000 of coverage
$100 Imputed income volume
x $.06 Rate for 28-year old employee
$6 unadjusted imputed (taxable) income per month
- $4 employee post-tax contribution per month
$2 adjusted imputed (taxable) income per month

Life insurance imputed income should be prorated if less than a full month of coverage is provided.

Step 5

BALANCE YOUR FINANCIAL BOOK

You have completed the study of personal finance 1.0. Congratulations! Now you are ready psychologically to handle the big stuff: how to balance your financial book. I am going to introduce you to goal setting, oath making, goal contracting, and advanced financial management. The purpose of this exercise is to enable you to establish goals and use the financial tools of money management to work toward your goals methodically. You will learn how to change your balance sheet from red to black; in essence, you will be learning how to balance your financial book that is out of joint now. You have to learn to pay much attention to the numbers in your financial book, your bottom-line; that is what millionaires and billionaires do; that is what big corporations in the S&P 500 do. Running your financial life like a business corporation is the sine qua non of financial success. Verily must I tell you: If you dream of becoming a millionaire, you must mimic the financial habits of millionaires. You must become like a great actor playing the part of a millionaire in a play or movie. All the world is a stage, and you are a player; you are playing the part of a millionaire, so do not only memorize your lines by rut, but you must get into the millionaire true character. So help you God!

GOAL SETTING

If you dream of becoming a millionaire, you must begin by defining your goals. You cannot just wish for horses to ride like beggars. You must understand how to design and implement your millionaire plan. In fact, that is what I did, and that is what you should do, too. The first empirical studies on goal setting were performed by Cecil Alec Mace in 1935. Edwin A. Locke began to examine goal setting in the mid-1960s and continued researching goal setting for thirty years. Locke derived the idea for goal-setting from Aristotle's form of final causality. Aristotle speculated that purpose can cause action; thus, Locke began researching the impact goals have on individual activity of its time performance. Goal setting involves establishing specific, measurable, achievable, realistic and time-targeted (S.M.A.R.T) goals. Work on the theory of goal-setting suggests that it is an effective tool for making progress by ensuring that participants in a group with a common goal are clearly aware of what is expected from them.

On a personal level, setting goals helps you work towards your own objectives—most commonly with financial or career-based goals. Goal setting features as a major component of personal development literature. Goals provide you a sense of direction and purpose. Goal setting helps you capitalize on the human brain's amazing, unlimited, and personal powers; for instance, in the lessons on NLP, neuro-linguistic programming, I told you that your brain works like a super computer; your brain is a problem-solving and goal-achieving machine. Hence, you must learn how to articulate your financial goal with a specific plan to achieve it. Indeed, goals that are difficult to achieve and specific tend to increase your peak performance more than goals that are not. Your goal can become more specific through quantification or enumeration (should be measurable), such as by demanding an increase in productivity of 50%, or by defining certain tasks that must be completed. Setting goals affects your outcomes in many ways. The choices you make enable you to define your goals, to narrow your attention and direct your efforts to goal-relevant activities and away from perceived undesirable and goal-irrelevant actions. As for personal effort, it can lead you closer to your goal; by making the undue effort to work toward your goals, that action can lead to more effort; for example, if you typically produce four widgets an hour, and you have the goal of producing six, you may work more intensely towards the goal than you would otherwise. As for persistence, you must know that winners are not quitters; you should become more prone to work through setbacks if pursuing your financial or other goals. NLP reminds you to take cognition into account, too; goals can lead you to develop and change your behaviour. Cognition is a group of mental processes that includes attention, memory, producing and understanding language, solving problems, and making decisions. In this instance, I am referring to the conceptualization of your goals as an information processing view of your psychological functions. I am focusing on social cognition to explain your attitudes, attribution, and group dynamics. You set your goals by processing the information available to you and the applying knowledge I am teaching you now. Your cognition, or cognitive processes, can be natural or artificial, conscious or unconscious.

GOAL SETTING IN BUSINESS

In business, goal setting encourages you to put in substantial effort at work. You are a member of a team of workers. Also, because every member has defined expectations for their role, little room is left for inadequate effort to go unnoticed. Your managers cannot constantly drive motivation, or keep track of your work as an employee on a continuous basis. Goals are, therefore, an important tool for managers, since goals have the ability to function as a self-regulatory mechanism that acquires an employee a certain amount of guidance. Below I am distilling four mechanisms through which goal setting can affect your individual performance at work:

--Goals focus attention towards goal-relevant activities and away from goal-irrelevant activities.
--Goals serve as an energizer; higher goals induce greater effort while low goals induce lesser effort.
--Goals affect persistence; constraints with regard to resources affect work pace.
--Goals activate cognitive knowledge and strategies that help employees cope with the situation at hand.

GOAL–PERFORMANCE RELATIONSHIP

In this regard, there is a relationship between a goal and the performance intended to achieve that goal. An examination of the behavioral effects of goal-setting, led to the conclusion that 90% of laboratory and field studies involving specific and challenging goals led to higher performance than did easy or no goals. This fact underlined the importance of establishing higher performance goals. It is not adequate for me to urge you to do your very best. I must provide you the specialized knowledge you need to begin setting goals. For this reason, this chapter furnishes you with specific information on goal setting. By reading it attentively, you will have a clear and precise view of what I expect from you. In my mind, goal setting is of value to you because it facilitates your effort in focusing your efforts in a specified direction. I am motivating you to participate in the goal setting discussion, but the goals must be challenging as well.

It is my belief that the more I motivate you the more you will be stimulated and interested in accepting the goal-setting materials I will present to you. I want you to become committed to the design of your goals; if you lack commitment to your millionaire goals, then, you will lack motivation to reach them. To commit to these goals, you must believe in their importance or significance. As for attainability, you must also believe that you can attain, or at least partially reach, these defined goals. If you think no chance exists of reaching the millionaire goals, you may not even try. The specialized knowledge that follows will give you the confidence and self-efficacy you need to achieve your goals. The higher your self-efficacy regarding the task of becoming a millionaire, the more likely you will set higher goals and the more persistence you will show in achieving them.

FEEDBACK

Unlike the other success gurus, I have made feedback the common-core of my wealth-building system. I do not want you to buy my book and be stuck with it like the confused buyer of a VCR in 1983. After reading the book, I encourage you to contact me. I will encourage you to undergo a five-step coaching program, depending on your level of maturity: observation of student, analysis of student performance, evaluation of the level of student's financial proficiency, feedback from student, and planning of student's individual progress. The enhancement of performance through goals requires feedback. Goal setting and feedback go hand in hand. Without feedback, your goal setting is unlikely to work. Providing feedback on short-term objectives helps you to sustain motivation and commitment to the goal of becoming a millionaire. Besides, I promise to provide feedback to you on the strategies followed to achieve the goals and the final outcomes achieved as well. Generally, feedback on strategies to obtain your goal is very important, especially for complex work like studying to become a millionaire, because challenging goals put focus on outcomes rather than on performance strategies, so they impair performance.

Proper feedback is also very essential, and the following hints may help for providing a good feedback:

--Create a positive context for feedback.
--Use constructive and positive language.
--Focus on behaviors and strategies.
--Tailor feedback to the needs of the individual student of $ucce$$tology.
--Make feedback a two-way communication process.

Goal-setting may have little effect if you cannot see the state of your performance with the goal. Note the importance of you knowing where you stand with achieving your goals, so you can determine the desirability of working harder or of changing your methods. Advances in our technology can facilitate providing feedback to you. My systems analysts have designed computer programs that track goals for any members of my organization. The computer systems maintain every club member's goals, as well as their deadlines. Separate methods may check the member or student's progress on a regular basis, and other systems may require perceived slackers to explain how they intend to improve on their learning. We maintain a simple focus on an outcome, but we also encourage openness to exploration and understanding to growth among our students.

So do you want to become a millionaire? I assume your answer is yes. Your dreams are closer than you think, but you must establish a plan of action to make these dreams come true. Most people are still poor because they dream about getting rich, but they do not take any concrete action to make their dreams come true. Procrastination or inaction is an unacceptable course of action. You must work on defining your goals; you must conceptualize a plan to realize your goal. I am ready and willing to assist you on this financial journey. Let us go!

There is more to personal finance than the drudgery of debts and budgets.

When I became to America, I did not simply state that I wanted to grow rich; indeed, I stated my goal, and I formulated a step-by-step plan to realizing my goal. I read many books on goal setting to learn how to proceed in formulating my goals. I learned about thinking about achieving my goals in the short-term and long-term. Although my financial goal was set for me to become a millionaire in 7 or 8 years, I had ancillary goals, too: physical, family, spiritual, and psychological.

ALL MY GOALS

Financial Goal=to become a millionaire entrepreneur specializing in the provision of computer-based personal services.
Physical Goal=to lose weight and become sexy and physically fit.
Family Goal=to get married and father 2 children
Spiritual Goal= to pray daily, read the bible, and maintain a close relationship with God.
Psychological Goal= to achieve profound peace of mind and be happy

BRAINSTORMING

How did I arrive at formulating these goals? I spent much time thinking about my predicament as a first generation African immigrant struggling to realize the American Dream of success. Instead of wasting my precious time lamenting on my calamitous life in America, I started spending much time brainstorming and free writing. I had learned about brainstorming from Dr. Judith Nembhard in my writing and English composition courses at Howard University. Brainstorming is a group creativity technique by which a group tries to find a solution for a specific problem by gathering a list of ideas spontaneously contributed by its members. Brainstorming was developed and coined by Alex Faickney Osborn in 1953 through the book *Applied Imagination*. In the book, Osborn not only proposed the brainstorming method but also established effective rules for hosting brainstorming sessions. Brainstorming has become a popular group technique and has aroused attention in academia.

Multiple studies have been conducted to test Osborn's postulation that brainstorming is more effective than individuals working alone in generating ideas . Some researchers have concluded that the statement is false (brainstorming is not effective), while others uncovered flaws in the research and determined that the results are inconclusive. Furthermore, researchers have made modifications or proposed variations of brainstorming in an attempt to improve the productivity of brainstorming. However, there is no empirical evidence to indicate that any variation is more effective than the original technique. Nonetheless, brainstorming can be of great utility when the group accounts for, and works to minimize the group processes that decrease its effectiveness.

FREE-WRITING

As for free writing, my first encounter with free writing dates back to 1979, when I took a course on the poetry of identity from Dr. Linda LaRue, an African-American Fulbright scholar. She had presented free writing to us as a technique used in Freudian psychoanalysis as a remedy for the neuroses of patients.

Free writing regards writing as a soothing balm for patients undergoing the problems of mental restlessness. Free writing, also called stream-of-consciousness writing, is a prewriting technique in which a person writes continuously for a set period of time without regard to spelling, grammar, or topic. It produces raw, often unusable material, but helps writers overcome blocks of apathy and self-criticism. It is used mainly by prose writers and writing. Free writing is an antidote of writer's block. It is used mainly by prose writers and writing teachers.

Some writers use the technique to collect initial thoughts and ideas on a topic, often as a preliminary to formal writing. However, free writing is not the same as automatic writing. Unlike brainstorming where ideas are simply listed, in free writing one writes sentences to form a paragraph about whatever comes to mind. Hence, by free writing and brainstorming, you can prepare a list of your goals: financial, physical, family, spiritual, and psychological. Do not forget to use heuristics in preparing for writing your goals in life. The most fundamental example of heuristic is the process of problem solving by asking questions in a trial and error sequence, which can be used in everything from matching nuts and bolts to finding the values of variables in algebraic problems. Below are a few other commonly used heuristics, from George Pólya's 1945 book, *How to Solve It*:

If you are having difficulty understanding a problem pertaining to goal setting, please, try drawing a picture. If you cannot t find a solution, try assuming that you have a solution and seeing what you can derive from that (working backward). If the goal-setting problem is abstract, try examining a concrete example. Try solving a more general problem first (the inventor's paradox: the more ambitious plan may have more chances of success).

In psychology, heuristics are simple, efficient rules, hard-coded by evolutionary processes or learned, which have been proposed to explain how people make decisions, come to judgments, and solve problems, typically when facing complex problems or incomplete information These rules work well under most circumstances, but in certain cases lead to systematic errors or cognitive biases.

Although much of the work of discovering heuristics in human decision-makers was done by Amos Televisionersky and Daniel Kahneman, the concept was originally introduced by Nobel laureate Herbert Simon. Gerd Gigerenzer focuses on how heuristics can be used to make judgments that are in principle accurate, rather than producing cognitive biases – heuristics that are fast and frugal.

In 2002, Daniel Kahneman and Shane Frederick proposed that cognitive heuristics work by a process called attribute substitution which happens without conscious awareness. According to this theory, when somebody makes a judgment, of a target attribute, which is computationally complex, a rather easier calculated heuristic attribute is substituted. In effect, a cognitively difficult problem is dealt with by answering a rather simpler problem, without being aware of this happening. This theory explains cases where judgments fail to show regression toward the mean. Heuristics can be considered to reduce the complexity of clinical judgments in healthcare.

READING MANY BOOKS ON GOAL SETTING

You should learn from my example of goal setting. I had read many motivational books on time management and goal setting. I started crafting my goals based on findings in my reading. It is beyond the scope of *The Miraculous Millionaire* to explore goal setting in detail. This topic has been explored in too many books, which you can ascertain on my web sites (princeojong.com, millionaireiuniversity.com) or http://www.amazon.com. Nonetheless, in step 12, attend Millionaire iUniversity, I have listed many books which I consider valuable for your erudition:

THE MILLIONAIRE ENTREPRENEUR'S OATH

Below is a copy of the oath I had written back on November 14, 1988, the day my father passed through transition:

On this 14th day of November 1988, the day my father Dr. Gabriel Ojong Ayuk passed through transition, I, Prince Ojong, solemnly swear before human kind and the almighty God, the maker of heaven and earth to use my divine and unlimited power for the pursuit of material and spiritual wealth. I have decided to become a do-it-yourself millionaire entrepreneur, the master of my destiny.

As a votary at the shrine of wealth, I affirm; I dedicate; I consecrate; I consent. Today marks an end as well as a new beginning; I am being born again, financially! Without contrition, I have renounced my reckless past. Thereupon, I promise to spend the rest of my earthly life, days and nights, doing God's will and fulfilling my ordained cosmic mission on earth. In this respect, I am embarking on a mystical search for the right vehicle that will take me to my financial goal. By the end of this year, 1988, I will possess assets worth $10,000. I will double and compound these assets every year for five years, so that by 2000 I will become a self-made millionaire. To guarantee my seriousness, I am a writing a check to myself with the face value of 1,000,000. The check and my oath will be posted conspicuously in my abode for me to see every morning and every evening.

As a provision of selflessness and gratitude, I make the following agreement: As soon as I liberate myself from the slavery of poverty, I will spend part of my life sharing these secrets with my fellow human beings who are less fortunate than me. At least, I promise to encourage my fellow beings to read Napoleon Hill's book entitled *Think and Grow Rich*.

I understand fully that the law of cosmic compensation and spirituality govern human affairs. Since I do not subscribe to the philosophy of something for nothing, I expect to use individual action to attune myself with the Infinite Force of Divinity. In other words, I comprehend that financial success is not as free as manna from heaven. Because heaven helps only those who help themselves, I shall work hard and smart to deserve cosmic blessing. So help me Jesus; so help me God!

Signature:..

Date:..

THE MILLIONAIRE ENTREPRENEUR'S GOAL CONTRACT

Below is a copy of the goal contract I had made with myself and my God.

Date:_____

By_____ I will have earned a minimum

of $_____

I will have earned this amount of money as a result of giving the most efficient computer-based

services of which I am capable, rendering the fullest possible quantity and the best possible

quality of service in the capacity of _____

This is an irrevocable contract I make with myself and my God, the infinite force of divinity.

My Name:_____   Date:_____

My Signature:_____

Name of God:_____   Date:_____

God's Signature:_____

MILLIONAIRE STUDENT WEEKLY ACTION (TO-DO) CHECKLIST

If you have proceeded this far, I must congratulate you again for taking the steps to become the next self-made millionaire. Once again, congratulations. I advise you to continue doing what has made it possible for me to rise to the top of the financial world. I encourage you to revisit all the actionable checklist items I have presented below. To motivate and assist you in comprehending and applying the instructions presented in the book, I have built Millionaire iUniversity around a weekly action checklist, which are a series of baby steps vital to your program of self-improvement. By using this to-do list every week, you have no choice but to take quick action to improve yourself financially. At the beginning of each week, you have to schedule and highlight all the activities of personal finance that you plan to undertake.

To populate this scheduler, ask yourself the following questions:

What do I have to do next week?
Who is it about?
What will happen?
Where will it take place?
When will it take place?
Why will it happen?
How will it happen?

This technique is called the five Ws. I use it when I am brainstorming and free writing ideas for a paper. I also use it when I am teaching my daughters the principles of English composition. Similarly, in journalism, the five Ws, also known as the five Ws and one H, or the Six Ws, is a concept in news style, research, and in police investigations that are regarded as basics in information-gathering. It is a formula for getting the full story on something. The maxim of the five Ws and one H, is that for a report to be considered complete it must answer a checklist of six questions, each of which comprises an interrogative word. Even if you are experiencing writer's block, the five Ws will assist you in compiling financial ideas for your checklist.

It suffices for me to introduce you to some ideas that can feature on your to-do list:

Say your morning prayers
Recite your afternoon prayers
Say your evening prayers
Perform your Sunday bible readings
Pay your tithes every week
Revise the literature of the millionaire's secret
Set personal and financial goals
Write your plan to build wealth
Buy insurance: life, health, property, and casualty
Balance your financial book
Compute and surf
Start a business

Decode the IRS tax codes
Play the stock market
Manage mutual funds
Invest in real estate
Take care of your health
Have fun
Accept the challenges of chasing the American Dream
Avoid procrastination
Support your plans with persistence and determination
Pray for divine blessings
Dream about money
Unlock your in-born creativity
Think about money
Get a well-paying job
Set your goals
Write your goals down on paper
Maintain your focus on your goals
Map out you clear sense of direction
Read a good book on personal finance
Teach yourself personal finance
Acquire marketable skills
Focus on continuous self-development
Concentrate on your pursuit of financial success
Take action to explore your world and your Maker
Be a good Samaritan; help someone in need humbly
Dedicate your life to serving others
Be impeccably honest with yourself and others
Network with others
Take good care of your health
Quit a slavish job
Work hard
Form your mastermind group
Leverage your strengths
Create a monthly budget
Explore avenues of self-employment
Control your expenses
Save your money
Optimize credit cards
Improve your credit history
Find great bank and negotiate away fees
Open a 401(K) and/or a Roth IRA
Draft a spending plan
Diversify your investment goal
Use asset allocation to minimize risks
Choose a hobby

There is more to personal finance than the drudgery of debts and budgets.

Have fun
Maintain self-discipline
Reaffirm success
Cancel the word failure from your vocabulary
Develop resilience and bounce back
Become an incurable optimist
Add the affirmation "great" to your daily vocabulary
Develop a stellar reputation for speed and dependability

By examining the chart listed below, you can evaluate your performance at the end of each week.

Week #	Date	Activity Description	Completed? Yes/No
1			
2			
3			
4			
5			
6			
7			
8			
9			
10			

MILLIONAIRE STUDENT DEBT REDUCTION CAMPAIGN

The following illustration shows how a fictitious you, Joe the Debt Eliminator, can get out of debt. Although he does not make much money, Joe gets out of debt by reading *The Miraculous Millionaire* and implementing my plans.

PLAN ONE: SAVE $1,000 CASH AS A STARTER EMERGENCY FUND

Now that you have started paying yourself second, please, begin your saving campaign right away! Before you do anything else, you must save a $1,000 emergency fund. This money is to be used only for emergencies such as car repairs, sickness, and medical bills. Do not skip this step. It only takes a few setbacks for you to realize the wisdom of setting this money aside. If you have a cash cushion, life's mishaps will not force you to sink deeper into debt. You are able to recover more quickly.

PLAN TWO: POWER UP THE DEBT DESTROYER MACHINE

Once you have been successful in accumulating some savings, it is the right time to tackle your consumer debt. You do this with the debt destroyer.

Here is how the death destroyer machine works: List your non-mortgage debts from lowest balance to highest balance. Pay the minimum payment on all debts except the one with the smallest balance. Throw every penny you can find at the smallest debt.

When that debt is gone, do not alter the monthly amount you used to pay debts, but pay all you can toward the debt with the next-lowest balance. By using the powerful debt destroyer machine to obliterate some of your consumer debts, you have programmed yourself to modify your spending behavior for the better. You will be flattered by your small and quick wins, and you will be prepared to initiate the process of tackling bigger debts.

PLAN THREE: FINISH THE EMERGENCY FUND

Joe the Debt Eliminator's $1,000 emergency fund was only a start. After he has erased his non-mortgage debt, it is now time for him to embark on heavy lifting--some serious saving. He should try as soon as possible to accumulate and reserve three to six months of living expenses. For most people, that is the equivalent of $5,000 to $10,000. The easiest way to implement this strategy is for Joe the Debt Eliminator to simply take the money he was applying to his debt destroyer machine and convert it into a savings machine. If he was paying $500 each month toward debt, now he can throw that money into a high-yield savings account. I can always research the best lending institutions in all the states of the union. For instance, Joe the Debt Eliminator is now on step three. He has two thousand dollars saved in the bank. His goal is to set aside $10,000 by the end of 2012. Because he will soon be acting in a blockbuster movie full-time, he is actually hoping to save $20,000, but that may be quite of a stretch.

PLAN FOUR: INVEST 10% OF YOUR INCOME IN RETIREMENT

While Joe the Debt Eliminator is completing the first three steps, especially the first two, I recommend that he should suspend all other investment activities, including automatic employee payroll deductions credited into a 401(K) with an employer match. In this wise, Joe the Debt Eliminator is saving investing for last, that is once he has learned how to cultivate good money habits. It is understandable that Joe the Debt Eliminator will lose a few years of compound returns in his retirement accounts, but that loss is fine in the long run. By following the first three debt elimination steps, Joe the Debt Eliminator will have developed smart money habits and a strong saving ethic. Hence, it will not take much effort for Joe the Debt Eliminator to catch up with his prior investment losses.

Now that Joe the Debt Eliminator has paid off his debt and saved adequate money for his emergencies, I recommend that Joe the Debt Eliminator should invest 10% of his income into mutual funds. Step 9 of *The Miraculous Millionaire* deals with the management of mutual funds and bonds. By investing in mutual funds, Joe the Debt Eliminator is reducing his risk through asset diversification. Risk minimization is the positive result of diversification, which enables assets to be spread evenly among several broad categories of funds. If you work for an employer who matches your automatic 401(K) payroll deductions, then, you should put some of your money into a Roth IRA; put the rest of the 1% wherever it makes the most sense to you.

There is more to personal finance than the drudgery of debts and budgets.

PLAN FIVE: SAVE FOR COLLEGE

The cost of college tuition in the USA has been rising astronomically. It is a pity to see college graduates with loans of over $200,000. Yet, I must point out that education is important; it is a determinant of success. It is the principal predictor of upward economic and social mobility in the USA. Almost every parent wants his or her child to attend an Ivy League school. While well-educated students tend to have bright career prospects, their poor peers are condemned to chaff and wallow in the mediocrity of blue collar jobs. It is important for you to begin saving for a college. Once you have already begun saving for your retirement, you can turn some of your attention toward your children. Saving for college ensures that a legacy of debt is not handed down your family tree. Other parents opt to finance their children's college education with saving accounts such as 529 plans. I still prefer cash-value insurance as the long-term vehicle to save for my children's college education.

My first piece of advice, however, is for you to seek scholarships. Back in the days when I was a struggling student at Howard University, I was able to secure a scholarship of $5,000 from a Massachusetts millionaire who did not want his name to be disclosed to the public; the millionaire wanted to help African students from a francophone country. I applied for the scholarship, and I was too happy to receive the news that I was one of the winners. Similarly, when my junior sister was attending pharmacy school at Howard University, she could not work because of her tight school schedule. Against her will, I managed to secure a $10,000 scholarship for her to cover tuition for two semesters at Howard University, Washington, DC. The donors were interested in assisting female students from developing countries in Africa; my sister fit the bill. Without the scholarship, my sister would have dropped out of school. Thanks for the scholarship. Today, she is a tenured professor of pharmacy at her alma mater. Since then, I have learned that many scholarship quotas are not satisfied because of the indolence of prospective students. Scholarships are still there, but you must use your research skills to uncover them. Financial aid counselors at major universities have asserted that it is mind-boggling how much scholarship money goes unclaimed every year. The students who know how to research sources of this money are able to fund most of their education through scholarships. The improvident and have-not students are condemned to rely on either student loans and payments by their parents. One of the seminars sponsored by my organization focuses on the inscrutable world of college education financing. If you are interested to learn more, please, call my office: (301) 593-4897. I can help.

As far as the private financing of college education is concerned, my recommendation is for you to rely on a permanent life insurance product known as equity indexed universal life option B increasing. What does EQUITY-INDEXED UNIVERSAL LIFE INSURANCE mean? It is a specially designed permanent life insurance policy that allows policyholders to tie cash accumulation values to a stock-market index such as the Standard and Poor 500. Indexed universal life insurance policies typically contain a minimum guaranteed fixed interest rate component along with the indexed account option. Indexed policies give policyholders the security of fixed universal life insurance with the growth potential of a variable policy linked to indexed returns.

If you establish this financial instrument early in your child's life, you will be astonished by the amount of money you can accumulate for your child's college education. Best of all, if the child does not use the money, you can reallocate it to other uses tax free. In fact, this is how I am looking forward to financing my children's college education. If you are interested in the details of how this policy works, I would be willing to share the details with you.

PLAN SIX: PAY OFF YOUR HOME MORTGAGE

Once you have taken care of all your other small consumer debts, and everything else, then, it is appropriate for you to focus your attention like a laser beam on your biggest debt of all: home mortgage. From the book titled *The Banker's Secret*, I had learned the value of prepaying my mortgage. Prepayment can reduce your mortgage principal and interest dramatically, thereby shortening the repayment period of your standard mortgage. I started by ensuring that I make 13 monthly mortgage payments per year instead of twelve. How does it work? Easy. To weaken the power of compounding, I divide my monthly mortgage amount by 12. Every month, as I am paying my regular mortgage, I apply the extra payment to reduce the principal. Imagine that your monthly mortgage payment is $1,000. In twelve months you have to pay $1,000 x 12, which is tantamount to $12,000. Mathematically, therefore, if you want to produce an extra 1 month of mortgage payment, which is $1,000, you prepay one lump sum of $1,000 before the end of the year or you divide $1,000 and be applying extra monthly principal payments of $84. This extra prepayment of $84 will ensure that you accumulate one extra monthly payment of $1,000. You do not have to throw money away to those bi-weekly mortgage companies that promise you heaven and earth to reduce your mortgage to zero. If you need more information on this subject of prepayment for mortgage debt elimination, join the Millionaire Club and attend Millionaire iUniversity.

PLAN SEVEN: BUILD WEALTH

If you have eliminated your debt, built emergency savings, invested 10% of your income in a 401(K) and Roth IRA, and paid off your mortgage, you can begin to build some serious wealth. True! How? It is not yet time for you to rest on your laurels. It is a big deal to pay off all your debts, but it is simplistic to think that you have become wealthy. Where my program beats Suze Orman, Dave Ramsey, and other gurus is the fact that I, Prince Ojong, outline a specific investing blueprint for you to follow after you have eliminated your debt. Now that you have found financial peace by paying off all your debts, you cannot make do with Dave Ramsey's vague affirmations of investing in the dark. He urges you to invest, but he does not teach you specifically how to invest; you will never be financially at peace if you put all your savings in a 401(K) or ROTH IRA. Dave Ramsey's investing advice reminds me of the vague exhortations of Primerica's insurance sales agents; these Primerica agents' mantra of "buy term and invest the difference" is idiotic like a song sang by a Shakespearean fool or an idiot. Investing requires more than just taking baby steps; investing is not kiddie stuff; it is a very risky business. The average person does not have a clue as to where Dave Ramsey or Primerica wants him or her to invest his or her growing treasury of savings. This is why *The Miraculous Millionaire* is different from the other books; my book narrates my investing adventures; it distills and instills the lessons I have learned and how the average person can model the excellence of my experience.

ACCOUNTING MBA FOR FREE

At this juncture, I want to share materials with you that will make you look and sound better than an MBA graduate from the Wharton School of business administration. So you want to become a millionaire entrepreneur? You must have a plan that will allow you to find good investments, reduce taxes, beat inflation, and properly manage money. In this chapter, you will comprehend why you need to become financially more literate. Whether you are new to accounting and financial planning or a seasoned veteran, I will provide you with the valuable information and techniques you can use to create and implement a consistent personalized financial plan. My plan will also take into consideration the new tax rules that affect home ownership, saving for college, estate planning, and many other aspects of your financial life. In fact, the only way you can get out of the rat race is to acquire the language of millionaires; you may not be aware that millionaires' lingua franca is accounting. If you are aspiring to communicate like a millionaire, you must acquire native fluency in the millionaire's linguistic code; in other words, I am stressing the requirement for you to become financially more literate than ever before; that is, when you will be ready to learn how rich people play and win the money game. In this chapter, I will teach you the advanced fundamentals of accounting and investing. I want you to start using big words such as cash, cash flow, credit, debit, debts, assets, equity, depreciation, balance, income, and liabilities with the facility of easy grace.

By the way, do you know the famous accountant's SECRET? No? You should. Seriously, if you want to take control of your financial future and unlock the doors to financial success, you owe it to yourself to know and apply the famous accountant's secret: Assets = Liabilities + Equity. In other words, Equity + Liabilities = Assets. I am going to break down this equation to the point that even a child in kindergarten can understand it fully. The best way for me to introduce you to the famous accountant's secret is to ask you to type the words "create a balance sheet" in your Google browser. The search results will yield a sample of the financial statement that accountants call a balance sheet. Simply, a balance sheet is a snapshot of your financial position. For a corporate entity, a balance sheet makes it easy for an accountant to share the pulse of the business with managers. In this vein, the accountant is functioning like a physician diagnosing the condition or the health status of the business. Most accounting balance sheets classify a company's assets and liabilities into distinctive groupings such as Current Assets; Property, Plant, and Equipment; Current Liabilities; etc. The grouping of equity comprises of items such common stocks and retained earnings, as these classifications make the balance sheet more useful. Personally, I like to update my personal balance sheet every three or six months. As my student, I advise you to follow suit; frequently updating your balance sheet is a fun and helpful way for you to gauge your progress.

Assets is anything you own of value that has an artificial lifespan of at least one year. The term liabilities refers to the debts you owe. If an asset is leveraged, such as a house, equity is the portion of the house that belongs to you after you have subtracted the amount of your mortgage. During the course of your life, you acquire many assets, for example: cash, petty cash, temporary investments, accounts receivable, inventory, supplies, pre-paid insurance, land, land improvements, buildings, equipment, goodwill, trade names, etc.

Your liabilities may comprise of notes payable, accounts payable, wages payable, interest payable, taxes payable, warranty liability, unearned revenues, and bonds payable; these are all debts you owe and have to pay. Generally, accountants will draw two cross lines on a sheet of paper that look like the letter T. Do you remember the T-square diagram? It is a technical drawing instrument used by draftsmen primarily as a guide for drawing horizontal lines on a drafting table.

On the left side of the diagram, the accountant presents information about your assets; on the right side of the diagram, the accountant displays your liabilities and equity. Take a short moment to peruse your balance sheet. If you look at the bottom line, you will notice the sum of assets is equal to the sum of liabilities and owner's equity. In both columns, the amount of liability on the left side of the chart must balance with the amount of equity and owner's equity on the right side of the chart. Indeed, that is why the document is called a balance sheet. If you have not grasped the sense of this explanation, please, do not worry; like a broken record, I will keep coming back to it to ensure your comprehension. It is easier than you think! I will prove to you that the concept of a balance sheet is not that difficult to grasp fully.

YOUR DYNAMIC BALANCE SHEET

Millionaires use the balance sheet as a dynamic tool for financial transactions and money management. Are you ready to take control of your finances? I will be your guide. Here, you will find tips and information to help you get organized. I must stress that it is easier than you think! When you are ready to get started, I have the tools that can show you exactly where your money's going. From the middle class to millionaires, everyone feels a few dollars short of comfort at times. But more money will not necessarily solve financial difficulties. The solution is to manage your money like the professionals. The key is to develop strong money management and computer skills that can help you use the money you have today to live the life you want. Plus, when your ship does come in, the great job, the winning lottery ticket or the inheritance from rich Uncle Billy, you will know how to handle it. People win the lottery every day, but they are broke soon because of the lack of proper money management skills. Their tragedy reminds you that people need to have a plan for their money. If you do not have a plan but the other person does have a plan, they are going to win because they have the discipline, goal and desire and you are just sort of playing by the ear. And who is the other person? Marketers and finance professionals hucking all kinds of slick stuff. It is true! It is not your imagination that is playing you false; in fact, finance professionals and other people are out to get you, or at least your money. Being prepared by becoming more literate financially will help you counter the very ferocious forces out there that want you to spend, spend, and spend.

A PENNY PINCHER OR CHEAPSKATE'S MONEY SAVING GUIDE

If you want to become a millionaire, you must learn the value of the good ole mighty dollar of the USA. I have summarized sixty ways I have been saving money every day; do you want to be like me? Then, imitate my frugal ways. You can use the money you save for your investment plans. Ok? As a bulwark against people who want you to spend foolishly, I am presenting you with a penny pincher or a cheapskate's money saving guide:

There is more to personal finance than the drudgery of debts and budgets.

AIRLINE FARES

1. Compare low-cost carriers with major carriers that fly to your destination. Remember, the best fares may not be out of the airport closest to you.

2. You may save money by including a Saturday evening stay-over or by purchasing the ticket at least 14 days in advance. Ask which days of the week and times of the day have the lowest fare.

3. Even if you are using a travel agent, check airline and Internet travel sites, and look for special deals. If you call, always ask for the lowest fare to your destination.

CAR RENTAL

4. Since car rental rates can vary greatly, compare total price (including taxes and surcharge) and take advantage of any special offers and membership discounts.

5. Rental car companies offer various insurance and waiver options. Check with your automobile insurance agent and credit card company in advance to avoid duplicating any coverage you may already have.

NEW CARS

6. You can save thousands of dollars over the lifetime of a car by selecting a model that combines a low purchase price with low depreciation, financing, insurance, gasoline, maintenance, and repair costs. Ask your local librarian for *Consumer Reports* or new car guides that contain this information.

TRANSPORTATION

7. Having selected a model and options you are interested in, you can save hundreds of dollars by comparison shopping. Get price quotes from several dealers (over the phone or Internet) and let each know you are contacting the others.
8. Remember there is no "cooling off" period on new car sales. Once you have signed a contract, you are obligated to buy the car.

USED CARS

9. Before buying any used car:
• Compare the seller's asking price with the average retail price in a "bluebook" or other guide to car prices which can be found at many libraries, banks, and credit unions.
• Have a mechanic you trust check the car, especially if the car is sold "as is."
10. Consider purchasing a used car from an individual you know and trust. They are more likely than other sellers to charge a lower price and point out any problems with the car.

AUTO LEASING

11. Do not decide to lease a car just because the payments are lower than on a traditional auto loan. The leasing payments are lower because you do not actually own the car.

12. Leasing a car is very complicated. When shopping, consider the price of the car (known as the capitalized cost), your trade-in allowance, any down payment, monthly payments, various fees (excess mileage, excess "wear and tear," end-of-lease), and the cost of buying the car at the end of the lease. A valuable source of information about auto leasing can be found in *Keys to Vehicle Leasing: A Consumer Guide*, which is published by the Federal Reserve Board and Federal Trade Commission.

GASOLINE

13. You can save hundreds of dollars a year by comparing prices at different stations, pumping gas yourself, and using the lowest-octane called for in your owner's manual.

14. You can save up to $100 a year on gas by keeping your engine tuned and your tires inflated to their proper pressure.

CAR REPAIRS

15. Consumers lose billions of dollars each year on unneeded or poorly done car repairs. The most important step that you can take to save money on these repairs is to find a skilled, honest mechanic. Before you need repairs, look for a mechanic who:
• is certified and well established;
• has done good work for someone you know; and
• communicates well about repair options and costs.

AUTO INSURANCE

16. You can save several hundred dollars a year by purchasing auto insurance from a licensed, low-price insurer. Call your state insurance department for a publication showing typical prices charged by different companies. Then call at least four of the lowest-priced, licensed insurers to learn what they would charge you for the same coverage.

17. Talk to your agent or insurer about raising your deductibles on collision and comprehensive coverage to at least $500 or, if you have an old car, dropping this coverage altogether. This can save you hundreds of dollars on insurance premiums.

18. Make certain that your new policy is in effect before dropping your old one.

HOMEOWNER/RENTER INSURANCE

19. You can save several hundred dollars a year on homeowner insurance and up to $50 a year on renter insurance by purchasing insurance from a low-price, licensed insurer.

There is more to personal finance than the drudgery of debts and budgets.

Ask your state insurance department for a publication showing typical prices charged by different licensed companies. Then call at least four of the lowest priced insurers to learn what they would charge you. If such a publication is not available, it is even more important to call at least four insurers for price quotes.

INSURANCE

20. Make certain you purchase enough coverage to replace the house and its contents. "Replacement" on the house means rebuilding to its current condition.
21. Make certain your new policy is in effect before dropping your old one.

LIFE INSURANCE

22. If you want insurance protection only, and not a savings and investment product, buy a term life insurance policy.
23. If you want to buy a whole life, universal life, or other cash-value policy, plan to hold it for at least 15 years. Canceling these policies after only a few years can more than double your life insurance costs.
24. Check the National Association of Insurance Commissioners website (www.naic.org/cis) or your local library for information on the financial soundness of insurance companies.

CHECKING ACCOUNTS AND DEBIT CARDS

25. You can save more than $100 a year in fees by selecting a free checking account or one with no minimum balance requirement. Request a complete list of fees that are charged on these accounts, including ATM and debit card fees.
26. See if you can get free or lower cost checking through direct deposit or agreeing to ATM only use. Be aware of charges for using an ATM not associated with your financial institution.

SAVINGS PRODUCTS

27. Before opening a savings account, find out whether the account is insured by the federal government (FDIC for banks or NCUA for credit unions). Financial institutions offer a number of products, such as mutual funds and annuities, which are not insured.

BANKING/CREDIT

28. Once you select a type of savings account, use the telephone, newspaper, and Internet to compare rates and fees offered by different financial institutions, including those outside your city. These rates can vary a lot and, over time, can significantly affect interest earnings.
29. To earn the highest return on savings (annual percentage yield) with little or no risk, consider certificates of deposit (CDs) or U.S. Savings Bonds (Series I or EE).

CREDIT CARDS

30. To avoid late payment fees and possible interest rate increases on your credit cards, make sure you send in your payment a week to ten days before the statement due date. Late payments on one card can increase fees and interest rates on other cards.

31. You can avoid interest charges, which may be considerable, by paying off your entire bill each month. If you are unable to pay off a large balance, pay as much as you can. Try to shift the remaining balance to a credit card with a lower annual percentage rate (APR). You can find listings of credit card plans, rates, and terms on the Internet, in personal finance magazines, and in newspapers.

32. Be aware that credit cards with rebates, cash back, travel awards, or other perks may carry higher rates or fees.

AUTO LOANS

33. To save as much as several thousand dollars in finance charges, pay for the car in cash or make a large down payment. Always get the shortest term loan possible as this will lower your interest rate.

34. Make certain to get a rate quote (or preapproved loan) from your bank or credit union before seeking dealer financing. You can save as much as $1000 in finance charges by shopping for the cheapest loan.

35. Make certain to consider the dollar difference between low-rate financing and a lower sale price. Remember that getting zero or low-rate financing from a dealer may prevent you from getting the rebate.

FIRST MORTGAGE LOANS

36. Although your monthly payment may be higher, you can save tens of thousands of dollars in interest charges by shopping for the shortest term mortgage you can afford. For each $100,000 you borrow at a 7% annual percentage rate (APR), for example, you will pay over $75,000 less in interest on a 15-year fixed rate mortgage than you would on a 30-year fixed rate mortgage.

37. You can save thousands of dollars in interest charges by shopping for the lowest-rate mortgage. with the fewest points. On a 15-year $100,000 fixed-rate mortgage, just lowering the APR from 7% to 6.5% can save you more than $5,000 in interest charges over the life of the loan, and paying two points instead of three would save you an additional $1,000.

38. Check the Internet or your local newspaper for mortgage rate surveys, then call several lenders. for information about their rates (APRs), points, and fees. If you choose a mortgage broker, make certain to compare their offers with those of direct lenders.

39. Be aware that the interest rate on most adjustable rate mortgages (ARMs) can vary a great deal over the lifetime of the loan. An increase of several percentage points might raise payments by hundreds of dollars a month, so ask the lender what the highest possible monthly payment might be.

There is more to personal finance than the drudgery of debts and budgets.

MORTGAGE REFINANCING

40. Consider refinancing your mortgage if you can get a rate that is lower than your existing mortgage rate and plan to keep the new mortgage for at least several years. Calculate precisely how much your new mortgage (including points, fees and closing costs) will cost and whether, in the long run, it will cost less than your current mortgage.

HOME EQUITY LOANS

41. Be cautious in taking out home equity loans. The loans reduce or may even eliminate the equity that you have built up in your home. (Equity is the cash you would have if you sold your house and paid off your mortgage loans.) If you are unable to make payments on home equity loans, you could lose your home.
42. Compare home equity loans offered by at least four reputable lending institutions. Consider the interest rate on the loan and the annual percentage rate (APR), which includes other costs, such as origination fees, discount points, mortgage insurance, and other fees. Ask if the rate changes, and if so, how it is calculated and how frequently, as this will affect the amount of your monthly payments.

HOME PURCHASE

43. You can often negotiate a lower sale price by employing a buyer broker who works for you, not the seller. If the buyer broker or the broker's firm also lists properties, there may be a conflict of interest, so ask them to tell you if they are showing you a property that they have listed.
44. Do not purchase any house until it has been examined by a home inspector that you selected.

RENTING A PLACE TO LIVE

45. Do not limit your rental housing search to classified ads or referrals from friends and acquaintances.
Select buildings where you would like to live and contact their building manager or owner to see if anything is available.
46. Remember that signing a lease probably obligates you to make all monthly payments for the term of the agreement.

HOME IMPROVEMENT

47. Home repairs often cost thousands of dollars and are the subject of frequent complaints. Select from among several well established, licensed contractors who have submitted written, fixed-price bids for the work.
48. Do not sign any contract that requires full payment before satisfactory completion of the work.

HOUSING

MAJOR APPLIANCES

49. Consult Consumer Reports, available in most public libraries, for information about specific appliance brands and models and how to evaluate them, including energy use. There are often great price and quality differences. Look for the yellow Energy Guide label on products, and especially for products that have earned the government's ENERGY STAR, which can save up to 50% in energy use.

50. Once you have selected a specific brand and model, check the Internet or yellow pages to learn what stores carry the brand. Call at least four of these stores to compare prices and ask if that is the lowest price they can offer you. This comparison shopping can save you as much as $100 or more.

HEATING AND COOLING

51. A home energy audit can identify ways to save up to hundreds of dollars a year on home heating (and air conditioning). Ask your electric or gas utility if they audit homes for free or for a reasonable charge. If they do not, ask them to refer you to a qualified professional.

52. Enrolling in load management programs and off-hour rate programs offered by your electric utility may save you up to $100 a year in electricity costs. Call your electric utility for information about these cost-saving programs.

TELEPHONE SERVICE

53. Once a year, review your phone bills for the previous three months to see what local, local toll, long distance, and international calls you normally make. Call several phone companies which provide service in your area (including wireless and cable), to find the cheapest calling plan that meets your needs. Consider a bundled package that offers local, local toll and long distance, and possibly other services, if you heavily use all the services in the bundle.

UTILITIES

54. Check your phone bill to see if you have optional calling features or additional services, such as inside wire maintenance, that you do not need. Each option you drop could save you $40 or more each year.

55. If you make very few toll or long distance calls, avoid calling plans with monthly fees or minimums. Or consider disconnecting the service altogether and use dial around services such as 10-10 numbers or prepaid phone cards for your calls. When shopping for dial around service, look for fees, call minimum, and per minute rates. Treat prepaid cards as cash and find out if there is an expiration date.

There is more to personal finance than the drudgery of debts and budgets.

56. If you use a cell phone, make sure your calling plan matches the pattern of calls you typically make. Understand peak calling periods, area coverage, roaming, and termination charges. Contracts offered by most carriers will provide you with a trial period of 14 days or more. Use that time to make sure the service provides coverage in all the places you will be using the phone (home, work etc.). Prepaid wireless plans tend to have higher per minute rates and fees but may be a better option if you use the phone only occasionally.

57. Before making calls when away from home, compare per minute rates and surcharges for cell phones, prepaid phone cards, and calling card plans to find how to save the most money.

58. Dial your long distance calls directly. Using an operator to place the call can cost you up to $10 extra. To save money on information calls, look the number up on the Internet, or in the directory.

FOOD PURCHASED AT MARKETS

59. You can save hundreds of dollars a year by shopping at lower-priced food stores. Convenience stores often charge the highest price.

60. You will spend less on food if you shop with a list, take advantage of sales, and purchase basic ingredients, rather than pre-packaged components or ready-made items.

61. You can save hundreds of dollars a year by comparing price-per-ounce or other unit prices on shelf labels. Stock up on those items with low per-unit costs.

PRESCRIPTION DRUGS

62. Since brand name drugs are usually much more expensive than their generic equivalents, ask your physician and pharmacist if a less expensive generic or an over the counter alternative is available.

63. Since pharmacies may charge widely different prices for the same medicine, call several. When taking a drug for a long time, also consider calling mail-order pharmacies, which often charge lower prices.

FUNERAL ARRANGEMENTS

64. Plan ahead, making your wishes known about your funeral, memorial, or burial arrangements in writing to save your family or estate unnecessary expense.

65. For information about the least costly options, which may save you several thousand dollars, contact a local Funeral Consumer Alliance or memorial society, which are usually listed in the Yellow Pages under funeral services.

66. Before selecting a funeral home, call several and ask for prices of specific goods and services, or visit them to obtain an itemized price list. You are entitled to this information by law.

66 Ways to Save Money was developed by a working group of representatives from government agencies, consumer groups, business organizations, and educational institutions that sought to develop and publicize money-saving tips. The initiative was managed by the non-profit Consumer Federation of America (CFA).

THE TEN COMMANDMENTS OF QUICK RICHES

Dear Prospective Millionaire:

Now you will see with your two naked eyes the wisdom of regular saving and investing. By adhering to the following steps, it is easy to put your plan in action.

Step #1: "Do-It-Yourself" investing is the best approach to building wealth. Avoid full-service brokers. Join the Millionaire Success Club and learn to invest on your own. It is easy to become a member, and investing is fun! Call (301) 593-4897.

Participate in the club's investment program monthly. Yes, you can do it. If not, then, ask a kid to show you how to save a dollar every day in a "piggy" bank. On the date of the meeting or at your earliest convenience, invest like other members. Benjamin Franklin said "A penny saved is a penny earned."

Step #2: Implement the "Pay-Yourself-Second" or ten-percent rule. Apportion at least 10% of your annual income for investing. Immediately you receive your pay check, write a check to yourself second; that is, before you write checks to pay other bills. If you lack the discipline, the Millionaire Success Club is ready to help you. Do not waste your time budgeting, if you dislike it. Like dieting, budgeting, which is boring, does not work for some people.

Step #3: Apply the "dollar-cost-averaging" principle. Invest the same amount of money on a regular basis. By using this principle, you benefit from price fluctuations in the capital markets. When stock prices appreciate, you buy less shares; when stock prices depreciate, you buy more shares. In fact, you win all the time. No more complaints about stock-price volatility and market corrections.

Step #4: Capitalize on the magic of compounding. Time is money. Time is your good buddy and slave. As you sleep, so does time grow your money on trees everywhere. Do you remember the simple and compound interest formulae you learned in primary school? It may sound like kiddie stuff, but it is the secret of growing your money. Albert Einstein called compounding the eighth wonder of the world. The surreal affluence of millionaires and billionaires shows Einstein is right.

Step #5: Pay zero taxes on your investments. Invest in tax-free or tax-deferred instruments. Ms. Leona Helmsley of New York said "Rich people do not pay taxes; small people do." She was thrown in jail. Why? She revealed a big secret of the rich and famous. Avoid capital gains by manipulating the income tax system adroitly. Recently, Warren Buffett begged President Barack H. Obama to stop cuddling America's rich and famous; the former encouraged the latter to sign new legislation to tax the rich more.

Step #6: Seek guidance from the guns and butter theory of spending. Buy goods that appreciate in value; minimize the purchase of items that depreciate in value. For example, while millionaires buy guns, the average Joe Blow squanders money on butter.

There is more to personal finance than the drudgery of debts and budgets.

Step #7: Invest in education. It is a smart move in 2012 and the future. Functional education will never disappoint you. We are living in an information era. Hence, it pays to acquire the right education or training. I am referring to self-education and specialized knowledge.

Step #8: Carry enough insurance: life, auto, and health. Trouble sounds no alarm bells. It never rains, but it pours. Do not be caught unprepared.

Step #9: Never finance a car with a 5 year loan. Buy a two-year old model and $ave a mighty bundle of dollars.

Step#10: Slash mortgage interest and build equity fast; that is, without converting to a bi-weekly mortgage program.

Besides, join a credit union. There are many benefits for you.

Armchair millionaire, good luck! These ten steps should be your awful watchword. See you at the top!

Contact: (301) 593-4897
             (301) 593-4879

Fax: (240) 241-5137

THE PRINCE-OJONG CHECKLIST TO FINANCIAL FREEDOM

I love checklists. I love checklists especially when I want to make progress in a particular area but I do not exactly know what steps to take. This is a personal financial checklist that covers all the steps I have taken over the last 5-28 years that have helped me move from being a financial mess to having a little bit of an idea of what is going on. Some of the listed items are bigger and will take a long time, and some of them are simple tasks that you can accomplish in a day. Some will be relevant to your situation and some will not; that is why it is called "personal" finance; everyone's situation is unique.

But, if you are just starting out and are trying to get yourself into a better position financially, I would suggest spending the next couple months and checking off as many things on this list as possible. If you do that you will be on your way to financial freedom!

This is not a chronological step-by-step process, but like the title suggests it is just a checklist. Some of the items can be done simultaneously, while others will require another item to be checked off first. Other than the first couple items, they are not listed in any particular order. If you are looking for a step-by-step process, I highly recommend this checklist:

START GIVING REGULARLY

Start giving regularly. Something! Anything! If you do not have money, give your time. Just get the sowing and reaping process started. The Holy bible says as long as the earth remains there will always be seedtime and harvest and you cannot reap what you do not sow. So just like a farmer would not expect crops without planting seed, we too must start sowing in the area that we want to reap.

MAKE A LIFELONG PROMISE TO YOURSELF TO SPEND LESS MONEY THAN YOU EARN

We could end this checklist right here and it would suffice. Just about everything listed below falls into this category. Spending less than you earn is the key to wealth building, and is the most important lesson when it comes to personal finance. You can do everything else right, but if you spend more money than you earn – you will not be in a good financial position. This is the simple rule that allows families living on a $40,000/year salary to retire with millions and that causes millionaires to go bankrupt. You have to decide that you will not spend more money than you earn.

PAY OFF ALL CONSUMER DEBTS

Proverbs 22:7 says that the borrower is a slave to the lender. Having been a slave and a free man in this area, I much prefer being free. A wonderful second benefit is that you have a lot more financial peace and can build wealth faster when you are out of debt. For paying off debts, I recommend many tools and resources to cut your debt.

NEGOTIATE A BETTER RATE WITH CREDIT CARD COMPANIES

While I was working to pay down my debt, I spent some time on the phone-negotiating with my credit card companies to get a better interest rate. It is not a guarantee, but I consistently would get off the phone with a better interest rate than when I called.

CREATE A BUDGET

I recognize the fact that some people dislike bugeting. Initially, I did not like establishing a monthly budget. When I realized that budgeting was a necessary exercise in personal finance, I had no other choice than to start budgeting. If budgeting was the cost of becoming a millionaire, so be it; I was willing to pay it. Creating a budget can be as simple or as difficult as you make it. I love having a budget in place – contrary to what I thought before I tried it; it does not feel like we are in handcuffs, but rather that we are more free to spend money in the areas we want to. There are lots of budgeting software options and other budgeting tools to help you. Having a budget has helped my marriage, saved us thousands of dollars, and given us so much more peace with our money.

There is more to personal finance than the drudgery of debts and budgets.

GET THE EMPLOYER MATCH ON YOUR 401(K)

If your employer has a matching program in your 401(K) or 403b (many of them do) you should try to take advantage of that if at all possible. My former employer had a 100% matching program. So if I put in $500, they put in $500. That is a 100% return on my investment. This is the easiest way to boost your retirement dollars.

START AN EMERGENCY FUND

This was another thing that we did to give us a lot more peace with our personal finances. It can be expected that unexpected things will happen. Creating an emergency fund is just proof that you are expecting them. We have since used our emergency fund to save us even more money.

SELL YOUR JUNK

Way too many of us have way too much stuff. A lot of it would never be missed if we got rid of it. I have sold a lot of stuff on Ebay and Amazon and it helped provide some extra cash to pay down my debt.

START LEARNING WHAT THE BIBLE SAYS ABOUT MONEY

The Holy bible really has a lot to say about our money. There are many biblical verses about money that every Christian should know.

START GIVING 10%

Giving 10% of your income to your local church is an important milestone. God was the original giver and we were created by Him to be givers as well. I have witnessed miracles in our life in the area of giving and it also happens to be the only place in the Holy bible where God says it is okay to test him – See Malachi 3:10.

ORGANIZE YOUR BANK ACCOUNTS

I discovered that having more than one checking account allowed us to manage our money much cleaner and with more efficiency. Here is a little on how we organize our bank accounts.

CUT YOUR EXPENSES

If you are really trying to save money or get out of debt, you need to thoroughly examine each of your monthly expenses. I wrote about 15 ways to cut expenses which will get you started, but always be asking yourself, "Is _____ really necessary?" or "Can I get _____ cheaper somewhere?"

SIMPLIFY YOUR BILL PAYING PROCESS

I created a simple system for paying my bills each month. It made my life a lot easier and eliminated a lot of stress. Read more: How to Pay Monthly Bills.

FIGURE OUT YOUR TRUE HOURLY WAGE

This is a fantastic exercise to help you more accurately know what your time is worth and whether or not that job you have is worth it. Try it here: How much are you really getting paid?

SET CAREER GOALS

Following up on the previous task, is the current job worth it? It is going to help you reach your career goals? If you continue doing what you are doing, where will you be in 5 years – or 20 years? Are you doing what you love? If not, find someone doing what you want to do, take them out to lunch, and ask them how they did it.

CREATE A WILL

Save your loved ones a headache and just do it. You can do it at LegalZoom.com in less than 30 minutes for $69 and be done with it. Nolo.com is another do-it-yourself source for writing a will.

EVALUATE YOUR CAR SITUATION

I am convinced that one of the biggest things that keeps most middle class Americans in the middle class is their insistence on spending way too much of their income on cars. I used to believe that I would always have a car payment. I was wrong and now I intend to never have a car payment because I will save up cash for whatever car I buy. Watch the car video on my web site for inspiration. For more information on this subject, please, learn how cars affect your financial freedom.

START SAVING FOR KID'S COLLEGE

If you have children you might want to start saving for their college education. Personally, I would not do this until I had my debt paid off and had a head start on saving for retirement. Your children can take a loan out for college, but the only loan you can get for retirement is on a credit card and that seems a bit foolish to me – do not you think so? Some argue that the 529 is the best college saving plan, but the Education Savings Account is a good option as well.

GET LIFE INSURANCE

When I started a family in 1997, I bought term life insurance for the very first time. I believe in buying term insurance over whole life. There are some cases where there could be an argument for choosing whole life, but generally term life seems to be a better purchase for most people.

There is more to personal finance than the drudgery of debts and budgets.

I recently signed up a friend for her first life insurance policy; I used Pacific to get a term life insurance quote and she was happy with the process. You can read more about the use of life insurance in step 3 of the book.

PAY OFF YOUR HOUSE EARLY

As part of getting out of debt, I want to live without a mortgage as well. Here are 4 ways to pay off your house early. Just imagine your electric bill being the most expensive bill each month. I cannot wait!

GIVE MORE THAN 10%

The more I understand stewardship, the more I realize that every dollar that is in my bank account is not mine – it is all God's. A big part of being a good steward is understanding this and never letting money get a hold on us. I am convinced that the most fulfilled people in the world are those who are always looking for ways to give of themselves. Time, energy, or money – it is in our DNA to be givers and like the parable of the talents teaches us, if we are faithful with small amounts we will be entrusted with more.

BUDGETING TIPS

Like most people I know, I hate budgeting. I have always regarded budgeting as painful drudgery. It is like a bitter pill I am forced to swallow against my will. In fact, after the failure of my magazine business, I had to learn how to prepare and maintain a monthly budget because of the necessity of getting out of debt. After I learned the essentials of budgeting, I bought a copy of Microsoft Money and Quicken software to automate the monotonous tasks of budgeting. For my businesses, I bought a copy of Peachtree and QuickBooks. Hence, if you like working with computers like me, I would advise you to do what I did to get a handle on budgeting. If you are still the old fashioned type, then, I still recommend the envelope system or budget worksheet.

Personal budget planning is one of the most painful-yet-essential financial skills you can possibly learn. Though it might hurt to ration out what you can and CANNOT spend, it will change your financial future forever. Planning your personal finances without a budget is like trying to make a map without a compass. Success just is not very plausible. You need a plan. As the old adage goes, "If you fail to plan, you plan to fail." So we have compiled the following articles to help guide you to creating the perfect budget for your life. Read on:

PLANNING YOUR BUDGET

Before you actually begin writing your personal budget, you will need to first analyze the principles of a sound budget. Remember, budgeting is not just about making ends meet before your next paycheck — it is also about making sure your debt and retirement are taken care of.

MAKING THE BUDGET

How to Budget For Free with Quicken Online
How to Budget with the Envelope System
How to Budget with Microsoft Excel

Though budgeting is absolutely critical to financial success, do not forget that it does not inherently mean you are going to follow through with it. A plan is just a plan — a plan without action is utterly pointless.

As William Feather humorously explained:
"A budget tells us what we cannot afford, but it does not keep us from buying it." Writing a personal budget is a great step forward, but remember: it is called budget planning for a reason. A budget is a plan — not an action. Unless you actively stick to your budget, it is simply a waste of time.

BEFORE YOU BEGIN

Before you write a budget, you first have to see your expenses. Mint Online is a free service that lets you track your money online. You can hook it up to your bank, track how much you spend on gas, check out your grocery bills — and no, you do not have to spend a dime. It USED to cost $36 per year, but they just released it for free. I'm surprised they did, to be honest. This is a great way to track your money with software, without counterproductively spending money. Mint is owned by the most trusted personal finance software provider out there — I'm surprised their letting their online software be used for free.

SIGN UP AND LOOK AROUND

It is a more fun way to get ready to track your expenses for your budget plan. Regardless of whether you use software or an old fashioned pencil and paper, you will need to find a way to track all of your expenses — otherwise, you will be budgeting blind. But Wait! There is More! Budgeting is just the first step. If you find that you are spending more than you earn, then you have two options:

SAVE MORE MONEY, OR MAKE MORE MONEY

It is literally that simple. Whether you are trying to save money for college, get out of debt, or plan for retirement, it does not matter. If your budget shows that you are spending more than you earn, you have to increase your savings or decrease your spending. There is no other way.

PURPOSE

Managing money means making choices. There is never enough money for all the things we would like. This game will help you decide what is most important to you. How to Play To start you will need a pencil with an eraser.

There is more to personal finance than the drudgery of debts and budgets.

You will be coloring in or writing an "X" to mark the squares.

ROUND #1 BUDGETING

Play the budget game. Today you have a 20 Square income. Look at all the categories in *The Budget Game*. Each item has a set number of squares which must be marked to select that item. First, you must select one item in each of the categories with the gold stars (Food, Housing, Furnishings, Transportation, Insurance and Clothing & Laundry). Once you have finished selecting items in the Check out these Budgeting TIPS Game Instructions required categories, continue selecting other items until you have used up your 20 square income.

ROUND #1 DISCUSSION QUESTIONS

Compare your spending choices to those of other players. What did you spend your money on? How do your values, goals, and past experiences affect your spending choices? What did you learn about yourself?

ROUND #2 RE-BUDGETING

Your income has just been cut to 13 Squares. What will you change or give up? Erase to remove some selections and mark your new ones. Make the changes until you have marked only 13 squares. Compare your budget-cutting decisions with other players. Why did you make a different choice?

Wants vs. Needs — A need is a necessity, such as housing or food. A want can be anything and may not be a necessity. Be careful when spending on wants.

10% saving solution — After budgeting for necessities and before spending anything for wants, always tuck away some money from each paycheck for emergencies into a rainy day savings account. Before Charging — Ask yourself: 1) Do I really need it? and 2) Will I still have this 5 years from now? If the answers are No, then wait until you can pay cash.

Rule of Percentages — A good rule of thumb for budgeting your salary is: 70% pay current bills, 20% save for future purchases, 10% invest for long term. Money Tracking —We often spend money without thinking about it. Keep track of all your expenditures (cash, checks, debit cards, ATM withdrawals and credit cards), even the smallest ones. Record them every time in a notebook or register. Review them regularly to make yourself aware of where your money goes. Fixed, Flexible or Luxury? – Categorize the expenses in your budget. Is it fixed, such as rent or a car payment? Is it flexible such as groceries, gas or long distance use? Or is it luxury, such as entertainment or going out to eat?

Rule of 72 (to double your money) — If you know the interest rate you can get, divide 72 by the known interest rate and it will give you how many years it will take to double your money.

If you know how many years you have, divide 72 by the number of years and it will tell you what interest rate you must have to double your money. Examples: If interest rate is 6%. 72 ÷ 6 = 12 years. If time is 10 years. 72 ÷ 10 = 7.2% interest rate needed.

SAMPLE MONTHLY BUDGET FOR ADULTS & FAMILIES

Making a budget is not as difficult as you think. Making a budget is the most important step in controlling your money. A budget allows you to track your Income (the money that you have) and your Expenses (the money you spend). By writing down your monthly income and expenses, you can see how much money you expect to have for the month and plan for how much you can spend.

THE FIRST RULE OF BUDGETING

The first rule of budgeting is simple: Spend less than you earn! If you earn $2,000 a month from your job, $50 from Interest on your savings account, then your income for the month is $2,050. Now you know that you have to spend less than $2,050 for the entire month.

STRUCTURING YOUR BUDGET

1: Determine your Income.
Estimate all "incoming" money, including Salary/Bonus/Commissions, Interest, Child Support, and other sources.

2. Estimate Required Expenses.
Required expenses include taxes and bills. Required bills include mortgage/rent, utilities, insurance, car maintenance, gas, groceries, credit card/debt payments and medical expenses. You should also include payment to your savings in the "Required Expenses" category. You should strive to save enough to cover three months of expenses. You can also save for vacations and Christmas gifts. It is critical that you get in the habit of paying yourself first! Even a few dollars each month helps build your savings.

3. Estimate Discretionary Expenses
After you have paid your Required Expenses, you can use the money left over for some discretionary expenses, like entertainment (movies and dining out), or new furniture. Review the following Sample Budget on page 2, and then make your own monthly budget using the worksheet on page 3. Stay within your budget, 10% saving solution, and you will always be in control of your Money and Stuff! For a sample monthly budget, proceed to my web site or check on Google.

GETTING OUT OF DEBT

CREDIT CARD DEBT

Unmanageable debt ranks high as a major life stressor. Thankfully, it is a stressor that can be

There is more to personal finance than the drudgery of debts and budgets.

eliminated and avoided in the future. A number of students will experience excessive credit card debt simply because they found it too easy to spend using plastic and because they did not differentiate between wants and needs.

It is a tough lesson to learn that the rush from spending recklessly soon dissipates when struggling to make even the minimum monthly payment (MMP) on a credit card account. Embarrassed that they got themselves into this situation, some teens hide their situation from others, which only adds to their stress level. Although saddled with unmanageable debt, young adults should remember that there is always a solution. Rather than hiding their problem, it is best to confide in a trusted adult who may be able to provide guidance to the situation. Through the use of common sense, applying some financial savvy, and by making some hard choices, the student will soon get a handle on the problem and can be debt free.

If you can identify with the credit card debt situation in question, the following is important information that will help you resolve your debt problem:

1.☐Do not deny you have a problem. If you are struggling to make the monthly mortgage payments (MMPs) on your account, you have a dilemma that must be addressed. If you remain complacent about your credit card debt, it will be with you for years.

2. Stop using your credit card(s). This financial advice might seem obvious to you, but it is important. It has worked for me and most of my students. You cannot continue to add to your credit card debt if you cannot even handle your current obligation.

3. ☐Contact your credit card issuer. If you are having difficulty making the MMP on your account, call your issuer and advise them of your problem. The front-line customer service agent may not be able to help you under these circumstances. Ask to talk specifically with someone who handles workout plans. Your issuer may be willing to waive late fees or over-credit-limit fees, or even be willing to reduce your annual percentage rate: APR.

4. ☐Make a budget. You need to know how your money is used. To start, keep a journal to see exactly how you are spending your money. This includes small expenditures. Separate essential items from non-essential items. The financial goal is to see if you can free up some money to pay down your credit card debt.

5. ☐Increase your income while reducing your expenditures. Make a commitment to do without those things that are not necessary.

6. ☐Find a job. If you are already employed, you may be able to find additional part-time work. Start moonlighting. If you are in doubt, contact my office for specific suggestions.

7. ☐Do not skip credit card payments. Make sure you pay at least the MMP on all accounts each month.

8.☐First pay down your card with the highest APR. Make the MMP on all of your cards except the one with the highest APR. Make the highest payment possible on this account until you get the balance down to zero. If you have several cards, follow this process until all your accounts have a zero balance.

9.☐Take advantage of a balance transfer offer. By transferring your balance which has a high APR associated with it to a card with a low APR, you will be able to pay off your debt faster. However, be sure you understand the terms. Is there a balance transfer fee? How much is it? How long does the transfer offer last? Typically, a balance transfer offer that lasts one year is better than a six month offer. What is the go-to rate? That is, at the completion of agreement, what will the new rate be? Does the low introductory offer apply to both the transferred balance as well as new purchases? If the low APR only applies to the transferred balance, it is best not to use the card for new purchases.

10.☐If all else fails, consider contacting a credit counselor for help. Be careful not to get scammed, especially by those late night offers to "get you out of debt." It is best for you to stick with the tried and true debt-counseling organizations. For instance, the National Foundation for Credit Counseling can be located at www.nfcc.org; you can reach them by phone by calling the following number: (202) 677-4300 or 1-800-388-2227. For the benefit of consumers living in the Washingon metropolitan area, proceed to NFCC, 2000 M Street, NW Suite 505, Washington, DC 20036.

GOOD PRACTICES

1.☐Make a commitment to yourself to spend less than you earn.

2.☐Call your issuer and ask for a lower APR. Even if you can manage your credit card payments, it is best to have the lowest APRs possible. A simple phone call could end up saving you high interest costs.

3.If you must use credit, use your cards that have the lowest APRs. Remove the others from your wallet and store them in a safe place.

4.☐Once you are out of debt, NEVER, EVER PAY JUST THE MINIMUM MONTHLY PAYMENT! When you make just the MMP, most of your payment goes towards interest. Your balance remains virtually untouched while revolving month after month generating more interest for your credit card issuer!

5.☐Make mini payments on your account. If you earn unexpected money, for example, from a garage sale or overtime, pay down your credit card account. Even if this is a small amount of money, it adds up. Other debts you might have may include the following: debit payments, loans, cash expenses, groceries and household items, auto maintenance, gasoline, personal care, hair, prescriptions, medical co-pay, clothing, dry cleaning, school expenses, other regular expenses, discretionary expenses, dining out, entertainment, movies, gifts, holidays, home furnishings, vacation, memberships, and others.

There is more to personal finance than the drudgery of debts and budgets.

GOAL SETTING

1. Set goals

Not all superfluous spending goes to shiny new toys and baubles. Money can be easily frittered away through expensive cable packages or restaurant meals, to name a couple of examples. Setting goals provides a mechanism for overriding the impulse to buy things that are not as important. In my debt-reduction workshop, I teach students how to mentally associate the pleasure of dreaming with the drudgery of budgets and spending plans. "People do not often associate spending plans with dreaming, but if you do it right, it is a key ingredient," says Steve Bucci. "You need a reason not to spend on things that do not matter. You decide that you have a goal in mind that is more important." Writing down your goals will help prioritize spending when it comes time to map out your plan. Steve Bucci recommends writing short-term, medium-term and long-term goals on note cards. If you have them, include children and the significant other in the process. "You make your choices, but you need to have the dream or the goal and the money plus knowing that you are going to be able to put the money aside," Steve Bucci says.

Who is Steve Bucci? Steve is the author of *Credit Management Kit for Dummies* and co-author of *Managing Your Money All-In-One for Dummies*. His weekly column is distributed nationally by the Scripps-Howard newspaper syndicate.

Steve Bucci is former president of Consumer Credit Counseling Service of Southern New England. He is the founder of the Consumer Credit Counseling Service of Rhode Island, developed in the wake of the 1991 Rhode Island banking and credit union crisis. Steve Bucci also founded and was the former managing director of the University of Rhode Island Center for Personal Financial Education. The center is a joint venture with the University of Rhode Island to raise the level of financial literacy through innovative mass education programs and research.

2. Track spending

"The only way to plug the leak is to know where the leak is," says Gail Cunningham, senior director of public relations for the National Foundation for Credit Counseling. Take some time to try to follow every cent spent: the rent payment, the $3.32 latte, the 50-cent newspaper, the 79-cent pack of gum -- everything. Do not judge yourself now or feel angst over purchases. Almost everyone can usually account for most of their spending with a cursory overview of their finances, says Steve Bucci. "Most people can get to 90 (percent), but the last 10 percent is a killer. "It disappears ... lattes, tips, food at work, allowances for the children.

Just write it down and by the end of the month you will have most of the 10 percent and know where almost all of your money goes," Steve Bucci says. Continue to take notes on spending after the first month. "Keep up with the balance in your checkbook, each time you make a deposit or withdrawal, reconcile or balance your checkbook and also reconcile your statement when it arrives," Cunningham says. "No one wants to do it, but it is important." "Even if you use a debit card, you have to write that down in your checkbook -- you should carry something around that is going to keep up with your balance."

3. Automate savings

"We are the only industrialized nation with a negative savings rate; people are spending more than they make," says Dave Jones, president of the Association of Independent Consumer Credit Counseling Agencies. To combat sluggish savings, earmark a certain percentage or dollar amount for a savings account. Savings accounts can be either specialized retirement accounts or regular deposit accounts. Start small to get into the routine of saving regularly. "When you are getting started, it is more important that you get in the habit of saving rather than that you save a lot," says Steve Bucci. Use income tax refunds, windfalls, and raises to jump-start savings as well.

Received a raise at work? "Put that money toward savings. You were living just fine without it," says Gail Cunningham, senior director of public relations for the National Foundation for Credit Counseling. Bucci recommends funneling half of the newfound income into savings. "The other half you get to spend," he says. "So you are not missing anything, you are not taking anything away from yourself. You are still getting more money then you had before, but now you are saving a little bit more."

4. Prepare a budget

"We all need to do what is right for us," says Gail Cunningham, senior director of public relations for the National Foundation for Credit Counseling. "Some people might want to use Quicken or another computer software program and others might want a pad and pencil. It is just a matter of knowing what works for them." If possible, send a set percentage of your income straight to a savings account and try to configure your budget as though that money does not even exist.

Cunningham recommends that people divide their spending plan into separate categories with necessities taking top priority. Necessities would include housing, utilities, medical insurance, food, child care, secured loans, car payments, insurance, and co-signed loans. Then comes the unsecured debt, miscellaneous and entertainment expenses -- plus any other applicable categories.

Plug in your income and the amount of money shuttled into each category every month. You may see areas where you can trim some fat. For instance, you could save hundreds of dollars a year by requesting lower interest rates on credit cards or shopping around for car insurance. Unnecessary drains on funds will become apparent and you have the foundation in place to take action. "A spending plan will let people understand exactly what bills need to be paid first -- or if they need to put a little extra cash toward a bill," says Dave Jones, president of the Association of Independent Consumer Credit Counseling Agencies.

5. Change behavior

Fundamental to debt elimination or reduction is the urgency to change your money behavior. You may have all the financial knowledge in the world, but you will never get out of debt if you

There is more to personal finance than the drudgery of debts and budgets.

do not change your money behavior. My personal finance workshop teaches students much about the application of money behavior modification. You must believe in change. You must change your spending habits.

Ideally everyone would have plenty of money leftover at the end of the month. But if necessities leave you tapped out by the 20th of the month, it may be time to take drastic steps such as getting a roommate or finding a second job. Sometimes a change could be as easy as not eating out twice a week. "If someone is spending $100 a month on pizza, then they might decide they want to look at that and say, 'Well it is fine to order pizza in, but we are only going to do it once a week instead of two times a week,'" says Gail Cunningham, senior director of public relations for the National Foundation for Credit Counseling. "I have found that it is more successful if a person cuts back rather than cutting out," she says. "So back to our pizza example, do not say, 'OK, no more pizza.' Just say, 'OK, let us be more judicious.'" Curtailing credit card usage -- especially on impulse -- might be the best behavioral change you can make, particularly if you already have a large amount of credit card debt.

Another thing to do: "Get organized," says Cunningham. "You are not going to believe it, but people walk into our centers carrying grocery sacks full of unopened bills. And in that grocery sack are unopened letters from their mortgage lenders." Use a filing cabinet or a simple box to keep financial documents in order. Bills should be kept handy in a designated box or basket. The important thing is to set up a system that works for you. "It will save you time and you will not have to look for misplaced documents," she says.

6. Borrow wisely

Credit can be a good thing. Loans allow people to buy cars, houses, boats and even help cushion the blow in emergencies." It is fine when it is used properly," says Bucci. "What you have to know is that you are taking from tomorrow's money today." On the other hand, people do not always make buying decisions rationally and can easily rack up thousands upon thousands of dollars in debt. "If you have a $10,000 credit card bill on an 18 percent interest rate credit card and you make the minimum payment of 2 percent -- though some companies have higher minimums -- it will take 40 years to pay off that bill," says Dave Jones, president of the Association of Independent Consumer Credit Counseling Agencies. "And that is if you never make another purchase on that card."

To keep a perspective on borrowing, match a loan to the life of the product. "If this is a purchase that is going to take you a long time to pay off, then you use long-term credit to pay it off -- not short-term credit," says Bucci.

"Use long-term credit for big purchases and short-term credit for purchases that you are going to pay off in a reasonable amount of time," he says. Extreme examples would be buying a car with a credit card or taking out a home equity loan to replace a sofa. "You look at the couch that you are going to buy, and think this couch is going to be trash in five years. You do not want to be paying for a couch you no longer have 15 years down the line," Bucci says. "The payments should not outlive the purchase."

7. Prioritize bills

Late fees and exorbitant interest rates can eat away at even well-stocked coffers. Whether you are juggling a lot of financial plates or have only a couple of monthly obligations, paying bills on time -- every time -- is essential. One of the great conveniences of modern life, online bill pay allows consumers to schedule bill payments without touching a checkbook or finding postage stamps.

Some people prefer the security of real-world actions to virtual ones, however, which means they need to plan ahead. "Payments need to be sent at least seven to ten days before the due date," says Gail Cunningham, senior director of public relations for the National Foundation for Credit Counseling. "Write the date that you are going to mail it in the upper right hand corner under where the stamp goes and then file those bills in chronological order so that anytime you sit down, you have at your fingertips which bills need to be paid."

She also advises that if money gets too stretched, necessities should always come before paying unsecured debt. "Last in line are the creditors, but often the consumer pays them first. I always say if your creditor is happy and your electricity has been cut off, you have done it backward. But really, though, the creditors put on the pressure."

BALANCING THE BALANCE SHEET

Have you ever taken a snapshot of your personal finances? What are you really worth financially? By answering these questions, you will learn to leverage unknown and untapped potentials in your personal balance sheet to increase your equity or cash flow. If you are going to grow rich by following my financial advice, you better begin thinking like a business or a corporation. Corporations utilize the balance sheet to gauge the financial health of the company at any point in time, so must you develop the mindset of a corporation. Prior to discussing the idea of creating a balance sheet to better ascertain your financial health, I would recommend that you establish a single point access for all your financial documents:

1. -wills, trusts, and deeds
2. -financial accounts
3. -insurance
4. -business interests
5. -real estate
6. -annuities
7. -IRA/ 401(K)

The challenge of keeping pace with an ever changing financial landscape can be difficult as personal financial information rests scattered among multiple advisors, institutions, and accounts. Clients often become confused and frustrated as they attempt to properly arrange the pieces of their financial puzzle. What is missing is a single platform that provides organization and easy access to a complete financial picture. The dynamic balance sheet is the winning solution to this ubiquitous challenge.

There is more to personal finance than the drudgery of debts and budgets.

ACHIEVING THE WIDE ANGLE VIEW WITH THE DYNAMIC BALANCE SHEET

What is a balance sheet? Central to understanding the meaning of a dynamic balance sheet is the key accounting concept of a balance sheet, a financial statement that summarizes a company's assets, liabilities, and shareholders' equity at a specific point in time. These three balance sheet segments give investors an idea as to what the company owns and owes, as well as the amount invested by the shareholders. A balance sheet, therefore, is a financial statement that must be in a balance; it is called a balance sheet because the two sides balance out. This makes sense: a company has to pay for all the things it has (assets) by either borrowing money (liabilities) or getting it from shareholders (shareholders' equity).

Mathematically, a balance sheet must follow the following formula:

Assets = Liabilities + Shareholders' Equity

Traditional balance sheets help determine net worth by subtracting liabilities from assets. A proprietary, secure, on-line tool, The dynamic balance sheet® adds protection and cash flow analyses, creating a wide angle view to 'stress test' financial services, products, and strategies. By monitoring changes in protection, assets, liabilities and cash flow, The Dynamic balance sheet® automatically anticipates and keeps abreast of all the changing pieces in the four critical financial domains.

The dynamic balance sheet is an adaptable, always evolving solution that will be there every step of the way. Here is some information that will help you prepare as you set out on your journey toward financial balance. There are many goals you plan to accomplish in this life. What if you had a personal financial planner who took a completely different approach to money management without increasing risk? Join the millionaire club today! A master financial planner, like me, uses revolutionary web technology to help you with budgeting money, protecting what is important to you at this moment in time. Would you like to achieve financial balance today? Can you guess what financial balance could help you accomplish? If you want to find out, please, call me.

The dynamic balance sheet is a holistic approach to helping you achieve financial balance, giving you a wide-angle view of every area of your finances: Assets, Liabilities, Cash Flow, and Protection. It combines my unique financial philosophy of $ucce$$tology with state-of-the-art wealth-building technology and the partnership of a financial representative to help you achieve the best possible results. Do you know what affects your wealth? A lot of people do. Then, what is the solution of financial imbalance? Please, continue reading the book. I want you to gain a clearer and precise understanding of the factors that affect your wealth. These are challenges you may not even be aware of that can slow your progress. These challenges of wealth building comprise of financial disorganization; being financially disorganized can increase your costs and risks; it can also decrease your chance of real success. Even when you think you have all your records in order, they may still be financially disorganized in the eyes of Prince Ojong, an experienced financial professional with the intellectual power of quantitative and qualitative analyses.

Many people who are knew to personal finance take a compartmentalized approach to making financial decisions, treating each compartment separately, as if it had no effect on the other areas of their finances. They do not know how to focus on the big picture. Quantitative and qualitative analyses, therefore, help you to focus on the big picture of your personal finances; by using complex mathematical and statistical modeling, measurement and research, we can take a good picture of your financial situation; by assigning a numerical value to many personal finance variables, my quantitative analysts try to replicate the reality of your dynamic balance sheet mathematically. In other words, quantitative analysis can be done for a number of reasons such as measurement, performance evaluation or valuation of a financial instrument such as your balance sheet. It can also be used to predict real world events such as cash-flow changes in that balance sheet. Qualitative analysis refers to the supplementing of the use of numerical ratios with my personal or subjective business insights. In addition to relying on the facts we gather from numerical analysis, you are afforded the unique opportunity of the review of your balance sheet done with my two human eyes.

MYTHS AND FAILED STRATEGIES

Before you read *The Miraculous Millionaire*, I apologize to you for using any myths or financial strategies that have failed you in the end. I blame the hucksters for your frustration. When it comes to the wisdom you need to balance your financial book, you must remember that there is no such thing as one size fits all persons. Generally, wisdom that is aimed at everyone to balance the balance sheet is not right for anyone because everyone's situation is unique. This is the reason why I would like to supplement the information in the book with insights into your particular financial situation. I invite you to communicate with me by phone, email, or fax to educate me on your unique circumstance.

I know you are bombarded every day on television and radio with half-baked financial messages; also, newspapers, magazines, zealous friends, and even financial advisors hawking bad money advice that can turn your balance sheet red are not too far behind. They are presenting terrible lies as if the lies are universal truths. Now that you have read my book, I will blame you if you pay attention to bad financial advice again. In reality, you know now that bad financial advice may not apply to your finances at all. These myths and failed strategies create yet another obstacle between you and your financial goals. Here are some examples of common financial myths:

"My money only needs to keep pace with inflation."

"I will be in a lower income tax bracket at retirement."

"My 401(K) plan creates tax savings that can be spent or invested."

"Compounding interest creates a financial miracle."

"I will not need life insurance when I retire."

When traditional strategies fall short, clearly it is time to try something else. But what is so revolutionary about my dynamic balance sheet philosophy? How does it help you get past financial disorganization and failed strategies to build your wealth? The answer is simple. My approach is a holistic or comprehensive financial model that makes it easy for you to recognize the long-term potential of every dollar you earn. My notion of the balance sheet is dynamic in nature because it changes every day; it is not dead or stagnant. The dynamic balance sheet takes the simple equation of Assets − Liabilities = Net Worth and turns it into a completely unique approach to your personal finances by adding cash flow and protection considerations all in the same view. This holistic financial model makes it easy for you to recognize the long-term potential of every dollar you earn, so that you can make decisions toward achieving improved financial balance. If you balance sheet is in the red, it is not good for you. You want to whittle way your debts, so that your net worth should be increasing. When your debt is zero dollars, then, you have become debt-free; a debt-free individual is an individual who is experiencing financial peace.

With my new approach to balancing your financial book, you have more power to accomplish the following objectives:

1. Address issues of inadequate financial protection
2. Enhance asset performance in the marketplace
3. Reduce unnecessary expenses and risks
4. Build savings aggressively
5. Enhance your lifestyle
6. Enjoy a true partnership and companionship with your spouse

Another key component that sets my dynamic balance sheet apart is that you are not left on your own to figure things out by yourself. Working with a financial representative is part of the solution. Your chosen financial representative acts as a true partner to help you gain insights and take action that creates results. Can you see how you can build your wealth and get what you want out of life? But what if there was another option? What if you could do more with your money without taking more risk than you are comfortable with? My core philosophy of investing is a combination of risk minimization and profit maximization. It is a different investing approach with better results. The low-risk high-reward wealth-building formula is not wishful thinking; rather, it is a matter of understanding what affects your wealth and making the different areas of your finances work together.

My dynamic balance sheet approach gives you a wide-angle view of your financial world by displaying your Assets, Liabilities, Cash Flow and Protection in one place. In the hands of the financial specialist you choose, this tool can help you bring your four financial domains into sync, increasing efficiency, and allowing you to do more with your existing cash flow. My dynamic balance sheet gives you a wide-angle view of your financial world. Your financial data is updated daily, and you have instant access to my site wherever you are via a computer or any mobile device. You can receive automatic alerts whenever anything in your balance sheet changes. With up-to-date information, you can spot opportunity and make the most of it.

By putting my dynamic balance sheet to work for you, you have more power to realize the following objectives:

1. Increase protection
2. Build savings
3. Enhance asset performance
4. Pay off your debts
5. Increase your tax efficiency
6. Manage cash flow
7. Reach your goals without having to increase your cash flow

In fact, you are our partner. A pipeline of love and interest binds us together. You should regard our relationship as a partnership that will stay with you for ever and ever. Life does not stand still, and the definition of financial opportunity keeps changing. One of the most powerful things about my dynamic balance sheet is that it is LIVING WITH YOU ENDLESSLY. Unlike financial planning setups where you may have one meeting to choose investments and then you are on your own, this is an ongoing partnership. Your chosen financial representative works with you to monitor your financial situation and make adjustments as your circumstances and goals change. Because while my dynamic balance sheet offers solutions, it also encourages you to keep asking the important questions: What do you want to achieve next? Are you creating the legacy you want to leave? What do you value most? In the end, you will put an end to financial disorganization. My dynamic balance sheet helps coordinate your financial instruments and advisors in a way that brings the most value to your decisions and strategies. Your aggregated financial data is regularly updated.

You have direct access to it, so you know where you stand financially. You get a wide-angle view of your finances, allowing you to see how all your strategies are working together and to adapt them as your circumstances and your wants and desires change. So you can achieve the best possible results.

The result? The result now is positive, of course. Unlike the trial-and-error approach of the past, where you grapple with the myriad details of your balance sheet and end up with failed strategies that are at odds with one another, my dynamic balance sheet approach empowers you to create a positive impact or a sense of financial balance on your balance sheet across the board. Once you achieve a balance, it is an ongoing and collaborative process to maintain it. That is why you will find a very different kind of commitment from any of my financial specialists you choose than from any other, alien, or typical financial planning outfit. In my organization, I must confess that your chosen financial specialist builds a true relationship with you, versus the mercenary approach of just executing your financial transactions by rote, working with you and even with your other advisors to develop strategies that bring you the most money value. In fact, you are successful in getting where you want to go not by looking ahead, but by taking full advantage of your financial opportunities today. Your financial representative, by using my dynamic balance sheet, helps you maintain efficiency and optimal financial balance, implementing strategies and products as the world and your life change.

There is more to personal finance than the drudgery of debts and budgets.

My philosophy of $ucce$$tology and the technology of the dynamic balance sheet are always evolving, staying ahead of trends, so you have a powerful solution that helps you accomplish what you want, now and in the future. Life does not stand still, neither should your financial strategies.

To move forward, you first need to understand where you are. My dynamic balance sheet, with insights from your financial representative, brings clarity to your financial picture. Building wealth is about more than numbers. Building wealth has a qualitative aspect. To assist you balance your financial book, I employ the dynamic balance sheet, which aggregates all your financial data in one place. So you have a wide-angle view of your finances and can see how your four financial domains (Assets, Liabilities, Cash Flow and Protection) are working together.

With insurance protection built into the process, you have the freedom of knowing you are prepared for the unexpected. But beyond that, you also have a powerful and adaptable solution to assist you in planning for the changes you can foresee. Each new financial milestone you approach brings new goals and new financial challenges. The financial specialist you choose, using my dynamic balance sheet, helps you anticipate these issues, evolving your financial strategies to keep up with your life. Now you have the strong financial foundation you need to continue moving forward.

AN ACCOUNTANT THOU SHALL BE!

I have taught you balance sheet basics. As a prospective small business owner, you need not be an expert in financial statements and accounting to operate a successful business. However, a working knowledge of basic accounting principles is useful to facilitate comprehension of the financial statements. The benefit is that, as a business owner you will be able to more efficiently score the financial health of your budding business. To appreciate the work you are doing with your accountant or financial advisor, you should be able to communicate with them in the language of personal finance. That is why it is important for you to grasp accounting lingo. You can do it. Trust me. Do not worry. I, myself, am not a math whiz; in fact, in high school, I was one of the dumbest guys in math class; I even flunked statistics in my organizational communications program. Today, I am not ashamed to tell you that I lack the confidence to handle even elementary school mathematics proficiently; for this reason, I rely on my wife and tutors to assist my two daughters: Lucielle and Alexia. Indeed, I just summoned the courage to teach myself personal finance because I was motivated by dollar signs. I was desperate to make big money, and I never wanted fear of math to stand on my way to wealth. I used NLP exercises and the love of money to achieve my goal of demystifying mathematical accounting. Similarly, in high school, I obtained an excellent pass in economics by steeling my courage to face econometrics and data response. I promise to present the accounting ideas to you in a very simple fashion.

ACCOUNTANT'S SECRET

What is the famous accountant's secret rule number 1? It is expressed in the equation presented below:

Assets = Liabilities + Equity

The equation means that you derive the value of an asset by summing liabilities with equity. Conversely, you determine the equity of an owner of an asset by subtracting liabilities from the asset; you calculate the liabilities of an asset by removing the equity from the asset.

BALANCE SHEET DEFINED

The balance sheet is commonly defined as the financial report that lists (quantifies) the total assets, liabilities, and owners' equity of a business on a specified date, usually the last day of the accounting period. The balance sheet is divided into three primary sections or categories: assets, liabilities, net worth or owner' equity. The liabilities of the company subtracted from the assets shows the net worth. Net worth can be a negative figure if the liabilities are greater than the company's assets. Visit any of my web sites for a precise sample of a balance sheet. Google searches can also yield the same information.

ASSETS

Assets are any items of economic value that can be converted into cash. Assets are shown on the debit side of the balance sheet while the credit side shows liabilities and owners' equity. The two sides must be equal, or balance which is why it is called a "balance sheet." Assets are listed in descending order of liquidity, from most liquid (cash) to the least liquid (property, facilities and equipment). They include current assets, which are cash in hand and cash equivalents such as T-bills and money market funds. Next are the accounts receivables, followed by inventories of supplies and materials including raw materials, work in progress and finished goods. Current assets are usually defined as assets that can be converted into cash within 12 months. The fixed assets are durable assets with a life span greater than 12 months. This category includes properties, facilities, equipment and machinery, and whatever else the company uses to conduct business. Fixed assets need to reflect depreciation in the value of equipment, such as machinery, that has a limited expected useful life

LIABILITIES

Liabilities include all outstanding debts payable to employees, suppliers and creditors. They may include taxes, interest payments, and other unpaid expenses that the company has incurred but has not been paid at the time the books were closed. The first category of liabilities is accounts payable. These are the assets the company has received that have not yet been paid for. As with assets, liabilities are subdivided into current liabilities, debt payable within 12 months, mostly comprised of accounts payable, and long-term liabilities, payable in the future, after 12 months. Liabilities are also listed in descending order of due dates.

NET WORTH (OWNERS' EQUITY)

Subtracting liabilities from assets shows the net worth or the owners' equity. This represents the investment in the business by the owners' including the original start-up investment plus subsequent investments such as retained earnings. A basic tenet of double-entry bookkeeping is that total assets, what a business owns, must equal liabilities, what the business owes, plus equity.

SIGNIFICANCE OF THE BALANCE SHEET

The balance sheet provides the business owner the tool to perform a quick and fairly accurate assessment of the state of the business at a given point in time. It is the first of the three most important financial statements for any business. The second is the income statement which reports on the company's activities over a period of time by presenting the net addition, net income, or subtraction, net loss, to owners' equity from operations. The third is the statement of cash flows that shows how changes in balance sheet accounts and the income statement affect the availability of cash in the business. The top portion of the balance sheet should list your company's assets in order of liquidity, from most liquid to least liquid. Current assets are cash or its equivalent or those assets that will be used by the business in a year or less.

They include the following:

Cash is the cash on hand at the time books are closed at the end of the fiscal year. This refers to all cash in checking, savings, and short-term investment accounts. Accounts receivable is the income derived from credit accounts. For the balance sheet, it is the total amount of income to be received that is logged into the books at the close of the fiscal year. Inventory is derived from the cost of goods table. It is the inventory of material used to manufacture a product not yet sold. Total current assets is the sum of cash, accounts receivable, inventory, and supplies. Other assets that appear in the balance sheet are called long-term or fixed assets because they are durable and will last more than one year. Examples of long-term assets include the following: capital and plant is the book value of all capital equipment and property: if you own the land and building, less depreciation.

Investment includes all investments owned by the company that cannot be converted to cash in less than one year. For the most part, companies just starting out have not accumulated long-term investments. Miscellaneous assets are all other long-term assets that are not capital and plant or investment. Total long-term assets refers to the sum of capital and plant, investments, and miscellaneous assets. Total assets is the sum of total current assets and total long-term assets.

After listing the assets, you then have to account for the liabilities of your business. Like assets, liabilities are classified as current or long term. Debts that are due in one year or less are classified as current liabilities. If they are due in more than one year, they are long-term liabilities. Here are examples of current liabilities: accounts payable include all expenses incurred by the business that are purchased from regular creditors on an open account and are due and payable. Accrued liabilities are all expenses incurred by the business that are required for operation but have not yet been paid at the time the books are closed. These expenses are usually the company's overhead and salaries.

Taxes are those payments still due and payable at the time the books are closed. Total current liabilities is the sum of accounts payable, accrued liabilities and taxes. Long-term liabilities include the following: bonds payable is the total of all bonds at the end of the year that are due and payable over a period exceeding one year. Mortgage payable is loans taken out for the purchase of real estate that are repaid over a long-term period. The mortgage payable is that amount still due at the close of the fiscal year.

Notes payable are the amounts still owed on any long-term debts that will not be repaid during the current fiscal year.

Total long-term liabilities is the sum of bonds payable, mortgages payable and notes payable. Total liabilities is the sum of total current and long-term liabilities. Once the liabilities have been listed, the owner's equity can then be calculated. The amount attributed to owner's equity is the difference between total assets and total liabilities. The amount of equity the owner has in the business is an important yardstick used by investors to evaluate the company. Many times, it determines the amount of capital they feel they can safely invest in the business.

BALANCE SHEET

The balance sheet shows what a company owns and what it owes; the difference is what the company is "worth", at least on paper. One huge problem is that the fair market value of many assets can be very different from the "book values" shown here. So people looking for "value" stocks need to do more research, beyond the balance sheet.

A SAMPLE OF A BALANCE SHEET

A balance sheet is a financial statement that lists the assets, liabilities and equity of a company at a specific point in time and is used to calculate the net worth of a business. A basic tenet of double-entry book-keeping is that total assets (what a business owns) must equal liabilities plus equity (how the assets are financed). In other words, the balance sheet must balance. Subtracting liabilities from assets shows the net worth of the business a basic tenet of double-entry bookkeeping is that total assets (what a business owns) must equal liabilities plus equity (how the assets are financed). In other words, the balance sheet must balance.

(dollar figures are in thousands)	1997	1996
Assets		
Current Assets:		
Cash and Equivalents	$ 2,738	$ 2,260
Accounts Receivable	1,175	996
Inventory	1,034	897
Total Current Assets	4,947	4,153
Real Estate (purchase price)	31,677	29,847
Equipment (depreciated value)	13,448	12,958
Goodwill (depreciated value)	3,167	3,334
Total Assets	53,239	50,292

There is more to personal finance than the drudgery of debts and budgets.

Liabilities		
Current Liabilities:		
Accounts Payable	1,488	1,092
Short-term Debt	123	147
Total Current Liabilities	1,611	1,239
Long-term Debt	245	267
Other Liabilities	122	101
Total Liabilities	1,978	1,607
Total Shareholders' Equity	51,261	48,685

QUICKEN SOFTWARE

I love using computers. I love the facility of automating routine tasks, such as the drudgery of managing my money as an individual. Intuit is the developer of Quicken software, a personal finance application that shows you a basic way to begin managing your money. Your life is better financially when you know the position where you are; it is even best when you know the destination where you are headed. I can assure you that Quicken will help you organize your personal finances today and plan for tomorrow. Join the millionaires and buy a copy of Quicken from my web site, and I will assist you in learning how to use it.

WHAT QUICKEN CAN DO FOR YOU

Intuit's Quicken helps you see your complete financial picture. With Quicken, you will be able to see all your checking, savings, credit card, loan, investments, and retirement accounts in one place: no more having to visit multiple websites. See exactly where your money's going. Get a clear picture of what you are spending your money on, and where you can save. Quicken automatically organizes your expenses into categories and keeps track of your spending. By tracking your expenses, setting home budget goals and cutting costs, you can avoid scrambling to make ends meet each month—and actually start saving money. Stop Living Paycheck to Paycheck. Pay bills on time and reduce debt. Indeed, a cash flow graph in Quicken shows you a clear picture of what is coming in, what is going out, and how much is left for you to spend or save. And you can easily use Quicken to implement or create a customized plan to reduce debt. Stay on a budget, painlessly. Quicken makes it easy for you to get on a budget you can live with. Quicken automatically sets up budget goals based on what you have spent in the past. You can customize your plan, and we will track your progress. Here is budgeting for your peace of mind! Are you still stressed about money? My simple budgeting plan combines with Quicken to put you at ease. After all, budgeting is simply a way to ensure that you have enough money to reach your goals

CHECK YOUR CREDIT SCORE

With Quicken, there are five ways for you to maintain a healthy credit score. Your FICO credit score is a number in the range of 300-850 that represents your ability to repay lenders. A score above 760 usually makes it easy for you to secure the best interest rate on loans. In contrast, if you slip under 700 by just a couple of points, you will be surprised to watch your interest jump high.

These days, credit scores are not only used by lenders but they are also used by everyone from landlords to prospective employers and lovers. What this means is that a bad credit score can keep you from getting an apartment, a mobile phone, a lover, or even a job.

How do you keep your credit score in good shape? First and foremost, pay your bills on time. The longer an account is open with no negative reports, the better the deals you will get. This information shows that you can handle debt well. Please, keep credit card balances well below maximums. Balances that are more than even 30% of the credit limit can hurt your score. Do not carry more credit cards than you need. Scores reflect total debt and total debt capacity, called credit utilization. Review your credit reports, periodically. In fact, TransUnion.com, Equifax. com, and Experian.com post records of payments and lapses for all debt obligations. If you spot an error on your credit report, please, alert the credit bureaus immediately. They must launch an investigation or reinvestigation promptly; they must inform you of results, usually within 30 days. If you are aspiring to get rich, remember, a good credit score is an asset you do not want to lose. So be vigilant.

SMALL AND SIMPLE COST-CUTTERS FOR USE WITH QUICKEN

Below are some small and simple cost-cutters you can use with Quicken. These cost-cutters will help you get started saving as soon as possible:

1. Give yourself a raise and bank it. Boost your take-home pay by adjusting your tax-withholding and have the difference in pay automatically transferred to an online savings account. Most Americans have too much withheld from their paychecks every payday. Correcting that over withholding by filing a new W-4 form with your employer can create an instant pay raise.

2. Enroll in a 401(K). If your employer offers a 50-cent match for every dollar you contribute, even adding $60 a month will net you over a grand a year. And remember, boosting your 401(K) contribution by $60 a month will not cut your pay by that much, since pre-tax dollars go into the account. If you are in the 25 percent tax bracket, a $60 contribution cuts your paycheck by just $45. The other $15 comes from Uncle Sam.

3. Raise your car insurance deductible. Upping your potential out-of-pocket outlay from $250 to $1,000 can save you 15 percent or more off your premium.

4. Pay off your credit card. Carrying a $1,000 balance at 18 percent blows $180 every year on interest that you could put to better use elsewhere.

5. Go green. Control energy costs with a programmable thermostat. Prices start around $50, but you will cut your heating-and-cooling bill by 10-20 percent.

There is more to personal finance than the drudgery of debts and budgets.

6. Bundle up. Getting a package of phone, Internet, and cable from one provider can save you about $50 a month.

7. Use your employer's FSA. Flexible spending accounts let you pay health care and child care costs with pre-tax dollars. If your company offers them, take advantage and save 33 percent or more.

8. Get a credit card with rewards. Spending $80 a week on gas and groceries? Putting it on a card with 5 percent cash rebates will earn you nearly $200 a year.

9. Kick the habit. Smoking is hard on your health and the wallet. Three packs a week averages $50 a month or more.

10. Brown-bag it. Instead of spending $8 on takeout every day at work, bring a bagged lunch for $5. You will save $60 a month and $720 a year. Do your own calculation at Feed the Pig.org.

11. Negotiate your rate. Instead of paying an APR of 18 percent on your credit card, call your issuer and ask for a lower rate. If you have good credit, your lender might consider it, particularly if you can cite a better offer you have received from another card company.

12. Travel on the cheap. Bypass the old trifecta of travel search engines (Travelocity, Expedia and Orbitz) and head straight for SideStep.com, which will search them all—saving you money and time.

13. Insure yourself. Even if your company has a health plan, you may be able to do better for yourself. Pairing a high-deductible medical policy with a health savings account—which lets you put away pre-tax dollars for out-of-pocket medical expenses—can save money on premiums. Shop around at eHealthInsurance.com.

14. Make media free. Dust off your library card and enjoy DVDs and books for free. If you would normally rent a movie a week and buy a book a month, you can cut costs by $30 a month.

15. Change your calling plan. The average wireless phone user spends about $60 a month, including taxes and fees. If you talk for 200 or fewer minutes per month, switching to a prepaid plan where minutes cost 25 cents a minute could save you $10 a month. Compare plans at MyRatePlan.com.

16. Park your car. Why pay $25 a week in gas when you could pay half that to use public transit? Or check out carpooling at eRideShare.com and CarpoolConnect.com.

17. Ditch your gym. Forget the $40 a month gym membership that'll cost you almost $500 a year, and check out community centers in your area. Some may be free or charge a minimal fee, such as $100 a year. Or buy a good pair of running shoes and work out the old-fashioned way.

18. Reship your auto insurance. Using a comparison site like InsWeb.com can help you determine if you have received the best deal. Re-shop at least once a year to make sure you have the best deal.

19. Learn to cook. Cooking at home saves on your food budget and it could even improve your dating prospects—who is not impressed by someone who can prepare a great meal?

20. Keep track of your money. The best way to save is to know what you spend. It might not be pretty, but detail every expense for a month to get an idea of where you can cut back. Nearly everyone has some fat they can trim from their spending to put toward a savings goal.

HOME BUDGETING--SAVING FOR A RAINY DAY

You can also use Quicken to automate your budgeting. A budget squeeze offers an easy excuse not to save. But when you are just making ends meet, you need a financial buffer even more than people who have cash left over after they pay their bills. That is why you should save in advance for unexpected expenses. It is okay to start small. For instance, start with $500 and add just $20 a week. If you earn just 3.5% interest, in three years you will have $3,649 on hand to fix a leaky roof or install a new furnace. So where do you find $20 a week? Bundle telephone, cable and Internet services. Host potluck dinners instead of going out to eat. Try a "stay-cation" to avoid airfares and hotel bills. Then bank the money you save in a savings account at your local bank. Certificates of deposit (CDs) pay higher rates of interest, but you may not have access to your funds for 90 days or longer. Money market funds are accessible and generally pay higher interest than a savings account but require high minimum deposits and charge fees. Do not wait for rain. Start saving today. Quicken can help you track your spending and set savings goals you will actually reach.

PERSONAL FINANCE FOR THE Y GENERATION

The most important step toward financial security is to translate it into your own terms. Find out now how to attain simple financial security. Are you young, smart, and broke? The following budgeting tips are for you, a member of the Y generation. Too many twenty-somethings are beginning their adult lives unprepared to make sensible financial decisions. But that does not have to be your story. Although you have a built-in disadvantage if you were not taught the basics of personal finance or how to budget in school, that does not mean you cannot learn how to do it now. As a young person, you should be comfortable with a personal computer and all the new communication and technology devices: ipad, ipod, cellular phone, and iphone, so here is an approach to managing a home budget for a generation just starting out with money management.

If you just purchased a home or moved into your first unfurnished apartment, you have already received the message. The common, taken-for-granted appliances mother and father always provided (refrigerator, stove, microwave, etc.) must now be purchased by you. When these necessities have been provided for most of your life, it can be difficult motivating yourself to buy them for yourself.

There is more to personal finance than the drudgery of debts and budgets.

Many younger adults make little effort to plan ahead or budget for these items. Instead, they just turn to credit cards and wash their hands of the matter entirely. According to MSN, the median credit-card debt of low-income and middle-income people aged 18 to 34 is $8,200; and that amount of money excludes student loans. However, this is hardly the type of intelligent spending that helps young adults get their financial life started on sure footing.

The correct approach is to acknowledge, preferably before moving out, that you will need home appliances and budget for them just as you would other expenses. Unless you are a complete financial wreck, we are willing to bet your cell phone bill, Netflix subscription and car insurance bill are paid like clockwork every month. That is because these bills carry direct, immediate consequences for not paying them. To properly budget for home appliances, it is best to save for them in this same way. That is, shop around for the appliances you will need to buy, gather prices, and save a certain amount each month toward the costs.

If you opt not to pay for appliances up front, many stores offer payment plans, you must still account for the monthly payments in all of your future spending. This action is called financial planning, and it is the kind of task software tools like Quicken or Mint.com can automate for you. These online personal finance tools can show you where you are spending your money and also help you set a realistic budget for the true necessities of everyday life. For instance, if the combined cost of bringing home a refrigerator and stove will add another $500 in monthly payments to your budget, this should be planned for in advance, rather than haphazardly adjusted to later on. It may turn out that these extra costs pinch your spending in other areas, like entertainment. You will be less likely to blow off your bills, and go into debt, if you are aware of this going in than if you fall out of bed one day and suddenly realize you cannot go out for drinks as much as you used to.

Other key items you will likely need to buy are housewares. Unless mother and father sent you packing with their stuff, you will need to budget to buy silverware, cookware, bowls, plates, and small appliances.

BUYING THESE ITEMS FOR LESS

Of course, not all of these major household items need to be purchased brand new from a store. In fact, this may not even be the preferred path for most members of the Y generation. For instance, SteadfastFinances.com reported that the Y generation is developing a preference for used stuff, citing a recent study which showed that the under-40 crowd was more likely to buy used laptops, buy used cars on Craigslist and hunt for deals online before dropping big bucks at a major retailer.

This news has definite and positive implications for you starting a home budget. As the age group more comfortable with the Internet and technology than any other, there is simply no excuse for members of the Y generation not to get good deals on housewares and home appliances. More often than not, a used product can be found on the Internet that performs just as well as a new one for much less money.

That said, it is important to do your homework before jumping on the first deal you see. This is often easier said than done. An eBay search for microwave returned over 7,000.

The main thing to be mindful of when searching for major household items on websites such as eBay and Craigslist is seller dishonesty. While it is possible to find amazingly low prices on brand new, premium items like flat-screen televisions and refrigerators, prices low enough to evoke suspicion can signal a scam. Stories about eBay and Craigslist sellers using inflated claims about their merchandise are less common than in past years, but it is still a concern. To avoid being swindled, examine two things.

First, evaluate the ratings of the seller. It is not a perfect indicator, nor is anything other than receiving the merchandise as promised, but a seller with pristine ratings from other buyers over a long period of time is probably trustworthy. The second thing to look for is the difference between the retail price of the item versus the seller's asking price. Again, it is possible that someone is willing to sell you a brand new stove for less than half its current retail price because he abruptly lost his job, but the greater the difference between the retail and selling prices, the more curious you ought to be.

TIMING YOUR PURCHASES TO KNOWN SALE MONTHS

It is important to time your purchases to occur during the months known typically for sales. If you are not comfortable making such weighty purchases on Craigslist, you should still approach retail buying intelligently. For example, a 2009 BillShrink.com article on the 14 BEST TIMES TO MAKE MAJOR PURCHASES reveals that the best time to buy appliances is September and October, when stores are under pressure to clear space for the new arrivals. Indeed, this article points out that settling for last year's model of an appliance can save hundreds of dollars, and knowing why these items are on sale gives you negotiating leverage with salespeople. Computers are said to be cheapest during July and August, when manufacturers are running back to school sales and the end of Japan's fiscal year coincides with pushing new products to store shelves. April, May, and December are the months to watch for cookware, while dining room sets are highly promoted in late October and early November and recliners and chairs see significant activity in May and June.

If you cannot wait until one of these times to buy the item in question (we'd hate for our readers to go without a stove until September!), it may be better to look around on eBay or Craigslist. Of course, many retailers still run sales throughout the year, due to everything from excess inventory to slowdowns in business in the store. The overall idea is planning your household purchases—whether that means waiting or buying used—rather than being bamboozled by salespeople or tempted by credit cards to "just buy whatever" and get it over with.

THE TAKEAWAY

We cannot exaggerate the importance of approaching a home budget with an overall game plan. But do not worry. Every last detail of your financial future does not have to be mapped out today. Do not feel guilty about spending money to enjoy yourself. But do have a realistic spending plan before your back is against the wall and you are forced to somehow find a way to purchase big items for the first time.

PERSONAL FINANCE AND MARRIAGE

Are you single or married? I want to share five secrets of a financially happy marriage. When it comes to money, few couples are soul mates. Typically, one of you is a saver and the other is a spender. One of you is more conservative and the other is more of a risk-taker. And both of you are convinced that your way is the right way. That is why conversations about money so often deteriorate into arguments. But it does not have to be that way. You can create a system for handling finances that will satisfy you both. The information below shows you how to do it:

First, you should agree to disagree about some things in your marriage. While it is true that marriage makes the two of you as one, there should be room for more than one attitude about money in a marriage. Recognize that both your viewpoints are valid. You do not have to see eye-to-eye on everything, but it is essential for you to respect your partner's feelings about money; otherwise, you will not be able to come up with a plan you are both comfortable with. If the saver's happiness depends on being able to feel financially secure and the spender's happiness depends on being able to feel free to enjoy life, it is a good idea to earmark some money every month for both savings and fun purchases. Establish a common ground by identifying the important financial goals you can agree on: funding retirement, paying for college, taking an annual vacation, and more.

Second, you should maintain multiple bank accounts. No matter how close you are, your marriage should allow some space for individual independence. It is important to have a little money you can spend or save without consulting each other. It is a good idea for each of you to have one bank account in your own name, even if you maintain joint checking and savings accounts for household expenses, and for long-term goals like retirement and college. It is also prudent for each of you to establish your own separate credit record; otherwise, you may find it difficult to borrow money independently. Hence, keep one credit card that is in your name only, even if you use a joint credit card for your household purchases.

Third, share the bills. You need a system for paying bills that feels fair to both of you. Some couples pay their household bills from a joint account to which both spouses contribute. Others divide the bills, with each partner paying his or her share from their individual accounts. What is important is to make it an equitable division. For example, if one of you earns $75,000 a year and the other earns $25,000 a year, divide your shared expenses proportionately: The high earner pays two-thirds and the low earner pays one third of the household expenses.

Fourth, you should invest as a team. If you and your spouse each have a workplace retirement savings plan, sit down together and decide on a portfolio mix that uses both plans' investment options. Once you have agreed on an overall allocation—say, 50% U.S. stocks, 15% international stocks and 35% bonds—implement your strategy by picking the best-performing funds from each plan.

Fifth, you should communicate well. This advice sounds easier than it really is. Most couples are so busy working, raising children and running a household that they hardly have time to talk to each other. You may have to go out of your way to schedule a conversation about your finances twice a year. Treat it like an important work-related appointment you must keep. Discuss whatever is on your minds, including your household budget, retirement portfolio, vacation expenses, the children' allowances, and college funding. Plan to have this conversation in as relaxed an atmosphere as possible (perhaps over a nice meal when the children are in school or at summer camp). In short, always remember that marriage is a financial partnership, and like any successful partnership of equals, its depends on compromise and mutual cooperation.

A CHECKLIST OF FINANCIAL PLANNING STAPLES

There are essential items you probably put on your grocery list every week—including bread, eggs and paper towels. There are also financial planning staples every family needs. Here is a breadwinner's checklist of seven financial essentials:

1. A will

This is where you name a guardian for your children and direct how your assets should be distributed when you die. If you do not have a will, state law decides who gets your estate, and it can often take years for it all to wind its way through the legal system. This can create problems for your survivors. In many states, for example, your surviving husband or wife would get only one-third to one-half of the assets that were in your name alone. Your children would get the rest. But if they are minors, their share is administered by a court-appointed attorney until they turn 18 or 21, depending on when your state's law says they are adults. If you do not want to hire a lawyer to write your will, Quicken Will Maker can help you create the legal documents you need to protect your family and assets. Nolo.com also sells a product called Willmaker; the application is very user-friendly. Please, do not forget to call me for assistance: (240) 330-0839.

2. An emergency savings account

This is money you will need if you are laid off from work or confronted with unexpected home repair or medical bills. Your priority for this money is safety! It belongs in a bank account or a money market fund, not in the stock market. Your emergency account should be big enough to cover at least six months of living expenses.

3. An employer-sponsored retirement account

If you have access to an employer-sponsored retirement account, it should be your first choice for your savings. Your company may also match your contribution—or part of it. The most common plans are the 401(K) and the 403(b), which is used by non-profit organizations like churches, schools, and hospitals, and the 457, which is used by governments and municipalities.

You owe no taxes on your contributions or on their earnings until you withdraw them. Every plan has its own rules on what percentage of your salary you are allowed to save each year. Federal law limits the dollar amount of your contributions. In 2010, this limit was $16,500, $22,000 if you are age 50 or older. The 2011 IRA contribution limits are unchanged from 2010. Since 2008, the most you may contribute to a regular IRA each year is $5,000. However, if you will be 50 or older by the end of the year, you can contribute an extra $1,000, for a $6,000 total IRA contribution limit. Keep in mind you and/or your spouse must have earned income at least as great as the amount you contribute. These limits apply to both regular and Roth IRAs. Although you may be eligible to contribute to both plans, your combined contribution to both accounts cannot exceed your above limit ($5,000 or $6,000). Please, do not forget to call me for assistance: (240) 330-0839.

4. An Individual Retirement Account (IRA)

The maximum 2010 contribution you can make to either one (or to both together) was $5,000; $6,000 if you are age 50 or older. Your traditional IRA contributions may be tax-deductible, depending on your income and on whether you (or your spouse) are covered by a retirement plan at work. Roth IRA contributions are never tax-deductible, but your withdrawals will be tax-free after you are age 59-1/2 and have owned the Roth IRA for at least five years. You will find more information on both types of IRAs here. Please, do not forget to call me for assistance: (240) 330-0839.

5. Homeowner's or renter's insurance

If you are a home owner, your policy should cover the cost of rebuilding your house if it burns down. That is its replacement value, which is not the same as its market value. If you are a renter, your policy should cover your possessions for their replacement value, not their actual cash-value. The two sound alike, but their meaning is very different. For example, if you sold your living room couch, you would get its actual cash-value, but that is probably a small fraction of what it would cost you to replace it with a new couch. Whether you own or rent, make sure your policy includes adequate loss of use coverage. This insurance feature reimburses you for your hotel and restaurant bills and other living expenses if you are forced out of your home by an uninsured event, such as a fire. Please, do not forget to call me for assistance: (240) 330-0839.

6. Health insurance

Single person coverage is very expensive. Group coverage is less costly than an individual policy, so if you are not covered at work, your first step should be to find out if you are eligible for a group plan through a trade or professional association. Until recently, the cost and availability of individual coverage has depended on where you live. In some states, you cannot be turned down for health insurance. In others, you may be uninsurable if you have serious health problems. But with the enactment of President Obama's federal health care reform, the issue of health insurance is a rapidly changing landscape. Within six months or so, insurers will no longer be able to exclude children from coverage due to pre-existing conditions, and dependent children will be able to stay on their parents' policy until age 26. Under state laws, children had usually been eligible for coverage as dependents only until age 18 or 21. The new law will not require insurers to accept adults with pre-existing conditions until 2014.

But between now and then, it requires the establishment of temporary 'high risk pools' to insure people with pre-existing conditions who cannot find coverage elsewhere. These high risk pools will not be permitted to charge more than standard insurance rates. You will find more information about the health care changes that will be phased in over the next four years at newyorktimes.com, ehealthinsurance.com and insure.com. As the presidential elections of 2012 grinds on, I am still wading through the Affordability Health-Care Act. The Patient Protection and Affordable Care Act (PPACA), informally called Obamacare, or simply the federal health care law, is a United States federal statute signed into law by President Barack Obama on March 23, 2010.

Together with the Health Care and Education Reconciliation Act, it represents the most significant regulatory overhaul of the U.S. healthcare system since the passage of Medicare and Medicaid in 1965. PPACA is aimed primarily at decreasing the number of uninsured Americans and reducing the overall costs of health care. It provides a number of incentives—including subsidies and tax credits—to employers and individuals to increase the coverage rate. Additional reforms are aimed at improving healthcare outcomes and streamlining the delivery of health care. PPACA requires insurance companies to cover all applicants and offer the same rates regardless of pre-existing conditions or gender. The Congressional Budget Office projected that PPACA will lower both future deficits and Medicare spending. On June 28, 2012, the United States Supreme Court upheld the constitutionality of most of PPACA in the case National Federation of Independent Business v. Sebelius. Please, do not forget to call me for assistance: (240) 330-0839.

7. Life insurance

Life insurance is the cornerstone of your financial house. Step three of *The Miraculous Millionaire* explores the subject of life and other types of insurance in great detail. It suffices for me to add here that if you have dependents, life insurance is a must-have possession. If you are worried about costs and affordability, I would tell you that for the biggest policy at the smallest cost, buy term insurance. It is pure insurance coverage with no investment component. However, if you have money to invest, please, research a favorable equity-indexed and tax-advantaged contract. I can help you if you need the services of a reputable agent. Please, feel free to call me for assistance: (240) 330-0839.

How much life insurance do you need? A commonly used rule of thumb is that your policy should be five to ten times your annual income. More precisely, it should be big enough to generate sufficient income for your survivors when they invest the proceeds. If you assume they can earn 4% a year after taxes, a $500,000 policy, for example, generates $20,000 a year. Remember, your insurance need is reduced by any sources of income your family will have from your savings, investments, spouse's salary and Social Security survivors' benefits.

There is more to personal finance than the drudgery of debts and budgets.

You can comparison shop online for a term policy at sites like insweb.com, selectquote. com, accuquote.com, and efinancial.com. If you have taken care of everything on this list, congratulations! Your financial house is in good order.

TEACH YOUR CHILDREN HOW TO SAVE AND SPEND WISELY

Part of my motivation for writing this section here is to make you identify with me as either a parent or a child. I have two children: Lucielle and Alexia. My two girls were born in January 2000 and November 2001 respectively. Before they were born, I had been grappling with questions pertaining to their finances. As I struggle with my wife to raise them properly, I remain engrossed in thoughts about their future: careers and life changes. My dream is that I want them to attend Ivy League colleges. Alexia has already expressed serious interest in medicine. She dreams of a career in neuro-surgery; indeed, her role model is Dr. Benjamin Carson of John Hopkins University, Baltimore, Maryland. She has already read all the books written by Dr. Carson. As she keeps on dreaming big, she is looking forward to a future encounter with her idol.

As for Lucielle, she had expressed interest in singing and art, initially, but I had to convince her to return to the drawing board. She does not like practicing her craft, so I do not see her as a true artist. She likes playing the part of a banker, saving money all the time and managing it well. When I suggested careers in investment banking and a role model such as Warren Buffett, she latched onto the idea quickly. I am planning to take Lucielle to New York again; this time, my plan is for her to watch the workings of the stock market. Lucielle is already setting her sights on the business school of Columbia University and Harvard University. I am happy my children are mapping their career paths happily, but I have to contend with the reality of shouldering the rising college costs. How would I pay for them? As for myself, I have chosen cash-value life insurance. As for my little angels, Quicken gives me the advice on how to turn two young consumers into smart consumers, penny-pinching savers, and savvy investors. Did you know that teenagers spend more than $100 billion a year? Children under the age of 12 spend $11 billion per year. How can parents teach children to spend and save wisely? Once your children can handle basic arithmetic, let them help you plan a grocery shopping trip. Decide how much to spend and then ask for their help in getting the most for your money.

Allowances are also a good way to introduce children to spending and saving their own money. Insist that they save a portion of it and put it in a glass jar so they can watch their savings grow. When your children reach middle school, open a savings account for them. Explain how money in a bank earns interest on the opening balance, plus interest on the interest, a process called compounding.

Children enjoy hearing that their money is working for them. Ask older children to write a budget with your help. Then step back. Monitor spending but do not manage it. They will learn from their own mistakes. When your children reach high school, open a checking or debit account for them. But saving should remain the watchword. By now they should start to grasp the difference between short-term saving for an iPod versus saving for long-term goals such as college. Supportive parents raise informed consumers.

ESTATE PLANNING BASICS

I will like to conclude the chapter on balancing your financial book by dropping a favorable term of millionaires and billionaires: estate planning. Do not be afraid. I will discuss only the basics. What is estate planning? It is about protecting the people you love; that is why everyone, not just the wealthy, needs an estate plan. The details of your plan naturally depend on your individual situation or circumstances, but there are essential components every estate plan should include.

A STRATEGY FOR YOUR SURVIVORS

No matter how long you live, one day others are going to inherit everything you own. The following documents help ensure that your assets are distributed according to your wishes. As for a will, if you die without one, state law dictates who will get your possessions. The state's one-size-fits-all plan may not match your needs. In many states, for example, if you die unmarried, childless and without a will, all your assets go to your parents. You might prefer to leave your possessions to a close friend or to one of your siblings. Your will does not only cover your material possessions. It is also the document in which you name a guardian for your minor children in the unlikely event you are not there to raise them yourself. If you choose not to have a lawyer draft your will, a do-it-yourself option like Quicken or Nolo's Will Maker can help you create all the legal documents you need to protect your family and assets. As for current copies of your beneficiary designation forms, by law, the beneficiary forms for your IRAs, 401(K) plans, and other retirement accounts override your will. If your IRA beneficiary designation form names your sister Besem, for example, and your will says you are leaving the IRA to your cousin Joe, your cousin Joe is out of luck. If your beneficiary forms are missing, your estate becomes your default beneficiary. In that case, these accounts are distributed according to the directions in your will, but on less favorable tax terms.

A person who is a designated beneficiary on a retirement account has his or her whole lifetime to empty the account. For a 40-year-old heir, that could be more than four decades. But a person who inherits a retirement account under your will must empty the account and pay taxes on the money much more quickly, sometimes within five years of your death, depending on your age when you pass through transition.

A STRATEGY FOR EMERGENCIES

Your estate plan should also include three documents that address issues your family will face should you ever become incapacitated:

A Durable Power-of-Attorney: This document allows a person of your choice to act for you (write checks on your bank account, pay your taxes, etc.) when you are unable to do so. Make sure it is "durable" because a power-of-attorney that is not "durable" is only valid until you are incapacitated; then it expires. In other words, a non-durable power-of-attorney would allow your agent to act on your behalf if you are out of town but would be invalid if you were under anesthesia in a hospital.

There is more to personal finance than the drudgery of debts and budgets.

A Health-Care Proxy: If you cannot speak for yourself, this document gives someone else the legal right to make medical decisions on your behalf. Otherwise, a hospital and doctors will make these choices, not your family. A health-care proxy does not state your preferences. It says your agent knows what you want and is entitled to speak for you. A living will states what medical treatments you want and do not want. Make sure your health-care proxy and your doctors have copies. A living will is important because it serves as a back-up for a health-care proxy: If anyone argues with your agent, then, your living will is written proof of your wishes.

A STRATEGY FOR SPECIAL FAMILY SITUATIONS

Sometimes, it is smart to leave assets to a trust for the benefit of your heirs, instead of directly to your heirs. A trust is a legal entity that holds assets and distributes them according to your wishes. Your estate plan may need to include a trust if:

First, you want to provide for a minor or disabled child. You can leave money to a trust and name a trustee who will oversee its investments and distributions to your heir. Make sure you name a trustee who is likely to survive you. Your trust instructions can spell out how the money is to be used and how long the trust is to last.

Second, you have children from a previous marriage. You want your spouse to be provided for, but you also want to ensure that after his or her death these children will inherit any remaining assets. One way to do this is with a Qualified Terminable Interest Property Trust, better known as a Q-Tip Trust: At your death, your assets go into this trust, which pays lifetime income to your surviving spouse. When he or she dies, the trust assets are paid to your children from your previous marriage. A sound estate plan helps you protect the people you care about most—both during and after your lifetime.

In sum, you have learned much about how to balance your financial book like a professional. Beware of credit power. Resist the temptation of using plastic cards for money. Credit cards are addictive and destructive as drugs, giving you a quick fix by satisfying temporary desires. Continue practicing the habit of saving money every day. The value of the habit of saving is that it makes you feel the Power of CASH. When you have cash reserves, it is easy for you to take advantage of an investment opportunity quickly. The secret of saving is smart budgeting. Experiment with the ideas I have presented to you; implement my proven plan for financial fitness. I have shown you the process of budgeting with datasheets.

If you are experiencing any difficulties, Quicken financial software will help you to get out of debt and grow your equity quickly; you will learn how to design your own sure-fire plan for paying off ALL debts automatically. You will recognize the most dangerous money myths; you will learn how to secure a big, fat nest egg for emergencies and retirement; in the end, you will positively change your life and your family tree!

Step **6**

COMPUTERIZE AND RESEARCH THE INTERNET

There is more to personal finance than the drudgery of debts and budgets.

In the previous chapter, balance your financial book, I stressed the necessity of employing Intuit's Quicken in managing your money like a professional of personal finance. In broaching the subject of the application of computer hardware and software in money management, I made the assumption that you have already computerized the basic elements of your life and work. If my assumption is false, then, I must say to you now that I am sorry. Yet, I must stress the importance of personal and business computerization. The teaching of personal or business computing is beyond the scope of *The Miraculous Millionaire*, but there are many places where you can acquire an introduction to computing. Join the millionaire club, and we shall make the necessary arrangements for you to begin learning basic computing.

Whether you like computers or not, you cannot question the self-evidence, veracity, and centrality of computing to modern living. I have a few words of advice for all individuals who are serious about thinking and growing rich today: Thou must computerize and surf the Internet! It is important for you to learn how to use hand-held or portable digital devices and personal computers effectively at home and at work. I belong to the old generation of Bill Gates' desktop computing, but I am struggling to make sense of the cataclysmic shift to the new communication technologies ushered in by the Internet and mobile computing. I have embraced the brave and new era of computing like an intrepid voyager.

Additionally, it is vital for you to learn how to use a computer as a research tool. For this reason, on my web sites, I have appended a long list of computer search engines you can use to surf and research the Internet: princeojong.com and millionaireiuniversity.com. The easiest way to research the Internet is surfing the world wide web and employing many search engines.

Do not worry if you do not have a formal computer education; in fact, I taught myself how to use computers the hard way; I learned personal and business computing by buying and reading books and magazines; I also learned computer applications by reading thick manuals and experimenting with computers at home. Are you shopping for a computer? For most kinds of purchases, you can get valuable advice and comparisons on the Internet. Ask a librarian or friends which Internet sites they think are helpful, or you can use a search engine like Google or Yahoo. Be aware that information you find is often biased. At many websites, the only products or sellers listed are the ones that pay to advertise. Before buying anything on the Internet, check several websites and make sure you deal with reputable dealers.

COMPUTERIZE C'EST QUOI?

What does computerize mean? My dictionary tells me that the term computerize means to furnish with a computer or computer system or to enter, process, or store information in a computer or system of computers. If you were an average American like me back in the early 1980s, you were not the progeny of a great fortune or financial heritage like the Kennedys, Rockefellers, and the Trumps. You could not boast of money, power, influence, or personal connections. You were not born with a golden spoon in your mouth. As a result, you had to work hard to make it big in America; you had to learn to earn. Even today it is difficult for you to become enterprising like the lucky and whiz children from Richistan, Affluenza Americana, and Silicon Valley because you lack the factors of production: capital, land, labor, and technology.

However, there is a new technology in Pax Americana that should not be beyond your reach or grasp: portable digital devices and the personal computer, which was invented by International Business Machines, Inc. (IBM) in 1980. Back then, a personal computer was a rare commodity in computer laboratories; today, however, sages like Steve Jobs, Paul Allen, and Bill Gates have worked hard to turn the personal computer into a low-prized commodity for the home and work. Bill Gates, for instance, became rich by making computers a ubiquitous presence of daily life. In fact, his vision was encapsulated in the following words: "When Paul Allen and I started Microsoft over 30 years ago, we had big dreams about software. We had dreams about the impact it could have. We talked about a computer on every desk and in every home. It has been amazing to see so much of that dream become a reality and touch so many lives. I never imagined what an incredible and important company would spring from those original ideas."

MY COMPUTER BACKGROUND

In the early 1970s, when I was growing up in Yaounde, Cameroon, I overheard the word computer for the very first time from the mouths of some government employees working at the presidency of the republic; on a luncheon date in my family home, these civil servants were struggling to describe intelligibly the strange operations of a human-like machine at the presidential palace that was imported from France and America. Indeed, as a little boy, I had never seen or heard about robots, but their conversation sounded to me like the stuff of science fiction; as a voracious reader or junkie of thrillers and abridged novels of the science fiction genre, my imagination roamed far and wide. I wondered about the robotics of the computer at Cameroon's presidency, a hermetic and occult place.

My first real encounter with a computer, however, was personal; the year was 1984; the setting was the campus of Howard University. As I was walking around Blackburn Center, a colorful poster of the advertisement of a seminar and workshop with the headline "Personal Computer: The Magic Page" arrested my attention; I stood by the bulletin board to read the entire advertisement copy. I was too excited not only to attend the seminar and workshop but also to grasp the impact and importance of the personal computer in the classroom. As a graduate student busy revising my thesis proposal, I could appreciate the fact that the personal computer would facilitate the task of writing, editing, and rewriting my actual thesis.

Besides, impressed by my personal interest in personal computers, Rosaline Alexander, a classmate and African-American student from Austin, Texas, invited me a few weeks later to her apartment located around Ontario Road and Mount Pleasant, Washington, D.C. She took some time to show me how she used her personal computer for home and work; she used the MultiMate word-processor to type her school papers; she also typed term papers for students on campus, in addition to her work in a law firm in downtown Washington, D. C. I was thrilled. The desire to own a personal computer was born in my soul. As I look back now, little did I know I was playing with a new technology that would change my future life in America forever. I was unaware that I was interacting with a technology that would help a poor and laboring African student build his human capital. I was poor in land, capital, and labor. However, I would become rich in technology. I would have no reason to envy the children from Richistan, Affluenza Americana, and Silicon Valley. Technology has become the great equalizer. Thanks!

There is more to personal finance than the drudgery of debts and budgets.

The computer would become the centerpiece of my academic and professional life. Therefore, the personal computer, according to me, was tantamount to a major factor of production—the creation of goods and services for the satisfaction of human wants. If I worked hard to acquire and polish my computer skills, I would be able to establish an information-based business. I did not mind whether I had no personal connections in America. As an experiment, in 1986, I did what Napoleon Bonaparte had left undone. I managed to use the sum of fifteen hundred dollars, a portion of my hard-earned savings as a security guard and graduate assistant, to buy a brand new IBM PC compatible computer; indeed, it was a clone described at that time as an XT, which means extended technology. I bought the computer from Sudhir Sumongkol, a Thai computer consultant who was referred to me by Elias KAWSAR KHAN, a Howard University PhD student from Bangladesh. I was ecstatic like a lottery or sweepstakes winner.

It did not take a long time for my ecstasy to wear off; I was frustrated by my inability to begin using the computer right out of the box. Although back in Cameroon I had used my father's old typewriter to teach myself touch typing, I still felt the computer keyboard of my XT clone was as abstruse as the cockpit of an airplane; I could not make sense of anything, so I could not use my computer for over three weeks. I was almost ashamed of my intellectual paralysis. I discovered, to my amazement, that almost all my friends and acquaintances who had professed to be computer experts were, actually, computer illiterates; whenever I invited them to come and practice problems on the computer with me, they declined my invitation or searched for an alibi. It did not take a long time for me to realize that spewing and dropping computer terms such as Apple, VisiCalc, modem, monitor, CPU, Lotus 123, WordPerfect, MultiMate, and DOS did not mean that the individual knew how to use the computer.

Psychologically, I was totally unprepared for the long curve of self-study that awaited me. After getting frustrated by the negative attitudes of individuals who had claimed to be computer experts, I decided to pull the bull by the horns; I turned back to a strategy of personal advancement that had served me in middle school and high school. What is it? Self-study. The term self-study may be defined as auto didacticism (also autodidactic); self-study is self-education or self-directed learning. An autodidact is a mostly self-taught person. Instead of relying on other people to teach me how to use the personal computer, I decided to teach myself whatever I wanted to learn about personal computing.

BOOKS AND MAGAZINES

To demystify the personal computer, I decided to buy and read books and magazines on the subject in question. The first book I bought to complement my WordPerfect software manual was an introductory text from Egghead Software company, Alexandria, Virginia. The purchase and reading of magazines such as PC Magazine, and Computer Shopper opened my eyes to a wonderful world of computing that had been awaiting me. Free local magazines introduced me to the presence of amazing and burgeoning community of computer enthusiasts and hackers. I subscribed to the monthly magazines and joined the Capital PC User Group that was headquartered in Rockville, Maryland. Because I did not have much money at the time, I spent more time in the Alexandria Public library located on Mount Vernon Avenue.

The public library gave me a free opportunity to read books and magazines on personal computing. Of all the magazines I read, the one that left an indelible mark on me was titled *Home-Office Computing*; it was a publication of Scholastica. De jure, this magazine taught me how to operate a computer-based business from home without spending hundreds and thousands of dollars on an MBA degree. Later on, I decided to subscribe to it; every month, I always awaited the receipt of this magazine. Particularly, I remember reading and rereading the insightful and practical articles of Paul and Sarah Edwards. I want you to know that this couple even wrote 3 good books that have remained a common fixture in my family library: *Working from Home, Getting Business to Come to You,* and *Best Home-Based Businesses.* Much later, I had bought and read their book titled *Home-Based Business for Dummies.* I liked and still like the books in the class of the Dummies or Idiot series. For someone like me who is new to a subject, the books explain concepts in elemental terms with a readability level that does not surpass a high-school's 12th grader. In fact, self-education is the technique I have used time and again to learn and untangle the mysteries of the personal computer. To appreciate my devotion to self-study, you need to examine my personal list of suggested readings in Step 12 of *The Miraculous Millionaire.*

SOFTWARE

Software is the set of instructions that make computers work. I ascribe fundamental importance to the value of software. When I bought my first personal computer in 1986, it did not take very long for me to realize that software was the brain of the personal computer. Not only did I teach myself how to use many software packages, but I also began learning how to program in DOS, Dbase III, Visual Basics, MS Access, ASP.Net and SQL. How do I teach myself? Unlike most people, I take it upon myself to read software manuals thoroughly; to complement my knowledge of a particular application, I buy books from either Amazon.com or Barnes and Noble. Whenever I am working on a new software, I follow the instructions of the manual verbatim first; indeed, I read from the first page to the last page of the manual. If I do not comprehend a concept, I call the software company's technical support department. I have discussed the details of how I study software in step 7, the next chapter exploring the acquisition of entrepreneurial skills. In fact, as I was reading computer magazines and books, I was privy of the fact that MS DOS, Windows, and MS Office software were the Master keys to Bill Gates' riches. Indeed, Bill Gates only lost the keys to Steve Jobs when the former failed to envision the imminence and ascendancy of the Internet era. In the chapter on stocks, step 9, you will read about my successful investment in Microsoft stock back in the mid-1980s; most people had not yet heard of Bill Gates. As a computer enthusiast, I was following Microsoft's growing dominance of the PC world through its WINTEL alliance. I was happy I made a lot of money from this software knowledge.   In the same fashion, I have had to change trains to Apple, so I owned many stocks of Apple before the public craze over iPhones, iPads, and iPods.

INTERNET

Bill Gates, my super hero, ended his computer career at Microsoft as a billionaire founder who was running the race but without accomplishing the mission to conquer cyberspace.

His Achilles heels were the denial of the emergence of the Internet era and late acknowledgment of the fact that Windows would be supplanted by a new and open-sourced technological order of the Internet. What is the Internet? The Internet is a global system of interconnected computer networks that use the standard Internet protocol suite (TCP/IP) to serve billions of users worldwide. It is a network of networks that consists of millions of private, public, academic, business, and government networks, of local to global scope, that are linked by a broad array of electronic, wireless and optical networking technologies. The Internet carries a vast range of information resources and services, such as the inter-linked hypertext documents of the World Wide Web (WWW) and the infrastructure to support electronic mail. Most traditional communications media including telephone, music, film, and television are reshaped or redefined by the Internet, giving birth to new services such as Voice over Internet Protocol (VoIP) and IPTELEVISION. Newspaper, book and other print publishing are adapting to Web site technology, or are reshaped into blogging and web feeds.

The Internet has enabled or accelerated new forms of human interactions through instant messaging, Internet forums, and social networking. Online shopping has boomed both for major retail outlets and small artisans and traders. Business-to-business and financial services on the Internet affect supply chains across entire industries. The origins of the Internet reach back to research of the 1960s, commissioned by the United States government in collaboration with private commercial interests to build robust, fault-tolerant, and distributed computer networks. The funding of a new U.S. backbone by the National Science Foundation in the 1980s, as well as private funding for other commercial backbones, led to worldwide participation in the development of new networking technologies, and the merger of many networks. The commercialization of what was by the 1990s an international network resulted in its popularization and incorporation into virtually every aspect of modern human life. As of 2011, more than 2.1 billion people – nearly a third of Earth's population – use the services of the Internet.

The Internet has no centralized governance in either technological implementation or policies for access and usage; each constituent network sets its own standards. Only the overreaching definitions of the two principal name spaces in the Internet, the Internet Protocol address space and the Domain Name System, are directed by a maintainer organization, the Internet Corporation for Assigned Names and Numbers (ICANN). The technical underpinning and standardization of the core protocols (IPv4 and IPv6) is an activity of the Internet Engineering Task Force (IETF), a non-profit organization of loosely affiliated international participants that anyone may associate with by contributing technical expertise.

STRUCTURE

The Internet structure and its usage characteristics have been studied extensively. It has been determined that both the Internet IP routing structure and hypertext links of the World Wide Web are examples of scale-free networks. Similar to the way the commercial Internet providers connect via Internet exchange points, research networks tend to interconnect into large sub networks such as GEANT, GLORIAD, Internet2, and the UK's national research and education network JANET. These in turn are built around smaller networks. Many computer scientists describe the Internet as a "prime example of a large-scale, highly engineered, yet highly complex system". The Internet is heterogeneous; for instance, data transfer rates and physical characteristics of connections vary widely. The Internet exhibits "emergent phenomena" that depend on its large-scale organization. For example, data transfer rates exhibit temporal self-similarity. The principles of the routing and addressing methods for traffic in the Internet reach back to their origins the 1960s when the eventual scale and popularity of the network could not be anticipated. Thus, the possibility of developing alternative structures is investigated. The Internet structure was found to be highly robust to random failures and very vulnerable to high degree attacks.

ICANN

ICANN is headquartered in Marina Del Rey, California, United States. The Internet is a globally distributed network comprising many voluntarily interconnected autonomous networks. It operates without a central governing body. However, to maintain interoperability, all technical and policy aspects of the underlying core infrastructure and the principal name spaces are administered by the Internet Corporation for Assigned Names and Numbers (ICANN), headquartered in Marina del Rey, California. ICANN is the authority that coordinates the assignment of unique identifiers for use on the Internet, including domain names, Internet Protocol (IP) addresses, application port numbers in the transport protocols, and many other parameters. Globally unified name spaces, in which names and numbers are uniquely assigned, are essential for the global reach of the Internet. ICANN is governed by an international board of directors drawn from across the Internet technical, business, academic, and other non-commercial communities. The government of the United States continues to have the primary role in approving changes to the DNS root zone that lies at the heart of the domain name system. ICANN's role in coordinating the assignment of unique identifiers distinguishes it as perhaps the only central coordinating body on the global Internet. On 16 November 2005, the World Summit on the Information Society, held in Tunis, established the Internet Governance Forum (IGF) to discuss Internet-related issues.

MODERN USES

There are many modern uses of the Internet, which is shared in many industries. An accountant sitting at home in the USA can audit the books of a company based in another country, on a server situated in a third country that is remotely maintained by IT specialists in a fourth country. These accounts could have been created by home-working bookkeepers, in other remote locations, based on information emailed to them from offices all over the world.

Some of these things were possible before the widespread use of the Internet, but the cost of private leased lines would have made many of them infeasible in practice. An office worker away from their desk, perhaps on the other side of the world on a business trip or a holiday, can access their emails, access their data using cloud computing, or open a remote desktop session into their office PC using a secure Virtual Private Network (VPN) connection on the Internet.

There is more to personal finance than the drudgery of debts and budgets.

This can give the worker complete access to all of their normal files and data, including email and other applications, while away from the office. This concept has been referred to among system administrators as the Virtual Private Nightmare, because it extends the secure perimeter of a corporate network into remote locations and its employees' homes.

INFORMATION

Many people use the terms Internet and World Wide Web, or just the Web, interchangeably, but the two terms are not synonymous. The World Wide Web is a global set of documents, images and other resources, logically interrelated by hyperlinks and referenced with Uniform Resource Identifiers (URIs). URIs symbolically identify services, servers, and other databases, and the documents and resources that they can provide. Hypertext Transfer Protocol (HTTP) is the main access protocol of the World Wide Web, but it is only one of the hundreds of communication protocols used on the Internet. Web services also use HTTP to allow software systems to communicate to share and exchange business logic and data. World Wide Web browser software, such as Microsoft's Internet Explorer, Mozilla Firefox, Opera, Apple's Safari, and Google Chrome, lets users navigate from one web page to another via hyperlinks embedded in the documents.

COMMUNICATION

Electronic mail, or email, is an important communications service available on the Internet. The concept of sending electronic text messages between parties in a way analogous to mailing letters or memos predates the creation of the Internet. Pictures, documents and other files are sent as email attachments. Emails can be cc-ed to multiple email addresses.

DATA TRANSFER

File sharing is an example of transferring large amounts of data across the Internet. A computer file can be emailed to customers, colleagues and friends as an attachment. It can be uploaded to a website or FTP server for easy download by others. It can be put into a "shared location" or onto a file server for instant use by colleagues. The load of bulk downloads to many users can be eased by the use of "mirror" servers or peer-to-peer networks. In any of these cases, access to the file may be controlled by user authentication, the transit of the file over the Internet may be obscured by encryption, and money may change hands for access to the file. The price can be paid by the remote charging of funds from, for example, a credit card whose details are also passed—usually fully encrypted—across the Internet.

The origin and authenticity of the file received may be checked by digital signatures or by MD5 or other message digests. These simple features of the Internet, over a worldwide basis, are changing the production, sale, and distribution of anything that can be reduced to a computer file for transmission. This includes all manner of print publications, software products, news, music, film, video, photography, graphics and the other arts. This in turn has caused seismic shifts in each of the existing industries that previously controlled the production and distribution of these products.

SOCIAL IMPACT

The Internet has enabled entirely new forms of social interaction, activities, and organizing, thanks to its basic features such as widespread usability and access. Social networking websites such as Facebook, Twitter and MySpace have created new ways to socialize and interact. Users of these sites are able to add a wide variety of information to pages, to pursue common interests, and to connect with others. It is also possible to find existing acquaintances, to allow communication among existing groups of people. Sites like LinkedIn foster commercial and business connections. YouTube and Flickr specialize in users' videos and photographs. In the first decade of the 21st century the first generation is raised with widespread availability of Internet connectivity, bringing consequences and concerns in areas such as personal privacy and identity, and distribution of copyrighted materials. These "digital natives" face a variety of challenges that were not present for prior generations.

BBS

Electronic bulletin boards are the precursors of the Internet, as we know it today. I cannot discount the value of electronic bulletin board systems to my computer education. Back in the 1980s, I depended on BBSs for a lot of information, especially the download of software based on the honor system, that is, you use it first; if you like the software, you pay for it.. What exactly is a BBS?. A Bulletin Board System, or BBS, is a computer system running software that allows users to connect and log in to the system using a terminal program. Once logged in, a user can perform functions such as uploading and downloading software and data, reading news and bulletins, and exchanging messages with other users, either through electronic mail or in public message boards. Many BBSes also offer on-line games, in which users can compete with each other, and BBSes with multiple phone lines often provide chat rooms, allowing users to interact with each other.

Originally BBSes were accessed only over a phone line using a modem, but by the early 1990s some BBSes allowed access via a Telnet, packet switched network, or packet radio connection. Ward Christensen coined the term "Bulletin Board System" as a reference to the traditional cork-and-pin bulletin board often found in entrances of supermarkets, schools, libraries or other public areas where people can post messages, advertisements, or community news. By "computerizing" this method of communications, the name of the system was born: CBBS - Computerized Bulletin Board System.

SOFTWARE AND HARDWARE

Unlike modern websites and online services that are typically hosted by third-party companies in commercial data centers, BBS computers (especially for smaller boards) were typically operated from the SysOp's home. As such, access could be unreliable, and in many cases only one user could be on the system at a time. Only larger BBSs with multiple phone lines using specialized hardware, multitasking software, or a LAN connecting multiple computers, could host multiple simultaneous users. The first BBSes used homebrew software, quite often written or customized by the SysOps themselves, running on early S-100 microcomputer systems

There is more to personal finance than the drudgery of debts and budgets.

such as the Altair, IMSAI and Cromemco under the CP/M operating system. Soon after, BBS software was being written for all of the major home computer systems of the late 1970s era - the Apple II, Atari, Commodore and TRS-80 being some of the most popular. A few years later, in 1981, IBM introduced the first DOS based IBM PC, and due to the overwhelming popularity of PCs and their clones, DOS soon became the operating system on which the majority of BBS programs were run. RBBS-PC, ported over from the CP/M world, and Fido BBS, created by Tom Jennings (who later founded FidoNet) were the first notable DOS BBS programs. There were many successful commercial BBS programs developed for DOS, such as PCBoard BBS, Remote-Access BBS, and Wildcat! BBS which had early roots from the Colossus BBS started by the author of the popular shareware communications program Qmodem. Some popular freeware BBS programs for MS-DOS included Telegard BBS and Renegade BBS, which both had early origins from leaked WWIV BBS source code. There were several dozen other BBS programs developed over the DOS era, and many were released under the shareware concept, while some were released as freeware including iniquity.

COMPUTER AND INTERNET TIMELINE

It is beyond the scope of this book to present the history of computing and the Internet. I have included a list of search engines you might use to study the history of computing and the Internet. Not only do I want you to know that the former vice president, Al Gore, did not invent the Internet, but I also want you to recognize the benefit of leveraging Internet resources for your own betterment. Because I have asked you to use search engines to research computing and the Internet, I do not want to waste your precious time talking about the history of the Internet; rather, I want to underscore the fact that the Internet is a relic of the Cold War that America's government has reconstituted for civilian applications. I do not remember a day that goes by without me surfing the Internet at home and at work. Every day I use the Internet at home to read emails on Yahoo.com and Aol.com; I download and listen to music; I watch music videos on Youtube.com; I read news from all over the world; I communicate with friends on Facebook and other social media sites. I help my daughters with their homework by relying on the Internet, and chat with friends from all over the world using SKYPE. I purchase books and supplies online. As for business application of the Internet, I will elaborate in the next chapter. It suffices to stress that I used the Internet a lot in my business life. My daily organizer is electronic and Internet based, so it is easy for me to update and synchronize my information. After preparing a report with any of the applications in Microsoft Office, I can email it to the recipient over the Internet. Before I continue my discussion of computerizing and the Internet, I would like to present to you a history of the development of the computer and Internet. De jure, computer history serves as a framework within which you can fully appreciate the insights I am going to highlight my analyses.

SEARCH ENGINES LISTING

On my web sites, I have secured a comprehensive list of Internet search engines you should use to surf and research the Internet: http://www.princeojong.com or http://www. millionaireiuniversity.com. On the next page, however, are my top ten list of search engines.

TOP TEN SEARCH ENGINES

01. Google
Google is the undisputed king of 'spartan searching'. While it does not offer all the shopping center features of Yahoo!, Google is fast, relevant, and the largest single catalogue of Web pages available today.

02. Yahoo!
Yahoo! is several things: it is a search engine, a news aggregator, a shopping center, an emailbox, a travel directory, a horoscope and games center, and more.

03. Ask Jeeves
The Ask/Aka Ask Jeeves search engine is a longtime name in the World Wide Web. The super-clean interface rivals the other major search engines, and the search options are as good as Google or Bing or DuckDuckGo.

04. Bing
Bing is Microsoft's attempt at unseating Google. Bing used to be MSN search until it was updated in summer of 2009

05. DuckDuckGo
At first, DuckDuckGo.com looks like Google. But there are many subtleties that make this spartan search engine different.

06. Webopedia
Webopedia is one of the most useful websites on the World Wide Web. Webopedia is an encyclopedic resource dedicated to searching techno terminology and computer definitions.

07. Mahalo
Mahalo is the one 'human-powered' search site in this list, employing a committee of editors to manually sift and vet thousands of pieces of content.

08. The Internet Archive
The Internet Archive is a favorite destination for longtime Web lovers.

09. Yippy
Yippy is a Deep Web engine that searches other search engines for you. Unlike the regular Web, which is indexed by robot spider programs, Deep Web pages are usually harder to locate by conventional search.

10. Dogpile
Years ago, Dogpile was the fast and efficient choice before Google. Things changed, Dogpile faded into obscurity, and Google became king. But today, Dogpile is coming back.

There is more to personal finance than the drudgery of debts and budgets.

Step 7

ACQUIRE ENTREPRENEURIAL SKILLS

"WE CANNOT SOLVE PROBLEMS BY USING THE SAME KIND OF THINKING WE USED WHEN WE CREATED THEM." -- ALBERT EINSTEIN

Where do the wealthiest 1% of Americans invest their financial resources? Studies of wealth building and accumulation in America reveal the following statistics presented below:

1—Corporate stock.................90%
2—Real estate........................50%
3—Pension funds..................20%
    Personal trusts
4—Cash................................20%
5--Insurance Equity..............20%
6—Bonds..............................15%
7. Notes & Mortgages............15%

What can you glean from the statistics displayed above? 90% of the wealth of America's rich and famous is derived from corporate stock. How? Like Warren Buffett, they buy the corporate stock of the business entities that have sterling financials on their balance sheets. Or like Bill Gates and Steve Jobs, they create a business that solves a human need by establishing a new social or economic paradigm shift. While Bill Gates dropped out of Harvard University to found Microsoft, a micro-computer and software company, Steve Jobs founded Apple Computers and later on in his career he gave the company a new lease on life by inventing hot products such as the IPHONE, the IPOD, and the IPAD. Hence, if you are dreaming to be the next Bill Gates, then, it behooves you to acquire entrepreneurial skills; if you want to be the next, soon-to-be, or new entrepreneur millionaire, then, you must learn the computer superstars' secrets of how to establish and manage a profitable and successful business.

You should thank God you are living in America, the best of all possible worlds; you can read all the good books that have been written on Bill Gates and Steve Jobs; in addition to my advice, a reading of these books will teach you the mindset of these miraculous millionaires and billionaires; you will learn how to model their mental syntax to perform your own millionaire miracle. Mark Zuckerberg did just that with Facebook, a company that has just gone public with much fanfare. Even if you are not a member of the Y generation, you ought to know that Facebook is a social networking service and website launched in February 2004, owned and operated by Facebook, Inc. As of May 2012, Facebook has over 900 million active users, more than half of them using Facebook on a mobile device. Users must register before using the site, after which they may create a personal profile, add other users as friends, and exchange messages, including automatic notifications when they update their profile. Additionally, users may join common-interest user groups, organized by workplace, school or college, or other characteristics, and categorize their friends into lists such as People from Work or Close Friends. The name of the service stems from the colloquial name for the book given to students at the start of the academic year by some university administrations in the United States to help students get to know each other.

Facebook allows any users who declare themselves to be at least 13 years old to become registered users of the site.

Let us get back to Bill Gates and Steve Jobs! Indeed, we can add a few more names on the list: Pierre Omidyar, Steve Case, Jim Clark, Michael Dell, Larry Ellison, and Jeff Bezos. Who are these guys? They are what I describe as successful computer entrepreneurs; they took the risk of starting a new computer-based enterprise, and the marketplace rewarded them handsomely for their entrepreneurial spirit, which is the heart and soul of a genuine business person. The entrepreneurial spirit of the average business person is expressed by the reflection of entrepreneurial skills. So what do I mean by acquire entrepreneurial skills? By acquire entrepreneurial skills, I mean you have to learn to mirror, imitate, or model the mental syntax, mindset, and physical behavior of successful computer entrepreneurs like Bill Gates, Steve Jobs, Pierre Omidyar, Steve Case, Jim Clark, Michael Dell, Larry Ellison, and Jeff Bezos; these business super heroes are known the world over for bootstrapping profitable computer businesses.

Today, by learning from the rich examples of these great entrepreneurs, you could become what I refer to as The Miraculous Millionaire, someone who creates his or her own business miracles; as a result of saying welcome to the $ucce$$tology system; you possess the spirit to undertake the risk of using the factors of production to fulfill a human need or want in the marketplace. All the above listed individuals are entrepreneurs because at one time or another in their lives they became a student of a self-help or motivational system like $ucce$$tology; they learned and mastered the art, science, and philosophy of success; in fact, their life stories relate that they have learned how to use self-mastery and intuition to create successful businesses. Therefore, as the personal and business experiences of Bill Gates, Steve Jobs, Pierre Omidyar, Steve Case, Jim Clark, Michael Dell, Larry Ellison, and Jeff Bezos relate, there is a oneness or commonality of values and vision germane to the principles of entrepreneurship: the process of identifying a problem or need in the marketplace; the development of a business plan to codify the service or product; and the campaign of execution to bring the business solution or a vision to life.

In the case of Bill Gates and the founding of Microsoft, the business vision is the innovative idea or revolutionary opportunity to change how we compute and process information as human beings; in the example of Steve Jobs, the vision is simply a better way of using mundane tools like the telephone, computer, and television: iPhone, IPAD, and IPOD. The end result of this visionary process is the creation of a new venture, formed under conditions of risk and considerable uncertainty. Throughout my reading, teaching, and coaching experience, I have noticed a particular millionaire mindset that helps to form the foundation from which this entrepreneurial spirit springs. One way of describing this millionaire mindset is concentration and visualization or internal focus. Internal focus means that what goes on inside of your head and your heart greatly effects what happens to you in the outside world. In this wise, there is an inside and an outside world; there is a physical world and a spiritual world.

Normally, mystical individuals and charismatic Christians who are spiritually attuned with the laws of the invisible cosmos of God transcend these two worlds effortlessly; unfortunately, the majority of human beings, who are dismissed by the Rosicrucians as the unworthy, are earth bound to the physical world because they can avail themselves of the use of only their five senses. In the holy Bible, for instance, Jesus Christ talks about this duality of being (the body and the spirit). Where is your holy Bible? Please, keep it close to you; we have introduced courses on religion at Millionaire iUniversity to assist you; we want you to develop a mystical vision, the power of concentration, visualization, and intuition. You get the specialized knowledge they do not teach in the best business schools in the country.

Hence, it is often not the external trappings, such as the MBA or the business seminars, that make or break an entrepreneur. In fact, it is the internal focus of believing in yourself, listening to your intuition and tuning into your emotions that allows the entrepreneurial spirit of dreaming BIG to spring forth. By managing fear so that it does not become an obstacle, you are able to harness opportunity. Self-trust is paramount for risk-taking. A healthy entrepreneurial spirit requires trust in yourself and your intuition, an ability to make clear choices, a flare for mobilizing resources, and a capacity to move beyond obstacles created by fear. Connect with your entrepreneurial spirit and see where it leads you. Are you one of those folks in America who are tired of living from paycheck to paycheck? Has frustration led you to join the Occupy Wall Street movement? Does the idea of tripling your yearly income sound good? Do you dream to become your own boss? Do you like the idea of spending more time with your family? Is the idea of working for yourself agreeable to you? Does the flexible idea of taking time off appeal to you? Would you like to make plans to control your financial destiny? Would you welcome new ideas that can put you on the way to financial independence with an open mind? If your answers to these questions are affirmative, then, I, Prince Ojong, am looking for you. You are the reason why I am writing this book. The purpose of this chapter is to assist you in acquiring the entrepreneurial skills required for business ownership. Contrary to what you must have been told, you do not have to have much money or connections to create a small business, especially if you already have some computer skills. I am willing to introduce you to the best home-based computer service businesses in America: low start-up fees, affordable software, free business intelligence, no inventory, free web page, free training, and support.

Frankly, to acquire entrepreneurial skills, you need $ucce$$tology, that is, new thinking (glasnost) and restructuring (perestroika). When Mikhail Sergeyevich Gorbachev wanted to overhaul the Soviet system, he decided to introduce new thinking and restructuring. De jure, he was aware that he could not solve the problems pertaining to communist lethargy and inefficiency by using the same old kind of thinking that his predecessors (Vladimir Lenin, Alexei Rykov, Joseph Stalin, Georgy Malenkov, Nikita Khrushchev, Leonid Brezhnev, Yuri Andropov, and Konstantin Chernenko) had used to no avail. Hence, if you dream about becoming a millionaire entrepreneur or superstar, the name of the vehicle that will take you to your destination is entrepreneurial skills. For this reason, I ascribe great importance to facilitate the process of you, my student, acquiring the tools that are the *sine qua non* of business success. As an element of $ucce$$tology, entrepreneurship is an art, a science, and a philosophy. Do not worry if you think you are deficient right now as an entrepreneur. As you will observe, prior to discovering $ucce$$tology, I was an inexperienced and unsuccessful entrepreneur. The good news is that you can learn from my experiences; you can master the ingredients of entrepreneurship from me. As an art, in this chapter, I, the master artist or craftsman, will teach you the universal magic secrets of the craft of launching a small enterprise on a shoestring either from your home or an inexpensive commercial location. In regard to philosophy, I, the philosopher king of entrepreneurship, will introduce you to the systems of thought that Bill Gates, Oprah Winfrey, and all of the world's greatest entrepreneurs live by. As for the scientific basis of entrepreneurship, I, the business architect and scientist, will take you on a great safari, a voyage of entrepreneurial discovery; I will show you the secrets of building a profitable business; indeed, running a business is a science; you have to proceed systematically and methodically. For instance, I will focus your attention on the importance of writing a winning business plan, even if you will not approach any individuals, banks, or angels for funding. A business plan is the map that will guide you to success. To succeed in business, you need new thinking; you have to get rid of your old system of thinking. Albert Einstein states it well when he makes the following assertion: "We cannot solve problems by using the same kind of thinking we used when we created them."

Entrepreneurship is a two-edge sword. On the one hand, entrepreneurship has its merits. On the other hand, entrepreneurship has its demerits. In this chapter, nevertheless, I am going to use the plethora of personal experiences to assist you in building a small business, either at your home or in a commercial location. Actually, my first foray into entrepreneurship dates back to my childhood days in Cameroon. How old was I then? Probably, I was five years old. I was living with Susannah, my paternal cousin who was married to Mr. Otto Nkeng Ashu, a teacher from Ossing village. I was attending the Presbyterian Primary School located in Ntenako, Manyu Division. I had this great idea to start making money; I established a lemonade and grenadine stand in front Mr. Ashu's house, which was located in the school compound.

In addition to lemonade and grenadine, I sold a candy known to the students as bonbon—a lexicon which is a compounding of the French word for "good." My business failed; in fact, I did not operate it for more than a month. Why? As much as I liked the opportunity to make money, I could not resist the urge to consume the candy, lemonade, and grenadine. By contrast, when I was attending Yaounde University, I was successful in assisting my father build a family home in Yaounde, Cameroon; my father was very proud of me; I was flattered whenever my father appreciated my display of the skills of entrepreneurship. Since I have already recounted these two experiences in detail in my upcoming memoir titled *Dreams of America*, I am not going to dwell on these topics very much here.

It suffices for me to underscore that building a successful home-based business is possible. You do not need any special magic to have this become a reality for you. All it takes is knowing the ingredients to the recipe of success. It is as simple as mixing the recipe to bake a cake. Notice that it is simple, not necessarily easy. With so many home business opportunities available, it can get overwhelming trying to decide where to get started. So let us look at a handful of key ingredients that will see you to the top of the success ladder.

As a nation of the free and the brave, America encourages its citizenry to become entrepreneurs. Thinking about starting a business? You are not alone. Every year, thousands of Americans catch the entrepreneurial spirit, launching small businesses to sell their products or services.

Some businesses thrive; other businesses fail; and many businesses struggle. The more you know about starting a business, the more power you have to form an organization that develops into a lasting source of income and satisfaction. For help with the beginning stages of operating a business, the following checklist is a great place to start.

A PORTRAIT OF A COMPUTER ENTREPRENEUR AS A YOUNG AFRICAN

You may soon notice that the personal computer represents the framework within which I build my businesses. If the reason is not obvious to you now, I will provide some explanations. Because of the paucity of capital, I have always had a fondness for computer-based businesses. As my personal story relates, I am a poor immigrant from Africa. I do not have any personal connections or rich uncles like the Kennedys; I do not have any contact with money angels either. I do not have much capital to start a business. Hence, I have to use what I have to get what I need. God has given me a mind; I have been fortunate to recognize the importance of the personal computer revolution. To compensate for the lack of capital, I prefer to start only service businesses.

From the lessons of economic theory my teachers had taught me in Africa, I had learned how to capitalize on the four essential factors of entrepreneurial production (land, capital, labor, and technology) for my own betterment in America. As a true entrepreneur, my decision to start a business involved risk. However, my risk was minimized by the fact that I did not have a lot of resources. As for labor, I did not have the money to hire any employees; I had to rely on my own self; I had to rely on the brain God had given me. As for technology, I had to depend on the XT IBM clone computer I had bought to type the thesis of my Master's degree. As for land, I had very little space; indeed, I had only a dining table in my small, crammed, and dingy apartment that was located at 511 Four Mile Road, Alexandria, Virginia 22305.

BUSINESS LEVEL 1: WORD-PROCESSING AND TUTORING

The first business I started in America involved the provision of writing, word-processing, and tutoring services to students in the Washington metropolitan area. Back then, 1986, I did not know I needed a legal name for my business until I spoke to Quentin Custis, an African-American friend who was living at the Olde Towne West apartment complex where I worked at night as a security guard. I had been seeing Quentin Custis with copies of a magazine titled Black Enterprise, but I was never interested in that magazine; in fact, the black magazines that had attracted my attention were Ebony and Jet. Nevertheless I appreciated the business insights of Quentin Custis that resulted in me choosing a name for my business (American Computer Data Tracking) and registering it at the county office on King Street, Alexandria, Virginia.

There is more to personal finance than the drudgery of debts and budgets.

Initially, I had wanted to operate the business as a partnership with my friend Ayodele I. Balogun; when he told me he was not interested in the computer business, I decided to create a sole-proprietorship.

When did I start American Computer Data Tracking? I started the business in 1986. I had just completed the course work of my Master's degree. A few months later, I had obtained a pass in my Master's degree comprehensive examinations, and I was busy developing my thesis proposal, which morphed into the actual writing of my Master's thesis. I was working as a tutor in the English laboratory of the University of the District of Columbia in Washington, DC; I was also working as a graduate assistant at the English department of Howard University in Washington, DC. Additionally, I moonlighted as a security guard in Alexandria, Virginia. Hence, why did I start American Computer Data Tracking? I needed to supplement my income to assist my mother and sisters financially back home in Africa. By tutoring students in the English laboratory and teaching Freshman English, I had become aware of the demand for my services. Since I did not have any formal business education or training, I was forced to respond to this business opportunity artlessly. I did not know how to charge customers for my services either. In fact, customer input was the gauge I had used to set up the price for my services; whatever the customer was willing to pay me, I accepted it quickly.

Most of my early customers were college students of the University of the District of Columbia and Howard University. My main source of business was the English laboratory of the University of the District of Columbia. It was a common occurrence for me to acquire a customer after serving four students in the laboratory. Similarly, one out of every ten students I taught English composition at Howard University became my customer for life. Besides, some of the students were referred to me by their peers, that is, fellow students. It might be interesting to note that most of these student customers were foreign students from Africa, India, and the West Indies. To most of these students, English was a foreign language. Hence, their ability to learn written English was hampered by linguistic interference or language transfer. In linguistics, interference or cross-meaning is said to be a phenomenon which refers to non-native speakers or writers applying knowledge from their native language to a second language. Linguistic interference is most commonly discussed in the context of English language learning and teaching, but it can occur in any situation when someone does not have a native-level command of a language, as when translating into a second language.

For instance, a Haitian student would be forced to introduce French syntax into English when he or she is building sentences. An African student from Nigeria, for example, would introduce words of Pidgin English in his paragraphs. African-American students, who are supposed to be native speakers of English, inject Ebonics into the English lexicon. My most memorable experience teaching college writing was the case of John Black, who could not identify the subject, verb, or object in the following famous grammatical sentence: "John kicked the ball." "John kicked the ball" is an example which recurs with fanatical regularity in every grammar textbook. When the SVO (subject-verb-object) structure challenged my poor student, I knew my word-processing, writing, and tutoring service would prosper. The campus of the University of the District of Columbia was the place for a hungry entrepreneur to be. There were students everywhere who wanted to use my services. I was thrilled to discover that I had started competing favorably with the established-off-campus resume and typing service businesses that had been catering to students for ages. I had culled their phone numbers from all their advertisements that were plastered on bulletin boards on the campuses of The University of the District of Columbia and Howard University. By playing detective and spy, I called every business whose phone number I had found on the bulletin boards. By playing the role of a new and prospective customer, I was able to garner the business intelligence I needed from the enterprise: office hours, services, prices, office equipment, and software. Based on the business intelligence, I reorganized my business to be more attractive than the off-campus outfits. In terms of dollars, the results were excellent! I was too thrilled to think that I was making more money in my business than either working as a desk clerk and security guard or moonlighting as a laboratory technician on campus. At that time, I charged customers $4.00 per page for typing term papers or research papers, and I always added an editing charge of $50.00. Indeed, on the average, my business commanded $ 75.00 to $100.00 for a word-processing project. As for writing, if I had to go to the college library to borrow and read books for a research paper, I charged the student $250.00. My private-tutoring rate was $50.00. 90% of my private tutoring took place on the college campus; 10% of my private tutoring was done in my apartment in Alexandria, Virginia.

On the whole, I started my business the wrong way. In retrospect, I was proud of my business achievements, but today I would not suggest to any individual to restart and operate a typing service in the same manner. I was in a hurry to launch my word-processing service. Why do I regret? I should have prepared a business plan to guide me step-by-step to business success. I did not know anything about business management. I was just rolling with the punches. I never prepared a plan of business action. But I had belief and passion, and, for whatever reason, God was on my side. Hence, I would attribute the success of my first business in America, American Computer Data Tracking, to divine providence.

BUSINESS LEVEL 2: MAGAZINE PUBLISHING, INFORMATION BROKERAGE, AND MEDICAL BILLING

There is an old English adage that says "pride goes before a fall." I think it applies to my experience of rushing to start a magazine. Unlike American Computer Data Tracking, *Black Shopper* magazine, my second business, was not successful. I was crushed by a deliberate attempt to replicate the positive results of my first business venture. By teaching myself how to operate a personal computer and leveraging that knowledge to operate a successful word-processing service, I was tormented by self-delusions and the illusions of grandeur. I was like a balloon filled with the hot air of my own self-importance. In fact, the headline of the press releases I had written to the mass media to promote the magazine told the story of my arrogance: Black Dishwasher Publishes New Shopper's Guide. In fact, without any solid marketing or business plan, I rushed to drop out of my PhD program in organizational communications to launch a magazine titled *Black Shopper*.

There is more to personal finance than the drudgery of debts and budgets.

Dr. Cecile Blake, a Howard University professor who served as my mentor, struggled in vain to dissuade me from abandoning my post-graduate studies. I was very stubborn; my mind was already made up, and I could not listen to any voice of reason. My mother and sisters cried in silence for me, but I was fired up .like a rocket after reading about two of my heroes who had to quit school to pursue their dreams of business enterprise: Bill Gates of Microsoft and Steve Jobs of Apple.

My attendance of a Russ Whitney's money-making seminar in Crystal City, Virginia, however, became the last straw that broke the camel's back. Entrepreneurship and financial freedom for everyman, the core message of Russ Whitney, struck a major chord in me. His story was compelling:

"... Russ Whitney's story is proof, which includes dropping out of high school ... barely earning enough money to pay his bills while working in a slaughter house ... to becoming a millionaire in just a few short years ..."

His words were reassuring and instructive. Whether your goal is to be your own boss, become financially independent or build a nest egg so you can enjoy your retirement years, real estate investing and training can help you reach your goal — even during the worst of times and best of times life has to offer. In addition to real estate, the seminar also presented money-making ideas in sales, mortgage, and personal finance.

Although I was prospecting to begin publishing a magazine like John H. Johnson's *Ebony* and Earl Graves' *Black Enterprise*, I had not spent much time to research my idea and write a business plan. I was just excited to become known as a magazine publisher. Although I owned a personal computer, I did not have adequate knowledge of the emerging products and services of desktop publishing. Neither did I secure any paid advertisements from local black businesses. I was desperate. Nonetheless, I was able to write stories for the magazine; I was able to motivate friends, family, and acquaintances to write articles for the magazine. Nevertheless, I was clueless when it came to business management, typesetting, photography, and printing. For this reason, I was forced to learn the fundamental elements of publishing and printing as I went along.

God was always with me. Through an Indian guy called Terry and an advertisement in *The Washington Post*, I was fortunate to make the acquaintance of two white employees of McGraw-Hill, a publishing company: James Cavender and Cindy Doe. James Cavender was a graphic artist; Cindy Doe was a typesetter and page-layout artist. I was successful in selling my big dreams of magazine publishing to Terry, James, and Cindy; they bought it. James produced a very beautiful color-separated artwork of the magazine's glossy cover; Cindy used Ventura's Publisher and Aldus' PageMaker to handle the desk-top publishing of the magazine. Like a miraculous act wrought by Jesus Christ, while awaiting payment from prospective advertisers, I succeeded in convincing a white printer in Woodbridge, Virginia, to print and deliver one thousand copies of the magazine to my office in the Landmark area of Alexandria, Virginia. For weeks, I was too embarrassed to think that I could not pay him, even though he was earnest in making several collection attempts. I could not pay my office rent of five hundred dollars.

De jure, I was hemmed in the throes of the economic quagmire orchestrated by the presidency of the first George Bush—Herbert Walker. I struggled to borrow my way into prosperity and continue publishing the magazine. Black retailers were stocking copies of the magazine in their stores, and readers identified with the magazine's message of Afrocentricity, but they were not paying me timely or at all. I started using all the credit cards I had obtained in the past as a result of my mastery of information culled from Russ Whitney's books and free or inexpensive US government publications from Pueblo, Colorado.

Finally, I had no other choice than the decision and action to investigate US bankruptcy laws and file for personal bankruptcy. I was making money as an information broker, but the amount of money I was making was too minute to make any significant difference in my cash flow; it was like the act of throwing a small stone in a big blue ocean and watching the ripple effect of your action. As I started packing my belongings to move out of my office space, I observed that someone had stolen some of my business equipment from the office. As it turned out, the mystery man was Joachim Nola, someone I had met as I was developing the magazine. For the meager sum of two thousand dollars, I was forced by my insolvency to look for a business partner. Yet, in the end, I began regretting why I had listened to my business partner Joachim Nola to rent an office space for magazine publishing, a service we could have provided from home without the overheard of a commercial space.

Additionally, I regretted why I had quit my postgraduate studies to launch a magazine which failed woefully. As I slept at night, I heard some noise wheezing in my head punctuated by the following refrain: "Pride goes before a fall." My business failed not just because of the bad economy; de jure, I became a statistic of business failure because I lacked management skills. If I were a good business manager, I would have spent much time and money developing a smart business plan for my magazine business. I should have exercised a great deal of commonsense and caution in spending other people's money. Yet, I had thrown all caution to the wind, and I had to pay a dear price for it. For this reason, if I were to restart a magazine today, I would apply the art, philosophy, and science of business management. In other words, I will research the feasibility of the business idea and write a winning business plan. Additionally, I would teach myself typesetting, page layout, and printing. I have sought to follow this advice gingerly in my new publishing project: *The Miraculous Millionaire*.

Perhaps the business failure that pained me the most was my adventure in medical billing. I became a victim of the hype surrounding the electronic healthcare revolution. Without conducting any research, I convinced a few friends and acquaintances to join me in launching a healthcare software business. For months on end, I had been transfixed by television shows, breaking news, and press reports heralding the new age of electronic healthcare records; according to the mass media, overwhelmed by mountains of paperwork, healthcare providers were scrambling to automate their business operations with software and hardware. Hillary Rodham Clinton, the first lady at the time, became the poster girl of healthcare reform. I was excited about the promise of healthcare reform; I saw dollar signs everywhere. After I caught the jungle fever of healthcare reform, I became a distributor of MediSOFT software, a medical office patient accounting application produced by The Computer Place, Tucson, Arizona.

There is more to personal finance than the drudgery of debts and budgets.

I was excited when a few medical doctors and new medical billing centers sought my services. I wanted to grow my healthcare consulting business by operating my own medical claims and billing center. Unfortunately, I did not have the money to accomplish my objective. I thought that by capitalizing on the concept of OPM (other people's money), it would be easy for me to achieve my business goal, so I campaigned for business partners. Indeed, I was successful in recruiting five partners: Aloys Nanga, John Ngu, Frida Ngam, Christine Tamajong, and Joseph Tambe. Each partner invested at least the sum of one thousand dollars in the business. Since I had many computer terminals in my apartment, we used the investment money to print business cards, brochures, and letterheads. I bought a mailing list from Info USA and obtained a bulk-mail permit from the US Post Office. Despite all our efforts and money invested, the results of our marketing campaign were negative. Initially, I could not understand why doctors were not clamoring to use our medical claims and billing services. At best these doctors would buy MediSOFT from me and pay me to install the software for them.

At worst, I was too stunned to realize that these doctors were simply not interested in my services. Worst of all, I had to deal with the guilt of making my friends and acquaintances lose money in a venture I had assured them of substantial returns of money. In fact, this failure was catastrophic to me. All what I have labored for in storm and stress has aborted. Indeed, it felt like I had committed an abortion procedure. I had lost faith in myself. I had disappointed my friends. I could not sleep at night. I wished I could die. Were it not that God is against self-murder, I do not want to speculate on my fate. So help me God!

Business level 3: Credit repair, debt collections, bankruptcy, and divorce filings

After my magazine business failed, I was not ready, psychologically, to start another business. I had too many credit problems; creditors were calling me every five minutes. I did not have the financial resources to repay my huge debts. Worst of all, I had lost my security guard job.

A few days later, I also lost my position as an English teaching assistant at the University of the District of Columbia. My only employment was the tutor position I had held in the English laboratory. After I had depleted my meager savings, I started using credit cards to buy groceries and take cash advances. Since reading has always been my hobby, I spent much time after job hunting reading the local newspapers. Once upon a time, I had stumbled upon a magazine advertisement purporting to show regular folks how to make money as a paralegal without a law degree. The mail-order company was called the American Institute of Consumer Credit, Coral Gables, Florida. From the catalog of the American Institute of Consumer Credit, I ordered many "how-to" course packages with the following pompous title beginning with "HOW TO BECOME" a consumer credit repair consultant, mortgage reduction consultant, debt collections consultant, bankruptcy filing consultant, and divorce filing consultant without a lawyer, and advertising consultant. After reading all these how-to packages, I decided to supplement my para-legal knowledge with more reading materials from Nolo.com. If you look at the list of books in my library today, you will find many books published by Nolo.com on divorce filing and forms preparation, bankruptcy filing, personal credit, and business formation.

From its very inception, Nolo.com has been leading a democratic revolution to make the complex American legal system accessible to non-lawyers. Nolo.com represents legal self-determination. The do-it-yourself point of view of Nolo.com appealed to me a great deal. It gave me a sense of self-empowerment; in fact, after reading Nolo's books, I decided to file for bankruptcy pro se, that is, on my own without a lawyer to defend me in court. Nolo.com presents complex legal material in a very simple and straight forward manner for the common man. Law for the people! That is a slogan that captures the essence of the Nolo.com campaign to make the law accessible to the average US taxpayer or citizen. In order to strengthen my paralegal knowledge, I proceeded to the Howard University law library to ascertain journal articles on the review of current bankruptcy filing software. An expert researcher, I found some good articles on the best bankruptcy software in less than thirty minutes. I settled for the best two applications: Mathew Bender Collier Top Form Bankruptcy Software and Best Case Bankruptcy form.

After mastering these applications, I was confident to attempt to file my own bankruptcy petition pro se, that is, without a lawyer and exorbitant fees. Indeed, after I visited the courthouse of Alexandria, Virginia, to collect information on local rules germane to bankruptcy filing, I returned to my apartment to review my paperwork. I heaved a sigh of relief when the bankruptcy court clerk checked my forms and approved them for filing without any complaints. Although my instructional materials had forewarned me accordingly, I awaited the meeting of creditors with great trepidation. I was ecstatic and relieved when the bankruptcy trustee examined my paperwork and praised me effusively for the immaculate forms; From that day on, I started providing services to my friends and acquaintances as a non-legal bankruptcy forms preparer. My worry was the fear of being accused of unauthorized practice of the law without a license (UPL).

Hence, to all my customers, I emphasized the need to buy Nolo.com's bankruptcy textbooks. Before I exhausted the list of my friends and acquaintances as prospective clients, I started running classified advertisements in *The Washington Post*. For a short a while, everything was fine. Not much later, lawyers began responding to my advertisements. When most of them frowned upon my business and trustees started complaining about my business, I decided to refer my clients to local lawyers who were my friends.

Credit repair, debt collections, and divorce filings replaced bankruptcy filing on my business menu Because most of my bankruptcy clients wanted to reestablish their consumer credit, I started beating the credit doctor in my local market. I decided to specialize on only LEGAL credit repair. Any customer who wanted my assistance had to accept to do the right thing: work with creditors directly to eliminate debt. At the same time, I was happy to assist clients who were undergoing the process of uncontested divorce with no assets. Whenever I had time to spare, I indulged in my passion: debt collections. I was passionate about debt collections to the extent that I was using Microsoft 's Visual Basic and Access to write a software application on it. As much as I was learning, I did not feel I was making enough money. Besides, I was looking for a more stable business. It dawned upon me that I needed to research better business opportunities. My investigations took me the realm of *Entrepreneur* magazine. I read the magazine from cover to cover and ordered some of the manuals that which were advertised in it.

There is more to personal finance than the drudgery of debts and budgets.

Best of all, I became convinced that there was a better way to start and run a business: ASP—art, science, and philosophy. To every business, there is an art; to every business there is a science; to every business, there is a philosophy. Since I did not have much money, I decided to exploit the facilities of the free public library near my apartment building. I made it a habit to spend much time every week in the public library reading my favorite finance magazines and newspapers: *Entrepreneur*, *Money*, *Black Enterprise*, *Ebony*, *Essence*, *Fortune*, *Forbes*, *The Wall Street Journal*, *USA Today*, *The Washington Post*, *New York Times*, and *The Alexandria Gazette*. I reinforced the reading of magazines with books. If the library did not carry a book, I was forced to buy it in a book store or order it by mail order. In fact, the list of books I have recommended for further study in Millionaire iUniversity should impress on you my efforts to tap into the eternal spring of book knowledge. For your information, all the money-making secrets in this world are hidden in books and magazines, so make it a habit to read books and magazines. Where else can an ordinary poor person discover the occult secrets to financial riches in America? Where? In fact, success comes to those who wait and master the art, science, and philosophy of entrepreneurship. I was hell bent to apply these new insights in my prospective businesses. When I look back now, I think I was actually ready.

BUSINESS LEVEL 4: INCOME TAX PREPARATION AND CHECK CASHING

All the businesses that I founded after step 3 have been successful. Why? The reason is obvious; it is no magic. I think I have been fastidious in doing my homework before launching a business. For instance, the launch of my income tax preparation business is a textbook example of how to start a successful business in America. In fact, every year since 1986, as a result of writing a winning business plan and executing the plan flawlessly, I have been humbled to gross over a six figure income in income tax preparation. Although I was alarmed by the attention the mass media paid to income taxes when I came to America in 1983, it never occurred to me at that time that I would become an official player in the USA's income tax industry. As such, some people might argue that I got into the industry by chance; others might argue that I had planned to enter the industry at the most opportune time.

When I was working at the English laboratory at the University of the District of Columbia, I had struck up a friendship with JF, a young Cameroonian student affectionately known as "Petit Petit." In the course of assisting him with his writing assignments, he suggested to me the idea of leveraging my home computer as an income tax preparation machine. At the time, I did not know how to prepare income taxes; indeed, I was using an African-American PhD student as my favorite income tax preparer. JF and I agreed on the need for us to build a team for a new income tax preparation business; two of us would handle marketing and sales while JJ would be responsible for the actual income tax preparation; JJ was an accounting major at the University of the District of Columbia. I ordered *Taxcut*, an income tax preparation software, from MECA, a company run by personal finance guru Andrew Tobias; Dan Caine, a Boston tax lawyer, actually had written the built-in expert module of the application. I also ordered an income tax preparation manual from Federated Tax Company, a correspondence course outfit located in Chicago, Illinois.

When I realized that the business could not be started because of inflexibility in JJ's schedule, I decided to establish alternative plans for myself. First, I decided to ascertain whether there was a market for a new home-based income tax service. As I had learned the hard way, the purpose of any business is to satisfy a human need or want. If H & R Block and Jackson Hewitt Tax Service exist, is there a need for a third tax service? To answer this question, I studied and researched the US market for income tax preparation. I taught myself income tax preparation by reading IRS publications and studying the course manual I had ordered from Federated Tax of Chicago. I developed a one-page questionnaire, which I distributed to my friends and acquaintances. I evaluated the competition and developed my business Idea by taking income tax preparation classes from H & R Block and Jackson Hewitt Tax Service. Additionally, I ordered franchise documents from the competition. What I found most helpful, especially when writing my business plan, was the document called "UFOC," uniform franchise offering circular.

What is a Uniform Franchise Offering Circular (UFOC)? This is a document that must be provided by the franchisor to the prospective franchisee at least ten business days before any agreement of sale is signed and finalized. What is the importance of this document? Well, it is considered a disclosure statement that covers such items as the franchisor's obligations, the franchisee's obligations, territory boundaries, and initial and ongoing fees to be paid. All in all, twenty three important subsets of information are included in this comprehensive disclosure statement about the franchise that the franchisee is about to invest in. Furthermore, since prospective franchisees need to have enough information to be able to compile a business plan for financing purposes, the franchisor must offer sufficient documentation for franchisees to forecast future expenses for the business.

The UFOC is non-negotiable, and it is written within a consistent or uniform set of criteria. Individual states are not afforded the opportunity to change the terms and conditions of a franchise agreement. The only items that have any flexibility are territory location and possibly extreme demographic disadvantages. Since 1995, the Federal Trade Commission (FTC) has required that this document be written in plain English rather than be full of legal terms that the layman cannot understand. The North American Securities Administrators Associations (NASAA) administers and monitors the UFOC.

Below is a full listing of the information that makes up the document called "UFOC," uniform franchise offering circular. Following is a list of the 23 categories included in the UFOC:

The Franchisor and Any Predecessors
Identity and Business Experience of Persons Associated with Franchisor
Litigation History
Bankruptcy (any franchisees who may have filed)
Listing of the Initial Franchise Fee and Other Initial Payments
Other Fees and Expenses
Statement of Franchisee's Initial Investment
Obligations of Franchisee to Purchase or Lease from Designated Sources
Obligations of Franchisee to Purchase or Lease in Accordance with Specifications or from Authorized Suppliers

There is more to personal finance than the drudgery of debts and budgets.

Financing Arrangements
Obligations of the Franchisor; Other Supervision, Assistance or Services
Exclusive/Designated Area of Territory
Trademarks, Service Marks, Trade Names, Logo types and Commercial Symbols,
Patents and Copyrights
Obligations of the Franchisee to Participate in the Actual Operation of the Franchise Business
Restrictions on Goods and Services Offered by Franchisee
Renewal, Termination, Repurchase, Modification and Assignment of the Franchise Agreement
and Related Information
Arrangements with Public Figures
Actual, Average, Projected or Forecasted Franchise Sales, Profits or Earnings
Information Regarding Franchises of the Franchisor
Financial Statements
Contracts
Acknowledgement of Receipt by Respective Franchises

Upon receipt of the UFOC, it is essential that the franchisee evaluate the entire document before
getting into the signing of an agreement. Also, it is important for you to note that although
the document is required by law, it has not necessarily been reviewed for accuracy by a legal
body. Therefore, it is highly recommended that a franchise attorney assess the document for
accuracy. If there is any hesitation on the part of the franchisor to provide you with the UFOC,
you may wish to consider a different opportunity.

Next was the need for me to address the issue of business suitability. I had to determine if the
type of income tax business suits me. I did not have money to rent a commercial location, so I
was happy with a home-based operation. Since I already had my computers, the new business
was right for me because I needed only to purchase software to get started on a low budget. The
plan was to invest in software application that was more robust than either Taxcut or Turbo
Tax software. When I was using Taxcut, I stumbled upon a great tax software from Universal Ta
Systems, Inc. called Taxwise. In fact, research and review of all tax software applications in the
USA led me to Taxwise. The problem, however, was the financing; I could not afford to buy the
software alone, so I asked my friend GA to get into the business with me. The plan was for each
of us to contribute $3,000 toward the purchase of the tax preparation application; I would give
GA cash of $3,000, and he would use his American Express card to charge the purchase.

When GA refused to proceed with the deal, I was forced to strike a deal with the Taxwise
company and buy the software at a discount. Universal Tax Systems, Inc. agreed to sell the
$6,000 application to me for $4,000 under the following conditions: I would send them the
$3,000 immediately; I would pay the balance of $1,000 within the next 30 calendar days. For a
cash-strapped new entrepreneur, it was a good deal; I agreed to make the deal right away.
In fact, I had to withdraw much of the meager savings I had in Lloyd's Bank of London to settle
Universal Tax Systems, Inc. So now I was guaranteed to start the business during the January
1987 tax season.

The IRS was launching the new program of electronic tax filing; I was too proud to be a pioneer electronic tax filer. Would the income tax preparation business make money for me? The goal of business is to use the factors of production to provide a service or product with the goal to make an unlimited amount of profit. In fact, I had spent much time struggling to quantify the answer to that question. At the time I had just learned much about the theory and practice of writing winning business plans, so I was aware of the concept of "break-even analysis." I decided to use a break-even analysis to determine if my idea of an income tax service can make money. In economics and business, specifically cost accounting, the break-even point is the spot at which cost or expenses and revenue are equal; ceteris paribus, there is no net loss or gain, and I have "broken even" in my business. A profit or a loss has not been made, although opportunity costs have been "paid," and capital has received the risk-adjusted, expected return.

The following is an interesting example of the working of break-even analysis in this regard. Time is of the essence during the income tax season, which runs each year normally from January 15 to April 15. If my tax business prepares fewer than 200 income tax returns each month, it will make a loss, if it prepares more income tax returns, it will make a profit. Armed with this information, I, as the business manager of the income tax service, will then need to see if I expect to be able to prepare only two hundred tax returns per month.

If I think I cannot prepare more than 200 tax returns per month, to ensure the viability of my new tax business, I could do the following: try to reduce the fixed costs (by renegotiating rent for example, or keeping better control of telephone bills or other costs); try to reduce variable costs (the price it pays for the software by finding a new supplier); increase the price of my tax preparation services. Any of the actions specified above would reduce the break-even point of my tax business. In other words, the business would not need to prepare so many tax returns to make money if it could pay its fixed costs. Therefore, the break-even analysis answers the following question: Will your new business make money any time soon? To answer this question, I decided to write a business plan, including texts and statistical charts showing a profit and loss forecast and a cash flow analysis. I cannot overemphasize the importance of writing an effective business plan. Business plan software makes the task of writing a plan very easy.

Although I have worked with many computer applications, my personal favorite is Business Plan Pro. Created by Palo Alto Software, Business Plan Pro has everything the beginner or entrepreneur needs to develop a professional business plan. Even more advanced users will find the added financial resources useful in developing business plans for a variety of business concepts. Business Plan Pro offers more than just the ability to print and publish professional-looking charts, graphs, and reports. The major weakness of the planning solution is that Business Plan Pro offers no option to import from Microsoft Excel, a major spreadsheet application. Business Plan Pro, however, is ideal for beginners who are not looking for advanced features. Generally, software use is personal. I might like an application, but you might not like it. Hence, below is a list of other business plan software for you to review: BizPlan Builder, Ultimate Business Planner, Business Plan Maker, Professional Deluxe, Plan Write for Business, Plan Magic Business, BizPlan|DB, and Venture Planning System Pro.

There is more to personal finance than the drudgery of debts and budgets.

START-UP FINANCING

Have you found sources of start-up financing? When I was thinking about establishing a professional income tax preparation service, the first hurdle I had to deal with was the issue of start-up financing. In addition to buying the software, I needed money for day-to-day operations. Where would the money come from? In my case, I was fortunate to raise start-up capital. After I had paid Universal Tax Systems, Inc. $4,000, the company shipped the 1986 version of their software to me. Before the end of October 1986, I began learning the application in the comfort of my dingy apartment in Alexandria, Virginia. I printed business cards, and I started looking for customers, and income tax preparation business prospects. From four of these prospects, I raised the sum of $4,000, the money I had already invested in the purchase of the Taxwise software. If you have not resolved the issues pertaining to business financing, loans, and capital, then, you are not ready for business.

My next business planning task was to set up a basic marketing plan. How would I market my services to potential customers? First, I created a contact list of all my family members, friends, and acquaintances in the USA. I called every individual on my contact list twice a month until the beginning of the 1987 income tax season. I presented myself as the good old medical doctor of income tax preparation. I sold them on the novelty and benefits of establishing a home-based professional income tax service that was better than either H&R Block or Jackson Hewitt: 24/7 hours of operation, express service, convenience, experienced staff, and individualized tax preparation, 24-hour quick turnaround for rapid tax refund checks, $20 referral fee, and free electronic filing.

Little did I know that I was a David building an army to take on the Goliath or national behemoth of US income tax preparation. My contacts took my message to their family members, friends, acquaintances, and community organizations. African cab drivers were not left behind. In fact, they facilitated the movement of documents from taxpayers to tax preparers and from tax preparers to taxpayers. Because I had limited financial resources, I had focused the advertising of my income tax business to local, college, and African community newspapers. I remembered the lessons my high-school economics teacher had taught me: economics is a study of limited resources; because our needs and wants are infinite and resources are limited, we have to contend with the issues of scarcity and choice. In short, that was how I had developed a winning marketing and advertising plan for my income tax business.

In developing a business plan for my income tax venture, I had to decide on a legal structure. What would be the best form of organization for the business? One-man business or sole-proprietorship? Partnership? Corporation? Limited liability company? A guiding principle of choosing a business form of organization is the composition of business ownership. Although I loved the idea of starting the business alone, the recognition of my weaknesses and limitations nudged me away from a sole-proprietorship. Yet, it was difficult for me to identify the number of owners of my tax business. From my study of economics, I disliked the partnership type of organization. When I considered the hazards and perils of operating a business in a litigious environment like America, I decided to calculate how much protection from personal liability I would need.

In other words, I had known that liabilities depended on my business's risks, so what were the risks of starting my own income tax business? To tell you the truth, the risks were many, and I sought ways to deal with them through insurance protections. I also had to decide how I would like the business to be taxed. As an income tax preparation firm, I should have known that the tax liability of a business entity is a function of its classification by the US' Department of the Treasury (Internal Revenue Service). In this regard, the government has established discrete categories for each business form of organization: 1040 Schedule C for sole-proprietorships; 1120 for C corporations; 1120S for sub chapter S Corporations; 1065 for partnerships; and 1041 for estates and fiduciaries. In step 8 of the book titled decode the IRS tax codes, I am going to present insights that will assist you in laying threadbare the labyrinth of the US tax codes.

In addition to the importance of tax information, you must consider whether your business would benefit from being able to sell stock. I will enthrall you with my discussion of US capital markets in step 9. For now, however, it suffices for you to understand the importance of incorporation. To incorporate a business means you want to create an artificial business entity that is mutually exclusive from you as a person. Since I decided to incorporate my tax business on my own, I spent much time researching the legal process of incorporating a business in the Commonwealth of Virginia. Here also, I sought the assistance of many professional sources listed in the Millionaire iUniversity reading list for further study. I was happy to research the various types of ownership structures: sole proprietorship, partnership, limited liability company, C Corporation, and S Corporation.

In addition to the use of *The Miraculous Millionaire*, you can also get more in-depth information from many self-help resources before you settle on a structure. If you are unsure about choosing a business form, please, talk to a lawyer. Nolo Store can also assist you in talking to a lawyer. There are many online business registration facilities. If you are looking to create an LLC or corporation, Nolo has great online applications that can make it easy. Check them out. Finally, do not ignore the resources of Millionaire iUniversity; we have many Online LLC and Online Corporation applications, as well as a suite of books on the subject. If you need consulting assistance, please, call me.

CHOOSE A NAME FOR YOUR BUSINESS

Now that I have impressed upon you the importance business planning, I would like to underscore the need to choose a good name for your business. Every time I have started a new business, I have spent much time on selecting a name that would be appropriate to the business. For instance, look at some examples of my businesses: American Computer Data Tracking, Computer Publishing Network, TLC Tax Express, PMCI Medical Claims, Prince Ojong Tax Service, BMI Tax Clinic of America, OverReacher Empire Corporation, and 24/7 Services. As you can see, I choose business names that might suit my company and its products or services. The name should communicate the products or services you are offering to the public. Since my businesses are always computer-based and I know I will do business online, I always check if my proposed business names are available as domain names. I go to search engines like Google and Yahoo or domain-name registrars (networksolutions.com, godaddy.com, and prehosting.com) to check for the availability of the business names.

There is more to personal finance than the drudgery of debts and budgets.

Next, I check with my local county clerk's office to see whether my proposed names are on the list of fictitious or assumed business names in my county. As for corporations and LLCs, I check the availability of my proposed names with the Secretary of State or other corporate filing office. Additionally, I proceed to government web sites to do a federal or state trademark search of the proposed names still on my list. If a proposed name is being used as a trademark, I eliminate it immediately; if my use of the name would confuse customers or if the name is already famous, I look for a better alternative. In fact, I always choose among the proposed names that are still on my list. The next step after choosing a name is to register it officially with a government entity.

Legally, by registering my business name, I get the peace of mind of knowing that I am the one entitled to use it. I advise you to register your business name with your county clerk as a fictitious or assumed business name, if necessary. Besides, register your business name as a federal or state trademark if you will do business regionally or nationally and will use your business name to identify a product or service. Last but not least, register your business name as a domain name if you will use the name as a Web address too. In today's business world, a web site is a *sine qua non* of existence and survival.

In regard to preparing your organizational paperwork, I cannot underscore the fact that meticulous attention should be paid to the writing of the following documents: Partnership Agreement, LLC Articles of Organization, Operating Agreement, C Corporation Pre-Incorporation Agreement, Articles of Incorporation, Corporate Bylaws, Buyout Agreement (also known as a buy-sell agreement or stock agreement), S Corporation Articles of Incorporation, Corporate Bylaws, Buyout Agreement (also known as a buy-sell agreement or stock agreement), IRS Form 2553, Election by a Small Business Corporation. If you have the money, you can hire a lawyer to assist you in preparing these documents; otherwise, you can avail yourself of the services of Millionaire iUniversity. We can help you in any state of the union. Please, call my office: (301) 593-4897.

FIND A BUSINESS LOCATION

A business location may be a zoned commercial space or your home. Depending on your choice, you need to identify the features and fixtures your business will need. You need to determine how much rent you can afford. You need to decide what neighborhood would be best for your business and find out what the average rents are in those neighborhoods. Please, make sure any space you are considering is or can be properly zoned for your business. Before signing a commercial lease, please, examine it carefully and negotiate the best deal. If working from home, my personal preference for a low start-up, make sure your business activities will not violate any zoning restrictions on home offices. I learned the hard way during my business career. I had started my business in my dingy apartment in Alexandria, Virginia. In addition to dealing with the county that required a permit for home business operation, I had to contend with a hostile landlord who forbade the practice of customers streaming into my apartment for business.

I had thought I had found a solution to my need of office space when I bought a single-family home and decided to use the whole basement as my office; I created a stone and brick pathway from the garage that led to the back door of my walk-out basement.

From 1997, as time wore on, I spent much money on grass-roots marketing, business networking, and advertising. By the end of April 2003, the number of my customers grew by leaps and bounds. My neighbors took a dim look at my home-business operation; they reported me to the homeowners' association. Indeed, matters came to a head when an official from the homeowners' association decided to investigate my neighbors' complaints. As the official was parking his car in front of my home, he noticed that two cars were driving off from my driveway. After he got out of his car, he observed that three cars were parking in front of my home. In the course of a fifteen-minute observation, the homeowners' association official calculated that fifteen cars had parked in front of my house.

In the end, I decided not to fight the homeowners' association; I wrote a letter of apology, and I promised to correct the problem by renting office space in a commercial center. As God would have it, I found a commercial space opposite the White Oak Shopping Center in October 2003. My customers have adequate parking night and day. I do not have to worry about breaking the rules and regulations of homeowners' associations. A favorite topic of discussion in my high-school economics class was the finding of a location suitable for a business. The factors that affect the location of a business include: availability of amenities, cheap land, labor, infrastructure, level of competition from similar vendors/businesses, availability or accessibility to customers, accessibility to raw materials and suppliers, customers or consumers demand of such a business in a certain locality, that is, if your business is the only coffee shop in town, you will get many customers. If your business is one of many coffee shops in a town or city, you will not get as many customers. The ability to expand the business might also affect the location of a business.

FILE FOR LICENSE AND PERMITS

After you have addressed the issues pertaining to business location, you are ready to obtain licenses and permits for your business. Most localities in the USA provide new entrepreneurs with a publication titled "a guide to doing business in ...." If this publication does not exist in your locality, please, contact us. We can assist you in complying with all local, state, and federal regulations, including obtaining a federal employment identification number by filing IRS Form SS-4 and completing state and local forms. We can help you obtain a seller's permit from your state if you will sell retail goods. We can help you obtain state licenses, such as specialized vocation-related licenses or environmental permits, if necessary. We can assist you in obtaining a local tax registration certificate, a.k.a. business license. We can help you obtain local permits, if required, such as a conditional use permit or zoning variance.

OBTAIN INSURANCE

Perhaps, insurance is where we are qualified to help you the most. As an insurance agent, I recognize the importance and complexity of risks, perils, hazards, security, and protection.

There is more to personal finance than the drudgery of debts and budgets.

By employing my insurance services, I would use a needs-assessment tool to establish a determination of the type of personal and business coverage you require. Hence, you do not have to contact another insurance agent or broker to answer any questions. In addition to giving you policy quotes, I would spend much time to educate you on the insurance secrets of rich business men and women. I will show you how to obtain liability insurance on vehicles used in your business, including personal cars of employees used for business; I will show you how to obtain liability insurance for your premises if customers or clients will be visiting; I will show you how to obtain product liability insurance if you will manufacture hazardous products. If you will be working from your home, I will advise you to make sure your homeowner's insurance covers damage to or theft of your business assets as well as liability for business-related injuries. I will advise you to consider health & disability insurance for yourself and your employees.

SET UP YOUR BOOKS

I am not an accountant by training, but I have spent much time educating myself on accounting systems for small business. The success of my business ventures is a testament to my mastery of small business accounting. Indeed, I am proud to say that I have more experience than the average accountant, including those who pride themselves to be CPAs. I have served more clients successfully, but I have not felt the need to allocate time from my busy schedule to prepare for the CPA exam. I promise to assist you in setting up your books. I will send you to our Millionaire iUniversity to learn Accounting 101. I will convince you to learn whether to use the cash or accrual system of accounting for recordkeeping. If your business qualifies, I will show you how to choose a fiscal year if your natural business cycle does not follow the normal calendar year. By using QuickBooks software from Intuit, I will show you how to create the chart of accounts of a new company record and set up an electronic recordkeeping system for all payments to and from your business. I will educate you on when to consider hiring a bookkeeper or accountant to help you get set up your books. I can help you select and purchase small business accounting software.

SET UP TAX REPORTING

Samuel T. Coleridge's *Rime of an Ancient Mariner* reminds me of the alliteration in taxes, taxes everywhere! Closely related to the task of setting up your books is the function of tax reporting. When I established my income tax preparation business, it occurred to me that I, like other small business folks, needed to familiarize myself with the general tax scheme for my business structure. Interestingly, the Internal Revenue Service has done a great job of standardizing the income tax code. It suffices for you to learn to identify where you belong in the tax superstructure; the Internal Revenue Service makes most of these forms, booklets, and books available to taxpayers free of charge. Would you like to familiarize yourself with the common business deductions and depreciation pertaining to your area of business operation? Then, stop at any IRS office in your area. As for the famous Blue Book, *Publication 17, Your Federal Income Tax Guide for Individuals*; obtain IRS Publications 334, Tax Guide for Small Business, and get a copy of *Publication 583, Taxpayers Starting a Business*; obtain the IRS' Tax Calendar for Small Businesses; this calendar will assist you in planning for different tax events.

CHECK-CASHING BUSINESS

As you can see from the foregoing discussion, starting a business involves making quite a few initial decisions and getting policies and paperwork in place. For more information about professional help in starting a business the right way, I urge you to learn from my mistakes and experience by adhering to the aforementioned steps. Similarly, my check-cashing business is a textbook example of how to start a successful business in America. Like my income tax business, my check-cashing business was built on the accumulation of my business experience. In the course of marketing my income tax preparation services, without any formal investigation or research, I stumbled upon the economic viability of check-cashing services. For example, an Indian check-cashing service that, like my tax service, was subleasing space from a GC Murphy store located around King Street, Alexandria, Virginia, drew my attention to the benefits of providing check-cashing services to my tax clients.

A cursory observation of the low-income population of taxpayers using my tax preparation services revealed that more than 80% of these folks wanted to cash their tax refund checks immediately. Rapid Refund, a 48-hour quick tax loan product pioneered by H&R Block, was not serving the needs of these taxpayers for immediate cash. The liquidity preference of these taxpayers was to be able to cash their tax refund loans as soon as they obtain the cashier checks from their tax preparer; even in cases where these taxpayers owned bank accounts, they preferred to cash their checks right away; that is why the services of a check-casher were sorely needed.

Larry Kalathia, a gentleman and an Indian check-casher, had struck a friendship with me because he wanted me to collaborate with him to cash the tax checks of my clients. When he became satisfied with our business relationship, Larry Kalathia introduced me to Vipul Kalathia, his son who was running another check-cashing store located in Manassas Park, Virginia. After I succeeded in driving hundreds of income tax clients to Vipul's store, some bad blood ruptured our relationship. For one, Vipul did not appreciate most of the changes I sought for him to implement in his store; I had made a few friends who were working at ACE Check-Cashing Company, and I had tried to encourage Vipul to model his store after ACE. I suggested the use of a computer database like Dbase III+ to resolve the problems of cashing bad checks. Vipul was an illiterate teenager from an Indian village; he was peculiar to me in the sense that most of the Indians I have met in the USA are college educated and smart. What made matters worse was the fact that Vipul's father never tried to conceal his admiration for me. As much as I got along great with Larry Kalathia, my relationship with Vipul deteriorated to the abyss of scorn and dejection. Hence, I begged Larry Kalathia for us to part ways amicably, but not without making a singular promise to myself before God and man: I plan to use the fruits of my research of the check-cashing business to open my own store. As I drove away on Centreville Road, I could hear the whole universe shaking and my mouth saying "technology, technology, technology, location, location, location."

In less than three months, I met David Solomon , a Jewish guy who agreed to lease to me the premises of an old check-cashing store located at 9th and N Street NW, Washington, DC, very close to the former Washington Convention Center.

There is more to personal finance than the drudgery of debts and budgets.

The store, which was dilapidated, was in a crime-infested area of Washington, DC. It was a moment of decision; I swallowed hard and went for the deal. The words an entrepreneur must bear risks were ringing a loud bell in the consciousness of my mind. Since I had spent many months, over a year, researching the check-cashing business and writing my business plan, it did not take me a month to build the new check-cashing store completely. I knew precisely what to do and where to get what I wanted; I had the money to implement my plan of action. Indeed, I had secured over the sum of $100,000 from my tax preparation service and personal savings to use for check-cashing purpose. I had already known the importance of creating many profit centers for my business. It did not take long for Western Union to approve me as a retail agent; this acceptance was soon followed by Verizon's installation of three phone bill payment terminals in my store.

Third was the arrival of food stamp vouchers from the government of the District of Columbia. I was happy to be full swing in business. Because Western Union, the DC Government, and Verizon were referring many clients to me, I did not feel like wasting my money on advertising. Because of my good location, I was also getting too many walk-in customers. The location was personally risky for me; I was worried about my safety. Yet, I decided to stay in the check-cashing business for at least two years.

On April 15, 1997, I bought a single-family home in Silver Spring, Maryland. The house purchase made me an overnight sensation among African immigrants from Cameroon; like my mother and sisters, they were too stunned to think how a common and laboring guy like Prince Ojong could buy a brand new house with a $125,000 down payment. For one, they knew I did not have a professional office job. My sister Patricia could not believe that an erstwhile school dropout has bought a house in America before a pharmacist. Initially, I had wanted my sister to purchase the house with me as a co-signer, but the loan officer told me that want was not necessary in light of my strong financials and substantial down payment. I felt like everybody was talking about me, Prince Ojong. I began receiving more positive overtures from the young ladies. Interestingly, most of these ladies had been ignoring me. Almost overnight I became their match. In their eyes, the purchase of a red brick front single family home was a feat that qualified a guy as husband material. I became a little bit paranoid. It seemed like somebody was always watching me. How did I become hot and attractive suddenly? My attractiveness was the new home purchase.

How did I do it? How did I pull this deal off? Those were the questions in every body's mouth. Instead of keeping up with the Jones, I had been saving my hard-earned money for an appreciably long time. In the beginning, I was saving a dollar per day; as I started making more money, I started saving more; I was moving my savings into DRIPS (dividend reinvestment plans), mutual funds, and stocks with the mechanical regularity of a robot. I was starving myself; I was living an austere life like a monk or an Oxford cleric. Although the furniture in my apartment was old and broken, I was not in a financial position to buy new ones. Rather, I was salivating and investing my money like Silas Marner in George Eliot's novel. After I sold my check-cashing business, I was ready to begin a new business chapter incorporating daily trading of Internet stocks and stock investing, real estate sales, mortgage loan origination brokerage, and title settlements.

BUSINESS LEVEL 5: STOCK TRADING AND INVESTING, REAL ESTATE SALES, MORTGAGE ORIGINATION BROKERAGE AND TITLE SETTLEMENTS

Because the chapter of the book titled Step 9 explores my entrepreneurial activities in the stock market in detail, I do not want to discuss these activities here. It suffices to note that my success in the US capital markets was the result of using a trial-and-error method to build a plan based on the quest for creating my own approach to Wall Street: statistically rational analysis. In addition to stock trading and investing, I was implementing a plan I had developed to get rich in real estate; you can peak into this plan by referring to step 10, the tenth chapter of the book describing my plan of investing in real estate; since my days of working as a security guard, I have been watching late-night infomercials claiming to show the average Joe Six pack how to make big money overnight in real estate; now I will show you the fiction and fact of real estate investing, in addition to how I researched and implemented a successful plan for myself and you. I will also teach you the secrets of finance and title insurance I had learned from some Jewish guys at a local country club.

I must point out that I remain proud of the business plans I wrote to justify my approach to these businesses. As for real estate, what appealed to me the most was the Long and Foster business model, a process business with profit centers at every phase; the company makes money in brokerage sales; the company makes me in mortgage financing; the company makes money in title insurance and settlement services.

BUSINESS LEVEL 6: LIFE AND HEALTH INSURANCE SALES

Insurance is the business I am operating now and preparing for my retirement. In step three of the book, I discussed insurance as the foundation of wealth. I have spent much time in that chapter showing how an average person can make a plan to use life insurance as a golden ticket to a life of financial security and riches. If you have missed this information, please, return to step 3.Before I became an insurance agent, I had spent much money buying books on the quintessence of insurance as a product and service. Indeed, I had used these books in my research efforts and business planning. I was happy to write insurance policies with premiums of over $500,000 in 2012; God rewarded me with my own insurance brokerage firm: Overreacher Empire Corporation.

BUSINESS LEVEL 7. BOOK PUBLISHING AND VIDEO EDITING/AUTHORING

As I prepare for retirement, I have been asking myself how I can stay active and busy. What happens if I live for too long and exhaust all my financial resources? What would I do then? The answer to this question led me to turn my hobbies (software, reading, writing, music, dance, and video) into a viable business. I have made elaborate plans to publish a good book, a bestseller, every two years. I intend to publish my first book, *The Miraculous Millionaire*, this year, 2012; I plan to spend 2013 marketing and selling my book. In 2014, I have already planned to publish an anthology of my poems titled *Valleys of My Mind*, a poetic evocation of my songs, art, ideas, convictions, beliefs, fears, dreams, hopes, and yearnings.

There is more to personal finance than the drudgery of debts and budgets.

As a poet, I express what I perceive to be my responses to different phenomena. Sometimes in my soul it is stormy; in the valleys of my mind, writing becomes a soothing balm. Paradoxically, if my poetic expression is sometimes unintelligible and profound, my interesting memoir, *Dreams of America*, due out in 2016, will be the key to decode my melancholic mystery. De jure, you cannot get rich without taming your demons; you cannot get rich without making peace with God. By researching the publishing business and choosing the option of independent publishing to the completion of this book successfully, I guess, I have succeeded. I am ready to assist you if you harbor any ambitions of writing a book.

MILLIONAIRE ENTREPRENEUR'S ACTION PLAN

I have spent much time introducing you to the basis of a business and the quintessence of a business plan. A business is established to fulfill a need, not just a want, in the marketplace. I provided many reasons why I have a preferment for information-based businesses. Besides, I stressed the value of writing a business plan. I can never start a new business again without preparing a strategic business plan. Book publishing is a new business for me. I can assure you, nonetheless, that as I am writing the book you are reading, I have already spent much time laying threadbare the building blocks of my marketing and business plan. My infrastructure of book promotion is an integrated and turn-key system consisting of online and offline strategies. My new marketing suite is a powerful, next-generation marketing experience that delivers leads, sales and new customers by integrating social media, Internet search, bulk or mass email, and publicity into one smart suite. The marketing system cost me over $10,000. It includes five primary components: a mass media contacts database, news monitoring and management, social media monitoring and management, reporting and analysis, and press release or pitch distribution.

Besides, I have spent over a year researching book publishing and printing; I have spent over five hundred dollars buying books on marketing and advertising for authors; I have spent thousands of dollars for my publishing infrastructure. That is why, at this juncture, I know to my fingertips how I intend to make my target audience aware of the existence of *The Miraculous Millionaire*; like the US Army preparing for the epic struggle of a battle, I have already mapped out my war plans. I am busy polishing the book's contents, and I am also playing many marketing war games. As soon as I release the electronic files of the book to the printer, I will commence pre-publication promotion in earnest. When *The Miraculous Millionaire* becomes a bestseller, my detractors may argue that I am fortunate. The truth of the matter is that I am the architect of my own success. I lighted the wildfire on the woods that set the whole publishing world ablaze.

For this reason, I am asking you to follow my example; duplicate the millionaire entrepreneur's action plan:

#1 SOLID BUSINESS PLAN

Are you ready to become a new entrepreneur? Do you have a big idea for a new business? Write a solid business plan. A business plan is how you will make your entrepreneurial dreams come true, that is, from the moment of inspiration to the reality of minting your very first one million dollars. Think about what I am telling you. How will you handle the hurdles that come your way in the business world? You have to design many successful outcomes, effective winning strategies; after crafting your strategies, you have to put them in place on a map.

Entrepreneurial business is a like a game or a voyage of discovery; you need a road map to resolve the puzzle; even my daughter Lucielle know this fact. When she was eight years old, I used to enjoy watching her get excited over Dora the explorer and the use of maps. Dora Marquez, the main character, is an eight-year-old girl who embarks on a trip in every episode to find something or help somebody. She asks the viewers at home to help her find new ways to reach places with the help of a map. She also teaches viewers Spanish, introducing them to short words and phrases. So how do you intend to leave from point A to point B? Like Dora Marquez, you need a map, that is, a roadmap of success: a business plan. You should plan well for business success. People do not plan to fail; rather, they fail to plan.

#2 PROVISION OF A PRODUCT OR SERVICE

The solid foundation of any business is the provision of a product or service that is sorely in great demand, so offer a product or service that can be used on a regular basis by your consumers. Please, ensure that you will have repeat business. The goal is to create a long-term consumer base so that you will have a mountain of residual and passive income. I started the tax business because in this America the only things that are certain are taxes and death. I focused on a tangible business service, not on a fad. After twenty-six years (from 1986 to 2012), I am still going on strong in the tax business. The tax industry has changed very much, but I have survived and prospered because I have grown more business roots in the local pipelines of need in Washington, DC, by diversifying my services.

#3 FIND A BUSINESS COACH

Behind every successful individual is a coach. Michael Jordan, the greatest basketball player, had a coach. Mike Tyson, the great heavyweight boxer, also had a coach. In fact, his career and life begam to spiral downward after the death of his coach, Cus d'Amato. Similarly, I had many coaches in the course of my career, so find a coach or mentor who will inspire and support you. Your coach or mentor should already be at the level that you are striving for. He or she will help you gain access to the blueprint of success in your particular industry. You will avoid time-wasting and money-wasting mistakes by having a good mentor. We would be glad to be your millionaire coach; welcome to Millionaire iUniversity! We do not want you to buy the book and go to sleep. We want to mentor you; we want you to succeed. Yes, you can! Dial the magic number: (301) 593-4897.

4 ESTABLISH YOUR BUSINESS SUCCESS NETWORK

Business is not a lonely sport. You have to build a winning team, a dream team of success-oriented folks. Collaborate with a good team of individuals with the same goals as you. This is especially important in your first few months to the first year in your learning phase. Having a support group will encourage you, and you will also be learning from others who are in the same situation you are in.

#5 MARKETING TOOLS

Use effective marketing tools. You will also need to implement online marketing systems that can work for you 24 hours a day and 7 days a week. One such tool is a web site or Google's Adwords.

#6 WAR ROOM

Select an area of your home in which to set up your home office, which will be the nerve center of your new business. You can convert a spare bedroom, shed or garage if need be. Plan to keep your business equipment, tools and supplies in there and not spread around the house. Be sure to purchase separate supplies for home and business, to discourage family members coming into your business space to search for items they need. Create a home office. This is not as difficult as one would think. Every home office's needs are different, but there are some fundamental staples that all require. You will want to have a clean, noise-free environment that has good lighting and is free from distractions. This will help keep you more focused and productive. You will need a desk and chair. The size of your desk will depend on what its function is. You will want a place to store all your information about your customers such as a computer and/or a filing cabinet.

You may also need meeting and storage space: If, like many home-based businesses, yours will focus on services or affiliate products, there will be no need, or very little need, for storage. However, if you are planning to sell stocked products and ship them yourself, then make sure you have room to store them all. If you plan on holding meetings outside of your home, there will be no need for a conference room. If you are going to be seeing clients in your home, and do not have a conference room, then be sure to keep your place clean and neat at all times.

#7 COMMUNICATIONS TOOLS

 You will also want a computer system, phone, facsimile machine, scanner, copier, Internet connection, and any other communication tools you might need at hand.

8 DRESS FOR SUCCESS

Success is in the mind. You want to make sure that whatever your mind can see should radiate success. It is important for you to dress for success. Even if you work from home, please, put together a business wardrobe. You need not be a fashion plate or break the bank, but you must have neat, clean attire appropriate to your industry. Make sure you attend to personal grooming before getting dressed for appointments.

9 RESEARCH TAX LAWS

Be sure you have researched the tax laws and requirements of your county and your local jurisdiction. Set up a bookkeeping system on your own, or you should be prepared to hire an accountant if necessary. Income taxes are our business, so we can help you.

#10 MAKE TIME FOR BUSINESS

Set time aside every day to work for your business. Plan your days off ahead of time so you are not temped to ignore work on any given day because you do not feel like it. You reap what you sow. You cannot sleep your way to financial prosperity.

#11 TO-DO LIST

Make a plan and work it. A to-do list is a great way to stay on task. A to-do list can help you stay on track by by systematizing your work.

#12 ESTABLISH RULES FOR YOURSELF

Make sure your family knows the office is a business and off limits. If you have family members, especially small children, let them know that they are only to interrupt you in an emergency. Establish rules, such as do not disturb daddy or mummy when he or she is on the phone, and do not come into the office without knocking. Do not talk to or yell at the children, the spouse or the dog while you are on a business call. First impressions say a lot about you.

13 NETWORKING

Network with other people to get the word out about your business and gain inspiration from like-minded people. There are online networking sites and usually locally based groups for business owners.

#14 DECIDE ON BUSINESS ADDRESS

Decide if you can use your home address and phone number for business, or if you will need a separate, dedicated business phone number and perhaps a post office box for work related mail.

#15 YOU MUST HAVE AN EMAIL ADDRESS EXCLUSIVE TO YOUR BUSINESS

When I started my business, I had an email address from America Online. Much later, I obtained a second email address from Yahoo.com. Regrettably, I have been commingling my personal and business emals. Now I have established a new email address for my personal matters only. When you build a business web site, use an email address associated with your domain name; for example, my new email address is contact@princeojong.com; it looks very professional.

There is more to personal finance than the drudgery of debts and budgets.

#16 PRINT BUSINESS CARDS AND POST CARDS

Create business cards, post cards, and stationery with your contact details if you have the skills to produce professional quality printed materials yourself, or order them and have them professionally printed. Office superstores, like Staples and Office Depot, offer graphic and other business services. I have discovered that many web companies offer great deals on printing. A good example is Vista Print. I am not shy to recommend Vista Print to my readers because the company does a good job at an affordable price. The service of Vista Print is great.

TOWARD A THEORY OF ENTREPRENEURSHIP

Generally, entrepreneurship is not synonymous with business leadership. Par excellence, in a narrow sense, entrepreneurship is not synonymous with business management. An entrepreneur is perceived to be a visionary who organizes all the factors of production. As I see it, the drawing of lines of demarcation among entrepreneurship, management, and leadership is a theoretical and fruitless exercise of academic scholarship. For all practical purposes, the three business terms straddle distinctions of a definite kind.

As a living entrepreneur, I am responsible as the manager of my business; I am also the leader of my business. In a bigger scheme of things, I may be forced to relegate or delegate the functions stipulated above. In fact, this situation has also been germane to entrepreneurial startups such as Wal-Mart, Microsoft, Apple, Hewlett-Packard, Oracle, Sun Microsystems, and many other companies. In the beginning, the entrepreneur wore many hats, but as the fortunes of the enterprise waxed, he or she chose to relegate or delegate functions. In today's world, realities remind us of the rapidly changing economy; the old ways of management no longer work and will never work again.

The magnitude and pressure of environmental, competitive, and global market change we are experiencing is unprecedented. It is a very interesting and exciting world, but it is also a volatile and chaotic planet. You cannot address these new challenges with more of the same old management solutions; there has to be a new paradigm shift; successful change requires new management and leadership. For instance, psychological research has shown that under circumstances of uncertainty or unusual challenge and difficulty, people look for help in understanding questions about what matters, what to do, what direction to take, and what they should not do. Providing people with the answers that help them with these difficult questions is the essence of business management and leadership today and tomorrow.

ENTREPRENEURIAL LEADERSHIP

Entrepreneurial leaders, like Steve Jobs and Bill Gates, have some specific leadership attributes. Entrepreneurial leadership is leadership that is based on the attitude that the leader is self-employed. If you are going to run your business enterprise successfully, it behooves you to become an entrepreneurial leader. If a leader possesses the skills or attributes of an entrepreneur superstar, then, we can use the term entrepreneurial leadership to describe that leader.

In the new era of rapid changes and knowledge-based enterprises, managerial work becomes increasingly a leadership task, so leadership is the primary force behind successful change. Leaders empower employees to act on the vision. They execute their goals through inspiration and develop implementation capacity networks through a complex web of aligned relationships. In the increasingly turbulent and competitive environment firms face today, a new type of entrepreneurial leader distinct from other behavioral forms of managerial leadership is required. Leaders of this type take initiative and act as if they are playing a critical role in the organization rather than a mostly important one and energize their people, demonstrate entrepreneurial creativity, search continuously for new opportunities and pursue them, take risk, venture into new areas and provide strategic direction and inspiration to their people, take responsibility for the failures of their team, learn from these failures and use them as a step to ultimate success and strategic achievement.

Entrepreneurial leadership involves instilling the confidence in employees to think, behaving and acting with entrepreneurship in the interests of fully realizing the intended purpose of the organization to the beneficial growth of all stakeholders involved. In short, a reading of the books on Steve Jobs and Bill Gates reveal their rules of success to be entrepreneurial leadership. You do not know what you can get away with until you try. Good leaders do not ask employees to wait for official blessing from the boss to experiment or try out new solutions. If you ask enough people for permission, you inevitably come up against someone who believes his job is to say no. So, the moral of my story is, do not ask! That is the essence of the entrepreneurial mindset. No pain no gain; nothing ventured, nothing gained; indeed, venture-capital values are different from established corporate shared values.

Entrepreneurial independence demands space for action and trust, while corporate independence, independence in a corporation, implies responsibility and control imposed from above. Entrepreneurial speed demands agility, experimentation, adaptation, and rapid response to be first to market. Corporate experimentation comprises analysis, review, sober consideration of facts, and willingness to sacrifice speed for thoroughness. In contrast, entrepreneurial paranoia, much exhibited by Andy Grove, the former chief executive officer of Intel Corporation, is reflected in the "competitors are catching up to us" mentality; with entrepreneurial leadership, there is no overshadowing by an essential need to build corporate consensus and minimize perceived risk.

CREATE AN INSPIRING VISION

As an entrepreneurial leader, please, create an inspiring vision for your followers. Inspiration and vision are important. Your vision statement should be short and inspiring. Look at President Barack Obama; in 2008, his vision statement was yes we can; in 2012 his new vision statement is forward. By contrast, Governor Willard Mitt Romney's is believe in America. Hence, your business should have a catchy vision statement; mine is your dreams are closer than you think. Your vision statement must set a challenging and stretching goal that gives employees enormous freedom in finding ways to achieve it. You have also to communicate the message that doing what you do now, only better, is not enough.

If you do what you always did then you will not even get what you always received as you have to keep growing to stay where you are. You have to do something different to get different results. You have to do something significantly smarter to get significantly better results. As Albert Einstein once said, "Insanity is doing the same thing, over and over again, but expecting different results."

ENTREPRENEURIAL CREATIVITY

In previous chapters, I drew your attention to the power of neuro-linguistic programming. I discussed the use of the five senses and the faculty of imagination. I compared the human mind to a supercomputer, but I highlighted also the superiority of the former over the latter: creativity. I introduced you to visualization and mental creativity. As such, entrepreneurial creativity is about coming up with innovative ideas and turning them into value-creating profitable business activities. Generally, as a strong breed of human beings, entrepreneurs live a life of what I call a conscious existence; unlike animals, entrepreneurs do not live life to eat food and sleep. They think and grow; they respond to the stimuli from their surroundings; what ordinary mortals dismiss categorically as a problem or a question, entrepreneurs use their intellectual curiosity to welcome it as an opportunity camouflaged in the form of a puzzle, a riddle, or an enigma. As such, entrepreneurial creativity, the product or solution to a business need, is a composite of creativity amplified by the quick action of an entrepreneur. In mathematics, the formulaic information above can be expressed with the following equation:

Entrepreneurial creativity = creativity × entrepreneurial action.

LEADING INNOVATION

If you aspire to be a miraculous millionaire, you should lead or recognize business innovation. Leading innovation is a delicate and challenging process. You need to encourage expansive out-of-the-box thinking to generate new ideas, but also filter through these ideas to decide which ones to commercialize. Use a balanced loose-tight style of leadership for this purpose; loose-tight leadership alternates the creation of space for idea generation and free exploration with a deliberate tightening that selects and tests specific ideas for further investment and development. Looseness usually dominates the early stages of the innovation process; in the later stages, tightening becomes more important to scrutinize the concepts and bring the selected ones to the market. A balanced approach is essential to loose-tight leadership. Those who remain loose too long generate plenty of ideas but have difficulty commercializing them. Those who lock into the tight mode choke off all but most obvious ideas, thus confining innovation to incremental line extensions of existing products that add little value.

Within entrepreneurial leadership are the principles for transforming your business from mediocre to great. For example, in Tom Peters and Robert H. Waterman, Jr.'s *In Search of Excellence*, the famous and fabled management consultants established the hallmark of leading a business from the abyss of mediocrity to the wuthering heights of greatness. The book explores the art, science, and philosophy of management used by leading 1980s companies with records of long-term profitability and continuing innovation.

Today, a sequel to *In Search of Excellence* will highlight cutting-edge companies such as Facebook, Google, Amazon.com, and Apple. Like the great innovative companies of the 1980s celebrated in Tom Peter's book, Facebook, Google, Amazon.com, and Apple have dared their mediocre competitors to be different. They have not rested on their laurels to be copycats. They have chosen to emerge as contrarian enterprises. In business, contrarians are the change agents of the world. In fact, wealth-building businesses, such as Facebook, Google, Amazon.com, and Apple, are not simply executing better than their competitors; indeed, they are radically changing the business rules of the success game in their field or industry. Think about your own business. Where in your business can you break the rules? How can you set yourself apart from the crowd in your industry? How? In all my businesses, in my own way, I have always struggled to define myself as different and better than the competition. What about you? Think about your own business. Will you make or mar?

CHARISMA

Are you a charismatic leader? What is charisma? Warren Bennis and Burt Nanus describe charisma as the result of effective leadership, not the other way around. When you look at leaders like Alexander the Great, Winston Churchill, Adolf Hitler, John F. Kennedy, Vladimir Lenin, and Barrack Obama, I am sure you conclude that they all have one common style of leadership - charismatic leadership. They stand out from the pack of leaders because of their extraordinary qualities that are rarely found among leaders. In 2008, although Senator Barrack Obama was relatively young and Senator John McCain was relatively old, people trusted and voted the former as the president of the United States of America because of his charismatic leadership. In 2012, it seems there is going to be a déjà vu of 2008. Barack Obama will win the presidential race by a landslide, almost as he had done in 2008. The American economy is still in the doldrums, yet most American voters will repudiate former Governor Willard Mitt Romney, the self-proclaimed turnaround artist; they will swarm to President Barack Obama like moths to a candle light. As another instance of the working of charisma, the solders of Alexander the Great blindly followed him because of his charismatic leadership.

Third, many soldiers marched towards victory during the Second World War under the charismatic leadership of Winston Churchill. Similarly, the Germans were inspired by the vision of Adolf Hitler. Most Americans were influenced by the charismatic leadership of John F. Kennedy who gave them a clarion call: "Ask not what your country can do for you; ask what you can do for your country." At the 2012 Democratic party convention in Charlotte, North Carolina, a former president, William Jefferson Clinton, used the magnetic aura of charisma to rally the masses for the cause of President Barack Obama.

WHAT IS CHARISMATIC LEADERSHIP?

In 1947 Max Weber identified three leadership styles: bureaucratic, traditional, and charismatic leadership. Weber defined charismatic leadership as authority resting on devotion to the exceptional sanctity, heroism or exemplary character of an individual person, and of the normative patterns or order revealed or ordained by him. As such, charisma is an imperceptible aura related to the extraordinary powers bestowed on an individual by divine means.

There is more to personal finance than the drudgery of debts and budgets.

It is the rarest of the rare qualities which are usually acquired through birth. However, Weber's research reveals that charisma is a skill that can be honed by training, experience, and practice. Charismatic leaders are treated as having supernatural powers and abilities by their followers. They are good at body language and communication skills as well. They impress people through usage of eye contact and hand shake.

Besides, Robert J. House has contributed to the theory of charismatic leadership. Charisma is a Greek word meaning a divinely inspired gift. Charismatic personalities are charming and colorful. They have a magnetic personality, and they appeal to their people. They know the pulse of their people. It is basically a trait supported by certain skills that can be honed. For instance, if you were not born with charisma, you can become charismatic by acquiring communication skills and the knowledge of human psychology. Charismatic leaders are human manipulators such as transformational leaders. Charismatic leadership and transformational leadership appear to be similar. However, they are different in the sense that charisma helps to transform average individuals as well extraordinary individuals.

CATEGORIES OF CHARISMA

Charismatic leaders are categorized into five types: socialized, personalized, office-holder, personal, and divine charismatic leaders. The socialized charismatic leaders utilize their powers for the benefit of others. The personalized charismatic leaders unitize their powers for their personal benefits. The office-holder charismatic leaders are powerful as long as they occupy the office. Once they resign, they lose their charisma. In contrast, the personal charismatic leaders are powerful forever whether they are in office or out of office because of their extraordinary qualities. Finally, the divine charismatic leaders are the ones where people think that they are god sent. Jane A. Halpert classifies charisma into referent power, expert power, and job involvement. Referent power is the ability to influence others because of one's desirable traits and characteristics. Expert power is the ability to influence others because of one's specialized knowledge, competencies, skills, or abilities. Therefore, to excel as a charismatic leader, the leader must have expert and referent power and he or she must be involved in jobs briskly. Charismatic leaders help tackle crises effectively. Once the crisis is blown out, these leaders may not be required to help the situation of things. These leaders energize their followers and excite them through their rhetoric and bring them close to organizational goals and objectives.

Characteristics of Charismatic Leaders:

What are the characteristic features of a charismatic leader?
He/She is the greatest game changer.
 He/She is a change agent and status quo ante.
He/She is a visionary.
He/She is a magnetic personality with lots of energy and enthusiasm.
He/She projects an exciting and colorful picture to us, his followers.
He/She is a great communicator who is good at emotional intelligence.
He/She loves to live on edge and he is a risk taker and thrives in risk.
He/She is a self-promoter.

He/She boosts and boasts about himself to get excitement.

He/She does not bother for fear of failure and fear of death.

He/She is highly emotional but he balances himself

He/She is good at storytelling.

He/She believes in the concept of management by anecdote.

He/She starts his speeches with anecdotes to connect with their audience quickly and effectively.

He/She follows his heart.

He/She develops vision for others

He/She is highly confident.

He/She is an optimist.

He/She networks with people and builds bridges.

He/She is honest and helps others.

He/She never gives up.

Marianne Williamson is a spiritual activist, author, lecturer and founder of The Peace Alliance, a grass roots campaign supporting legislation currently before Congress to establish a United States Department of Peace. Marianne Williamson states that charisma is a sparkle in people that money cannot buy. It is an invisible energy with visible effects. Certainly, Jesus Christ, the man, is the most charismatic human being to have walked the earth.

Nonetheless, charisma is not exclusive to men. Truly, the world is replete with female paragons of charisma: the Virgin Mary, Miriam Makeba of South Africa, Helen of Troy, Cleopatra of Egypt, Joan D'Arc, Princess Diana of Wales, Margaret Thatcher of Great Britain, and Benazir Bhutto of Pakistan.

HOW DO YOU BECOME A CHARISMATIC LEADER?

The easiest way for you to become a charismatic leader is to model the life and times of our master Jesus Christ. Pick up a copy of your holy Bible. Read it from Mathews to Revelation. These biblical books will teach you many lessons on the charisma of Jesus Christ. Another book that sheds much light on the charisma of our Lord is titled *Jesus Christ CEO*; definitely, the book reminds you that Jesus Christ, as the incarnation of man, is the most charismatic human being to have walked on the face of the earth. It is a truth universally asserted that Jesus Christ has changed the world in a way that no other human being ever will. How do we measure time today? We reckon the nativity of Christ (BC) and the crucifixion of Christ (AD). I challenge you to show me a leader of any religion who has manifested absolute power over all the forces of nature. Show me any religious leader who has made his or her spiritual power evident by performing miracles. If I have to coach you to create your own financial miracles, you have to acknowledge that the power comes from heaven above, from Jesus Christ.

Hence, throw away those self-help books and motivational cassettes you bought on inspirational leadership. Send those consultants packing. Ask them to become Christians. Follow the examples of Jesus Christ listed above. Your mission is the job of following Christ. Know your job; set a good example for the people under you to emulate and follow; put results over politics. That is all the charisma you will really need to succeed in this life.

There is more to personal finance than the drudgery of debts and budgets.

Smile with the people you meet cheerfully from your heart; praise your peers and workers liberally, but you should criticize them sparingly; maintain eye contact with people; shake hands with them firmly; when in the midst of people, you should demonstrate positive body language; treat others with respect; always remember the names of people you meet; I had learned this lesson in Africa from Dale Carnegie's book titled *How to Win Friends and Influence People*. Improve your communication skills and acquire domain competency; that is, master both soft and hard skills. According to Dale Carnegie, that is what you need to do if you aspire to acquire charisma and make other people like you as a leader:

1. Begin with praise and honest appreciation.
2. Call attention to people's mistakes indirectly.
3. Talk about your own mistakes before criticizing the other person.
4. Ask questions instead of giving direct orders.
5. Let the other person save face.
6. Praise every improvement.
7. Give the other person a fine reputation to live up to.
8. Use encouragement.
9. Make the fault seem easy to correct.
10. Make the other person happy about doing what you suggest.

CRITICISM OF CHARISMATIC LEADERS

Although charismatic leaders drive others with their energy and enthusiasm, they believe more in themselves rather than others. They treat themselves as puppeteers and their followers as puppets. Once the charismatic leaders depart, the work comes to a grinding halt, thus leading to a leadership vacuum. They make their absence felt more. The charismatic leaders could not deliver the goods properly when viewed from historical leaders. They come, conquer and leave the world without any takeaways except showing a colorful and magical world to their followers: Nelson Mandela and John F. Kennedy. Jesus Christ seems to be the only charismatic leader who does not let down his followers; he does not want his followers to hit the rock bottom. He will come back again; he does not have to worry about being forced to oblivion. Other leaders have been thrown into the dustbins of history. For instance, Garry Winnick, the former chairman of Global Crossing Ltd is an example who let down his followers. Both Barack H. Obama and Osama bin Laden are charismatic leaders; while the former is using charisma for a great cause, the latter is using it for evil activities. Thank you, Navy Seals! I want to thank you again for scorching the serpent.

Winston Churchill was a charismatic leader with a complex personality. His leadership traits are a blend of intuition, invention, emotion, hedonism, nationalism, humor, reformist with a strong internal locus of control. Charismatic leaders like Josef Stalin and Adolf Hitler elevated themselves above criticism. It proved counterproductive for them as well as for their people. Therefore, there is danger involved in charismatic leadership. A good example of this danger is Jim Jones of Jonestown who misled 909 of his religious followers to commit revolutionary suicide; another instance of charisma gone amok is David Koresh, the religious leader of the Branch Davidians sect of Waco, Texas.

In conclusion, charisma depends on the mindset of the leader. If you were not born with it, how can you have charisma? By becoming more concerned about making others feel good about themselves than you are making them feel good about you. Charisma needs substance than style. Charisma presupposes that you have knowledge and content to speak and connect with others. Charismatic leaders are known for walking the talk. They go to any extent to please their followers. They have passion to serve their people. Therefore, the world needs charismatic leaders to address several leadership challenges globally.

ANATOMY OF THE CHARACTERISTICS OF SUCCESSFUL ENTREPRENEURS AND LEADERS

"Success is going from failure to failure without loss of enthusiasm."
—Sir Winston Churchill

To keep going despite setbacks is the hallmark of all successful entrepreneurs and leaders. While much has been written about the managerial challenges of running a business, less has been written about the characteristics underlying great leadership. I want to describes nine psychological characteristics of great leadership.

Leadership Characteristic 1: Self esteem

Underlying everything is a high sense of one's own self-worth. Without that, individuals will never undertake tough challenges. If one does not have it, it is important to develop self-esteem.

Leadership Characteristic 2: Need to achieve

The need to achieve has been associated with entrepreneurs and leaders who constantly seek to perform at their best. For example, this leadership characteristic would have described Oliver Cromwell (1599 to 1658) the Lord Protector of England, who once remarked, "He who stops being better, stops being good."

The great Harvard psychologist David McClelland is most associated with the need for achievement, a need learned by children primarily from their parents (McClelland, 1965). Individuals high in this need are open to feedback, are goal oriented, seek to be unique, and strive for accomplishments based on their own efforts—characteristics important to effective leadership. They also take risks, not extreme risks, but moderate ones. And what is moderate risk? Moderate risk means you have the ability to influence events, but do not have complete control. The key is that you believe you will be successful, but it is not a sure thing.

Leadership Quality 3: Screening for opportunity

Like all individuals, leaders screen incoming information to separate the useful from the useless. However, successful entrepreneurs and business leaders screen incoming information to constantly seek new growth opportunities. They act like gold miners who must shift through tons of dirt to find a few precious golden nuggets.

There is more to personal finance than the drudgery of debts and budgets.

Unfortunately, the vast majority of business people seem blind to new opportunities and so continually miss new ways to grow the business. Is that not the way Bill Gates overlooked the emergent Internet revolution? Some people would argue that it is not really finding opportunity, but getting lucky. Of course, there are individuals who seem to have the knack of being in the right place and at the right time. Create your own luck; develop an extremely successful business; become a millionaire many times over. If you want to create your own luck, prepare yourself before opportunity knocks on your door. Capitalize on an opportunity missed by your peers and competitors.

Leadership Characteristic 4: Locus of control

Successful leaders and entrepreneurs typically show a high internal locus of control. In many different studies done over the years, those with a high internal locus of control are more likely to experience success, than individuals who are high on the external locus of control. When someone perceives events as under the control of others, fate, luck, the system, their boss, etcetera, they have an external locus of control.

Individuals high on the internal locus of control have a different assumption about how the world works. They practice NLP without knowing it; they assume that any success they experience is due to their personal efforts and that they have the ability to influence events. Interestingly, internal also assume failure was also their fault.

Leadership Characteristic 5: Goal orientation

Businesses come and go, but those that last always share a common characteristic with their founder: a relentless drive to accomplish goals. They understand what the priorities are and continue to work toward that goal, day in and day out. For many, the leadership characteristic of staying focused on a goal is a very difficult thing to do since life in the world of business tends to distract us.

Leadership Characteristic 6: Optimism

Underlying successful entrepreneurial leadership is a boundless font of optimism that never seems to end. As Napoleon Hill relates the mindset of entrepreneurs, when faced with a problem, they view it as a challenge; when faced with a setback, they view it as a new direction; when told no, they say, "Maybe not now, but I know you will change your mind later." This characteristic contrasts sharply with the vast majority of people who project a more pessimistic, defeatist quality.

For the millionaire mind, it is this belief in the positive that serves as the foundation for dealing with the many set-backs one will inevitably encounter in the world of business. Young children naturally have a positive view which seems to turn more negative as they age. Parents can easily test this in children by asking the question, "What will you be when you grow up?" Young children confidently say, exactly what they want to be. However, ask a teenager the same question and they are not so sure.

Leadership Characteristic 7: Courage

Many professors talk about entrepreneurs as risks takers. But this leadership characteristic is like saying snow is cold; it is accurate, but it is missing something. Another way is to say the same thing is that one must have guts. It requires a great deal of courage to build a company from the ground up. Someone once explained that large organizations function like wombs protecting employees from a harsh and unforgiving environment. It takes a great deal of courage to leave a corporate or government womb and strike out by oneself into the cold, cruel world of business. When one first starts a business, one is alone.

Leadership Characteristic 8: Tolerance of ambiguity

This term refers to a person's tolerance of uncertainty and risk. As human beings, we are creatures of habit; we like being robotic, repeating the same processes every day. Entrepreneurs generally score high on this scale. As we age, we have a tendency to be more comfortable repeating a relatively small set of behaviors. For example, we eat pretty much the same food, shop in the same stores, watch the same programs, have lunch with the same people, listen to the same music.

One may change jobs, but rarely does one change industries. It is amazing how many people end up retiring in the same industry in which they received their first job. If one's tolerance of ambiguity is low, one will gravitate toward large, established organizations; better still, one would work for the government where things change little if at all. In contrast to older, established organizations, entrepreneurial start-ups exist in an environment where almost everything is new and many things have not been done before. For example, no policies exist to guide action and start-ups typically lack the old timers who serve as the voice of experience.

Leadership Characteristic 9: Strong internal motivation.

You must have the fire inside your soul burning brightly like Satan in hellfire. As NLP shows, the motivation that drives our behavior comes from two sources: internal (intrinsic) and external (extrinsic). Intrinsic factors (internal representations) include constructs such as needs, desires, motives, and will power.

Extrinsic factors (physiology) include any type of motivational influence from the environment such as rewards and punishments. For entrepreneurs, the most important motivational factor is the intrinsic one. Entrepreneurs keep going despite the fact that employees tell them they are foolish, friends say they are wasting their time, and family tells them to get a real job. When the intrinsic drive goes away, so does any chance of success.

To wrap-up the discussion of leadership characteristics, I have some good news for you; many of the leadership characteristics listed above are learnable. For example, you can think and train your mind to recognize business opportunity; NLP and psychology tell me that optimism or pessimism is a controllable state of mind, so too is a positive or negative mental attitude.

By using NLP to manipulate your physiology and internal representations, you can increase the need for achievement or you can decrease your potential of achievement. The reality is what you may perceive to be bad news: it is not easy for you to do so without much private practice or some formal coaching from me. After all, you cannot build a strong and solid financial foundation without some hard work and sacrifice. It suffices for you to conclude that where there is the will, there will be a way.

WARNINGS OF ENTREPRENEURIAL LEADERSHIP

1. Delegation of duties

With the number of tools available on the Internet, it is quite possible that a new entrepreneur, like you, can build a successful business online. You can even build a media empire. However, if you expect to expand, you will need to delegate tasks at some point. You simply cannot do everything yourself and also expect to grow. That means you need to hire people and inevitably deal with normal work situations in the corporate world. I urge you to forget about traditional business leadership. Since I came to America, I have only had very few bosses who were good business leaders: Cynthia Fletcher, David Miller, Peter Simmons, Chris Wydeck, Carl Mayse, and David Seaman. I learned much about business management and leadership because they were charismatic, personable, and forward-thinking. Above all, they taught me the value of team work.

2. Wisdom from work

I am ready to share some of their wisdom with you. They had distilled these perspectives in me while we were working together.

3. Workforce blame

Never blame your peers or employees. At least, do not blame an employee in front of another employee. If you have to reprimand an employee, please, do it in private. Doing it in public sets a bad tone in the workforce. You lose respect with all employees because such bad management behavior spreads fast like bad gossip.

4. Avoid conflict

As a manager, always do your very best to avoid conflict. Do not create adversarial situations. Do not pit one employee against another employee or ask them to snitch on others. Healthy competition at work is fine, but tale bearing, slander, back-stabbing, and character assassination are like corporate cancer.

5. Understand the work

Be prepared to learn new skills. Be a life-long and constant learner. Always make sure you understand the work your boss entrusts you to do. As a boss, you should always have at least a fundamental understanding of the work you are expecting your employees to do. This understanding makes it easier on everyone when they try to tell you why something cannot be done, or that it will cost more.

6. Weigh and consider

You should always weigh and consider situations logically and empathically. Do not put square pegs in round holes. Basically, assign the right work to the right people, to allow them to work optimally. Do not be like those companies whose names I want to remain anonymous for security reasons; the managers were always excited to challenge me with a job they knew I could not handle; as a consequence, they crushed my morale and spirit for their own sport. Hence, I swore never to be mean to any employee.

7. Lead by example

Brainstorm with your employees. As Christ leads his disciples, so shall you lead your employees. The first shall be the last, and the last shall be the first. If your company encounters a problem that covers new ground, do not expect your employees to know how to solve it. If you know the solution to a business problem, give your employees a crash course; they can take things from there. Leading by example does not mean that you should treat your workers like a pets or puppies. If they still have trouble solving a new problem, brainstorm with them.

Proper brainstorming requires that at least the moderator of the meeting does some legwork beforehand. Record all ideas without censorship, or you might miss the best solution, which might be unfamiliar and thus seem odd. Ask questions; do not shout commands. Communicate well and clearly. In an entrepreneurial startup company with a positive environment and a healthy spirit of competition, most people want to be asked questions; they want to be challenged. Announce the day or week's assignments, and let your employees pick them by lottery. In other words, if you are not yet a big company, you need to define every employee's role. Do not underestimate any employee. You might be surprised to discover the hidden potential of your employees. Challenges also weed out the lazybones.

8. Be decisive

Be a decisive leader. The buck stops with you. The business is your business. Always have a strategy ready. If business problems crop up and employees are aware of them, they will be thinking about their bills, their mortgages, etcetera, not your bills. Consider profit-sharing or bonuses. In fact, bonuses go a long way toward building employee loyalty, passion, and creativity. . If your company is still young, there is only so far you can go with bonuses, so also consider profit-sharing or private equity sharing. Give employees incentives to motivate them to have a sense of belonging, but you should remain the decision-maker; publicize what needs to be done; then ask for volunteers or assign tasks if necessary. Sure, there will still be stragglers, but a creative bonus matrix weeds them out. Talk to a good accountant about the best way to implement these incentives. If you still need assistance, contact me.

There is more to personal finance than the drudgery of debts and budgets.

9. Be sympathetic.

Your workers are human beings, not machines. Working with them means you have to contend with their emotional baggage. Be sympathetic toward your employees, or, at least, be courteous. It is only human to not always be in top form, even with incentives. Talk to your employees, understand them, and give them some leeway whenever possible. Have some redundancy in job descriptions, right from the beginning, to allow someone to temporarily take up the slack. Be firm. Being sympathetic is all well and good, but you do have a business to run. Be firm when it is necessary.

THE 60-MINUTE MBA

MBA is an acronym for a master's degree in business administration. It is the official and upper echelon qualification of most of the talented and educated people managing and leading corporate enterprises in America today. Who needs an MBA in 60 minutes, anyway? You do. Do you want to swim with the sharks and be eaten alive? Without a doubt, if you aspire to bootstrap and operate your own business, it is important for you to know in a nutshell what these big guys studied in some of the top business schools in two years. As a professional or new budding entrepreneur, I know you do not have the luxury of time to learn business administration. That is why I have summarized the following content for you to consume in sixty minutes.

Whether your business is a small (mom-and-pop) venture or a growing corporation, management is fundamental to the health and survival of your enterprise. Statistics have shown that the cause or factor of most business failures is management. You can have all the beautiful ideas on earth, but your business will fail if you lack managerial skills. In fact, the recognition of this fact is attributable to the national popularity of graduate programs in business management. Many students, supported by their families and loved ones, spend over one hundred thousand dollars to buy MBAs from Ivy League institutions, such as Harvard University or the University of Pennsylvania (Wharton School of Business).

What are they getting in return? Not much: history of business management, quantitative analysis, and qualitative analysis. Certainly, the MBA programs give students an ornate certificate that you could use your computer and laser printer to design and print online. Aware of this weakness, many schools, taking their cues from Harvard Business School, are revamping their MBA programs to reflect the complex reality of the modern-day world of work. As for you, I am offering the 60-minute MBA, the quintessence of what you need to know to manage your own enterprise or a bigger corporation. To this compendium of knowledge, I plan to add theoretical and practical instruction from the Millionaire iUniversity. You will learn how business managers set precise goals for their enterprises; you will learn the techniques effective managers use to praise and motivate their employees to become more efficient and productive; you will learn how to reprimand employees respectfully to improve on work performance. De jure, you do not need an MBA to be the master or mistress of the business universe. If you have a couple of years to spare, you can sit in business school seminar rooms. No problem! I rest my case. If not, I bring to you the essential MBA course manual. I have done the hard work for you. What you have to do now is read and come to the Millionaire iUniversity.

IDEA OF BUSINESS MANAGEMENT

The verb manage comes from the Italian "maneggiare," that is, to handle, especially tools, which in turn derives from the Latin manus, that is, hand. The French word for management is "gestion"or "menagement," later management, which influenced the development in meaning of the English word management in the 17th and 18th centuries. Some definitions of management are: organization and coordination of the activities of an enterprise in accordance with certain policies and in achievement of clearly defined objectives. Like entrepreneurship, management is often included as a factor of production along with machines, materials, and money.

According to the management guru Peter Drucker (1909–2005), the basic task of a management is twofold: marketing and innovation. Directors and managers have the power and responsibility to make decisions to manage an enterprise when given the authority by the shareholders. As a discipline, management comprises the interlocking functions of formulating corporate policy and organizing, planning, controlling, and directing the firm's resources to achieve the policy's objectives. The size of management can range from one person in a small firm to hundreds or thousands of managers in multinational companies. In large firms, however, the board of directors formulates the policy which is implemented by the chief executive officer.

In the beginning, it is important to point out that the idea of leadership is not synonymous with management. In all business and organizational activities, management is the act of getting people together to accomplish desired goals and objectives using available resources, such as the factors of production, efficiently and effectively. As such, a manager sees new opportunities, plans, organizes, measures, and improves the organization. Management comprises planning, organizing, staffing, leading or directing, and controlling an organization, that is, a group of one or more people or entities, or effort for the purpose of accomplishing a goal. That is what MBA students refer to as the 5 Ms of management. Resourcing encompasses the deployment and manipulation of human resources, financial resources, technological resources and natural resources. Therefore, your role, as a manger of a business, is to operate the organization for an unlimited amount of profit.

Your personal experiences can also serve as your teacher of good management principles. The reading of old and current management literature can also be a good teacher of sound management principles. Success in business management is like the art of making friends. If your employees are like you, they will be motivated by guilt to make you happy; if your employees are afraid of you, like Machiavelli's The Prince, then, they will be afraid to displease you, the corporate king. Hence, you have to choose between love and fear. Nonetheless, do not forget the golden rule which states that the customer is king; learn what customers want and give it to them. Establish a weekly plan to acquire new customers, and work your plan daily. Work hard to grow your customer base, and be prepared when opportunity knocks on your heaven's door. Always remember that customers buy benefits, not pedantic scholarship. To succeed in customer sales, you must love people; you must have empathy; you must be willing to help people solve their problems. Listen to your employees attentively. Please, read Thomas J. Peters' book titled *In Search of Excellence: Do it; Fix it; Try it.*

There is more to personal finance than the drudgery of debts and budgets.

LEVELS OF MANAGEMENT

Generally, there are three levels of management below operatives or operating employees:
1—Top management
2—Middle management
3—Bottom or First-Line management

MANAGERIAL ISSUES

The 5 Ms of management that an organization uses to succeed and grow are machinery, manpower or woman power, materials, money, and markets. Yet, the management must pay particular attention to the following issues listed below:

Planning and decision making
Organizing and staffing
Leading and controlling
Production and operations
Consumers and products
Distribution and pricing
Advertising and personal selling
Accounting and budgeting
Obtaining financial resources
Using financial resources
Managing risk
Understanding financial markets
Computers and their use in business
Small business and franchising
Government and business law
Unions and the American worker

CORPORATE CULTURE

Corporate culture is the way of life of a business organization. It is the heart and soul of a corporation. Is the heartbeat of the company formal or informal? To discover the culture of a corporation, you have to examine the documents, activities, actions, and opinions of the company. Perhaps more important are codified corporate documents, such as manuals, courses, letters, web sites, and books. Corporate or organizational culture is the collective behavior of humans that are part of an organization, it is also formed by the organization values, visions, norms, working language, systems, and symbols; it includes beliefs and habits. It is also the pattern of such collective behaviors and assumptions that are taught to new organizational members as a way of perceiving, and even thinking and feeling. Organizational culture affects the way people and groups interact with each other, with clients, and with stakeholders. Organizational culture is a set of shared mental assumptions that guide interpretation and action in organizations by defining appropriate behavior for various situations.

At the same time, although a company may have its own unique culture, in larger organizations, there is a diverse and sometimes conflicting cultures that co-exist due to different characteristics of the management team. Organizations often have very differing cultures as well as subcultures. Thus, organizational culture may also have negative and positive aspects.

HAWTHORNE EFFECT

What is the Hawthorne effect? The term received its name from a factory called the Hawthorne Works, where a series of experiments on factory workers was carried out between 1924 and 1932. The central idea behind the Hawthorne effect, a term used as early as 1950 by John R. P. French, is that changes in participants' behavior during the course of a study may be related only to the special social situation and social treatment they received. John R. P. French applied the term in reference to a set of studies begun in 1924 at the former Hawthorne (Cicero, Illinois) Works of the Western Electric Company, the manufacturing arm of AT&T. From the Hawthorne effect, you can learn to manage people by giving them personal attention: listening to them; welcoming their complaints; and expressing praise to them as recommended by Kenneth Blanchard's *The One Minute Manager*. In this wise, the manager focuses his attention on employee morale and efficiency.

MANAGEMENT BY OBJECTIVES

Management by objectives (MBO) is a process of defining objectives within an organization so that management and employees agree to the objectives and understand what they need to do in the organization. The term management by objectives was first popularized by Peter Drucker in his 1954 book titled *The Practice of Management*. The essence of MBO is participative goal setting, choosing courses of actions and decision making. An important part of the MBO is the measurement and the comparison of the employee's actual performance with the standards set by the management of the enterprise. Ideally, when employees themselves have been involved with the goal setting and choosing of the course of action to be followed by them, they are more likely to fulfill their responsibilities. According to George S. Edirne, the system of management by objectives can be described as a process whereby the superior and subordinate jointly identify the organization's common goals, define each individual's major areas of responsibility in terms of the results expected of him or her, and use these measures as guides for operating the unit and assessing the contribution of each of its members.

Conversely, management by objectives does not mean setting quotas. It means the definition of objectives that need to be achieved by the business organization. It means using time management to establish to-do lists and the choice of managers or employees to whom tasks are assigned or delegated. Management must measure results timely: daily, weekly, monthly, or yearly. Formal research, meetings, and reports can also be used to justify results. Ideas must be tested; ideas must be targeted; ideas must be measured; if the results are negative, the ideas must be rejected.

There is more to personal finance than the drudgery of debts and budgets.

SCIENTIFIC MANAGEMENT

Management theory posits that the operation of a business is a science. For this reason, business events and activities must follow a scientific process. One of the concepts you might overhear MBA students bragging about is scientific management Also called Taylorism, scientific management was a theory of management that analyzed and synthesized industrial workflows. Its main objective was the improvement of economic efficiency, especially labor productivity. Scientific management marks one of the earliest attempts to apply science to the engineering of processes and to business management. Its development began with Frederick Winslow Taylor in the 1880s and 1890s within the manufacturing industries. Its peak of influence came in the 1910s; by the 1920s, it was still influential but had begun an era of competition and syncretism with opposing or complementary ideas. Although scientific management as a distinct theory or school of thought was obsolete by the 1930s, most of its themes are still important parts of industrial engineering and management today. These include analysis, synthesis, logic, rationality, empiricism, work ethic, efficiency, elimination of waste, standardization of best practices, disdain for tradition preserved merely for its own sake or merely to protect the social status of particular workers with particular skill sets, the transformation of craft production into mass production, and knowledge transfer between workers and from workers into tools, processes, and documentation.

SYSTEMS THINKING

One of the concepts you might overhear MBA students bragging about is systems thinking. Systems thinking is the process of understanding how things influence one another within a whole. In nature, systems thinking examples include ecosystems in which various elements such as air, water, movement, plants, and animals work together to survive or perish. Correspondingly, in organizations, systems consist of people, structures, and processes that work together to make an organization healthy or unhealthy. Systems thinking has been defined as an approach to problem solving, by viewing problems as parts of an overall system, rather than reacting to a specific part, outcomes or events and potentially contributing to further development of unintended consequences. Systems thinking is not one thing but a set of habits or practices within a framework that is based on the belief that the component parts of a system can best be understood in the context of relationships with each other and with other systems, rather than in isolation. Systems thinking focuses on cyclical rather than linear cause and effect. Since business organizations can be viewed as systems, management can also be defined as human action, including design, to facilitate the production of useful outcomes from a system. This view opens the opportunity to manage oneself, a pre-requisite to attempting to manage an organization or others.

HIRING AND FIRING OF PERSONNEL

Even if you are a charismatic leader, you do not have to be too friendly with employees. As the saying goes, familiarity breeds contempt. Hiring is a tough business. It takes patience, proper screening, and careful analysis. Are you in the process of hiring new employees? The economy is still slow.

With so many talented individuals out of work right now, it is going to take some time for you to find an ideal job prospect, the one candidate who really fits the bill.

HIRING RIGHT

Yet, it incumbent upon you to hire the right prospects for your enterprise. Any mistakes will cost you dearly. Below is a hiring process that you should weigh and consider:

1. Say the Lord's prayer
2. Post a job description for prospects to see
3. Advertise the position in the mass media
4. Get responses and referrals from your employees
5. Schedule the first get-to-know-you interview
6. Read resume and check references
7. Screen job applicant by using a testing tool: DISC TEST
8. Judge the extent to which you like the applicant
9. Ascertain whether applicant is a team player
10. Find out if applicant is enthusiastic about the job
11. Evaluate applicant's mission statement
12. Review applicant's balance sheet
13. Check applicant's credit report
14. Calculate applicant's employee benefits
15. Interview spouse of job applicant
16. Handle 90-day job probation review

FIRING EMPLOYEES

As much as you hire employees, an occasion may arise when you have to fire them. In order not to create unintended consequences, it is important for you to fire employees in the right way. Please, fire employees with dignity. Do not relish the prospect of firing people like a friend of mine who brags that he likes firing people who work for him. If you have to fire an employee, please, start with reprimands; proceed with more reprimands, and end by sanctioning the employee's incompetence. In short, there are three main reasons why you should fire people:

1. Job performance failure
2. Personal problems affecting job performance
3. Job incompetence

MARKETING

If you are running a business, you have to market your product or service. If you have followed my advice, you should have written a business plan, which normally contains a marketing plan. In preparing your marketing plan, you should have raised many questions. Where is my target market? How does my target market become aware of the existence of my product or service? How do I reach my potential customers? By conducting market research, you would obtain good answers to these questions. Stay close to your customer; listen to the customer. You need to make an effort to market your product or service methodically. I am assuming that you have already written your winning business plan, and you are following your marketing plan step-by-step.

Develop an appropriate marketing mix: product, place, promotion, and price. I call them the 4 Ps of marketing. Develop the right product that satisfies human wants or needs; ascertain the right place or channels of distribution such as retail or wholesale; design the right personal selling or advertising program; and price your product or service to reflect what the customer perceives to be the right price, which must reflect true value. You do not want your customer to feel that you are cheating or overcharging them. In our telegenic society, image sells; looks are important, so dress for success and hit the pavement daily; or begin cold calling with a phone list from Sales Genie or Info USA. Do not shy away from advertising in college or local newspapers. Join the chamber of commerce or a country club. As a small business person, the marketing books I found the most useful are the following: Paul and Sarah Edwards, *Getting Business To Come to You* and Jay Conrad Levinson *Guerrilla Marketing: Easy and Inexpensive Strategies for Making Big Profits from Your Small Business*. These two books taught me how to use low-cost but effective tools to market my products and services: word of mouth, referrals, business cards, postcards, thank-you cards, birthday cards, church bulletins, yellow pages, direct mail, and the Internet. Finally, I am inviting you to join the Millionaire Club, where I will coach you. You will learn and master time-tested strategies to develop an effective marketing plan.

ADVERTISING

You need to advertise your business. Please, do not confuse advertising with marketing. Advertising is a paid campaign involving the use of different mass-media tools; by contrast, marketing is the use of personal and promotional approaches to create awareness about the existence of your products in the marketplace. Good examples of advertising comprise of the following: newspapers, magazines, television, and the Internet. Marketing may take the forms of personal selling, emails, phone calls, direct-mail letters, and public relations. Much of my business success is attributable to the effective use of low-cost advertising. My advertising campaign always resembles guerrilla warfare.

I set my goals and a small budget; I identify my emotional appeal to my prospects or customers; I write my advertising copy by paying attention to the acronym AIDA: attention, interest, desire, and action.; I choose the media where I will advertise my products and services; I set the time schedule my advertising will run; and I run the advertising and track its effectiveness weekly. I use advertising for three purposes: to inform, to persuade, and to remind. My primary goal of using advertising is to inform prospective customers that I have a product or service for sale. My secondary goal of using advertising is to persuade the prospect to choose my services or products over those of my competitors. My tertiary goal of using advertising is to remind customers that I am still in business, and I am ready to serve them. People are too busy to remember all the time that you are still in business. Hence, it makes sense for you to remind them constantly of your presence.

SALES, SALES, SALES

It is the sale, stupid! That is what business success is all about. You can be a technical guy, but you cannot succeed in business if you do not know how to sell your product or service. Take the example of Apple, Inc. In the old days, Steve Wozniak was the guy who built the computers, but it took the sales genius of Steve Jobs in order for Apple Computer to make it into the big time. If you are wondering how to sell your product or service, please, adhere to the following four steps:

1—Greet your prospective customer warmly and enthusiastically.
2—Present the benefits of the service or product informatively.
3—Close the sale artfully and persuasively.
4—Congratulate the customer for doing business with you.

ANATOMY OF A SALE

Most people do not like selling things. In fact, that is why there are relatively fewer salespersons in the world. Although, generally, sales positions offer more generous compensation benefits than other job positions, most people still shy away from sales jobs because they acclimated to the security of a weekly paycheck.

If at all they have to accept a full-time sales position, they always require their new employer to pamper them with the diapers of a weekly pay that is as much as the regular pay of an employee in another department. Today, I am going to teach you the dynamics of selling, that is, the art, science, and philosophy of making the sales deal. Selling a product or a service is a psychological process of communication involving qualification, rapport, education or information, and the close. I am going to show you how I use the anatomy of a sale in my insurance business.

My first marketing task is qualification. I begin by asking questions and using mental notes to address the questions with an answer: Is the prospect qualified to be my customer? Ceteris paribus, do they have the money to buy what I am selling? It is inadequate for a sales prospect to want something without the ability to demand it. If wishes were horses, then, beggars would ride. I use questions to engage sales prospects in a game of elimination. For instance, I have had much success selling a life insurance product called IRS Code Section 79 because I am always at great pains to qualify my prospect. In the beginning, I make sure the sales prospect owns a small business, or he or she is amenable to the idea of spending money to create a new C corporation.

Because I am worried about customer chargebacks, I encourage most of my clients to sign a contract and pay for their first annual premium in full, as opposed to making small monthly payments. After the sales prospect passes the qualification test, I proceed to the second phase of establishing rapport. By borrowing and implementing the neuro-linguistic programming techniques of mirroring and mutual identification, I always succeed in building rapport with my prospective customer. I use verbal cues to imitate the language of the prospect; I imitate the posturing and sitting positions of the sales prospect. In the long run, I hypnotize the prospect to feel and think that we are a pair of similar characters who could be friends; I identify with him or her, and he or she ends up sharing my values.

There is more to personal finance than the drudgery of debts and budgets.

After I succeed in building rapport with the prospect, I spend time to educate them on the tangible and intangible benefits of the life insurance product I am selling; I try as much as possible not to appear professorial to the customer; after studying the prospect, I look for emotional triggers that would persuade him or her to say yes to me. Finally, I close the sale by presenting a compelling argument that the prospect can relate to 100%.

CHANNELS OF DISTRIBUTION

Normally, there are at least four channels of distribution of a product or service:

1. Manufacturer to consumer
2. Manufacturer to retailer and then to consumer
3. Manufacturer to wholesaler to retailer to consumer
4. Manufacturer to wholesaler to wholesaler to retailer to consumer

PRODUCT LIFECYCLE

If you are going to be a great marketer, you better start imbuing your product with the characteristics of biology. Like a living organism such as an amoeba, a commercial product generally goes through stages of life. Any living organism has a lifecycle, stages of life and death: introduction, growth, maturity, and decline. A product is in the introduction phase when it is newly launched into the market. Sales are rising, and customers are accepting and using the product. Growth, the second stage of the product, is marked by a period of extremely rapid sales expansion because of advertising, word of mouth, and referrals. Maturity denotes the stage where the product has peaked and aged. Sales growth is slowing down probably because of the new entry of competitors into the marketplace and the availability of substitute products. The decline phase is marked by the sales and profits of the product falling as the product is being edged out of the market by competitors.

FRANCHISING

To franchise, or not to franchise, that is the question? Why reinvent the wheel? If the system is not broken, why fix it? Entrepreneurship is not the sole path to business ownership. If you are not comfortable with the idea of being in business for yourself on your own terms, then, you may want to explore franchising. What is franchising? Franchising is the practice of starting a business by licensing the use of another firm's vaunted successful business model. The word franchise is of Anglo-French derivation - from franc - meaning free, and is used both as a noun and as a transitive verb. For the franchisor, the franchise is an alternative to building chain stores to distribute goods and services that avoids the investments and liability of a chain. The franchisor's success depends on the success of the franchisees. The franchisee is said to have a greater incentive than a direct employee because he or she has a direct stake in the business. Thirty three countries, including the United States, China, and Australia, have laws that explicitly regulate franchising, with the majority of all other countries having laws which have a direct or indirect impact on franchising.

The following U.S. listing tabulates the early 2010 ranking of major franchises along with the number of sub-franchisees or partners from data available for 2004. As can be seen from the names of the franchises, the USA is a leader in franchising, a position it has held since the 1930s when it used the approach for fast-food restaurants, food inns and, slightly later, motels at the time of the Great Depression. As of 2005, there were 909,253 established franchised businesses, generating $880.9 billion of output and accounting for 8.1 percent of all private, non-farm jobs. This amounts to 11 million jobs, and 4.4 percent of all private sector output. Below is a listing of the top ten franchises in America:

1. Subway (sandwiches and salads)
2. McDonald's (fast food)
3. 7-Eleven Inc. (convenience stores)
4. Hampton Inns & Suites (mid-price hotels)
5. Great Clips (hair salons)
6. H&R Block (tax preparation and now e-filing)
7. Dunkin' Donuts (donuts and breakfast)
8. Jani-King (commercial cleaning)
9. Servpro (insurance and disaster restoration and cleaning) |
10. MiniMarkets (convenience store and gas station)

Generally, the start-up fees of these franchises are prohibitive. If you do not have the money in the bank, it means you have to become a huge debtor again. By using the consulting services of the Prince Ojong organization, we can help you secure the market intelligence required to duplicate and replicate any franchise system in America without the risk of going broke by borrowing much money from the bank. By capitalizing on local demographics and psycho-graphical research and loopholes in the federal and franchise reporting systems, we can furnish you with the tools and knowledge you need to operate a new business service like a turn-key franchise outfit. You will feel like you are reading an espionage novel. Come and let us show you how we play dirty and little spy tricks on franchisors; by law, franchisors are required by Federal and state regulations to send franchise documents to prospective franchisees; we trade the places of new prospects and order these documents and turn the tables against franchisors. Do you want to know our business secrets? Then, join the Millionaire Club! If you do, we shall send you to our financial boot camp at Millionaire iUniversity, where you will learn all the secrets.

FRANCHISE KILLER APPLICATION

Beware of the Ides of franchises! Most of them are rip offs! Come to Millionaire iUniversity! We are the franchise killer application. We are the University of Hard Knocks, the MBA mint and the heart and soul of today's business. We offer you well-researched business plans; we are the playbook of millionaire success, the blueprint of good leadership. Good business involves you, the owner, employees, and your local community. Here is your prophetic breakthrough of financial education! Please, surrender to the will of God! Establish your faith in the Lord Jesus Christ. Stop wasting time negotiating corny contracts with the devil or Judas Iscariot. Sign the contract now with Prince Ojong, the apostle of Jesus Christ of Nazareth.

There is more to personal finance than the drudgery of debts and budgets.

LAUNCHING YOUR BUSINESS ENTERPRISE

Are you ready to launch your own business enterprise? Even if you have much startup capital, my advice would be for you to start small. After you have tested your entrepreneurial skills, you could spread your wings and fly like a bird in the blue sky. Running a business is analogous to learning how to drive an automobile. It takes practice for a while in order for you to become proficient. Allow yourself time to make mistakes; learn from your mistakes and the mistakes of others.

Remember, the most successful computer entrepreneurs started their business in a garage. Do you remember Hewlett Packard? Who is the maker of the best laser printer in the world? For your information, it was started in a garage. I told you I started my business part-time in my apartment on a dining table I shared with my junior sister. Start your business on a part-time basis, that is, while you continue doing what you are already doing. You will know when to quit your full-time job and spend all your time running your new business venture on a full-time basis. You will also know when the time is right for you to expand your business. If you can avoid it, please, do not get an SBA (Small Business Administration) loan! Do not worry about buying a franchise. I know many friends who bought franchisees and their businesses did not pan out. I will not call names. These friends had assumed that the mere idea of buying a big-name franchise was tantamount to financial success. They were wrong, absolutely. Many franchisors are serious about running veritable business operations, but some franchisors play games with the US government and franchisees. In fact, these franchisors know that their business systems are either overvalued or impractical. Yet, they dumb their worthless ware on unsuspecting franchisees. I am sorry to tell the truth that some franchises are scams. Beware of scams!

I am warning you: do not get involved with Zeek Rewards or multi-level marketing businesses. Always do your diligent homework! Needs assessment is the origin of a new business. The purpose of a business is to fill a need or want that heretofore is unfilled or unmet in the marketplace. Look around you. Drive around your local area. What do you see? You can turn your hobby into a business. According to me, selecting a good business means matching your business idea or vision with needs, questions and answers, problems and solutions, skills and abilities, hobbies and personality traits, values, dreams, and your passions. Show your passions.

Finally, when you start your business, let your employees know that you are a passionate big boss. Use your feelings and emotions to inspire them. Show them that you care about them. Build a tribe of loyal followers who are passionate about your business enterprise; be the next Steve Jobs. Treat people nicely, that is, the way you would like them to treat you. In this wise, establish an employee business model based on biblical principles and entrepreneurship. Use the knowledge you obtain from this book to teach your employees how to achieve and live the American dream. Teach them financial literacy and the principles of business operations. Be fair in managing your employees. If you are nice to them, they will be nice to you and your customers; as a result, your business will prosper. Accept your employees as champions, teachers, leaders, partners, associates, or members of your dream team. Let employees contribute to the team.

BECOME AN ENTREPRENEURIAL LEADER

Your dreams are closer than you think, so act now to make your dreams come true. As your business thrives, my advice is for you to become an entrepreneurial business leader. Manage your business enterprise with the spirit of an entrepreneur: courageous, creative, determined, driven, good work ethic, impulsive, maverick, motivated, passionate, quick learner, quick action, risk taker, unconventional, and visionary. Like charismatic leaders, use the power of persuasion. Like the good old doctor, believe in the provision of excellent service to your fellow man or woman. Like Jesus Christ washing the feet of his disciples, show humility and simplicity to your customers and business associates or employees. Believe in hard work. Think big! Demonstrate the magic of thinking big to your employees. Show them that they can become what they think and dream about every day. If you aim very high, you will hit what you aim at. If you aim at nothing, you will hit nothing.

BUSINESS OPPORTUNITY GALORE

Come to Prince Ojong! Hearty welcome to Prince Ojong's business opportunity! If you have been searching for the perfect business opportunity, then, you have come to the right place. Feel free to take a good look at Millionaire Club, an ideal money-making system that gives you the opportunity to establish your own business without a lot of money or connections. You can set your own hours; you do not have to worry about employees and payroll; you are free to market all over the world without territorial restrictions; your earning potential is dependent upon your own abilities. In a word, hearty welcome to the easiest and simplest business to start today. Here is a chance for you to leverage your potential and open a business of your dreams.

Are you experiencing many difficulties? Are you having money problems? Are you still running the rat race of survival living from paycheck to paycheck? I, Prince Ojong, can help you now! Stop! Stop suffering in silence! Come to me, Prince Ojong. I am waiting anxiously for you: Come to me, all you who are weary and burdened, and I will give you financial peace and rest. There are financial solutions here, so come to my financial paradise. You do not have to be a victim of financial circumstances; let Prince Ojong show you how to be the master of your personal finances. With Prince Ojong, many solutions are possible. With ordinary men and women things are impossible, but with God's son, all things are possible. You see, Prince Ojong is the pope of the American Dream; his detractors dismiss him as a modern day Robin Hood of personal finance. Prince Ojong is a wonderful boy. He wants to be your financial savior. This guy can turn you green with envy or just turn you off. Prince Ojong is the name! Playing and winning the money game is the game! My mission is to help you live the American Dream. I want to help you identify and resolve critical personal financial matters that you have not yet addressed and of which you may not even be aware.

My financial roots in America date back to 1988, when the untimely loss of my father and the need to assist my mother and sisters forced me to start an apartment-based tutoring, research, and word-processing service business. Later, I experimented successfully with the ideas of electronic medical billing and IRS electronic tax filing and refund anticipation loans. Afterward, I bought my first home in 1997 and set my sights on Wall Street and electronic stock trading.

There is more to personal finance than the drudgery of debts and budgets.

When I began a revolutionary crusade to transform the real-estate industry, little did I know that I would soon smell the sweet scent of millionaire financial victory. Then insurance became the crown jewel in my financial arsenal. In African immigrant communities all across the USA, I, Prince Ojong, popularized the terms millionaire and millionaire club.

THE OPPORTUNITY

Knock on the door of financial opportunity. Ask and it will be given to you; seek and you will find; knock and the door will be opened to you. Change your life! Come and build your future with me! A historic shift is taking place in the business world today. More than ever, people are striking out on their own and starting their own businesses. The old idea of working a 9-to-5 job until you are age 65 is out and a new age, the age of the entrepreneur, is dawning. Will you be there? With the assistance of Prince Ojong you can be there in a hurry! Prince Ojong is calling all the angels and dreamers in America!

Be your own boss! Work on YOUR schedule! Own your own business! Earn unlimited income! Best of all, you do not have to quit your full-time job. The Millionaire Club's part-time business option allows you to continue bringing home a steady paycheck while earning extra cash part-time. Let me show you a better way to do business. At the Prince Ojong organization, you are in business FOR yourself but not BY yourself. I provide all the support and training you need! Plus, you have the freedom and flexibility to build your business with your own style. You can make a change in your own life while helping other people change their lives. Tell me. What could be better than that?

Join the Millionaire Club and start your business today! As a Prince Ojong representative, you will offer families real solutions to their financial problems. You will feel great about what you do. In addition, you will have a flexible business opportunity that allows you to work as your schedule allows. As my personal example shows, you do not need a background in financial services to become successful financially. I am an English major; I have never taken a college course on either accounting or finance. Yet, I am cruising to success. I am offering you a turn-key system to help you learn the business and succeed:

1. No large capital investment required
2. No inventory to maintain
3. Unlimited territory — we never restrict your market[1]
4. Comprehensive training, marketing and operations support
5. Start your business part-time[2]
6. No business experience or degree required
7. Earn income while you learn
8. You can OWN your business

I am offering you real life success. All the people you see with me today started with a dream, and they have changed their lives in the process. What about you? The Prince Ojong organization is a dream factory, a place where, with hard work, anyone can make their dreams come true. The people you see with me were very hungry. They wanted to succeed financially. I could see the fire of hunger in their eyes. When they discovered me, they decided to go for it. Today, with much money in the bank, they have the kind of freedom that they never dreamed possible. What about you? With commitment and hard work, so can you be like them. Long live Prince Ojong!

BUSINESS STEPS

As the writing of a business plan reveals, there are four steps to starting a business: ideation, assessment, implementation, and iteration. Ideation refers to the process of conceptualizing an idea (need or want) that answers a question or solves a problem in the marketplace. Assessment pertains to the research of the feasibility of the market question, problem, or idea intended to be solved by stressing significant trends, market size, impact areas, window of opportunity, growth rates, and resources. Implementation is the process of rolling out the prototype of the product or service. Iteration is the critical review of the business model for congruence with the competition and market. Why do most entrepreneurs fail? They do not spend an adequate amount of time planning the launch of their business; by planning your business startup, you immediately put the odds in your favor.

EXPERIMENT TO ACQUIRE ENTREPRENEURIAL SKILLS

A CAPITALIST THOU SHALL BE! Capitalism is a system of private enterprise that believes in the employment of capital with other factors of production to produce unlimited profits. I am motivating you to MIND YOUR OWN BUSINESS; I want you to be like me; model rich people; rich people do not work for the CORPORATION; they OWN the corporation; they are employers who control their own destiny; they are self-reliant; rich people are entrepreneurial; they take risks; they learn to make up their mind decisively; take advantage of opportunity when it knocks By contrast, poor people enjoy working as slaves for the corporation. Reminiscent of the system of chattel slavery in the Old South, poor people are afraid of what they perceive to be the nightmare of freedom. The dramatic irony is that they complain daily that they dislike their jobs and they hate rich people for no good reason. No! No! No! You do not want to be like them.

Why did I become an entrepreneur in America? As my story relates, I was responding to the reality of living in a capitalist environment. After living in America for three years, it dawned upon me that the best way to survive in the U.S.A. was to become an entrepreneur. Indeed, in my mind, entrepreneurship offered the surest way to the American dream of success. I was a wage slave. Entrepreneurship represented the noble act of buying my freedom. I was born an African prince, so I did not want to be a slave of wages. I wanted the unfettered opportunity to determine my own destiny in the U.S.A. Certainly, it was a risk, but I have made a career in life by taking calculated risks. It all started from childhood. In fact, the decision to come to America was a risk. As I have made it abundantly clear already, I had perceived coming to America as an experiment. I had made the calculation that the United States was the only country on earth that offered the opportunity for me to realize my fullest human potential as an individual. By coming here, I was testing the idea whether an African with no connections can survive or endure in the nation built on the ideal of freedom. I must confess that prior to coming to America, I had spent at least two days a week at the American cultural center in Yaounde. It may sound funny today.

There is more to personal finance than the drudgery of debts and budgets.

If I was not thumping through many volumes of books in the air-conditioned and clinically clean library, I was watching American films such as Alex P. Haley's *Roots*, Richard Wright's *Almost a Man*, or Lorraine Hansberry's *A Raisin in the Sun*. Another favorite activity of mine was the pastime of watching video casts of current US news and world reports from the CBS television channel. Once again, I would like to give special thanks to Dr. George Hagerty, a US Fulbright professor. He had inspired me to dream BIG of America.

TEN-QUESTIONS TEST

Are you ready to become a do-it-yourself, super entrepreneur? What does the label millionaire superstar sound like? Good, right? While there is no single entrepreneurial archetype, there are certain character traits that indicate an entrepreneurial personality. If you have ever wondered whether or not you have what it takes to be an entrepreneur, here is your chance to find out.

Take the following test consisting of ten simple questions:

1. Do you enjoy selling new ideas to your friends and family members?   YES/NO
2. Do you cherish working independently?   YES/NO
3. Do you have the capability to multitask?   YES/NO
4. Do you often find more than one solution to a problem?   YES/NO
5. Do you think you are smarter than most of your bosses?   YES/NO
6. Do you have an interest in working long hours?   YES/NO
7. Do you have a discovered God-given talent or skill?   YES/NO
8. Do you like life-long learning?   YES/NO
9. Do you exhibit persistent behavior?   YES/NO
10. Do you feel you have the power to shape your destiny?   YES/NO

The correct answer to each question is YES. If you get 7 or more questions correctly, then, you fit the entrepreneurial profile. You are creative, bold, and independent. You are willing to work hard in return for being personally and financially rewarded for your efforts. Congratulations! By being self-motivated and determined, you are now ready to get on the good foot of private business enterprise. However, if you answered less than 7 correctly, you are more of a team player or a manager of the corporation. You do not savor the relationship of owning your own business.

DREAMS AND MORE ENTREPRENEURIAL TESTING

I want to test you some more. On my web site are more questions for you to answer. Your answers will help me know how to tailor a personal-finance solution germane to your unique circumstances. I want you to photocopy the pages containing the questions and your answers. Fax them to me using the number I have provided below: (240) 241-5137. Please, include your name, email address, and phone number, so that I can contact you. Menawhile I want to encourage you to live your dreams today; you might reach for the stars. America is still the land opportunities. Do not listen to naysayers! Dare to dream the American Dream. Dr. Martin Luther King, jr, had a dream; I had a dream; you have the right to have a dream, too.

Step 8

DECODE THE IRS TAX CODES

"Only two things in life are certain -- death and taxes."
Benjamin Franklin

TAX SECRETS OF THE RICH AND FAMOUS

There is more to personal finance than the drudgery of debts and budgets.

In this chapter, I will dissect and simplify the superstructure of America's income taxes. You will discover how the rich and famous use their knowledge of the US taxation system to pay zero or lower taxes legally and how you can do it, too! When I came to America back in 1983, I was taken aback by the sight of newspapers and magazines emblazoning the topic of income tax with joyful abandon. In retrospect, during the American colonial period, Benjamin Franklin, an eminent patriot who used his many talents to become a wealthy man, famously said that the only things certain in life were death and taxes. Today, nevertheless, Governor Willard Mitt Romney's 2012 presidential candidacy has reinvigorated the age-old debate over the burden of taxation and income tax fairness. Shy and scared of rerunning for the presidency on either Barack Obama's record performance since his ascendancy into the White House, or on his positive YES WE CAN MANTRA, the Barack Obama campaign has settled desperately and successfully on the kitchen sink strategy of lynching his opponent in public and reminding Americans that Governor Willard Mitt Romney was unqualified to be president of the USA; as President Barack Obama argued incessantly, like the refrain of a sad song, Governor Willard Mitt Romney belonged to the class of the rich and famous. So the latter must be punished for the success of leveraging the knowledge of the US taxation system to pay zero or lower taxes legally.

In this wise, Bain Capital, a wildly profitable franchise founded by Governor Willard Mitt Romney, became the albatross of President Barack Obama's negative campaigning. Wake up folks! We are not living in the USSR; we are still living and working in the good old USA. Whatever happened to the American Dream? Do not allow self-serving politicians brainwash you to become jealous of rich folks in America. The rich are not responsible for the calamity of the middle class. We do not need class warfare in the USA; keep it in the USSR or Russia! If you really want it, you can become rich in America, too. The rich are not different from you and me; the only way the rich are different from you and me is that they apply the principles of $ucce$$tology to their daily lives; they run their personal finances like a corporate behemoth such as IBM or Microsoft. If, like Governor Willard Mitt Romney, they cannot prepare their own income tax returns, they are smart enough to hire professionals to assist them in this effort. In regard to taxes, please, do no worry about millionaires and billionaires; they have the resources to take care of their interests; in fact, as far as playing and winning the money game is concerned, they are always many steps ahead of the average Joe Six Pack. Romney, for instance, has not committed any crime; rather, the democrats are chastising him for doing the right thing. Hence, it behooves you to acquire the tax knowledge that they already possess. Do not envy the rich folks, like Romney, whose tax rate is less than 14%.

Corporate taxes today are at a 40-year-low, even as the executive suites at big corporations have become throne rooms where the crown jewels wind up in the personal vault of the CEO. The American taxation system is a complex superstructure, but why envy Governor Willard Mitt Romney for doing a good job of keeping abreast with implementing tax strategies? Why is he to blame for conveniently capitalizing on loopholes and overseas investment and governments that conveniently look the other way? Similarly, in a story headlined "*For Big Companies, Life Is Good,*" the WALL STREET JOURNAL reports that big American companies have emerged from the deepest recession since World War II more profitable than ever: flush with cash, less burdened by debt, and with a greater share of the country's income.

But, the newspaper notes, "Many of the 1.1 million jobs the big companies added since 2007 were outside the U.S. So, too, was much of the $1.2 trillion added to corporate treasuries." Is it true that Warren Buffett pays less taxes than his secretary? So is this Governor Willard Mitt Romney's fault? Save the drama of the embarrassment of riches to hypocritical democrats. Who are they fooling? They are deceiving the gullible group of individuals who are a slave to skin color and chattel slavery. Interestingly, an examination of President Obama's 2011 and 2010 taxes show that his adjusted gross income (AGI) of 2012 will almost cross the millionaire income line. The fact is that while most of President Obama's cheerleaders are clapping for him, he is busy making his ascent into the orbit of millionaire space. His life will never be ordinary again; after he leaves the White House, he stands to begin making an obscene amount of money every year. In fact, he has the potential to overtake Romney. Who says politics and public service do not pay well? In America career politics pays huge dividends. Democracy is on sale.

WHAT IS TAXATION?

To tax is a Latin word for "to estimate," that is, to impose a financial charge or other levy upon a taxpayer, an individual, or legal entity, by a state or the functional equivalent of a state such that failure to pay is punishable by law. Taxes are also imposed by many administrative divisions. A tax may be defined as a pecuniary burden laid upon individuals or property owners to support the government; it is a payment exacted by legislative authority. A tax is not a voluntary payment or donation, but an enforced contribution, exacted pursuant to legislative authority and is any contribution imposed by government, whether under the name of toll, tribute, tillage, impost, duty, custom, excise, subsidy, aid, supply, or other name. Taxation, therefore, is the act or principle of levying taxes on an individual, business, or corporate entity, or the condition of being taxed.

DIRECT AND INDIRECT

Taxes consist of direct tax or indirect tax, and may be paid in money or as its labor equivalent (often but not always unpaid labor). Taxes are sometimes referred to as direct taxes or indirect taxes. The meaning of these terms can vary in different contexts, which can sometimes lead to confusion. An economic definition states that direct taxes may be adjusted to the individual characteristics of the taxpayer, whereas indirect taxes are levied on transactions irrespective of the circumstances of buyer or seller. According to this definition, for example, income tax is direct, and sales tax is indirect. In law, the terms may have different meanings. In U.S. constitutional law, for instance, direct taxes refer to poll taxes and property taxes, which are based on simple existence or ownership. Indirect taxes are imposed on events, rights, privileges, and activities. Thus, a tax on the sale of property would be considered an indirect tax, whereas the tax on simply owning the property itself would be a direct tax.

PRINCIPLES OF TAXATION

Most governments collect funds from different sources to provide public services or to finance transfer payments. Of all the methods of raising resources, taxation constitutes the most important one in mixed economies.

THEORIES OF TAXATION

These are two theories of taxation: the benefit theory and the ability theory.

THE BENEFIT THEORY

The benefit theory of taxation has two merits. First, it is considered fair. The beneficiaries of government expenditure pay proportionately for these benefits through taxation. Second, the benefit approach determines simultaneously the tax levels and public services of different governments

THE ABILITY THEORY

The most important principle of taxation is the ability-to-pay approach, which treats revenue and expenditure of the government separately. In this case, taxes are imposed on the basis of tax payers' ability to pay. The ability to pay principle is conceived in terms of sacrifice on the part of the taxpayers.

The questions in this regard are: what should be the sacrifice of each taxpayer and how should this sacrifice be measured? This sacrifice is the argument of the Obama campaign of 2012, which involves the rich being taxed more heavily than the poor. Equal marginal sacrifice implies that the rich should sacrifice a greater proportion of their utility. The person with higher income will bear the most burdens. This rule recommends that taxes should be raised in such a manner that after tax everyone has the same income.

TAX RATES

Taxes are most often levied as a percentage, called the tax rate. An important distinction when talking about tax rates is to distinguish between the marginal rate and the effective (average) rate. The effective rate is the total tax paid divided by the total amount the tax is paid on, while the marginal rate is the rate paid on the next dollar of income earned. There are six income tax rates in place for the 2012 tax year: 10%, 15%, 25%, 28%, 33%, and 35%. A taxpayer's tax rate is a function of his or her income tax filing status and amount of yearly income.

PURPOSE AND EFFECTS OF TAXATION

Money provided by taxation has been used by governments and their functional equivalents throughout history to carry out many functions: war, the enforcement of law and public order, protection of property, economic infrastructure (roads, legal tender, enforcement of contracts, etcetera), public works, social engineering, and the operation of government itself. Governments also use taxes to fund welfare and public services. A portion of taxes also go to pay off the state's debt and the interest this debt accumulates. These services can include education systems, health care systems, pensions for the elderly, unemployment benefits, and public transportation.

PROPORTIONAL, PROGRESSIVE, REGRESSIVE, AND LUMP-SUM TAXES

An important feature of tax systems is the percentage of the tax burden as it relates to income or consumption. The terms progressive, regressive, and proportional are used to describe the way the rate progresses from low to high, from high to low, or proportionally. The terms describe a distribution effect, which can be applied to any type of tax system (income or consumption) that meets the definition.

PROGRESSIVE TAX

A progressive tax is a tax imposed so that the effective tax rate increases as the amount to which the rate is applied increases.

REGRESSIVE TAX

The opposite of a progressive tax is a regressive tax, where the effective tax rate decreases as the amount to which the rate is applied increases.

PROPORTIONAL TAX

In between the progressive and regressive tax is a proportional tax, where the effective tax rate is fixed, while the amount to which the rate is applied increases. For instance, taxpayers are levied in proportion to their income: fraction, section, percentage, share, part, quantity, and amount.

LUMP SUM TAX

A lump-sum tax is a tax that is a fixed amount, no matter the change in circumstance of the taxed entity.

GENERALITIES OF TAXATION

Many jurisdictions tax the income of individuals and business entities, including corporations. Generally the tax is imposed on net profits from business, net gains, and other income. Computation of income subject to tax may be determined under accounting principles used in the jurisdiction, which may be modified or replaced by tax law principles in the jurisdiction. The incidence of taxation varies by system, and some systems may be viewed as progressive or regressive. Rates of tax may vary or be constant (flat) by income level. Many systems allow individuals certain personal allowances and other nonbusiness reductions to taxable income. Personal income tax is often collected on a pay-as-you-earn basis, with small corrections made soon after the end of the tax year. These corrections take one of two forms: payments to the government, for taxpayers who have not paid enough during the tax year; and tax refunds from the government for those who have overpaid. Income tax systems will often have standard and itemized deductions available that lessen the total tax liability by reducing total taxable income. They may allow losses from one type of income to be counted against another. For example, a loss on the stock market may be deducted against taxes paid on wages.

INCIDENCE OF TAXATION

The incidence of taxation refers to the recognition of the entity that bears the burden of taxation. The theory of tax incidence has a number of practical results. For example, the United States' Social Security payroll taxes are 6.2%, paid half by the employee and half by the employer. However, I think that the worker is bearing almost the entire burden of the tax because the employer passes the tax on in the form of lower wages. The tax incidence is thus said to fall on the employee. This is what economists define as a shift in the incidence of taxation. The employer shifts the burden of taxation to the employee.

TAXATION USA

The nation had few taxes in its early history. The American economy during the revolutionary period was mostly agrarian. From 1791 to 1802, the United States government was supported by internal taxes on distilled spirits, carriages, refined sugar, tobacco and snuff, property sold at auction, corporate bonds, and slaves. The high cost of the War of 1812 brought about the nation's first sales taxes on gold, silverware, jewelry, and watches. In 1817, however, Congress eliminated all internal taxes, relying instead on tariffs on imported goods to provide sufficient funds for running the government.

In 1862, to support the Civil War effort, Congress enacted the nation's first income tax law. It was a forerunner of our modern income tax system in that it was based on the principles of graduated or progressive taxation, and of withholding income at the source. Additional sales and excise taxes were added, and an inheritance tax also made its debut. In 1866, internal revenue collections reached their highest point in the nation's 90-year history. The Act of 1862 established the office of Commissioner of Internal Revenue. The Commissioner was given the power to assess, levy, and collect taxes, and the right to enforce the tax laws through seizure of property and income and through prosecution. The powers and authority remain very much the same today.

IDEA OF INCOME

What is income? The term denotes money that is derived by a taxpayer in a particular tax year. The US possesses an income tax system. As you will soon learn, income can be earned or unearned. While the income of employees can be described as earned, the income of rich folks like Romney is unearned. Yet, all income is presumed to be taxable, but America's tax laws provide that income is taxed in a variety of ways.

Wages, for example, are subject to several different types of tax rates. Dividends and capital gains, in contrast, may be taxed at a lower rate, and some income might be partially taxable or even non-taxable. The income of millionaires tends to be unearned; the income of working-class folks tends to be earned. As a bonus feature of *The Miraculous Millionaire*, upon request, I am ready to provide you with a comparative analysis of the tax returns of President Barack H. Obama and Governor Willard Mitt Romney; the analysis explains the difference between earned income and unearned income; it is a tax study in contrasts, but Obama is gaining ground fast.

RECOGNITION OF INCOME AND RELATED ISSUES

A major challenge to most US taxpayers is recognition of income. For those taxpayers who are at the bottom of the totem pole, income recognition is an easy affair; they work one or two jobs with no investments to show for it; in contrast, recognition of income is complicated for taxpayers who are working hard and acting smart about the manner in which they plan their personal finances. I want to highlight some sources of income:

INCENTIVE STOCK OPTIONS

Look at your income tax return. Do you have incentive stock options? If not, you should! Incentive stock options enjoy favorable tax treatment compared to other forms of employee compensation reported on the W2 form. Income from wage and salary income persons working as employees means the taxpayer receives compensation in the form of wages, salary, and/or tips. Compensation for an employee's labor is taxed partly to the employee and partly to the employer. There are at least four federal taxes imposed on wage and salary income, plus any state and local taxes. Income from incentive stock options is taxable for federal income tax (including the alternative minimum tax), but are not taxable for Social Security and Medicare taxes.

SELF-EMPLOYMENT INCOME

Self-employed persons incur three federal taxes on their earnings: federal income tax, Social Security tax, and Medicare tax. These taxes are imposed on net self-employed income, after various work-related expenses have been subtracted. State and city taxes, and various local business taxes may also apply. Most self-employment income of sole proprietorships is calculated on either IRS Schedule C-EZ or Schedule C; the result is transferred to IRS Form 1040. Self emloyment income of partnerships is reported on IRS Form 1065; the self employment income of corporations is calculated on IRS Form 1120C or 1120S.

COMMUNITY PROPERTY INCOME

As for filing income tax returns using the status of married filing separately, spouses living in community property states will need to follow state law to determine how much income to include on each spouse's separate federal tax return. There are some broad, general rules for determining community income, which must be split equally between the spouses, and for determining separate income.

IRS COMMUNITY PROPERTY RULES FOR GAY COUPLES

The IRS has released new guidance on allocating the community property of gay couples who are married or registered domestic partners. These new community property rules affect how same sex couples in three states prepare their federal tax returns and could reduce federal taxes for some gay couples. For more information, please, refer the web site of the Internal Revenue Service: http://www.irs.gov.

There is more to personal finance than the drudgery of debts and budgets.

TAX TREATMENT OF CREDIT CARD REWARDS AND FREQUENT FLYER MILES

Rewards and discounts issued by credit card companies and frequent flyer miles are not considered taxable income. However such rewards and discounts can reduce the cost of a tax-deductible expense.

CANCELED MORTGAGE DEBT AND TAXES

Normally, debt that is forgiven or canceled by a lender is considered taxable income to the debtor. But there are exceptions in the case of mortgages under the Mortgage Forgiveness Debt Relief Act. Learn more about the exclusions for mortgage debt.

CANCELED DEBT AND MORTGAGE FORGIVENESS

With the debacle of the housing market of 2007 and the rise in foreclosures and short sales, IRS Form 1099 C has made a ubiquitous appearance on the income tax scene. Anytime a lender cancels, or forgives, your debt, that is considered income to the debtor. Canceled debt on a main home may be tax-free, providing welcome tax relief to people who have lost their homes through foreclosure.

WAGE AND SALARIES

Wage information for the whole year is recorded on the W-2 tax form. Wages and salaries are reported on Form 1040 Line 7. I teach how to read your Form W-2 Wage and tax statement at my seminar and workshop. Some backstreet income tax preparers do not know how to interpret codes on IRS Form W2. If you have not yet received your W-2 form by January 31, 2013, please, report your employer to the IRS: 1-800-829-1040.

INTEREST INCOME AND THE REPORTING OF INTEREST AND TAX-EXEMPT INTEREST

Interest income from banks, money market funds, and tax-exempt bonds are reported on your tax return. Later, I will show you how to report your interest income on Form 1040 Line 8.

DIVIDEND INCOME AND THE REPORTING OF DIVIDENDS AND QUALIFIED DIVIDENDS

Dividends from stocks and mutual funds are reported on your tax return. Fill out Schedule B; the amounts of ordinary dividends go on Form 1040 Line 9a; and the amounts of qualified dividends go on Form 1040 Line 9b.

TAXABLE REFUNDS AND FIGURING THE TAXABLE PORTION OF STATE TAX REFUNDS

Generally, for most low-income taxpayers, if they itemize their deductions, you report their last year's state tax refund on this year's tax return on Form 1040 Line 10. When you are in doubt, please, use the worksheet to do your calculations. Taxcut or Turbo Tax software can come to your rescue here.

ALIMONY RECEIVED AND TAX REPORTING

Report the full amount of alimony, or separate maintenance, you received in 2012. However, do not report any amounts you received for child support. Likewise, your ex-spouse must report alimony paid to you along with your social security number to the IRS.

BUSINESS INCOME REPORTING

Report business income or loss from self-employment on Form 1040 Line 12. When you come to my seminar and workshop, I will share many tips for reporting your net profit or loss from self-employment on Schedule C. The IRS is auditing many tax returns with a Schedule C. Be careful!

ORDINARY GAINS / LOSSES

You report ordinary gains on Form 1040 line 14. Figure and report your ordinary gains and ordinary losses from the sale of business assets.

IRA DISTRIBUTIONS

You report IRA distributions on Form 1040 Line 15. I will share many tips for figuring and reporting non-taxable and taxable Individual Retirement Account distributions, withdrawals, and rollovers.

IRA WITHDRAWALS

A distribution is synonymous with a cash withdrawal. You report IRA withdrawals on Form 1040 Line 15. There are many tricks in figuring out and reporting non-taxable and taxable Individual Retirement Account withdrawals, distributions, and rollovers.

PENSIONS AND ANNUITIES REPORTING

Reporting the taxable portion of pension and annuity income can get a little tricky. When do you use the simplified method? When must you use the general rule? The secret key is to pay attention to the contents of Form 1099-R. What is the distribution code in box 7? The code should shed light on the appropriate tax treatment.

RENTAL INCOME AND LOSS

Rental income and loss goes on Form 1040 Schedule E. The key to mastering the Schedule E is to organize your income and expenses using a spreadsheet like Microsoft Excel or personal finance software such as Intuit's Quicken. Better still, there is the QuickBooks application for those who are serious about managing their rental activities like a business. In reality, in my tax preparation and consulting experience, I have observed that clients who keep detailed summaries of their rental property expenses are the ones who benefit most at tax time from the generous tax rules regarding rental income.

S-CORPORATION PROFITS

What about reporting 1120S Schedule K-1 income? Shareholders receiving a Schedule K-1 must report the amounts on IRS Form 1040 Schedule E, page 2. Generally speaking, ordinary net business income or loss is reported on Schedule E. Other income items are reported in the appropriate part of the 1040 tax return.

PARTNERSHIP INCOME

Partners receiving a Schedule K-1 must report the amounts on IRS Form 1040 Schedule E, page 2. Generally speaking, ordinary net business income or loss is reported on Schedule E. Other income items are reported in the appropriate part of the 1040 tax return.

FARM INCOME

Farmers report their net profit or loss from farming on IRS Form 1040 Schedule F. This form reports income and expenses for self-employed farmers. Tax tips for farmers can be gleaned from links to essential IRS resources: http://www.irs.gov.

UNEMPLOYMENT COMPENSATION

Back in 1986, unemployment compensation was exempt from income taxation. That is not the case today, so report unemployment compensation as taxable income on Form 1040, 1040A, or 1040EZ.

SOCIAL SECURITY BENEFITS

Social Security benefits are taxed depending on your total income from all other sources. I will show you how to calculate how much of your Social Security benefits are taxable. You can rely on Taxcut software or Turbo Tax software. Both applications have been designed for the tax novice. Yet, an income tax professional can use these programs to review the content of new changes in US tax laws. At the beginning of every income tax season, I buy both applications for my tax preparation business; I like to know what do-it-yourself taxpayers using.

FOREIGN INCOME

Did you work abroad? Did you invest money in a foreign country? Switzerland? Cayman Islands? Please, do not forget to report foreign unearned and earned income and wages on IRS Form 2555.

OTHER INCOME

Generally, I prefer not to use the other-income section of Form 1040 to report prizes, awards, gambling winnings, jury duty, and other income; I prefer the use of Schedules A and C; it seems the IRS also manifests this preference.

TAXABLE OR NON-TAXABLE INCOME

Generally, income may be taxable or non-taxable. An item is taxable when it is subjected to taxation. Income, food, property, and merchandise are some examples of items that are considered taxable. A governing agency usually determines the percentage of taxes that need to be paid on a specific item or service. By contrast, non-taxable means an item, such as cash-value life insurance, is not subjected to taxation.

TAXABLE INCOME

Taxable income refers to the base upon which an income tax system imposes tax. Generally, it includes some or all items of income and is reduced by expenses and other deductions. The amounts included as income, expenses, and other deductions vary by country or system. Many systems provide that some types of income are not taxable and some expenditures not deductible in computing tax. Some systems base tax on taxable income of the current period, and some on prior periods. Taxable income may refer to the income of any taxpayer, including individuals and corporations, as well as entities that themselves do not pay tax, such as partnerships. Some systems allow tax deductions for certain non-business expenses. Such deductions may include personal expense items, such as a home mortgage interest deduction, and vary widely by jurisdiction. In addition, many systems allow deductions for personal allowances or a minimum deemed amount of personal deductions. The United States Federal system allows a deduction for personal exemptions, as well as a minimum standard deduction in lieu of other personal deductions. Some states in the United States allow few personal deductions. Generally, most income you receive is considered taxable, but there are situations when certain types of income are partially taxed or not taxed at all.

To help taxpayers understand the differences between taxable and non-taxable income, the Internal Revenue Service offers these common examples of items not included as taxable income:

--Adoption expense reimbursements for qualifying expenses
--Child support payments
--Gifts, bequests, and inheritances
--Workers' compensation benefits
--Meals and lodging for the convenience of your employer
--Compensatory damages awarded for physical injury or physical sickness
--Welfare benefits
--Cash rebates from a dealer or manufacturer

WARNING!

If you aspire to become a wealth builder, you must comprehend the dichotomy taxable and non-taxable income. Some income may be taxable under certain circumstances, but not taxable in other situations. Below are some examples of items that may or may not be included in your taxable income:

--Life insurance
If you surrender a life insurance policy for cash, you must include in income any proceeds that are more than the cost of the life insurance policy.

-- Life insurance proceeds, which were paid to you because of the insured person's death, are not taxable unless the policy was turned over to you for a price.

--Scholarship, fellowship, or grant
 If you are a candidate for a degree, you can exclude amounts you receive as a qualified scholarship or fellowship. Amounts used for room and board do not qualify.

--Non-cash income
Taxable income may be in a form other than cash. One example of this is bartering, which is an exchange of property or services. The fair market value of goods and services exchanged is fully taxable and must be included as income on Form 1040 of both parties.

However, all other items—including income such as wages, salaries, tips, and unemployment compensation — are fully taxable and must be included in your income unless it is specifically excluded by law. I want to remind you that the examples stipulated above are not all-inclusive. For more information, see IRS Publication 525, Taxable and Nontaxable Income, which can be obtained at http://www.irs.gov or by calling the IRS at 800-TAX-FORM (800-829-3676).

TAX DEDUCTION

Most income tax systems, generally, allow a tax deduction, that is, a reduction of the income subject to tax, for various items, especially expenses incurred to produce income. Often these deductions are subject to limitations or conditions. Tax deductions, generally, are allowed only for expenses incurred that produce current benefits, and capitalization of items producing future benefit is required, sometimes with exceptions. Most systems allow recovery in some manner over a period of time of capitalized business and investment items, such as through allowances for depreciation, obsolescence, or decline in value. Many systems reduce taxable income for personal allowances or provide a range of income subject to zero tax. In addition, some systems allow deductions from the tax base for items the tax levying government desires to encourage. Some systems distinguish among types of deductions: business versus non-business deductions. If you are running a small business, you are allowed to deduct the majority of your expenses as business deductions; however, the deductiions of salaried employees are limited severely.

IDEA OF EXPENSES

In order for you to benefit from tax planning like the rich and famous folks, you need to understand the precise definition of expenses. Simply, expenses are the economic costs that a business incurs through its operations to earn revenue. To maximize profits, businesses must attempt to reduce expenses. Because expenses are such an important indicator of a business' operations, there are specific accounting rules on expense recognition, in addition to accrual and cash methods.

The expenses of an enterprise can be perceived to be money spent or costs incurred that are tax-deductible and taxable-income reducing. Expenses are the opposite of revenues. Examples of expenses include payments to suppliers, employee wages, factory leases and depreciation. An income tax authority, such as the IRS, has very specific regulations that allow taxpayers to deduct certain expenses if used for business-related activities.

For example, the IRS allows a traveling salesperson to deduct traveling expenses (fuel expenses and car rental costs) as a business deduction, because those costs are an integral part of the job. Nearly all jurisdictions that tax business income allow tax deductions for expenses incurred in trading or carrying on the trade or business. Technical details of the allowance vary, and may be very general for all expenses, or very specific in respect of certain expenses. The amount of particular deductions may be limited based on character or amount, or deductions in aggregate may be limited or reduced. To be deducted, the expenses must be incurred in furthering a business. Generally, a business includes only those activities undertaken for profit.

What constitutes a trade or business? A hobby is not a business. A hobby is an activity you engage in for pleasure or entertainment. It is possible, nevertheless, for your hobby to become a business. Generally, a business must be regular, continuous, substantial, and entered into with an expectation of profit. Expenses must be ordinary and necessary. What expenses are ordinary and necessary? The phrase deals with what expenses are appropriate to the nature of the business, whether the expenses are of the sort expected to help produce income and promote the business, and whether the expenses are not lavish and extravagant. Note that under this concept the same sorts of expenses are generally deductible by business entities and individuals carrying on a trade or business. To the extent such expenses relate to the employment of an individual and are not reimbursed by the employer, the amount may be deductible by the individual.

ACCOUNTING METHODS

One important aspect of determining tax deductions for business expenses is the timing of such deductions. The method used to account for these expenses is commonly referred to as an accounting method. Accounting methods, for tax purposes, may differ from applicable generally accepted accounting principles (GAAP). Some examples of the application of accounting methods include timing of recognition of cost recovery deductions (such as depreciation), current expensing of otherwise capitalizable costs of intangibles, and rules related to costs that should be treated as part of cost of goods not yet sold. Further, taxpayers often have choices among multiple accounting methods permissible under GAAP and tax rules. Examples include conventions for determining which goods have been sold (such as first-in-first-out, average cost, etcetera), whether or not to defer minor expenses producing benefit in the immediately succeeding period, etcetera.

DEPRECIATION AND AMORTIZATION

Many systems require that the cost of items likely to produce future benefits be capitalized. Examples include plant and equipment, fees related to acquisition of property, and costs of developing intangible assets (e.g., patentable inventions). These are called depreciation systems.

Such systems often allow a tax deduction for cost recovery in a future period. A common approach to such cost recovery is to allow a deduction for a portion of the cost ratably over some period of years. The U.S. tax system, for instance, refers to such a cost recovery deduction as depreciation for costs of tangible assets and as amortization for costs of intangible assets.

NON-BUSINESS EXPENSES

Some tax systems distinguish between an active trade or business and the holding of assets to produce income. In such systems, there may be additional limitations on the timing and nature of amounts that may be claimed as tax deductions. Many of the rules, including accounting methods and limits on deductions, that apply to business expenses also apply to income producing expenses.

LOSSES

Many tax systems allow a deduction for loss on sale, exchange, or abandonment of both business and non-business income producing assets. This deduction may be limited to gains from the same class of assets. In the U.S., a loss on non-business assets is considered a capital loss, and deduction of the loss is limited to capital gains. Also, in the U.S. a loss on the sale of the taxpayer's principal residence or other personal assets is not allowed as a deduction except to the extent due to casualty or theft.

PERSONAL DEDUCTIONS

Many jurisdictions allow certain classes of taxpayers to reduce taxable income for certain inherently personal items. A common such deduction is a fixed allowance for the taxpayer and certain family members or other persons supported by the taxpayer. The U.S., for example, allows such a deduction for personal exemptions for the taxpayer and certain members of the taxpayer's household. In addition, many jurisdictions allow reduction of taxable income for certain categories of expenses not incurred in connection with a business or investments. In the U.S. system, these (as well as certain business or investment expenses) are referred to as itemized deductions for individuals. These deductions include, for example, the following tax benefits for U.S. residents:

--Medical expenses (in excess of 7.5% of adjusted gross income)
--State and local income and property taxes
--Interest expense on certain home loans
--Gifts of money or property to qualifying charitable organizations
--Losses on non-income-producing property due to casualty or theft
--Contribution to certain retirement or health savings plans
--Certain educational expenses
--Job expenses and cerain miscellaneous expenses

The US tax systems provide that an individual may claim a tax deduction for personal payments that, upon payment, become taxable to another person, such as alimony. The US systems generally require, at a minimum, reporting of such amounts, and may require that withholding tax be applied to the payment.

IRS TAX COMMUNITIES

Taxes may be imposed on individuals (natural persons), business entities, estates, trusts, or other forms of organization. Taxes may be based on property, income, transactions, importation of goods, business activity, or a variety of factors, and are generally imposed on the type of taxpayer for whom such tax base is relevant. Thus, property taxes tend to be imposed on property owners. In addition, certain taxes, particularly income taxes, may be imposed on the members of organizations for the organization's activities. Thus, partners are taxed on the income of their partnership. With few exceptions, one level of government does not impose tax on another level of government or its instrumentalities. Below is a succinct presentation of the organization of IRS tax communities as presented on the web site of the US tax authority:

Individuals—the provision of tax information for individuals
Businesses-- the provision of tax information for businesses
Charities /Non-profits-- the provision of tax information for charities and non-profits.
Government entities-- the provision of tax information for governmental entities.
Tax professionals-- the provision of tax information for tax professionals
Retirement plans-- the provision of tax information for retirement plans.

TAX REDUCTION STRATEGIES

CASH-VALUE INSURANCE

In writing about tax reduction strategies, the millionaire money secret that has been hidden under the sun for many centuries, far away from the madding crowds of poor people in America, is cash-value life insurance optimized to capitalize on IRS MEC limits. While millionaires and billionaires on Wall Street are exploiting cash-value life insurance to create multi-generational wealth for themselves and their families, the poor Americans on Mean Street are still wallowing in the stupor of ignorance and financial illiteracy. You can use cash-value insurance, especially products of the equity indexed universal life variety, as a winning income tax reduction strategy in the form of private equity banking, employee benefits, loans, or cash withdrawals.

LOANS

Most universal life policies come with an option to take a loan on certain values associated with the policy. These loans require interest payments which are paid to the insurance company. The insurer charges interest on the loan because they are no longer able to receive any investment benefit from the money that has been loaned to you. Repayment of the loan principal is not required, but payment of the loan interest is required. If the loan interest is not paid, it will be deducted from the cash-value of the policy. If there is insufficient value in the insurance policy to cover interest, the policy will lapse.

Loans are not reported to any credit agency and payment or non-payment against them will not affect the policyholder's credit rating. If the policy has not become a modified endowment contract, the loans are withdrawn from the policy values as premium first and then any gain. Taking loans on universal life policies will affect the long-term viability of the plan. The cash-values removed by loan are no longer earning the interest expected, so the cash-values will not grow as expected. These distributions will shorten the life of the policy. Usually those loans will cause a greater than expected premium payment as well as interest payments. Outstanding loans will be deducted from the death benefit at the death of the insured.

WITHDRAWALS

If withdrawals are effectuated in accordance with IRS regulations, an equity indexed universal life policy can provide income that is tax-free. Withdrawals should not exceed the total premium payments made into the policy. Also, tax-free withdrawals can be made through internal policy loans offered by the insurance company, against any additional cash-value within the policy. This withdrawal can exceed policy premiums and still be taken 100% tax-free. If the policy is set up, funded, and distributed properly, according to IRS regulations, an equity-indexed universal life insurance policy will provide an investor with many years of tax-free income. This vehicle can significantly outperform traditional investments such as stocks, bonds, mutual funds, CDs or variable annuities that are placed in taxable and tax-deferred accounts such as an IRA, 401(K), or 403(b). Most universal life policies come with an option to withdraw cash-values rather than take a loan. The withdrawals are subject to contingent deferred sales charges and may also have additional fees disclosed in the contract. Withdrawals will permanently lower the death benefit of the contract at the time of the maturity. Once the amount of withdrawals has been calculated, the insurer reckons the result of subtracting the loan withdrawals from the death benefit.

Next, is the amount of gain paid to the insured's beneficiary, so it is possible to take a tax-free withdrawal from the cash values of the policy. This supposition assumes, however, that the policy is not a MEC, that is, modified endowment contract. Withdrawals are considered a material change and cause the policy to be tested for compliance with MEC limits and rules. If cash withdrawals from the policy are not managed well, in effect, the policy may become a MEC, and the insured could lose his or her tax advantages. Indeed, the real worth of cash-value life insurance to a taxpayer is the building of wealth in a tax-free environment. It is important to respect IRS rules and regulations. In preparing a new insurance policy for my clients, I spend much time to ensure that the policies are IRS compliant. I love obeying the laws of this great country of ours. You should, too.

COLLATERAL ASSIGNMENTS

Collateral assignments will often be placed on life insurance to guarantee the loan upon the death of debtor. If a collateral assignment is placed on life insurance, the assignee will receive any amount due to them before the beneficiary is paid. If there is more than one assignee, the assignees are paid based on date of the assignment, that is, the earlier assignment date gets paid before the later assignment date.

THE EDIFICE OF IRS TAXATION

The Internal Revenue Service, a division of the US Department of the Treasury, is responsible for administering the revenue laws of the United States of America. In fact, as a result of the needs for uniformity, compliance, and standardization, the American taxation system is a monolithic superstructure grafted on a complex architecture consisting of the following elements:

Form 1040—Individual
Form 1041—Fiduciary
Form 1065—Partnership
Form 1120C—C Corporation
Form 1120S—S Corporation
Form 5500—Employee benefit
Form 706—Estate tax
Form 709—Gift tax
Form 990—Exempt organization
Form 480.10—Puerto Rico Corporaciones
Form 480.20—Puerto Rico Sociedads
Form 482—Puerto Rico—Individual

Form 1040 deals with income taxes for individuals; Form 1041 consists of income taxes for fiduciaries; Form 1065 deals with income taxes for partnerships ; Form 1120C comprises of income taxes for C Corporations; A C-corporation refers to any corporation that, under United States federal income tax law, is taxed separately from its owners. A C-corporation is distinguished from an S-corporation, which generally is not taxed separately. Form 1120S is the income tax standard of an S or Sub Chapter S Corporation.

Most major companies, and many smaller companies, are treated as C-corporations for U.S. federal income tax purposes. Form 5500 consists of income taxes involving employee benefits. Form 706 deals with income tax for dead persons, estate tax; Form 709 pertains to income taxes comprising of gift taxes; Form 990 comprises of income taxes for non-profit or tax exempt organizations, such as 501 (C) (3) or 501 (C) (7).

PUERTO RICO TAXES

However, do not forget Puerto Rico. Officially, the Commonwealth of Puerto Rico is an unincorporated territory of the United States, located in the northeastern Caribbean, east of the Dominican Republic and west of both the United States Virgin Islands and the British Virgin Islands. Below are three income tax divisions of Puerto Rico:

480.10—Puerto Rico Corporaciones
480.20—Puerto Rico Sociedads
482—Puerto Rico—Individual

There is more to personal finance than the drudgery of debts and budgets.

ANATOMY OF FORM 1040

I want to demystify IRS Form 1040. It is beyond the scope of this book to dwell on the entire architecture of the American taxation system. However, I want you to punctuate the discussion on income tax reduction strategies with a thorough examination of the IRS Form 1040. Familiarity with the income tax form under review is important. Before I discuss the income tax reduction strategies favored by America's rich and famous, I want you to proceed to the IRS' web site and download one tax form: Form 1040. Although there are Forms 1040EZ and 1040A, I prefer to use Form 1040, the long income tax form exploited by America's millionaires and billionaires. I would like you to become familiar with this form. Why? It holds the secret treasures of income tax deductions, credits, shelters, and withholdings. For the purpose of simplicity, I shall draw your attention to each line and number of the IRS Form 1040.

Do you plan to itemize your deductions? Do you have many income adjustments? Do you owe, or have you paid, taxes in addition to your income taxes? Can you claim several tax credits? Then hearty welcome to Form 1040, the personal grandfather of all federal income tax returns. If this is the first time you have filed a 1040 instead of the shorter 1040A or 1040EZ forms, you will immediately see the differences. Do not be intimidated; Form 1040 is longer than Form 1040EZ and Form 1040A, but you will also find many similarities to the simpler forms, especially the Form 1040A. The good news I have for you is that the Form 1040 gives you more income tax saving opportunities than the other forms; read Form 1040 to reduce your income tax bill today.

Below is a line-by-line explanation of Form 1040. Are you ready to rock and roll? Hence, sharpen your pencils, and let us get to work. I am going to teach you the art of war. Have you been opportuned to read *The Art of War*? It is an ancient Chinese military treatise attributed to Sun Tzu, also referred to as "Sun Wu" and "Sunzi," a high-ranking military general, strategist and tactician, and it was believed to have been compiled during the late Spring and Autumn period or early Warring States period. The old rule of battle urges us to divide and conquer, so if we want to conquer IRS Form 1040, we must break it into many meaningful portions. IRS Form 1040 is a two-page form. I am going to enumerate the various sections of the form to you: Label, Filing status, Exemptions, Income, Adjusted gross income, Tax and Credits, Other taxes, Payments, Refund, Amount you owe, Third party designee, Sign here, and Paid preparer use only.

Let us begin by analyzing page one.

LABEL

At the top of page one is a mailing label. If you received a tax package from the IRS with a peel-off label, just stick it on here. If any of the information is incorrect, make the corrections, clearly and directly, on the label. If you did not receive a tax package from the IRS, then, fill in the information requested by hand, including your first name, middle initial and last name. Joint filers must each fill in this information.

Then add your home address, including ZIP code. Do not forget to write your social security number (numbers, for married couples) in the boxes provided at the upper right-hand corner of the Form 1040. Even if you are married and decided to file separately, you must enter your spouse's social security number or tax identification number underneath yours. Check to ensure your entry is correct. The Internal Revenue Service will not process a tax return that is missing a social security number. The missing or omission of a social security number could mean the payment of a penalty and interest by you.

You also get the chance to contribute $3 to the presidential election campaign fund. It does not matter if you, and your spouse, check YES or NO. The checking will not affect your tax liability either way.

FILING STATUS (LINES 1-5)

You are now at the filing status section of the Form 1040. There are five choices, one each on lines 1 through 5: single, married filing jointly, married filing separately, head of household, and qualifying widow or widower with a dependent child. Each choice has specific requirements and offers different tax advantages.

Also, the standard deduction amount for each filing status is different, as is the final tax due. Please, review your filing status and select the one that fits your needs and gives you the best tax result.

EXEMPTIONS (LINES 6A-6D)

Next, you start whittling away at your impending tax bill. The exemptions section of the Form 1040, line 6 and all its sub-lines below, lets the IRS know how many individuals depend on you for support. Technically, if your filing status is married filing jointly, then, your spouse is not your dependent.

But when you file your income taxes, each of you is counted as an exemption, so check boxes 6a and 6b, accordingly. Later in the filing process, this computation of exemptions will help reduce your taxable income. Your other dependents are, in most cases, individuals who live with you, but there are instances where you can provide substantial support and claim a person as a dependent even if they lived elsewhere.

It is important to accurately claim dependents so that you get the full benefit of the exemptions. The IRS also will check to ensure your dependents are valid. To that end, the agency requires you to enter their names on line 6c, along with their social security numbers and relationships to you.

On the extreme right, you will see several lines regarding your dependents. Enter the appropriate numbers on each line. At line 6d add these up and put the total in the box; this is the number you will eventually multiply by $3,700 and subtract to get your taxable income amount.

There is more to personal finance than the drudgery of debts and budgets.

INCOME (LINES 7-22)

Now let us proceed to the main reason the IRS wants the Form 1040 from you: Just how much was your earned and unearned income? How much money did you make last year? To make these monetary entries a little easier, on you and the IRS tax examiner who will be reviewing your return, the IRS allows you to round off cents to whole dollars; drop amounts under 50 cents to the last dollar and increase amounts from .51 to .99 to the next dollar. If you are rounding off one entry, you must round off all entries.

WAGES (LINE 7)

Most people will enter on line 7 the amount shown in box 1 of the W-2 wage statement they received from their employers. If you had more than one job, you should have multiple W-2s. Add them all up and enter the total here. If you received other types of income, such as tips or money for household work you did, that goes on line 7, too, even if you did not get an official statement. Remember to attach copy B of all your W-2s here.

INTEREST INCOME (LINE 8A-8B)

On line 8 you report what you earned in interest. The IRS wants to know about all of it, even if you do not owe taxes on it. Taxable interest amounts, generally from bank accounts and similar savings instruments, go on line 8a. This money usually is reported to you, and the IRS, in box 1 of the 1099-INT form sent by your financial institution. If your total taxable interest exceeds $1,500, then, you will have some more paperwork to complete; use part 1 of Schedule B to enter the details of your earnings. But if the interest is less than $1,500, just enter it directly on the Form 1040 line 8a. If you received any tax-exempt interest, again usually delineated on financial statements, put that on the Form 1040 line 8b. There is no threat of an extra form for this money, regardless of the amount.

DIVIDEND INCOME (LINES 9A-9B)

If you received ordinary dividends, you will get a Form 1099-DIV showing the dividend amount. It goes on line 9. If the total dividend is more than $1,500, or if you received ordinary dividends as a nominee, that is, they were registered in your name but the actual money belonged to someone else, you must fill in and attach part 2 of Schedule B. Because of tax-law changes, you will see a new line on the 2011 Form 1040. The new line 9b is where you will enter qualified dividends; these will appear in box 1b on your 1099 statement. Qualified dividends now are taxed at 15 percent (or 5 percent for taxpayers with lower incomes).

Details on what constitutes a qualified dividend can be found on the Form 1040 instructions. You will also notice that the area on line 9b where you enter qualified dividends is inset, meaning that this amount is not included when you total your income in a few more lines. Do not worry; the IRS will get back to it. You will have a special worksheet to account for these earnings and to ensure that you pay the appropriate, lower tax on them.

TAXABLE REFUNDS (LINE 10)

Did you receive any 1099-G forms? These statements are issued by governments to report money you received. The most common example is a state tax refund. If you used your state income tax payments as an itemized deduction to lower your federal tax bill, any state refund you get usually is taxable. Enter the amount on line 10.

ALIMONY RECEIVED (LINE 11)

Divorce has many financial implications, including taxes, for both parties. If you receive alimony payments, they are taxable and you need to enter the amount you received on line 11.

BUSINESS INCOME (LINE 12)

Self-employed taxpayers, whether it is a main job or a little freelance work on the side, must report that income and expenses on either Schedule C or C-EZ. The profit reflected on either of those forms is entered on line 12 of Form 1040. If you recorded a business loss instead, then, put the loss amount in parentheses on line 12.

CAPITAL GAIN OR LOSS (LINE 13)

If you sold a stock, regardless of whether you made or lost money on it, you have to file Schedule D. This two-page form can be confusing, but it also can save you some tax dollars. It allows you to calculate any long-term gains at a lower tax rate. If you sold an asset at a loss, that bad investment could help reduce any gains, or even part of your other taxable income. After you figure your gain or loss on Schedule D, transfer the final amount from there to Form 1040's line 13. Again, put parentheses around any loss amount; that is an American convention in accounting. Investors who received capital gains distributions from mutual funds but had no other capital gains transactions to report do not have to worry about Schedule D. These distributions are reported on the 1099-DIV statements you get from your mutual fund managers. If this situation applies to you, simply put the distributions amount on line 13 and check the small box on that line.

OTHER GAINS OR LOSSES (LINE 14)

Line 14 is only for taxpayers who sold or exchanged assets they used in their trade or business. In this case, you will also have to file Form 4797 along with the 1040.

IRA DISTRIBUTIONS (LINE 15A-15B)

IRA distributions stand for individual retirement account money. If you took money from an individual retirement arrangement, you report the distribution on line 15. This is from any IRA: traditional, Roth, or a self-employed IRA plan. This rule also applies to retirement money you rolled over into another tax-deferred account. Put the total distribution, money you took out or rolled over, on 15a and the taxable amount on 15b. You should have a 1099-R showing the amount distributed and whether it was taxable or non-taxable.

PENSIONS AND ANNUITIES (LINE 16A-16B)

Similarly, you should have a Form 1099-R if you received any pension money. This includes transfers of 401(K) accounts from one employer to another. The total distribution goes on line 16a, with the taxable amount on 16b. You do not have to enter anything on line 16a if your pension payments are fully taxable.

If your pension or annuity is partially taxable and your Form 1099-R does not show the taxable part, it is up to you to figure the taxable part. The IRS provides details on how to do this in Publication 939. Even if your 1099-R shows a taxable amount, it may be to your advantage to check out this publication as well as the worksheet on page 26 of the 1040 instructions. The computations may give you a lower taxable pension amount. Also, if any tax was withheld from your pension or IRA, attach the 1099-R forms that show that amount along with your W-2s.

RENT, ROYALTIES, AND OTHER INCOME (LINE 17)

Income from the house you rent goes on line 17, after you have figured the exact amount by completing Schedule E. Earnings from royalties, partnerships, S corporations, or trusts also are reported on this schedule and the appropriate Form 1040 line.

FARM INCOME OR LOSS (LINE 18)

Farmers must use Schedule F to report income gained or lost from that operation. Attach it and put the final amount on line 18.

UNEMPLOYMENT COMPENSATION (LINE 19)

Back in the early 1980s, unemployment compensation was exempt from income taxation. The rules for taxing unemployment have changed again since 2009. For 2009 only, the first $2,400 of unemployment income was not counted as taxable income. For 2011, however, all unemployment income is subject to tax, so nowadays, unemployment compensation is subject to tax. If you received these benefits, you should have received a Form 1099-G. Enter the total on line 19.

SOCIAL SECURITY BENEFITS (LINE 20A-20B)

Did you reap some of your well-earned federal retirement benefits last year? Then you should have received a Form SSA-1099. Railroad retirement benefits treated as social security are reported on the similar Form RRB-1099. Use these statements and the worksheet on page 28 of the Form 1040 instructions to figure if any of your benefits are taxable. Report the total distributions on line 20a and the taxable portion on line 20b.

OTHER INCOME (LINE 21)

Line 21 is where you enter any other taxable income you have not yet told the IRS about. This is not self-employment earnings. Rather, it includes prizes, awards, gambling winnings, jury duty fees, Alaska Permanent Fund dividends, qualified state tuition program earnings, and reimbursements or other amounts received for items deducted in an earlier year. List the type and amount of income, using a separate sheet if necessary, and attach it to your return. As I have made abundantly clear, I do not like the other income portion of Form 1040, so do not get carried away with the use of other income.

Believe it or not, not all income is taxable. As a smart taxpayer, your right is to investigate and isolate those particular items that are not taxable. Child support, money or property you inherit or receive as a gift and life insurance proceeds you receive as a beneficiary are some of the few items that escape IRS attention.

TOTAL INCOME (LINE 22)

Do you want to know exactly how much you received last year from all these various income sources? So does the IRS. Add lines 7 through 21 and enter the sum of your total income on line 22. Now let us get to work cutting that amount! This next section of the 1040 allows you to adjust your income by taking several above-the-line deductions. They get their name because they are listed at the bottom of page one of the Form1040. By taking all these deductions you can and you will reduce your adjusted gross income, which, in turn, cuts your overall income tax bill because figuring your AGI is the first step in arriving at your final taxable income amount.

EDUCATOR EXPENSES (LINE 23)

Line 23 is a tax break for teachers and other public and private school employees who spent their own money on classroom materials and supplies. Up to $250 of qualifying purchases may be claimed here. If both you and your spouse are teachers, you can claim up to $500, but only if each of you spent the maximum credit amount.

CERTAIN BUSINESS EXPENSES OF RESERVISTS, PERFORMING ARTISTS, AND FEE-BASIS GOVERNMENT OFFICIALS. ATTACH FORM 2106 OR 2106-EZ (LINE 24)

HEALTH SAVINGS ACCOUNT DEDUCTION. ATTACH FORM 8889 (LINE 25)

If you had a health savings account, you can take the deduction.

MOVING EXPENSES 3903 (LINE 26)

The IRS gives taxpayers a break for some moving expenses, as long as the move is connected with work. Form 3903 details allowable moving expenses. Once you complete it, enter the amount on line 26 of Form 1040 and attach Form 3903 to your return.

DEDUCTIBLE PART OF SELF-EMPLOYMENT TAX. ATTACH SCHEDULE SE (LINE 27)

Being your own boss has a lot of appeal. It also means more tax obligations, including self-employment taxes. But on line 28 you get half of these payments back.

SELF-EMPLOYED SEP, SIMPLE, AND QUALIFIED PLANS (LINE 28)

Retirement accounts are a great way to prepare for your golden years as well as reduce taxes. Self-employed workers have several options, including Keoghs, simplified employee pensions (SEPs) and SIMPLE plans. If you contributed to such an account, deduct the amount on line28.

SELF-EMPLOYED HEALTH INSURANCE DEDUCTION (LINE 29)

If, as a self-employed worker, you paid for health insurance for yourself, your spouse, or dependents, you now can deduct 100 percent of those costs on line 29. Use the IRS worksheets and Form 1040 instruction booklet to figure the amount you can enter here, especially if at any time you also were eligible for an employer-provided health care plan.

PENALTY ON EARLY WITHDRAWAL OF SAVINGS (LINE 30)

Your Uncle Sam can be a softie. Here Uncle Sam gives you a tax break for doing something that originally got you in trouble. If you took money from a savings account and had to pay a penalty for that, you can deduct that fee on line 30. You should get Form 1099-INT or Form 1099-OID showing just how much money you can enter.

ALIMONY PAYMENTS (LINE 31A-31B)

This is a favorite tax deduction of America's rich and famous folks. Do you remember Tiger Woods? How much did he pay in alimony? He paid a lump sum of $100,000,000.00! It is probably no fun writing that big alimony check every month, but on line 31a he can deduct them from his total income. The deduction for alimony payment is not the preserve of rich folks. You can take it, too. Do not forget, however, to enter your ex-spouse's social security number on line 32b, or the IRS could take this deduction away from you.

 IRA DEDUCTION (LINE 32)

The next adjustment is for any deductible contributions you made, or will make by the filing deadline, to a traditional individual retirement account. The 2011 IRA contribution limits are unchanged from 2010. Since 2008, the most you may contribute to a regular IRA each year is $5,000.

However, if you will be 50 or older by the end of the year, you can contribute an extra $1,000, for a $6,000 total IRA contribution limit. Keep in mind you and/or your spouse must have earned income at least as great as the amount you contribute. An alternative tax-free investment vehicle is the purchase of a cash-value life insurance policy with a high MEC limit.

STUDENT LOAN INTEREST DEDUCTION (LINE 33)

If you paid interest on a student loan, you may be able to deduct up to $2,500 of it on line 33. The loan money had to be used to pay for higher education expenses, including tuition, room and board and books, for yourself, your spouse or one of your dependents. To figure the exact amount you can enter here, use the worksheet on the Form 1040 instruction book.

TUITION AND FEES. ATTACH FORM 8917 (LINE 34)

If you continued your education but did not have to go into debt to do so, line 34 offers you a way to write off some of your schooling costs. You can claim here up to $3,000 in eligible tuition and fees. As with the student loan deduction, there are limits.

And if you claim the Hope or Lifetime Learning tax credits to pay some school costs for a student named as a dependent on your return, you cannot use the tuition and fees adjustment for that same student.

Similarly, you cannot use this deduction against expenses you paid with tax-free scholarship, fellowship, grant, or education savings account funds, such as a Coverdell education savings account, tax-free savings bond interest or employer-provided education assistance.

Uncle Sam does not like taxpayers double-dipping in the tax-break pool.

DOMESTIC PRODUCTION ACTIVITIES DEDUCTION . ATTACH FORM 8903 (LINE 35)

Use Form 8903 to figure your domestic production activities deduction (DPAD). Your DPAD is generally 9% of the smaller of your qualified production activities income (QPAI), or your adjusted gross income for an individual, estate, or trust (taxable income for all other taxpayers) figured without the DPAD.

ADD LINES 23 THROUGH 35 (LINE 36)

These are the final adjustments. The next line, number 36, is a sneaky one. It is not actually labeled final adjustments. Rather, it tells you to add lines 23 through 35.

However, if you read the 1040 instruction book, you will find that here is where you can take several specific, although uncommon, tax breaks ranging from performing arts expenses to jury duty pay given to your employer.

SUBTRACT LINE 36 FROM LINE 22. THIS IS YOUR ADJUSTED GROSS INCOME (LINE 37)

This is your famous AGI, that is, adjusted gross income. It is now time for adjustments payoff with line 34. Subtract line 33 from line 22 and enter the amount here. This is your adjusted gross income.

AMOUNT FROM LINE 37 (ADJUSTED GROSS INCOME) (LINE 38)

Please, turn to Form 1040 page 2. We have to whittle away at your AGI en route to your taxable income. Re-enter your AGI from the last line of the front page on line 38.

BIRTH AND BLINDNESS (LINE 39A)

There are four boxes that need to be checked if:

1--you were born before January 02, 1947
2--your spouse was born before January 02, 1947
3—you are blind
4—your spouse is blind

If you are 65 or older or visually impaired of any age, you need to pay special attention to the boxes on line 39a. These boxes could allow you to increase your standard deduction substantially.

Please, refer to the IRS instructions booklet or your income tax preparer. Turbo Tax and Taxcut are two software packages you could use to simplify the income tax preparation process. If you need help with your taxes, please, do not hesitate to contact us; our Millionaire iUniversity can be of immeasurable assistance to you. If you are a couple who is filing your income taxes jointly, please, note that there are two boxes for each spouse.

SPOUSE ITEMIZATION OR DUAL-STATUS ALIEN (LINE 39A)

Are you married but filing your income taxes separately from your spouse? If you are one of the small groups of taxpayers who are married but you and your spouse file separately, please, ensure that you do not overlook line 39b. Since you are filing the long form, it is likely you will both be itemizing deductions. However, if your spouse is doing so on a separate return, check this box. The IRS wants to know this information so it can check that you both are not claiming the same write-offs.

ITEMIZED DEDUCTIONS OR STANDARD DEDUCTION (LINE 40)

On line 40 you enter either your standard deduction amount or the deductions you itemized on Schedule A; I shall walk you through Schedule A during one of our workshops. The standard amounts allowed for each filing status are listed on the left side of the form, or in the instruction book for filers who checked boxes on line 39a.

Be sure the deduction method you choose is the most tax advantageous. Deductions help you get to the lowest possible taxable income amount, so pick the larger amount. If you are 64 years old and blind but itemizing provides you with more deductions than the increased standard amount, then, please, itemize. Itemized deduction is favored by taxpayers who can claim many tax deductible items: mortgage interest, health insurance premium, medical expenses, and more.

SUBTRACT LINE 40 FROM LINE 38 (LINE 41)

After you have entered your deductions (line 40), subtract them from your AGI (line 38) and put the amount on line 41.

EXEMPTIONS (LINE 42)

Exemptions reduce your taxable income. You can deduct $3,700 for each exemption you claim in 2011. If you are entitled to two exemptions for 2011, you can deduct $7,400; that is $3,700 × 2. There are two types of exemptions you may be able to take: personal exemptions for yourself and your spouse and exemptions for dependents, dependency exemptions. While each is worth the same amount ($3,700 for 2011), different rules, discussed later, apply to each type. Let us return to page one of Form 1040; take an exemption for yourself, your spouse, and those dependents you can claim as tax exemptions. Take the number you placed on line 6d and multiply it by $3,700. This dollar amount goes on line 42. It is important to note that high-income taxpayers may not be able to get the full benefit of their exemptions.

TAXABLE INCOME (LINE 43)

Subtract your exemption amount (line 42) from your income total (line 41). This is your taxable income, the amount that the IRS uses to compute precisely what you owe, and it goes on line 43. If your deductions are more than your income, then, you have no taxable income, so enter zero on line 43. Lucky you! You have no tax due! But do not stop. If you had taxes withheld, you must file a return to get that money back. And if you are eligible for any tax credits, coming up in just a few lines, you could get an even bigger refund.

TAX (LINE 44)

This is the amount of tax that has been computed for you to pay the IRS. Most of us, however, will enter a taxable income amount, so now we go to the heart of this process: determining what is owed the IRS. That amount goes on line 44. But as is generally the case when it comes to taxes, figuring your bill is not a one-size-fits-all step.

ALTERNATIVE MINIMUM TAX (AMT) (LINE 45)

Just when you thought it was safe, here comes the alternative minimum tax on line 45. The Alternative Minimum Tax (AMT) is an income tax imposed by the United States federal government on individuals, corporations, estates, and trusts. AMT is imposed at a nearly flat rate on an adjusted amount of taxable income above a certain threshold (also known as exemption). This exemption is substantially higher than the exemption from regular income tax. Regular taxable income is adjusted for certain items computed differently for AMT, such as depreciation and medical expenses. No deduction is allowed for state income taxes or miscellaneous itemized deductions in computing AMT income. Taxpayers with incomes above the exemption whose regular Federal income tax is below the amount of AMT must pay the higher AMT amount.

ADD LINES 44 AND 45 (LINE 46)

In addition to the amount of computed tax on line 44, add the amount of alternative minimum tax on line 46.

FOREIGN TAX CREDIT. ATTACH FORM 1116 IF REQUIRED (LINE 47)

You can claim a credit only for foreign taxes that are imposed on you by a foreign country or US possession. Generally, only income, war profits, and excess profits taxes qualify for the credit. Largely, the following four tests must be met for any foreign tax to qualify for the credit:

1. The tax must be imposed on you.
2. You must have paid or accrued the tax.
3. The tax must be the legal and actual foreign tax liability.
4. The tax must be an income tax or a tax in lieu of an income tax.

CREDIT FOR CHILD AND DEPENDENT CARE EXPENSES (LINE 48)

You may be able to use line 48 if you paid someone to care for your child or other dependent who could not care for himself or herself. The key requirement for this tax credit is that the care was necessary so you could work or look for work. If you are eligible for the child and dependent care credit, you will also need to fill out and attach Form 2441.

EDUCATION CREDITS FROM FORM 8863, LINE 23 (LINE 49)

There are two education credits that could save you tax money. You enter them on line 49. The Hope Credit helps pay for expenses during a student's first two years of college and could shave $1,500 per student off your tax bill.

The Lifetime Learning Credit can be used for undergraduate, graduate and professional degree courses for anyone and offers a maximum annual $2,000 savings. You can claim both in the same year, but not for the same expenses. Because of the many incidents of fraud and abuse, for the 2012 tax year, the IRS requires taxpayers claiming the benefit of education credit to present a copy of Form 1098-T from a recognized institution.

Form 8863 details both these credits and requirements. And if you claimed the tuition and fees deduction for a dependent student, you are not allowed to take either credit for the same student.

RETIREMENT SAVINGS CONTRIBUTIONS CREDIT. ATTACH FORM 8880 (LINE 50)

The retirement savings contributions credit on line 50 is a tax break designed to reward lower-wage earners who contribute to retirement accounts. An eligible filer could use the credit to reduce his or her tax bill by as much as $1,000. The actual tax break depends upon a worker's income, filing status and just how much he puts into a retirement plan.

Basically, the lower the income, the bigger the credit. Of course, any offer of a smaller tax bill generally involves a bit more work on the taxpayer's part. To see if you can claim the saver's credit, check out the IRS instruction booklet. If you are eligible, you will need to complete Form 8880 to determine the amount to enter on line 50 of Form 1040.

CHILD TAX CREDIT (LINE 51)

The child tax credit, claimed on line 51, can cut your tax bill by $1,000 per child. There are certain eligibility tests both you and your child must meet and a worksheet to complete before you can claim this credit. The IRS 1040 instruction booklet contains details and the worksheet you can use to calculate the child tax credit. The worksheet is especially important this filing season for the nearly 24 million parents who received an advance payment of this credit last year.

RESIDENTIAL ENERGY CREDITS. ATTACH FORM 5695 (LINE 52)

The non-business energy property credit is aimed at homeowners installing energy efficient improvements such as insulation, new windows, and furnaces. The credit is more limited than in the past years, but it can still provide substantial tax savings.

OTHER CREDITS FROM FORM 3800/8801 (LINE 53)

Form 3800 is used to claim any of the general business credits. Use Form 8801 if you are an individual, estate, or trust: to figure the current year nonrefundable credit, if any, for alternative minimum tax (AMT) you incurred in prior tax years, to figure the current year refundable credit (individuals only), if any, for any unused credit carry forward, and to figure any credit carry forward.

ADD LINES 47 THROUGH 53 TOTAL CREDITS (LINE 54)

Now add up all the credits you qualified for -- lines 47 through 53 -- and enter the sum on line 54. This number represents your total nonrefundable credits, meaning these credits can get your bill down to nothing. If they total more than your owe, the excess credit is of no use to you.

SUBTRACT LINE 54 FROM LINE 46 (LINE 55)

Then subtract line 54, total credits, from line 46 (regular tax and AMT due) and enter the amount on line 55. If your credits are greater than the tax you owe, enter zero here.

SELF-EMPLOYMENT TAX (LINE 56)

Taxpayers who worked for themselves, either as their full-time job or as a side endeavor to make a little extra money, must pay self-employment tax toward Social Security and Medicare. The amount is figured on Schedule SE and entered on line 56 of Form 1040 page 2.

There is more to personal finance than the drudgery of debts and budgets.

UNREPORTED SOCIAL SECURITY AND MEDICARE TAX FROM FORM 4137/8919 (LINE 57)

As for tip income taxes, if you received tips of $20 or more in any month last year and did not report the full amount to your employer, you must pay the Social Security and Medicare or railroad retirement tax on it here on line 57. To figure the tax, use Form 4137.

Additional tax on IRAs, other qualified retirement plans, etc. Attach Form 5329 if required (Line 58)

If the income tax withheld on Form 1099R for IRAs, or other qualified retirement plans, is inadequate, you use Form 5329 to calculate the additional tax you owe; you enter the result on Form 5329, and you also report the result on Form 1040 line 58.

HOUSEHOLD EMPLOYMENT TAXES FROM SCHEDULE H (LINE 59A)

Are you a household employer? You may not feel like a household employer, but you might be one. You have a household employee if you hired someone to do household work and that worker is your employee. The worker is your employee if you can control not only what work is done, but how it is done. If the worker is your employee, it does not matter whether the work is full time or part time or that you hired the worker through an agency or from a list provided by an agency or association. It also does not matter whether you pay the worker on an hourly, daily, or weekly basis, or by the job. If you paid a household employee $1,400 or more last year, you must pay Social Security and Medicare taxes for that employee. For instance, you pay Betty Nanny to babysit your child and do light housework 4 days a week in your home. Betty follows your specific instructions about household and child care duties. You provide the household equipment and supplies that Betty needs to do her work. Betty is your household employee. Fill out Schedule H and put the amount you owe on the Form 1040 line 59a.

FIRST-TIME HOMEBUYER CREDIT REPAYMENT ATTACH FORM 5405 IF REQUIRED (LINE 59B)

You may be able to take the first-time homebuyer credit if you were an eligible buyer who purchased a home as your primary residence in 2008, 2009, or 2010. Eligibility varies depending upon the year of your home purchase.

OTHER TAXES. ENTER CODE(S) FROM INSTRUCTIONS (LINE 60)

If the amount is zero or small, hold the celebration for a few minutes. What the IRS gives, it also (and more frequently) takes. The next section of Form 1040 is Other Taxes.

ADD LINES 55 THROUGH 60. THIS IS YOUR TOTAL TAX (LINE 61)

Add lines 55 through 60 to find your total tax amount. This number goes on line 61. Now we get to see how much of that amount you have already paid.

FEDERAL TAX WITHHELD FROM FORMS W2 AND 1099 (LINE 62)

This is the most common tax payment. Almost everyone who has a job sees a big chunk of cash subtracted from each paycheck to send to Uncle Sam. That federal withholding is reported on your W-2. It also can be found on various 1099 forms that detail other income you earned. Total them all and put the amount on line 62.

2011 ESTIMATED TAX PAYMENTS AND AMOUNT APPLIED FROM 2010 RETURN (LINE 63)

If you made estimated tax payments last year, that total goes on line 63. You also enter here any overpayment from your 2010 return that you applied to your 2011 estimated tax bill.

EARNED INCOME CREDIT EIC (LINE 64A)

Low-income workers who did not get advance payments of the earned income credit through their pay should explore whether they can claim it here. Eligibility guidelines, worksheets and EIC tax credit tables are in the Form 1040 instructions booklet. When you figure how much you can claim, enter the amount on line 64.

NONTAXABLE COMBAT PAY ELECTION (LINE 64B)

You can elect to include your nontaxable combat pay in earned income for the earned income credit. If you make the election, you must include in earned income all nontaxable combat pay you received. If you are filing a joint return and both you and your spouse received nontaxable combat pay, you can each make your own election. The amount of your nontaxable combat pay should be shown on your Form W-2 in box 12 with code Q.

Be forewarned; electing to include nontaxable combat pay in earned income may increase or decrease your EIC. Figure the credit with and without your nontaxable combat pay before making the election. Whether the election increases or decreases your EIC depends on your total earned income, filing status, and number of qualifying children.

If your earned income without your combat pay is less than the amount shown below for your number of children, you may benefit from electing to include your nontaxable combat pay in earned income and you should figure the credit both ways. If your earned income without your combat pay is equal to or more than these amounts, you will not benefit from including your combat pay in your earned income.

ADDITIONAL CHILD TAX CREDIT. ATTACH FORM 8812 (LINE 65)

You may be able to get even more of a tax break for your children through the additional child tax credit on line 65. Like the earlier child tax credit, you have to meet eligibility standards. And you must take the child tax credit first (line 51). Complete Form 8812 to claim the additional credit, which could give you a refund even if you do not owe any tax.

AMERICAN OPPORTUNITY CREDIT FROM FORM 8863, LINE 14 (LINE 66)

The American opportunity credit is a partially refundable tax credit detailed in Section 1004 of the American Recovery and Reinvestment Act of 2009.

FIRST TIME HOMEBUYER CREDIT FROM FORM 5405 LINE 10 (67)

People who claimed the first-time homebuyer credit on their federal income tax return in 2008 will need to begin repaying that tax credit on their 2010 tax return. The homebuyer credit is still available until April 2011 for military personnel.

AMOUNT PAID WITH REQUEST FOR EXTENSION TO FILE (LINE 68)

If you requested an extension to file your return, you had to estimate your tax bill and pay it with that request. Enter that amount on line 68, regardless of whether you paid by credit card, check, or money order. If you did use your credit card, do not include the convenience fee you were charged as part of your tax payment. That went to the private company handling the transaction, not Uncle Sam.

EXCESS SOCIAL SECURITY AND TIER 1 RRTA TAX WITHHELD (LINE 69)

If you, or your spouse if you file a joint return, had more than one employer and your combined income last year was more than $87,000 last year, too much Social Security tax may have been withheld from your paychecks. You can get back the amount over $5,394 that was withheld from you by noting the excess on line 69. Some railroad workers could be in similar straits. Line 69 is for this excess railroad tax, too.

CREDIT FOR FEDERAL TAX ON FUELS. ATTACH FORM 4136 (LINE 70)

Use Form 4136 to claim a credit for certain nontaxable uses (or sales) of fuel during your income tax year. Also use Form 4136 if you are claiming the alternative fuel credit, a blender claiming a credit for a diesel-water fuel emulsion, or a producer claiming a credit for an alcohol fuel mixture, a biodiesel or renewable diesel mixture, or an alternative fuel mixture.

The following lines are self-explanatory:

CREDITS FROM FORM 2439, 8839, 8801, 8885 (LINE 71)

LINE 71 REPORTS REFUNDS FROM FORMS 2439, 8839, 8801, AND 8885

TOTAL PAYMENTS (LINE 72)

Add lines 62, 63, 64a, and 65 through71. The sum goes on line 72 as the total tax you have already paid.

OVERPAYMENT (LINE 73)

If line 72 is more than line 61 (total tax due), you are going to get some cash back from the US Internal Revenue Service. Subtract line 61 from 72 and enter your overpayment amount on line 73.

REFUND AMOUNT. ATTACH FORM 8888 (LINE 74A-74B—74C-74D)

As silly as it seems, line 74a asks the amount of your overpayment you want refunded to you. Most of us want it all. If you do not, decide how much you do want now and enter it here. If you want your refund to go directly to a bank account, fill in the routing number on line 74b. If you have any questions about the nine digits to enter here, contact your financial institution. Line 74c lets the IRS know if it is a checking or savings account. And do not forget to enter your full bank account number, which can be up to 17 letters and numbers, on line 74d. If you are copying the number from a check, be careful not to include the check number here.

REFUND APPLIED TO ESTIMATED TAXES (LINE 75)

If you are among the few people who do not want a full refund, you have the option to apply part or all of your refund toward 2012 estimated tax payments. That amount goes on line 75. Be sure this is what you want to do. Once you tell the IRS to use the money toward estimated taxes, you cannot change your mind and get a full refund.

AMOUNT YOU OWE (LINE 76)

If you had to skip the three lines discussed above, it is because line 61 is larger than line 72. Sorry. That means you have a tax bill due. Subtract line 72 from line 61 and enter the amount you owe on line 76.

ESTIMATED TAX PENALTY (LINE 77)

You also might owe a penalty if you owe at least $1,000 and the amount due is more than 10 percent of your total tax due. A penalty could also be assessed if you did not make timely estimated tax payments. Complete Form 2210 to find out if you owe the penalty. If so, enter the penalty on line 77, and do not forget to add it to your taxes due amount on the line above. Because Form 2210 is complicated, you can leave line 77 blank, so that the IRS will figure any penalty and send you a bill. You will not be charged interest on the penalty if you pay by the date specified on the bill. When you have figured your final tax bill and want to pay by check or money order, make it out to the United States Treasury, not the IRS.

THIRD PARTY DESIGNEE

The third-party designee section of Form 1040 allows you to name someone else to handle any questions about your return.

There is more to personal finance than the drudgery of debts and budgets.

By checking the YES box here, you allow the IRS to contact your tax professional, father, CPA, mother, cousin, or anyone else you want to solve problems related to your return. Details on naming a designated tax representative can be found on the pages of the Form 1040 instructions. But folks who did turn their taxes over to a professional should have noticed a new section this year on the Form 1040, just in the third-party designee area; you can give the IRS permission to go directly to your tax preparer if the agency has any questions about your return. The goal is to shorten the time it takes to get tax problems resolved.

SIGN HERE

Finally, whether you are getting a refund or paying Uncle Sam, you have reached the end of the long Form 1040. Sign your name and write in the date, your occupation, and your daytime telephone number. If you are filing a joint return, your spouse must sign and provide the same information as well. Since you have read this far, we are going to assume you are preparing your income taxes yourself, so you do not need to worry about the paid preparer's signature block below.

Now, gather all your supporting attachments and forms, assembling them in order of their attachment sequence number shown in the upper right corner of each and attach them to the Form 1040. Also attach the first copy or Copy B of your various W-2 and, if taxes were withheld, your 1099 forms, too. Enclose your payment with your income tax return, but do not attach the check or money order to the form. Make sure you have the correct envelope that came with your tax package. One is designated for returns getting a refund, the other for those paying tax. Then double check your Form 1040 one more time for errors before sealing the envelope and heading to the US post office to get it on its way by April 15. Good luck. You are now a tax preparer. During my seminar and workshops, we shall work on completing Schedule A and state income tax returns. For students who cannot attend the seminars and workshops, I will encourage them to take advantage of our distance or online learning resources located at http://www.millionaireiuniversity.com. Additionally, I am looking forward to introducing you to the business of electronic income tax filing. You must have already heard names such as H&R Block, Jackson Hewitt, and Liberty Tax Service. I will show you how to start an income tax return preparation service without spending a fortune on junk and franchise fees. I have been a player in the tax industry since 1986, when the IRS introduced electronic tax filing as a pilot program.

INCOME TAX REDUCTION STRATEGIES

At this juncture, since you have a good understanding of Form 1040, I think you are ready to receive the unknown or little-known tax tips favored by America's rich and famous folks from me. The 2012 tax season has come and gone, and now it is November 2012. We are preparing already for the next income tax season; in fact, soon you may be in a position to pick up a copy of official IRS tax forms and booklets at your local U.S. post office, or the Internal Revenue Service will mail a package to the address you used on your 2011 income tax return. If you are like an average taxpayer, you are worrying about either getting a fat and quick refund or paying Uncle Sam a big chunk of money.

Do not worry. You may not be in a good mood to be thinking about a dull subject such as income taxes now. If you want to be rich and famous like the Joneses and the Smiths, you better get into the robotic habit of thinking about income taxes daily. Your rich and famous neighbors are wealthy because they have taught themselves the habit of predicating almost all their financial decisions on income taxes. Hence, you should be thinking about income taxes now. Good cheer!

My objective in step 8 is to assist you in learning and applying what rich guys like Governor Willard Mitt Romney and Warren Buffett know about income taxes. Help is right here! Like the good and old doctor, I am the humble or accidental tax expert who is here to educate you on the subject of income taxes and wealth building. Income tax season is supposed to be a pleasurable time, a stress-free tax season. Even if you do not want to join the Millionaire Club, please, call my office at (301) 593-4897. I can help you immeasurably.

LIKE AMERICA'S RICH AND FAMOUS, WOULD YOU LIKE TO LEARN HOW TO PAY ZERO OR LITTLE TAXES? Then, here is your 2012 tax guide to every significant tax break that the U.S. Internal Revenue Service allows! Indeed, decoding the American tax code is not an exercise for the faint of heart. In fact, the American tax system is very complex for ordinary mortals to comprehend and implement. Thank God I have come to your rescue. To pay zero or little taxes, you need to pay special attention to the following: tax planning, tax strategies, and tax preparation.

TAX PLANNING

Have you ever developed a tax plan? If not, please fire your income tax professional and hire the experts recommended by my Taxzero1 outfit from Millionaire iUniversity. Unlike most governments, the US administration has been at great pains to standardize and codify the American tax system, so it behooves you to cultivate the good habit of planning an effective income tax strategy. In fact, most of the income tax publications and forms of the IRS are free like the air that you breathe every day. People who do not plan hardly ever achieve good tax results. A great income tax preparation and consulting service, such as Taxzero1 from Millionaire iUniversity, should provide you with tax planning tips.

Taxzero1 consultation is free of charge. A smart individual starting a new business needs to write a business plan, so you, an income taxpayer, need a tax plan that can serve as your blueprint of success in personal finance. Tax planning involves articulating and setting goals and developing a plan to achieve those goals. The following list of tax issues and events that should assist you to begin brainstorming and free-writing prior to meeting your accountant or tax preparer for tax planning:

Adoption, Alimony, Alternative Minimum Tax, Annuity, Awards, Bartering Agreement, Bonds, Births, Business/ Self Employment, Capital Gains, Cash Contribution, Casino, Casualty, Charity, Child Care, Children, Church, College Planning, Death, Dependents, Disability, Disaster, Distributions, Dividends, Divorce, Domestic production, Education, Equipment, Estate Sales, Exemptions, expense acceleration, Farm Income, Filing Status, Fire, Foreign Tax Credit,

Gambling, Health Insurance, Home Use, Income shifting, index options, Interest, Itemized Deduction, IRA, Jury Duty, KEOGH, Land, Lottery, market discount, Marriage, Medical bills, Mortgage, Moving Expenses, Non-Cash Contribution, Options, original issue discount, Pension, Personal Residence, Prizes, purchases, purchase of Aircraft, purchase of Boat, Purchase of Car, Purchase of Motor, Home, Raffles, Railroad Retirement, Real Estate, Rental Property, Retirement, Royalties, sales, Salaries, savings, SEP, short sales, Social Security, Standard Deduction, State Tax Refund, stocks, Student Loan, swaps, tax deference, Theft, timing techniques, Tips, Tuition and Fees, Trust, Unemployment Compensation, Use of Personal Automobile at work, Wages, salaries, and wash sales.

TAX STRATEGIES

By tax strategies, I am referring to tax plans, policies, approaches, tactics, stratagems, and schemes favored by America's rich and famous folks. Millionaires and billionaires hire the big brains of the smartest accountants and lawyers to assist them in implementing strategies of income tax minimization. Similarly, as a student of Millionaire iUniversity, you could hire a great income tax preparation firm, such as Taxzero1, to provide you with the income tax strategies that, until now, have been the preserve and exclusive privilege of millionaires and billionaires; that is, you can begin to exploit hundreds of tips and techniques to shield your income through exclusions, credits, deductions, shelters, smart investments, and loopholes. Millionaires and billionaires exploit income reduction strategies; you, too, can exploit the strategy of income reduction by strategizing to lower the amount of income reported on your tax return; for example, on your Form 1040, you can plan to lower the income you report on lines 8a to 21. Millionaires and billionaires understand the American income tax system. As a result of this understanding, they exploit all the loopholes available in order to reduce their taxable income. By reducing their taxable income, they are reducing their tax liability. By contrast, as Leona Helmsley, America's Queen of Mean, once said, little people who are ignorant bear the brunt of taxation in America:

I said: "You must pay a lot of taxes." She said: "We don't pay taxes. Only the little people pay taxes." –Elizabeth Baum, former housekeeper to Helmsley (October 1983).

Why is Warren Buffett paying less income taxes than his secretary? The US government loves to pamper and cuddle tax-savvy rich folks. Instead of sitting still like ducks and be eaten alive by dirty Washingtonian politicians for supper, millionaires and billionaires are too smart to be alert and mobile. Even the famous investigative reporters from *Forbes* magazine cannot quantify their income accurately; millionaires and billionaires have a fondness for privacy and secrecy; they like to hide or reduce their income so that they should pay little or no taxes to the government. In contrast, the income of most members of the struggling American middle class or the poor is exposed on line 7 of Form 1040 page 1; the rich have stopped working for money. As a result, money works for them; that is why the sources of their income tend to be the following: taxable interest, tax-exempt interest, ordinary dividends, capital gains, alimony received, business income, rental real estate, royalties, partnerships, S corporation, trusts, and farm income. Please, I am urging you to approach income taxes like the rich and famous folks.

As a case in point, I want to draw your attention to the 2012 presidential candidate of the Republican Party; recently, Governor Willard Mitt Romney was coerced to release his income tax returns. Finally, I have downloaded and studied his income taxes of 2010 and 2011 tax years. I remember what I saw in his income taxes of 2010 and 2011 very well; then, it is noteworthy for you to know that his income came principally from unearned income sources: capital gains from his ownership of stocks in Bain Capital, the venture capital firm he had founded. The company, Bain Capital, and its actions during its first 15 years, have become the subject of political and media scrutiny as a result of co-founder Governor Willard Mitt Romney's 2012 presidential campaign. Romney's opponents have thrust Bain Capital into the consciousness of the average American. In spite of all the spin and hype, it suffices for you to know that Bain Capital is a capital and positive force for good in the country. Headquartered in Boston, Massachusetts, Bain Capital is an alternative asset management and financial services company that specializes in private equity, venture capital, credit and public market investments.

Bain Capital invests across a broad range of industry sectors and geographic regions. As of the beginning of 2012, the firm manages approximately $66 billion of investor capital across its various investment platforms. The firm was founded in 1984 by partners from the consulting firm Bain & Company. Since inception it has invested in or acquired hundreds of companies including such notable companies as AMC Entertainment, Aspen Education Group, Brookstone, Burger King, Burlington Coat Factory, Clear Channel Communications, Domino's Pizza, DoubleClick, Dunkin' Donuts, D&M Holdings, Guitar Center, Hospital Corporation of America (HCA), Sealy, The Sports Authority, Staples, Toys "R" Us, Warner Music Group, and The Weather Channel. As of the end of 2011, Bain Capital had approximately 400 professionals, most with previous experience in consulting, operations, or finance. As you can see from the presentation above, there is nothing wrong with Bain Capital. The purpose of unfettered capitalism is the production of unlimited value for shareholders of a corporation. It is dramatic that it took Governor Willard Mitt Romney, a rich man running for president of the USA, for the average American to learn much about how rich folks use complicated vehicles and strategies to legally pay zero or a litlle taxes on their income. I wish America can have more events to propel the subject of taxation into the public domain.

MILLIONAIRES AND BILLIONAIRES EXPLOIT EXCLUSIONS

Exclusions comprise of tax-free money or alternatives to earned income such as the following: hospitalization premiums, group life insurance premiums, group legal services plans, accident and health plans, employee death benefits, merchandise distributed to employees on holidays, expenses of your employer, meals and lodgings, employee discounts, workers' compensation, cafeteria plans, dependent care assistance program, employer educational assistance, employee awards, miscellaneous fringe benefits, donatives items (gifts, bequests, inheritances, scholarships, fellowships, prizes, and awards), investor specials such as interest on state and municipal obligations, benefits for the elderly (public assistance payments, social security and other retirement benefits, retirement annuities, sale of home). Miscellaneous individual exclusions consist of carpool receipts, damages, divorce and separation arrangements, life insurance, and schedule of excludable items.

MILLIONAIRES AND BILLIONAIRES CAPITALIZE ON TAX CREDITS

The average taxpayer knows about earned income tax credit, child tax credit, American opportunity credit, and first-time homebuyer credit. Millionaires and billionaires know more about arcane income tax credit; typically, income tax credits result in dollar-for-dollar tax reduction or big tax refunds: earned income credit, excess social security, child and dependent care credit, credit for real estate taxes and mortgage interest paid, targeted jobs credit, research tax credit, orphan drug tax credit, and adoption assistance. Please, pay much attention to the following IRS forms: 4136, 2439, 8839, 8801, and 8885. I will discuss them in detail in my tax workshops. I invite you to attend my seminars and workshops; please, feel free to call my office and invite me to your city: (301) 593-4879 or (301) 593-4897. My mission is to stamp out financial illiteracy in America; my goal is to demystify personal finance; I want the average American to be educated on tax subjects. I have prepared many documents that can simplify the task of learning for you. Please, take advantage of my tax materials. I want to hold your hand.

MILLIONAIRES LOVE DEDUCTIONS

Millionaires love tax deductions. By keeping good income tax records, millionaires try as much as possible to maximize their business deductions. At the very heart of income tax deductions is the concept of deductibility; this idea refers to knowing all the tax items that you are eligible to deduct legally; deductible items are found in the maze of the IRS form known as Schedule A. By turning most of their personal deductions into business deductions, millionaires increase their aggregate deductions; thus, they reduce their taxable income and pay less income tax.

As far as the income tax code goes, deductions are my favorite tax-saving tools. Deductions are the tax secrets the rich folks do not want you to know. At the center of rich folks' tax strategy is the maximum exploitation of the concept of income tax deductions: standard deduction, itemized deductions, business, trade, employee, alimony, retirement plan, self-employment tax, health insurance, moving expenses, medical, income taxes, real-estate and personal property tax, interest, charitable contributions, casualty, theft losses, miscellaneous trade and business deduction of employees, travel expenses, transportation, meals and entertainment, gifts, reimbursable employee business expenses, and educational expenses.

MILLIONAIRES AND BILLIONAIRES LOVE TAX SHELTERS

Millionaires love tax shelters. They use tax shelters to hide their money from the prying eyes of the IRS. Traditional tax shelters include the following: real estate, fees in public real estate partnerships, oil and gas, equipment leasing, single-premium life insurance, cattle feeding program, tax straddles, art reproduction, non-cash gift shelters, and municipal bond swaps. Indeed, the tax professionals of Millionaire iUniversity can show you how to observe, classify, and analyze tax shelters for the purpose of income tax reduction. Some of their favorite schemes involve unearned income of minors, outright gifts, Clifford trusts, interest-free loans, gift leasebacks, family partnerships, family member employment, and business establishments such as offshore finance schemes and bank accounts to hide assets in the Cayman Islands, Bermuda, Switzerland, and New Zealand.

TAX PREPARATION

Your income tax preparer should be in a position to assist you in implementing most of the ideas discussed in this chapter. If not, I will help you. I have a great income tax preparation firm behind me that can provide you with tax assistance. For immediate help, please, call (301) 593-4879.

MORE INCOME TAX TIPS FOR 2012

As I write this chapter, I am worried because soon it will be the end of the year. I wonder whether you have had much time to plan your financial affairs. Below is some food for thought:

--Write a will. Do not make any excuses. If you can afford it, please, ask your attorney to assist you in this effort. Otherwise, I can recommend that you do it yourself by using a user-friendly software from Nolo.com: Willmaker. Intuit, the publisher of Quicken, the best-selling financial software, also sells this product. Take advantage of it; if you need assistance, I am ready to assist you; please, call (301) 593-4879.

--Plan to make most of your consumer purchases income tax deductible. You do this by distinguishing between personal expenses and business expenses. Do not commingle your funds; maintain separate bank accounts for business and individual use.

--Use your personal residence as an income tax haven. Use the IRS tax form known as Schedule A to deduct mortgage interest and real estate taxes. Additionally, start a new business at home and profit from many business-use-of-the-home deductions. When you start a business from home, you are entitled to deduct direct and indirect expenses.

--Establish a Roth IRA if you are still working a job. For income tax purposes, it is better than the traditional IRA. To shield much of your income from taxation, maximize your IRA contribution to the legal limit of your filing status.

--Travel the world in 90 days on Uncle Sam's dollar. You can deduct travel expenses as either an employee or employer. As an employee, you can deduct travel expenses on Form 2106; in contrast, as a self-employed individual, you can deduct travel expenses on page two of Schedule C. For an elaborate explanation of how to benefit from travel as a work expense, please, join the Millionaire Club. We will teach you how to use your job to create legitimate income tax deductions.

--To the best of your human ability, make all your assets income tax deductible: cars, boats, airplanes, and recreational vehicles.

--Take advantage of the investment potential of life insurance. Why not create a million-dollar retirement plan? In this endeavor, equity-indexed universal life insurance is preferred because it avails you the opportunity to capitalize on the index crediting strategies of the S&P 500.

As an alternative to an IRA, life insurance produces the best returns if you take advantage of the MEC limits, that is, without the insurance policy becoming a modified endowment contract. In fact, a tax exempt investment vehicle, universal life is a class of life insurance product that allows policy owners to enjoy a partial, special, and favorable tax treatment. However, changes to the US tax law in 1988 resulted in certain insurance policies that were funded too rapidly (generally in one lump sum payment) being classified as modified endowment contracts (MECs).

Thus, the use of such insurance policies as short-term savings and investment vehicles was eliminated; the government imposed stiff penalties as a form of deterrence. Prior to enactment of the MEC rules, it was possible to place large amounts of cash into a single premium life insurance policy where the inside buildup grew tax deferred; at death the proceeds of the policy passed tax free to the beneficiary. If the policy owner needed the money, the cash-value was accessible to the policy owner through tax-free lifetime loans or cash withdrawals. By themselves, these policies were being used in place of other investment vehicles whose earnings would have been subject to income taxes.

--Set up a blind trust to protect your assets. What is a blind trust? A blind trust is a trust in which the fiduciaries, namely the trustees or those who have been given power of attorney, have full discretion over the assets, and the trust beneficiaries have no knowledge of the holdings of the trust and no right to intervene in the management of the trust. Blind trusts are generally used when a settlor (sometimes called a trustor or donor) wishes to keep the beneficiary unaware of the specific assets in the trust, such as to avoid conflict of interest between the beneficiary and the investments. Politicians, like Governor Mitt Romney and others in sensitive positions, often place their personal assets (including investment income) into blind trusts, to avoid public scrutiny and accusations of conflicts of interest when they exercise power or direct government funds to the private sector.

--Use a living trust to avoid probate hoax, gift tax, and estate tax. That is what the rich and famous folks do. What is a living trust? Generally, a trust is an arrangement under which one person, called a trustee, holds legal title to property for another person, called a beneficiary. You can be the trustee of your own living trust, keeping full control over all property held in trust.

A living trust, also called an inter vivo trust, is simply a trust you create while you are alive, rather than one that is created at your death. Different kinds of living trusts can help you avoid probate, reduce estate taxes, or set up long-term property management. I cannot give you legal advice on trusts because I am not an attorney; I do not want any court in the USA to charge me with a crime such UPL: unauthorized practice of law. Nonetheless, I can refer you to many competent lawyers who work for me in the field of estate planning. If you have a need for legal advice, please, call me for some references: (301) 593-4879.

--Exploit tax lien certificates as an investment. The first time I actually grasped the tax lien concept was when I ordered a course from John Beck. I will teach you much about it. So come to me! Here is your opportunity to make money by trading in the payment of real-estate tax for the taxpayer or homeowner in default; in return, you acquire the privilege or the right to own the property or earn substantial interest in the process.

A tax lien sale is the sale, conducted by a governmental agency, of tax liens for delinquent taxes on real estate. It is one of two methodologies used by governmental agencies to collect delinquent taxes owed on real estate, the other being the tax deed sale. In a tax lien sale, the lien (for delinquent taxes, accrued interest, and costs associated with the sale) is offered to prospective investors at public auction.

Traditionally, auctions were held in person; however, Internet-based auctions, especially within large counties having numerous liens, have grown in popularity as this method allows for bidders from outside the area to participate.

In the event that more than one investor seeks the same lien, depending on state law, the winner will be determined by one of five methods: bid down the interest, premium, random selection, rotational selection, and bid down the ownership.

TAX BONUS FEATURE

To make it possible for you to learn much about taxes, I have a special gift for you: Barack Obama and Mitt Romney tax returns. I have spent much time analyzing the income taxes so that you can see for yourself how the big guys use the tax system. To collect your gift, please, come to any of my digital platforms: princeojong.com or millionaireiuniversity.com. If you need assistance, please, call my office: (301) 593-4879 or (301) 593-4897. Good luck to you!

Step 9

PLAY AND WIN THE STOCK MARKET GAME

We mint millionaires one person at a time.

As I was editing this chapter of *The Miraculous Millionaire*, I came across a book I plan to review for you in a blog or newsletter: The author is Robert Frank, an erstwhile writer of *The Wall Street Journal*. The book's title is *Richistan: A Journey Through the American Wealth Boom and the Lives of the New Rich*. As much as it chronicles the life and times of millionaires and billionaires, my only fascination with the book was with the portrayal of the language of millionaires and billionaires. Hence, before we embark on stock investing fundamentals, please, accompany me on a crash course in linguistics, the scientific study of language. Noam Chomsky, an American linguist I have admired for many decades, agrees that language may refer either to the specifically human capacity for acquiring and using complex systems of communication, or to a specific instance of such a system of complex communication. The scientific study of language in any of its senses is called linguistics. In fact, I agree with Franz Fanon when he says in his book titled *Black Skin White Masks* that he ascribes fundamental importance to the phenomenon of language. Back in my undergraduate days, that is, from 1979 to 1982, I was taught language and communication in linguistics classes; the recurrent theme of my linguistic lectures was the idea that language is a code. Since we shall draw analogies between stock investing and English, you will agree that stock investing is the secret code of millionaires and billionaires; if you cannot the decipher the stock investing code of millionaires and billionaires, you cannot comprehend the subject of their conversation.

By understanding the language of stock investing and speaking it fluently, I have prepared myself for the critical task of building many small businesses and ensuring a comfortable retirement for myself; by the same token, I have been planning for the financing of my daughters' college education; I want my children to have a career that is better than mine. Therefore, I implore you to learn to read, write, and speak the language of stock investing. I will teach you about dialects, cognates, and language varieties. I will show you how to invest in stocks without risks. If you are foolhardy, I will show you how to calculate your risks. If you have already learned how to save your money, I will show you how you can make it grow. You will happy to become wealthy. You will speak in tongues, the global language of stock investing, and you will translate it for your loved ones. Trust me; when I teach you how to trade and invest in stocks, you will be very happy. It is easier to learn how to trade and invest than you might think.

I understand you are scared or confused about how to handle your investments and fed up with advice from stock brokers, financial planners, insurance advisors, and media darlings that has cost you huge sums of money, pain, and suffering. Stop placing your financial security at risk; indeed, the cure is in your hands. I, Prince Ojong, a street-smart individual equity investor with more than two decades of experience, reveal the one investment goal you should have, the two obstacles you will face, and why you have been failing with your investment strategies. Above all, I will share the secret to successful investing with you; I will even include a special section for those who are already retired. Hence, rescue yourself today from the pain of watching your life savings go down the drain. Regain the confidence that your investments can provide you with lifelong financial security and prosperity. Get a great night's sleep by not having to lie awake worrying about your investments.

There is more to personal finance than the drudgery of debts and budgets.

STOCK INVESTING AS THE MILLIONAIRE'S SECRET LINGUISTIC CODE

I became aware of the existence of stocks and the capital markets in 1976, when I was a young middle-school student taking classes in economics. Of all the chapters in my economics textbooks, none was as unintelligible and impractical as the one discussing the operations of the stock market. Back then, my country, Cameroon, did not have an equity market, so I was reading textbooks and drawing examples exclusively from the air or the far-removed British economy. To simplify the learning process, I decided to begin my economics studies by reading *Ordinary Level Economics of West Africa*, an abridged textbook from Olayiwola Adejare Lawal, a Nigerian author. Next, I read Geoffrey Whitehead's textbook titled *Economics Made Simple*, what my peers had dismissed pejoratively as *Economics Made Difficult*. I culminated my studies with another British textbook from a verbose author by the name J.C. Hanson.

To this day, I cannot forget the incessant use of the term "the Chancellor of the Exchequer," which continues to reverberate in my head like the refrain of a love song or the chorus of a Greek tragedy. The Chancellor of the Exchequer is the title held by the British Cabinet minister who is responsible for all economic and financial matters. Often simply called the Chancellor, the office-holder controls HM Treasury and plays a role akin to the posts of Minister of Finance or Secretary of the Treasury in other nations. The position is considered one of the four Great Offices of State and in recent times has come to be the most powerful office in British politics after the Prime Minister. It is the only office of the four Great Offices not to have been occupied by a woman. By comparison, in the American financial system, the closest position to the Chancellor of the Exchequer is the chairman of the Federal Reserve. The Chairman of the Board of Governors of the Federal Reserve System is the head of the central banking system of the United States. Known colloquially as chairman of the fed, or in market circles fed chairman or fed chief, the chairman is the active executive officer of the Board of Governors of the Federal Reserve System. As stipulated by the Banking Act of 1935, the president of the USA appoints the seven members of the Board of Governors of the Federal Reserve System; they must then be confirmed by the US Senate and serve for 14 years. Once appointed, governors may not be removed from office for their policy views. The chairman and vice-chairman are chosen by the president from among the sitting governors for four-year terms; these appointments are also subject to Senate confirmation. By law, the chairman reports twice a year to Congress on the Federal Reserve's monetary policy objectives. He or she also testifies before Congress on numerous other issues and meets periodically with the Secretary of the Treasury.

Currently, the chairman is Ben Bernanke, a South Carolina macro economist nominated by George W. Bush and sworn into office on February 1, 2006, for a term lasting until January 31, 2010. He was nominated for a second time by President Obama in 2009. In 2010 he was confirmed by the senate for a second term, ending January 31, 2014. Bernanke succeeded Alan Greenspan, who served for more than 18 years during the terms of four U.S. presidents. The law applicable to the chairman and all other members of the Board provides, in part: No member of the Board of Governors of the Federal Reserve System shall be an officer or director of any bank, banking institution, trust company, or Federal Reserve bank or hold stock in any bank, banking institution, or trust company; and before entering upon his duties as a member of the Board of Governors of the Federal Reserve System he shall certify under oath that he has complied with this requirement, and such certification shall be filed with the secretary of the Board. Generally speaking, the function of the US Federal Reserve is to be either the policeman or pilot of the US economy, which operates like a child's balloon. When it is necessary, the child can pump air into the balloon; similarly, the child can release air out of the balloon. As such, Bernard Bernanke, the chairman of the US Federal Reserve, is our big money pilot; he can use interest rates to stimulate the economy or to slow down the economy. In recessionary times like the ones we are living in now, Bernard Bernanke's goal is to stimulate the economy so that the US economy should not lapse quickly into another recession; thus, he increases the money supply in the financial system by reducing the discount rate the Federal Reserve charges commercial banks; by contrast, during the heydays of Internet stocks, Alan Greenspan, Bernard Bernanke's predecessor, raised interest rates to discourage investors from engaging in irrationally exuberant trading behavior; by raising the discount rate, in effect, the Federal Reserve is making it expensive for investors to borrow money; for instance, stock traders who were using margin accounts to borrow money for trading were slammed with the heavy burden of higher trading costs. When the Federal Reserve increases the discount rate they charge member banks to borrow money; these banks, in turn, transfer these costs of borrowing money to their customers. In short, the operaton of the Federal Reserve system reflects the working of the economic concepts of demand and supply.

ALIEN IN AMERICA

Although I knew about the existence of Wall Street when I came to America, ignorance and many preconceptions prevented me from playing and winning the stock market game. For one, most of the individuals I was interacting with on a daily basis at that time gave me the impression that the stock market was the preserve of America's millionaires and billionaires, a casino of rich and famous folks toasting champagne wishes and caviar dreams. Additionally, I was a functional illiterate in stock-market terms; I could not understand the symbolic language of stocks, as they were presented on either television or in daily newspapers. Moreover, some of my acquaintances had discouraged me from learning how to read stock tables, which they had dismissed as exercises and experiments in financial futility.

When I started working as a desk clerk or security guard in country clubs and luxury high-rise apartments for the rich and elderly, I challenged myself to demystify the working of the American capital markets; I decided to use some of the tenants and residents of the posh buildings where I worked as tutors or study guides. I had observed that many affluent residents were fond of coming to the front desk to check on their newspaper deliveries. I always asked, "Why?" I had observed that they were curious to ascertain how their stock investments were performing. I started asking them to show me how to read a stock table in a newspaper; others showed me how to read the ticker tape on television. While my friends picked up the newspaper to read about sports, I started reading stock tables voraciously; I started flipping the remote control to watch television channels displaying a ticker tape at the bottom of the screen. However, the day I watched a television show presenting the Beardstown Ladies, I experienced an epiphany. Eureka! I felt I had discovered the millionaire's money language. Here I was wondering why I, a Ph. D candidate with tremendous research and analytical skills, could not beat a group of old white women with very little, if any, formal college or graduate education.

There is more to personal finance than the drudgery of debts and budgets.

I decided to order all their books to learn how to model their mindset and excellent stock market performance: *The Beardstown Ladies' Common-Sense Investment Guide: How We Beat the Stock Market-And How You Can, Too; The Beardstown Ladies' Pocketbook Guide to Picking Stocks*; The Beardstown Ladies' *Stitch-In-Time Guide to Growing Your Nest Egg: Step-By-Step Planning for a Comfortable Financial Future*. From the first book, I started learning to decode the abstruse language of stock investing for my personal, professional, and business betterment. I started speaking and writing the language of money and stock investing. I had to learn quickly. Why not? I was tired of being poor and making dumb excuses for myself. Money was the lingua franca of millionaires and billionaires, so if I wanted to obtain membership into that exclusive club of rich and famous folks, I had to learn how to communicate with them. The use of money for stock investing is the world's most universal and important language. It is written everywhere; it is spoken everywhere. By understanding how to speak and write about money and stocks investing, I was afforded an opportunity to follow the secret conversations of the rich and famous folks in politics, business, and at work.

STOCK MARKET 101

The stock market is a place where money is sold. Central to the idea of the existence of a market is the availability of space or location, sellers, buyers, and prices determined by the interplay of the mechanism of demand and supply. In an economic sense, therefore, the stock market is a market like any other. In fact, we can compare the stock market to a supermarket like Giant Food, Safeway, and Shoppers Food Warehouse. Just as the stock market is replete with all types of stocks, these retail supermarkets are full to the brim with products. Do not be surprised to observe supermarkets now sporting not only automated teller machines but the branches of popular banks and chemists or pharmacies. Like supermarkets, the stock market is a part and parcel of our daily life; today, most television channels feature stock news and analyses.

STOCK OWNERSHIP

Who owns stocks? Individuals, investment clubs, and institutions own stocks. Why do people buy and sell stocks? There are two main reasons why people trade stocks. For one, people anticipate to make big and quick money from the stocks' performance. Second, people are interested in exercising shareholder rights and privileges.

LOCATION, LOCATION, LOCATION

Where is the stock market? First, the premier stock exchange was established in Philadelphia, PA, in 1790. Second, there is the big apple, New York city, the home of the present and traditional arm of the stock market on Wall Street, Manhattan, New York; indeed, it was started in 1792. Third, there is also the NASDAQ: the acronym stands for the National Association of Securities Dealers Automated Quotations. NASDAQ is really just the system that brokers use to identify different stocks and how much they are worth. Unlike the big exchange board, that is, the New York Stock Exchange, the NASDAQ has no physical existence; in fact, it has no physical trading floor, only a virtual or computer presence. Above all, there are smaller exchanges such as the American Stock Exchange (AMEX) and over-the counter (OTC).

A DAY ON WALL STREET

What is a day on Wall Street like? On the New York Stock Exchange, trading begins Monday through Friday from 9:30 a.m. to 4:00 p.m. The exchange rents booths to trading houses. Stock orders are placed when a brokerage firm's broker takes the order to a stock specialist on the trading floor. The specialist is like a dealer, who keeps track of orders from brokers

RITUAL OF IPOS

Before a company begins trading on Wall Street, the company must make a transition from being a private entity to a public company. This conversion process is technically defined as an IPO, initial public offering; that is, this is the very first time that the company is coming to the public to raise funds from the public; in return, members of the public, either directly or indirectly through their investment bankers, are given the unique opportunity to buy shares in the new public company. Before a private company can become public, the company needs to hire the services of a prestigious Wall Street investment bank. The following are the largest full-service global investment banks; full-service investment banks usually provide both advisory and financing banking services, as well as the sales, market making, and research on a broad array of financial products, including equities, credit, rates, currency, commodities, and their derivatives:

- Bank of America Merrill Lynch
- Barclays Capital
- BNP Paribas
- Citigroup
- Credit Suisse
- Deutsche Bank
- Goldman Sachs
- HSBC
- JPMorgan Chase
- Morgan Stanley
- Nomura Securities
- RBC Capital Markets
- UBS

PRIMARY MARKET

When Wall Streeters refer to the existence of the primary market, they are discussing the new IPO market. An initial public offering (IPO) or stock market launch is a type of public offering where shares of stock in a company are sold to the general public, on a securities exchange, for the first time. Through this process, a private company transforms into a public company. Initial public offerings are used by companies to raise expansion capital, to possibly monetize the investments of early private investors, and to become publicly traded enterprises. A company selling shares is never required to repay the capital to its public investors. After the IPO, when shares trade freely in the open market, money passes among public investors.

Although an IPO offers many advantages, there are also significant disadvantages. Chief among these are the costs associated with the process, and the requirement to disclose certain information that could prove helpful to competitors, or create difficulties with vendors. Details of the proposed offering are disclosed to potential purchasers in the form of a lengthy document known as a prospectus. Most companies undertaking an IPO do so with the assistance of an investment banking firm acting in the capacity of an underwriter. Investment banks, working as underwriters, provide a valuable service, which includes help with correctly assessing the value of shares, share price, and establishing a public market for shares, initial sale. Alternative methods, such as the Dutch auction have also been explored; the most notable recent example of this method is the Google IPO. China has recently emerged as a major IPO market, with several of the largest IPO offerings taking place in that country.

FACEBOOK IPO

The social networking company Facebook, Inc. held its initial public offering (IPO) on May 18, 2012. The IPO was one of the biggest in technology, and the biggest in Internet history, with a peak market capitalization of over $104 billion. Media pundits called it a cultural touchstone. Facebook's founder and chief executive Mark Zuckerberg had for years been unwilling to take the company public, and he resisted a number of buyout offers after Facebook's founding. The company did, however, accept private investments from companies, often technology firms. When the number of shareholders crossed the 500 threshold, Facebook had to take the company public. Zuckerberg retains immense control over the company, despite the fact that Facebook is a public entity.

Facebook's long-anticipated initial public offering was ultimately plagued by a series of problems: with its exchange, NASDAQ, which suffered a paralyzing computer malfunction during the first hours of the IPO, leading to tens of millions of dollars in trades being wrongly placed; with its underwriter, Morgan Stanley, over claims of an initial price that was too high and too many shares, leading; and with some Facebook executives, who were accused of alerting industry insiders to Facebook's earnings before they were public. Facebook, Morgan Stanley, and NASDAQ are facing litigation over the matters. The problems also led the stock to lose over a quarter of its value in less than a month, although it went on to regain some of its losses.

SECONDARY MARKET

Small investors who could not pluck Facebook shares during the IPO phase now have their opportunity grab on to those shares in the secondary market, where the stock begins trading normally. The secondary market, also called aftermarket, is the financial market in which previously issued financial instruments such as stock, bonds, options, and futures are bought and sold. Another frequent usage of the term secondary market is to refer to loans which are sold by a mortgage bank to investors such as Fannie Mae and Freddie Mac. The term secondary market is also used to refer to the market for any used goods or assets, or an alternative use for an existing product or asset where the customer base is the second market; for example, corn has been traditionally used primarily for food production and feedstock, but a second or third market has developed for use in ethanol production. With primary issuances of securities or financial instruments, or the primary market, investors purchase these securities directly from issuers such as corporations issuing shares in an IPO or private placement, or directly from the federal government in the case of treasuries. After the initial issuance, investors can purchase from other investors in the secondary market. The secondary market for a variety of assets can vary from loans to stocks, from fragmented to centralized, and from illiquid to very liquid. The major stock exchanges are the most visible example of liquid secondary markets - in this case, for stocks of publicly traded companies. Exchanges such as the New York Stock Exchange, NASDAQ and the American Stock Exchange provide a centralized, liquid secondary market for the investors who own stocks that trade on those exchanges. Most bonds and structured products trade over the counter, or by phoning the bond desk of one's broker-dealer. Loans sometimes trade online using a loan exchange.

THIRD MARKET

The third market, as in finance, refers to the trading of exchange-listed securities in the over-the-counter (OTC) market. These trades allow institutional investors to trade blocks of securities directly, rather than through an exchange, providing liquidity and anonymity to buyers. Third market trading was pioneered in the 1960s by firms such as Jefferies & Company although today there are a number of brokerage firms focused on third-market trading, and more recently dark pools of liquidity.

DISCOUNT BROKERS

Distinct from a full-service stock broker, a discount brokerage is a business that charges clients significantly lower fees than a traditional brokerage firm, typically offering comparatively fewer services and support. In the securities industry, a discount brokerage helps clients buy and sell securities on a stock exchange. Discount brokerages usually allow their clients to trade for their own account with little or no action with a live broker. Some brokers, like Bank of America, have now offered no-commission trades to their clients that have a specific amount of money with them. Discount brokers, like TD Ameritrade, PTI Securities & Futures and E-Trade, also provide advanced trading systems, which is why they appeal most to frequent and active traders. Beginner investors may turn away from discounted brokers because of the advanced systems and terms, and instead go to traditional brokers. Whether you deal with a discount brokerage, a full-service discount brokerage, or a traditional brokerage, most brokers are regulated and licensed by a local authority. In the U.S., the Financial Industry Regulatory Authority (FINRA) oversees brokerages, and consumers can do an online search to check the broker's standing.

Below is a list of discount brokers:

- ☐ Charles Schwab Corporation
- ☐ E-Trade
- ☐ PTI Securities & Futures
- ☐ Scottrade
- ☐ Interactive Brokers

- ☐ TD Ameritrade
- ☐ Hargreaves Lansdown
- ☐ Clubfinance
- ☐ Bestinvest
- ☐ Fidelity Investments
- ☐ Firstrade
- ☐ TradeKing
- ☐ Vanguard Brokerage Services

PRICE THEORY

Although market imperfections and inefficiencies affect stock price occasionally, demand and supply are the true determinants of stock price. The stock market represents the working of almost perfect competition. For this reason, the price of a stock tends to be determined by the demand and supply mechanism. Supply and demand is an economic model of price determination in the stock market. It assumes that in a competitive stock market, the unit price for a particular security will vary until it settles at a point where the quantity demanded by consumers, at current price, will equal the quantity supplied by producers, at current price, resulting in an economic equilibrium of price and quantity.

The following are the four basic laws of supply and demand:

1. If demand increases and supply remains unchanged, then it leads to higher equilibrium price and higher quantity

2. If demand decreases and supply remains unchanged, then it leads to lower equilibrium price and lower quantity.

3. If supply increases and demand remains unchanged, then it leads to lower equilibrium price and higher quantity.

4. If supply decreases and demand remains unchanged, then it leads to higher equilibrium price and lower quantity.

PRICE ELASTICITY OF DEMAND (PED OR E_D)

Price elasticity of demand was devised by Alfred Marshall. Price elasticity of demand (PED or E_d) is a measure used in economics to show the responsiveness, or elasticity, of the quantity demanded of a good or service to a change in its price. More precisely, it gives the percentage change in quantity demanded in response to a one percent change in price, holding constant all the other determinants of demand, such as income. Price elasticities are almost always negative, although analysts tend to ignore the sign even though this can lead to ambiguity. Only goods which do not conform to the law of demand, such as Veblen and Giffen goods, have a positive PED. In general, the demand for a good is said to be inelastic, or relatively inelastic, when the PED is less than one, in absolute value; that is, changes in price have a relatively small effect on the quantity of the good demanded. The demand for a good is said to be elastic, or relatively elastic, when its PED is greater than one, in absolute value; that is, changes in price have a relatively large effect on the quantity of a good demanded. Revenue is maximized when price is set so that the PED is exactly one. The PED of a good can also be used to predict the incidence, or burden, of a tax on that good. Various research methods are used to determine price elasticity, including test markets, analysis of historical sales data, and conjoint analysis.

PRICE ELASTICITY OF SUPPLY (PES OR E_s)

Price elasticity of supply (PES or E_s) is a measure used in economics to show the responsiveness, or elasticity, of the quantity supplied of a good or service to a change in its price. When the coefficient is less than one, the supply good can be described as inelastic; when the coefficient is greater than one, the supply can be described as elastic. An elasticity of zero indicates that the quantity of a good supplied does not respond to a price change; it is fixed in supply. Such goods often have no labour component or are not produced, limiting the short run prospects of expansion. If the coefficient is exactly one, then, the good is said to be unitary elastic. The quantity of goods supplied can, in the short term, be different from the amount produced, as manufacturers will have stocks which they can build up or run down.

BID: A bid is the price offer of a buyer in the auction-like marketplace of the stock market.

ASK: ASK is the price the seller of a security is willing to accept from the buyer.

SPREAD: Spread or of Bid-Ask Spread is the amount by which the ask price exceeds the bid. This is essentially the difference in price between the highest price that a buyer is willing to pay for an asset and the lowest price for which a seller is willing to sell it. For example, if the bid price of a stock is $20 and the ask price is $21 then the bid-ask spread is $1. The size of the spread from one asset to another will differ mainly because of the difference in liquidity of each asset. For example, currency is considered the most liquid asset in the world and the bid-ask spread in the currency market is one of the smallest: one-hundredth of a percent. On the other hand, less liquid assets, such as a small-cap stock, may have spreads that are equivalent to one percent or two of the asset's value.

GLOBAL VILLAGE

Let us name the continents: North America, South America, Europe, Central America, Africa, Australia, and Asia. Today, we live in a global village. We live in an entirely networked world, so no man or country is an island anymore. If you like it, you can trade in international stocks. It suffices for you to know that most foreign markets are not as perfect or regulated as the US stock markets. Besides, although you have the potential to earn superior returns from international stocks, expectations of those high returns must be balanced with the risk or reality of political, social, and economic turmoil. Please, review the current problems with the Eurozone: Greece, Spain, and Italy. There are also the issues of currencies. Every country uses its own currency. Generally, a currency is a unit of exchange; a currency is a form of money and medium of exchange. Currency includes paper, cotton, or polymer banknotes and metal coins. Countries generally have a monopoly on the issuing of currency, although some countries share currencies with other countries.

Today, currencies are the dominant means of exchange. Different countries may use the same term to refer to their respective currencies, even though the currencies may have little else to do with each other; a place that is technically part of another country sometimes uses a different currency from that of the parent country. There are over 182 current official, or de facto, currencies of the 193 United Nations member states: one UN observer state, nine partially recognized states, one unrecognized state, and 33 dependencies. There are also the issues of languages. Do you speak any foreign language? Voulez vous investir en France? Est ce que vous parlez francais? Möchten Sie in Deutschland investieren? Sprechen Sie deutsch? ¿Le gustaría invertir en España? ¿Hablas español?

INVESTING IN INTERNATIONAL STOCKS

If you are not one of the faints of heart, then, you might still be interested in investing in overseas stock markets. Below are four ways for you to accomplish your goals:

1--MNC: You can buy and sell the stocks of multi-national corporations on US exchanges.
2—Invest in a mutual fund that has a global or international focus.
3—Purchase ADRs, that is, American Depository Receipts
4—Buy and sell shares in foreign companies' trades on the big board—NYSE.

For more details on investing in international stocks, please, come to our investing workshop; call (301) 593-593-4879.

MARKET RISK

I would like to stress that stock investing is not kiddie stuff. If you make foolish mistakes, you can get hurt seriously. Before you invest your hard-earned money in the stock market, please, define you risk-taking potential:

1. High Risk
2. Moderate Risk
3.Limited Risk
4. Low Risk
5. No Risk

For more information on the calculation of investment risks, please, come to our investing workshop; call (301) 593-593-4879.

INFLUENCES ON STOCK MARKET

Generally, all American stock exchanges are regulated by the SEC, Securities and Exchange Commission. However, the dominant influence on the stock market is exerted by the US government under the aegis of the Federal Reserve. Although the government does not police the behavior of investors, the Federal Reserve makes a concerted effort to orchestrate the proper functioning of the capital markets. Investors make choices and decisions in the market, and the stock market affects the emotions of these investors. Generally, there are positive and negative influences on the stock market. Positive events include the following: ample money supply, tax cuts, low interest rates, political stability or domestic and international expectation of stability, and full or high employment. By contrast, negative stock market factors comprise of the following: tight money supply, increased taxes, high interest rates offering investors better returns in less risky investments, political unrest or turmoil, and low employment or high unemployment.

Stock market cycles mirror general business cycles. Periods of boom are punctuated by periods of bust. Bull market is a term that refers to positive market expansion; bear market is a term that defines recessionary market cycles.

READING A STOCK TICKER TAPE ON TELEVISION

You have seen them on business programs or financial news networks: a flashing series of baffling letters, arrows and numbers scrolling along the bottom of your television screen. While many people simply block out the ticker tape, others use it to stay on top of market sentiment and track the activity of certain stocks. What exactly is that cryptic script reeling by? It obviously tells us something about stocks and the markets, but how does one understand the ticker tape and use it to his or her advantage?

BRIEF HISTORY

Firstly, a tick is any movement, up or down, however small, in the price of a security. Hence, a ticker tape automatically records each transaction that occurs on the exchange floor, including trading volume, onto a narrow strip of paper or tape. The first ticker tape was developed in 1867, following the advent of the telegraph machine, which allowed for information to be printed in easy-to-read scripts. During the late 19th century, most brokers who traded at the New York Stock Exchange (NYSE) kept an office near it to ensure they were getting a steady supply of the tape and thus the most recent transaction figures of stocks. These latest quotes were delivered by messengers, or pad shovers, who ran a circuit between the trading floor and brokers' offices. The shorter the distance between the trading floor and the brokerage, the more up-to-date the quotes were.

READING THE TICKER TAPE

It is easy to read the ticker tape, but you have to know the precise information represented on the ticker tape. Let us use a stock quote of Microsoft Corporation as an example: MSFT is the ticker symbol, which is a four-letter identifier for Microsoft Corporation; next is a display of the number of Microsoft shares traded; then you have the share price of Microsoft; what follows is a sign showing that the price of the stock is falling; and finally we know the exact dollar amount of the price decrease. For example, go to http://www.marketwatch.com; enter the ticker symbol of Microsoft Corporation: MSFT. What do you see? It is that simple. Another favorable web site of mine is http://www.cnnfn.com. You can use it to track information about your stocks. In the back of the book, I have compiled a long list of my favorable web sites.

CNBC

Another web site popular with small investors is CNBC. What about the CNBC ticker? It is a computer simulation of ticker tapes shown as a crawl on the lower part of the television screen. The CNBC ticker shows security and index symbols just like old ticker tapes that received information by telegraph. The ticker is shown during the national commercial breaks.

There is more to personal finance than the drudgery of debts and budgets.

During the heydays of the dot.com fever, for example, enthusiastic investors flocked to television screens of CNBC reporting stock news. CNBC's major attraction was also Maria Bartiromo, the so-called money honey. She is the anchor of the Closing Bell program and the host and managing editor of *The Wall Street Journal Report*. She is also credited for becoming the first reporter to broadcast live from the floor of the New York Stock Exchange. She has appeared on various television shows and been the recipient of various journalism awards including being inducted into the Cable Hall of Fame.

READING A STOCK TABLE IN A NEWSPAPER

Almost any mass-circulation or financial newspaper in the USA has a table of stock quotes. I want to give you an assignment. You have to use the stock tables in these newspapers to learn how to research stocks. Initially, the information may appear intimidating, but I will make it look like a piece of cake. Most stock tables in newspapers summarize and present stock information in the following manner in columns: Company Name, Ticker, 52 Week High, 52 Week Low, P/E, Yield, Dividend, High, Low, Close, and Net Change:

Company stands for the name of the corporation. This column lists the name of the company. If there are no special symbols or letters following the name, the security in question is common stock. Different symbols imply different classes of shares. For example, pf means the shares are preferred stock.

52-Week High and Low represents the highest and lowest prices at which a stock has traded over the previous 52 weeks, that is, one calendar year. This information typically does not include the previous day's trading.

Ticker symbol is the unique alphabetic name which identifies the stock. If you watch financial television news, you have seen the ticker tape move across the screen, quoting the latest prices alongside this symbol. If you are looking for stock quotes online, you always search for a company by the ticker symbol. If you do not know what a particular company's ticker is you can search for it at http://www.finance.yahoo.com. I have also given you the domain names of other web sites you can use for stock study.

Dividend per share indicates the annual dividend payment per share. If this space is blank, the company does not currently pay out dividends.

Dividend yield is the percentage return on the dividend. It is calculated as annual dividends per share divided by price per share.

Price/Earnings Ratio (PE) is calculated by dividing the current stock price by earnings per share from the last four quarters. Of all financial ratios, PE is the most important one; it tells you the plain truth about the cost of a stock relative to other stocks in the market. This importance is why stock investors are always asking for the PE of a stock. For more details on how to interpret or calculate the PE ratio of stocks, come to our stock-investing seminar and workshop. Come!

Trading Volume shows the total number of shares traded for the day, listed in hundreds. To get the actual number traded, add 00 to the end of the number listed.

Day High and Low indicates the price range at which the stock has traded at throughout the day. In other words, these are the maximum and the minimum prices that people have paid for the stock.

The Close is the last trading price recorded when the market closed on the day. If the closing price is up or down more than 5% than the previous day's close, the entire listing for that stock is bold-faced. Keep in mind that you are not guaranteed to get this price if you buy the stock the next day because the price is constantly changing, even after the exchange is closed for the day. Later, I will introduce you to after-hour trading. The close is merely an indicator of past performance and except in extreme circumstances serves as a ballpark of what you should expect to pay.

Net Change is the dollar value change in the stock price from the previous day's closing price. When you hear investors talking about a stock being up for the day, it means the net change was positive. By contrast, if you hear investors talking about a stock being down for the day, it means the net change was negative.

QUOTES ON THE INTERNET

Nowadays, it is far more convenient for most of us to get stock quotes off the Internet. This new method of stock quotation is superior to the old-fashioned one because most web sites update their information throughout the day; indeed, these financial web sites give you more information, news, charting, and research. To get stock quotes, simply enter the ticker symbol into the quote box of any major financial site like CNNFN, YAHOO! FINANCE, MARKETWATCH, or MSN MONEYCENTRAL. If you do not know the ticker symbol of a stock, please, enter the full legal name of the stock. Because of the wired nature of our brave new world, I have provided you with many company names and domains relevant to stock investing.

TRIAL-AND-ERROR EXPERIMENT OF STOCK INVESTING

In retrospect, my foray into stock investing was a trial-and-error experiment to discover or build an original, unique, and winning system. As the list of books on my reading list shows, I made an effort to read many books and materials on stock investing. The authors who made the most impression on me included the following: The Beardstown Ladies, Peter Lynch, Warren Buffett , William O'Neill, and George Thompson.

Similarly, I experimented with many investment software packages: NAIC's stock selection guide, Peter Lynch's Stock Shop, Windows on Wall Street software by Windows on Wall Street, Wall Street Analyst by Omega Software, Omnitrader by Nirvana Systems, Value Line Investment Survey by Value line, Telechart 2000 by Worden Brothers, Indigo Investor by Microstar, and Wizetrade by WGAL, LLC.

There is more to personal finance than the drudgery of debts and budgets.

SRA (STATISTICALLY RATIONAL ANALYSES)

SRA reflects the story of discovering my own approach to trading stocks. It shows you how I jettisoned the trial-and-error approaches of investing in favor of inventing my own miracle trading system. How can I create a truly sensible stock picking method? This is a question that has bedeviled me as I made progress to establish myself as a small investor on Wall Street. Today, I am happy, however, that it motivated me to create SRA, that is, Statistically Rational Analyses. The following is a succinct presentation of SRA, which I have christened "the Prince Ojong stock investment guide." You, too, should be contented because after many futile attempts of research and trading, finally, I created SRA, statistically rational analyses for everybody to use and make big money in the stock market. SRA is based on the art, science, and philosophy of studying the US stock market and researching what worked on Wall Street yesterday, what works today, and what will work tomorrow.

The "S" in statistics underpins my objective in adopting a scientific method that depended on the study of a population of stocks; the "R" in rational explains the relevance in combining the strengths of the two dominant investigative approaches on Wall Street: fundamental analysis and technical analysis. In the course of my studies, I realized that both approaches have weaknesses and strengths; I sought to discard the weaknesses of these approaches and incorporate only their strengths. For instance, I realized that fundamental analysis advises me if the economics of the company whose stock I am interested in is sound; by contrast, technical analysis tells me the right time to establish a purchasing or selling position in the stock. Hence, unlike most Wall Streeters who have been wasting precious time fighting each other, I have the best of the two worlds. The "A" in analyses refers to the value of dissecting the stocks for a thorough and objective examination; in applying the scientific method to my stock picking, I undergo three processes: observation, classification, and analysis.

SRA IN PRACTICE

I have created my own investment system like an auto-pilot. In practice, the SRA system of stock investing is a process that consists of three steps germane to the application of the scientific method: observation, classification, and analysis.

STEP 1: OBSERVATION

In phase one, observation, I spend much time using statistical techniques to create a long list or a population of stock candidates for examination and investigation. Why? This observation serves as the first stage of identifying a list of stocks to buy or sell. Below, I am going to enumerate my common tools of stock observation:

52-Week Highs
52-Week Lows
Acquisitions
After-Hours Trading
Analyst Downgrades

Analyst Upgrades
Analyst Research
Annual Earnings Report
Breaking News
Buyback/Repurchase of shares
Conference Calls
Discussion Boards
Earnings Calendar
Forums
Gaps
Guidance
Internet
IPOs
Largest Price Gain
Largest Price Loss
Lowest Price Gain
Lowest Price Loss
Magazines
Mergers
Most Actives
Most Viewed
Newspapers
Newsletters
Press Releases
Quarterly Earnings Report
Reissue of Shares
Stock Splits
Whispering Calls

I am going to give you an assignment. Go to a search engine, such as Yahoo! or Google; enter the terms listed above one-by-one. What kind of information did you get? Which stocks look like interesting candidates for you to study in detail? Put the stocks on a paper list or a spreadsheet like Microsoft Excel.

STEP 2: CLASSIFICATION

Move to the second stage of the stock study. In phase two of SRA, I spend much time on stock organization and classification. I classify the stocks I have listed above into small and manageable groups for further study. I also pay attention to the kinds of stock. Generally, a stock is a unit of ownership of a company. There are two main classifications of stocks: common stocks and preferred stocks.

CLASSIFY STOCK SECTORS

After I have completed the preliminary study of the population of stocks, I proceed to classify them into sectors. I do not want to put all my eggs in one basket; I want to maintain a balanced portfolio and spread my risk across many sectors, industries, or types of business. For example, stock classification by industry may include retail, gaming, lodging, computer, telecommunications, pharmaceuticals, and financials. Stock classification by type of business is also good. Do you remember the concept of crop rotation in elementary school? Crop rotation is the practice of growing a series of dissimilar types of crops in the same area in sequential seasons. Crop rotation confers various benefits to the soil. A traditional element of crop rotation is the replenishment of nitrogen through the use of green manure in sequence with cereals and other crops. Crop rotation also mitigates the build-up of pathogens and pests that often occurs when one species is continuously cropped, and can also improve soil structure and fertility by alternating deep-rooted and shallow-rooted plants.

Most savvy investors, like smart money managers, perceive their role in the stock market to be analogous to the part played by farmers; in this regard, stock picking is like farming; stocks are like crops; farmers have to rotate them seasonally to turn a profit. The idea of stock rotation is to put companies in similar industries together for comparison purposes. Indeed, most analysts and financial media call these groupings sectors, and you will often read or hear about how well certain sector stocks are doing. One of the most common classifications of stocks divides the market into eleven different sectors. Investors consider two of these sectors defensive and the remaining nine cyclical. Let us look at these two categories and see what they mean for the individual investor. Stocks are broken up into different categories. The highest level category is a sector.

The sectors most people are familiar with are:

1. Transportation
2. Consumer non-cyclical
3. Health care
4. Conglomerates
5. Technology
6. Services
7. Capital goods
8. Financial
9. Consumer cyclical
10. Utilities
11. Basic materials
12. Energy

Each sector is further broken into several Industry Groups. For instance, Energy is typically broken into the industry groups:

1. Oil and gas – integrated
2. Coal
3. Oil well services and equipment
4. Oil and gas operations

DEFENSIVE STOCKS

Defensive stocks include utilities and consumer staples. These companies usually do not suffer as much in a market downturn because people do not stop using energy or eating food. Hence, defensive stocks provide a balance to portfolios and offer protection in a falling market. However, for all their safety, defensive stocks usually fail to climb with a rising market for the opposite reasons they provide protection in a falling market: people do not use significantly more energy or eat more food. Defensive stocks do exactly what their name implies, assuming they are well run companies. They give you a cushion for a soft landing in a falling market.

CYCLICAL STOCKS

Cyclical stocks, on the other hand, cover everything else and tend to react to a variety of market conditions that can send them up or down; however, when one sector is going up another may be going down. Here is a list of the nine sectors considered cyclical:

- Basic materials
- Capital goods
- Communications
- Consumer cyclical
- Energy
- Financial
- Health care
- Technology
- Transportation

Most of these sectors are self-explanatory. They all involve businesses with which you can readily identify. Investors call them cyclical because they tend to move up and down with businesses cycles or other influences. Basic materials, for example, include those items used in making other goods –lumber, for instance. When the housing market is active, the stock of lumber companies will tend to rise. However, high interest rates might put a damper on home building and reduce the demand for lumber.

TRACK STOCK SECTORS

What is the rationale of providing this information to you? This information will make you a better stock picker like Peter Lynch, Warren Buffett, and me. Unlike the foolish trading crowd watching CNBC and assuming that the stock market knows no seasons, you know fully well that the opposite is true; you understand that seasonal changes affect the physics, biology, and chemistry of stocks, so you choose to be alert and trade strategically; stocks are like human beings; they assume the personalities of their owners, so you choose not to follow the herd mentality. I want you to be smart; I want you to emulate me; I want you to use this information to track stock sectors and prefigure your entrances into the stock market and your exits.

Above all, as a small investor, the only way for you to make big money in the market is to mimic the actions of the big players in the stock market; personally, I know a stock sector is out of favour if the readings of my trading instruments confirm that the big boys on Wall Street are selling or moving their money out of that sector. In fact, by examining stock sectors, such as a large group of stocks, I can get a fairly accurate and decent view of the big money flow. What I mean by big money flow is the direction where big market makers, such as investment banks and mutual funds, the true drivers of stock prices, are doing with their big money. As a small investor, I tend to buy or sell lots of only one hundred shares at a time; by contrast, institutional investors buy or sell lots of many shares; hence, they make the market; they rule the market. For your assignment, I would like you to use many search engines and web sites presented in steps 6 and 12 to take a good look at a list of stock sectors and some information pertaining to performance.

Additionally, there are a few key pieces of information I like you to pay attention to when you look at the lists stipulated above:

1. --The ratio of new highs to new lows in the sector. Right now, the services sector is showing an 11 to 1 ratio of new lows to new highs. This is a good indication that the services sector is getting hit hard, and could be ripe with stocks to short.

2. --RS (Relative Strength) rank is the rank of each sector versus every other sector. I actually keep a weekly log of these ranks. If you see a trend of a particular sector dropping in rank, that is a sign that big money is moving out.

3. --13-Week % versus S&P 500 is a pretty simple measure of how each sector is performing against five hundred of the biggest companies in the US, that is, the entire market as a whole.

INVESTOR'S BUSINESS DAILY (IBD)

Again, the best way to use this data is to track it over time. If you see a pattern of decline by a particular sector versus the market, it is usually a good place to start shorting. Stocks sectors are helpful stock sorting and comparison tools. As a beginner, you can get reliable information on stock sector rotation from the newspaper or online edition of William J. O'Neill's *Investor's Business Daily* (IBD). I love reading IBID because it provides all this information to me in a concise format. IBD saves me much time. But do not get hung up on using just one organization's set of sectors, though. For instance, *MorningStar.com* uses slightly different sectors in its tools, which let you compare stocks within a sector. This information is extremely helpful, since one of the ways to use sector information is to compare how your stock or a stock you may want to buy, is doing relative to other companies in the same sector. If all the other stocks are up 11% and your stock is down 8%, you need to find out why. Indeed, the why question is the role of fundamental analysis. Likewise, if the numbers are reversed, you need to know why your stock is doing so much better than others in the same sector: maybe its business model has changed and it should not be in that sector any longer. All of the preceding concepts are methods I use daily to track stock sector rotation. Similarly, stock sector rotation is the favourite action of mutual fund and portfolio managers whose past time is shifting assets from one stock sector of the economy to the other. In the final analysis, these stock sector rotations are key indicators as to the state of the economy. You never want to be making investment decisions in a vacuum. By using sector information, you can see how a stock is doing relative to its peers. That information will help you understand whether you have a potential winner or loser. Armed with that intelligence, you can know when it is the most opportune time to buy or sell the stock. In addition to classifying stocks for study by sector rotation, I also investigate equities by understanding their personalities or idiosyncratic features. As far as I am concerned, stocks behave like human beings; behind every stock on Wall Street is a human buyer or seller; hence, as a stock scientist, I like to discover their chemistry, biology, and physics, which I have often subsumed in the following manner:

Big cap stock
Blue chip stock
Cyclical stock
Defensive stock
Dividend stock
Growth stock
Income stock
Large cap stock
Mid cap stock
Momentum stock
Multinational stock
Non-cyclical stock
Rolling stock
Small cap stock
Small company stock
Value stock
Volatile stock
Undervalued stock

Further, I put my stocks in four discrete groups: growth stocks, value stocks, income stocks, and momentum stocks. My cardinal rule is to weigh my stock purchases, sales, and portfolio in the following manner:

40%......growth stocks
30%......value stocks
20%..... income/dividend stocks
10%......momentum/swing stocks

40%......GROWTH STOCKS

PETER LYNCH

I believe in success modeling. I like to invest like the masters. In this category, I apply the theory and practice of Peter Lynch. From reading Peter Lynch's books and using his Stock Shop software, I have mastered a common-sense approach to stock investing. Money is a valuable asset, so I have learned that as a small stock investor, I have to manage my money well or seriously; or else, I will lose it in the stock market. Additionally, I have learned that a stock is not just a stock; a stock represents a business. By buying a stock, I am voting with my hard-earned money to invest in that business.

Who said you could not learn to manage your own money? Is it the white-shoe Wall Street guys or some MBA brats from the Ivy League schools? I am giving you an opportunity to prove them wrong like my hero, Peter Lynch; as the legendary manager of the famous Fidelity Magellan mutual fund, Peter Lynch created a superlative and unbeatable record. Peter Lynch has written three good books that I consider invaluable to small investors: *Beating the Street, Learn to*

Earn: a Beginner's Guide to the Basics of Investing and Business, and *One Up on Wall Street: How to Use What You Already Know to Make Money in the Market*.

Additionally, he has developed software that mimics his investment approach. If you want to find growth stocks, or ten baggers, you owe it to yourself to emulate Peter Lynch's investment approach. His ideas sound very simple, but they work very well. He encourages you to question and challenge the conventional wisdom of the Wall Street crowd He advices small investors to research their local area to discover new and great businesses for stock investment; in fact, that is how I stumbled upon the ten baggers known as Google, Apple, Ebay, Amazon, Yahoo!, Best Buy, and Chipotle. Peter Lynch encourages small investors to invest in what they know; this advice helped me establish winning positions in Microsoft before the words *Windows* and Bill Gates became household names in America.

Why not research the products you use every blessed day as a consumer. Chances are the company behind the stock is doing very well; if you do not do your diligent homework, you will never know it; similarly, you pay many utility bills every end of the month. Who are these companies? You must seek hidden gems in the neighborhood that the Wall Streeters are unaware of. According to Peter Lynch, a great business must have the following four qualities:

1. --sustainable competitive advantage
2. --plenty of cash on the balance sheet
3. --little or no debt
4. --strong leadership or management

Above all, you must learn to diversify your investments. I like to use options to protect my positions, but I use them sparingly. They are not a source of making big money for me.

30%......VALUE STOCKS

I believe in success modeling. I like to invest like the masters. In this category, I apply the theory and practice of Warren Buffett and Value line Investment Survey. Nicknamed the Oracle of Omaha, Nebraska, Warren Buffett is the most famous investor in the whole world. A former student of Benjamin Graham, Warren Buffett applies what he has learned from his master at Columbia University, New York. Like Graham, Buffett espouses the value stocks approach to investing. He advises you to maintain a good temperament; when investing in stocks, you should master your emotions. When making investment decisions, you must control the feelings of greed and fear. Time is your friend, so you must be patient to maintain a long-time horizon for investing. "Do not sell [a stock] too soon," he warns. According to Buffett, the singular purpose of buying a stock is to invest in a great business for profit maximization. It is better to buy great brand businesses when these enterprises are out of favor with the foolish Wall Street folks. Be contrarian; buy undervalued companies that Wall Street big shots are running away from; invest in the stock or company for the long haul. Interesting examples in this regard are Warren Buffett's acquisition of the following companies: Coca Cola (KO), Johnson & Johnson (JNJ), and Procter & Gamble Company (PG). In this wise, Buffett invests only in companies he would like to be in business with for the long haul. Value investing is like a marriage in the old days.

LESSONS FROM THE MASTER

What lessons did Warren Buffett learn from his master Benjamin Graham? To ascertain the answer, I decided to read Benjamin Graham's two books: *The Intelligent Investor* and *Security Analysis*.

THE INTELLIGENT INVESTOR

Graham advises stock investors to adhere to a long-term perspective. He emphasizes that stock investing is the antithesis of speculation. The intelligent investor studies a security thoroughly to discover its PE ratio and true value. The intelligent investor perceives trading securities to be analogous to the ownership of a business franchise; he or she has to analyze the financial state of the business; he or she ignores erratic and short-term fluctuations in stock market prices. The intelligent investor ignores the emotions of fear and greed, whims, sentiments, and caprices of the moment. The intelligent investor knows that short-term the stock market is stupid and erratic like a political voting machine; long-term the stock market is like a weighing machine that reads true value. As such, Graham questions the hypothesis of the efficiency and perfection of the stock market; markets are neither efficient nor perfect; the theory of efficiency or perfection is either a fallacy or a figment of the trader's barren imagination. De jure, as much as economics expects human behavior to be rational, most investors in the stock market are not acting rationally or intelligently; rather, they are ruled by emotion and a crowd mentality.

Faced with this reality, each time the stock market swoons, investors in the mold of Warren Buffett capitalize on the correction as a unique buying opportunity; intelligent investors perceive market corrections as the right time to buy premium companies that have been on their watch list for a long while. Market corrections are analogous to sales in a department store. Whoever gets angry when Best Buy, Macy's, or JC Penny announces a sale? Then, why do Wall Street big shots and foolish investors decry market corrections?

SECURITY ANALYSIS

In *Security Analysis*, Benjamin Graham encourages all intelligent investors to use fundamental analysis to isolate underpriced securities in the stock marketplace. By following this advice, I buy stocks at a discount to book value; interesting examples in this regard are GE, IBM, GMC, and Coca Cola. I exploit market fluctuations to discover discounted stocks. For preliminary assistance in using fundamental analysis, I advise you to examine *NAIC's Stock Selection Guide*; a second source of stock research assistance is the web site of Millionaire iUniversity; if you need help, we could organize a workshop in your city; please, let us know much about your needs..

VALUE LINE INVESTMENT SURVEY

Value line Investment Survey is a publication I depend on all the time. The Beardstown Ladies introduced me to this pearl-like publication. In their stock-investment guide, they made many references to *Value line Investment Survey*. I will discuss *Value line Investment Survey* in detail soon. For now, it suffices for you to know and appreciate this treasure trove of investing.

There is more to personal finance than the drudgery of debts and budgets.

20%..... INCOME/DIVIDEND STOCKS

I believe in success modeling. I like to invest like the masters. In this category, I apply the theory and practice of the Dogs of the DOW. Before investing in volatile stocks, it is important to dress up your stock portfolio with the 30 securities that are a component of the Dow Jones Industrial Average. Certainly, these stocks will not make you rich, but they can provide a stream of income and dividends.

COMPANIES IN THE DOW JONES INDUSTRIAL AVERAGE

Below is a list of companies belonging to the DOW Jones Industrial Average.

MMM 3M Co
AA Alcoa Inc.
AXP American Express Co
T AT&T Inc.
BAC Bank of America Corporation
BA Boeing Company
CAT Caterpillar Inc.
CVX Chevron Corp
CSCO Cisco Systems Inc.
DD E. I. du Pont de Nemours and Company
XOM Exxon Mobil Corporation
GE General Electric Company
HPQ Hewlett-Packard Company
HD Home Depot Inc.
INTC Intel Corporation
IBM International Business Machines Company
JNJ Johnson & Johnson
JPM JPMorgan Chase and Company
KFT Kraft Foods Inc.
MCD McDonald's Corporation
MRK Merck & Co Inc.
MSFT Microsoft Corporation
PFE Pfizer Inc.
PG Procter & Gamble Company
KO The Coca-Cola Company
TRV Travelers Companies Inc.
UTX United Technologies Corporation
VZ Verizon Communications Inc.
WMT Wal-Mart Stores Inc.
DIS Walt Disney Company

There are many ways I use the stocks in the DOW 30 for investment purposes. First, I research and identify companies with a long history of paying dividends or increasing their dividend such as Winn-Dixie, which is not part of the DOW 30 today. You can glean this information from online research sources: NAIC's resources and Value Line Investment Survey. Second, within the 30 companies in the DOW, I select the 10 companies that are paying the highest dividend and invest in them. In fact, on Wall Street, these 10 companies are referred to as the Dogs of the DOW. Conversely, I identify 10 companies in the DOW with the lowest yielding dividend; I buy them and hold for one year. After one year, I sell them.

If I cannot afford to buy these stocks in lots of 100, I use the strategy of DRIPS, dividend reinvestment plans. When I was starting out as a small investor, I did not have much money to invest in the stock market, but I had the desire and ambition to get started. DRIPS provided a vehicle for me to use; I did not have to deal with a traditional or full-service stock broker, so I did not have to pay a heavy load. Chuck Carlson is the author who introduced me to the concept of investing in DRIPS. http://ww.dripinvestor.com. Another good web site for information on DRIPS is *The MoneyPaper*'s http://www.directinvesting.com. The web site sports the following slogan: helping self-reliant investors since 1981.

10%......MOMENTUM/SWING STOCKS

I normally allocate 10% of my investing to trading momentum or swing stocks. My father used to tell me that too much work without play makes Jack a dull boy. Why should I be a dull boy? Why should the big guys on Wall Street have all the fun? Indeed, I like working hard and smart to invest my money, but I also like playing with swing trading to exploit the turbulent market of momentum stocks. Momentum is the rate of acceleration of a security's price or volume. The idea of momentum in securities is that their price is more likely to keep moving in the same direction than to change directions. In technical analysis, momentum is considered an oscillator and is used to help identify trend lines.

Once a momentum trader sees acceleration in a stock's price, earnings or revenues, the trader will often take a long or short position in the stock in the hope that its momentum will continue in either an upward or downward direction. This strategy relies on short-term movements in a stock's price, unlike fundamental value. Momentum stocks are stocks with high returns over the past three to 12 months. Momentum investors seek out stocks with the potential to double or triple within just a few months. Momentum investors generally hold a stock for a few months and monitor their holdings daily. They tend to sell their stocks within a few months after acquiring it. There are many stocks in the market that accelerate in price that go on to make 100% to 300% returns in less than year or even in a few months. Netflix is an example.

However, for the investors who are just starting, momentum investing can be a confusing and frustrating experience to find these stocks. I do not recommend momentum plays or swing trading for novice investors. Let me come to your rescue. Here are some keys to spot momentum stocks. One of the first signs you can use to spot momentum stocks is the relative strength of the stock compared to the overall market over a specific timeframe. Most momentum investors seek a stock which has outperformed at least 90% of all stocks over the past 12 months. When major indices decline, a great momentum stock exhibits strength, by holding or even exceeding their highs.

When the major indices rally, momentum stocks typically lead the rally and make new highs outpacing the market. Potential momentum stocks should show in their balance sheet that they are growing at an accelerated rate.

Another factor is the Earnings per Share (EPS) growth. At least a 15% year-over-year earnings per share growth is needed to qualify as a momentum stock. Stocks with accelerating rates of EPS growth over previous quarters are also considered. In addition, positive forecasts by many analysts regarding the company's earnings are necessary for identifying momentum stocks. Further, momentum investors also look at whether the reported earnings exceeded the analysts' forecasts compared to the last quarter. A company cannot grow its earnings faster than its Return on Equity (ROE), which is the company's net income divided by the number of shares held by investors, without raising cash by borrowing or selling more shares. Many companies raise cash by issuing stock or borrowing, but both alternatives reduce earnings-per-share growth. For momentum investors, a potential stock should show an ROE of 17% or better. The share price and trading volume of the stock are also factors to spot a momentum stock. The only reason for stocks that trade at very low prices is that they are already out of favor with the market. Avoid stocks trading below US$5.

Momentum investors seek stocks that have high trading volumes, the number of shares traded daily on the average. Very low trading volumes indicate the market's lack of interest. Generally, momentum investors seek companies with a minimum volume of 100,000 shares, or at least, momentum investors like to see the average daily volume increases as the value of the stock rises. Start keeping a list of potential momentum stocks and track their performance in the market. In time, you will be able to spot the stocks that go on to make 100% to 300% returns in less than year or even in a few months. My special preferences of momentum stocks are Internet stocks, securities of new companies that cater to an Internet market niche. Facebook (FB) is an interesting example in this regard.

TRACKING MOMENTUM/SWING STOCKS

JACK D. SCHWAGER

I rely on two tools to track and research momentum and swing stocks: Jack D. Schwager's book titled *Getting Started in Technical Analysis* and the Worden Brothers' amazing software known as *Telechart 2000*. Schwager's book is a lucid introduction to technical analysis. Revered by many, reviled by some, technical analysis is the art and science of deciphering stock price activity to better understand market behaviour and identify trading opportunities. In this accessible guide, Jack Schwager, perhaps the most recognized and respected name in the field, demystifies technical analysis for beginning investors, clearly explaining such basics as trends, trading ranges, chart patterns, stops, entry, and exit and pyramiding approaches.

USING TELECHART 2000

I have simplified and automated my use of Telechart 2000. First, I focus my attention on swing stocks that have been listed most active. You can find this list on many web sites or Telechart

2000 can provide you with this information. Second, I use the online version of William J. O'Neill's Investors Business Daily (IBD) to confirm the direction of money flow for everything stock on the most active list. If IBD shows that the institutional investors on Wall Street are buying a stock heavily, I prepare to establish a buy position in the stock; by contrast, I prepare to establish a sell position in the stock if IBD shows that the big money is flowing heavily out of the stock. Third, I mark a band which delineates the daily support and resistance levels of the stock. Fourth, I program my computer to loop and automatically execute a trade each time the price point hits either the support level or the resistance level. Telechart 2000 is a good stock tool. Wade Cook introduced me to Telechart 2000. Offered by Worden Brothers, Inc., Telechart 2000 is a stock charting platform. The company supports its product by providing live seminars in major cities across the USA. The company also posts news of webinars on its website to help users utilize the program and learn about using charts and indicators for successful trading.

STEP 3: ANALYSIS

Analysis is the third and final stage of my stock evaluation exercise. I have chosen to combine the two, heretofore, diametrically opposing approaches to investing on Wall Street: fundamental analysis and technical analysis. In the analysis phase, I use fundamental analysis to tell me the stock I should buy or sell. After perusing documents, such as 10-Ks, annual reports, philosophy, operations, balance sheet, and auditor's letters, I raise and answer the following questions:

1. Who is the manager of the business?
2. What has happened to the stock and company?
3. Where do the company's operations take place?
4. Why should I, or we, buy or sell the stock?

INTERNET RESEARCH

If I think I cannot answer the questions listed above satisfactorily, I decide to pursue additional Internet research, which is the second phase of fundamental analysis. I have enumerated my most popular Internet research sources below:

AlphaChart
American Association of Individual Investors
Bank Rate Monitor
Barrons
Bonds Online
Bruce Babcock's Reality Based Trading Company
Bureau of Public Debt
Calvert Group
CBS Marketwatch.com
Chicago Board of Trade
Chicago Board of Options
CNNfn.com

Dogs of the DOW
Fidelity Investments
Fortune.com
Fundalarm
Google Finance
INO Global Markets
Investors.com
Money.com
Morningstar
MSN Money
Mutual Funds magazine Online
NAIC Software—betterinvesting.org
Networth Mutual Fund Market Manager
NumaWeb
Reuters
The New York Times
The Wall Street Journal
The Washington Post
Vanguard Group of Funds
Yahoo Finance
Zacks

ADDITIONAL INTERNET RESEARCH SOURCES

I do not want you to complain about the lack of research sources. Below is another list of Internet sources you might find useful for research purposes:

Anderson Investor's Software
Applied Derivatives Trading
Board of Governors of the Federal Reserve
Campbell Harvey Hypertextual Finance Directory
Closing Bell from Mercury Mail
Consumer Information Center
CPAdvisor
Deja News
Deloitte and Touche Peerscope
Duff & Phelps Credit Rating Company
Edustock
FX Week
Gamelan Official Directory for Java
Great Pacific Trading Company
Interactive Quote
Internal Revenue Service
Investment FAQ Home Page
Investools

IRA Epstein & Company Futures
Kiplinger's 101: Investment Terms You Should Know
Lebenthal & Company
Lind-Waldock & Company
Misc.invest.stocks
Money.com
Money Minds
Munder Funds
NASDAQ
Netstock Direct
Nuveen Research
Olsen and Associates
PC Financial Network
PC Quote Europe Investor's Emporium
Quote Ticker Bar
Robertson, Stephens & Company
Roger Engemann and Associates
Savoy Discount Brokerage Investment Glossary
SEC Edgar
Smith Barney
Strong Funds
The Holt Stock Report
The Insurance News Network
The Option Fool
The Pitbull Investor
The Small Cap Investor
Think Quest International
Trader Gizmos
Traders' Library
US Securities and Exchange Commission (SEC)
Wall Street Directory

THE VALUE LINE INVESTMENT SURVEY

The use of *The Value Line Investment Survey* is my third stage of the fundamental analysis of a stock. The Value Line Company publishes many products: the stock survey, small and mid-cap edition, mutual fund advisor, special situation service, select, and convertible online. *The Value Line Investment Survey*, however, is the product that I use a lot. Initially, I used to read the hard-copy of the survey in the public library. In 1997, when I founded the Millionaire Club, I decided to subscribe personally to the desktop version of the survey. I was making more money, but I did not have the time to spend at the public library anymore. Later, with the mass popularity of the world wide web, I decided to switch to the online version of The Value Line Investment Survey. Why do I like *The Value Line Investment Survey* very much? The service is like a small investor affording to hire hundreds of analysts to study the stock market and report on the business model of many companies on one page consecutively. I am going to give you another assignment; for your appreciation, log on to Google.com; enter the following words, verbatim: a sample of a one-page Value Line report on Johnson and Johnson (JNJ). Choose the report appearing as the third item.

I WANT TO DISSECT A VALUE LINE REPORT FOR YOU

I assume that you have downloaded and printed a copy of the Value Line report on Johnson and Johnson (JNJ). I assume that you have read the report in its entirety. I assume that you are still looking at the report right now.

VALUE LINE RANK OF TIMELINESS

The timeliness rank is Value Line's measure of the expected price performance of a stock for the coming six to 12 months relative to the population of approximately 1,700 stocks. Stocks ranked 1 (Highest) and 2 (Above Average) are likely to perform best relative to the approximately 1,700 stocks we follow. Stocks ranked 3 are likely to be average performers. Stocks ranked 4 (Below Average) and 5 (Lowest) are likely to underperform stocks ranked 1 through 3 in Value Line's universe. At any one time, there are 100 stocks ranked 1; 300 ranked 2; approximately 900 ranked 3; 300 ranked 4; and 100 ranked 5. Value Line has published timeliness ranks for more than 33 years. Twice a year, in January and July, the results of the performance of the timeliness ranks are published in Selection & Opinion.

Overall, the results have been truly outstanding. Mark Hulbert, a Forbes columnist who studies the performance of investment publications, has written that over a 17-year period, *The Value Line Investment Survey* is in first place for risk adjusted performance. The most important factor in determining the timeliness rank is earnings growth. Companies whose earnings growth over the past 10 years has been greater than their stocks' price appreciation tend to have high scores.

In addition, the ranks take into account a stock's recent price performance relative to all approximately 1,700 stocks in the Value Line universe. A company's recent quarterly earnings performance and any recent earnings surprises caused because a company reported results that were significantly better or worse than expected are also factors. They are combined to determine the timeliness rank. Here is just one word of caution. Stocks ranked 1 for timeliness are often more volatile than the overall market and tend to have smaller capitalizations (the total value of a company's outstanding shares, calculated by multiplying the number of shares outstanding by the stock's price per share). Conservative investors may want to select stocks that also have high Safety ranks because they are more stable issues.

INDUSTRY

Value Line also publishes industry ranks which show the timeliness of each industry. This industry ranking is analogous to the concept of crop rotation. The Industry ranks indicate how Value Line believes the prices of stocks within 90 or more industries will perform relative to each other. These ranks are updated weekly and published on the front cover and inside the

Summary & Index. They also appear at the top of each Industry Report in Ratings & Reports. The Industry rank is calculated by averaging the Timeliness ranks of each of the stocks assigned a Timeliness rank in a particular industry.

SAFETY RANK

The Safety rank is a measure of the total risk of a stock compared to others in the population of approximately 1,700 stocks. As with the timeliness rank, Value Line ranks each stock for risk safety from 1 (Highest) to 5 (Lowest). However, unlike timeliness, the number of stocks in each category from 1 to 5 may vary. The Safety rank is derived from two measurements, weighted equally, found in the lower right hand corner of each page: a company's financial strength and a stock's price stability. Financial strength is a measure of the company's financial condition, and is reported on a scale of A++ (highest) to C (lowest). The largest companies with the strongest balance sheets get the highest scores. Price stability is based on a ranking of the standard deviation, a measure of volatility, of weekly percent changes in the price of a company's own stock over the last five years, and is reported on a scale of 100 (highest) to 5 (lowest) in increments of 5. Generally speaking, stocks with Safety ranks of 1 and 2 are most suitable for conservative investors. A stock's price growth persistence and a company's earnings predictability are also included in the the Safety rank stipulated above, but they do not factor in the calculation of Safety rank; however, they are useful stock statistics.

TECHNICAL RANK

The technical rank is primarily a predictor of a stock's short term, three to six months, relative price change. It is based on Value Line's proprietary model, which examines ten relative price trends for a particular stock over different periods in the past year. It also takes into account the price volatility of each stock. The Technical ranks also range from 1 (Highest) to 5 (Lowest). At any one time, about 100 stocks are ranked 1; 300 ranked 2; 900 ranked 3; 300 ranked 4; and 100 ranked 5.

BETA

Beta is a measure of volatility and is calculated by Value Line. While it is not a rank, we do consider it important. Please, momentum players take note of beta.

ANALYST'S COMMENTARY

The stock analyst's written commentary is in the lower half of the page. Many readers think this is the most important section of the page. In the commentary, the analyst discusses his or her expectations for the future. There are times when the raw numbers do not tell the full story. The analyst uses the commentary to explain why the forecast is what it is. The commentary is also particularly useful when a change in trend is occurring or about to occur. As an example, a stock may have a poor timeliness rank but the analyst thinks earnings could turn around in the future. In this case, the analyst may use the commentary to explain why he or she thinks conditions are likely to get better, thus giving the subscriber insight into what is happening and why.

FINANCIAL ESTIMATES

The estimates of sales, earnings, net profit margins, income tax rates, and so forth are all derived from spreadsheets maintained on every company and printed in bold italics. The numbers are based on an analyst's latest thinking about where a company may be in the future. Value Line's analysts regularly review their projections with the company's management. Afterwards, they make whatever adjustments they believe are warranted.

HISTORICAL FINANCIAL DATA

Many investors like to use the statistical array to do their own analysis. They, in particular, use the historical data in the centre of each report to see how a company has been doing over a long time frame. It is worth pointing out that while all of the data are important, different readers find different data items to be most useful. The numbers are probably most helpful in identifying trends. For example, look at sales per share to see if they have been rising for an extended period of time. Look at operating margins and net profit margins to see if they have been expanding, narrowing, or staying flat. Also check the percentages near the bottom to see if the return on total capital or the return on shareholders' equity have been rising, falling, or remaining about the same.

ANNUAL RATES OF CHANGE

The annual rates box is located in the left-hand column. This box shows the compound annual growth percentages for sales, cash flow, and other items for the past 5 and 10 years and also Value Line's projections of growth for each item for the coming 3 to 5 years. Trends are also important here. Check whether growth has been increasing or slowing and to see if Value Line's analyst thinks it will pick up or fall off in the future.

TARGET PRICE RANGE

In the upper right-hand section of each report is a target price range for each stock. This is the range in which the price is likely to fall during the period 3 to 5 years hence. The range is based on the analyst's projections in the period 3-5 years out for earnings multiplied by the estimated price/earnings ratio in the statistical array for the same period. The width of the high-low range depends on the stock's safety rank. A stock with a high Safety rank has a narrower range, one with a low Safety rank, a wider one.

3- TO 5-YEAR PROJECTIONS

In the left hand column of each report, there is also a box which contains 3- to 5-year projections for a stock price. There you can see the potential high and low average prices we forecast, the % price changes we project, and the expected compound annual total returns, price appreciation plus dividends. To make these calculations, analysts compare the expected prices out 3 to 5 years into the future, as shown in the target price range and projections box, with the recent price shown on the top of the report.

Investors whose primary goal is long-term price appreciation should study the 3- to 5-year projections carefully and choose stocks with above-average appreciation potential. For comparative purposes, you can find the estimated median price appreciation potential for all approximately 1,700 stocks on the front page of the Summary & Index.

PRICE/EARNINGS RATIOS

Information about Price/Earnings ratios appears at the very top of the Value Line page as well as in the statistical section in the center. A Price/Earnings ratio, often referred to as a P/E ratio or simply a P/E, is probably the most widely used statistic in investing. It is calculated by dividing the price of a stock, usually the current price, by twelve months of earnings. If, for example, a stock is selling at $40 a share and its annual earnings are $2.00 a share, its P/E is 20. Few investors will buy a stock without knowing what its P/E is. Most frequently, investors will compare the P/E of one stock with that of another before making a decision to purchase or sell.

WILLIAM J. O'NEILL'S TECHNICAL ANALYSIS AT WORK

In his book *How to Make Money in Stocks: A Winning System In Good Times or Bad*, William J. O'Neill introduces CANSLIM, a growth stock investment strategy he formulated from his study of the 500 best performing stock market winners dating back to 1953. Although CANSLIM uses a sprinkling of fundamental analysis, its technical analysis focus cannot be disputed. In fact, technical analysis is the second component of my stock analysis exercise. After I have used fundamental analysis to select my potential buy and sell candidates, I always like to get a confirmation signal prior to the execution of a buy or sell order. Here is the question I would like to address: When should the buying or selling of the stock take place? I use William J. O'Neill's CANSLIM to obtain the answer. First, I read, study, and interpret the daily, weekly, and monthly price and volume charts that can tell me if a stock is behaving properly or not and if the stock is under accumulation, institutional buying, or not. Stock charts measure the actual demand and supply equation for a stock in the real marketplace, that is, Wall Street. From William J. O'Neill's CANSLIM and the cup-with-a-handle pattern, I am closer to identifying good trading candidates.

CANSLIM

What is CANSLIM? It is not a new fad or diet plan. If you are trying to lose weight, please, look elsewhere. Although *The Miraculous Millionaire* covers the subject of financial fitness, CANSLIM is impertinent to weight loss. CANSLIM is an acronym. CAN SLIM refers to the seven-pronged mnemonic publicized by the American newspaper *Investor's Business Daily*, which claims to be a checklist of the characteristics performing stocks tend to share before their biggest gains. It was developed by *Investor's Business Daily* editor William J. O'Neil who has reportedly made several hundreds of millions of dollars by consistently using its approach.

The seven parts of the CANSLIM mnemonic are as follows:

--C stands for current earnings. Per share, current earnings should be up to 25%. Additionally, if earnings are accelerating in recent quarters, this is a positive prognostic sign.

--A stands for annual earnings, which should be up 25% or more in each of the last three years. Annual returns on equity should be 17% or more.

--N stands for new product or service, which refers to the idea that a company should have a new basic idea that fuels the earnings growth seen in the first two parts of the mnemonic. This product is what allows the stock to emerge from a proper chart pattern of its past earnings to allow it to continue to grow and achieve a new high for pricing. A notable example of this is Apple Computer's iPod.

--S stands for supply and demand. An index of a stock's demand can be seen by the trading volume of the stock, particularly during price increases.

--L stands for leader or laggard? O'Neil suggests buying the leading stock in a leading industry. This somewhat qualitative measurement can be more objectively measured by the relative price strength rating (RPSR) of the stock, an index designed to measure the price of stock over the past 12 months in comparison to the rest of the market based on the S&P 500.

--I stands for institutional sponsorship, which refers to the ownership of the stock by mutual funds, particularly in recent quarters. A quantitative measure here is the Accumulation/ Distribution rating, which is a gauge of mutual fund activity in a particular stock.

--M stands for market indexes, particularly the Dow Jones, S&P 500, and NASDAQ. During the time of investment, O'Neil prefers investing during times of definite uptrends of these three indices, as three out of four stocks tend to follow the general market pattern.

Ceteris paribus, I have established my method of applying CANLSIM. When the stock forms a cup-with-a-handle pattern and the price of the stock crosses above the 50 day moving average, I establish a buy position in the security; by contrast, I sell when the stock price falls below the 50-day moving average.

PRINCE OJONG'S TIME-TESTED RULES OF STOCK INVESTING

Finally, I have shared with you the fundamental information you need to play and win the stock market game. When you attend my money-making seminar and workshop, I promise to give you practical and survival stock tips and techniques. For now, however, I would like to tell you that a word to the wise is sufficient. I do not want to pummel you with more stock advice, but, please, I am exhorting you to pay much attention to the following think points:

--Pay God first, not the piper. If you are in doubt, please, reread step 1 of the book. After paying your maker, you can be whittling away at your debt. High interest and fees are drags on your wealth, so struggle to pay off credit card debt; this is the best investment you will ever make.

Save to the maximum that you can afford; invest for the long term; you need to be in the market all the time.

--Pay off credit card debt and establish cash reserves before investing. I may sound like a broken record, but you cannot build under the heavy weight of debts. I do not mind repeating the idea that debt is bad, so pay off your credit cards and plan to save money for a rainy day.

--Start saving now, not later. Do not worry about whether the market is high or low; just begin investing. Trust in time rather than timing. The secret to getting rich easily and quickly is, surely, the miraculous power of compounding, that is, compound interest. Keep a steady course. The most important driver in the growth of your assets is how much you save, and saving requires discipline. To develop discipline, I recommend that you begin to pay God first; then begin saving your money, at least 10%. Save your money after paying God; then, invest before anything else, even paying bills that are not on your budget; implement a budget, change your spending habits, and pay off your debt. Do not be caught empty-handed. I recommend that you open an emergency fund. I do not specify how much you should set aside, but I do cover a variety of places to put the cash: money market accounts, certificates of deposit, and online savings accounts. I also recommend purchasing cash-value life insurance for tax-free retirement.

--Stiff the tax collector. Make the most of tax-advantaged savings: Open an Individual Retirement Account, contribute to your company's retirement plan, take advantage of tax-free savings for your child's education, and buy your first home rather than rent. All of these things help to reduce the bite that taxes take out of your money.

--Match your asset mix to your investment personality. Based on your risk tolerance and your investment horizon, choose the best mix of cash, bonds, stocks, and real estate. I encourage investors to buy each of these through cash-value insurance or mutual funds.

--Never forget that diversity reduces adversity. Do not just buy stocks — buy stocks, bonds, and other investments classes. Within each category, diversify further. And do not just buy one stock

— Buy mutual funds of many stocks. Finally, I recommend diversification over time, that is, making investments at regular intervals using dollar-cost averaging.

--Avoid expensive mutual funds. The only factor reliably linked to future mutual fund performance is the expense ratio charged by the fund. In fact, I am advising you that costs or loads matter for all financial products.

--Bow to the wisdom of the market. Forget about market timing because no one can time the market. The market is too unpredictable. Professional money managers cannot beat the market; financial magazines cannot beat the market; in fact, nobody can beat the market on a regular basis. The best way to earn consistent gains is to invest in broad-based equity index funds using a non-MEC universal life insurance contract. It may sound boring, but it works.

--Automate your trading with stock or options software. I recommend Telechart 2000 for stocks, and I recommend Charles Schwab's OptionsXpress for trading options. Educate yourself; education shall set you free. Invest regularly, that is, monthly. Beware of bad advice. Stay away from it and old wives' tales. Tailor your portfolio for your situation. Do not invest in hot tips.

--Be disciplined like an American soldier. Keep accurate and good records. Exercise patience; do not try to make money too fast. Diversify your assets. Rebalance your portfolio periodically. Risk is as important as return, so diversify your investment portfolio among all asset classes: cash, certificate of deposits, stocks, mutual funds, annuities, and bonds. Even if you are not averse to risk, I am advising you that it is important to subscribe to the policy of portfolio diversification. Do not put all your eggs in one basket; diversify, diversify, and diversify!

--Do not be greedy. Greed is a bad emotion; control it; otherwise you will make bad decisions. Be an intelligent investor. Use your God-given talent. Move your 401(K) to an IRA when leaving your job; do not cash out.

--Explore the opportunities to invest in annuities: fixed and variable. Variable annuities may not be good for some people. I have saved many documents that can educate you on the basics of annuities. Call my office for these documents: (301) 593-4897.

--Do not let taxes dictate all your investment moves. Be realistic about how much you will need in retirement. Assume modest returns when calculating how much you might have in the future.

--Use Dollar-Cost Averaging. Dollar cost averaging (DCA) is an investment strategy that may be used with any currency. It takes the form of investing equal monetary amounts regularly and periodically over specific time periods, such as $100 monthly for 10 months, in a particular investment or portfolio. By doing so, more shares are purchased when prices are low and fewer shares are purchased when prices are high. The point of this exercise is to lower the total average cost per share of the investment, giving the investor a lower overall cost for the shares purchased over time. Dollar cost averaging is also called the constant dollar plan (in the US), pound-cost averaging (in the UK), and, irrespective of currency, as unit cost averaging or the cost average effect.

--Use hedging to offset the risk of losing your money. A hedge is an investment position intended to offset potential losses/gains that may be incurred by a companion investment. In simple language, a hedge is used to reduce any substantial losses/gains suffered by an individual or an organization. A hedge can be constructed from many types of financial instruments, including stocks, exchange-traded funds, insurance, forward contracts, swaps, options, many types of over-the-counter and derivative products, and futures contracts. Public futures markets were established in the 19th century to allow transparent, standardized, and efficient hedging of agricultural commodity prices; they have since expanded to include futures contracts for hedging the values of energy, precious metals, foreign currency, and interest rate fluctuations.

--Use arbitrage to make money in the global marketplace. Arbitrage is a strategy that involves the simultaneous trading (buying and selling) of the same security in different markets to take advantage of price disparities between the two markets.

--Watch your bucket of gold. Keep a watchful eye on expenses and margin trading; use margins only for momentum plays.

MUTUAL FUNDS

Did you know that nearly half the households in the U.S.A. invest in mutual funds? In the following section, I will ask you to play and win the stock market game by investing also in mutual funds. I want you to use your hard-earned money to back only proven stock winners. After I have preached the virtues of stock investing and insurance, I want to introduce you to index mutual funds, presumably converting you to my religion of risk-free investing. First, I will explain what mutual funds are; in the end, I will suggest possible index funds and asset allocations. Do not be your own worst enemy. Keep trying to learn. I admonish you to stay the course; learning about mutual funds is a form of self-reliance. A good understanding of mutual funds will be a hedge against dependence, faulty thinking, overconfidence, herd behavior, and the sunk-cost fallacy. Even if you enjoyed my discussion on stock investing, I am encouraging you to explore mutual funds, too.

Whenever I raise the subject of mutual funds, my customers begin raising many questions: Mutual funds? What are they? How many types of mutual funds exist? How do mutual funds work? What is the anatomy of the prospectus of a mutual fund? What are the advantages of investing in mutual funds? What are the disadvantages of mutual funds? Without much ado about nothing, on the following pages, I am ready to address these questions and other issues you might have on the subject of mutual funds. I will do it right now! Generally, many investors choose mutual funds, over individual stocks, because they do not have the expertise to research individual stocks all the time. This is fine, but mutual-fund investors need to realize that mutual funds also require research to pick the best of mutual funds as well. The world of mutual funds is wide and complex; not all mutual funds are created equal and if you are like me, you want to find mutual funds that are top performers over the long run to best make your money work for you.

For this reason, investing your hard earned money in mutual funds comes with some big decisions. So, before you invest, you need to ask yourself a simple question: What am I investing for? Unfortunately, it is not enough for you to say "I want to get rich quick in mutual funds." You need to define your financial goals and decide on your financial objectives, the steps you are taking to achieve your goals. Your goals could be to build wealth over time, to use the money as an income stream, to pay for your children's education, or simply to pass on wealth to future generations. But having clear objectives is just the start of your goal definition. Where to put your money in mutual funds is your next objective; as I will show you, you have so many investment choices, and the process can be confusing for many people. That is why mutual-fund investing can make all the difference. Luckily, the only investment you need to make right now is some time to learn the basics of mutual-fund investing.

WHAT ARE MUTUAL FUNDS?

Simply put, mutual funds are pools of money from many different people which are then invested in portfolios of stocks, bonds, or other investments to meet specific financial objectives. They are very attractive to the average person because you can actively participate in a wide range of investments which would be prohibitively expensive on your own. Because mutual funds are managed by professional money managers, you only need to know which funds are consistent with your own goals and tolerance for risk. While the notion of pooling money to make investments is centuries old, the first official mutual fund was launched in 1924. Obviously, the idea caught on, and today there are literally thousands of different funds catering to every kind of investment style and objective, and they are very popular for retirement plans like the IRA and 401(K).

HOW DO MUTUAL FUNDS WORK?

Instead of buying individual stocks or bonds, for instance, when you invest in a mutual fund you are purchasing shares of the fund, making you a shareholder. You can buy and sell shares in mutual funds and while you hold your shares you can participate in the fund's rewards, increase in value, and risks, decrease in value. Mutual funds are very easy to invest in, although I must warn you, fees and costs can vary widely. Hence, you must do your homework before you invest your money.

A FEW WORDS ABOUT DIVERSIFICATION AND ASSET ALLOCATION

Before I get into the thick of things, I would like to stress the significance of diversification and asset allocation. In fact, for the sake of beginners, I have included a glossary at the end of this discussion because mutual-fund investing can seem like speaking a whole different language from the American English variety. Two of the most common terms you are going to read and hear, and the most important to understand as well, are diversification and asset allocation. The term diversification reminds everyone about an old phrase: "never put all your eggs in one basket." Well, that is what diversification is all about. Some mutual funds can do this for you because they spread your money across many different investments, perhaps hundreds or thousands, under the theory that if one stock, or other asset class, is down another might be up. The goal is to help you reduce your exposure to risk and increase your potential for rewards. By choosing different styles of mutual funds, you can accomplish the goal of diversification.

I want you to set your sights now on asset allocation. While diversification means to spread your money among different types of investments, allocation means how much money to allocate or put in each type or class of asset. The basis of asset allocation is that different asset classes, for instance stocks, bonds, and others, will perform differently from each other. In other words, when stocks are up bonds may be down, and vice versa. That is why, depending on your objectives, it is important to consider just how much money you want to commit to each type of asset. For instance, if your goals are long range, you may have a bigger percentage invested in stocks; by contrast, if you want to live on the money you have invested, bonds may be the way to go. It all depends on your risk tolerance and your goals.

But be aware that as much as asset allocation and diversification may help you in minimizing market risk, they do not assure either a profit or a guarantee against loss.

WHAT KINDS OF MUTUAL FUNDS ARE OUT THERE?

With over 10,000 mutual funds in existence today, you certainly have a wide range to choose from to meet your specific needs. While I cannot recommend which ones are right for you, knowing the general types available will give you a good grounding to begin narrowing down your search. What follows is a list of the four broad categories of mutual funds, each with its own risk and reward potential, along with a short investor profile of those who would find them attractive. Bear in mind these are just representative groups; indeed, there are many more specialized funds and subcategories. Your financial representative can help you determine what makes the most sense for you. When you decide to join the Millionaire Club, you will have access to the finest financial representatives in the high-finance industry.

EXCHANGE-TRADED FUND (ETF)

An exchange-traded fund (ETF) is an investment fund traded on stock exchanges, much like stocks. An ETF holds assets such as stocks, commodities, or bonds, and trades close to its net asset value over the course of the trading day. Most ETFs track an index, such as the S&P 500 or MSCI EAFE. ETFs may be attractive as investments because of their low costs, tax efficiency, and stock-like features. ETFs are the most popular type of exchange-traded product. Only so-called authorized participants, typically large institutional investors, actually buy or sell shares of an ETF directly from or to the fund manager, and then only in creation units, which are large blocks of tens of thousands of ETF shares, usually exchanged in-kind with baskets of the underlying securities. Authorized participants may wish to invest in the ETF shares for the long-term, but usually act as market makers on the open market, using their ability to exchange creation units with their underlying securities to provide liquidity of the ETF shares and help ensure that their intraday market price approximates to the net asset value of the underlying assets. Other investors, such as individuals using a retail broker, trade ETF shares on this secondary market. An ETF combines the valuation feature of a mutual fund or unit investment trust, which can be bought or sold at the end of each trading day for its net asset value, with the tradability feature of a closed-end fund, which trades throughout the trading day at prices that may be more or less than its net asset value. Closed-end funds are not considered to be "ETFs," even though they are funds and are traded on an exchange. ETFs have been available in the US since 1993 and in Europe since 1999. ETFs traditionally have been index funds, but in 2008 the U.S. Securities and Exchange Commission began to authorize the creation of actively managed ETFs.

BOND OR INCOME FUNDS

Bond or income funds are made up primarily of bonds, so here is a quick explanation of a bond. Basically, bonds are a way for a company, or government or agency, to borrow money, so they owe whoever buys that bond. Bonds are issued with specific face values and interest rates called "yield." That is why bonds are known as "fixed-income." Bonds are generally also sold with a specific maturity date, meaning they have to be purchased back at a certain time at face value. This can make them stable, lower risk investments depending on the issuer. As mentioned earlier, stocks and bonds do not behave the same way so having some money invested in bond or income funds – which can be lower risk – can be a good way to balance your risk and rewards. Just as in stock funds, there are many different kinds of bond funds. Some invest only in corporation-issued bonds; others concentrate on government bonds or agencies and some invest in a mixture of the two categories. The choices multiply from there, because corporations and governments issue different kinds of bonds. Different companies will be considered higher or lower risk for instance. Some funds concentrate on different industries or regions. It all sounds a little complicated, but relax. The mutual funds do all the research for you, and there are many sources to help you match specific mutual-fund choices to your financial goals. Certain bond or income funds can be good for investors who are looking for a stream of income and prefer less risk.

STOCK OR EQUITY FUNDS

The beauty of stock funds is that they instantly give you access to a wide range of different company stocks which most people could not afford on their own, with the added plus that the mixture of stocks within a fund is managed by a finance professional. Stocks are shares of ownership in a company, so if that company does well the stock will do well: increase in value. But, if that company does poorly, or even in the industry it is in does poorly, that stock may lose value. This means that stock funds offer the potential for higher rewards than bond or money market funds, but they also come with more risk as well. Depending on your tolerance for risk, stock funds can be ideal for individuals with long-term investment goals. That is often why they are so popular for retirement funds and pensions. Just as with bond funds, there are many different kinds of stock funds catering to all styles of investors and financial objectives. This variety of choice is good, because it means you can find just the right ones for you, but it also means there are a mind-boggling array of choices.

POPULAR MUTUAL-FUND STRATEGIES

Some of the more popular fund strategies available include the following list below:

Growth funds – Stocks of companies considered to be fast growing.

Value funds – Stocks of companies generally considered to be undervalued.

Large-cap funds – Stocks of very large blue chip companies that tend to pay dividends.

Balanced funds – A combination of stocks and bonds to achieve some growth while attempting to manage risk.

International funds – Mostly foreign-owned company stocks, or a combination of U.S. and foreign stocks. International securities are subject to political influences, currency fluctuations and economic cycles that are unrelated to those affecting the domestic financial markets and may experience wider price fluctuations.

Of course there are many other investments, along with mutual funds that can provide a mixture of different strategies. The important thing for you to remember is to always choose mutual funds with your financial goals in mind.

Particularly, stock or equity mutual funds can be good for the following group of investors:

1. -- Generally have a longer-term timeline
2. --Do not mind taking some risk
3. --Want to increase diversification
4. --Like having lots of choices

INDEX FUNDS

Index funds are designed to mimic or replicate the returns of a specific stock or bond index or benchmark, such as the following: DOW 30, S&P 500, the Russell 2000, and the NASDAQ. DOW 30 is the Dow Jones Industrial Average; the mutual fund invests your money in thirty of the top large capitalization firms monitored by the Dow Jones company. The S&P 500 is an index that tracks the stock performance of 500 companies widely regarded by investors to be representative of 500 large company stocks in general. The Russell 2000 is an index that measures the performance of the small-capitalization segment of the U.S. equity universe. What about the NASDAQ? It is an index that tracks the performance of specific technology-laden companies in the USA.

As a small investor, you can match an investment directly into an index; in fact, there are many mutual funds you can use to match almost every kind of stock index available, that is, from small-capitalization indices to large or foreign entities. Index funds hold the same stocks in the same proportions regardless of how the individual stocks are doing. This is why index funds are called passive funds; the fund manager is not actively managing the stocks in the mutual fund in an attempt to outperform what the market is doing, but simply trying to get as close to the index as possible. What is interesting to many investors is that index funds, generally, do better than most other funds, and for that reason index funds have become very popular. Index funds can be good for investors who can tolerate some risk and prefer, principally, lower fees. Most mutual funds that are actively managed charge their customers too many junk fees. Run away from these types of investments. Choose no or low load index funds; you will build wealth faster.

MONEY MARKET FUNDS

When you want to keep a certain amount of cash on hand, whether for emergencies, purchases, or simply while you decide how to invest it, money market funds make an ideal choice. These funds generally invest in short-term, high-quality stable securities, including U.S. Treasury bills and certificates of deposit, and these funds are highly liquid, meaning you can cash out of them quickly. Some money market funds allow you to write checks on them as well. They have, by far, the lowest risk of all styles of mutual funds, but the lowest potential reward as well. Generally, a money market fund offers returns higher than those of typical checking or savings accounts.

Money market funds can be good for the following group of investors:

-- Have almost no tolerance for risk and prefer stability
-- Have a short-term investment objective
-- Have a preference to maintain liquidity to cash out easily
--Have a want to generate income

In general, money market funds are offered to meet the liquidity needs of clients, but unlike bank deposits, money market funds are not insured or guaranteed by the Federal Deposit Insurance Corporation (FDIC) or any government agency. Although money market funds seek to preserve the value of your investment at $1.00 per share, it is possible to lose money by investing in a money market fund.

HOW TO BUY A MUTUAL FUND

When you have done your homework and found a mutual fund or two that look interesting to you, there are some specific steps and pieces of information that you will want to know before you make a purchase. They are the following:

1. GET A PROSPECTUS

By law, before you invest, the mutual-fund company is required to send you a prospectus, which details a plan of the fund's objectives and how these objectives will be achieved; the prospectus also includes information on the mutual fund's past performance, fees, management, risk, and so forth. Please, do not gloss over or ignore the prospectus; the document can look daunting, but you must read it; in fact, it tells you everything you need to know before you spend a dime, so do not skim over the mutual fund's prospectus. If you cannot read it from cover to cover, please, call my office for assistance. For a modest fee, we will read and summarize the benefits of the mutual fund for you. We can make things easy for you to choose a mutual fund. Hence, there is no reason for you to complain. How else should we encourage you to begin investing today? The merit of mutual funds is that they shield new investors from the risk of picking stocks. Yet, you have to research mutual funds before you buy them. Right?

2. WHERE TO PURCHASE

Mutual funds can be bought from a variety of sources, including: banks, insurance companies, stock brokers, investment advisors, discount brokers, online sources, and the mutual fund companies themselves. Who you ultimately choose to go with depends on many variables such as fees, costs, variety, and level of advice you want and expertise. Ask many questions and get clear answers. Consider a fund's objectives, risks, charges and expenses carefully before investing. Read the prospectus thoroughly; the prospectus contains this and other information and is available from your advisor. If you are in doubt, please, feel free to call my office for referral information. Please, it is important for you to understand that mutual funds are not without the risks of capital; hence, you must read the prospectus carefully before you invest in a mutual fund.

MUTUAL FUND FAMILIES

Mutual funds are so many like stars in the sky above. Today, we speak of mutual fund tribes and families. Below are some big mutual-fund families. Before I provide the listing to you, I would like to proffer a warning. It is important for me to underscore the fact that I am neither recommending them nor am I providing any financial or legal advice to you. Rather, I want you to use this information as a starting point for intensive study. If you need referrals, I can contact my associates who are qualified by law to sell mutual funds to members of the public.

THE VANGUARD GROUP

The Vanguard Group is an American investment management company based in Malvern, Pennsylvania, that manages approximately $1.7 trillion in assets. It offers mutual funds and other financial products and services to retail and institutional investors in the United States and abroad. Founder and former chairman John C. Bogle is credited with the creation of the first index fund available to individual investors. He has also been credited with the popularization of index funds generally, and driving costs down across the mutual fund industry. The Vanguard Group is owned by the funds themselves, with each fund contributing a set amount of capital towards shared management, marketing, and distribution services.

JOHN CLIFTON BOGLE

If there is one name you should remember in mutual-funds investing, it is John Clifton Bogle. He was born in Montclair, New Jersey, on May 8, 1929. Like my customer Donji Finch, Bogle's family was affected by the Great Depression. He attended Blair Academy on a full scholarship, and he earned an undergraduate degree from Princeton University in 1951, and he attended evening and weekend classes at the University of Pennsylvania. For pushing down the long and concrete walls of mutual fund junk fees, he deserves to my hero. He is the founder and retired CEO of The Vanguard Group. He is known for his 1999 book titled *Common Sense on Mutual Funds: New Imperatives for the Intelligent Investor*, which became a bestseller and is considered a classic. Bogle is famous for his insistence, in numerous media appearances and in writing, on the superiority of index funds over traditional actively-managed mutual funds. He believes that it is folly to attempt to pick actively managed mutual funds and expect their performance to beat a well-run index fund over a long period of time. Bogle argues for an approach to investing defined by simplicity and common sense. Below are his eight basic rules for investors:

1. Select low-cost index funds

2. Consider carefully the added costs of advice

3. Do not overrate past fund performance

4. Use past performance to determine consistency and risk

5. Beware of stars, that is, popular mutual-fund managers

6. Beware of asset size

7.   Do not own too many funds

8.   Buy your fund portfolio - and hold it for the long haul

I follow John C. Bogle's advice to the letter. Even though I pick individual stocks, I am still weighted heavily in equity-indexed mutual funds. Please, begin making regular investments to a diversified portfolio of index funds. Be patient. The simplicity of John C. Bogle's message does not detract from its value. I recommend that you should read his excellent book on mutual funds. In fact, the book sticks to the basics; it is short; it is well written in plain English; it contains no jargon; it is easy to understand; John C. Bogle simplifies the concepts so the average person can grasp them. It is filled with great advice. Though the advice may seem elementary, it is advice that works.

FIDELITY INVESTMENTS

Fidelity Investments (FMR LLC) is legally known as Fidelity Management and Research; it is an American multinational financial services corporation. It is one of the largest mutual fund and financial services groups in the world. It was founded in 1946 and serves North American investors. Fidelity Ventures is its venture capital arm. Fidelity International Limited (FIL) was an international affiliate founded in 1969, serving most countries in the rest of the world. In September 2011, FIL was rebranded as 'Fidelity Worldwide Investment. As you can see, Fidelity Investments manages a large family of mutual funds, provides fund distribution and investment advice services, as well as providing discount brokerage services, retirement services, wealth management, securities execution and clearance, life insurance, and a number of other services.

AMERICAN FUNDS

American Funds is a family of 33 mutual funds managed by Capital Research and Management, part of the Capital Group Companies. Capital Research and Management serves as the investment advisor to the 33 American Funds. The company does not advertise and shuns publicity, preferring to rely on brokers' recommendations to their clients. With over $1 trillion in assets under management (as of November 2010), American Funds is the third largest behind Fidelity and The Vanguard Group.

PIMCO

Pacific Investment Management Company, LLC., commonly called PIMCO, is an investment firm headquartered in Newport Beach, California. PIMCO is led by co-founder William H. Gross, usually known as Bill Gross, who serves as Co-Chief Investment Officer, and Mohamed A. El-Erian, the other Co-CIO as well as the firm's CEO. It is the world's largest bond investor. Gross manages the Total Return Fund, the world's largest mutual fund with assets of $242.7 billion as of June 30, 2011. He co-founded the firm in 1971, launching with $12 million of assets. Previously, PIMCO had functioned as a unit of Pacific Life Insurance Co., managing separate accounts for that insurer's clients. In 2000, PIMCO was acquired by Allianz SE, a large global financial services company based in Germany, but the firm continues to operate as an autonomous subsidiary of Allianz. PIMCO oversees investments totalling more than $1.7 trillion on behalf of a wide range of clients, including millions of retirement savers, public and private pension plans, educational institutions, central banks, foundations and endowments, among others.

FEES AND COSTS

Mutual funds can cost a lot or a little depending on what you buy and where. Fees generally break down into two categories: ongoing, or maintenance, fees and purchase and sales charges called loads. Loads are sales commissions which come in several forms: a front-end load means you pay the fee when you purchase the fund; a back-end load means you are charged fees when you sell the mutual fund. The amount of fees you pay depends on how long you hold your mutual-fund shares. In contrast, no-load funds do not charge fees either; they make money from management fees.

RESEARCHING MUTUAL FUNDS

To facilitate the task of researching mutual funds, I have attempted to do some homework for you; I have highlighted four important sources, but you have to continue conducting research for your own betterment.

1. MORNINGSTAR, INC.

In researching mutual funds, your primary destination should be the web site of Morningstar, Inc. Traded on the stock exchange called NASDAQ with the four letter symbol MORN, Morningstar Inc. is a financial data provider based in Chicago, Illinois, USA. Morningstar provides data on more than 380,000 investment offerings, including stocks, mutual funds, and similar vehicles, along with real-time global market data on more than 8 million equities, indexes, futures, options, commodities, and precious metals, in addition to foreign exchange and Treasury markets.

Morningstar also offers investment management services through its registered investment advisor subsidiaries and has more than $190 billion in assets under advisement and management as of March 31, 2012. The company has operations in 27 countries. Morningstar created the Morningstar Rating, Morningstar Style Box, and other proprietary measures.

2. WALL STREET JOURNAL ONLINE

The Wall Street Journal Online is a virtual extension of the famous *Wall Street Journal*. Back in the heydays of the dot.com era, I could not imagine a day of waking up from sleep without the treasury of my delivered copy of *The Wall Street Journal*. As a premier American English-language international daily financial newspaper, *The Wall Street Journal* is published in New York City by Dow Jones & Company, a division of News Corporation, along with the Asian and European editions of the Journal. *The Wall Street Journal* is the largest newspaper in the United States, by circulation.

According to the Audit Bureau of Circulations, it has a circulation of 2.1 million copies (including 400,000 online paid subscriptions), as of March 2010, compared to USA Today's 1.8 million. Its main rival, in the business newspaper sector, is the London-based *Financial Times*, which also publishes several international editions. This online publication can be a very useful research resource on mutual funds.

3. INVESTOR'S BUSINESS DAILY

Investor's Business Daily (IBD) is a national newspaper in the United States, published Monday through Friday, that covers international business, finance, and the global economy. Founded in 1984 by William O'Neil, it is headquartered in Los Angeles, California. IBD provides detailed information about stocks, mutual funds, commodities, and other financial instruments aimed at individual investors. The newspaper provides detailed, concise statistics using earnings, stock price performance, and other criteria to help investors find quality stocks. Detailed index and stock charts are present throughout the newspaper. The stock and mutual fund information is designed to be used along with the founder William O'Neil's book titled *How to Make Money in Stocks: A Winning System in Good Times or Bad.* In William O'Neil's book, you can learn more about CANSLIM, an acronym for what he claims to be a checklist of the characteristics performing stocks tend to share before their biggest gains. I love the online version of IBD; the online publication can be a very useful research resource on mutual funds.

4. YAHOO FINANCE

Yahoo! Finance is a service from Yahoo! that provides financial information. It is the top financial news and research website in the United States, with more than 23 million visitors in February 2010, according to Comstore. Yahoo! Finance offers information including stock quotes, stock exchange rates, corporate press releases, financial reports, and popular message boards for discussing a company's prospects and stock valuation. It also offers some hosted tools for personal finance management. Yahoo! Finance Worldwide offers similar portals localized to assorted large countries in South America, Europe, and Asia. This online publication can be a very useful research resource on mutual funds.

MUTUAL FUND CHECKLIST OR SPREADSHEET

The easy or best way for you to implement the results of your mutual-fund research is to create a checklist that serves as a framework for you to compare and contrast the mutual funds you are considering seriously. De jure, your checklist might include the following five headers:

1.   --5-year performance of the mutual fund
2.   --10-year performance of the mutual fund
3.   --Manager tenure
4.   --Minimum initial investment
5.   --Expense ratio

MUTUAL FUND WARNINGS

--Always look for mutual funds with no load, meaning there is no sales charge when you put your money in or when you take it out. One of the reasons I take a dim look at mutual funds is the excessive fees the customer has to pay. Interestingly, most of the mutual-fund managers underperform the market. In fact, this reason explains why I have a preferment for no-load and index mutual funds. Once again, I am advising you that we should all learn from John C. Bogle of The Vanguard Group. For his undergraduate thesis at Princeton University, John C. Bogle conducted a study in which he found that around three quarters of mutual funds did not earn any more money than if they invested in the largest 500 companies simultaneously, using the S&P 500 stock market index as a benchmark. In other words, three out of four of the managers could not pick better specific winners than someone passively holding a basket of the 500 largest public U.S. companies. The managers could pick specific stocks which would do as well as picking the 500 largest stocks, essentially doing as well as random chance would dictate, but the cost to pay their expenses, as well as the high taxes incurred through active trading, resulted in underperforming the index. These results explain why I encourage most of my customers to concentrate on no-load mutual funds or equity-indexed universal life contracts, that is, cash-value life insurance policies that mimic the S&P 500 index.

--Be careful of investing in a mutual fund that your local bank, bank teller, or advisor suggests to you without the benefit of your own research. I respect the work of bank tellers, but I must acknowledge that these essential bank employees are functional financial illiterates. I talk to bank tellers daily. Today, many banks are acting like the middlemen of mutual-fund companies; they have made arrangements with security brokers to use their facilities to sell mutual funds to the banks' customers; in return, the mutual-fund companies give the banks big money in the form of commissions or kickbacks. Is that not the reason why many mutual funds have to charge exorbitant fees? Caveat emptor; let the buyer beware! These mutual funds can have very high expense ratios that drag down your investment returns quickly. On the one hand, banks operate legitimate businesses; on the other hand, banks are cut-throat competitors. Banks are like Ali Baba, a cabal of thieves whose penchant for stealing from the innocent and poor American people is expressed by the joyful abandon of Shylock, a character in William Shakespeare's *The Merchant of Venice.*

A SHORT GLOSSARY OF MUTUAL FUND INVESTOR TERMS

I recognize the fact that investing in mutual funds is akin to traveling to a foreign land like Pandora in James Cameron's movie titled *Avatar.* I want you to enjoy your new adventure; I want you to become fluent in the language of mutual funds. Hence, I have appended a short glossary of investor terms for the benefit of new mutual-fund investors.

Allocation: Dividing investment assets according to an individual's goals, risk tolerance and timeline to balance risk and reward.

Asset: Any item of value that can be converted to cash, including stocks and bonds.

Bond: A debt security issued by a corporation or government office. The issuer agrees to pay the bondholder a predetermined interest rate for a specified length of time and promises to repay the bond in full on the maturity date.

Cap: Short for "capitalization," or the sum of a company's debt, stock and earnings.

Capital Gain: The amount that an asset's selling price exceeds the buying price.

Certificate of Deposit (CD): Certificates offered by banks which pay a higher level of interest than regular checking/savings accounts in exchange for tying up money for a specific time.

Debt: Amount owed by an organization, usually represented as "bonds."

Dividend: The payout of part of a company's earnings as a return on investment in its stock.

Diversification: The practice of attempting to reduce risk by spreading investments across asset classes like stocks, bonds and cash, because they generally do not behave the same way in the market.

Equity: Ownership of a company, most often in the form of shares of stock.

Growth: An investment strategy that seeks stocks with strong earnings and/or potential for growth.

Income: Money earned through employment or investment returns.

Index: A representation of the value of a certain set of securities which acts as an indication of the health and direction of the market as a whole (see S&P 500).

IRA: Individual Retirement Accounts are a tax-deferred way to put aside a specific amount of money each year until withdrawals can begin at age 59. The money is often invested in mutual funds.

Large Cap: A company with more than $5 billion in capitalization.
Load: Loads are the fees charged for buying or selling a mutual fund. They can be charged upfront.
(front-end load) or upon the sale (back-end load). No-load funds do not charge a commission.

Market: This term generally refers to the securities market as a whole (in the U.S. this is often interchangeable with "Wall Street" or "the Street").

Mid Cap: A company with a capitalization of $1 billion to $5 billion.

Portfolio: An investor's total collection of investments, including stocks, bonds, cash and more.

Prospectus: A legally required document that provides all the details and facts about an investment so investors can make informed choices.

Return: The amount that an investment earns annually, usually shown as a percent.

Risk: The likelihood that an investment will or will not lose value.

S&P 500: A group of unmanaged securities widely regarded by investors to be representative of large-company stocks in general. An investment cannot be made directly into an index.

Security: A generic term for any investment instrument issued by a corporation or government that represents equity or debt.

Share: A unit of ownership in a corporation or mutual fund.
Small Cap: Generally a company with market capitalization between $300 million and $1 billion.

Stock: An investment instrument that shows ownership in a corporation, usually expressed in "shares." Also called equity securities.

Timeline: The length of time money is expected to be invested, also known as "horizon." Most investments are either short-, medium- or long-term.

Value: An expression relating to the relative worth of an investment.

Volume: The number of securities traded (bought and sold) during a specific time period for a specific market, region or stock exchange.
Yield: The annual rate of return on an investment expressed as a percentage.

Step 10

INVEST IN REAL ESTATE

Real-estate investing offers many benefits to savvy investors like me, Prince Ojong, the Lord and Savior of the 99% of the masses of America: income, capital gains, leverage, and taxation. If you manage your real-estate investing like a small business, you can, certainly, make much money in a short time; that is the income potential of real-estate investing. A second profit center of real-estate investing is capital gains. Third, leverage is a powerful investing tool you can wield with joyful abandon. Fourth, real-estate investing offers you many opportunities of income tax elimination, reduction, or minimization. In short, the four benefits stipulated above constitute the joys of investing in real estate. If I, a new immigrant from Africa, can do it, you can do it, too. I am offering a push-button real-estate investing system to you, but you must work hard and smart to make my system work for you. My system is high-tech but semi-automatic. Please, I do not want you to use it like a remote control; my system is still manual. I want you to use your brains to follow the system manually; I do not want to hear that it does not work; in fact, that is why I have insisted on combining my seminars with workshops that take into account the particular problems that my students might be having in different parts of the country. I do not want you to be disappointed and throw away *The Miraculous Millionaire* or my home-study workbook; I am willing to work with you patiently, until you get things right. I am ready to coach you. I will prove to you that real-estate millionaires and billionaires like Donald Trump, Ted Turner, Jorge Perez, Mortimer Zuckerman, and Samuel Zell are not any smarter or happier than you are. They simply know a few powerful success secrets that have allowed them to win the money game. How would you like to learn these money making secrets and live a life filled with extraordinary possibilities of happiness?

CHOOSE PRINCE OJONG AS YOUR REAL-ESTATE COACH

CHOOSE A COACH WHO HAS DONE IT WELL, NOT JUST TALKED ABOUT IT! There are too many armchair real-estate success gurus out there; unfortunately, most of them are not intelligent enough to pass the Federal and State exam, even after fifteen tryouts. Fortunately, you should be happy I am not one of them. There is too much physical evidence to prove to you that I have made too much money buying and selling real estate successfully as a private investor and Maryland salesperson. In addition, paper trails show that I have held a Maryland title insurance license. Hence, if you plan to play and win the real-estate investing money game, you need more than a huckster of junk cars or boiler-plate gibberish that does not work and will never work; you need me, a God-fearing individual who has done it successfully; you need someone who genuinely cares about working-class people on your side; your need a mentor or a coach who can improve your financial welfare.

That individual is me, Prince Ojong. Hire me as your personal coach; come to my seminar, and invest in one of my coaching packages to support your studies. Tiger Woods, the greatest golfer that ever lived, has a coach. Michael Jordan attributes his high school coach as the greatest contributor to his success in sports. To achieve extraordinary results today most experts agree that you need a coach. With a good coach like me, your dreams can be closer than you think. If you believe in your dream of getting rich quickly and easily, hire me. In retrospect, when I look back at my progress in real-estate investing, I do not regret the decision to abandon my PhD studies to research how an average individual in America, with either no money or no connections, can learn and master the secrets of the art, science, and philosophy of building wealth using real estate as a vehicle of choice. My primary philosophy of real-estate investing is centered on a very simple idea: "work smart, not hard." Please, jot this idea down: "Work smart, not hard." My mission is to give good hope to you; I am motivating you to believe that you could make easy money in America by using real estate.

Unlike fly-by-night real-estate gurus, I do not make my money from selling get-rich-quick books or peddling seminars and useless home-study courses. I write books that have excellent content. I am an average person who has been investing profitably in real estate. In fact, I have held a mortgage, real-estate, and title insurance license since the year 2000. Initially, I was investing as a private investor; later, I became a realtor because I wanted to have access to the multiple-listing service (MLS), a database of houses available in the Washington, DC, metropolitan area for sale. My real-estate system maybe a turn-key program; yet, I am here to warn you that it is incredibly difficult to invest in real estate, if you do not have the right knowledge: specialized knowledge. The purpose of this chapter, therefore, is to prepare you like the good soldier for war in the trenches of real-estate investing. I want to share my specialized knowledge with you.

GENESIS: APPRECIATING THE SO-CALLED REAL ESTATE GURUS

First, I must pay respect to my beloved real-estate gurus; second, I will present my most memorable or sweetest real estate transactions. Third, I will end the chapter with many articles designed to increase your knowledge of real-estate investing. As a born-again Christian, the fairest way to begin the chapter on real estate is by expressing my sincere appreciation for a group of valuable entrepreneurs often derided in the mass media and the Internet as "real-estate gurus." In normal American parlance, the term guru is a pejorative one. In this vein, it is disrespectful and irresponsible to associate real-estate pioneer educators for the masses with it. Certainly, I am not arguing that all real-estate motivational educators deserve much respect; rather, my point of contention is that we should not lump all of them in the same column of vice; let us disparage the bad ones, but let us also respect and salute those who have contributed immensely to the education of many unwary students.

Students need to accept responsibility for implementing the strategies they have learned from every home-study real estate course; as a perfect example, whenever I attended real-estate seminars in the past, I was critical in analyzing the information I had received from the motivational speakers; as a student, I saw my role as a researcher or scientist; since I was a new immigrant, I did not understand much about the lessons; I had to research everything for myself; yet, I appreciated the opportunity to sit in a beautiful hotel room and learn the subject of real-estate investing in America free of charge; I had noticed the real-estate courses lacked a sense of completeness; if the seminar promoter hailed from Florida, for example, he or she provided cases that could not, at all, be duplicated in the Washington, DC, metropolitan area. Hence, instead of complaining that the material does not work or heaping much blame on the motivational speaker, I had to adapt the real-estate instruction to reflect the realities of my home environment. As an example, I always used Baltimore city, Maryland, as the best testing ground of most of the ideas I had read in creative real-estate investing, especially the infamous no-money down technique. In addition to the MLS, I depended on *The Baltimore Sun* paper and a coterie of friends to navigate through the maze of this particular real-estate market.

ED BECKLEY

"ONE DECISION IN THIS PRESENT MOMENT COULD CHANGE YOUR FINANCIAL DESTINY FOREVER." --Ed Beckley

Perhaps it is fitting to introduce my appreciation for Ed Beckley with the kind words of Anthony Robbins, who is also my hero.

"Ed, when I first got started, I learned so much from you. You were definitely one of my early heroes. I just wanted to tell you how grateful I am."
— Anthony Robbins, best-selling author and world renowned speaker

I heard the name Ed Beckley for the very first time in my life when I was working as a security guard at Olde Towne West, a high-rise apartment complex in downtown Alexandria, Virginia. At the time, money was very tight. I was also struggling to complete my master's degree at Howard University, Washington, D.C. That was when Norman Shepherd, an African-American acquaintance who used to live around Olde Towne West, introduced me to Ed Beckley's seminar and home-study course. In fact, he invited me to a motivational seminar in Crystal City, Virginia, but I refused to go to the seminar by giving him an alibi. I was perplexed when Norman Shepherd returned to my security post a few days later with Ed Beckley's real-estate home study course.

He attempted to negotiate a deal with me; if I was willing to share the cost of the program with him, we could begin investing in real estate together. As I have said earlier, money was tight; I was making less than $350 per week working as a security guard. How could I spend $250.00 or $125.00 on Ed Beckley's course. Before I met Norman Shepherd, I had never heard about motivational seminars. Much later, Norman Shepherd had complained to me about the difficulty of applying Ed Beckley's ideas; most of the home owners in Virginia he had contacted had less than twenty percent equity in their houses; in other words, banks still held a mortgage or deed of trust on their houses. For this reason, even if they had wanted to get rid of their homes, their lenders had to be contended with drastically. Hence, the no-money-down technique could not work in Alexandria, Virginia.

As time wore on, I stumbled upon the television infomercials of Ed Beckley. I decided to buy his books. The cover of the first book of Ed Beckley that I read showed him well attired in a three-piece suit and posing in front of a Rolls Royce automobile with the following words emblazoned as the title: A self-made millionaire tells you his secrets of real estate success; No Down Payment Formulas; Over 100 ways to buy real estate for little or nothing down by Ed Beckley.

JOHN POLK

I appreciate John Polk for introducing me to the real-estate investment strategy of tax liens and certificates. After reading the booklets that he gave to us, his prospective students, I spent much time researching the workings of tax liens and sales in the state of Maryland. Back in 1987, I attended his real-estate money-making seminar in a posh hotel in Crystal City, Virginia.

There is more to personal finance than the drudgery of debts and budgets.

JOHN BECK

In 1997, I bought my first home in Silver Spring, Maryland, for the sum of $250,000. In the same year, I learned about John Beck, and I ordered his "free and clear real-estate system," which focused on tax liens and certificates; I remember I spent less than $150.00. Principally, John Beck's system consisted of three CDs:

CD1--Real Estate for Pennies on the Dollar: Cash in on Government Tax Deed Sales
CD2—Internet Resources and Making Money Links: find, purchase and resell properties from your computer
CD3—North American Tax Sale Directory: locate and buy tax sale properties all over the United States and Canada

DAVE DEL DOTTO

What is it about Dave Del Dotto? Let me try to name it: style, charm, acting, and good looks? At first, I was captivated by his infomercial. The real-estate guru, decked out in a white linen suit and perched on a stage at a swank Hawaiian resort, made it all sound so easy. To his right sat eight of his disciples, from bricklayer to barrister, all of whom told of amassing great wealth after buying their master's $297-collection of inspirational tapes and books. I decided to buy his book entitled *How to Make Nothing But Money: Discovering Your Hidden Opportunities for Wealth*. I found the book immensely useful; the book suggested simple ideas I used to make money on the side, especially trading in properties acquired at different kinds of auctions.

As for Dave Del Dotto's complete seminar and training package, I did not want to part away with the kind of money he was asking me to pay him. As luck would have it, Antony K. Ndikum, a high-school friend, offered me the same package of six manuals he had bought at Dave Del Dotto's seminar:

1. Creating cash flow now
2. The United States directory of government auctions
3. How to make a fortune in foreclosures
4. 101 Purchase Offers Sellers Can't Resist
5. Dave Del Dotto's success express: How to start and profit from your own business,
6. Dave Del Dotto's How to Make a Fortune in Foreclosures with No Money Down

I will never forget Antony K. Ndikum because of his kindness. The receipt of a package consisting of the books mentioned above made me feel like a real sweepstakes winner. I hunkered down in my apartment and read all of Dave Del Dotto's books. Certainly, much of the material was neither comprehensive nor all-encompassing, but I used my own initiative to conduct some research. Whenver an idea in the books aroused my curiosity and interest, I spent much time in the public library gathering information on the subject. In fact, some of the ideas I had used in my real-estate investing were fashioned from a reading of Dave Del Dotto's books. In this regard, I was unlike the average student who complained about real-estate home study courses or books he or she had not read. Thanks a million, Antony K. Ndikum.

RUSS WHITNEY

In the beginning of *The Miraculous Millionaire*, I mentioned the huge impact Russ Whitney had on me. I was so captivated by Russ Whitney to the extent that I decided to drop out of my PhD program to start a business. Russ Whitney is a high school drop-out who became a self-made millionaire by building a money-making business in real-estate renovations. What was his initial business? Well, Russ Whitney explains it in the following manner:

"I ordered a book that had a couple of ideas that made sense. I finally found something that I could do that did not require a lot of money to start, and in 3 weeks, I made $11,000..."

He and his family celebrated his initial financial success with a commitment to use that money to make more money. He quickly invested it in another money-making vehicle. A little over a year later, at the age of 22, he had racked up $117,000 in profits. Actually, that is not bad for a guy who used to work at a slaughter house.

CARLETON SHEETS

I had been watching Carleton Sheets on television for a considerably long while. Before I became a realtor in 2000, I decided to supplement my real-estate education with Carleton Sheets' course. Carleton H. Sheets is a real estate investor and television pitchman who was notable for television infomercials which targeted real estate business opportunities for amateurs. The frequency of the Carleton Sheets infomercials increased throughout the late 1990s in response to rising values in real estate. Carlton Sheets published *The World's Greatest Wealth Builder* in 1998. Carleton Sheets was born on August 25, 1939, in Illinois. He moved to Delaware, Ohio, where his father worked for Procter & Gamble. One of his early jobs was marketing soft-drink bottle caps and was later became director of marketing for a Florida company that was a major processor of orange juice. In the 1970s, he started investing in real-estate properties; in the early 1980s, he worked as a pitchman for a company that represented the real estate authority Robert G. Allen, an early advocate of the "no-money-down" path to financial success. In the early 1980s, Carleton Sheets teamed up with businessmen from Chicago, Mark S. Holecek and Donald R. Strumillo, to form the venture known as Professional Education Institute.

CIRCLE OF INFLUENCE

Probably, the first step to start your own real-estate investing business is to cultivate a circle or sphere of influence. You live in a social-media world, so take quick action to engage your family, friends, and acquaintances. In his book titled *7 Habits of Highly Effective People*, Steve Covey underscores the importance of being proactive. In fact, proactive people focus their efforts on their circle of influence, a database of all the people that they know. If you want business to come to you, you are obliged to nurture your circle of influence. You work on the things you can do something about: pertaining to the problems of marketing your real-estate investing business. I am Prince Ojong. I am an extremely successful real estate investor because I pay unusual attention to members of my circle of influence. When I forget them, they forget me, too. As the saying goes, out of sight; out of mind. My banner year was 2004. I made much money.

There is more to personal finance than the drudgery of debts and budgets.

I can tell you what you need to do to succeed like me: build a network money machine of referrals. You need to leverage the real-estate knowledge that I am inculcating into you to recruit and develop a network of people from your sphere of influence that you live or work with who can make you strong where you are weak. That is your real-estate money machine. To make big money in real estate, you have to cultivate people to serve you, the king or queen, as either big or small players: friend, partner, associate, marketer, cheerleader, fanatic, referrer, buyer, seller, appraiser, inspector, public adjuster, banker, priest, pastor, realtor, loan officer, settlement agent, abstractor, renter, homeowner, termite inspector, and lawyer.

 If you are being mentored by another individual or group in my organization or if you have gone through the course after attending my seminar and workshop course and have tried in vain to succeed but you are still having difficulties, please, give me a call at (301) 593-4897; if I am not available, please, e-mail me at theafricannation@yahoo.com. I promise to contact you at my earliest convenience to discuss your problem. My mission is help; I want to use my program to assist you. I cannot afford to make false promises to you like the bad apples; I also cannot tell you about bird-dog programs, that is, the false promises that I have money available for financing and fixer uppers so that you can succeed. I already have many students that I am helping. Frankly, my capacity is limited, so I am very selective in marketing and selling my coaching program. So contact me later to see if you qualify.

THE ART OF MY SWEETEST DEALS

Unlike real-estate gurus, who do not practice what they preach, I am going to show you a few of my favorite real-estate deals. You will get a unique opportunity to examine my mindset. The structure of real-estate investing resembles the biology of a life cycle. I was not the brightest biology student in high school, but I remember my teacher explaining the idea of a life cycle in the following manner: the continuous sequence of changes undergone by an organism from one primary form, as a gamete, to the development of the same form again. For example, human beings undergo many developmental transitions in their lifetimes; let me take the case of a new baby or you. Can you imagine the changes you undergo? As an example, you go through a series of stages: childhood, adulthood, middle age, and old age.

Similarly, a real-estate investing transaction is characterized by five stages:

1. Decision
2. Analysis
3. Purchase
4. Management
5. Sale

DECISION

First, you have to make the decision to invest in real estate; you have to consider all the general dynamics and variables: attractiveness of the location, return on investment, cash flow, capital gains, inflation, equity appreciation, drawbacks, and risks.

ANALYSIS

Second, you have to spend much time working on the numbers. You have to analyze the deal; you have to conduct some feasibility studies; you have to inspect and appraise the property; you also have to consider financing issues. Will you be interested in seller financing? Is it available as an option? What about OPM—other people's money? Or do you have the cash to put on the table? Do the numbers tell you that the deal is a good one? What is the character of the local economy or the market? Is it a buyer's market? Or is it a seller's market? What is the demand and supply equation?

PURCHASE

Third, you have to make an offer to buy the property; if the seller likes your sales offer, he or she will ratify it promptly; however, if there is competition with multiple offers, the deal may become a little bit tricky. You have to exercise your negotiation skills to the limit. Before you buy a property, you have to decide what you want to do with it. Are you planning to use the property as a personal residence or a second home? Do you plan to lease the property? Have you calculated how much rent tenants are willing to pay for the possession and enjoyment of the property? Are you satisfied with the physical state of the property?

MANAGEMENT

The fourth phase entails managing the property. Are you ready to become a landlord? Or do you plan to outsource operational management to a third party? I am a veritable do-it-yourselfer; I always prefer to manage my own properties. It is economical for me to manage my properties. Before I bought my first investment property, I had spent quality time studying the fundamentals of property management. Most new property owners are worried about finding good tenants for their vacant properties. I have developed a simple plan that works well: first, I prepare the property for showing to prospective tenants; second, I put a captivating classified advertising in the real-estate section of the most popular newspaper in my local area; third, I manage the showing of the property to prospective tenants; fourth, I ask serious prospects to complete an application for rent form and a credit check form; from the list of multiple prospects, I select the best prospects; fifth, I prepare a lease agreement; I ask the customer to sign it and pay me the security deposit and first month's rent; I hand the keys of the property to the renter. I say, "Thank you for your business."

SALE

Fifth, you have to sell the property. When do you sell a property? Why do you sell the property? How do you sell a property? Generally, I sell a property after I have accomplished the objective for which I had bought it. The most common reason I sell a property is to recover the basis of my investments and capital gains; sometimes I sell a property for income tax reasons; I make the sale to coincide with the period I want to recognize losses from tax shelters, for example. I love selling my properties through the MLS, real-estate multiple listing service. I always engage realtors and folks in my circle of influence in the process of selling.

There is more to personal finance than the drudgery of debts and budgets.

LIST OF MY POSSIBLE REAL-ESTATE-INVESTMENT STRATEGIES

There are three broad categories of investment strategy that I advocate:
1. bargain purchase
2. increase value
3. double-digit cap rate

In fact, I am going to use my favorite transactions to assist you in learning how I had made my investment decisions.

VIGNETTES OF BEST DEALS

Stratford Garden Drive, Silver Spring, MD

When I started making much money in my income-tax-preparation and check-cashing business, I started harboring the thought of buying my own home for the very first time. Many years of watching late-night real-estate infomercials and dreaming about homeownership were followed by self-study of the complete process of buying and selling a personal residence. Yet, I decided to defer the decision to buy a home until I was getting ready to get married and start a family; according to my thinking, a family man needed much living space. For this reason, a townhouse was out of the question for me. I spent much time cogitating on most of the thorny issues of buying a brand new single-family home. I discovered that being an informed individual about the home buying process is empowering. Hence, you are lucky to have come to me, the right place. Let me get you started on the process of buying your first home!

Hickory Leaf Way, Silver Spring, MD 20904

This was my first investment deal. I bought this distressed property for $90,000 as a foreclosure from HUD, the Department of Housing and Urban Development. The offering price of the property was $105,000. The property needed some work, so I hired a home inspector for $250 to evaluate the amount of work I needed to do to bring it up to living standards; a home renovation specialist who studied the inspection report assured me that the property needed only cosmetic changes for $8,500. I saw the potential of renting the unit for $1,200. I had excellent credit, but my personal funds were limited, so I had to rely on creative financing. I signed the sales offer, and I handed an earnest-deposit check of $5,000 to the realtor. The deal had to be completed in forty-five days. My initial plan of financing the purchase of the house was to use a home-equity line of credit. I had equity of $125,000 in my primary residence.

A newspaper came to my financial rescue like a deus ex machina. While reading *The Wall Street Journal* on a Monday morning, I came across an article discussing the advent of a new generation of financial institutions called Internet banks; unlike their brick-and-mortar peers, Internet banks were virtual; of all the Internet banks mentioned in *The Wall Street Journal* article, none was as exciting as Deep Green Bank (http://www.deepgreenbank.com). I applied for a home-equity line of credit, and on Wednesday, I was stunned to see a deposit of $35,000 in my checking account at M&T Bank, Silver Spring, Maryland.

Immediately, I bought a certified check from my local bank; I made it payable to the settlement company that was to handle my real-estate closing in Alexandria, Virginia. Three weeks later, after I had signed the home-equity loan documents in my home in the presence of a notary, I received a check for the rest of the money ($90,000). I rushed to Virginia to close the deal. It was the quickest real-estate settlement I had ever experienced because there were no mortgage papers for me to sign; in fact, there was no lender involved in the transaction. Before I closed the deal, I had many prospective tenants angling like fish to lease the property for $1,200.

Lisage Way, Silver Spring, MD 20904

This was my second rental property. I decided to collaborate with my wife and sister-in-law to purchase the property. After the real-estate closing, I began looking for tenants; I put a classified advertising in *The Washington Post*. I invited serious prospects to come and look at the property. Those who were interested in the property had to complete a rental application and pay a processing fee of $50. From the information on the application and credit report, I chose the most ideal rental prospect, and I asked for 2 months security deposit.

East Nolcrest Drive, Silver Spring, MD 20901

This was an investment property I wanted to use for the operation of an assisted living home. My research had revealed that the Food and Drug Administration (the FDA), a US government agency, was planning to relocate adjacent to the area; I was expecting real-estate prices to soar in the next nine months. In fact, all my price predictions came to pass miraculously. But there were some bumps on the road. Some things did not work out exactly as I had planned, so I resolved to rent rooms to different individuals who later bought homes from me.

Old Gun Powder Road, Beltsville, MD 20705

This project was my nightmare. I must confess that I made many mistakes in building three single-family luxury homes on a big lot with the expectations of a net profit of at least $100,000 per house. When the real-estate market collapsed, I could not sell the houses. In fact, I lost everything. Unfortunately, I had spent over $100,000 paying mortgages in the anticipation of a market recovery that, until now, has not happened. The location of the property was an ideal one. The construction of the houses was on schedule, and I was negotiating with the builder to construct eleven more single-family homes in Laurel, Maryland. Had it not been the builder's avarice, I would have signed the new deal, a deal of my death. The market collapsed in my face. I am still recovering from the huge financial losses I had incurred at this project.

Clematis Road, Gaithersburg, MD 20882

This is my biggest investment to date. I bought a distressed property worth $1,500,000 for $1,200,000. I used equity from four homes to acquire this property. It was like I was anticipating the economic meltdown in real estate; I sold most of my rental properties in 2004; I did not want to be carrying so much real-estate debt. I was beginning to take a very dim look at overleverage in 2003. Finally, I, the prince, have built the royal palace of my dreams.

There is more to personal finance than the drudgery of debts and budgets.

Ivanhoe Avenue, Baltimore, Maryland 21228

I bought this property in 2004 at an Alex Cooper auction for $35,000. I spent $5,000 to fix it up, and I sold it in 2007 for $75,000. I made a profit of $35,000 from this deal. For students in the Washington, DC, metropolis, a visit to the offices of Alex Cooper is worth its weight in gold and silver. The following is the company's street address: 908 York Road Towson, Maryland 21204. (410) 828-4838 is the company's phone number; the company's domain name is alexcooper.com. I stumbled upon this company by accident; I was looking for a place to buy quality oriental rugs for my new home at an affordable price; a mutual real-estate investor referred me to Alex Cooper. Are you looking to invest in real estate? You will enjoy doing business with this company.

Multi-family rental property / Pine Avenue, Takoma Park, Maryland

When I felt the need to get involved heavily in the property rental business, I decided to obtain a real-estate salesperson license. My first deal was located at Pine Avenue, Takoma Park, Maryland. I was looking for a multi-family property with opportunities for tax write-offs and income. Eureka! I found it! It was a unique property. It was a fully rented 10-unit building in Takoma Park, Maryland. The property had a large additional structure which could be used for future development as a duplex home or workshop. I was thrilled by the fact that the building was in an ideal location; it was easy to rent; the numbers told me there was a very high demand for accommodation in the area.

The property was located in a historic district with ample parking a walking distance to a recreation center and the metro. I was also happy to meet the proverbial motivated seller I have been hearing about from real-estate gurus; the financing was right; it was an assumable loan with seller/owner financing. I checked county real-estate records, and I asked my abstractor to furnish me with the chain of title. I obtained the property price and tax history data from public records, but the MLS feed gave me more information about the property; I researched the local jurisdiction in which the applicable property was located. As you know, the MLS cannot guarantee that all public records and MLS data are accurate and error-free; it was important for me to rely on my expertise as a local realtor to obtain the most up-to-date information available on the property.

Mangum Road, College Park, Maryland 20740

I bought a property adjacent to the University of Maryland, College Park Campus. I like the University of Maryland at College Park very much; indeed, I wanted to enter a PhD program there, but the school did not offer organizational communications. I am thinking that in the future one of my children might go there if she cannot get into an Ivy League institution like Princeton, Harvard, MIT, or Yale. Right now, I am leasing the unit to college students. I am happy because the rents I receive monthly pay the mortgage and the maintenance of the house. Besides, I make a profit of five hundred dollars monthly; this profit contributes to the payment of the equity indexed universal life insurance policies I had bought for my two daughters.

NEWSPAPERS, NEWSPAPERS, NEWSPAPERS

Today, I like to shout the words INTERNET, INTERNET, INTERNET! The late Don Lapri used to shout on television, "Newspapers, newspapers, newspapers." I had bought his program because of the compelling power of his television infomercials. I was disappointed to find out that the program was too sketchy to be useful to any individual who is serious about making big money. However, to every cloud, there is a silver lining; I must confess that Don Lapri motivated me to focus my passion and attention on the investment potential of newspapers. I read and aggregate news on the world wide web, yet I use newspapers to run classified advertisements. It is their role as a goldmine of information, however, that makes them indispensable to me as a real-estate investor. I have cultivated the habit of reading newspapers to the extent that I wake up in the morning looking for them. I may read news stories online, but I enjoy holding newspapers in my hands. As a personal rule, whenever I travel to a new city, I buy its popular newspaper before I proceed to my hotel room; newspapers provide a window for me to explore new investment opportunities. Julius Achere Ntui, my childhood friend, was stunned when, during a week-end trip to Los Angeles, I used newspapers to make some sweet deals in Bakersfield, California. I have also used newspapers to identify investment opportunities in Virginia Beach.

When I was working as a security guard at Campbell Heights, a retirement apartment community in Washington, DC, I observed that the aged residents loved reading newspapers; similarly, when I was working as a security guard at The Representative, a luxury high-rise condominium owned by affluent residents including congressmen and senators, I observed firsthand the residents' love affair with newspapers. Newspapers can be vital to your life as a real-estate investor. I love reading newspapers. Some people dismiss newspapers as old fashioned in the new wired world. I beg to differ. Hence, I encourage you to subscribe to the major newspaper in your locality. You can use newspapers to scout new real-estate deals. All major newspapers have at least one section devoted to apartments and houses for lease, trade, or sale.

In addition to *The Washington Post*, I have always made good use of *The Baltimore Sun*. The newspaper covers news, business, sports, arts, lifestyle, opinion, archives, classifieds, food, travel and subscription and advertising information for THE BALTIMORE region. When I realized that the Washington, DC, real-estate market was very pricey, I turned my attention to Baltimore City and County because of the information I had discovered in *The Baltimore Sun*. Instead of complaining that the methods of real-estate gurus did not work, I sought to fill in the gaps in their programs on my own. Today, I know the geography of Baltimore City and County appreciably well. I have done real-estate deals from Milford Mill to Middle River; I have scouted for real-estate opportunities from Ellicott City to Essex. Back then, there were no GPS navigational systems, so I got lost too many times with maps in my car that I had bought at 7-11 store. Hence, things are easy for new real-estate investors. If money is tight, you can begin doing what I had done; you can start real-estate investing by profiting from Baltimore City and County sales of tax liens certificates. When assigning a certificate, the City or County must collect the total liens against the property, plus interest accruing from the date of tax sale to the date of assignment. For investors in tax liens, the annual rate of return is 20%; banks offer 1% or less.

There is more to personal finance than the drudgery of debts and budgets.

ESTABLISH A TITLE SETTLEMENT COMPANY

My next tip is for you to establish your own real-estate closing and title insurance company. At some point in your real-estate investing career, you will realize the need to establish your own real-estate escrow company. If you are busy making many deals, there will be pressure from customers and other real estate players for you to close those deals quickly and timely. It will dawn on you sooner or later that the lily-white real-estate settlement companies cannot accommodate you anymore; they may not be willing to schedule your settlement transaction on a short notice; they may be asking you to wait for weeks to close your deals. Even though you do not like to wait, you have no choice.

Your refinance clients want to close their deals during the week end, but all the lily-white firms in your town or city are closed; they open only from Monday through Friday. What is the answer? To tell you the truth, the answer is for you to form your own real-estate company; in fact, that is what I did in 2005. Tired of waiting for established firms, such as RGS Title, Paragon Title, and Universal Title to conduct my closings, I started giving my business to any settlement company that was flexible enough to accommodate the needs of my customers. For instance, my customers used to wonder why I would leave Silver Spring, Maryland, to close deals in Baltimore. In the end, I formed ABC Standard Settlements, Inc. in Hyattsville, Maryland, prior to the reception of a title agency appointment from CONESTOGA TITLE Insurance Company of Lancaster, Pennsylvania. My business model was John Davison Rockefeller's company known as Standard Oil; established in 1870 as a corporation in Ohio, Standard Oil was the largest oil refiner in the world. I had big dreams to change the real-estate escrow business in America.

I must acknowledge that my title agency's early appointment was as a factor of the strength of the business plan I had written using Palo Alto's software known as *Business Plan Pro*. To polish up on my real-estate knowledge and demystify the work of my processors, settlement agents, and attorneys, I decided to obtain a title insurance license. I ordered many books on title insurance from Amazon.com and other online sources. After I had read these books, I registered and attended a two-day course taught by experienced real-estate attorneys and title insurance executives at the Maritime Conference Center, 692 Maritime Boulevard. Linthicum, Maryland 21090. Three of my employees had accompanied me to take the PSI title insurance exam; I was the only one who passed the exam on a first trial. Officially, I never settled any real-estate cases in my real-estate office in the capacity of a settlement agent, but I used my knowledge to disarm arrogant attorneys and serve my customers well. If you have the time or need, please, obtain a title insurance license and form your own real-estate settlement enterprise.

REASSIGNMENT

Reassignment has been my favorable real-estate technique. In fact, I have used it extensively in the Baltimore market. Reassignment means to assign or transfer real-estate ownership rights for a second time. An assignment, Latin cessio, is a term used with similar meanings in the law of contracts and in the law of real estate. In both instances, it encompasses the transfer of rights held by one party, the assignor, to another party, the assignee. The legal nature of the assignment determines some additional rights and liabilities that accompany the act.

I have used the reassignment technique with joyful abandon in auction deals in the Baltimore real-estate market because of lower prices.

Essentially, the strategy involves going to an auction, bidding on deals, and winning from five to ten bids; the technique also involves using at least $5,000 in earnest-deposit money to secure each property, and transferring my ownership interest to a third party for a reassignment or finder's fee. To facilitate the transaction, I assist the new owner to obtain financing and close the deal. When I am buying a property at an auction, I present myself as the new buyer. Since I do not want to own five or ten new properties at once, I look for third parties who can assume the ownership from me; thus, I am transferring my rights of potential property ownership to another individual. So long as the individual pays me a reassignment fee and refunds the earnest-deposit money I paid at the auction, I am ready to relinquish my potential rights as a buyer/owner. In this wise, if I had bought ten properties at the auction, and I charged a two thousand dollars reassignment fee, I stood to make a cool twenty thousand dollars.

What I normally do when I return from the auction is to contact all individuals who are in my circle of influence. If none of them is interested in reassignment, then, I turn my sights to *The Baltimore Sun* for advertising the properties. Whenever I secure a buyer, I draft a reassignment contract, a simple form for both parties, the assignor and the assignee, to sign. I am the assignor; the third party to whom my rights are transferred is the assignee. I take the cash or certified funds straight to the bank. The assignor remains liable unless there is an agreement to the contrary. An agreement must manifest intent to transfer rights; it may not necessarily be in writing; words will do, and the rights assigned must be certain. The effect of a valid assignment is to extinguish privity between the assignor and the obligor and create privity between the obligor and the assignee.

LEASE OPTION CONTRACTS

I hate lease option contracts, but they are popular with some real-estate investors. A lease option, more formally known as a lease with the option to purchase the property, is a type of contract used in both residential and commercial real estate. In a lease-option deal, a property owner and tenant agree that, at the end of a specified rental period for a given property, the renter has the option of purchasing the property. A lease option is different from a lease purchase, in that a lease purchase binds both parties to the sale, whereas in a lease-option transaction the buyer has the option but the seller does not. In fact, many sellers renege on their commitment to the buyers; they prevent the buyers from exercising the option to buy the property at the previously agreed upon terms.

USE OPM

OPM is an acronym which stands for other people's money. One of the realities you will experience in the course of your real-estate investing career is the paucity of capital. You have scouted and researched a nice property for sale, but you do not have the funds to buy it outright. You have tried all the no-money-down and bird-dog programs, but they have not worked for you. What should you do? OPM might come to your rescue. OPM means you have to rely on the financial resources of others. If you do not have something, please, do not be cynical to think that other people are destitute or broke like you. Present them with your business plan, and ask them for financial assistance. They maybe your angel, father, mother, brother, sister, cousin, uncle, aunt, nephew, niece, son, or daughter. Just ask! It does not hurt to ask for money. I have asked for money from total strangers by running classified advertising in local newspapers. When the prospects showed up, I presented my business plan to them. Sometimes some of them took a chance on me; others declined to assist me.

Do not be shy; ask for help! Why should you suffer in silence? Pray and ask for help. A miracle always happens to those who pray and believe in our Lord, Jesus Christ. The holy Bible encourages you to ask:

Matthew 7:7:
Ask, and it shall be given you; seek, and ye shall find; knock, and it shall be opened unto you.

Psalm 34:4:
I sought the LORD, and he answered me; he delivered me from all my fears.

Matthew 18:19:
Again, I tell you that if two of you on earth agree about anything you ask for, it will be done for you by my Father in heaven.

MASTERMIND

Your mastermind is your brain trust, your dream team of experts, so it is important for you to create your own mastermind group. No man is an island. Business is a contact sport. You cannot afford to do business alone. Even organized criminals are smart enough to know that you need to have a dream team to succeed. Hire many professionals to join your dream team of real-estate investing: painters, home renovation specialists, appraisers, and inspectors. Since you are giving them business, please, encourage them to give you referrals, a list of people who need or might need your services.

BUYING LAND AND BUILDING

Buying land and building houses may sound romantic, but it is a very complex process. I have tried it. It is not for the faint of heart. After conducting adequate research, I made the initial foray into buying land and building houses in 2006. Guided by listings I had pulled from the MLS, I drove to remote areas of Howard County, Montgomery County, and Prince Georges County. I presented my selection of potential purchases to surveyors, engineers, and land professionals; in fact, I spent over $15,000 paying engineers and surveyors to investigate the potential of the land for construction. I do not regret the fact that I lost $15,000 because my accurate homework insured me from losing hundreds of thousands of dollars. Additionally, I became aware of issues pertaining to blemishes on the chain of title. A CHAIN OF TITLE is the sequence of historical transfers of title to a property. The chain runs from the present owner back to the original owner of the property, such as Lord Baltimore in Maryland.

OVERLEVERAGE

My investment project on Old Gunpowder Road, Beltsville, Maryland, taught me bitter lessons pertaining to the use of excessive leverage in real-estate investing. Please, resist and avoid the temptation of overleverage. Leverage is good sometimes, but overleverage is bad. In 2008, my real-estate business almost went more than six feet under because of the demerits of overleverage. I was working hard. The deals were coming to me like the flow of water from a stream. The good Lord was blessing me; I was living like the real prince who I am; my admirers had nicknamed me the crowned prince of real estate, but I lost my magic touch because of greed and overzealousness.

Three single-family units I was building around Old Gunpowder Road, Beltsville, Maryland, tested my mettle as a smart investor. Normally, I would make $100,000 from a new construction unit; my calculation was that I was going to make at least $300,000 from the big Old Gunpowder Road project. As the market started turning southward or down, I had the inkling that I was going to be buried by an avalanche of mortgage debt. I had partnered with friends and relatives to build three custom single-family houses. Like I usually did, I was hoping to sell these homes quickly for big profit. As the saying goes, man proposes, but God disposes. In life we often make plans for the future. We may decide on what to do in future and how something should turn out. But the fact is that things may not happen the way we expect them to unfold, despite our honest intentions, best wishes, and unstinted efforts. The lucid explanation of this phenomenon is that God has a contrarian plan for us. That was my horrific experience with the grand Old Gunpowder Road project. The collapse of the real-estate project meant I could not find buyers for three units.

Yet, I had to begin and continue servicing three mortgages. After one year of paying three huge mortgages, in addition to my offices and luxury home, I had exhausted my life's savings. It was not difficult for me to jettison any notion of deriving profit from the three houses. My biggest worry was that I had disappointed friends and relatives who had unshaken belief in me as a real-estate high roller. My brother-in-law who had sought to bail me out financially by assuming mortgage payments for two of the houses was forced to learn a very bitter lesson in mortgage relief; in fact, after making mortgage payments of almost one hundred thousand dollars in a climate of persistent economic paralysis with no buyers in sight, he resolved that we should cut our losses; I acquiesced to throw in the towel. I am not quitter, but I had to quit. From then to this day, I have signed legislation to banish leverage forever. I have decided to avoid real-estate speculation. As I see it now, mortgage debt is a cancer; I do not want to handle any more leverage in my life. In this context, Dave Ramsey is right in advocating for a regime of debt elimination and financial fitness.

PREPAYMENT OF MORTGAGE

I advise you to work hard to reduce mortgage debt. I have closed almost all my home-equity lines of credit. I use only debit cards because I hate borrowing money now. I make an unusual effort to prepay all my mortgages. I always ensure that my mortgage instrument does not contain any negative prepayment clause. Most mortgages on income-producing real estate, as distinct from owner-occupied housing, contain clauses restricting early payment of the loan. These clauses are highly controversial, and borrowers like me often resist their enforcement. In the past, I have employed statistics to analyze the cumulative effect of the presence in the same mortgage documents of both a clause imposing a fee upon prepayment of the loan and a clause accelerating the loan in the event of default, sale, eminent domain taking, or hazard insurance payoff. I always try to refinance my mortgages to eliminate the pre-payment clause provision or obtain a lower rate of interest.

USE A REAL-ESTATE TRUST

A real estate trust can be set by a family. In this regard, a FAMILY TRUST is a trust set up to benefit members of your family. Almost any real-estate assets can be held by the trust. A trust is a clever tool you can use to own property or transfer its ownership. By law, you can own real estate as a person. Otherwise, you can own it as a corporate entity such as a real-estate trust. In my seminars and workshops, through my powered attorneys, you will become acquainted with the secrets of using real estate trusts to build and protect wealth. Rich folks use it as part of their estate planning; you can use it, too. For starters, I recommend resources published by Nolo.com; even if you will be hiring an attorney to assist you in drafting your trust instrument, it makes much sense for you to begin researching the basics of living trusts.

REIT

REIT is an acronym for a real-estate investment trust. A real estate investment trust or REIT is a tax designation for a corporate entity investing in real estate. The purpose of this designation is to reduce or eliminate corporate tax. In return, REITs are required to distribute 90% of their taxable income into the hands of investors. The REIT structure was designed to provide a real estate investment structure similar to the structure mutual funds provide for investment in stocks. REITs can be publicly or privately held. Public REITs may be listed on public stock exchanges. My advice is that you should investigate profitable properties such as nurseries.

REMIC

After you have risen from the low rank of a bit player to the high rank of a tycoon, you may want to explore investment opportunities in REMIC, which refers to a real estate mortgage investment conduit, or, sometimes also called collateralized mortgage obligations. It is a type of special purpose vehicle used for the pooling of mortgage loans and issuance of mortgage-backed securities.

REAL ESTATE SWAPPING

Real estate swapping comprises the exchange or trading, for example, of like-kind of real estate. Real-estate trading, also referred to as permanent real-estate swapping, is a type of I-buy-yours-you-buy-mine arrangement. It is distinct from vacation-home swapping. The deteriorating real-estate market around 2007 has led many people to realize that trading may be an extremely viable approach to selling their real estate. This approach only works if the seller is also looking to buy another property, such as a move or relocation. But it is possible to move up or down in price, size, etc., or even trade to another city or state entirely. Real-estate trades fall under the 1031 exchange tax loophole. 1031 exchanges are a legal way to defer capital-gains tax on investment properties. 1031 exchanges do need to involve an actual trade of real estate between two parties.

REAL ESTATE STOCKS

Real-estate stocks are securities derived from the domain of real estate. Below are some ticker symbols of real-estate stocks for you to study:

ARE, AVB, FCE-A, GRT, HT, LXP, RPT, RYN, HOT, DCT, GSPC, IYR, VNQ, OFC, BRE, PPS, UDR,CBL, PEI, TCO, MAC, SPG, SKT, WDC.AX, AAPL, BEE, AHT, CLDT, PEB, CHSP, HPT, PKY, CLI, HIW, PDM, HPP, MPG, SLG, BXP,CDR, DDR, BFS, KRG, AKR, EQY, IRC, PCH, PCL, MAR, FR, FPO, TRNO

REAL ESTATE TAX SHELTER

When most real-estate investors think about tax shelters, their minds go to the practical application of depreciation, which makes real estate a great investment choice because it is also treated as an expense for tax purposes. The concept of real-estate tax shelter is very intriguing. De jure, as it relates to the Internal Revenue Code, there is an incredible benefit to using IRS Schedule E and successfully filing your tax return as a professional real-estate investor. The secret of tax shelter is the depreciation of real estate. Because of the progressive tax system used in the United States, it is extremely difficult for most people to accumulate any real savings from their work salary alone. Real estate tax shelters can come to your rescue. You can create a limited liability company in order to capitalize on real-estate tax shelters. Traditionally, most real-estate investors have a fondness for the use partnerships as a business structure. I, Prince Ojong, prefer the LLC, limited liability company. We live in a society in which litigation has run amok, so I like to protect myself legally and take advantage of real estate tax shelters simultaneously; I use the LLC structure to achieve both business and personal objectives.

IT IS ECONOMICS, STUPID!

Although I was involved in the home building and construction business in Cameroon, that particular experience did not prepare me for the vision of real-estate investing as the pathway to the American Dream. When I was growing up in Yaounde, all around me I saw Bamileke people buying land from the Betis and building houses for rent. I saw landlords making much money from petty rental units, but I never saw the big deals, the kind that real-estate gurus, such as Ed Beckley, Dave Del Dotto, John Polk, Robert Allen, Russ Whitney, and Carleton Sheets talked about all the time. Additionally, I was awestruck by the convertibility and liquidity of American real estate. In America, for instance, houses are commodities like cars and boats. These commodities can be financed and refinanced with joyful abandon. By contrast, in much of Africa, it is very difficult, if not uncommon, to sell a house.

There is more to personal finance than the drudgery of debts and budgets.

As a result, real-estate capitalism succeeds in America and fails in Africa because of the lack of convertibility and liquidity. Yet, African entrepreneurs or homeowners would love to have the flexibility to be able to build, buy, or sell a house. Right now, these Africans lack liquidity preference. In economic theory, liquidity preference refers to the demand for money, considered as liquidity. The concept was first developed by John Maynard Keynes in his book *The General Theory of Employment, Interest and Money* to explain determination of the interest rate by the supply and demand for money.

HERNANDO DE SOTO

The existence of title insurance in Western countries provides a valid argument why real-estate capitalism succeeds in the Western world but fails in developing countries. In *The Mystery of Capital*, Hernando de Soto, the world-famous Peruvian economist takes up the question that, more than any other, is central to one of the most crucial problems the world faces today: Why do some countries succeed at capitalism while others fail? In strong opposition to the popular view that success is determined by cultural differences, de Soto finds that it actually has to do with the legal structure of property and property rights. Every developed nation in the world at one time went through the transformation from predominantly informal, extra-legal ownership to a formal, unified legal property system, but in the West we have forgotten that creating this system is also what allowed people everywhere to leverage property into wealth. This persuasive book has revolutionized our understanding of capital and point the way to a major transformation of the world economy.

It is against this backdrop of economic theory that I want to impress the importance of real-estate ownership on you. Real-estate millions are everywhere. Learn how you can get your fair share. I want you to capitalize on what you have learned in the preceding pages about creating wealth by buying a BIG chunk of America; the information reflects accurate knowledge of the real-estate industry in America and the strategies you can use to make more money with less pain. In fact, I have addressed every issue private investors consider critical completely: the fundamentals of real-estate investment, understanding real-estate jargon, the smartest way to buy real-estate, sources of financing, no money-down deals, common-sense mortgage reduction techniques, real-estate property development, tax secrets, tips, and tricks for property owners, and more.

INVEST IN REAL-ESTATE NOW

So you are thinking about investing in real estate? Great! As you are probably aware, some of the world's richest people have made their fortunes by investing in real estate. Investing in real estate is a great way to generate passive income, which, if done properly, would allow you to quit your job and live off the residual income from your investment properties. Most people think that they need much money, a good credit score, and substantial savings to invest in real estate. This is simply not the case. Why should you invest in real estate now? I have to harp on the theme of transience. Time is of the essence! You can model the business excellence of America's real-estate moguls and invest your way to the top echelon. The biggest secret of America's superrich and famous individuals is the reliance on real-estate investing to build large fortunes.

My favorite past time is reading. I enjoy reading books about the creation of wealth. As an example, this week, I was gleefully thumbing through the pages of *Forbes* magazine's 2012 list of America's billionaires. The following statement in the magazine confirmed what many of us may not be aware of: A report released by the National Association of Realtors last year pointed out that in the U.S., about a fifth of a household's wealth is composed of home equity.

What is home equity? Home equity is the residual value of a real-estate property beyond any mortgage thereon and liability therein; in other words, home equity is the market value of a home less any debt incurred by the homeowner. The following example will shed more light on the meaning of home equity: John and Mary bought a single-family home in April 1997 in Silver Spring, Maryland, for four hundred thousand dollars. In April 2012, an appraiser told them that their property was worth seven hundred and fifty thousand dollars. The balance on their mortgage is two hundred thousand dollars. What is their home equity? Their home equity is five hundred and fifty thousand dollars, the difference between the mortgage balance and the market value of the home. That is the magic of compounding; that is the miracle of real-estate in wealth-building.

You may want to attend my real-estate seminar and take my course on real-estate investing. You will also benefit when I come to your town for a seminar and workshop. I never had the opportunity to take a real estate course until I decided to become a realtor; nevertheless, I spent much time attending real-estate money-making seminars, and I learned from many gurus: Ed Beckley, Dave Del Dotto, John Polk, Robert Allen, Russ Whitney, and Carleton Sheets.

How should you invest in real estate now? I cannot make specific recommendations without knowing you personally. The limitation of a book, such as *The Miraculous Millionaire*, is the difficulty of adapting the information to meet the unique needs of every reader in my target market. How can you apply the investing principles of real estate to your own situation? You have no choice but to come to my real-estate investing seminar and be empowered by an action plan designed just for you. The action plan takes you, step by step, through the goal-setting process to identifying specific investments that could help you meet each goal. To every working-class individual in America, here are the awful watchwords: to realize the American Dream, you must grow into a genuine capitalist with many interests in real-estate. You can begin your real-estate investing by acquiring your own abode, a personal residence that can be a condominium, townhouse, or single-family home. You can graduate by working with my real-estate team to make quick and sweetheart deals. As an experienced real-estate salesperson, I can help you make the right decisions.

What about people with bad credit and low-income levels, or little in the way of savings? Fine! Today, more than ever before, a whole world of opportunity has opened up for the beginner real-estate investor. Regardless of your income levels, credit history or real-estate investment experience, there exist real-estate investing opportunities for you. Unfortunately, most beginner real-estate investors feel like they will be limited because of low-income levels, not enough savings or bad credit. For the beginning real-estate investor, there are many investment strategies, not just one.

There is more to personal finance than the drudgery of debts and budgets.

For example, there are short sales, foreclosure opportunities, lease options, rent to own options, real-estate flipping opportunities, real-estate control strategies, government-sponsored programs, For-Sale-By-Owner (FSBO) options, and a host of other investing strategies for beginner real-estate investors. As a beginner, it is important that you understand all of these options and then narrow them down to a real-estate investing strategy that best suits your needs. The Prince Ojong real estate program is the best program to help you, the beginner real-estate investor. I want you to learn how to invest in real estate regardless of your income, credit, or savings! In the next chapter, I will introduce you to my coaching programs. I will explain how you can register to capitalize on all our wealth-building resources.

IS REAL ESTATE A SAFE INVESTMENT?

As with any investment idea, you are going to have many so-called specialists who focus on the risks associated with such investments. Real-estate investing is no exception to this rule. There are countless people who claim that real-estate investing is a poor investment choice. However, I believe that the numbers should speak for themselves. Real-estate prices have continued to rise over the long run by substantial amounts, and they continue to grow at a rate faster than inflation. Informed investors realize that it is never too late to start investing, but the earlier you start, the harder and smarter your money can work for you. When you reinvest the earnings on your investment, you can take advantage of the power of compounding — the growth of earnings on earnings.

Take quick action to become a smart or commonsense real-estate investor. Informed investors select investments that can potentially help them meet specific investment goals. Identifying your investment goals is the first step in financial planning. All investments involve some level of different kinds of risk, including market risk and inflation risk. In general, making an informed decision to assume more risk can create the opportunity for greater reward. Informed investors take their own risk tolerance into consideration when making investment decisions. Informed investors develop realistic expectations about both long-term market performance and short-term market movements. They base these expectations on historic averages and evaluate current market performance against those averages when monitoring their progress toward long-term goals. So you are still thinking about investing in real estate? Great! Invest in real estate now!

LEARN HOW TO LEVERAGE THE INTERNET IN YOUR REAL ESTATE INVESTING

When I started investing in real estate in the good old days, the wired world was still in its infancy. Every tool was very primitive. Today, however, the world wide web, as a component of the Internet, has made the task of researching investment opportunities really easy. Prior to the introduction of bulletin board systems, such as CompuServe, public libraries were the only means of investigating real-estate investments. I want to draw your attention on how you can leverage the Internet in your real-estate investing:

Millionaire iUniversity.com:
http://www.millionaireiuniversity.com

The centerpiece of my real-estate networking is the masterpiece web site describe above. I am the Robin Hood of real estate. I am here to help you! Whether you are new to the market, thinking of moving up, or you are an experienced investor, I have the expertise, proven track record, and resources to help you buy or sell your next home. Enthusiasm, knowledge of the area and personal concern for the clients' interests combine to make me an outstanding resource for your real estate transaction. I work extensively to help buyers and sellers meet their real estate goals. When you need the services of a realtor, why not hire someone that will make you and your real estate goals #1?

Home buyers are using the Internet in increasing numbers each day to research information on properties. Reports state that approximately 80% do their initial home search on the web. The Internet now outpaces classified advertising for attracting buyers to properties. My website provides invaluable information on the buying and selling process and is intended to be easy to use and consumer friendly. The site makes it convenient for you to preview available properties and narrow your search before feeling pressured to contact a realtor. Of course, when you are ready to discuss your real estate needs and goals, or if you have any questions, I am always available to help:

Prince Ojong:
http://www.princeojong.com
Direct: (240) 350-1131
Office: (301) 593-4897 or (301) 593-4897
Fax: (240) 241-5137

Other sites that may be of informational value to you comprise of the following:

Commercial real estate listings:

Adam A. Weschler and Sons, Inc.
http://www.artfact.com/features/selectHouse.cfm

Alex Cooper.com:
http://www.alexcooper.com

A.J. billig.com:
http://www.ajbillig.com

BNI Building News:
http://www.bni-buildingnews.com
BNI Building News provides the most accurate and easy-to-use cost estimating data available anywhere. Choose from 8 separate volumes covering General Construction, Public Works, Electrical, Facilities, Home Remodeling, and more.

Costar.com:
http://www.costar.com

There is more to personal finance than the drudgery of debts and budgets.

Express Auction.com:
http://www.expressauction.com
Are you interested in information about upcoming real-estate auctions? Join their mailing list to keep informed of latest offerings.

Harveywest.com:
http://www.harveywest.com

HomeSource.com
http://www.homesource.com

HMBI:
http://www.hmbireo.com
HMBI is dedicated to providing highly trained professionals to market and manage numerous single-family homes across the country for the Department of Housing and Urban Development and other government and independent agencies.

Investing for Success:
http://www.icief.com
The Investing for Success web course is an educational program jointly sponsored by the National Urban League (NUL) and the Investment Company Institute Education Foundation (ICIEF). This program responds to research showing that, when it comes to investing, African Americans lag behind other groups with similar incomes. The reason most often cited is lack of knowledge. NUL, ICIEF, and the mutual fund industry have joined forces to help address this "knowledge gap."

Ocwen Financial Corporation:
http://www.ocwen.com
Formed in 1988, Ocwen Financial Corporation ("Ocwen") is a vertically integrated multi-billion dollar, publicly traded (NYSE: OCN) financial services holding company, engaged in a variety of businesses related to mortgage servicing, real estate asset management, asset recovery and technology. Headquartered in West Palm Beach, Florida, Ocwen is dedicated to becoming a global leader in providing asset management services and advanced technology solutions to selected financial markets. Ocwen pursues its goal of being an industry-leading mortgage servicer, real estate and technology provider by focusing on globalization, Six Sigma process improvements and enabling technology.

Tidewaterauctions.com:
http://www.tidewaterauctions.com
This site is a treasure trove of information for real-estate investors. The discussion of the pitfalls of buying condominiums and what to look out for in terms of owner occupancy rates and reserves is required reading for anyone who is thinking about buying a condo. Generally, most realtors do not tell people about the issues with condo ownership. I own five condos and love condos, but you really have to research the HOA and junk fees before buying. This site provides some useful information, but my seminars can show you how to invest in condos.

SUCCEED IN REAL ESTATE BY SETTING THE RIGHT GOALS

The typical real estate investor's net-worth goal is a million dollars. In the preceding pages, I have presented an outline or sketch of strategies, tactics, tips, and tricks on how to succeed in real-estate investing; they are lessons I had learned the hard way in my 15-plus years odyssey on the real planet. My real-estate investing system focuses on locating and choosing the right deals. Perhaps more important than the deals is the importance of setting the right goals. Unlike most motivational new seminar promoters who encourage you to choose whatever extremely high goals your heart desires, I emphasize the importance of choosing the right goals. If you choose your goals carefully, you are far more likely to achieve them and far more likely to be happy when you do. Choosing the wrong goals will greatly lessen your chances of success, waste years of your life, and can cause serious problems like family or health difficulties

READ OR PERISH

Above all, if you want to succeed in real-estate investing, you have to sharpen your blades every day. How can you remain creative? You remain creative by reading about the experiences of other small investors; you can have the ideas; you can experiment with daily. I advise you to take the real estate sales and investing course we are offering at Millionaire iUniversity.

Step 11

JOIN THE MILLIONAIRE CLUB

Where Your Dreams Are Closer Than You Think

MISSION

Life is a mission. Therefore, our mission in life is to help you, a self-reliant individual, make your financial dreams come true.

MOTTO:

God first; family second; business third.

We mint millionaires one person at a time.

JOIN THE MILLIONAIRE CLUB

The success train is leaving the station, so I am calling all the dreamers out there. Today, I am urging you to board the train of financial success, which is about to leave the station. To all the dreamers out there, the following is the awful watchword, the millionaire manifesto: Get rich or perish! The going may be tough, but do not give up on your dreams. When you do, they die like raisins in the sun. Old dreams may fade away, but they never die. Indeed, they lie buried in the ash heap of despair, forgetfulness, and neglect.

Dear Soon-to-be-Millionaire, I thank you very much for taking the eleventh step on the journey of financial freedom. It is an honor, indeed, that you are following my footsteps. In fact, it was only a few years ago that I, too, decided to fight for my economic independence. As the founder of the Millionaire Club, I would like to welcome you to the mountain top of personal finance. Fervently do I hope that you will live by the secrets of rich and famous folks that the club will expose to you; specialized knowledge, desire, and action are the objects and tools that distinguish millionaires from you. If you are reading this chapter, then, the odds are for some time you may have been trying to achieve the American Dream of financial independence, but perhaps without much success and with limited funds. Perhaps you are wondering how an average individual with big dreams can start making big money. Well, the Millionaire Club will provide the answer to all your money questions; the club will present solutions to your problems.

The Millionaire Club is on a crusade to make all its members wealthy. So will you make or mar it? It all depends on you. Is financial success not a personal choice? Some people do not care about the future. They do not worry because they think the future will never come. But it will! Do not be like them. Let them continue to have fun hitting the financial iceberg like the Titanic! Let them have the desire to follow foolish money crowds. Birds of the same feather flock together, so vote to be with millionaires; choose to become a member of the Millionaire Club, which will show you, practically, how to win God's love, think like millionaires, capitalize on insurance secrets of the rich, master the rudiments of personal finance, increase your computer literacy, start a small business, benefit from the IRS tax codes, win in the stock market, and profit from real estate. Above all, the club will encourage you to set and meet your financial goals, such as planning to retire rich before age 65 and avoiding the landmines of success: inertia, procrastination, desire for instant gratification, and temptation to get rich quickly. See you in paradise God bless you.

NEOPHYTE'S WELCOME

Dear Partner in $ucce$$, I am happy to welcome you formally to the Millionaire Club, doing business as OverReacher Empire Corporation. Come and see American wonders! As I consider you a neophyte, I am writing to congratulate you for crossing the threshold from financial illiteracy to financial education. By joining the Prince Ojong organization, you have chosen a date with financial destiny; you have elected to join the rank of a class of human beings distinguished from the unworthy, every-day, or ordinary folks. I salute you well; you are now worthy. I encourage you to continue your voyage of self-discovery and financial mastery. Since I embarked on that journey many years ago, I have not turned back. I also urge you to walk on the way to wealth courageously. Please, do not be tempted by the devil to turn or look back. Keep on walking forward faithfully.

THE AMERICAN DREAM

You believe in the great American Dream. Do not you? By joining the Millionaire Club, you are demonstrating that you believe in the American Dream; you are patronizing your own business; you are buying your freedom from wage slavery; you are supporting your American dream. Many years ago, when I was a little boy of five, I had an American Dream, too. In Malende, a little village located in the African nation of Cameroon, a young couple unwittingly and unknowingly introduced their young son to the ideal of the American Dream. Every week end, they took their son to a Cameroon Development Corporation (CDC) camp to watch the movies of Charlie Chaplin and other movie stars. The couple anchored the week-end film outings on a gift to their lone son of a kiddie slide projector, which became their son's most-prized possession. Their son named his toy "fine country," a Pidgin English word for America the beautiful land. Their son's fascination with the images of a beautiful America gave birth to his burning desire to come to America, the wonderful land of his dreams. Then the young man came to America; he started a new life in the land of opportunity. Like a tragic hero, he conquered the American Dream. The son is Prince Ojong, the founder of the Millionaire Club.

THE DECLARATION OF FINANCIAL INDEPENDENCE

Below is the preamble of the Millionaire Club:

We are votaries at the shrine of the Magna Charta and the Constitution of the United States of America. Like Thomas Jefferson of yore, we consecrate; we dedicate; we pledge; and we submit. When in the course of personal, spiritual, and financial events it becomes necessary for a group of success-oriented individuals to dissolve the physical and psychological ties that bind them to a life of financial mediocrity, and to assume among the powers of the earth, the separate and equal station to which the Laws of Nature and Nature's God entitle them, a decent respect to the opinions of humankind requires that they should declare the causes which compel them to the separation. We hold these truths to be self-evident, that all men and women are created equal, that they are endowed by their Creator with certain unalienable Rights, among these are prosperous Life, economic Liberty, and the lustful pursuit of financial Happiness. That to secure these personal, spiritual, and financial rights, OverReacher Empire Corporation organized the Millionaire's Club.

PURPOSE OF THE MILLIONAIRE CLUB

a)   To maintain and promote the values of independent education in personal finance, business, and investing.
b)   To establish a world-wide channel of communication which individuals who are serious about getting ahead financially can receive positive programming and participate in interactive discussions.

c)   To contribute to the enhancement of the social, cultural, educational, and economic life of members.

d)   To provide the moral and material support necessary for members to realize their financial goals and economic pursuits.

e)   To create a framework that facilitates the process of networking with other individuals who are serious about financial success.

MEMBERSHIP

The Millionaire Club ascribes fundamental importance to membership. In conformance with the ideals of equality, prosperity, and freedom aforementioned, members are the nucleus of the Millionaire Club, which is an organization of members, by members, and for members. Although the organization is not a religion, it preaches a qualitative, practical, and do-it-yourself philosophy of financial independence. The network of self-reliant members is the medium through which the club's gospel of financial success is disseminated worldwide. In other words, the club perceives its members to be akin to Jesus' disciples, "who go and tell it on the mountain, over the hills and everywhere" that the dream of financial freedom is REAL for those who believe in God and are born again. In respect to membership, the Millionaire Club does not discriminate against individuals on the basis of creed, race, color, religion, gender, nationality, or education. In other words, any individual who is serious about getting ahead financially can apply for membership. After the individual in question pays a non-refundable membership fee, the club accords the individual member a ranking commensurate with the amount of the membership fee. The club has eight levels, so choose your appropriate status below. For detailed information on the Millionaire Club, please, call (301) 593-4879, (240) 330-0839, or (301) 593-4897

THE MILLIONAIRE CLUB MEMBER RANKS

The Millionaire Club is not good for all persons. I am calling many dreamers to join the club, but few of them deserve to be members. How do you begin? In the Millionaire's Club, there are eight levels of membership. A member's entitlements are derived from the amount of the membership fee and the business performance of the member. The club's entry level is IBS, independent business solicitor; by contrast, the club's highest echelon is IMD, international marketing director. Within the club's structure, there are two roads to wealth: Service America and Business America.

Service America presents a shopping-mall concept where members and consumers buy products and services at a discount; the highest discounts are given to international marketing directors; by contrast, Business America presents an opportunity for a member to start his or her own business on a shoestring budget.

 In this wise, any member is allowed to benefit from our discounts automatically, that is, without joining the Millionaire Club as international marketing director. Non-members can only purchase products or services from the club. As for parties interested in getting compensation from us, they must be members who have chosen to join the Millionaire Club at a specific compensation level.

COMPENSATION LEVELS

IBS—Independent Business Solicitor	10%
AMR—Area Marketing Representative	15%
CMR—City Marketing Representative	20%
LMR—Local Marketing Representative	25%
CME/CET---County Marketing Executive/County Executive Trainer	35%
SMD—State Marketing Director	40%
NMD--National Marketing Director	45%
IMD—International Marketing Director	50%

IBS—Independent Business Solicitor   10%

First, you can pay the sum of $499.99 to join the business at the starting point of an IBS, that is, Independent Business Solicitor. All IBSs (Independent Business Solicitors) have the privilege and right to market and sell the products and services of OverReacher Empire Corporation to their customers in return for the compensation of 10% commission from the company's SERVICE AMERICA client referral network.

AMR—Area Marketing Representative   15%

Second, you can elect to pay the sum of $699.99 to join the club at the higher echelon of an AMR-- Area Marketing Representative. All AMRs (Area Marketing Representatives) have the privilege and right to market and sell the products and services of OverReacher Empire Corporation to their customers in return for the compensation of 15% commission from the company's SERVICE AMERICA client referral network.

You begin your business by prospecting for consumers (referral business customers) and developing producers (customers who can sign up as IBSs in your sales dream team). Additionally, IBSs who raise their business production volume to the aggregate sum of $15,000 in less than 12 months qualify to be promoted as AMRs—area marketing representatives.

CMR—City Marketing Representative   20%

Third, you can elect to pay the sum of $999.99 to join the business at the higher echelon of a CMR. An AMR qualifies to be promoted to the rank of a CMR—City Marketing Representative when the AMR in question raises his or her business production volume to the aggregate sum of $20,000 in less than 12 months.

All City Marketing Representatives have the privilege and right to market and sell the products and services of OverReacher Empire Corporation in return for the compensation of 20% commission from the company's SERVICE AMERICA client referral network. You begin your business by prospecting for consumers (referral business customers) and developing producers (customers who can sign up as IBSs in your sales dream team).
.

LMR—Local Marketing Representative   25%

Fourth, you can elect to pay the sum of $1,299.99 to join the business at the higher echelon of a LMR. An CMR qualifies to be promoted to the rank of a Local Marketing Representative when the CMR in question raises his or her business production volume to the aggregate sum of $25,000 in less than 12 months All LMRs (Local Marketing Representatives) have the privilege and right to market and sell the products and services of OverReacher Empire Corporation in return for the compensation of 25% commission from the SERVICE AMERICA referral network. You begin your business by prospecting for referral business and developing both customers who can sign up as IBSs.

CME/CET---County Marketing Executive/County Executive Trainer   35%

Fifth, you can elect to pay the sum of $1,599.99 to join the business at the higher echelon of a CME. A LMR (Local Marketing Representative) qualifies to be promoted to the rank of a County Marketing Executive/County Executive Trainer when the LMR in question raises his or her business production volume to the aggregate sum of $35,000 in less than 12 months All CME/CETs (County Marketing Executive/County Executive Trainer) have the privilege and right to market and sell the products and services of OverReacher Empire Corporation in return for the compensation of 35% commission from the company's SERVICE AMERICA client referral network. You begin your business by prospecting for referral business and developing both customers who can sign up as IBSs. Additionally, the successful completion of the building of a 3 member team is a sine qua non for LMRs aspiring to the elevation as County Marketing Executive/County Executive Trainer.

SMD—State Marketing Director   40%

Sixth, as a SMD, you can elect to pay the sum of $1,999.99 to join the business at the higher echelon of a SMD. A CME/CET (County Marketing Executive/County Executive Trainer) qualifies to be promoted to the rank of a State Marketing Director when the CME/CET in question raises his or her business production volume to the aggregate sum of $40,000 in less than 12 months All State Marketing Directors have the privilege and right to market and sell the products and services of OverReacher Empire Corporation in return for the compensation of 40% commission from the SERVICE AMERICA referral network.

You begin your business by prospecting for referral business and developing both customers who can sign up as IBSs. Additionally, the successful completion of the building of a 12 member team is a sine qua none for CME/CET-- County Marketing Executive/County Executive Trainer aspiring to the elevation as State Marketing Director.

NMD--National Marketing Director   45%

Seventh, you can elect to pay the sum of $2,999.99 to join the business at the higher echelon of a NMD. A SMD (State Marketing Director) qualifies to be promoted to the rank of a National Marketing Director when the SMD in question raises his or her business production volume to the aggregate sum of $45,000 in less than 12 months All National Marketing Directors have the privilege and right to market and sell the products and services of OverReacher Empire Corporation in return for the compensation of 45% commission from the SERVICE AMERICA referral network. You begin your business by prospecting for referral business and developing both customers who can sign up as IBSs.

Additionally, the successful completion of the building of a 27 member team is a sine qua none for SMD-- State Marketing Directors aspiring to the elevation as National Marketing Director.

IMD—International Marketing Director   50%

Eighth, you can elect to pay the sum of $3,999.99 to join the business at the higher echelon of a IMD. A NMD, National Marketing Director, qualifies to be promoted to the rank of an International Marketing Director when the NMD in question raises his or her business production volume to the aggregate sum of $50,000 in less than 12 months All International Marketing Directors have the privilege and right to market and sell the products and services of OverReacher Empire Corporation in return for the compensation of 50.00% commission from the SERVICE AMERICA referral network. You begin your business by prospecting for referral business and developing both customers who can sign up as IBSs. Additionally, the successful completion of the building of an 81 member team is a sine qua none for NMD-- National Marketing Directors aspiring to the elevation as International Marketing Directors.

MILLIONAIRE CLUB GLOSSARY

Customers

Customers are the people who buy the MILLIONAIRE CLUB products and services from you. Customers may or may not be members of the Millionaire Club organization. One of your best sources for building a customer base is a group of people you already know. These are acquaintances who try MILLIONAIRE CLUB products and services and they become your customers as they use and reorder various MILLIONAIRE CLUB items. However, we have found out that people everywhere need our high-quality products and services.

IBSs

IBSs are people who have evaluated the Millionaire Club and elected to join the business. The most successful Millionaire Club businesses enjoy a balance of merchandising MILLIONAIRE CLUB products and sponsoring IBSs. Growth in your business comes from sharing the Millionaire Club business with others and helping them decide if it is right for them. This is called sponsoring. Millionaire Club IBSs who sponsor others generally have higher average sales volumes than those who do not sponsor.

Group/Team

No man is an island. You succeed in your Millionaire Club business by building a dream team. What can you learn from Jesus Christ? Although he was divine, to conquer the world, he built a fantastic group of 12 disciples. Similarly, in order for you to succeed, you are obliged to recruit a team of fantastic salespeople. Your "team" is the group of IBSs and AMRs you have sponsored. Many individuals you have sponsored personally proceed to sponsor others people into the Millionaire Club business for your betterment. You train and motivate your group—your down line-- and, as a result, you earn extra income when they earn income. As you continue to grow your business and they continue to grow theirs, you both benefit.

$1,000 BONUS

OverReacher Empire Corporation pays you the sum of $1,000 bonus whenever you accomplish any of the following feats in 30 consecutive calendar days:

1. Acquisition of 20 new customers who purchase any of the services promoted by our Service America referral network.
2. Recruitment of 20 new IBSs into your dream team or marketing group.
3. Recruitment of 10 new AMRs into your dream team or marketing group.

QUARTERLY INCENTIVES

Every quarter (Summer, Fall, Winter, and Spring), OverReacher Empire Corporation recognizes the marketing and sales achievements of its all-star and top performers. The weights considered are customer production, trainer production, and total revenue.

Additionally, award recipients are classified in the following order:

Founder's Inner Circle
1,000 Customers' Club
500 Customers' Club
250 Customers' Club
100 Customers' Club
75 Customers' Club
50 Customers' Club
25 Customers' Club

Like any other business, your Millionaire Club business needs frequent input and activity to grow. However, whatever your goals, you control how quickly or how slowly you build your business. After all, it is your independent Millionaire Club business. Over time, a Millionaire Club business can grow considerably. The more IBSs in your group who become successful in the Millionaire Club business, the stronger your business will become, and the higher the pin levels you can qualify for. We call them pin levels because you earn incentive pins at the various achievement levels of the business. Each pin level features a set of incentives and rewards for being successful.

The Millionaire Club offers IBSs many benefits. Some are financial; others are intangible, such as peer recognition, pride in achievement, the joy of helping others, working with family, and the esteem of owning your own business.

CONTACT INFORMATION OF THE MILLIONAIRE CLUB

White Oak Professional Park
11231 Lockwood Drive
Silver Spring, MD 20901
Phone: 301-593- 4897
Fax: 240-241-5137
Email: theafricannation@yahoo.com
Web: http://www.princeojong.com

BUSINESS AMERICA

Did you know we could train you to offer many computer-based services? While several of my early business ventures were successful, my greatest lesson came from the use of referral, network, or affinity marketing in my income tax preparation business. I am a self-taught tax consultant. Before I took the income tax preparation course from Jackson Hewitt Tax Service, I had already utilized a home-study package from Federated Tax Service, Inc., 4751 South Central Avenue, Chicago, Illinois, 60638, to teach myself how to prepare income tax returns from home. By engineering a grass-roots campaign and multi-level marketing, in the form of word-of-mouth appeals and $10-referral coupons, I grew my income tax business quicker than most CPA firms and national tax franchise companies. For example, this reality stunned me when I drove to Virginia Beach, Virginia, to attend a John-Hewitt seminar designed for new franchisees. It was heartening to discover that my tax office had prepared more income tax returns than any Liberty Tax franchisee. I did not have the benefit of radio and television advertising. Hence, it was insensible for me to buy the Liberty Tax franchise. I had read many inexpensive manuals from *Entrepreneur* magazine on how to operate and market a tax office. Hence, I quickly realized that anyone who was willing to work hard could have a tax business of their own through this direct person-to-person marketing method. People trust their friends more than radio or television.

There is no need to reinvent the business wheel. Network marketing works. We have learned much about the business model of multi-level marketing from the 1980s to present day. We have understood the failings of these enterprises; we have comprehended their successes, too. Unlike the competition, we have decided to be very fair and generous in compensating and motivating our business partners. Besides, we do not encourage them to waste their precious time marketing products and services that, sorely, do not fulfill the dire needs of customers in today's marketplace. Therefore, we have fashioned the Millionaire's Club business paradigm on the strengths of existing networking marketing companies. By using a shopping mall model, we specialize on marketing the products and services customers need desperately every day. We have simply changed the channel of distribution to get rid of middlemen and women and provide customers with lower prices every day. Show us a customer who is not interested in saving time and money today, and I will show you Wal-Mart. Indeed, with the Millionaire's Club

Business Opportunity Kit being the only start-up cost, virtually anyone can own a Millionaire Club business. Compared to other business opportunities, initial costs for starting a Millionaire Club business is intentionally low, priced affordably for nearly anyone with a desire to invest in their future.

SERVICE AMERICA

Who Cares About You? We do! We are your ubiquitous business service referral center. Because we worry about helping you satisfy personal, spiritual, and financial needs, we have established a one-stop referral shopping center for you called SERVICE AMERICA. You talked, and we listened. Now you can make money by referring your friends and family to the increasing menu of services and products offered by OverReacher.com. For each service or product, you earn a commission based on your compensation level in our organization. To initiate a referral, call the following phone numbers: (301) 593-4897 or (301) 593-4879. Or you can fax the referral service form to us at 240-241-5137.

COMMUNICATION

Hearty welcome to the information age! We are poised to capitalize on the "power shift" wrought by the new-wealth revolution of information and communication technologies. America, as an economy, has undergone many cataclysmic changes. Starting with an agrarian economy, America morphed into the industrial age after World War II. The advent of the 1980s catapulted America into the jazzy information era. Specifically, the 1980s ushered in the personal computer revolution; the explosive 1985 brought in its awake the telecommunications revolution; the 1990s were marked by the race to commercialize and popularize the Internet and the world wide web. Now the race is to leverage the benefits of Internet technologies for voice over Internet protocol—VOIP and the videophone. All along, I have been strategically situated to capitalize on these emergent opportunities. In fact, from the early 1980s, I had taught myself how to use a personal computer; I had used my pioneer company known as "American Computer Data Tracking" to be at the forefront of the information revolution in communication technologies. While my competitors had succumbed to the vagaries of the stormy business weather, I had endured in the desert like an oasis of prosperity.

It should come, therefore, as a surprise to no one today that our growing list of communication products and services comprises of the following:

Calling/Phone Cards
High-Speed Internet Service
In Bound International Numbers
Satellite TELEVISION
Video Phone--VOIP Digital Home Phone Service
Video Phone--VOIP Digital Small Business Phone Service
USB Phone
WI FI Phone
Wireless Phone (cellular)

There is more to personal finance than the drudgery of debts and budgets.

COMPUTER CONSULTING

We have come a long way, baby! Did you know computer consulting is one of the first services we offered the public? Back then, there was no Microsoft WINDOWS; there was just plain old DOS and no hard drives. Those pioneer days are gone, but we have kept up with the times. Using the OverReacher.com brand, we collaborate with our computer experts to meet the challenges you face in automating your home or office.

CREDIT REPAIR/DEBT COUNSELING

Is credit repair a myth or reality? Learn the fact and fiction about personal credit restoration. The truth will enthrall you, and you will be happy to work with our credit repair consultants. I am not surprised by the fact that too many people have bad credit. I live in the real world. I understand the predicament of ordinary working folks. America is a forgiving society; there is life for you after debt. Do not despair. You can always make a fresh start.

ENTREPRENEURSHIP

Let us coach you to go into business for yourself. Learn how to bootstrap and manage your operation to success. Statistics show that 4 out five 5 businesses fail every year. Do not be part of the negative statistics. Come to the business masters of OverReacher.com; ride the waves of success.

FRANCHISING

Franchising has become a very attractive route to entrepreneurship. We can give you a lending hand! We can use our prodigious resources to research franchising opportunities for you. There is no business under the sun that we do not know much about. When exploring the idea of investing in a franchise, our critical assessment of the opportunity in question will lay threadbare the positives and the negatives. In short, our leg work can save you headache, time, and money.

INCOME TAX PREPARATION

By using the TaxZero1.com brand, we provide income tax preparation services 24/7 and 365 days per year. Located in medical suites, generally, we perceive income taxes to be analogous to the provision of medical services. No matter the state of the union where you live, we are flattered you have given us the opportunity to serve you better. If you are interested in establishing a tax service, we can assist you to become successful.

INSURANCE

Because we know that you matter most, we worry about your insurance needs: health, life, property, and casualty. Using the umbrella of our corporate contacts, we have developed solutions to all your insurance problems. Become an insurance salesperson today. Call us now!

MORTGAGE

By using the American Dream brand, we help you obtain the common-sense loan to buy or sell the property of your dreams. Mortgages cost too much, and mortgage professionals enjoy mystifying their business. We decided to demystify and streamline the entire mortgage process. Who is benefiting? You! We can also help you obtain a license in your state to operate a mortgage brokerage. I was the business architect of Rockefeller Finance and American Dream Mortgage. During that time, I organized seminars and workshops to train new loan officers.

MORTGAGE REDUCTION

How can you accelerate the building of home equity? The solution is mortgage reduction. Our strategies of mortgage reduction work in all types of markets. The cornerstone of our debt management and elimination program is mortgage reduction. We have an arsenal of nuclear tools designed debt elimination. Do you dream of becoming mortgage free?

MUSIC/VIDEOS

Work without play makes Jack a dull boy. It is true. In fact, that is why we have introduced entertainment in our business. The American way is to work hard and play hard. As a means of giving back to the community, we sponsor and promote local artists. You can buy their work in our store. POP stands for Prince Ojong Production. We offer music and video production services to fresh, new, and undiscovered talent. We specialize on the production and distribution of African CDs and DVDs. Using the Nollywood moniker, we have strategically created awareness about the existence of Nigerian, Ghanaian, Cameroonian, and other African movies and videos in the United States of America. We are forging better ties with artists around the globe.

REAL ESTATE

As a realtor, I have worked with the following prestigious brands: Long and Foster Realtors, Fairfax Realty, and RE/MAX; I am proud to have satisfied the real-estate needs of many taxpayers. When I became disenchanted with the working of our real-estate referrals, I sought to make the buying and selling of real-estate a pleasant experience. By building on knowledge derived from your tax records, I tailor our real-estate services to meet your particular need. I am capable of handling out-of-state and international real-estate transactions.

SOFTWARE SALES

We have acquired the expertise to design and build custom computer programs. Our present area of specialization includes the following: medical software, dental software, debt-collection software, and income tax preparation software. If you are shopping for custom software, do yourself a big favor; call us for free and serious consultations. We have also been involved with offshore software development: India, Russia, and other places. Our challenge is to engineer a homegrown solution: to design and produce software in America at a very competitive price.

There is more to personal finance than the drudgery of debts and budgets.

STOCK TRADING/INVESTING

We can show you how to open a window on Wall Street. Learn the money secrets of the big boys on the Stock Market. Learn how to trade and invest like a child learning the alphabets of ABC. Tycoon Prince Ojong exposes the secrets of making millions on Wall Street!!! Learn to play the stock-market game like the professionals. Make some magic; deal yourself a winning hand. Stop complaining that the big guys have all the luck and fun. There is free lunch on Wall Street for everybody. Just hurry and ask for your fair share of giveaways today. For the first time, the stock-market secrets of the rich and famous are revealed in black and white: Benjamin Graham, Warren Buffet, Charles T. Munger, Peter Lynch, Michael Price, Bill Gates, and others. A regular person has many advantages that make Wall-Street professionals truly envious and bitter. Let Prince Ojong help you CAPITALIZE on these advantages and fabulous deals!

TITLE CLOSING/SETTLEMENT

You told us you were tired and frustrated by big closing companies that were insensitive to your needs. As usual, we listened to you; we decided to do something about it. By using the ABC Standard Settlement and Title brand, we provided closing services in our premises.

TRAINING

We are, fundamentally, a direct-sales and training organization. Prince Ojong, the founder of the organization, has spent his entire life in the classroom. His father was a university professor. Similarly, like Bill Gates of Microsoft fame and fortune, Prince Ojong dropped out of a PhD program in organizational communications to start his first business enterprise on a full-time basis. As a result, Prince Ojong perceives OverReacher.com to be a knowledge organization, and training is an adjunct of the common core knowledge products of OverReacher.com. Our training encompasses many disciplines.

WORD PROCESSING/GRAPHIC DESIGN/PUBLISHING

Our business started small in 1986 as a word-processing service catering to the needs of students and small business persons. Back then, computers were an uncommon commodity found mostly in laboratories and offices. We have changed with the times. Today, we can help you with reports, flyers, business cards, letterheads, newsletters, resumes, term papers, dissertations, research, and theses. So what do you want to do today?

CONTACT

OverReacher.com
(P.O Box 10334, Silver Spring, MD 20914)
11231 Lockwood Drive, Silver Spring, MD 20901
Phone: 240-350-1131   301-437-3130
Fax: 240-241-5137

MEMBERSHIP APPLICATION OF THE MILLIONAIRE CLUB

This agreement is made by and between OverReacher Empire Corporation (hereinafter called "MILLIONAIRE CLUB") and

....

....

....

(hereinafter called "Member") on this ....day of.........................20   ....

Whereas MILLIONAIRE CLUB is a book publisher, comprehensive personal-finance coach, and computerized service bureau that offers education and marketing through the medium of the Millionaire Club to individuals and

Whereas SERVICE AMERICA and BUSINESS AMERICA, their incredible work from home business opportunities, provide individual sales training and consulting support, they require no previous experience and no employees.

Whereas Member wishes to realize increased revenue, savings, net worth, wealth, financial literacy, and efficiency through the use of the services and products of the Millionaire Club.

The parties (MILLIONAIRE CLUB and Member) hereto agree as follows:

1.0   Services/Products
That Member agrees to welcome with an open mind new ideas concerning the nature and causes of the wealth of individuals, American capitalism, common-sense investing, and creative wealth-building strategies.

That MILLIONAIRE CLUB gives Member the privilege to affiliate with individuals who are serious about thinking and growing rich.

That Member agrees to abide by the rules of Millionaire Club.
That Member agrees to capitalize on the two club programs: SERVICE AMERICA and BUSINESS AMERICA.

2.0   Payment or/Compensation
Member agrees to pay MILLIONAIRE CLUB a non-refundable, one-time membership fee within the range of $499.99 and $3,999.99), in advance for direct and indirect costs associated with running the business and investment club: computer software, research fees, marketing expenses, sponsor commissions, and more.

There is more to personal finance than the drudgery of debts and budgets.

Member has chosen the membership level checked below:

IBS—Independent Business Solicitor	10%/$499.99_____
AMR—Area Marketing Representative	15%/$699.99_____
CMR—City Marketing Representative	20%/$999.99_____
LMR—Local Marketing Representative	25%/$1,299.99_____
CME/CET---County Marketing Executive/	
County Executive Trainer	35%/$1,599.99_____
SMD—State Marketing Director	40%/$1,999.99_____
NMD--National Marketing Director	45%/$2,999.99_____
IMD—International Marketing Director	50%/$3,999.99_____

Member, if he or she is interested in the BUSINESS AMERICA program, agrees to pay MILLIONAIRE CLUB additional fees for advanced business training and consulting. On the other hand, MILLIONAIRE CLUB, through the medium of SERVICE AMERICA, agrees to pay Member a commission for all the latter's business referrals. MILLIONAIRE CLUB has the full discretion to introduce new business services to Member.

TERMS OF AGREEMENT

This agreement may be terminated by either party upon submission of a thirty (30) day notice. Member agrees to waive the right to use litigation to terminate this agreement. Warranties under this agreement, expressed or implied, are abrogated. The parties agree that the foregoing constitutes the exclusive available guarantee.

CODE OF ETHICS

It is mutually understood that MILLIONAIRE CLUB and Member maintain and operate under a code of ethics to ensure the integrity and confidentiality of club business secrets. This ethical code, therefore, includes responsibilities, protection of the public interest, maintenance of objectivity and impartiality, and professional due care and competence.

The parties hereto have executed this agreement as of the day and year first written above.

....Date:...............
Representative for Member

....Date:...............
Representative for MILLIONAIRE CLUB

NB: Member's personal Info:

Member's Sponsor:...

Member's ID information:...

....

Member's Home Phone #:...

Work #:...

A Division of OverReacher Empire Corporation
11223 Lockwood DR, Silver Spring, MD 20901
Phone: (301) 593-4897 or (301) 593-4879
Fax: (240) 241-5137

Our Bu$ine$$ i$ to $ave You Time and Money!

Step 12

ATTEND MILLIONAIRE IUNIVERSITY

"You develop millionaires the way you mine gold. You expect to move tons of dirt to find an ounce of gold, but you do not go into the mine looking for the dirt--you go in looking for the gold." ---Andrew Carnegie

CONVOCATION DAY

[Self-reliance is the awful watchword of a true do-it-yourselfer. Therefore, on the formal occasion of the convocation of The Millionaire iUniversity, Prince Ojong is too proud to deliver Ralph Waldo Emerson's Self-Reliance address before the entire student body of The Millionaire iUniversity.]

We mint millionaires one person at a time.

A VIRTUAL VARSITY

Chasing your millionaire dreams can be a daunting challenge. That is why I wrote *The Miraculous Millionaire*. I wanted to demystify the process of making a transition from poverty to riches. I have used the word millionaire in book so many times. In fact, the use is voluntary and deliberate. At this juncture, the word millionaire should not sound strange in your ears any more. Even though I have provided you with the knowledge you need to design and build your millionaire dreams, I feel confident that you will appreciate the practical and immeasurable benefits of attending Millionaire iUniversity, a virtual university. I recognize the fact that the book is inadequate in helping you set and meet your financial goals. If you are like most of my students, you still need some form of handholding. Gone are the days when you were pumped up after reading a book, only to realize that you need a coach to guide you in your studies; gone are the days when you attended a money-making seminar and lost the feeling of exhilaration upon arrival at home. No longer will you be excited to read a book on personal finance only to be frustrated because you cannot implement the advice of the author. For this reason, I created Millionaire iUniversity to supplement my ideas with the realities of your circumstances; Millionaire iUniversity tailors the advice in the book to reflect your idiosyncratic needs.

If you need any assistance, personal help is just a phone call away. You can also reach me by email, Internet, and snail mail. In fact, Millionaire iUniversity is the online and offline workshop of all my millionaire apprentices. Millionaire iUniversity is a virtual room, area, or establishment where you can join us to do manual, automatic, or light work pertaining to wealth building. At Millionaire iUniversity, you have come to an educational institution where you can learn the theory and practice of wealth-building technologies; you will attend a series of meetings emphasizing interaction and exchange of information among a usually small number of participants: a group of individuals who are serious about practicing the gospel of wealth-building. Millionaire iUniversity is a goldmine of minting new millionaires; in fact, to borrow the words of Andrew Carnegie, a robber baron, "You develop millionaires the way you mine gold. You expect to move tons of dirt to find an ounce of gold, but you do not go into the mine looking for the dirt--you go in looking for the gold." Andrew Carnegie, America's first great industrialist, nearly 100 years ago had forty-three millionaires working for him. That was an unheard-of occurrence in those days. A reporter asked him how he managed to hire forty three millionaires. Carnegie responded that none of them were millionaires when he hired them.

MILLIONAIRE IUNIVERSITY'S GOAL

The goal of Millionaire iUniversity is to coach you to implement all the materials you have learned from *The Miraculous Millionaire* so that you should become the next millionaire. After you pay the membership fee to join the Millionaire Club, we begin by asking you to collaborate with us in evaluating your present circumstance; the self-evaluation procedure helps us uncover your dreams, fears, passions, ambitions, goals, strengths, and weaknesses. As your personal coach, I work with you on many exercises to establish a millionaire plan of action. You have to imagine that you are a millionaire architect in training; my role is to hold your hands, until you have learned how to design and build the money mansion on your own. I can boast that no other company offers this kind of service in the world today! Trust me! Hence, as a reminder, call my office and complete the process of joining the Millionaire Club; automatically, you will be admitted into Millionaire iUniversity. Are you ready? Oh Yes! Then, hearty welcome to Millionaire iUniversity!

ENTREPRENEURIAL EDUCATION

The purpose of founding Millionaire iUniversity is to create a learning environment that can be conducive to the promotion of entrepreneurial training. The hallmark of training at Millionaire iUniversity is the creation of a genuine entrepreneur, not just an MBA manager. In step seven of *The Miraculous Millionaire*, I distilled the general knowledge of an average MBA graduate. Like Henry Mintzberg, my argument is that that knowledge is inadequate; it will not make you a millionaire, so I have created Millionaire's iUniversity to give you a unique opportunity to learn how to implement most of the ideas discussed in *The Miraculous Millionaire*. While American universities and business schools churn out MBA management or administration graduates, Millionaire's iUniversity's products are real entrepreneurs who for pennies on the dollar dazzle and bamboozle the world with the sheer greatness of their creative talents in the marketplace.

EXPLANATION OF ENTREPRENEURIAL EDUCATION

What is entrepreneurial education? Entrepreneurial education may be defined as the act of imparting general and practical knowledge that is known to be the privy of an entrepreneur. The word entrepreneur is derived from the French word for an undertaker, someone or a person who organizes all the factors of production and manages any new enterprise, especially a business, usually with considerable individual initiative and start-up risks. Hence, an entrepreneur is an employer or contractor of labor. De jure, the word entrepreneur entered the English lexicon after the Norman Conquest. Therefore, as a citadel of entrepreneurial studies, Millionaire iUniversity prides itself in training students to develop the mindset, powers of reasoning, character, and judgment of a typical entrepreneur, as opposed to an MBA manager of a corporation.

Unlike present day business schools that focus on teaching the fundamental skills of managing an existing corporation, Millionaire's iUniversity underscores the teaching of the creative strategies for harnessing the factors of production: technology, land, capital, labor, and entrepreneur. Millionaire iUniversity reflects what it takes to attend a non-traditional, cyberspace institution. Millionaire iUniversity provides intensive training and technical assistance to people with a promising business idea or a desire to start their own businesses. The curriculum includes workshops and seminars on business startups, market research, marketing tools, strategic planning, networking and community resources, sales techniques, presentation skills, and financial management as well as legal, insurance, human resource, time management, and commercial real-estate issues. A business' use of technology and the Internet is also explored thoroughly.

The objective of the coaching program is to assist participants in the preparation and implementation of a specific, comprehensive business plan tailored to each individual entrepreneur's needs. Another important component of the program is to facilitate connections between the entrepreneur and all of the resources and services he or she may need to successfully launch and sustain a business. In the final analysis, the purpose of these programs is to create many jobs, which contribute to the economic development of the United States of America.

Depending on the student's membership status in the Millionaire Club, the program coaching is structured to include approximately 4 to 12 weeks of intensive online and offline classroom training followed by an additional 4 to 12 weeks of one-on-one consulting to help each entrepreneur through the start-up phase of his or her business. At the conclusion of the classroom portion of the program, each entrepreneur is expected to present his or her business plan to a panel of bankers, consultants, and other business-planning experts for some real-world feedback on the business concept. Development and presentation of a business plan is among the requirements for successful completion of the coaching program.

Millionaire iUniversity differs from other business assistance programs in several key ways. Using an established and tested curriculum, the program ties all of the various aspects of the plan together in an integrated fashion; financial basics are stressed, enabling participants to gain the financial knowledge necessary to effectively control their businesses; program staff have cultivated partnerships with many community, business, and government entities so that program participants can be linked to the resources they need to establish and grow their businesses. Each instructor is or has been a successful business owner providing an important perspective on the unique issues faced in start-up and growth situations.

ON THE EDUCATION OF MILLIONAIRES

As I was researching how to organize Millionaire iUniversity, I came across *The Education of Millionaires: It is Not What You Think and It is Not Too Late*, a book written by Michael Ellsberg that reinforced my faith in entrepreneurial education. Fundamentally, the book explores the following myth: "If you get into a good college, study hard, and graduate with excellent grades, you will be pretty much set for a successful career." The author concludes by presenting what he perceives to be the reality: "The biggest thing you will not learn in college is how to succeed professionally." You will learn how to manage a corporation, but you will never learn how to think like an entrepreneur.

Unlike Michael Ellsberg, I do not want to engage in college education bashing; I do not want to deceive any one into thinking that it is worthless to go to college today. I know that Michael Ellsberg heaps much praise on self-made individuals who have educated themselves and become experts or broke new ground in technology, finance, and other fields: "Some of the smartest, most successful people in the country did not finish college. None of them learned their most critical skills in an institution of higher education. And like them, most of what you will need to learn to be successful you will have to learn on your own, outside of school." You should understand that the goal of a business school MBA program is to train corporate managers and administrators. By contrast, the goal of Millionaire iUniversity is to nurture prospective entrepreneurs, enterprising individuals whose thinking can crystallize big ideas into the action of establishing new small or one-man businesses.

There is more to personal finance than the drudgery of debts and budgets.

If you examine Michael Ellsberg's success formula, you will observe that the author regurgitates many simple ideas:

1. Get your head out of your ass.
2. Find people that inspire you and help them.
3. Learn what people want.
4. Show them that you can deliver.
5. Invest in yourself and build little by little, keep teaching yourself.
6. Own the impact you are making in the world, under your own name.
7. And really, get your head out of your ass, stop being a victim and own your life. Dead-end jobs are not forever. If you want different, make it so, because the education structure as we know it may be the next bubble.

Michael Ellsberg states that he set out to fill in the gaps of college education by interviewing a wide range of millionaires and billionaires who do not have college degrees, including fashion magnate Russell Simmons, Facebook cofounder Dustin Moskovitz and founding president Sean Parker, WordPress creator Matt Mullenweg, and Pink Floyd songwriter and lead guitarist David Gilmour.

Where I agree with Michael Ellsberg is on the need for colleges and universities to begin teaching many courses on entrepreneurship, a guide for students to develop practical success skills required in the real world. Ellsberg concludes that learning the skills in his book well is a necessary addition to any college education, whether you are a high school dropout or a graduate of Harvard Law School:

1.   --how to find great mentors
2.   --how to build a world-class network
3.   --how to learn real-world marketing and sales
4.   --how to make your work meaningful
5.   --how to build your brand of you
6.   --how to master the art of bootstrapping, and more

STREET SMARTS

Success today depends on street smarts, not just college theory or garbage book smarts. It has to do with your motivation, network, passion, and the ability to make others believe in you. You will learn a lot of academic stuff in college, but you will not develop these entrepreneurial skills, which are requisite for success in life. Whether you go to college or not, my coaching program will help you learn what it takes to succeed in today's entrepreneurial economy. I call it the magic-cards factor, what you need to play and win the money game. Your success in a specialized-knowledge society depends on mastery of soft skills and practical intelligence; yet they do not feature in college or high-school curriculums. Make your education a life-long process. Your education starts in the crib and ends when you take your final breath. Entrepreneurial education is self-education, which is the key to upgrading your mind and your life. I, an entrepreneur, am the one running Millionaire iUniversity, instead of administrators and bureaucrats; in fact, that is why, the school is teaching most of the skills and mindsets found among millionaires and billionaires. In fact, Millionaire iUniversity is a necessary antidote to a traditional college education.

SELF-EDUCATION AS A QUICK FIX FOR THE BROKEN AMERICAN EDUCATIONAL SYSTEM

My friend, you do not have the luxury of time to lament the calamity of the breakdown of the American education system and the ascendancy of other countries. Politicians can talk and squabble over how to fix the broken American education system to restore the reality of the American Dream, but you have an emergency crisis: fix your own education first. You are the man and woman in the mirror. I am asking you to look at yourself and make the change to entrepreneurial education. Educate yourself; do not limit your education to what you learn formally in the classroom; start by taking the time to educate yourself in skills needed in many areas of the work world. Do not waste your time watching junk shows on television every day; if you enjoy watching television, please, allocate much of your time only to educational programming. Acquire the specialized knowledge that will give you upward job mobility in society. Aspire to live the American Dream. In fact, the American Dream is not dead. When people complain about the death of the American Dream, I get the impression that these people are still stuck in the time warp of Arthur Miller's *Death of a Salesman*. What they actually intended to say was the gradual erosion of financial opportunities in America that used to result from the attainment of quality higher education.

By contrast, other nations are leading America in reading, mathematics, and science. If America is declining, the cause of the decline is the dwindling number of people who are using quality education as the fastest ticket to betters jobs and income opportunities. American inventors like Bill Gates have acknowledged that their financial prowess is attributable to the fact that they were very good in science, mathematics, and reading. I agree with Bill Gates completely. For much of the American century, functional education has served as the engine of the ease of upward social mobility, what we refer to generally as the American Dream. Please, inculcate the habit of self-study. If you want to feed your mind with positive information, please, develop the habit of studying new subjects on your own, that is, without a formal instructor or classroom. You may begin self-study by introducing yourself to the fundamentals of economic theory. Make financial topics relevant to your daily life.

A possible point of departure is the reading of your town's daily newspaper. Make an effort to read the newspaper from cover to cover. Do not be like those guys who pick the paper and concentrate only on the pages of cartoons and sports. What about the finance pages? What about the stock tables? What about the legal announcements? I love reading newspapers. Even though I get much of my news online, I still subscribe to my metro newspaper, *The Washington Post*. *The Wall Street Journal* and *Investor's Business Daily* are my prime jewels, too. I love the feel of holding the newspaper in my hands. Even when I travel out of town, I make a habit of picking the most popular papers in the city I am visiting. Make your self-education go beyond the bounds of newspapers. What about books? If you do not have money to buy books, please, cultivate the habit of spending much time in your local public library.

There is more to personal finance than the drudgery of debts and budgets.

Read the newspapers and books! They are free to you, the taxpayer. Stop taking your government for granted; the government is providing facilities and services that are in dire need in other countries, but Americans take these resources for granted. Ah! A reading of newspapers will help you answer questions such as the following: Where does money come from? Why are some people rich and others poor? How is government regulation relevant to markets? What is the climate of entrepreneurship in my local area? What is the state of employment, growth, and taxes in my local areas? Is globalization good for my local area?

MILLIONAIRE iUNIVERSITY

Listed below are the Millionaire iUniversity Colleges. The virtual presence of this institution of higher learning is http://www.millionaireiuniversity.com. Please, choose a college to attend from the list below:

College of Insurance
College of Real Estate & Mortgages
College of Entrepreneurship
College of Accounting & Taxation
College of Personal Finance

LIST OF BUSINESSES YOU COULD START

Below is a list of small-business opportunities for you to consider. We can assist you in starting any of these businesses. We shall be be adding more businesses on this list.

Accountant
Bankruptcy Petition Preparer
Book Sales
Bulk Mail Processing Agent
Business Incorporation Consultant
Business Planning Consultant
Bulk Mail Processing Agent
Check-Casher
Computer Consultant
Credit Consultant
Credit Repair Consultant
Debt Collection Consultant
Graphic Design Consultant
Health Insurance Agent
Insurance Agent
Income Tax Consultant
IRS 501 (C) (3) Consultant
Lawn and Landscaping Consultant
Marketing and Sales Consultant
Medical Biller

Mortgage and Loan Consultant
Notary Public
Para-Legal
Phone Card Vendor
Photographer
Publisher
Real Estate Agent
Real Estate Investor
Travel and Ticketing Agent
Used Car Sales Consultant
Settlement/Title Agent
Stock Trader/Investor
Video Editor

COURSES RECOMMENDED FOR FURTHER STUDY

Miraculous millionaires are students for life. Miraculous millionaires are never contented with the level of their present knowledge. As votaries at the eternal spring of knowledge, they are as thirsty as travelers in the desert. As such, the suggested reading list below is, actually, my family library collection; I can reassure you that I have read all the books in my library. For your personal development and improvement, I have organized the list of books in order of courses you should take from Millionaire iUniversity today. As you browse the collection of books, please, feel free to select the books that appeal to you. I have made arrangements for you to purchase the books from my web site: http://www.millionaireiuniversity.com or princeojong.com.

ACCOUNTING, ECONOMICS, AND SOCIAL STUDIES COURSE

Ayittey, George B. N. Africa in chaos.
    Africa unchained: the blueprint for Africa's future.
    Defeating Dictators: Fighting Tyranny in Africa and Around the World
Blanchard, Kenneth and Margaret McBride. The one minute apology.
Blanchard, Kenneth and Spencer Johnson. The One minute manager.
Bohannon-Kaplan, Margaret. The role of personal responsibility in balancing individual liberty and the common good.
Duffy, Conviser. CPA review: Accounting & reporting
    CPA review: Audit.
    CPA review: Financial.
    CPA review: Law.
Duke University. Mediterranean Quarterly.
Fanon, Frantz. Black Skin, White Masks
    The Wretched of the Earth.
Finkler, Steven A. The complete guide to finance and accounting.
Fox, Jack. Accounting and recordkeeping made easy for the self-employed.
    Starting and building your own accounting business.

Heilbroner, Robert and William Milberg. The making of economic society.
Hurdle, Tim Berry. The book on business planning.
Kottak, Conrad Philip. Cultural anthropology.
Landrum, R. Eric. Introduction to psychology.
Lewis, Gordon P. Bookkeeping and tax preparation.
Mazrui, Ali Al'amin. The Africans: A triple heritage.
         The Trial of Christopher Okigbo.
Towards a Pax Africana: A Study of Ideology and Ambition.
World Culture and the Black Experience.
McConnell, Campbell R. and Stanley L. Brue. Economics: principles, problems, and policies.
Parker, Johnny. Blueprints for marriage.
Powell, Jewell R. Marriage 101.
 Ragan, Robert C. Step-by-step bookkeeping.
Schnepper, Jeff A. How to pay zero taxes.
Thomson, Alex. An introduction to African politics.
Tuccille, Jerome. The optimist's guide to making money in the 1980s.
Villalon, Leornardo A. and Peter VonDoepp. The fate of Africa's democratic experiments.
Walstad, William B. and Robert C. Bingham. Economics study guide.

AMERICAN/BRITISH ENGLISH AND LITERATURE COURSE

Ali, Shahrazad. The blackman's guide to understanding the blackwoman.
Ashbery, John. The best American poetry.
Baldwin, James. Go tell it on the mountain.
Bevilacqua, Michelle. More words you should know.
Bevington, David. The complete works of William Shakespeare.
Bradbury, Malcolm and James McFarlane. Modernism.
Britannica. Encyclopedia.The great books.
         The great conversation.
Brown, Peter Harry and Patte B. Barham. Marilyn: the last take.
Camus, Albert. Caligula.
         The plague.
         The myth of Sisyphus.
         The rebel.
         The stranger.
Cather, Willa. Alexander's bridge.
         A lost lady.
         Death comes for the archbishop.
         Five stories.
         Lucy Gayheart.
         My Antonia.
         My mortal enemy.
         Obscure destinies.
         One of ours.
         O Pioneers!

Sapphira and the slave girl.
Shadows on the rock.
The old beauty and others.
The professor's house.
The song of the lark.
Youth and the bright medusa.

Cervantes. Don Quixote.
Chadwick, Jennifer and Oliver Chadwick. 50 ways to meet your lover.
Clark, Mary H. Weep no more, my lady.
CliffNotes. Mythology.
Clinton, Bill. My life: early years.
      My life: the presidential years.
Corder, Jim W. Handbook of current English.
Cowley, Malcolm. Exile's return.
Crane, Stephen. The red badge of courage.
Crowell. Roget's international thesaurus.
Cruz, Nicky and James Buckingham. Run baby run.
Dabney, Lewis M. The portable Edmund Wilson.
Danziger, Marlies K. and W. Stacy Johnson. An introduction to the study of literature.
Day, Martin S. A handbook of American literature.
Defoe, Daniel. Moll Flanders.
      Robinson Crusoe.
Dickens, Charles. A tale of two cities.
      Bleak house.
      Christmas carol.
      David Copperfield.
      Great expectations.
      Hard times
      Little Dorrit.
      Nicholas Nickleby.
      Oliver Twist.
      Our mutual friend.
      The old curiosity shop.

Dipoko, Mbella Sonne. Because of women.
      Black and white in love.
Dictionary project. A student's dictionary.
Dos Passos, John. Manhattan transfer.
Dostoevsky, Fyodor. Notes from underground.
Dunbar, Paul L. The sport of the gods.
Eastman, Richard M. A guide to the novel.
Elliot, George. Adam Bede.
      Daniel Deronda.
      Middlemarch.

There is more to personal finance than the drudgery of debts and budgets.

Romola.

Silas Marner.

The mill on the floss.

Elliot, T.S. Murder in the cathedral.

Ellison, Ralph. Invisible man.

Faulkner, William. Absalom, Absalom.

Fitzgerald, Scott. The Great Gatsby.

Fogelin, Robert J. Understanding arguments: an introduction to informal logic.

Fowler, H. Ramsey and Jane E. Aaron. The Little, Brown handbook.

Fruehling, Rosemary T. and N.B. Oldham. Write to the point.

Frye, Northrop. Anatomy of criticism.

Frye, Northrop et al. The practical imagination.

Government Printing Office. Word division.

Graham, Sheila Y. Harbrace college workbook.

Grosse and Dunlap. The American tradition in literature.

Hacker, Diana. Rules for writers.

Haggard, H. Rider. Montezuma's Daughter.

Hawthorne, Nathaniel. The scarlet letter.

Hemingway, Ernest. A farewell to arms.

For whom the bell tolls.

In our time.

The old man and the sea.

The sun also rises.

Holman, C. Hugh. A handbook to literature.

Horton, Rod W. and Herbert W. Edwards. Background of American literary thought.

Houghton Mifflin. The American heritage dictionary.

Howells, William D. The rise of Silas Lapham.

Huxley, Aldous. Brave new world.

James, Henry. Roderick Hudson.

The American.

The portrait of a lady.

Washington Square.

Jewett, Sarah Orne. The country of the pointed firs.

Jones, LeRoi. Dutchman and the slave.

Joyce, James. A portrait of the artist as a young man.

Dubliners.

Exiles.

Finnegans wake.

Ulysses.

Kazin, Alfred. On native grounds.

Kolln, Martha and Robert Funk. Understanding English grammar.

Kondo, Baba Zak. The black student's guide to positive education.

L'Amour, Louis. Haunted mesa.

Leary, lewis. American literature: a study and research guide.

Lewis, Sinclair. Babbitt.

Lodge, David. 20th century criticism.
Malveaux, Julianne et al. The paradox of loyalty: an African-American response to the war
          on terrorism.
McClester, Cedric. Kwanzaa.
Melville, Herman. Billy Budd.
          Moby Dick.
Merriam Webster. A pronouncing dictionary of American English.
          Ninth new collegiate dictionary.
Microsoft. Encarta dictionary.
Miller, Perry. Major writers of America II.
MLA. MLA handbook for writers of research papers.
Molloy, John T. Dress for success.
Myers, L.M. and Richard L. Hoffman. The roots of modern English.
Nadell, Judith et al. The McMillan reader.
Norris, Frank. The Octopus.
Norton. The Norton anthology of American literature.
          The Norton anthology of English literature I.
          The Norton anthology of English literature II
Ojong, Ayuk George. The use of the American pioneer past in Willa Cather's novels.
O'Neil, Russell. The choice.
Orwell, George. 1984.
Penney, Alexandra. Great sex.
          How to make love to a man.
Pope, John C. Seven old English poems.
Prescott, Frederick C. An introduction to American prose.
Ravitch, Diane. The American reader.
Ross-Larson, Bruce. Edit yourself.
Runciman, Lex and Francine Weinberg. The Everyday writer.
Schweik, Robert C. and Dieter Riesner. Reference sources in English and American literature.
Seyler, Dorothy U. Read, reason, write.
Solzhenitsyn, Aleksandr I. The cancer ward.
          The gulag archipelago.
Sparknotes. Ultimate style.
Steel, Danielle. Fine things.
Stevenson, Robert Louis. Treasure island.
Strunk, Jr., William and E. B. White. The elements of style.
Thoreau, Henry David. Walden and civil disobedience.
Thorpe, James. The aims and methods of scholarship in modern languages and literatures.
Tibetts, Charlene and Arn Tibbetts. Strategies: a rhetoric and reader with handbook.
Updike, John. The coup.
Voeks, Virginia. On becoming an educated person.
Wald, Susan. Spanish for dummies.
Walker, Alice. The color purple.
Webster. Dictionary.
          New college dictionary.

New Webster's dictionary.
Spanish/English dictionary.
The new international Webster's pocket reference library.
Third new international dictionary.
Wells, H. G. The invisible man.
Wharton, Edith. The house of mirth.
Whitfield, Jane S. University rhyming dictionary.
Woodson, Carter. The miseducation of the negro.
Wright, Richard. American hunger.
      Native son.

BIOGRAPHY, AUTOBIOGRAPHY, AND MEMOIR COURSE

Barrett, Wayne. Trump: the deals and the downfall.
Blair, Gwenda A. The Trumps: three generations that built an empire.
Carroll, Diahann and Ross Firestone. Diahann!
Chernow, Ron. Titan: the life of John D. Rockefeller, Sr.
 Chiu, Tony. Ross Perot: in his own words.
Ebony Magazine. John H. Johnson.
Farman, Irvin. Tandy's money machine
Getty, J. Paul. How to be rich.
Goldman, Albert. Elvis.
Graham, Billy. Just as I am.
Gross, Daniel. Forbes' greatest business stories of all time.
Jackson, Latoya. Starting over.
Johnson, John H. Succeeding against the odds.
Langley, Monica. Tearing down the walls.
Lewis, Reginald F. and Blair S. Walker. Why should white guys have all the fun?
Kennedy, John F. Profiles in courage.
Kessler, Ronald. The richest man in the world: the story of Adnan Khashoggi.
Mansfield, Stephanie. The richest girl in the world: the extravagant life and fast times of
      Doris Duke.
Morella, Joe and Edward Z. Epstein. Rita: the life of Rita Hayworth.
O'Neill, George and Dick Lehr. The underboss: a dramatic inside look at the rise and fall
      of a mafia family.
Palin, Sarah. Going Rogue: An American Life.
Stevens, Mark. King Icahn: the biography of a renegade capitalist.
Taraborrelli, J. Randy. Call her Miss Ross: the unauthorized biography of Diana Ross.
Trimble, Vance H. Sam Walton: the inside story of America's richest man.
Trump, Donald J. Trump: the art of the comeback.
Trump, Donald J. and Meredith McIver. Trump: think like a billionaire.
Walton, Sam and John Huey. Sam Walton: made in America my story.
Washington, Booker T. Up from slavery.
Young, Jeffrey S. Steve Jobs: the journey is the reward.

BUSINESS FUNDAMENTALS COURSE

American Institute of Consumer Credit. Become a certified consumer credit consultant.
    Become a certified mortgage reduction consultant without a computer.
    Become rich by buying profitable bankrupt businesses with little or no money down.
    How to become an advertising marketing consultant.
    How to get free government loans, guarantees and grants in 3 weeks with no hassles.
    The real entrepreneur's guide to free money.
Arden, Lynie. The work at home sourcebook.
Charter Financial. Building wealth.
Cochran, Gary. Cashing in on direct marketing.
    Finding and funding direct marketing products.
    Making it big with mail order.
Collins, Eliza G.C. and Mary Anne Devanna. The portable MBA
Cook, James R. The start-up entrepreneur.
Deutsch, Donny. The Big Idea.: How to make your entrepreneurial dreams come true, from the AHA motherent to your first million.
Edwards, Paul and Sarah Edwards. Getting business to come to you.
    The best home businesses for the 1990s.
    Working from home.
Entrepreneur Magazine. Business start-up guides.
    Check cashing start-up guide.
    Collection agency start-up guide.
    Flat fee real estate agency start-up guide.
    Loan brokering start-up guide.
    Medical claims services start-up guide.
    The guide to credit counseling.
Fritz, Roger. Nobody gets rich working for somebody else.
Gateways Research Institute. The prosperity solution.
Ginsburg, Carol M. and Robert Mastin. Money making 900 numbers: how entrepreneurs use the telephone to sell information.
Halloran, James W. The entrepreneur's guide to starting a successful business.
Hansen, Nancy Edmonds. How you can make $20,000 a year writing: no matter where you live.
Harvard Business Review. Business classics: fifteen key concepts for managerial success.
Hausaman, Carl. Moonlighting: 148 great ways to make money on the side.
Hicks, Tyler G. How to start your own business on a shoestring and make up to $500,000 a year.
Inc. Magazine. Sprint's business success series.
Kahn, Sarah and the Philip Lief Group. 101 Best businesses to start.
Kishel, Gregory and Patricia Kishel. How to start and run a successful consulting business.
    How to start, run, and stay in business.
Lesko, Mathew. Lesko's info-power: information USA.
Lewsi, Jerre G. and Leslie D. Renn. How to start and manage a travel agency.
Loeb, Marshall. 1990 money guide.
McQuown, Judith H. Inc yourself: how to profit by setting up your own corporation.

Minars, David. Your business your money.
Monaghan, Kelly. Home-based travel agent.
Nelson, Billy and Peter Economy. Consulting for dummies.
Ramsey, Dan. The upstart guide to owning and managing a travel service.
Rudelius, William and W. Bruce Erickson. An introduction to contemporary business.
SBA. (Small Business Administration). Financial management: how to make a go of
      your business.
Seglin, Jeffrey L. Financing your small business.
Shenson, Howard L. How to develop and promote successful seminars and workshops.
Simon, Alan R. How to be a successful computer consultant.
Thompson, Douglas. How to open your own travel agency.
Veblen, Thorstein. The theory of the leisure class.

COMMUNICATIONS FUNDAMENTALS COURSE

Battle, Stafford L. and Rey O. Harris. The African-American resource guide to the Internet and online services.
Boothman, Nicholas. How to Make People Like You.
Collier, Marsha. Ebay business all-in-one for dummies.
      Ebay for dummies.
      Starting an Ebay business.
Coombs, Jason. And Ted Coombs. Setting up an Internet site for dummies.
Davidson, Jeffrey P. Blow your own horn.
Dern, Daniel P. The Internet guide for new users.
Emery, Vince. How to grow your business on the Internet.
Griffith, Jim. The official Ebay bible.
Hill, Brad. Internet directory for dummies.
Laermer, Richard. Full Frontal PR.
Levine, John R. The Internet for dummies.
Love, Doug. Internet explorer for dummies.
Oliver, Dick. Teach yourself HTML 4.
Pearlman, Leah and Carolyn Abram. Facebook for Dummies.
Helmstetter, Shad. You can excel in time of change.
Warner, Janine. Web Sites for Dummies.
      What to say when you talk to yourself: powerful new techniques to program your
      potential for success.
Wolff, Michael. Burn rare.
Zimmerman, Jan and Doug Sahlin. Social Media Marketing for Dummies.

COMPUTERS, COMPUTING, AND PROGRAMMING COURSE

Angermeyer, John et al. The Waite Group's tricks of the MS-DOS masters
Barker, F. Scott. Access 97 power programming.
Bigelow, Stephen J. PC drives and memory systems.
Boillot, Michael. Understanding Fortran 77: with structured problem solving.

Bove, Tony et al. The art of desktop publishing: using personal computers to publish it yourself.

Bowen, Charles and David Peyton. The complete electronic bulletin board: starter kit.

Boyce, Jim. Understanding Visual Basic 3 for Windows.

Bretz, Jeff and John Clark Craig. 100 ready-to-run programs and subroutines for the IBM-PC.

Brumm, Penn. 80386: a programming and design handbook.

Burns, Diane et al. The electronic publisher.

Byers, Robert A. dBase III plus for every business.

Cassel, Paul. Teach yourself Access 95 in 14 days.

Chen, Steven. The IBM programmer's challenge.

Cobb, Douglas. Douglas Cobb's 1-2-3 handbook.

Corel Gallery. 10,000 clip art images.

Cowart, Robert. Microsoft Access 2.00: quick and easy.

Crane, Mark W. and Joseph R. Pierce. Laserjet companion.

Cusuman, Michael A. and Richard W. Selby. Microsoft secrets.

DiGiovanna, Ed. DOS shareware utilities.

    Programming tools shareware.

DiGiovanna, Jennifer Holt and Ed DiGiovanna. Business applications shareware.

Everett, John H. and Elizabeth P. Crowe. Information for sale.

Frank, Judith M. Managing business microcomputer systems.

Getz, Ken. et al. Microsoft Access developer's handbook.

Gookin, Dan. DOS for dummies.

Gookin, Dan and Andy Townsend. Hard disk management with MS-DOS and PC-DOS.

Harvey, Greg. DOS for dummies.

Jantz, Richard J. Ventura publisher for the IBM PC.

Jennings, Roger. Using Access 95.

Johnson, Robert H. MVS: concepts and facilities.

Kaufeld, John. Access for Windows 95 for dummies.

Kaufman, Milton and Arthur H. Seidman. Electronics sourcebook for technicians and engineers.

Kleper, Michael L. The illustrated handbook of desktop publishing and typesetting.

Kriya Systems. Typing tutor IV.

Krumm, Robert. Getting the most from utilities on the IBM PC.

Krumm, Ron. Access programming for dummies.

Lai, Robert S. Writing MS-DOS device drivers.

Lord, Kenniston W. Office automation systems handbook.

Lubow, Martha and Jesse Berst. Publishing power with Ventura.

  Style sheets for business documents.

Lubow, Martha and Polly Pattison. Style sheets for newsletters.

Manes, Stephen and Paul Andrews. Gates: how Microsoft's mogul reinvented an industry and made himself the richest man in America.

Margolis, Art. Troubleshooting and repairing the new personal computers.

Martin, James. Local area networks: architecture and implementation.

Mayo, Jonathan L. Computer viruses.

McClelland, Deke and Craig Danuloff. The PageMaker companion.

Medrcado-Gardner, Juanita. "No code" database design with Access 2.0.

Microsoft. Access developer's toolkit

There is more to personal finance than the drudgery of debts and budgets.

Getting results with Microsoft Office for windows 95.
Microsoft Access Language reference.
Office 95 data access reference.
Visual Basic.
Middleton, Robert G. Troubleshooting electronic equipment without service data.
Millman, Jacob, and Arvin Grabel. Microelectronics.
Murray, Katherine. Using PFS first publisher.
Norton, Peter. Inside the IBM PC.
Norton, Peter and Robert Jourdain. The hard disk companion.
Oxner, Ed. Designing with field-effect transistors.
Parker, Sybil P. McGraw-Hill encyclopedia of electronics and computers.
Perry, Gary. Visual Basic starter kit.
Perry, Paul et al. Insider's guide to software development.
Pilgrim, Aubrey. Build your own 80286 IBM compatible and save a bundle.
  Build your own multimedia PC.
Prague, Cary N. et al. Access for Windows 95 secrets.
Prague, Cary N. and James E. Hammitt. The dBase III programming handbook.
Prague, Cary N. and James E. Hammitt. The dBase III programming: tips and techniques.
Prague, Cary N. and Michael R. Irwin. Access for Windows 15 Bible.
Richardson, Ronny. MS-DOS batch file programming.
Rimmer, Steve. Mastering CorelDraw.
Sawusch, Mark R. The best shareware.
Schaffer, Clifford A. Working with Focus: an introduction to database management.
Scott, D.F. Programming illustrated.
Seidman, Arthur H. Ivan Flores. The handbook of computers and computing.
Simpson, Alan. Understanding dBase III plus.
Smith, David N. Concepts of object-oriented programming.
Sipolt, Michael J. and Thomas Sheldon. Hard disk management in the PC and
        MS-DOS environment.
Socha, John and Devra Hall. Teach yourself Visual Basic 3.0
Ullman, Larry. MySQL: visual quick start guide.
Viescas, John L. and Jeff Conrad. Microsoft Office Access 2007: inside out.
Wallace, James. Hard drive.
        Overdrive: Bill gates and the race to control cyberspace.
Will-Harris, Daniel. Typestyle: how to choose and use type on a personal computer.
Wolverton, Van. Running MS-DOS.

FRENCH LITERATURE

Camus, Albert. La peste.
L'Etranger.
De Musset, Alfred. On ne badine pas avec l'amour.
Flaubert, Gustav. Madame Bovary.
Larousse de poche

INSURANCE FUNDAMENTALS COURSE

A.D. Banker and Company. Maryland life and health insurance.
Enterprise Insurance Training. Life and health pre-licensing manual.
Hastings, Jeff. So you want to be an insurance agent: a step-by-step approach to a
        successful insurance agency
Holliday, Nick. Internet Marketing for insurance agents
Kelley, Patrick. Tax-free Retirement.
Kessler, Ronald, The Life Insurance Game
Kravitz, Seth and Lev Barinskiy. Mastering Insurance Marketing: how to move your agency
forward in the new media age.
Pierre, Sr., Melvin. Increase your insurance sales, retention, & referrals now!!!
Rossi, Rick et al. Saving Middle America: Securing Financial Dreams

LAW, MEDICINE, AND HEALTHCARE

Adamec, Chris. The unofficial guide to eldercare.
Alexandra, Bliss. Divorce: a New York's guide to doing it yourself.
APA. The pharmacy technician.
        The pharmacy technician workbook and certification review.
Burke, Barlow. Law of title insurance.
Canter, Laurence A. and Martha S. Siegel. US Immigration made easy: the insider's guide.
Clifford, Denis. Make your own living trust.
Deutsch Howard D. Immigration the easy way.
Doran, Kenneth J. Personal bankruptcy and debt adjustment: a fresh start; a step-by-step guide.
Gadow, Sandy. The complete guide to your real estate closing.
Gosdin, James L. title insurance: a comprehensive overview.
Hennin, S. Real estate title search abstractor basics.
Irwin, Robert. Home closing checklist.
Kochanski, David M. and Eric M. Schneider. The essential title examination guide for
        Maryland paralegals.
Kougler, Karen E. Closing concepts: a title training manual.
        Title basics: a search and exam manual for beginners.
Lewis, Loida N. and Len T. Madlansacay. How to get a green card: legal ways to stay in the USA.
Lieberman, Trudy et al. Consumer reports: complete guide to health services for seniors.
Lorman Education Services. Fundamentals of real estate closings in Maryland.
Mancuso, Anthony. How to form a nonprofit corporation.
        How to form a nonprofit corporation in all 50 states.
MLTA. Title insurance pre-licensing course.
National Business Institute. Maryland real estate title law: problems and solutions.
        Mastering real estate titles and title insurance in Maryland.
        Real estate title examination in Maryland.
Nolo Press. Willmaker.
Oltmanns, V.R. Going into escrow: escrow knowledge to enhance one's estate.
Perez-Salva, Abilio. Title insurance 101.

Powers, Mary F. and Janet B. Wakelin. Pharmacy Calculators.

Redmond Consulting Group. Real estate settlement processing manual.

Reich, Lawrence R. and James P. Duffy. You can go bankrupt without going broke: an essential guide to personal bankruptcy.

Rothenbers, Robert E. The new American medical dictionary and health manual.

Schreuder, Sally Abel. How to become a United States citizen: a step-by-step guidebook for your self-instruction.

The Computer Place. Med iSOFT patient accounting.
     Practisoft patient accounting

Warner, Ralph. The independent paralegal's handbook: how to provide legal services without becoming a lawyer.

White, Donald A. Maryland real estate: practice and law.

Wilkin. Noel E. Journal of pharmacy teaching.

Woodhouse, Violet et al. Divorce and money: how to make the best financial decisions during divorce.

MOTIVATIONAL LITERATURE FUNDAMENTALS COURSE

Barnhart, Tod. The Five Rituals of Wealth.

Bettger, Frank. How I raised myself from failure to success in selling.

Clason, George S. The richest man in Babylon.

Corey, Stephen R. The 7 Habits of highly effective people.

Cypert, Samuel A. Believe and achieve.

Davies, Dave. Mind Over Money

Fisher, Mark. The instant millionaire.

Haroldsen, Mark O. The common man's guide to uncommon success.
     How to wake up the financial genius inside you.
     The courage to be rich.

Hill, Napoleon. Think and Grow Rich.
     Success through a positive mental attitude.
     The master key to riches.

Jackson, Sr., Reverend Jesse L. and Jesse L. Jackson, Jr. with Mary Gotschall. It is About the Money! The Fourth Movement of the Freedom Symphony: How to Build Wealth, Get Access to Capital, and Achieve Your Financial Dreams

Kimbro, Dennis. Think and Grow Rich: A Black Choice

Korda, Michael. Power.
     Success.
     Worldly Goods.

Lee, Dwight R and Richard B. McKenzie. Getting Rich in America:
8 Simple Rules for Building a Fortune and a Satisfying Life.

Mackay, Harvey. Swim with the sharks without being eaten alive.

Robbins, Anthony. Unlimited Power.
     Awaken the giant within.

Schwartz, David J. The magic of thinking big

Stanley, Thomas J. and William D. Danko. The Millionaire Next Door:
The Surprising Secrets of America's Wealthy.
Trump, Donald J. Think Like Billionaire.

MUSIC AND ENTERTAINMENT COURSE

Brae, C. Michael and Damean V. Russell. Music distribution: selling music in the
    new entertainment marketplace.
Chappell, Jon et al. home recording studio basics: what you need to know to build a
    home studio.
Colier, Maxie D. The ifilm digital video filmaker's handbook.
 Cool, Benjamin. Sex and camcorders.
Cooper, Jeff. Building a recording studio.
Coryat, Karl. Guerrilla home recording: how to get great sound from any studio.
Dawes, John and Tim Sweeney. The complete guide to the Internet promotion for
    artists, musicians, and songwriters.
Frascogna, Jr., Xavier M. and H. lee Hetherington. This business of artist management.
Galper, Hal. The touring musician: a small business approach to booking your band on the road.
Gervais, Rod. Home recording studio: build it like the pros.
Goldstein, Jeri. How to be your own booking agent and save thousands of dollars.
Halloran, Mark. The musician's business and legal guide.
Harrison, Mark. All about piano.
Hooper, David and Lee Kennedy. How I make $100,000 a year in the music business
    without a record label, manager, or booking agent.
Kalmer, Veronika. Label launch.
Lathrop, Tad and Jon Pettigrew. This business of music marketing and promotion.
Macdonald, Ronan. The billboard illustrated home recording book.
Machlis, Joseph and Kristine Forney. The enjoyment of music.
Newell, Philip. Recording studio design.
Newton, Dale, and John Gaspard. Digital filmmaking 101: an essential guide to producing
    low-budget movies.
Passman, Donald S. All you need to know about the music business.
Price, Zack. The beginner's guide to computer-based music production
Shirley, John and Richard Strasser. The savvy studio owner.
Schwarts, Daylle D. Start and run your own record label.
Schonbrun, Marc. The everything home recording book.
Sight and Sound. Country pops: A-B-C music for beginners.
        Creating sounds on your electronic keyboard.
        Films of the 1980s: A-B-C music for beginner
        Hot country: A-B-C music for beginners.
        Letter music; country favorites.
        Music video hits: A-B-C music for beginners.
        Superstar hits: A-B-C music for beginners.
Sweeney, Tim. Guide to releasing independent records.
        Guide to successfully playing LIVE: an in-depth two hour workshop with Tim Sweeney.

There is more to personal finance than the drudgery of debts and budgets.

Volinchak, Tom. Make money with your studio.
West, Ray. Adult video business: how you can find attractive women to star in your own
        adult films, make money, and quit work in 7 weeks.
White, Paul. Basic home studio design.

PERSONAL FINANCE FUNDAMENTALS COURSE

Bach, David. Automatic millionaire.
                Smart couples finish rich.
                Smart women finish rich.
Belsky, Gary and Thomas Gilovich Why Smart People Make Big Money Mistakes (and How to
Correct Them).
Berman, Daniel K. The credit power handbook.
Black Enterprise.
Boardroom Classics. The complete book of money secrets.
Clyatt, Billy. Work Less, Live More: The Way to Semi-Retirement.
Crockett, Marilyn. The money club: how we taught ourselves the secret to a secure financial
future—and how you can, too.
Dacyczyn, Amy. The Complete Tightwad Gazette.
Dave Del Dotto. A treasury of government loans.
        Government auctions.
        How to make nothing but money.
        National foreclosure network.
Edelman, Ric. The Truth about money.
Eden press. Credit improvement and credit cards ... loans and leases.
Eisenson, Marc. The Banker's Secret.
Entrepreneur Magazine.
Forbes Magazine.
Fortune Magazine.
Freeman, Harrine. How to get out of debt.

Gilles, Jerry. Money love.
Givens, Charles. Financial self-defense.
        More wealth without risk.
        Wealth without risk.
Gorchoff, Louis R. The insider's guide bankcards with no credit check.
Hammond, Billy. Credit secrets: how to erase bad credit.
        Life after debt: the complete credit restoration kit.
Harris Publications. Small Business Opportunities.
Hunt, Mary. The best of the cheapskate monthly: simple tips for living lean in the 1990s.
Kiyosaki, Robert T. Rich father poor father.
Leonard, Robin. Money troubles: legal strategies to cope with your debts.
Malkiel, Burton G. The Random Walk Guide to Investing
McCarthy, Ed. The fast forward MBA in financial planning.

Molles, Cris. 60 ways to raise cash fast.

Money Magazine.

Mundis, Jerrold. How to Get Out of Debt, Stay Out of Debt, and Live Prosperously

Newsweek Magazine.

Phillips, Wayne. How to start your own business by doing business with the government.

Quinn, Jane Bryant. Making the most of your money.

Ramsey, Dave. Financial Peace: Putting Common Sense Into Your Dollars and Cents
> Financial Peace Revisited
> The Total Money Makeover: A Proven Plan for Financial Fitness

Scholastic. Family computing.
> Home Office computing.

Sethi, Ramit. I Will Teach You to Be Rich.

Simmons, Barbara. Penny-pinching: how to lower every day expenses without lowering
> your standard of living.

Stanley, Thomas and William Danko The Millionaire Next Door.

Success Magazine.

The Beardstown Ladies. Stitch-in-time guide to growing your nest egg: step-by-step planning
> for a comfortable financial future.
> Smart spending for big savings: how to save for a rainy day without sacrificing
> your lifestyle.

The Wall Street Journal. Guide to planning your financial future.
> Guide to understanding money and investing.
> Guide to understanding personal finance.

Thomson Financial Publishing. Key to routing numbers.

Tilford, Monique. Your Money or Your Life by Vicki Robin, Joe Dominguez.

Warren, Elizabeth and Amelia Warren Tyagi. All Your Worth: The Ultimate Lifetime
> Money Plan

White, J. Arlene. Credit mechanic: the poor man's guide to credit repair.

REAL ESTATE SALES AND INVESTING COURSE

Allen, Robert G. Creating wealth.
> Nothing down.

Ambalal, Purandar. Foreclosures: how to prevent, stop, beat, and survive.

Badt, Evan. Unlocking the mystery of foreclosures.

Becker, Norman. Home inspection checklists: Illustrated checklists and worksheets you
> need before buying a home.

Berges, Steve. The complete guide to flipping properties.

Bergsman, Steve. Maverick real estate investing.

Boog, Billy. Selling homes 123.

Bronchick, William. Financing secrets of a millionaire real estate investor.

Bronchick, William and Robert Dahlstrom. Flipping properties: instant cash profits in
> real estate.

Cauldwell, Rex. Inspecting a house.

Condon, Chris. Building real estate riches: how to invest in new homes for maximum profit.

Cook, Frank. 21 things I wish my broker had told me: financial advice for new real estate professionals.

Cross, Carla. The real estate agent's business planning guide.

Cummings, Jack. Investing in real estate with other people's money: proven strategies for turning a small investment into a fortune.

Dallow, Theodore J. How to buy foreclosed real estate for a fraction of its value.

Decima, Jay P. investing in fixer-uppers.

Dennis, Marshall W. and Michael J. Robertson. Residential mortgage lending.

Dotto, Dave Del. Cash flow expo library.
Creative financing.

Dulworth, Mike and Teresa Goodwin. Renovate to riches: buy, improve, and flip houses to create wealth.

Dworin, Lawrence. Profits in buying and renovating homes.

Eldred, Gary W. make money with fixer-uppers and renovations.

Evans, Blanche. The hottest e-careers in real estate.

Ferry, Mike. How to develop a six figure income in real estate: superstar selling the Mike Ferry way.

Friedman, Jack P. and Jack C. Harris. Keys to investing in real estate.
Keys to mortgage financing and refinancing.

Galaty, Fillmore W. et al. Modern real estate practice.

Garton-Good, Julie. All about mortgages: insider tips to finance or refinance your home.
Real estate licensing super course.

Gerisilo, Phil and Rob Lebow. Succeed in real estate without cold calling.

Grogan, D.L. and M.C. Buzz Chambers. California mortgage loan brokering and lending.

Hamilton, Katie. Fix it and flip it: how to make money rehabbing real estate for profit.

Harkins, Phil and Keith Holliman. Everybody wins: the story and lessons behind RE/MAX

Herd, Robert L. How to become a mega-producer real estate agent in five years.

Hicks, Tyler. How to borrow your way to real estate riches.

Hopkins, Tom. How to master the art of listing and selling real estate.

Hoven, Vernon. Real estate and taxes: what every agent should know.

Johnson, Deborah and Steve Kennedy. How to farm $uccessfully by phone.

Keller, Gary. The millionaire real estate agent.

Klein, Saul D. et al. Real estate technology guide.

Kollen, Melissa S. Buying real estate foreclosures.

McLean, Andrew J. Buying real estate for pennies on the dollar" how to make a fortune in foreclosures.

Miller, Peter G. Successful real estate investing: a practical guide to profits after tax reform for the small investor.

Miller, Peter G. The common sense mortgage: how to cut the cost of home ownership by $100,000 or more.

Misko, James A. How to finance any real estate any place any time.

Murphy, Terri. E-listing and e-selling secrets for the technologically clueless.
Listing and selling secrets.

Myers, Kevin C. Buy it, fix it, sell it, profit: a comprehensive guide to no-sweat money-making home rehab.

Pashkow, Sidney A. and Victoria A. Jackson. Focusing on foreclosures: a step-by-step primer in the art of acquiring foreclosure properties.

Pestrak, Debra. Playing with the big boys and girls in real estate.

Polk, John. High yield low risk.

RE/MAX. Welcome home: thoughts to celebrate your work and your dreams.

Reynolds, Monica. Multiply your success with real estate assistants.

Richard, Dan Gooder. Real estate rainmaker: successful strategies for real estate marketing.

Rider, Stuart Leland. The complete idiot's guide to investing in fixer-uppers.

Roos, Dolf De. The insider's guide to 52 homes in 52 weeks: acquire your real estate fortune today.

Ross, George H. Trump strategies for real estate: billionaire lessons for the small investor.

Sager, Lawrence. Guide to passing the PSI real estate exam.

Sheets, Carlton. How to buy your first home or investment property with no down payment. Real estate forms portfolio.

Sparta, Kelle. The consultative real estate agent.

Steinmetz, Thomas C. The mortgage pit.

Stone, Barry. The consumer advocate's guide to home inspection: avoiding the nightmare of purchasing a money pit.

Summey, Mike and Roger Dawson. The week-end millionaire's secrets to investing in real estate.

The Home Depot. Decks 1-2-3

Thomas, Ted. Big money in real estate foreclosures.

Warda, Mark. Essential guide to real estate contracts.

Weiss. Mark B. Real estate Flipping: grow rich buying and selling property.

Wiedemer, James I. The smart money guide to bargain homes: how to find and buy foreclosures.

Wittenmeyer, Bryan C. Real estate business and investment opportunities: the complete guide to starting a high-profit business.

Zagaris, Michael P. The PMZ way: strategies of highly successful real estate agents.

RELIGION, MYSTICISM, AND PHILOSOPHY COURSE

AMORC. Mystics at prayer.
    Rosicrucian Digest.
    Rosicrucian Monograph.
    Sepher Yezirah.
    The mastery of life.

Bonhoeffer, Dietrich. The prayer book of the bible.

Browne, Sylvia. About the paranormal.
    Contacting your spirit guide.
    Phenomenon: everything you need to know.

Candlewick Press. Egyptology.

Cerve, Wishar S. Lemuria: the lost continent of the Pacific.

Claremont, Lewis. The 7 keys to power.

Dorene Publishing. The 6th & 7th Books of Moses.

Dover Publications. The book of psalms.

Dubin, Reese P. Telecult Power: the amazing new way to psychic and occult wonders.

Edwards, Lonnie C. Spiritual Laws.

Freemantle, James S. The psalms of David.

Gamache, Henri. The 8th 9th & 10th Books of Moses.

Goldschneider, Gery. The secret language of luck.

Gramercy Books. The lost books of the bible.

Hewitt, William W. Psychic development for beginners.

Hohman, John George. Pow-wows or long lost friend.

Inserra, Rose. Dictionary of Dreams.

Isopanisad, Sri. Discovering the original person.

Jones, Laurie B. Jesus CEO: using ancient wisdom for visionary leadership.

Lee, Edward. Practical mysticism.

Lewis, C.S. Reflections on the psalms.

Lewis, Harvey Spencer. Mansions of the soul: the Cosmic Conception.
        Mental poisoning.
         Rosicrucian Principles for home and business.
        Self-mastery and fate with the cycles of life
        The mystical life of Jesus.
        The secret doctrines of Jesus.

Lewis, Ralph M. Cosmic mission fulfilled.
         Sanctuary of Self.
         Whisperings of self.
         Yesterday has much to tell.

Lushena Books. The 6th & 7th Books of Moses.

Magnus, Albertus. Egyptian secrets: or white and black art for man and beast.

Malbrough, Rev. Ray T. The magical power of the saints.

Meyer, Marvin W. The ancient mysteries.

Miller, Stephen M. The complete guide to the bible.

Oribello, William Alexander. The sealed magical book of Moses.

Oribello, Willaim Alexander. Candle burning magic with psalms

Ramatherio, Sri. Unto thee I grant.

Rivas, Anna. Candle burning magic.
        Powers of the psalms.
        Secrets of magical seals.

Russell, Bertrand. A history of western philosophy.

Selig, Godfrey A. Secrets of the psalms

Seventh-Day Adventists. Minister's handbook.

Sumner, Tracy Macon. How did we get the bible?

The Holy Bible

The Jewish Publication Society. The book of psalms.

Torrey, R.A. How to pray.

US News & World Report. Secrets of Christianity.

Warren, Rick. The purpose-Driven life.

Warren, Rick. The Purpose-Driven Life Journal

Whitney, Russ. Building wealth: how anyone can make a personal fortune without money, credit, or luck.

White, Ellen G. Pastoral ministry.

Wippler, Migene Gonzalez. The new revised 6th & 7th Books of Moses and the magical uses of the psalms

SALES, MARKETING, AND COMMUNICATIONS COURSE.

Arnold, Hugh J. and Daniel C. Feldman. Organizational behavior.

Blatner, David. QuarkXPress.

Carnegie, Dale. How to win friends and influence people.

Dizard, Jr., Wilson P. The coming information age.

Devito, Joseph A. Essentials of human communication.

El-Nawawy, Mohamed. Aljazeera.

Feldman, Daniel C. Managing careers in organizations.

Gallegos, Frederick et al. Audit and control of information systems.

Gitomer, Jeffrey. Little Red Book of Selling.

Goldhaber, Gerald M. organizational communication.

Goldstein, Irwin L. Training in organizations: needs assessment, development, and evaluation.

Green, Gordon W. Getting straight As.

Hiebert, Ray E. et al. Mass media III: an introduction to modern communication.

Howard, Michael C. and Patricia C. Mckim. Contemporary cultural anthropology.

Howard University. Howard journal of communications.

Lau, James B. and A.B. Shani. Behavior in organizations.

Levinson, Jay Conrad. Guerrilla marketing.

Littlejohn, Stephen and Karen A. Foss. Theories of human communication.

Laudon, Kenneth C. and Jane Price Laudon. Management information systems: a contemporary perspective.

McClelland, Deke. Photoshop for dummies.

McPhee, Robert D and Phillip K. Tompkins. Organizational communications: traditional themes and new directions.

Mandell, Maurice L. Advertising.

Minium, Eward W. Statistical reasoning in psychology and education.

Naisbitt, John and Patricia Aburdene. Megatrends 2000.

Nyamnjoh, Francis B. Africa's Media: democracy and the politics of belonging.

Page, Roy A. Our way of life: the odyssey of a farm family.

Page-Jones, Meilir. Practical project management.

Poe, Richard. Wave3: the new era in network marketing.

Roberts, Ralph R. and John Galagher. Walk like a giant sell like a madman.

Rubin, Rebecca B. et al. Communication research: strategies and sources.

Tofler, Alvin. Powershift.

Tubbs, Stewart L. A systems approach to small group interaction.

Tubbs, Stewart L. and Sylvia Moss. Human communication.

Williams, Frederick. Technology and communication behavior.
     The communications revolution.

Yin, Robert K. Case study research: design and methods.

Software online and offline Course
4DCD LLC, Social Media Marketing.
Adobe. Acrobat professional
Indesign
Photoshop
Premiere
Reader
Anderson, Andy. Final Cut Pro 7. Video Training DVD
Avanquest. My Maillist and Postage Saver
        Webeasy 8 professional.
Barrons. Pronounce it perfectly in English.
Bellamy, Seamus. Joomla! For Dummies.
Bestcase.com. Best case bankruptcy software.
Brenneis, Lisa. Final Cut Pro 7
Bricklin, Dan. Demo it!
Broderbund. Clickart.
        PrintMaster.
Calyx Software. Point.
Chicago Board Options Exchange. The index toolbox.
        The options toolbox.
Comtronic. Debtmaster.
            Property manager.
Corel. Gallery magic.
Cosmi Corporation. English: learn to speak English today.
Cosmi Software. 1000 Best Fonts.
        Deluxe Wills and trusts.
         Print Perfect.
        Stationery & Brochure Maker.
Criss Cross. Criss Cross plus real estate.
Cybermedia. First Aid.
Davidson. Ultimate speed reader.
Drake Software. Drake tax software.
Expert Software. Travel planner CD.
E-Z Legal Software. Incorporation.
Getgood, Susan J. Professional blogging for dummies.
H & R Block. Taxcut.
Hussey, Tris. Create your own blog.
Individual Software. Anytime Organizer.
        Web pages and graphics.
Intuit. Quicken.
        QuickBooks.
Kobler, Helmut. Final Cut Pro HD for Dummies.
Lynch, Peter. The stock shop.
Made Easy Products. Buying and selling a home.
        Employee policies and manuals

Personal legal forms and agreements.

Mathew Bender. Colier Topform bankruptcy software.

McAfee. VirusScan.

Microsoft. Access

Frontpage

Office Professional.

Plus!

Publisher.

Visual Basic.

Windows.

Microstar. Indigo investment software.

Mindware. IQ builder.

Miser, Brad. MacBook Pro.

Mymortgagetrainer.com. Financial strategies.

Namo. Web editor professional.

Nolo Press. Willmaker.

Winning in small claims court.

Norton, Peter. PC Anywhere.

Nova Development. Print Artist.

Omega Research. Wall Street analyst.

Palo Alto Software. Business plan pro.

Sales and Marketing Pro.

Perry, Greg. Access 95.

Phone Disc. Powerfinder.

Pro One. Grammar.

MBA

Prospectplus.com Prospectplus!

Quark. QuarkXpress.

Rackham, Neil. Spin Selling.

Rightsoft. Right writer.

Select Phone. Select Phone.

Serif.com. Webplus x4.

Socrates. Credit repair.

Employee and policies manuals.

Estate planner library.

Human resource library.

Personnel forms.

Success. The powerful business plan writer.

The powerful marketing plan writer.

Swift Software. Web site promoter.

Title Software Corporation. Title Express.

Tobias, Andrew. Taxcut

Transparent Language. Easy translator.

Turbo Tax

Universal Systems. Taxwise.

There is more to personal finance than the drudgery of debts and budgets.

White Smoke.com. Grammatik.
Windows on Wall Street. Windows on Wall Street.
Winway. Resume.
Wizetrade.com. Wizetrade
Wolsky, Tom. Finalcut Pro 7
Zipforms.com

STOCKS FUNDAMENTALS COURSE

Baker, Deborah Rosen and Julie Behr Zimmerman. Julie and Debbie's guide to getting rich on just $10 a   week: how we are making a fortune and you can too using dividend reinvestment plans.

Buffett, Mary and David Clark. Buffettology: the previously unexplained techniques that have made Warren Buffett the world's most famous investor.

Carlson, Charles B. Buying stocks without a broker.

Chuck Carlson's 60-second investor: 201 tips, tools, and tactics for the time-strapped   investor. Drip investor.

Darvas, Nicolas. How I made $2,000,000 in the stock market.
       Wall Street: the other Las Vegas.

Fisher, Philip A. Common stocks and uncommon profits.

Gardner, David and Tom Gardner. The motley fool investment guide: how the fools beat wall street's wise men and how you can too.

Gallea, Anthony M. and William Patalon III. Contrarian investing: buy and sell when others will not and make money doing it.

Gerlach, Douglas. Investor's web guide: tools and strategies for building your portfolio.

Graham, Benjamin. The intelligent investor: a book of practical counsel.

Greenblatt, Joel. You can be a stock market genius even if you are not too smart: uncover the secret hiding places of stock market profits.

Hagstrom, Jr., Robert G. The Warren Buffett way: investment strategies of the world's greatest investor.

Helly, Jason. Neatest little guide to stock market investing.

Lichello, Robert. How to make $1,000,000 in the stock market automatically.

Littauer, Stephen. How to invest the smart way in stocks, bonds, and mutual funds.

Lowe, Janet. Warren Buffett speaks: wit and wisdom from the world's greatest investor.

Lowenstein, Roger. Buffett: the making of an American capitalist

Lynch, Peter and John Rothchild. Beating the street.
       Learn to earn: a beginner's guide to the basics of investing and business.
       One up on wall street: how to use what you already know to make money in the market.

Malkiel, Burton G. A random walk down wall street.

Mature, Richard J. Stock picking: the 11 best tactics foe beating the market.

O'Hara, Thomas E. and Kenneth S. Janke, Sr. Starting and running a profitable investment club.

O'Shaughnessy, James. How to retire rich: time-tested strategies to beat the market and retire in style.
       Invest like the best.
       What works on wall street.

Seto, Matt and Steven Levingston. The whiz kid of wall street's investment guide.

Sivy, Michael. Michael Sivy's rules of investing: how to pick stocks like a pro.

Skousen, Mark and Jo Ann Skousen. High finance on a low budget: build wealth regardless of your income.

The Beardstown Ladies. The Beardstown ladies' common-sense investment guide: how we beat the stock market-and how you can, too

The Beardstown Ladies' pocketbook guide to picking stocks

The Beardstown Ladies' Stitch-In-Time Guide to Growing Your Nest Egg: Step-By-Step Planning for a Comfortable Financial Future.

Tobias, Andrew. The only investment guide you will ever need.

Tyson, Eric. Mutual funds for dummies.

Vujovich, Dian. 10 minute guide to the stock market.

Wade, Cook. Cash flow and beyond.

Stock market miracles.

Wall street money machine

Walden, Gene. The 100 best stocks to own in America.

STOCKS TECHNICAL ANALYSIS COURSE

Abell, Howard. Digital day trading.

The day trader's advantage: how to move from one winning position to the next.

Allrich, Ted. The on-line investor: how to find the best stocks using your computer.

Bittman, James B. Options for the stock investor.

Dell, Robert. The strategic electronic day trader.

Downs, Ed. Nirvana's omnitrader.

Farrell, Christopher A. Day trade online.

The day trader's survival guide: how to be consistently profitable in short-term markets.

Gonzalez, Fernando and William Rhee. Strategies for the online day trader: advanced trading techniques for online profits.

Investor's Business Daily. Guide to high performance investing.

Kiev, Ari. Trading to win: the psychology of mastering the markets.

Klein, Andrew D. Wallstreet.com: fat cat investing at the click of a mouse.

Koppel, Robert and Howard Abell. The inner game of trading: creating the winner's state of mind.

Lefevre, Edwin. Reminiscences of a stock operator.

Lukeman, Josh. The market maker's edge: day trading tactics from a wall street insider.

McCafferty, Thomas. All about options: the easy way to get started.

Moreland, Jonathan. Profit from legal insider trading.

Murphy, John J. The visual investor: how to spot market trends.

New York Institute of Finance. Technical analysis: a personal seminar.

O'Neill, William J. How to make money in stocks: a winning system in good times or bad.

24 essential lessons for investment success: learn the most important investment techniques from the founder of Investor's Business Daily.

Sethna, Dhun H. Investing smart: how to pick winning stocks with Investor's Business Daily.

Oz, Tony. The stock trader: how I make a living trading stocks.

There is more to personal finance than the drudgery of debts and budgets.

Pistolese, Clifford. Using technical analysis: a step-by-step guide to understanding and
      applying stock market charting techniques.
Rubenfeld, Alan. The supertraders: secrets and success of wall street's best and brightest.
Schwager, Jack D. Getting started in technical analysis.
                  The new market wizards: conversations with America's top traders.
Sarkovich, Misha T. Electronic day trading made easy.
                  Electronic swing trading for maximum profit.
Schaeffer's Investment Research. The option advisor.
Sincere, Michael and Devon Wagner. The after-hours trader.
The Options Industry. Understanding stock options: a classroom manual.
Thomsett, Michael C. Getting started in options.

SEMINARS AND WORKSHOPS

The Miraculous Millionaire is not just the book you are reading now. It is more than a book;
it is $ucce$$tology: a philosophy, a science, and an art. In fact, no book, except probably
one written by deus ex machina, can adequately teach you how to get rich without additional
support materials in the form of seminars, workshops, and coaching. In light of this fact, I have
developed the seminars and workshops listed below to hold your hand and guide you on the
path of financial success:

1. THE MONEY GAME SEMINAR: HOW YOU TOO CAN PLAY AND WIN BIG

Making big money is a game. I can compare it to football, soccer, basketball, tennis, and
baseball. To every game, there are referees, players, and spectators. To every game, there are
owners and two teams: a winning team and a losing team. Similarly, you can choose to remain
a spectator or player of the money game. If you choose to join the winning team, the seminar
reveals how wealth is created in a capitalist economy. It also stresses how shifts from
agrarian and industrial production to the information-service economy have revolutionized
the methods of generating wealth in contemporary America. The seminar also shows
students more than twenty ways of raising money to finance business projects that suit
their personalities. Ultimately, the discussion of the 101 best businesses to start in the new
millennium has long been considered America's best-kept secret.

2. "TAKE- IT-OFF" PSYCHOANALYTIC CLINIC

This is a workshop you do not want to miss. Why have you been unable to plan to become
financially successful? What is holding you back in the bondage of economic slavery?
What is still making you a coward of financial freedom? Fear? Friends? Family? Excuses?
Procrastination? Social distress? Schizophrenia? Hypnosis? Suicide? Anxiety? Guilt? Who is
sabotaging your chances of success? How can you unfetter the chains that ensnare you? When
shall you declare your financial freedom? People get confused sometimes. The mind that solves
our problems and sets up a balance between us and the outside world is distorted, basically
angry or afraid, the two main drives that propel people to act. It is the purpose of the take-it-off
clinical workshop to give you an impetus to act for your own financial success. Driving down to

the inner recesses of your being, I will use psychoanalysis to flush out the waste that is blocking the arteries of your body. You will feel good and rejuvenated when you experience the thrill of recapturing lost opportunities. No longer will you feel guilty for not succeeding financially.

I will work with you, one on one, to develop your financial success plan. Through your actions, you tell a story of past actions that have been successful in resolving the imbalances you have found or successful in the opposite. That story can be told if you are convinced that you should make the effort. In your personal story are the precious metals that can be mined out patiently to tell us what happened, what factors were involved in our confusion. Hence, as your financial psychoanalyst, I am someone who does just that; I prompt you to tell your story, and I find out who you truly are. I unearth the millionaire inside you. In addition to psychoanalysis, I avail myself of the following tools for your betterment: neuro-linguistic programming, praying, imagining, breathing, visualizing, meditating, exercising, invoking, concentrating, affirming, attuning, and divining.

Are you worthy of divine help? If yes, then, let the light of God, the light of cosmic consciousness, shine into your spirit; cosmic consciousness is God's court of last appeal. The receipt of divine favor is conditional upon pleasing God with our thoughts and actions. By developing the habit of thinking ennobling and positive thoughts, you make the greatest approach to spiritual purity; by praying daily and acting according to God's will, you secure a key to heaven. In so thinking and acting, you will be emulating Jesus Christ, our greatest master, who taught us all the first lessons in the art of living a practical and useful life among men and women on earth.

3. HOW YOU CAN RAI$E YOUR$ELF FROM MEDIOCRITY TO $UCCE$$ WORKSHOP

The course does two things. First , it recounts the fascinating story of my life, the rise from complete obscurity to financial prominence. Second, the course reveals the belief and monetary system I developed in order to achieve my goals in life. Third, the course shows how you can succeed by modeling my belief system, mental syntax, and physiology. I will introduce you to the idea of the modeling of excellence. If you subscribe to my prevailing school of thought that the best way to learn something is by picking the brains of the best masters, then, this course is an absolute must for you. You cannot understand and master the $ucce$$tology system without it .

4. FREE MONEY FOR COLLEGE WORKSHOP

Every year thousands of scholarships go unclaimed because many students do not know they exist. It is underestimated that the monetary value of these scholarships is $6.6 billion. Curiously, good academic standing and family income are not the criteria for the award for some these scholarships. Believe it or not, almost every student is eligible for some type of financial aid. If you would like to help a "child," why not use this information to change his or her life? Perhaps there is someone in your family considering college education. Do not wait until he or she is admitted before worrying about financial aid; get a head start; send for a gold mine of information today.

There is more to personal finance than the drudgery of debts and budgets.

5. CREDIT POWER WORKSHOP

The workshop reveals top secrets for building your own quick cash flow system. The course is the most comprehensive information organized to solve the financial problems of individuals who belong to three distinct categories: credit consumers who want to build their borrowing power to the potential level of a millionaire, individuals who want to establish credit for the first time, and people who want to learn how to legally erase or repair bad credit.

OPM! Creative applications of other people's money will be explored with credit and financing. OPM! You must have heard people use that acronym. But do you remember what it stands for? Perhaps you already remember that I have already used the term in step 10, the earlier chapter on investing in real estate. OPM denotes other people's money. But do you know how it works? That is the function of this workshop. Are you really serious about becoming wealthy? Then this workshop is all the information you need to leverage your way to affluence like the Donald Trumps of America. Remember an important fact about credit: banks lend money only to people who want it, but not to those who need it; strike-up friendships with bankers before you need them, not after. You can get rich quickly by learning how to use other people's money, but not their taxes, which is living on welfare.

6. FREEBIE$ FROM UNCLE $AM

Forget President Barack Obama and Governor Willard Mitt Romney playing the game of politics. America is an individualistic society, yet individuals must appreciate the almost invisible hand of the US government in their success. I am not a politician, but, as an economist, I must underscore the role of the U.S. government in wealth creation. Generally, Americans, especially those who have never ventured abroad, take the US government for granted. A visit to a dictatorial den in Africa, for example, might compel the average American to appreciate the freedom he or she enjoys every day. Without the fertile or good soil of democracy, an entrepreneur cannot plant the seeds of a business; otherwise, the entrepreneur will be like the character in the parable of the sower who sows seeds on clay, sandy, or rocky soil. Unbeknownst to the general public, smart people in America get rich by relying on government programs.

The U.S. government is a great benefactor. If you have a mind for success, you can use the government to become a multimillionaire. Many Americans have done it; others are doing it now; and you can do it too. What you really need is someone to show you how to do it. And that is exactly what this course does; it shows you the process of benefiting from a variety of government programs. Incredibly, not many people are asking for these freebie$. Even billionaires such as Donald J. Trump capitalize on the US government's largesse or wealth fare. I will teach you everything you should know about auctions, contracts, free services, giveaways, grants, loans, and more. First, these freebie$ are unadvertised. Second, many people are ignorant about them. Third, some people who have heard about these freebie$ think the offers are too good to be true. As a result, this money accumulates and waits for someone to take it eventually. And the few individuals who know about these opportunities, such as H. Ross Perot and Donald Trump, have been laughing to the bank. Why should you not be one of them?

7. FREEBIE$ BUT GOODIE$ WORKSHOP

This workshop is an Authoritative Source of Thousands of Things You Can Get For Free. Have you attended this workshop before? You should! You have heard people say in America nothing is for free, right? Well, sometimes that generalization does not hold. By authorizing you to operate private foundations and public charities, the US government, virtually, gives you a license the print money. Corporations will be begging you to take their money; also, there are many organizations in the good old USA willing to give away their products. This amazing course shows you how to exploit the non-profit organization tax structure; the workshop is organized in a format which reveals lists of thousands and thousands of free items anyone can get free of charge from America's corporations. If you can write a simple letter, then, you can benefit from hundreds of a dollar's worth of freebies from government agencies, trade associations, and famous companies with brand-name products: cosmetics, shampoos, film, cheese, vitamins, and recipes. Remember, these companies are not stupid; according to them, freebies and giveaways are a calculated strategy to introduce their products or establish and maintain brand loyalty in a market as competitive and perfect as the American one. When companies want to get rid of surplus items, what do you expect them to do? Think about it. Take the course and learn how to write for these freebies.

EPILOGUE

To conclude, seek education. Ignore the lottery. Specialized knowledge, issuing from financial education, is better insurance than the lottery. I know what it feels like to be a sweepstakes or lottery winner, but the high is only momentary. Lottery winners and their money are soon and easily parted. Lottery winners lose their money because of financial illiteracy; they cannot read; they lack financial intelligence: specialized knowledge. If you want to be rich, and stay rich, you are obliged to read, interpret, and comprehend numbers and words; if you want to be rich, you need to be financially literate. Financially-literate individuals have mastered the famous accountant's secret code: assets=liabilities + owner's equity; in other words, financially literate individuals show a preferment for assets over liabilities.

Join the Millionaire Club and learn how you should incorporate businesses. Incorporating is the way rich people play and win the big money game. They capitalize on the power of the legal

We mint millionaires one person at a time.

structure of a corporation to benefit from asset accumulation, distribution, estate planning, asset protection, and tax reduction.

As for the 10% saving solution, whenever you receive your pay check, please, apply the 10% principle of tithing by the holy Bible; allot another 10% of your current earnings to create your own savings and wealth, not only to pay bills. Read books and magazines on earned income, passive income, and portfolio income. Be like rich folks. Like a good actor, affect the habits and manners of America's rich and famous folks. Rich people capitalize on the following investment strategies: stocks, bonds, mutual funds, real estate, notes, and royalties; I enjoy emulating them! What about you? Understand basic economics, especially the notion of markets, the forces of supply and demand, accelerator, multiplier, and compounding.

Choose to be rich! There is a millionaire giant inside you. Awaken the sleeping giant of personal-finance within you. Specialized knowledge is power. Financial literacy is a form of specialized knowledge. Financial literacy will give you the powerful knowledge you need to multiply your assets. Riches will make you to become powerful in society. Feed your mind with positive energy; as the NAACP says, "A mind is a terrible thing to waste." God has given you a mind; use it to acquire wealth. Register and attend Millionaire iUniversity; invest in your financial education. Learn new technologies. Read and make yourself a financial genius. That is the secret of America's rich and famous folks. That is why only 5% of Americans are rich and 95% of Americans are running the rat race of poverty. Keep learning how to read. Come to the seminars and workshops of $ucce$$tology; call (301) 593-4897.

Ultimately, my financial advice to you can be stated in a few short words: worship and glorify the Lord, your God. Educate yourself financially every day for life; acquire computer skills to make yourself marketable. Eliminate your debts and save at least 10% of your money; establish a financial and investment plan and execute it. As you can see, your financial future is in your hands. You are the architect of your own destiny. Please, do not rely on the US government to take good care of you. The US government has made the country to get heavily into debt; the country does not have a lot of financial resources again. This negative change in the fortunes of the USA is responsible for the recent downgrade of its credit rating. The country is almost broke, so, please, do not count on safety nets such as Medicare benefits, social security benefits, and 401(K). If you are aware of the details pertaining to the national debt, then, you would hearken to the clarion call of lifting yourself up from poverty. When you verify statistics on the US national debt (http://www.usdebtclock.com), you will comprehend the folly of people who are still relying on the US government to guarantee them a safe and secure retirement.

There is a better way to a safe, tax-free, and secure retirement. The better way is the application of the proven and winning system of $ucce$$tology. Will you ever give up the lifestyle of living from pay check to paycheck? In fact, living in poverty is no longer a viable financial option. I am here to spread a message of hope, the good news for all the 99% folks living in Middle America. I am a savior; I am a teacher; I am a missionary. I am on a mission to change you and the next generation of Americans struggling to make it into the big time today. I am unashamed to be a Christian; I am a crusader; I am on a crusade to bring to you a Christian-centered approach to wealth-building. My mission is to inspire you; my mission is to motivate you into financial action; my mission is to eradicate financial illiteracy, the major cause of poverty in Middle America. Do you know how money works like the rich and famous? Do you care about improving your financial situation? Are you concerned about retirement, long-term care, disability, and life insurance? Yes? Then, it is time for you to change your life, so make that change now! Where are you now? Where do you want to go today? Get started! Stop standing on the sidelines of life like a spectator at the super bowl!

Join the grass-roots revolution! Participate in the new financial movement. Join the Millionaire Club; attend Millionaire iUniversity. Learn how to save and invest your money; establish an emergency fund. Apply the common-sense money-management techniques discussed in the book. If you have forgotten the step-by-step plan I have presented in the book, please, I have summarized it below for your erudition. Dream and aspire. Define your goals. Make your financial plan! Prepare your budget. Become an entrepreneur today. Decide on a business need. Communicate your business vision to the whole wide world. Register your business with your state and the Internal Revenue Service. Open a business bank account. Automate your accounting system or hire an accountant to do it for you. Serve your customers, contractors, and debt collectors.

As you can see, $ucce$$tology works well in all economic climates; do not worry whether the market is bullish or bearish. Here is a simple experiment for you: Do you have a mirror in your house? Look at the mirror. What do you see? Do you see your reflection? Look at your reflection, the man or woman in the mirror. Tell him or her to accept responsibility for past irresponsible behavior. Advise him or her to change old spending habits; advise him or her to adopt the new success system presented in the book. Ask him or her to swear aloud in the following manner:

"I thank God for the system of $ucce$$tology; I am ready to change my life today; I promise to learn from Millionaire iUniversity, the university of hard knocks; I am born again; never again will I want to be broke and in debt."

Good luck! If you are still having problems developing your financial plan or establishing your goals, then, I urge you to join the Millionaire Club and attend Millionaire iUniversity. Call my office, and order your ticket to financial success now: call (301) 593-4897. Re-read the book seven times. Introduce yourself again to Prince Ojong. FOLLOW PRINCE OJONG! He will prove to you that your dreams are closer than you think. He will show you how to create wealth without risk. He will assist you in drawing up a winning financial plan you can implement to change your life for the better. He will present a platform for you to start your own business. Instead of flip flopping like a puppet of fate, you will be in control of your financial destiny. There has been a massive wealth shift from agrarian and industrial economies to an information economy. You can ride the waves of modern wealth by capitalizing on your God-given talents, self-study, and computer literacy. In fact, that is my thesis. In America, there is an opportunity for the ordinary person to achieve financial independence. By applying my principles, you do not have to depend on other people; rather, you have to depend on yourself. It will always be up to you to think and grow rich in America; nobody can do it for you; you have to carry your own cross.

Follow the sensible and twelve-step plan to financial freedom listed below:

Step 1 Pay God first
Step 2 Discover the millionaire's secret
Step 3 Use insurance as your foundation of wealth
Step 4 Teach yourself personal finance
Step 5 Balance your financial book
Step 6 Computerize and research the Internet
Step 7 Acquire entrepreneurial skills
Step 8 Decode the IRS tax codes
Step 9 Play the stock market game
Step 10 Invest in real estate
Step 11 Join the Millionaire Club
Step 12 Attend the Millionaire iUniversity

In twelve chapters, I have given you the blocks you need to build your financial house, the millionaire mansion. I have armed you with a truly divine formula for building bullet-proof wealth. Act now! What you have to do now is muster some courage to master your insecurities, anger, and fears. Be decisive! Build some momentum! I have given you the architectural blueprint you need to construct your edifice; I have given you the map you need to tread upon the road to financial freedom.

Come to my seminar, and I will show you how to leverage the use of the truckload of information presented in *The Miraculous Millionaire*. Personally, I am dying to prove to you that $ucce$$tology works in good times and bad times, so, please, look forward to the future with confidence. In the course of attending my workshops, I will teach you how to discern and set your goals now on the wheel of life: spiritual, physical, career, financial, intellectual, social, and family. Your goals must be written, personal, specific, time-limited, and measurable. I will help you to analyze the immediate and remote cause of your money problems: ignorance, competition, fear, procrastination, bad luck, insomnia, and more. Please, count on me to offer solutions appropriate to your circumstances. Imagine the reality of living a better life: nurturing relationships, transformed marriages, debt-free life, and money invested for college, and prosperous retirement.

Like my students and clients, if you follow my professional advice, you can start living the good life today. You can stop worrying about money and personal debts. What does becoming rich sound like to you? Are you ready to be wealthy? Of course, there is a catch! You have to pay the price for success: effort, sacrifice, perseverance, character, diligence, vision, knowledge, positive mental attitude, and responsibility. It is unfathomable for you to remain a victim of circumstances; you can become the architect of your destiny. Capitalize on the new knowledge you have acquired this book, a turn-key or push-button wealth-building system. My program is the true gospel of millionaire money-making secrets. Like Jesus Christ, I have only a three-year ministry to evangelize the good news of wealth-building with Christ. Learn; to be the master of your destiny, you have to learn; earn; to obtain what you desire, you have to earn. Farewell.

There is more to personal finance than the drudgery of debts and budgets.

GLORIA

Gloria
Glory to God in the highest,
and on earth peace to people of good will.
We praise you,
we bless you,
we adore you,
we glorify you,
we give you thanks for your great glory,
Lord God, heavenly King,
O God, almighty Father.
Lord Jesus Christ, Only Begotten Son,
Lord God, Lamb of God, Son of the Father,
you take away the sins of the world, have mercy on us;
you take away the sins of the world, receive our prayer.
you are seated at the right hand of the Father, have mercy on us.
For you alone are the Holy One, you alone are the Lord, you alone are the
Most High,
Jesus Christ, with the Holy Spirit, in the glory of God the Father.
Amen

THE LORD IS MY SPHEPHERD

BULK ORDERS/DISCOUNTS

For bulk orders, you can receive substantial discounts off the cover price of the book. We have special deals for churches, schools, government agencies, non-governmental organizations, classes, workshops, seminars, contests, giveaways, and businesses.

For information or details on bulk orders and discounts, please, feel free to contact us using the information:

OverReacher Empire Corporation
11231 Lockwood Drive
Silver Spring, MD 20901
Office #: (301) 593-4897
          (301) 593-4879

Fax #: 240-241-5137
Email: theafricannation@yahoo.com

WEB: http://www.princeojong.com
http://www.miraculousmillionaire.com
http://www.millionaireiuniversity.com

MONEY-MAKING SEMINARS & WORKSHOPS

We use our seminars and workshops to illuminate the rich content of *The Miraculous Millionaire*.

List of Seminars and workshops:

1. The Money Game Seminar: How You Too Can Play and Win Big

2. "Take- It-Off" Psychoanalytic Clinic

3. How You Can Rai$e Your$elf from Mediocrity to $ucce$$

4. Free Money for College Workshop

5. Credit Power Workshop

6. Freebie$ from Uncle $am

7. Freebie$ But Goodie$

For information or details on sponsoring a seminar or workshop, please, feel free to contact us using the information:

OverReacher Empire Corporation
11231 Lockwood Drive
Silver Spring, MD 20901
Office #: (301) 593-4897
        (301) 593-4879

Fax #: 240-241-5137
Email: theafricannation@yahoo.com

WEB: http://www.princeojong.com
http://www.miraculousmillionaire.com
http://www.millionaireiuniversity.com

562 The Miraculous Millionaire

JOIN THE MILLIONAIRE CLUB

The best way for you to benefit from the wealth of our knowledge system is to join the Millionaire Club. Then, you will be given the unique opportunity to attend Millionaire iUniversity, our virtual institution of higher learning.

Choose your membership level below:

IBS—Independent Business Solicitor	10%/$499.99_____
AMR—Area Marketing Representative	15%/$699.99_____
CMR—City Marketing Representative	20%/$999.99_____
LMR—Local Marketing Representative	25%/$1,299.99_____
CME/CET---County Marketing Executive/	
County Executive Trainer	35%/$1,599.99_____
SMD—State Marketing Director	40%/$1,999.99_____
NMD--National Marketing Director	45%/$2,999.99_____
IMD—International Marketing Director	50%/$3,999.99_____

OverReacher Empire Corporation
11231 Lockwood Drive
Silver Spring, MD 20901
Office #: (301) 593-4897
         (301) 593-4879
Fax #: 240-241-5137

Email: theafricannation@yahoo.com

WEB: http://www.princeojong.com
http://www.miraculousmillionaire.com
http://www.millionaireiuniversity.com

READER FEEDBACK

OverReacher Empire Corporation
11231 Lockwood Drive
Silver Spring, MD 20901
Office #: (301) 593-4897
         (301) 593-4879

Fax #: 240-241-5137
Email: theafricannation@yahoo.com

WEB: http://www.princeojong.com
http://www.miraculousmillionaire.com
http://www.millionaireiuniversity.com

Hearty welcome to *The Miraculous Millionaire* guest book and reader feedback form. Please, use this form to send messages to us, to suggest changes, and to request more information about our financial services. Should you prefer a rapid contact mode, you may reach us by emailing us at theafricannation@yahoo.com.

We would appreciate your honest feedback to *The Miraculous Millionaire*.

How did you first find out about the book?

How do you like it?

What do you like most about the book?

What do you like the least about the book?

Is there anything that you would change?

Desiderata

Go placidly amid the noise and the haste, and remember what peace there may be in silence. As far as possible without surrender be on good terms with all persons.

Speak your truth quietly and clearly; and listen to others, even to the dull and the ignorant, they too have their story. Avoid loud and aggressive persons, they are vexations to the spirit.
If you compare yourself to others, you may become vain and bitter; for always there will be greater and lesser persons than yourself.

Enjoy your achievements as well as your plans. Keep interested in your own career, however humble; it is a real possession in the changing fortunes of time.

Exercise caution in your business affairs, for the the world is full of trickery. But let not this blind you to what virtue there is; many persons strive for high ideals, and everywhere life is full of heroism.

Be yourself. Especially do not feign affection. Neither be cynical about love; for in the face of all aridity and disenchantment it is as perennial as the grass. Take kindly the counsel of the years, gracefully surrendering the things of youth.

Nurture strength of spirit to shield you in sudden misfortune. But do not distress yourself with dark imaginings. Many fears are born of fatigue and loneliness.

Beyond a wholesome discipline, be gentle with yourself. You are a child of the universe, no less than the trees and the stars; you have a right to be here. And whether or not it is clear to you, no doubt the universe is unfolding as it should.

Therefore, be at peace with God, whatever you conceive him to be, and whatever your labors and aspirations in the noisy confusion of life, keep peace in your soul. With all it's sham drudgery and broken dreams; it is still a beautiful world.

Be cheerful. Strive to be happy.

Index

Symbols

$ucce$$tology 564
$ucce$$tology as an Art 56

A

Abraham Maslow 109
Academc Knowledge 564–578
Accountant's Secret 564
Accounting 280
Action Plan 564
Actions and Decisions 564
Adjustable Rate Mortgage 564
Adolf Hitler
  Charisma 367
Advance Fee Loan Scams 564
Adverse Possession 208
Advertising 564
Affirmations 564
Afformations 564
Age of Enlightenment 101
AIDAS 564
Albert Einstein
  Compounding 289
Alexander Graham Bell 257
Alexander the Great
  Charisma 367
Alex Faickney Osborn 270
Alfred Marshall 440
Amazon.com
  Steve Bezos 367
A.M. Best Company
  Insurance Rating Service 196
American Dream 564
American Express 564
American Frontier 564
American Funds 564
American Institute of Consumer Credit 346
American Pioneer 564
American Professors 564
American Stock Exchange 27
Amos Televisionersky 271
Anatomy of a Sale 564
Anchor 101
Andrew Carnegie 118

Andrew Tobias
  Taxcut 348
Andy Grove
  Intel Corporation 365
Angels 79
Annual Percentage Rate 564
Anthony Robbins 564
Apple 564
Appreciation 98
Architect 78
Aristotelian 136
Aristotle
  Final Causality 267
Obstacles
  Fear
    Cynicism
      Laziness 223
Art 564
Assets 564
AT&T 564
Attend Millionaire iUniversity 564
Attribute Substitution 271
Auto and Home Loans 564
Auto Insurance 564
Automatic Millionaire 469
Auto Suggestion 564
Avoiding Scams 564

B

Balance Sheet 281
Balance Your Book 564
Banker's Secret
  Own Your Own Bank 252
Bank of America 167
Bank Owned Life Insurance 564
Bankruptcy 564
Barack Obama
  Change
    Forward 365
BBS 564
Behavioral Guideposts 116
Belief 564
Benazir Bhutto 369
Benjamin Franklin 392
Benjamin Graham 452
Benson and Hedges 564
Bentley 153
Berkshire Hathaway 98
Bernard Bernanke 564

There is more to personal finance than the drudgery of debts and budgets.

There is more to personal finance than the drudgery of debts and budgets.

There is more to personal finance than the drudgery of debts and budgets.